101

MICROSOFT
VISUAL BASIC .NET
APPLICATIONS

Sean Campbell, Scott Swigart,
Bob Carver, Patrick Barnes, Jim Pragit,
Oz Rugless, Kris Horrocks

PUBLISHED BY
Microsoft Press
A Division of Microsoft Corporation
One Microsoft Way
Redmond, Washington 98052-6399

Library of Congress Cataloging-in-Publication Data
    101 Microsoft Visual Basic .NET Applications / 3 Leaf Solutions.
        p. cm.
    Includes index.
    ISBN 0-7356-1891-7
    1. Microsoft Visual BASIC.   2. BASIC (Computer program language).
    3. Microsoft .NET.   I. 3 Leaf Solutions (Computer Firm).

    QA76.73.B3A18   2003
    005.2'768--dc21   2003043639

Printed and bound in the United States of America.

1 2 3 4 5 6 7 8 9   QWE   8 7 6 5 4 3

Distributed in Canada by H.B. Fenn and Company Ltd.

A CIP catalogue record for this book is available from the British Library.

Microsoft Press books are available through booksellers and distributors worldwide. For further information about international editions, contact your local Microsoft Corporation office or contact Microsoft Press International directly at fax (425) 936-7329. Visit our Web site at www.microsoft.com/mspress. Send comments to: *mspinput@microsoft.com*.

Acquisitions Editor: Danielle Voeller
Project Editor: Lynn Finnel
Technical Editor: Dail Magee Jr.
Copyeditor: Roger LeBlanc
Electronic Artist: Michael Kloepfer
Desktop Publisher: Gina Cassill

Body Part No. X09-39044

Contents at a Glance

Table of Contents

Acknowledgments

Many people came together to create this book and the samples associated with it, and we would like to thank them for their help. First, we would like to thank Mike Iem and Duncan MacKenzie, who conceived the original concept of the samples and sponsored the original samples project for Microsoft. We would also like to thank the developers who authored the initial samples: Micah Clymer, Gary Gumbiner, Oz Rugless, Kris Horrocks, Steven Borg, Jim Pragit, Patrick Barnes, Brian Randall, Sean Campbell, Scott Swigart, and Bob Carver.

We would also like to thank Tommy and Danny Ryan, who were responsible for much of the testing work that ensured all the samples you receive with this book run on Microsoft Visual Studio .NET 2002 and 2003.

No book can be created and brought to market without the help of a great publishing company, and we found that in Microsoft Press. Specifically, we would like to thank Danielle Bird and Lynn Finnel, who helped bring this book to fruition.

Finally, all the authors would like to give thanks to their families and others who supported them throughout the writing of the code and text that makes up this book.

About the Applications

The 101 sample applications that make up this book contain code that answers many common questions a beginner-to-intermediate-level Microsoft Visual Basic .NET developer is faced with when building Microsoft .NET applications.

Each sample application was developed using a set of coding conventions (which you'll find in this book), and each sample shares a common look and feel, as much as possible. Each sample also includes a readme.htm file that explains some basics of the application in case you're reviewing a sample without having the book close at hand.

The samples in this book are ready to be run in either the Microsoft Visual Studio .NET 2002 or 2003 development environment. You can find the Visual Studio .NET 2003 files in Chapter folders within the \101VBApps folder; look inside the VS2002 folder within the \101VBApps folder for the Visual Studio .NET 2002 files.

Finally each application is designed to be "F5-able," meaning that they should all run out of the box, without any special configuration. Any circumstances for which specific software or setup is needed is fully documented in the readme. The only general requirement is that you have Microsoft SQL Server installed either as a default instance or an instance installed with the name NETSDK. You can easily install a version of SQL Server by installing the version of MSDE that ships with the .NET Framework quickstarts.

Objectives

In broad terms, the objectives of this book are

- To provide you with a wide range of sample code that you can directly use to build Visual Basic .NET applications using known best practices

- To provide you with sample applications that can educate you on nearly all aspects of the .NET Framework that are commonly used in day-to-day development

- To give you a set of F5-able sample code

Target Audience

This book targets the following three types of developers:

- Beginning .NET developers
- Intermediate .NET developers
- Visual Basic 6 developers

Beginning developers can quickly ramp up to .NET by initially leveraging the many samples found in the Visual Basic .NET Language, Data Access, and Windows Forms user interface (UI) chapters. These chapters and associated samples provide a firm foundation for any .NET Framework developer.

Intermediate developers can benefit from the variety of sample code found in the more intermediate to advanced chapters (for example, those that cover security, enterprise services, GDI+, and advanced .NET Framework subjects). This code will help intermediate developers better understand the .NET Framework.

There are millions of Visual Basic 6 developers who know exactly how to get things done using Visual Basic 6, but who have not yet learned how to accomplish the same tasks using the Microsoft .NET Framework. We think that these 101 samples are probably the quickest route to learning the .NET Framework that a Visual Basic 6 developer could find. The samples are designed to cover the most common programming tasks, in detail, and serve as a bridge for Visual Basic 6 developers who are migrating their skills to the Framework. All the samples follow specific coding conventions, and the samples share a similar UI. The code samples are discussed extensively in the book, and all code is designed to be F5-able. This helps to flatten the learning curve that a Visual Basic 6 developer typically has to endure when moving to the .NET Framework.

This book doesn't target the following types of developers:

- Web developers
- Developers of mobile applications

This book takes a distinctly Windows Forms view of .NET Framework development, targeting developers who build mainly rich-client applications. The book does provide a limited number of samples for Web sites and Web services, but these samples are designed to augment the skills of a rich-client developer rather than provide exhaustive coverage of Web development.

Our hope is that these samples will help jump-start your rich-client development on the Microsoft .NET Framework.

Structure

Each chapter has a standard format it follows when describing each sample application. First a set of related applications is shown at the beginning of each sample. Next, new concepts in the given sample are outlined. If you're reading the book from front to back, you'll see the new topics introduced prior to each sample. If you're using the book as more of a reference, the "New Concepts" sections provide an abstract for the sample, allowing you to skip to the specific samples that illustrate that concepts that interest you. The majority of the text for each sample consists of a detailed code walkthrough. The code walkthrough explains the key concepts the sample is designed to illustrate. Finally, a conclusion for each sample gives some final points to think about for each application.

Installing the Sample Files

The sample code used in this book is available on the book's Web site at *http://www.microsoft.com/mspress/books/6510. asp*. To download the sample files, click the Companion Content link in the More Information menu on the right side of the Web page. This will load the Companion Content page, which includes the link for downloading the sample application files. To install the sample application files, run the executable file downloaded from the link and accept the license agreement that is presented.

By default, the files will be copied to the folder [My Documents] \MicrosoftPress\101VBApps.

System Requirements

To use the sample code provided at the Web site, you'll need a computer with the following configuration:

■ Microsoft Windows 2000 (SP3 or later recommended), Windows XP Professional, or Windows Server 2003, Web Edition.

■ Microsoft Internet Explorer 5.5 or later.

■ The .NET Framework SDK, which you can download from the MSDN Web site at *http://msdn.microsoft.com/netframework/downloads /default.asp*. (Because Microsoft Visual Studio .NET includes the SDK, you don't need to install the .NET Framework SDK separately if you install Visual Studio .NET.) Note that Windows Server 2003 comes with the .NET Framework version 1.1 preinstalled, so you do not need to install this separately.

- Visual Studio .NET 2003 or Visual Studio .NET 2002, Professional Edition or higher.
- 128 MB of RAM or higher.
- 800 MHz processor or higher.

Corrections, Comments, and Help

Every effort has been made to ensure the accuracy of this book and the contents of the sample files. Microsoft Press provides corrections and additional content for its books through the World Wide Web at the following address:

http://www.microsoft.com/mspress/support

To connect directly to the Microsoft Press Knowledge Base and enter a query you have, visit the following address:

http://www.microsoft.com/mspress/support/search.asp

If you have problems, comments, or ideas regarding this book or the sample files, please send them to Microsoft Press. Send an e-mail message to mspinput@microsoft.com, or send postal mail to the following address:

Microsoft Press
Attn: *101 Microsoft Visual Basic .NET Applications* Editor
One Microsoft Way
Redmond, WA 98052-6399

Please note that product support is not offered through the preceding addresses. For help with Visual Basic .NET, you can connect to Microsoft Product Support Services on the Web at *http://support.microsoft.com*; for additional developer information about Visual Basic .NET, go to *http://www.microsoft.com/net* and search on Visual Basic .NET.

Visit the Microsoft Press World Wide Web Site

You are also invited to visit the Microsoft Press World Wide Web site at the following location:

http://www.microsoft.com/mspress

You'll find descriptions for the complete line of Microsoft Press books, information about ordering titles, notice of special features and events, additional content for Microsoft Press books, and much more.

1

Working with Microsoft Visual Studio .NET 2003 and Microsoft .NET Framework 1.1

This chapter discusses some of the new functionality of Microsoft .NET Framework version 1.1 and how the .NET Framework has changed from .NET Framework version 1.0. First, however, we'll look at some productivity enhancements found in Visual Studio .NET 2003.

Visual Studio .NET 2003

Visual Studio .NET 2003 is an incremental release over Visual Studio .NET 2002, yet it still contains numerous enhancements of interest to developers.

Changes to Add Web Reference

One of the first changes you come across when working with Visual Studio .NET 2003 is the improved Add Web Reference dialog box. This dialog box is shown in Figure 1-1.

The Add Web Reference dialog box in Visual Studio .NET 2003 posseses capabilities beyond those that were offered with the Add Web Reference dialog box found in Visual Studio .NET 2002. First, the new Add Web Reference dialog box can easily browse local Web services. In addition, when viewing Web Services Description Language (WSDL) documents for Web services, the Add Web Reference dialog box now applies a simple style sheet instead of only showing the user the raw WSDL document for the Web service. This makes it easier to find the actual methods exposed by the Web service. Also, you can now easily change the name of the proxy class before actually adding the Web reference. This new feature saves the previously required step of renaming the proxy after it was created by Visual Studio .NET 2002. You can see the formatted WSDL described in Figure 1-2.

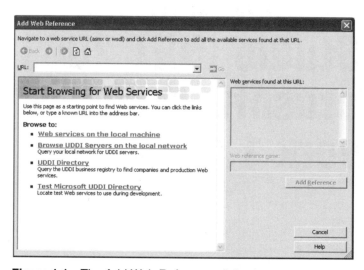

Figure 1-1   The Add Web Reference dialog box.

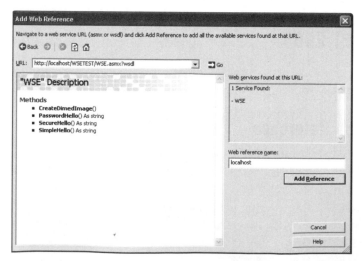

Figure 1-2   Formatted WSDL in the Add Web Reference dialog box.

The new Add Web Reference dialog box also lets you easily navigate to and browse local, Microsoft, and test Universal Description, Discovery, and Integration (UDDI) nodes. From these nodes, you can query for existing Web services and add them to your project. Figure 1-3 shows the Add Web Reference dialog box at the Microsoft UDDI node.

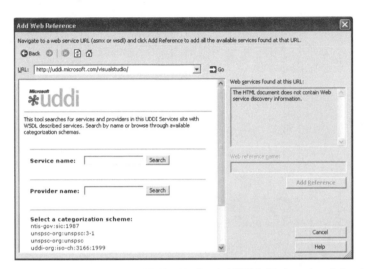

Figure 1-3   Browsing UDDI with the Add Web Reference dialog box.

Coding Enhancements

In this section, you'll learn about the various coding enhancements that have been added to Visual Studio.NET 2003. The most significant of these are detailed below.

Auto-Stub

One of the nicest new features that helps you to write code using Visual Studio .NET 2003 is the Auto-Stub feature. Auto-Stub takes methods that are declared as *MustOverride* and automatically adds procedure stubs for you when you specify the base class for a new class you are creating. In Figure 1-4, a custom trace listener is being created. Notice that no members are specified for the class.

After adding an *Inherits* statement and then hitting the Enter button, the two *MustOverride* members are automatically added to the class definition. Even though you still have to write the implementation code for these members, this new Auto-Stub feature eliminates some boilerplate coding and mouse-clicking that was previously required to achieve the same objective. This also works if you implement an existing interface for a class you're creating. In Figure 1-5, you can see what Auto-Stub does.

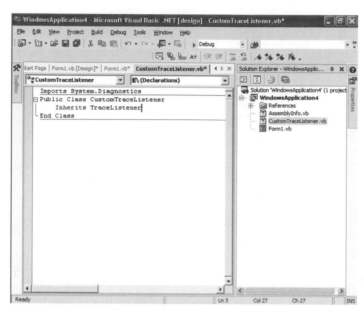

Figure 1-4 The world before Auto-Stub.

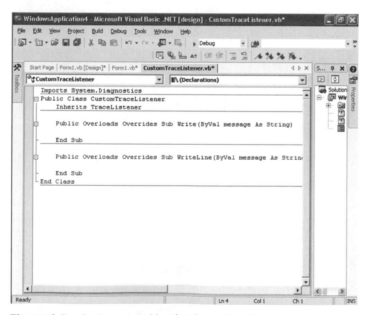

Figure 1-5 Code created by the Auto-Stub feature.

Most Recently Used IntelliSense

The Visual Studio .NET 2003 version of IntelliSense now keeps track of items you've used most recently and displays them first in IntelliSense—no more scrolling to find *StreamWriter* every time you need it when it's the thing you most recently used in the *System.IO* namespace.

Procedure Separators

Another new coding enhancement is the use of procedure separators. These separators have been in view in most of the screen shots used so far in this chapter.

Track Active Item

Another new option in Visual Studio .NET 2003 is to have Visual Studio .NET automatically track and open the folder tree that contains the file you're currently working on in the editor. You no longer have to manually open a folder in the Solution Explorer to access a file in that window. This quick access is useful when working with objects such as Web service proxy classes that are always a few folder levels down. Selecting Environment, and then Projects And Solutions in the Visual Studio .NET Options dialog box allows you to access the Track Active Item In Solution Explorer check box, which allows you to specify whether you want this tracking done automatically. This option is enabled by default.

Debugging Enhancements

You can once again use IntelliSense in the Immediate window. This useful feature that you probably greatly missed when it was gone is now back in Visual Studio .NET 2003. Now it's very easy to drill into an object's properties and methods using IntelliSense in the Immediate window. In Figure 1-6, the properties and methods of the *Me* object are shown.

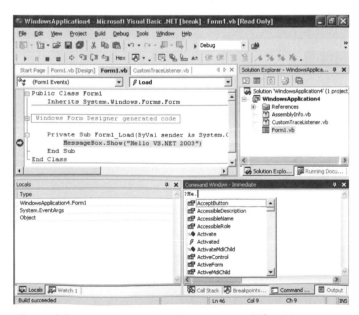

Figure 1-6   The Immediate window and IntelliSense.

In addition, some nice changes were made to the way certain debugging windows display information. For example, members are now displayed in alphabetical order. Also, private members are not shown by default, which greatly cleans up the list of members.

Easy Access to the Object Browser

You can now simply double-click an assembly in the Solution Explorer window and be taken directly to the Object Browser window with the focus placed on the assembly you double-clicked. This step-saver is one more small productivity difference between Visual Studio .NET 2002 and Visual Studio .NET 2003.

Changes to the Start Page

The start page has two enhancements in Visual Studio .NET 2003. First, it's much faster to load. So those of you who disabled the start page in Visual Studio .NET 2002 because it caused Visual Studio .NET to load slowly can now re-enable it. Also, the start page now contains valuable links to community and technical information that are regularly updated. Figure 1-7 shows the improved start page.

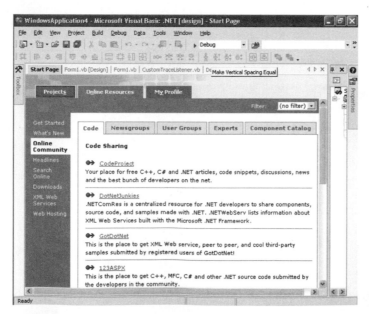

Figure 1-7   The changes to the start page.

Code and Project Migration

Visual Studio.NET 2003 also includes some tools to aid in migration tasks. Tools exist to help with the migration of Visual Basic 6 code as well as the migration of solutions and projects built with Visual Studio .NET 2002.

Project Migration

Visual Studio .NET 2002 projects and solutions are automatically upgraded to the Visual Studio .NET 2003 project and solution file format when opened in Visual Studio .NET 2003. When you open a project file in this way, a prompt appears asking whether you are sure you want to upgrade the project.

An important point to remember is that there is a supported process that uses the integrated development environment (IDE) to migrate project and solution files to the Visual Studio .NET 2003 format. Once migrated, though, they can no longer be opened in Visual Studio .NET 2002.

You can, however, make a manual change to a project or solution file once it's upgraded to open it again in Visual Studio .NET 2002. In the .sln file, you need to change File Version 8.00 to 7.00. In the .vcsproj file, you need to change ProductVersion 7.10.2215 to 7.0.9466 and Schema Version 2.0 to 1.0. Keep in mind that this manual change is not officially supported and might not work in the future.

A final point, and an important one, concerning project migration is that when the upgrade is performed, the migration process does not create a backup of the project and solution files in the Visual Studio .NET 2002 format. So if you want to open the project and solution files in Visual Studio .NET 2002 after the migration, you need to manually create a backup of the files prior to performing the migration.

The Visual Basic 6 Code Snippet Tool

Visual Studio .NET 2003 contains a Visual Basic 6 to Visual Basic .NET Code Snippet tool that allows you to easily migrate snippets of code instead of entire projects. The Code Snippet tool is easy to use and can be found by selecting Upgrade Visual Basic 6 Code from the Tools menu when you are viewing a code window. Figure 1-8 shows the tool.

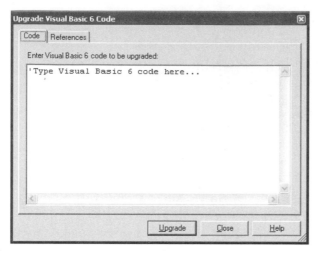

Figure 1-8   The Visual Basic 6 Code Snippet tool.

Significant Framework Changes

If someone told you that they made more than 1000 changes to something, your first thought typically would be that a great deal of changes were made. Although a great many changes were made to .NET Framework in the move from 1.0 to 1.1, many of them are minor or have limited benefit. However, there are changes that can have a positive impact on your development efforts. Those changes that have the most impact are detailed in this section.

Trust Levels

In this case, what is old is new again. For those who were familiar with .NET Framework 1.0 during its beta period, the concept of trust levels should be nothing new. The ability to set trust levels for ASP.NET applications was disabled in the .NET Framework 1.0 release just prior to the release to manufacturing (RTM). Now with the release of .NET Framework 1.1, the ability to select trust levels is back and fully enabled. Before we dive into trust levels, though, you need to have some background on Code-Access Security.

Code-Access Security

Code-Access Security describes a way of securing applications so that applications are granted or denied certain permissions based on permissions granted to the code itself. For ASP.NET applications, these grants and denials of permissions for an application are accomplished via the use of trust levels. For Windows Forms applications, these grants and denials can be generated declaratively via attributes and imperatively via method calls on permission objects. Some default trust levels for ASP.NET sites are initially defined in a set of configuration files found in the C:\%windir%\Microsoft .NET\Framework\%FrameworkVer%\Config directory. If you view the contents of this directory, you find configuration files for the trust levels listed in Table 1-1.

Table 1-1   Trust Levels

Trust Level	Description
None	No privileges are granted.
Minimal	This level merely grants the ability to execute. It doesn't provide the ability to access protected resources.
Low	An application has the ability to read its own resources but not those of other applications.
Medium	Read and Write privileges are granted to an application's own directories. The application can also interact with Microsoft SQL Server.
High	Most .NET Framework classes can be accessed.
Full	Applications can essentially execute any managed or native code they want to.

Each trust level grants and/or denies certain permissions to the code of the ASP.NET application. For example, with the trust level set to Medium, the ASP.NET application can read and write to its own directories only and not to those of other ASP.NET sites on the same machine. For a detailed list of the permissions granted by default to a given trust level, you can simply open in Notepad the file that represents the trust level. In Notepad, you'll see the XML representation of the permissions granted to an ASP.NET application running under the given trust level.

To begin to work with trust levels is easy. First create an ASP.NET application using Visual Studio .NET 2003. Then open the web.config file for the site. In between the *<system.web>* elements inside web.config, add the following code.

```
<trust level="high" />
```

The value for the *level* attribute can initially be any one of the predefined trust levels (None, Minimal, Low, Medium, High, or Full). When this *<trust>* element is placed in web.config, the associated ASP.NET site is constrained by the permissions granted or denied in the given trust level.

You can also modify the existing trust level definitions or create new trust levels. All you need to understand is the code-access security permissions defined in the trust-level configuration files.

The simplest way to create a custom trust level would be to copy one of the existing files and then modify it as you see fit by adding new permissions or removing permissions from the file. Once you have modified the file and given it a new name, you then have to modify machine.config. The machine.config file is found in the same directory specified earlier: C:\%windir%\Microsoft .NET\Framework\%FrameworkVer%\Config.

After opening machine.config in your favorite text editor, you'll find the following section:

```
<location allowOverride="true">
<system.web>
    <securityPolicy>
        <trustLevel name="Full" policyFile="internal"/>
        <trustLevel name="High" policyFile="web_hightrust.config"/>
        <trustLevel name="Medium" policyFile="web_mediumtrust.config"/>
        <trustLevel name="Low" policyFile="web_lowtrust.config"/>
        <trustLevel name="Minimal" policyFile="web_minimaltrust.config"/>
    </securityPolicy>
    <!-- level="[Full|High|Medium|Low|Minimal]" -->
    <trust level="Full" originUrl=""/>
</system.web>
</location>
<system.web>
```

Here you can see the individual trust level configuration files associated with their friendly name. To add another custom trust level, all you need to do is add another element between the *<securityPolicy>* elements. The new element should have the friendly name for your trust level as well as the name of the file that represents it.

```
<securityPolicy>
    ⋮
    <trustLevel name="CustomLevel" policyFile="web_customlevel.config" />
    ⋮
</securityPolicy>
```

At this point, you can use the simple trust element specified earlier in a web.config file, and your custom trust level is then used to define the permissions granted or denied to the given ASP.NET Web site.

```
<trust level="CustomLevel" />
```

Services Without Components

In the previous release of the .NET Framework, working with COM+ services from managed code was possible. However, doing so entailed many boilerplate steps and a decent amount of repetitive coding to simply work with distributed transactions or other frequently used COM+ services. The release of .NET

Framework 1.1 removes the need for much of this coding when your application is running on .NET Framework 1.1 and running atop the Windows Server 2003 operating system.

Applications built on top of .NET Framework 1.0 required you to first create a class that inherited from the *ServicedComponent* base class. This class was found in the *System.EnterpriseServices* namespace. Next you had to strongly name your component by generating a public/private key pair with the *sn.exe* command-line utility and then signing your assembly. Finally, you registered your class (and associated assembly) with COM+ services with one of two methods. The first method required a user to have administrative rights on his box when the application was first run. If the user had administrative rights, the serviced component would be automatically registered with COM+ services. If it could not be guaranteed that the first user to run the application would have administrative rights, the *RegAsm.exe* command utility could be used to preregister the serviced component with COM+ services prior to application execution.

All these steps and considerations for utilizing commonly used COM+ services (such as transactions) are no longer necessary with the release of .NET Framework 1.1. Two new classes eliminate the need for such complexity. The first of these classes is the *ServiceConfig* class; the second is the *ServiceDomain* class. In the following code snippet, you can see how they work together:

```
Dim config As New ServiceConfig
config.TrackingEnabled = True
config.TrackingAppName = "EntSrv"
ServiceDomain.Enter(config)
'COM+ available here
ServiceDomain.Leave()
```

The *ServiceConfig* class encapsulates many tasks you would typically perform by decorating your code with attributes when building Serviced Components with the 1.0 release of the .NET Framework. Using this class, you can specify transaction attributes and other essential metadata. Here two configuration options are specified. First, tracking is enabled for the application. Enabling tracking allows the component to be visible as a running process in the Component Services snap-in while the application is running. Second, a friendly name is specified for the application so that it can be more easily recognizable in the Component Services snap-in.

The real magic begins after the call to the *Enter* method of the *ServiceDomain* class. The *ServiceConfig* instance is passed as an argument to this method, and when the method is done executing, everything after it has access to COM+ services until a call to the *Leave* method of the *ServiceDomain* class is made.

It's as simple as that.

No more specifying a strong name for the component. No more inheriting from Serviced Component. And, in many cases, no more need to use additional attributes. The additional attributes used in Framework 1.0 applications to note things such as whether tracking was enabled or whether the *TransactionOption* enumeration was used are now merely specified by passing values to properties of the *ServiceConfig* class.

To see how this might work with distributed transactions, we'll walk through a slightly more lengthy example.

> **Note**   We're beginning at the end with "Application #101: New for 2003." We thought it best to begin the book by introducing all the .NET Framework 1.1 news that's fit to print. You can continue on with Chapter 1 and run Application #101 or jump ahead to other chapters and applications that interest you.

Application #101: New for 2003

In Application #101, the sample application associated with this chapter, there is a tab named Services Without Components. On this tab, you'll find a button named Using Transactions. A portion of the code for the click event handler for this button is as follows:

```
Dim config As New ServiceConfig
config.Transaction = TransactionOption.Required
config.TrackingEnabled = True
config.TrackingAppName = "EntSrv"
config.TrackingComponentName = "EntSrvComponent"
ServiceDomain.Enter(config)

Try
    ' Update Product Prices
    scmd.CommandText = "UPDATE PRODUCTS SET UNITPRICE = " & _
        "UNITPRICE * 1.12 WHERE UNITPRICE > 15"
    Dim recordsAffected As Integer = scmd.ExecuteNonQuery()

    ' Write out the number of changed records to an audit table
    scmd.CommandText = "INSERT PriceAudit VALUES(1.12," & _
        recordsAffected & ")"
    scmd.ExecuteNonQuery()
Catch ex As Exception
    ContextUtil.SetAbort()
    MsgBox("A error occurred when processing the " & _
        "transaction", MsgBoxStyle.OKOnly, Me.Text)
Finally
    ServiceDomain.Leave()
    scnnNorthwind.Close()
End Try
```

Notice a couple of things about this code. First there is the creation of a *ServiceConfig* object, and this object is passed as a parameter to the *Enter* method of the *ServiceDomain* class. In this case, one additional property is set on the *ServiceConfig* class. This *Transaction* property specifies the type of transaction you want to use. These are the standard transaction options that have been used for some time now when developing applications that leverage COM+ distributed transactions. In most cases, the *TransactionOption.Required* enumeration value will suffice.

Next, note the execution of two different SQL statements. The first statement updates product prices in the Northwind database. The second statement takes the number of products that were updated and records this value in the audit table named PriceAudit.

Next, note the call to the *SetAbort* method of the *ContextUtil* object in the *Catch* portion of the *Try/Catch* exception handling block. By calling this method in the case of an exception, both the modifications of the INSERT and UPDATE statements are rolled back. This rollback happens because both T-SQL statements are part of a distributed transaction. A distributed transaction is brought about by simply wrapping the two *ExecuteNonQuery* method calls in between the calls to the *Enter* and *Leave* methods of the *ServiceDomain* class.

Side-By-Side Execution

Side-by-side execution is the phrase used to describe the ability to install and use two distinct versions of .NET Framework on the same machine. Currently, only two distinct versions exist, .NET Framework versions 1.0 and 1.1. When both versions are installed simultaneously on the same machine, it is important to understand the effect this has on .NET applications already installed on the machine.

Windows Forms Applications

The first rule to remember is that a Windows Forms application compiled against .NET Framework version 1.0 will *float up* to run against .NET Framework version 1.1 if version 1.0 isn't present. While this behavior can be modified through the use of configuration files, note that this is the standard default behavior for Windows Forms applications. However, applications built with Visual Studio .NET 2002 and compiled against .NET Framework 1.0 assemblies will choose to run against the .NET Framework 1.0 if both versions of the framework are present on a machine. The floating-up behavior occurs if only .NET Framework 1.1 is present. This means that if a version 1.0 application is moved to or installed on a machine that contains only .NET Framework 1.1, the application attempts to execute against the 1.1 version of Framework without any prompt or notification that it is doing so.

If you want to change this default behavior, the first step you need to take is to create a configuration file. Visual Studio .NET 2003 makes it easy to create configuration files for this purpose.

Simply access your project's Property Pages dialog box and choose the Build property page, as shown in Figure 1-9.

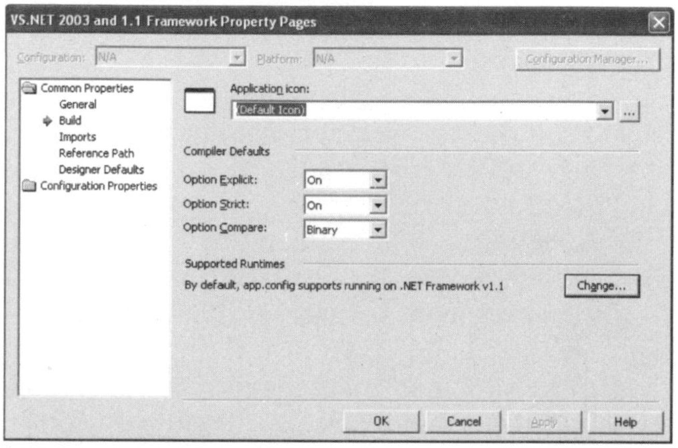

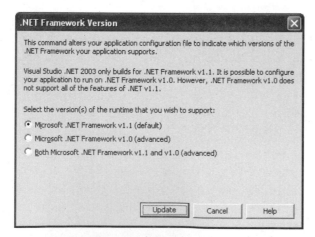

Figure 1-9 Build properties.

Then click the Change button. You'll see a dialog box like the one shown in Figure 1-10.

.NET Framework Version

This command alters your application configuration file to indicate which versions of the .NET Framework your application supports.

Visual Studio .NET 2003 only builds for .NET Framework v1.1. It is possible to configure your application to run on .NET Framework v1.0. However, .NET Framework v1.0 does not support all of the features of .NET v1.1.

Select the version(s) of the runtime that you wish to support:

- Microsoft .NET Framework v1.1 (default)
- Microsoft .NET Framework v1.0 (advanced)
- Both Microsoft .NET Framework v1.1 and v1.0 (advanced)

Update   Cancel   Help

Figure 1-10 Choosing a framework version.

In the dialog box shown in Figure 1-10, you can choose from three different options for creating configuration files. You can create a configuration file that causes your application to target only .NET Framework 1.1, a configuration file that causes your application to target both versions of the .NET Framework, or a configuration file that forces the application to run against version 1.0 only.

These configuration files give you the flexibility you need to ensure that your application runs against only the version of .NET Framework you intend it to be run against. However, you need to remember that the default behavior when a configuration file is not present is for your application to try to run against a later version of .NET Framework if the version the application targets is not available. Therefore, many times the best approach is to include a configuration file with your application. Doing so gives you control over which version of .NET Framework your application runs against. This configuration file should allow your application to run only against the .NET Framework versions you've done sufficient testing against with your application.

Additional Scenarios

Table 1-2 details some interesting implications of side-by-side execution for Windows Forms applications.

Table 1-2 Side-By-Side Execution and Windows Forms Applications

Application Compiled Against	Machine Configuration	Result	Messages
.NET Framework 1.0	.NET Framework 1.1 only	Application runs against .NET Framework 1.1.	No notification is given that the application is running against .NET Framework 1.1 assemblies.
.NET Framework 1.0	1.0 Framework and 1.1 Framework Installed	Application runs against the 1.0 Framework.	No notification is given that the application is running against .NET Framework 1.0 assemblies.
.NET Framework 1.1	.NET Framework 1.0 only	Application runs against .NET Framework 1.0 if a configuration file is present that redirects the application to use .NET Framework 1.0.	An error message is raised if the configuration file is not present at first execution of the application. The application fails to execute.

ASP.NET Applications

ASP.NET applications have a slightly different set of rules than Windows Forms applications. Because all your ASP.NET applications run from the single instance of Internet Information Server (IIS) installed on the local machine when the .NET Framework 1.1 is installed, all the Web sites are upgraded to use the .NET Framework 1.1 by default. This is because the default Web site is upgraded to version 1.1. Because all the other Web sites inherit from the default Web site, they are then upgraded to run against version 1.1 as well. If you want to change the version of .NET Framework your Web site is running against, you need to use the *aspnet_regiis* utility:

```
aspnet_regiis -s w3svc/1/root/MyWebApp
```

This example changes the Web site MyWebApp so that it runs against the .NET Framework 1.0 assemblies. The *aspnet_regiis* application is .NET Framework specific, and one is included with each version of .NET Framework. To have a Web site target a given .NET Framework version, you merely run the command just shown with the version of the *aspnet_regiis* application that matches the version of .NET Framework you want a given site to run against. You can find *aspnet_regiis* in the C:\%SystemRoot%\Microsoft.NET\Framework\%FrameworkVer% directory.

Finally, if you are installing .NET Framework version 1.1 by itself, you can also use the following command-line switch to prevent the upgrade of ASP.NET applications to 1.1:

```
dotnetfx.exe /q:a /c:"install /noaspupgrade /l /q"
```

No-Touch Deployment

No-Touch deployment refers to running a Windows Forms application from a URL. By executing a Windows Forms application from a URL, you can gain ease of deployment and still retain the rich user interface people have come to expect from Windows Forms applications. While the purpose here is not to rehash issues surrounding the implementation of a No-Touch application deployment as a whole, it's important to touch on the impact of side-by-side .NET Framework installations when you are using this deployment strategy.

Fundamentally, the issues that affect a No-Touch deployed application are the same as those that affect applications that are deployed via more traditional means. Therefore a configuration file must be present in a given side-by-side scenario for an application to succesfully execute. For example, if a Windows Forms application is compiled against the 1.1 Framework assemblies and is placed on a Web server for clients to retrieve, what happens if a client machine only has the .NET Framework 1.0? The answer is the application fails to execute. This result is exactly what one would expect if a locally installed copy of the application was being executed.

What makes No-Touch applications different is that by default ASP.NET applications do not allow configuration files to be accessed from client machines. Specifically the serving of files with a .config extension is prohibited.

Therefore, you must configure a Web site to allow clients to download configuration files so that machines that don't have .NET Framework 1.1 and have only .NET Framework 1.0 can succesfully run your application. You could also choose not to deploy the No-Touch application to these machines until they have been upgraded to .NET Framework 1.1. Or you could choose to create an additional copy of your application that has been tested and compiled against .NET Framework 1.0 and install it on machines that have only .NET Framework 1.0 installed. However, the point to remember is that the issue of having to have the appropriate configuration file present on the client machine does not go away in a No-Touch deployment scenario.

Components

I've saved the discussion of components for last because, honestly, there isn't anything you can do to change the default behavior of a given component. Components associated with a given application run against the .NET Framework version chosen by the application. There is no configuration file you can create for a component that ensures it runs against a given version—and only that version—of .NET Framework. This means you have to take special care to inform users of your component what framework versions it has been tested against. You also have to take considerable care when leveraging features found only in version 1.1. If a 1.0 Windows Forms application attempts to use a component that was originally compiled against version 1.1, and this component leverages features found only in .NET Framework 1.1, serious problems could arise from the use of the component. At best, a simple error message is raised and certain features are disabled in the application. At worst, data corruption or inconsistent application behavior occurs. It all depends on how your component was constructed, whether it was leveraging functionality found only in .NET Framework version 1.1, and so on.

Until configuration files exist for components, the safest approach when you don't have compete control over the .NET Framework versions installed on a client is to compile against the earliest version of .NET Framework your client base could have.

Framework Configuration

.NET Framework version 1.0 installs a Framework Configuration tool that can be found by opening Administrative Tools in the Control Panel. With the release of version 1.1, there are now two different .NET Framework configuration tools you need to use. One targets .NET Framework 1.0, and the other targets .NET Framework 1.1. Functionality between the two is identical, and if you're familiar with setting configuration settings using the .NET Framework 1.0 tool, you should find no challenges in using the .NET Framework 1.1 tool.

Language Changes

Compared to the sweeping changes to the Visual Basic language brought about by the first release of the .NET Framework, the changes to version 1.1, although beneficial, are minor. There are two changes: an easier way to declare a loop variable, and the use of BitShift operators.

Loop Variable Declaration

In Visual Basic .NET, you can now easily declare a loop variable as part of a *For* or *For Each* loop. This makes coding *For Each* loops much easier, as you don't have to declare the variable before entering the *For Each* loop. Here's an example:

```
Dim sqlDA As New SqlDataAdapter( _
    "select firstname, lastname from employees", scnnNorthwind)
Dim dsEmployees As New DataSet
sqlDA.Fill(dsEmployees)

Dim sb As New StringBuilder
Dim fullName As String

For Each dr As DataRow In dsEmployees.Tables(0).Rows
    fullName = CStr(dr("FirstName")) & " " & CStr(dr("LastName"))
    sb.Append(fullName & vbCrLf)
Next

MsgBox(sb.ToString(), MsgBoxStyle.OKOnly, "Northwind Employees")
```

Note that in this example, the variable named *dr* is not declared as being of type *DataRow* except within the declaration of the *For Each* loop itself. If you attempt to write this exact code and compile it against .NET Framework 1.0, you would recieve a compile error. To fix the error, you would have to declare the variable named *dr* and specify its type as *DataRow* before declaring the *For Each* loop.

Here's an example of the appropriate syntax for the .NET Framework 1.0:

```
Dim sqlDA As New SqlDataAdapter( _
    "select firstname, lastname from employees", scnnNorthwind)
Dim dsEmployees As New DataSet
sqlDA.Fill(dsEmployees)

Dim sb As New StringBuilder
Dim fullName As String
Dim dr as DataRow
```

```
For Each dr In dsEmployees.Tables(0).Rows
    fullName = CStr(dr("FirstName")) & " " & CStr(dr("LastName"))
    sb.Append(fullName & vbCrLf)
Next

MsgBox(sb.ToString(), MsgBoxStyle.OKOnly, "Northwind Employees")
```

Simply put, Visual Basic .NET's new loop-variable declaration feature just makes your life a bit easier when writing *For* and *For Each* loops.

BitShift Operators

Visual Basic .NET now supports BitShift operators. So now you can write statements such as the following:

```
Dim i1 as Integer = 1
Dim i2 as Integer

i2 = i1 << 2 'i2 would equal 4
i2 = i1 << 4 'i2 would equal 16

Dim i3 as Integer = 16
Dim i4 as Integer

i4 = i3 >> 2 'i4 would equal 4
i4 = i3 >> 4 'i4 would equal 1

Dim i5 as Integer = 23334
Dim i6 as Integer

i6 = i5 << 4 'i6 would equal 373344
```

Additional Framework Changes

While some of the most significant .NET Framework and tool changes have already been detailed, there are a few more changes of interest in version 1.1. What follows is not an exhaustive list of changes by any means, but merely changes that might be of most interest to the majority of developers.

The ODBC Namespace

The Open Database Connectivity (ODBC) data provider is now included in .NET Framework 1.1. While not entirely new—as it has been available as a separate download for some time—it's now included in the .NET Framework 1.1 installation. The ODBC namespace gives .NET Framework applications more ability to consume data from additional legacy data sources such as mainframes.

Enabling Windows XP Theme Support

One of the sample applications in this book covers how to support Microsoft Windows XP themes in such a way that your application can be used on machines whether they have only version 1.0 or both .NET Framework 1.0 and .NET Framework 1.1 installed. However, if you're sure that all machines you will deploy have version 1.1 installed, you can enable Windows XP theme support in a much easier way than the use of the manifest files detailed in the sample application.

The .NET Framework 1.1 *Application* object contains a method not found in the *Application* object found in version 1.0. This additional method is named *EnableVisualStyles*. Calling this method at the proper place in your application enables Windows XP theme support for your application.

To use the *EnableVisualStyles* method appropriately, your Windows Forms application needs to call the method before calling the *InitializeComponent* method.

Note that all the standard rules apply for Windows XP theme support. The need to set the flat-style property for some controls and the fact that some controls still do not support Windows XP theming is still true even with the use of the *EnableVisualStyles* method. For details on these additional restrictions, turn to Chapter 4 and see Application #43: XP Theme Support.

Folder Browser

The folder browser is not exactly a new control, but being able to get to it easily from managed code is what has changed with the release of .NET Framework 1.1.

The folder browser is now available through the toolbox in Visual Studio .NET 2003. It can also be easily displayed by instantiating the control in code:

```
Dim fldBrwse As New FolderBrowserDialog
fldBrwse.Description = "The New Folder Browser Control"
fldBrwse.ShowNewFolderButton = True
fldBrwse.RootFolder = Environment.SpecialFolder.MyComputer
If fldBrwse.ShowDialog() = DialogResult.OK Then
    MsgBox("You selected: ", _
        fldBrwse.SelectedPath, _
        MsgBoxStyle.OKOnly, Me.Text)
End If
```

Working with the folder browser control is similiar to working with the *OpenFileDialog* or *SaveFileDialog* controls. First you create an instance of the control. Next, you specify the default properties you want. In this case, a description is set for the dialog box, the new folder button is enabled, and the dialog box's default location is set to the *MyComputer* location through use of the *RootFolder* property.

The dialog box is then shown to the user by calling the *ShowDialog* method. The return value of this method call is of type *DialogResult*. In this case, if the return value is equal to *DialogResult.OK*, the folder the user selected is displayed in a Message Box.

SpecialFolder Enumeration

.NET Framework 1.0 provided easy access to special folder locations—for example, accessing the Desktop folder with an enumeration named *Special-Folder*. The paths for these folders can be obtained by calling the *GetFolderPath* method of the *Environment* class and passing as a parameter to this method call one of the *SpecialFolder* enumerations, as shown here:

```
MsgBox(System.Environment.GetFolderPath _
    (Environment.SpecialFolder.Desktop), _
    MsgBoxStyle.OKOnly, Me.Text)
```

.NET Framework 1.1 extends this ability by adding two more folders to the *SpecialFolder* enumeration. The first is *MyMusic*, and the second is *MyPictures*.

```
MsgBox(System.Environment.GetFolderPath _
    (Environment.SpecialFolder.MyMusic), _
    MsgBoxStyle.OKOnly, Me.Text)

MsgBox(System.Environment.GetFolderPath _
    (Environment.SpecialFolder.MyPictures), _
    MsgBoxStyle.OKOnly, Me.Text)
```

As you can see in this code, the *MyPictures* and *MyMusic* folders can be easily retrieved by passing the appropriate enumeration to the *GetFolderPath* method of the *Environment* class.

System.IO

Another useful change is the ability to get and set UTC datetimes for files and directories. The following code illustrates how this is accomplished with the *File* and *Directory* classes found in .NET Framework 1.1.

```
Dim msg As String
msg = "UTC Creation Time: " & _
    CStr(File.GetCreationTimeUtc("..\ReadMe.htm")) & vbCrLf
msg &= "UTC Write Time: " & _
    CStr(File.GetLastWriteTimeUtc("..\Readme.htm")) & vbCrLf
```

(continued)

```
MsgBox(msg, MsgBoxStyle.OKOnly, Me.Text)
Dim msg As String
msg = "UTC Creation Time: " & _
    CStr(Directory.GetCreationTimeUtc("..\ReadMe.htm")) & vbCrLf
msg &= "UTC Write Time: " & _
    CStr(Directory.GetLastWriteTimeUtc("..\Readme.htm")) & vbCrLf
MsgBox(msg, MsgBoxStyle.OKOnly, Me.Text)
```

Conclusion

The .NET Framework 1.1 and Visual Studio .NET 2003 contain a moderate number of enhancements over their predecessors. Considering the incremental nature of the release, it would be unreasonable to expect more changes to the framework and Visual Studio .NET. Taken as a whole, the changes that were made are a nice, solid set of enhancements to the framework and development tools. I've found each one of the enhancements to be useful in a variety of cases in my development projects.

The remainder of the book introduces you to the 101 sample applications that shipped with this book. You'll find versions of the samples built for .NET Framework 1.0 and Visual Studio .NET 2002 as well as .NET Framework version 1.1 and Visual Studio .NET 2003. I encourage you to work with both versions of the sample code. You'll probably find that your development machines contain both frameworks. Knowledge of the differences between .NET Framework version 1.0 and version 1.1 will be a good skill to have moving forward as you do more .NET Framework development.

2

Working with the Microsoft Visual Basic .NET Language

Visual Basic .NET is a significant enhancement over Visual Basic 6. For one thing, it is a truly object-oriented language. For another, it has the benefit of full access to the .NET Framework and its huge class library, reducing the amount of code you have to write.

The following applications illustrate many of the features of Visual Basic .NET that give you more power and convenience than ever before, including string manipulation, structured exception handling, walking the stack, working with text files, and a variety of other features.

Application #1: Use Arrays

This sample shows you how to create, search, and sort arrays. Arrays are commonly used for grouping similar items, such as employee names in a list. Arrays provide a convenient container in which to store items, and they make it easy to manipulate those items using a single set of code.

New Concepts

To create an array, you declare a variable with a number in parentheses after it—for example, *Dim Employees(4) As String*. This example creates an array that will hold not four but five *String* elements because .NET arrays are always zero-based. This means that the first element has an index of zero and the fifth element has an index of 4. You use the index to refer to a particular element, such as *Employees.GetValue(2)*.

You can find out how many elements are in an array with the *Length* property (*Employees.Length*), and the *GetUpperBound* method reveals the upper bound (the highest index) of the array *Employees.GetUpperBound(0)*.

> **Caution**   The upper bound of an array is always one less than the number of elements because the array is zero-based. Don't confuse the *Length* with the upper bound. The *Length* is the actual number of elements. The upper bound is the highest index.

You can also create and populate an array all at once, like this:

```
Dim Employees() As String = {"Andrew Fuller", "Nancy Davolio"}
```

Sometimes you don't know ahead of time how many elements you'll need in an array. For instance, you might be reading data from a database into an array and not know how many records there are. This situation is perfect for a dynamic array. You declare a dynamic array without an upper bound—for example, *Dim Employees()*. Later, when you know how big you need the array to be, you *ReDim* the array with the desired upper bound—for example, *ReDim Employees(4)*.

You can *ReDim* as many times as you care to—enlarging or shrinking the array even after it has data in it—but each time you do, the array gets released and re-created. If you want to keep the existing values when you *ReDim*, use the *Preserve* keyword—for example, *ReDim Preserve Employees(6)*.

A matrix array (also known as a rectangular array) has multiple dimensions, or *ranks*. You can think of a matrix array as a combination of rows and columns, like a spreadsheet. For example, an array of employee names might have a row for each employee and two columns, one for first names and one for last names.

To create a matrix array, you declare it with two upper bounds, one for each rank—for example, *Dim Employees(3,1) As String*. This matrix array has four rows and two columns. You access each element in the array by using a separate index for each rank—for example, *Employees.GetValue(2,0)* would access the element in row 3, column 1.

As with single-rank arrays, you can short-circuit the creation process by declaring and populating the array all at once, as in the following example.

Notice the comma between the parentheses to indicate two dimensions and the curly braces around each pair of array items and around the entire set.

```
Dim Employees(,) As String = {{"Fuller", "Andrew"}, {"Davolio", "Nancy"}}
```

You'll often want to sort your arrays, and the good news is that it's a piece of cake. Just use the following structure: *Array.Sort(Employees)*. *Sort* is a *Shared* method, which means you invoke it on the class itself (*Array*), not on an instance of the class (*Employees*). Figure 2-1 shows a before-and-after view of a sorted array.

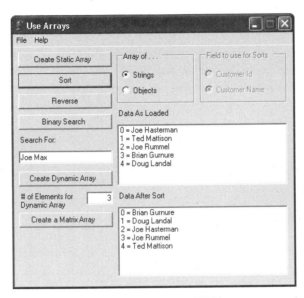

Figure 2-1   With Visual Basic .NET, it's easy to create, sort, and search arrays.

You'll need to sort your array if you want to search it because the items must be in sequence for the very efficient *BinarySearch* method to work. Be aware, however, that both *Sort* and *BinarySearch* work only with one-dimensional arrays.

Code Walkthrough

The sample application demonstrates the use of static arrays of value types and of object types as well as dynamic arrays. The sample also includes code for sorting and searching an array and for implementing matrix arrays.

Static Arrays of Value Types

To examine the concepts mentioned in the previous section in action, run the sample, select Strings from the Array Of group box, and click the Create Static Array button. The application creates an array of type *String* with five elements and displays the elements in the first list box on the form.

In this snippet from *btnCreateStatic_Click*, as the *peopleList* array is populated, its upper bound is automatically set to 4 because five names are passed to it.

```
Dim peopleList() As String = {"Joe Hasterman", "Ted Mattison", _
    "Joe Rummel", "Brian Gurnure", "Doug Landal"}
```

The contents of the array are displayed using the *DisplayArrayData* procedure, which adds each array element to a *ListBox* control. The heart of the display procedure is in the following three lines, in which the *GetValue* method retrieves the array element whose index is *i*, and returns it as a *String,* using the *ToString* method. The variable *i* is simply a counter, and *u* contains the array's upper bound, which was set earlier with the statement *Dim u As Integer = (arr.Length - 1)*.

```
For i = 0 To u
    lst.Items.Add(String.Format("{0} = {1}", i, _
        arr.GetValue(i).ToString()))
Next
```

Static Arrays of Object Types

Now click Objects in the Array Of group box and, once again, click the Create Static Array button. This time, the application creates an array of five *Customer* objects. The *Customer* class has a parameterized constructor, so we can pass data (in this case an *Id* and *Name*) to each new *Customer* instance as it is instantiated. Note that because this is an array of objects, you must instantiate each item with the *New* keyword.

```
Dim custData() As Customer = {New Customer(3423, "Joe Hasterman"), _
    New Customer(9348, "Ted Mattison"), New Customer(3581, _
    "Joe Rummel"), New Customer(7642, "Brian Gurnure"), _
    New Customer(2985, "Doug Landal")}
```

Once again, the application displays the contents of the array as strings. However, the *Customer* class has its own version of *ToString*, which formats and returns the *Id* and *Name* in a single string.

Dynamic Arrays

The *btnCreateDynamic_Click* event procedure demonstrates how to create a dynamic array: declare it, *ReDim* it, and populate it.

```
Dim dynamicData() As String
ReDim dynamicData(System.Convert.ToInt32(Me.txtLength.Text) - 1)
```

```
Dim i As Integer
For i = 0 To dynamicData.Length - 1
    dynamicData(i) = InputBox("Enter a string", i.ToString(), _
        "None " & i)
Next
```

Creating a dynamic array of objects is equally easy. In a loop, you instantiate new objects one by one, setting properties of each one as needed. In this example, the *Id* and *Name* properties are set for each new customer:

```
Dim dynamicData() As Customer
ReDim dynamicData(System.Convert.ToInt32(Me.txtLength.Text) - 1)

Dim i As Integer
For i = 0 To dynamicData.Length - 1
    dynamicData(i) = New Customer()
    dynamicData(i).Id = ((i + 1) * 10)
    dynamicData(i).Name = InputBox("Enter a string", ("Item " & _
        (i + 1)), ("None " & i + 1))
Next
```

Sorting an Array

As the *btnSort_Click* event procedure shows, you need just two lines of code to create and sort either a value-type array or an object-type array:

```
Dim peopleList() As String = {"Joe Hasterman", "Ted Mattison", "Joe Rummel", _
    "Brian Gurnure", "Doug Landal"}
Array.Sort(peopleList)
⋮
Dim custData() As Customer = {New Customer(3423, "Joe Hasterman"), _
    New Customer(9348, "Ted Mattison"), New Customer(3581, "Joe Rummel"), _
    New Customer(7642, "Brian Gurnure"), New Customer(2985, "Doug Landal")}
Array.Sort(custData)
```

If you take a look at the *Customer* class, you'll notice that right after the class declaration is the statement *Implements IComparable*. Because the class implements that interface and also has a *CompareTo* procedure, an array of *Customer* objects is both sortable and searchable. The class also has a mechanism for selecting which field to sort on, either *Name* or *ID*. If you're creating a class and want it to permit sorting, searching, or both, you need to follow this pattern.

Searching an Array

Finding an item in your array is slightly more challenging than sorting, but the very efficient *BinarySearch* method makes it almost a breeze. First, for the search to work correctly, the array must be sorted. Then you call the *Binary-Search* method as shown in the *btnBinarySearch_Click* event procedure. The method returns an *Integer* value that represents the position in the array where the item was found.

```
position = Array.BinarySearch(strData, strDataToFind)
If position >= 0 Then
    formattedMsg = String.Format("The value {0} was found in the array at " & _
        "position {1}.", dataToFind, position.ToString())
```

If the *BinarySearch* method doesn't find the search item, it returns a negative number that's the bitwise complement for the location where the item would have been if it existed. So a return value of -4 means that the item would have belonged at position 3 (the fourth element) if it actually existed. A return value of -6 would mean position 5 (the sixth element), and so on. To flip the negative number to its corresponding positive number, you use the *Not* operator.

```
Else
    Dim bWC As Integer = (Not position)
```

If the result of *Not* is zero, the item you didn't find would have been before the first item in the array if it existed. If the result is one greater than the upper bound of the array, the missing item would have been last in the array. If the result of *Not* is anything else, you can figure out which items it would have fitted between.

```
If bWC = 0 Then
    formattedMessage = String.Format("The value {0} was NOT found in " & _
        "the array. If it did exist it would be at position {1} " & _
        "before {2}", dataToFind, bWC.ToString(), peopleList(0))
ElseIf bWC = UBound(peopleList) + 1 Then
    formattedMessage = String.Format("The value {0} was NOT found in " & _
        "the array. If it did exist it would be at position {1} " & _
        "after {2}", dataToFind, bWC.ToString(), _
        peopleList(UBound(peopleList)))
Else
    formattedMessage = String.Format("The value {0} was NOT found in " & _
        "the array. If it did exist it would be at position {1} " & _
        "between {2} and {3}.", dataToFind, bWC.ToString(), _
        peopleList(bWC - 1), peopleList(bWC))
End If
End If
```

Matrix Arrays

Creating a matrix array (rectangular array) is simple, as you can see in the following *btnCreateMatrix_Click* event procedure:

```
Dim strMatrix(,) As String = {{"Bob", "Carol"}, {"Ted", "Alice"}, _
    {"Joe", "Lisa"}}
```

If you want to access all the values in a matrix array, you'll need two loops, one inside the other. The outer loop cycles through the rows, and the inner loop cycles through the columns. Note the use of *GetLength(n)* to retrieve the length of each dimension. Also note *GetValue(n, n)* to access each array element in turn.

```
For i = 0 To (arr.GetLength(0) - 1)
    For j = 0 To (arr.GetLength(1) - 1)
        lst.Items.Add(String.Format("({0}, {1}) = {2}", i, j, _
            arr.GetValue(i, j).ToString()))
    Next j
Next i
```

If you really have to, you can consider creating arrays with more than two dimensions, but be aware that managing such arrays is challenging.

Conclusion

Arrays make it simple to work with multiple objects as if they were a single object while allowing you easy access to the individual objects. .NET arrays make operations such as sorting and searching easy.

Application #2: Use *DateTimes*

This sample introduces you to most of the properties and methods of the *DateTime* and *TimeSpan* classes, and it allows you to work interactively with them.

New Concepts

The *DateTime* structure in .NET is different from the *Date* type in Visual Basic 6. Unlike the Visual Basic 6 *Date*, which was really a *Double* type in disguise, *DateTime* is a value type defined in the Microsoft Windows .NET Framework library and is available to all .NET languages. You can instantiate and initialize a *DateTime* class like this

```
Dim myDate As New DateTime (2004, 9, 15)
```

and it becomes September 15, 2004.

A *TimeSpan* object represents a period of time, measured in *ticks*, 100-nanosecond intervals. *TimeSpan* values can be positive or negative and can represent up to one day. The *TimeSpan* structure is useful for setting and manipulating periods such as time-out intervals or expiration times of cached items. *TimeSpan* structures can also be initialized like *DateTime* structures.

Code Walkthrough

This sample application illustrates the use of the *DateTime* and *TimeSpan* classes.

DateTime Shared Members

The shared *DateTime* properties and methods are demonstrated in the *Load-CalculationMethods* procedure. Shared properties include:

- **Now**   The current date and time as set on your system. Similar to the Visual Basic 6 function of the same name.

- **Today**   The current date as set on your system.

- **UtcNow**   The current date and time as set on your system, expressed as coordinated universal time (UTC), also known as Greenwich Mean Time.

- **MinValue**   The smallest possible value a *DateTime* can have.

- **MaxValue**   The largest possible value a *DateTime* can have.

```
lblNow.Text = DateTime.Now.ToString
lblToday.Text = DateTime.Today.ToString
lblUtcNow.Text = DateTime.UtcNow.ToString
lblMinValue.Text = DateTime.MinValue.ToString
lblMaxValue.Text = DateTime.MaxValue.ToString
```

Shared methods include:

- **DaysInMonth**   Given a year and month, returns the number of days in that month.

- **FromOADate**   Returns a *DateTime* value that corresponds to the provided Ole Automation Date, which is a floating-point number representing the number of days from midnight, December 30, 1899. Use this method to convert dates stored in Microsoft Excel—for example, to .NET *DateTime* format.

- **IsLeapYear**   Given a four-digit year, returns *True* if it is a leap year and *False* otherwise.

```
lblDaysInMonth.Text = DateTime.DaysInMonth( _
    CInt(txtYear.Text), CInt(txtMonth.Text)).ToString
lblFromOADate.Text = _
    DateTime.FromOADate(CDbl(txtFromOADate.Text)).ToString
lblIsLeapYear.Text = _
    DateTime.IsLeapYear(CInt(txtIsLeapYear.Text)).ToString
```

Figure 2-2 shows the wide variety of *DateTime* properties you can access.

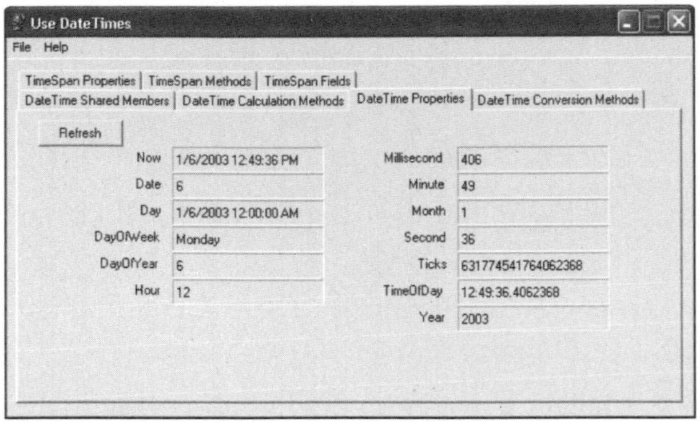

Figure 2-2   *DateTime* properties include just about any date-related or time-related information you might need.

DateTime Calculation Methods

DateTime instances permit a variety of calculations whose methods begin with *Add*. To subtract, simply pass a negative number as the parameter (or use the *Subtract* method). Most of the calculation methods are self-explanatory and most require a *Double* data type as a parameter, which means you can add or subtract fractional numbers—such as adding 1.5 hours to the current time. The exceptions are *AddMonths* and *AddYears*, which require *Integers*, and *AddTicks*, which accepts a *Long* value. (See the *LoadCalculationMethods* procedure for these examples.)

```
Dim dt As DateTime = DateTime.Now
lblNow3.Text = dt.ToString

lblAddDays.Text = dt.AddDays(CDbl(txtDays.Text)).ToString
lblAddHours.Text = dt.AddHours(CDbl(txtHours.Text)).ToString
lblAddMilliseconds.Text = _
    dt.AddMilliseconds(CDbl(txtMilliseconds.Text)).ToString
lblAddMinutes.Text = dt.AddMinutes(CDbl(txtMinutes.Text)).ToString
lblAddMonths.Text = dt.AddMonths(CInt(txtMonths.Text)).ToString
lblAddSeconds.Text = dt.AddSeconds(CDbl(txtSeconds.Text)).ToString
lblAddTicks.Text = dt.AddTicks(CLng(txtTicks.Text)).ToString
lblAddYears.Text = dt.AddYears(CInt(txtYears.Text)).ToString
```

DateTime Properties

In addition to the *DateTime* shared properties, you can access a number of useful properties specific to a particular *DateTime* instance: instance properties. First, you declare and assign a value to a *DateTime* variable, as shown in the following code, taken from the *LoadProperties* procedure in *frmMain*.

```
Dim dt As DateTime = DateTime.Now
```

Once you have the object variable, you can access a variety of properties, including the following ones. (See the *LoadProperties* procedure for implementation of these properties.)

■ **Date**   The date that *dt* contains.

■ **Day**   An integer between 1 and 31, representing the *dt* day of the month.

■ **DayOfWeek**   An enumerated constant that indicates the day of the week in the *dt* date, ranging from Sunday to Saturday.

■ **DayOfYear**   An integer between 1 and 366, representing the *dt* day of the year.

■ **Hour**   An integer between 0 and 23, representing the *dt* hour of day.

■ **Millisecond**   An integer between 0 and 999, representing the millisecond of the *dt* time.

■ **Minute**   An integer between 0 and 59, representing the minute of the *dt* time.

■ **Month**   An integer between 1 and 12, representing the *dt* month of the year.

■ **Second**   An integer between 0 and 59, representing the second of the *dt* time.

■ **Ticks**   A *Long* containing the number of *Ticks* in the *dt* date and time, counting from 12:00 A.M., January 1, 0001. A *Tick* is a 100-nanosecond period of time.

■ **TimeOfDay**   A *TimeSpan* that represents the fraction of the day between midnight and the *dt* time.

■ **Year**   An integer that represents *dt* year, between 1 and 9999.

DateTime Conversion Methods

Various instance methods let you convert *DateTime* instances. For example, you might have data gathered from a Web service using Coordinated Universal Time (UTC) and find that you need to convert to local time. These *Date/Time* conversion methods, demonstrated in the *LoadConversionMethods* procedure, provide just the capability you need:

■ **ToFileTime**   A system file time is a *Long* representing a date and time as 100-nanosecond intervals since January 1, 1601, 12:00 A.M.

■ **ToLocalTime**   Assumes that the parameter passed to it represents UTC time, and returns a *DateTime*, converted to local time, allowing for daylight savings time. The opposite of *ToUniversalTime*.

- ***ToLongDateString***   If the current culture is us-EN, returns a *String* with the date in the form: Monday, November 15, 2004. The format of the string varies depending on the current culture.

- ***ToLongTimeString***   If the current culture is us-EN, returns a *String* with the time in the form: 5:03:29 PM. The format of the string varies depending on the current culture.

- ***ToOADate***   Converts a *DateTime* to its OLE Automation date equivalent.

- ***ToShortDateString***   If the current culture is us-EN, returns a *String* with the date in the form: 11/15/2004. The format of the string varies depending on the current culture.

- ***ToShortTimeString***   If the current culture is us-EN, returns a *String* with the time in the form: 5:03:29 PM. The format of the string varies depending on the current culture.

- ***ToString***   Presents the *DateTime* value as a string, with many formatting choices.

- ***ToUniversalTime***   Assumes that the parameter passed to it represents local time, and returns a *DateTime*, converted to UTC time. The opposite of *ToLocalTime*.

Here is how these properties are accessed in the *LoadConversionMethods* procedure:

```
Dim dt As DateTime = DateTime.Now

lblNow2.Text = dt.ToString
lblToFileTime.Text = dt.ToFileTime.ToString
lblToLocalTime.Text = dt.ToLocalTime.ToString
lblToLongDateString.Text = dt.ToLongDateString
lblToLongTimeString.Text = dt.ToLongTimeString
lblToOADate.Text = dt.ToOADate.ToString
lblToShortDateString.Text = dt.ToShortDateString
lblToShortTimeString.Text = dt.ToShortTimeString
lblToString.Text = dt.ToString
lblToUniversalTime.Text = dt.ToUniversalTime.ToString
```

TimeSpan Properties

In the *btnRefreshTSProperties_Click* procedure, you establish a *TimeSpan* by subtracting a beginning *DateTime* from an end *DateTime*. The *Duration* method returns an absolute value for the *TimeSpan*, even if its value had been negative.

```
Dim ts As TimeSpan
Dim dtStart As DateTime
Dim dtEnd As DateTime
```

(continued)

```
' Parse the text from the text boxes.
dtStart = DateTime.Parse(txtStart.Text)
dtEnd = DateTime.Parse(txtEnd.Text)
ts = dtEnd.Subtract(dtStart).Duration
```

You can also create a *TimeSpan* from raw text, like "5.10:27:34.17". The *TimeSpan Parse* method interprets this as "5 days, 10 hours, 27 minutes, 34 seconds and 17 fractions of a second." See the *btnCalcParse_Click* procedure for a demonstration of the *Parse* method.

You can access the properties of *TimeSpan* as demonstrated in the *Display-TSProperties* procedure, which dissects and displays the individual parts of the *TimeSpan*. The property names are self-explanatory.

```
lblDays.Text = ts.Days.ToString
lblHours.Text = ts.Hours.ToString
lblMilliseconds.Text = ts.Milliseconds.ToString
lblMinutes.Text = ts.Minutes.ToString
lblSeconds.Text = ts.Seconds.ToString
lblTimeSpanTicks.Text = ts.Ticks.ToString
lblTotalDays.Text = ts.TotalDays.ToString
lblTotalHours.Text = ts.TotalHours.ToString
lblTotalMilliseconds.Text = ts.TotalMilliseconds.ToString
lblTotalMinutes.Text = ts.TotalMinutes.ToString
lblTotalSeconds.Text = ts.TotalSeconds.ToString
```

TimeSpan Methods

Most *TimeSpan* methods are shared methods. Those illustrated in the *LoadTS-Methods* procedure are among them. They each produce a *TimeSpan* from a *Double* (except *FromTicks*, which accepts a *Long*). This allows you to accept a value from a user or use the output of a previous operation, and it allows you to turn the value in that string into a *TimeSpan* object representing that value. For example, *FromDays* will produce a *TimeSpan* based on the number of days passed to it. *FromHours* turns a number into a *TimeSpan* with that many hours, and so on.

```
lblFromDays.Text = TimeSpan.FromDays(CDbl(txtFromDays.Text)).ToString
lblFromHours.Text = TimeSpan.FromHours(CDbl(txtFromHours.Text)).ToString
lblFromMilliseconds.Text = _
    TimeSpan.FromMilliseconds(CDbl(txtFromMilliseconds.Text)).ToString
lblFromMinutes.Text = _
    TimeSpan.FromMinutes(CDbl(txtFromMinutes.Text)).ToString
lblFromSeconds.Text = _
    TimeSpan.FromSeconds(CDbl(txtFromSeconds.Text)).ToString
lblFromTicks.Text = TimeSpan.FromTicks(CLng(txtFromTicks.Text)).ToString
```

TimeSpan Fields

The fields of a *TimeSpan* are all either read-only or constants. *MinValue* and *MaxValue* represent the smallest and largest values, respectively, that a

TimeSpan can hold, and they're read-only. All the fields beginning that start with *TicksPer* are constants representing the number of ticks in a given period of time. The *Zero* field is a constant intended to give you a convenient source for 0 in time calculations. Examples are:

```
lblMaxValueTS.Text = TimeSpan.MaxValue.ToString
lblMinValueTS.Text = TimeSpan.MinValue.ToString
lblTicksPerDay.Text = TimeSpan.TicksPerDay.ToString
lblTicksPerHour.Text = TimeSpan.TicksPerHour.ToString
lblTicksPerMillisecond.Text = TimeSpan.TicksPerMillisecond.ToString
lblTicksPerMinute.Text = TimeSpan.TicksPerMinute.ToString
lblTicksPerSecond.Text = TimeSpan.TicksPerSecond.ToString
lblZero.Text = TimeSpan.Zero.ToString
```

Conclusion

In this sample application you've seen that working with dates and times is greatly simplified in the .NET environment. Adding and subtracting days, hours, minutes, and so on, is intuitive and easy to do. *DateTime* has a number of other methods, such as *Compare*, which accepts two *DateTime* instances and returns a value indicating whether they are equal, whether one is greater than the other, and so on. You've also seen that working with time intervals for timeouts and expiration times is convenient with the new *TimeSpan* structure.

Application #3: String Manipulation

This sample demonstrates many methods of the Visual Basic .NET *String* class. The sample form divides the methods into three groups: methods that return strings (such as *Insert* and *Remove*), methods that return information (such as *IndexOf*), and shared methods (such as *String.Format*). In addition, the demonstration introduces two other useful string handling classes: *StringBuilder* and *StringWriter*.

New Concepts

The *String* class, part of the *System* namespace, provides the data type for all strings. A *String* object is truly an object: it's allocated on the heap like all other objects, and it's subject to garbage collection. The *String* class offers a variety of methods for string manipulation, comparison, formatting, and so forth. Characters in a *String* object are always Unicode.

String manipulation is one of the most expensive operations you can perform, in terms of system resources. This is even more true in .NET, where all strings are immutable—that is, once you create a string, you can't add to it, subtract from it, or change its value in any way. When you append a string to another, for example, the .NET runtime actually creates a new string with the old and new strings combined, and then it makes the original string available for garbage collection.

To the rescue comes the *StringBuilder* class, which is not a string but an object in its own right. It has a special internal buffer for manipulating a string far more quickly and efficiently than you could do otherwise. *StringBuilder* is most useful when you need to do repeated or large-scale manipulating of strings. It has methods for inserting, appending, removing, and replacing strings—and when you're done, you extract the result with the *ToString* method. *StringBuilder* is part of the *System.Text* namespace.

The *StringWriter* class is an implementation of the abstract *TextWriter* class, and its purpose is to write sequential character information to a string. It writes (under the hood) to an underlying *StringBuilder* object, which can already exist or be created automatically when the *StringWriter* is initialized. With a *StringWriter*, you have, in effect, an in-memory file to which you can write at will. *StringWriter* belongs to the *System.IO* namespace. Figure 2-3 shows the String Manipulation sample application in action.

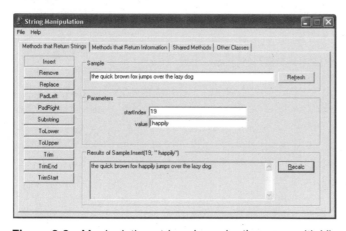

Figure 2-3   Manipulating strings is easier than ever with Visual Basic .NET.

Code Walkthrough

For clarity in this walkthrough, we'll present the code slightly modified to show the actual strings and numbers being passed as parameters, rather than the code's *CInt(strParam1), strParam2,* and so forth. We'll examine each method in the sequence presented on the form's tabs. Unless we say otherwise, the original sample string is "the quick brown fox jumps over the lazy dog". Keep in mind that the indexes used are zero-based.

Methods that Return Strings

Some methods of the *String* class return a string. These methods are:

- *Insert*   To insert one string into another, use the *String* class *Insert* method, specifying where to insert and what to insert. (In this case, insert the phrase " happily"—note the space—at index 19.) *Result below*: "the quick brown fox happily jumps over the lazy dog".

  ```
  txtResults.Text = sampleString.Insert(19, " happily")
  ```

- *Remove*   To remove a string from within another, use the *Remove* method, specifying the start point for removal and how many characters to remove. (In this case, remove 6 characters beginning at index 10.) *Result below*: "the quick fox jumps over the lazy dog".

  ```
  txtResults.Text = sampleString.Remove(10, 6)
  ```

- *Replace*   To replace a part of a string with some other string use the *Replace* method, providing the old value and the new. *Result below*: "the quick brown fox leaps over the lazy dog".

  ```
  txtResults.Text = sampleString.Replace("jumps", "leaps")
  ```

- *PadLeft/PadRight*   Sometimes you want to pad a string, ensuring that it's at least *n* characters long. The *PadLeft* method lets you pick a character and use it to pad your string. If you don't provide a padding character, it defaults to the space character. *PadRight* is just like *PadLeft*, except that the padding characters are added to the end of the string. *Original*: "123.45", *Result 1*: "   123.45", *Result 2*: "$$$123.45".

  ```
  txtResults.Text = sampleString.PadLeft(10)
  txtResults.Text = sampleString.PadLeft(10, "$")
  ```

- *Substring*   This method is similar to the old Visual Basic 6 favorite *Mid*. It lets you extract a portion of a string. You provide a start index and specify how many characters you want. If you don't specify a length, *Substring* returns all remaining characters. But be careful: whereas the *Mid* index starts at one, the *Substring* index, like everything else in .NET, is zero-based. *Result 1 below*: "own fox jumps over the lazy dog". *Result 2*: "own f".

  ```
  txtResults.Text = sampleString.Substring(12)
  txtResults.Text = sampleString.Substring(12, 5)
  ```

■ ***ToLower/ToUpper***   To transform a string to lowercase or upper-case, invoke the *ToLower* or *ToUpper* method, neither of which takes any parameters. *Original*: "This Sample has SOME mixed-CASE Text!", *Result 1 below*: "this sample has some mixed-case text", *Result 2*: "THIS SAMPLE HAS SOME MIXED-CASE TEXT!".

```
txtResults.Text = sampleString.ToLower
txtResults.Text = sampleString.ToUpper
```

■ ***Trim***   One of the best things you can do when you accept input from a user is to trim it, removing unintended white space at the beginning and end of the input. The *Trim* method lets you do that and more: it lets you provide an array of characters to be removed. *Original*: " the quick brown fox jumped over the lazy dog ". *Result 1*: "the quick brown fox jumps over the lazy dog". *Result 2*: " quick brown fox jumps over the lazy ". Note that in the second example the characters to be removed include both letters and a space. Also note that the characters must be submitted as a character array.

```
txtResults.Text = sampleString.Trim()
txtResults.Text = sampleString.Trim("the dog".ToCharArray())
```

■ ***TrimEnd/TrimStart***   These are just like *Trim*, except they work on the end and start of the string, respectively.

Methods that Return Information

The *String* class has a number of methods that help you get information about a string, including:

■ ***IndexOf***   If you need to find the location of a character or string within another string, *IndexOf* does the job. It also lets you choose where to start looking and how many positions to examine. It returns the index of the found item if it succeeds, or -1 if it fails. *Example 1 below*: Find "brown" beginning at index 4, and examine 20 characters. *Result 1*: 10. *Example 2*: Find "brown" beginning at index 4, examining all remaining characters. *Result 2*: 10. *Example 3*: Find "brown" anywhere in the string. *Result 3*: 10.

```
txtResults.Text = sampleString.IndexOf("brown", 4, 20).ToString
txtResults.Text = sampleString.IndexOf("brown", 4).ToString
txtResults.Text = sampleString.IndexOf("brown").ToString
```

■ ***IndexOfAny***   Let's imagine that you want to locate any one of a series of characters in a string, and you just need to know the first spot where any of them occurs. You'd use the *IndexOfAny* method in much the same way as you use *IndexOf* except that you pass a character array as the first parameter. Each of the following code snippets will return 7 as the index where one of the letters "a," "b," or "c" was found.

```
txtResults.Text = _
    sampleString.IndexOfAny("abc".ToCharArray, 4, 12).ToString
txtResults.Text = _
    sampleString.IndexOfAny("abc".ToCharArray, 4).ToString
txtResults.Text = _
    sampleString.IndexOfAny("abc".ToCharArray).ToString
```

■ ***LastIndexOf/LastIndexOfAny***   These methods are like *IndexOf* and *IndexOfAny*, but they report on the last occurrence of a string or character instead of the first.

■ ***StartsWith/EndsWith***   These methods return *True* or *False* if the target string starts or ends with a specified string. The comparison is case-sensitive. The following example returns *False* because "The qui" doesn't match "the qui".

```
txtResults.Text = sampleString.StartsWith("The qui").ToString
```

■ ***Split***   This method is handy for taking a string and slicing it into substrings based on one or more separators you provide. It returns an array containing the separated substrings. The first argument for *Split* is an array of separator characters, and the optional second argument is the maximum number of substrings you want. If you pass an empty string for the first parameter, *Split* will use white-space characters as separators. *Result 1 below*: An array containing "the qui", "k", "rown fox jumps over the l", "zy dog". *Result 2*: An array containing "the qui", "k", "rown fox jumps over the lazy dog".

```
Results = sampleString.Split("abc".ToCharArray)
Results = sampleString.Split("abc".ToCharArray, 3)
```

Shared Methods

In all the previous examples, a method was invoked on an instance of a string, *sampleString*. In these examples, we're demonstrating shared methods, which are methods that don't need an instance of a string but are invoked on the *String* class itself.

■ ***Compare***   When you want to compare two strings, the *Compare* method offers a variety of ways to do it. In addition to specifying the two strings to be compared, you can optionally specify whether to ignore case, where to start comparing, how many characters to compare, and which culture information to use. *Compare* returns a negative number if string A is less than string B, a positive number if it's the other way around, and a zero if they're equal. The comparison is lexical and takes into account the current culture. An uppercase "A" is considered greater than a lowercase "a". *Result 1 below*: (ignores case): 0. *Result 2*: (uses default case sensitivity): 1.

```
txtResults.Text = String.Compare("This is a test", _
    "this is a test", True).ToString
txtResults.Text = String.Compare("This is a test", _
    "this is a test").ToString
```

- **CompareOrdinal** This method does its comparison checking without considering the local culture. It's actually considerably faster than *Compare* because it doesn't have to translate each character to a number representing the character's position in the local alphabet. Like *Compare*, it allows comparison of substrings but has no other overloads. *Result below*: -32, because an uppercase "T" is lower in the ASCII collating sequence than a lowercase "t".

```
txtResults.Text = String.CompareOrdinal("This is a test", _
    "this is a test").ToString
```

- **Concat** You can concatenate up to four strings with the *Concat* method, which also lets you pass it objects and *ParamArrays* of objects or strings. *Result below*: "This is a test of how this works when you concatenate".

```
txtResults.Text = String.Concat("This is a test",
    " of how this works", " when you concatenate").ToString
```

- **Format** The *Format* method lets you apply a variety of standard and custom formats to strings, numbers, dates, times, and enumerations. The items in curly braces in the following code are replaceable parameters, which will be filled by 12 and 17.35, respectively. The first item, "{0:N0}", means "display item zero as a number with zero decimal places." The second item, "{1:C}", means "display item one as currency." The *Format* method has several other numeric format specifiers, including: d (decimal), f (fixed), as well as date/time specifiers, like d (short date). You can also specify your own custom formats. *Result below*: "Your 12 items total $17.35.".

```
txtResults.Text = _
    String.Format("Your {0:N0} items total {1:C}.", 12, 17.35)
```

■ *Join*   When you have an array that you want to convert into a single string, *Join* fills the bill. It lets you specify a separator character between the joined elements. *Result below*: "item1/item2/item3/ item4".

```
Dim values() As String
values = "item1,item2,item3,item4".Split(", ".ToCharArray)
txtResults.Text = String.Join("/", astrValues)
```

The *StringBuilder* Class

As we mentioned earlier, the *StringBuilder* class streamlines your string handling. In the following example, we insert a new word at index 19, take out six characters beginning at index 10, replace one word with another, and add a string to the end of the original one. *StringBuilder* has an *Append* method, but because we want to format the number of minutes, we use the *AppendFormat* method, which mimics the *Format* method of the *String* class.

```
Dim sb As New StringBuilder("The quick brown fox jumps over the lazy dog")
sb.Insert(19, " happily")
sb.Remove(10, 6)
sb.Replace("jumps", "leaps")
sb.AppendFormat(" {0} times in {1:N1} minutes", 17, 2)
```

Now if you wanted to add a comma after the word "dog," you would first need to locate the word and then insert a comma after it. *IndexOf* would be perfect for locating "dog," but unfortunately *StringBuilder* doesn't have an *IndexOf* method. Your solution: use *ToString* to get a copy of the string from *StringBuilder*, use *IndexOf* to locate the position of "dog," and then use the *StringBuilder Insert* method to put the comma where you want it in the original string. Once you're done, you extract the final string from *StringBuilder* with the *ToString* method.

```
Dim position As Integer
position = sb.ToString.IndexOf("dog")
If position > 0 Then
    ' Insert the comma at the position
    ' you found + the length of the text "dog".
    sb.Insert(position + "dog".Length, ", ")
End If
txtResultsOther.AppendText("StringBuilder output: " & sb.ToString)
```

The same actions using the *String* class would look like the following code. Note that this code causes the .NET runtime to create a new string five separate times.

```
Dim sampleString As String = "The quick brown fox jumps over the lazy dog"
sampleString = sampleString.Insert(19, " happily")
sampleString = sampleString.Remove(10, 6)
sampleString = sampleString.Replace("jumps", "leaps")
sampleString &= String.Format("{0} times in {1:N1} minutes", 17, 2)
position = sampleString.IndexOf("dog")
If position > 0 Then
    sampleString = sampleString.Insert(position + "dog".Length, ", ")
End If
txtResultsOther.AppendText("String output: " & sampleString)
```

The *StringWriter* Class

With its ability to write and to store sequential information in a *StringBuilder* using its *Write* and *WriteLine* methods, the *StringWriter* class makes assembling an output string easy.

Let's imagine that you have an array of strings containing address information and you want to create an address formatted for mailing. You could do it with a *String* object, concatenating with "&" and "&=". But the *StringWriter* class offers another way, utilizing its under-the-hood *StringBuilder* object. Here's how:

```
Dim sw As New StringWriter()
Dim addressInfo() As String = {"John Smith", "123 Main Street", _
    "Centerville", "WA", "98111"}

' Write the name and address lines to the StringWriter:
sw.WriteLine(addressInfo(0))
sw.WriteLine(addressInfo(1))
```

You could use *String.Format* to create the final line of the address, but here's how you'd do it with the *StringWriter Write* and *WriteLine* methods. *Write* simply appends data. *WriteLine* appends the data along with a line-termination character.

```
sw.Write(addressInfo(2))
sw.Write(", ")
sw.Write(addressInfo(3))
sw.Write(" ")
sw.WriteLine(addressInfo(4))

' Or, perhaps more efficiently:
'sw.WriteLine(String.Format("{0}, {1} {2}", addressInfo(2), _
'   addressInfo(3), addressInfo(4)))
```

If you used the *String* class, the code would be considerably less elegant, as the following example shows:

```
Dim str As String
str = addressInfo(0) & Environment.NewLine
str &= addressInfo(1) & Environment.NewLine

' Add the city/region/postal code values:
str &= addressInfo(2) & ", "
str &= addressInfo(3) & " " & addressInfo(4)
```

```
str &= Environment.NewLine

' Or:
' str &= String.Format("{0}, {1} {2}{3}", addressInfo(2), addressInfo(3), _
'       addressInfo(4), Environment.NewLine)
```

Conclusion

In this application you've seen that you can use the wide variety of methods of the *String* class to insert, remove, modify, locate, pad, trim, and otherwise manipulate strings. You've also seen that you can use shared methods of *String*—such as *Compare*, *Concat*, *Format*, and *Join*—directly on the *String* class without first instantiating a *String* object.

It's recommended that you use the *StringBuilder* class for efficiently manipulating large strings or to manage repeated manipulation of smaller strings. When you need to output a string, the *StringWriter* class offers the convenience of an in-memory file to which you can write repeatedly, while it uses a *StringBuilder* for efficient string concatenation.

Application #4: *Try...Catch...Finally*

No matter how carefully you write your code, errors are bound to happen. One sign of a well-written application is graceful handling of such errors. This sample demonstrates the new *Try...Catch...Finally* exception handling in Visual Basic .NET.

New Concepts

You're probably accustomed to writing error handlers in your Visual Basic 6 applications, using *On Error GoTo*. You can still do that in Visual Basic .NET, but this sample application demonstrates a better way.

Visual Basic .NET introduces a new concept to Visual Basic developers: *structured exception handling* (SEH). An exception is simply an anomaly—an error—in the execution of your application, and in keeping with the concept that everything in the .NET world is object-based, structured exception handling allows you to access a specific object associated with each kind of error (exception) that can occur. You can respond to an exception based on its specific type, or you can handle all exceptions generically.

The way you write your exception-handling code is different, too. In Visual Basic 6, you probably constructed your error handlers something like this:

```
Sub Foo()
    On Error GoTo ErrHandler
```

(continued)

```
          ' Code that could fail
    ExitHere:
          ' Close database connections, delete temp files, etc.
          Exit Sub
    ErrHandler:
          'Handle the error
          Resume ExitHere
End Sub
```

This is a classic example of spaghetti code. First you jump to the *ErrHandler* label if there's an error, and then after handling the error, you jump back to *ExitHere* to make sure you clean up any resources in use. Finally, you exit the procedure with the *Exit Sub* statement.

Another limitation of the *On Error GoTo* construct was that you could have only one active error handler per procedure. That meant that a second *On Error GoTo* statement would inactivate the first one.

Typically, your error handler block would include an *If/Then* or *Select Case* construct for handling different errors, based on *Err.Number*. At times, the error-handling code was greater in size than the code it was protecting.

The following sample application (shown in Figure 2-4) demonstrates how structured exception handling takes a different approach. This new approach is based on a specific *Exception* object for each kind of error and the use of the *Try/Catch* exception-handling code. The sample code that follows Figure 2-4 shows a *Try/Catch* block in its simplest form.

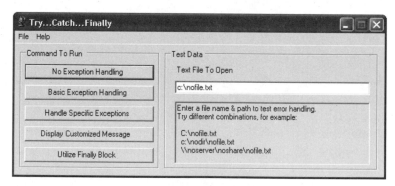

Figure 2-4 Structured Exception Handling gives you more control over errors than *On Error GoTo*.

```
Try
    ' Code that could fail (the protected block).
Catch exp As Exception
    ' Handle the exception.
Finally
    ' Code that gets executed regardless.
    ' Finally is optional.
End Try
```

The *Try/Catch* concept is superior to *On Error GoTo* in a number of ways, and key advantages of using SEH include:

■ Exceptions are generated and raised by the .NET runtime, which means not only that you don't have to write a lot of code to use SEH, but also that client applications written in another .NET language can catch and respond to exceptions generated in your Visual Basic .NET application.

■ Because each exception comes with its own object, you no longer have to write lengthy *If* or *Select Case* statements to check for specific error numbers. Instead, you can respond to each exception type in its own *Catch* block. (See the "Handling Specific Exceptions" section later in the chapter.)

■ You can have multiple *Try/Catch* blocks within the same procedure, one for each piece of code you want to protect.

■ You can nest *Try/Catch* blocks. For example, if a database connection fails in a *Try* block, your *Catch* block can have a nested *Try/Catch* that attempts to connect to an alternate server.

■ The *Try/Catch* construct has an optional *Finally* block, in which you can place all your clean-up code. You don't have to jump to it, it runs automatically.

Structured Exception Handling Specifics

As we just mentioned, you use a *Try/Catch* construct for working with exceptions. When an error occurs within the protected block, control passes to the *Catch* block, where you handle the exception—perhaps by simply notifying the user of the problem via a message box, perhaps by trying an alternative such as connecting to a different database server, or by whatever other action you consider appropriate.

The *Exception* object provides a number of informative properties, including:

■ *Message*   A description of the error.

■ *Source*   The name of the object or application that generated the error.

■ *StackTrace*   A list of the frames on the call stack at the time the exception was thrown. The *StackTrace* property includes information Visual Basic 6 developers have craved for years: the name of the original procedure where the exception was triggered, and the line number of the offending statement.

Other features of SEH include:

- The *ToString* method combines the name of the exception, the error message, the stack trace, and more.

- There's no equivalent for *On Error Resume Next*.

- You can jump out of a *Try/Catch* with an *Exit Try* or *GoTo* statement, but code in your *Finally* block will still be executed.

- You can omit the *Catch* block if you have a *Finally* block.

- You can create your own exceptions. (See the Custom Exceptions sample later in the chapter.)

- SEH can even handle exceptions generated by unmanaged code.

- Like Visual Basic 6, when an exception occurs in a procedure without a *Try/Catch,* the .NET runtime walks back up the call stack looking for an active exception handler. If it finds one, it passes control to it; otherwise, it generates a default exception response.

Code Walkthrough

Let's examine structured exception handling in action. We'll cover each option as reflected in the buttons on the sample form.

No Exception Handling

Without exception handling, an exception such as a file not being found results in a message box generated by the .NET runtime that invites the user to either ignore the error and continue or quit. The following example produces such a result because there's no exception handling in place:

```
Private Sub btnNoTryCatch_Click(...
    ⋮
    Dim fs As FileStream
    ' This command will fail if the file does not exist.
    fs = File.Open(Me.txtFileName.Text, FileMode.Open)
    MessageBox.Show("The size of the file is: " & fs.Length, Me.Text, _
        MessageBoxButtons.OK, MessageBoxIcon.Information)
    fs.Close()
    ⋮
End Sub
```

Basic Exception Handling

To implement basic exception handling, you add *Try/Catch/End Try* to the procedure, placing the code that could fail in the protected area between the *Try* and the *Catch*. If the file isn't found, control passes to the *Catch* block, where you can inform the user of the problem. In this case, we've chosen to refer to the *Exception* object as *exp*, but you can choose any name you care to. Note also that the message box displays the exception's *Message* property, which is a description of the error—much like *Err.Description* in Visual Basic 6.

```
Private Sub btnBasicTryCatch_Click(...
    Dim fs As FileStream
    Try
        ' This command will fail if the file does not exist.
        fs = File.Open(Me.txtFileName.Text, FileMode.Open)
        MessageBox.Show("The size of the file is: " & fs.Length, Me.Text, _
            MessageBoxButtons.OK, MessageBoxIcon.Information)
        fs.Close()
    Catch exp As Exception
        MessageBox.Show(exp.Message, Me.Text, MessageBoxButtons.OK, _
            MessageBoxIcon.Stop)
    End Try
End Sub
```

Handling Specific Exceptions

The .NET Framework provides a specific exception object type for every kind of exception. Whenever you can, you should code for specific exceptions, taking the appropriate action depending on which exception occurred. In the following example, we're able to notify the user with a precise message when either the file doesn't exist or the directory doesn't exist. We can also handle generic exceptions such as *IOException*, which could include a *FileLoadException*, a *PathTooLongException*, or the ultimate generic exception, *Exception*.

When you're handling specific exceptions, as we're doing here, be sure to sequence your *Catch* blocks from most specific to most general. For example, the last *Catch* block shown in the following code segment handles any exceptions not specifically handled earlier. Because it's the most generic of the *Catch* blocks, it needs to be last; otherwise, it will catch all exceptions, and the specific *Catch* blocks will never see them.

```
Private Sub btnSpecificTryCatch_Click(...
    Dim fs As FileStream
    Try
        ' This command will fail if the file does not exist.
        fs = File.Open(Me.txtFileName.Text, FileMode.Open)
        MessageBox.Show("The size of the file is: " & fs.Length, Me.Text, _
            MessageBoxButtons.OK, MessageBoxIcon.Information)
        fs.Close()
    Catch exp As FileNotFoundException
        ' Will catch an error when the file requested does not exist.
        MessageBox.Show("The file you requested does not exist.", _
            Me.Text, MessageBoxButtons.OK, MessageBoxIcon.Stop)
    Catch exp As DirectoryNotFoundException
```

(continued)

```
            ' Will catch an error when the directory requested does not exist.
            MessageBox.Show("The directory you requested does not exist.", _
                Me.Text, MessageBoxButtons.OK, MessageBoxIcon.Stop)
        Catch exp As IOException
            ' Will catch any generic IO exception.
            MessageBox.Show(exp.Message, Me.Text, MessageBoxButtons.OK, _
                MessageBoxIcon.Stop)
        Catch exp As Exception
            ' Will catch any error that we're not explicitly trapping.
            MessageBox.Show(exp.Message, Me.Text, MessageBoxButtons.OK, _
                MessageBoxIcon.Stop)
        End Try
End Sub
```

Displaying a Customized Message

You can take advantage of the wealth of information that the *Exception* object offers in its properties and methods, by creating custom messages that are formatted as you choose, including just the information you want to present. For example, the following procedure responds to an *IOException* by notifying the user that the file could not be opened and adding the message, source, and stack trace information provided by the *Exception* object:

```
Private Sub btnCustomMessage_Click(...
    Dim fs As FileStream
    Try
        ' This command will fail if the file does not exist
        fs = File.Open(Me.txtFileName.Text, FileMode.Open)
        MessageBox.Show("The size of the file is: " & fs.Length, Me.Text, _
            MessageBoxButtons.OK, MessageBoxIcon.Information)
        fs.Close()
    Catch exp As IOException
        ' Will catch any generic IO exception
        Dim sb As New System.Text.StringBuilder()
        With sb
            .Append("Unable to open the file you requested, ")
            .Append(Me.txtFileName.Text & vbCrLf & vbCrLf)
            .Append("Detailed Error Information below:" & vbCrLf)
            .Append("   Message: " & exp.Message & vbCrLf)
            .Append("   Source: " & exp.Source & vbCrLf & vbCrLf)
            .Append("   Stack Trace:" & vbCrLf)
        End With
```

This example also shows a nested *Try/Catch* block, something that you simply couldn't do with the Visual Basic 6 unstructured *On Error/GoTo* error handling.

```
        Dim strStackTrace As String
            ' Accessing an exception object's StackTrace could cause an
            ' exception so we need to wrap the call in its own Try..Catch
            ' block.
```

```
        Try
            strStackTrace = exp.StackTrace()
        Catch stExp As Security.SecurityException
            ' Catch a security exception
            strStackTrace = "Unable to access stack trace due to " & _
                "security restrictions."
        Catch stExp As Exception
            ' Catch any other exception
            strStackTrace = "Unable to access stack trace."
        End Try
        sb.Append(strStackTrace)
        MessageBox.Show(sb.ToString, Me.Text, MessageBoxButtons.OK, _
            MessageBoxIcon.Stop)
    Catch exp As System.Exception
        ' Catch any other exception
        MessageBox.Show(exp.Message, Me.Text, MessageBoxButtons.OK, _
            MessageBoxIcon.Stop)
    End Try
End Sub
```

Using the *Finally* Block

If you want certain code—such as code for closing database connections—to run whether there was an exception or not, you include a *Finally* block, which is always executed. *Finally* is optional, but if it's present, it runs immediately after the *Try* block if there was no error or immediately after the *Catch* block if there was. This is roughly analogous to using *Resume ExitHere* in Visual Basic 6, which was used to ensure that cleanup code would always run. But *Finally* is superior because it doesn't require you to write spaghetti code to jump to it. Instead, the .NET runtime ensures that the *Finally* block gets executed every time.

```
Private Sub cmdTryCatchFinally_Click(...
    Dim fs As FileStream
    Try
        ' This command will fail if the file does not exist.
        fs = File.Open(Me.txtFileName.Text, FileMode.Open)
        MessageBox.Show("The size of the file is: " & fs.Length, Me.Text, _
            MessageBoxButtons.OK, MessageBoxIcon.Information)
    Catch exp As Exception
        ' Will catch any error that we're not explicitly trapping.
        MessageBox.Show(exp.Message, Me.Text, MessageBoxButtons.OK, _
            MessageBoxIcon.Stop)
    Finally
        ' Clean up, if we did open the file successfully.
        If Not fs Is Nothing Then
            fs.Close()
            MessageBox.Show("File closed successfully in Finally block", _
                Me.Text, MessageBoxButtons.OK, MessageBoxIcon.Information)
        End If
    End Try
End Sub
```

Conclusion

This application has shown you that structured exception handling provides a more robust environment for handling errors than was available in Visual Basic 6, and that you can protect any code that could generate an exception with a *Try/Catch* block. You can, and should, write your code to respond to specific exceptions with a separate *Catch* block for each kind of error you want to handle.

Because exceptions are generated by the run time, you write less code and your application's exceptions are available to other client applications written in other .NET languages. You can use the *StackTrace* property to pinpoint where the error occurred in your code.

One final note: *On Error GoTo* is supported in Visual Basic .NET for backward compatibility, primarily for applications migrated from Visual Basic 6. It has been updated so that it actually generates exceptions and is fully integrated into the .NET Framework. You might be tempted to use it, but don't do it. Structured exception handling is infinitely superior and is compatible with cross-language development. Stick with SEH.

Application #5: Custom Exceptions

Even though the .NET Framework provides scores of exception types, seemingly one for every possible kind of exception, they might not be enough for you. This sample demonstrates how to create and use custom exceptions in Visual Basic .NET, as well as how to set up a global exception handler.

Building Upon...

Application #4: *Try...Catch...Finally*
Application #7: Object-Oriented Features

New Concepts

Creating custom exceptions to enhance those already provided by the .NET Framework is easy. We'll show you uses for such exceptions and how to create them.

Uses for Custom Exceptions

The .NET Framework class library provides more than 100 built-in exception types, covering almost every imaginable error. Why would you consider creating custom exceptions? Primarily for handling situations that break business rules or for situations in which you want to provide the client with more information than one of the built-in exceptions might provide.

In addition to the properties common to all exceptions—such as *Source*, *Message*, and the like—you will likely want to provide additional properties unique to your custom exception. These properties can offer detailed information to a client using your application or component. You should document your exception so that a developer will know under what circumstances the custom exception will be thrown, and what information he can gather from it.

Some guidelines on using custom exceptions include:

■ Think carefully before you create a custom exception, and do so only if you're sure there isn't already a built-in one that meets your needs.

■ Trigger your custom exception only when there's an exceptional event, not for common errors, such as a failed *File.Open* statement.

■ Don't use a custom exception for controlling program flow.

Creating Custom Exceptions

To create a custom exception, you must create a class that defines the exception. All exceptions inherit directly or indirectly from the *System.Exception* class. Two subclasses of *System.Exception* serve as the base classes for most other exceptions: *System.SystemException* and *System.ApplicationException*. You should inherit from *System.ApplicationException*, which represents exceptions thrown by applications, as opposed to *System.SystemException*, which represents exceptions thrown by the common language runtime itself.

In the sample application (shown in Figure 2-5), the class library project contains a variety of exception classes, arranged in the inheritance hierarchy depicted in Figure 2-6.

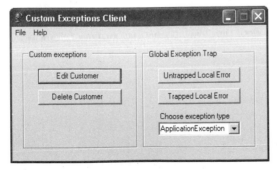

Figure 2-5   You can easily create your own custom exceptions with Visual Basic .NET. You can also set a global exception trap by attaching your own handler to the *Application.ThreadException* exception.

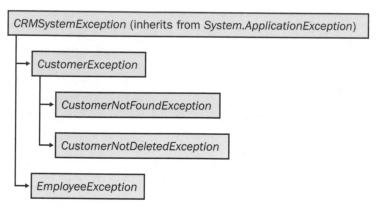

Figure 2-6   The sample application, Custom Exceptions Client, includes several custom exceptions arranged in an inheritance hierarchy.

Code Walkthrough

Let's examine the *Customer* class and the custom exceptions designed to work with it, all of which are defined in *Customer.vb*.

Creating the *Customer* Class

This class exposes two shared methods, *EditCustomer* and *DeleteCustomer*, as well as three public fields, *Id*, *FirstName*, and *LastName*. *EditCustomer* is designed to return a *Customer* object based on a supplied ID. The code in the sample simulates a failed database search for a customer, and then creates and throws an exception of type *CustomerNotFoundException*.

```
Public Shared Function EditCustomer(ByVal Id As Integer) As Customer
    ⋮
    Dim msg As String
    msg = String.Format("The customer you requested by Id {0} " & _
        "could not be found.", Id)
    Dim ex As New CustomerNotFoundException(msg)
    Throw ex
End Function
```

The *DeleteCustomer* method simulates finding customers, but it doesn't delete them. It demonstrates one of the benefits of creating your own exception—the ability to add methods like *LogError* (described later).

```
Public Shared Sub DeleteCustomer(ByVal Id As Integer)
    Dim c As New Customer()
    ⋮
    Dim msg As String
    msg = String.Format("The customer '{0} {1}' could not " & _
        "be deleted. Your account '{2}' does not have " & _
        "permission.", c.FirstName, c.LastName, user)
```

```
    Dim ex As New CustomerNotDeletedException(msg, c, user)
    exp.LogError()
    Throw ex
End Sub
```

Creating Custom Exceptions

The first custom exception is *CRMSystemException*, which is the base class for the other custom exceptions in the class library. Like all exceptions, it requires a *Message* parameter, which is a description of the exception. Its constructor then invokes the constructor of its base class, *System.ApplicationException,* passing the *Message* object to it. *CRMSystemException* exposes a *LogError* method, which makes an entry in the Application log. Finally, it exposes an *AppSource* property, which defaults to *"SomeCompany CRM System"* (set in the constructor), but this can be overridden by derived classes. Both *AppSource* and *Message* are used to identify the log entry.

```
Public Class CRMSystemException
    Inherits System.ApplicationException

    Private m_AppSource As String

    Public Sub New(ByVal Message As String)
        MyBase.New(Message)
        Me.m_AppSource = "SomeCompany CRM System"
    End Sub

    Friend Sub LogError()
        Dim e As System.Diagnostics.EventLog
        e = New System.Diagnostics.EventLog("Application")
        e.Source = Me.AppSource
        e.WriteEntry(Me.Message, _
            System.Diagnostics.EventLogEntryType.Error)
        e.Dispose()
    End Sub

    Public Overridable ReadOnly Property AppSource() As String
        Get
            Return m_AppSource
        End Get
    End Property
End Class
```

From this base exception class, the first derived class is *CustomerException*, which requires not only a *Message* but an object representing the customer whose account is being accessed when the exception occurs (*reqCustomer*). When this exception is thrown, the client application has access to the customer information through the *CustomerInfo* property. In some cases, such as when the customer is not found (as seen in *CustomerNotFoundException* later in this section), *reqCustomer* might be *Nothing*. Finally, the *AppSource* property of the class overrides its parent's *AppSource*, returning *"SomeCompany CRM Customer Module."* This means that when *LogError* gets called, it will use this *AppSource* property, not the *AppSource* property of the parent class.

```
Public Class CustomerException
    Inherits CRMSystemException

    Private m_AppSource As String
    Private m_Customer As Customer

    Public Sub New(ByVal Message As String, ByVal ReqCustomer As Customer)
        MyBase.New(Message)
        Me.m_Customer = ReqCustomer
        Me.m_AppSource = "SomeCompany CRM Customer Module"
    End Sub
    Public ReadOnly Property CustomerInfo() As Customer
        Get
            Return MyClass.m_Customer
        End Get
    End Property
    Public Overrides ReadOnly Property AppSource() As String
        Get
            Return Me.m_AppSource
        End Get
    End Property
End Class
```

From the *CustomerException* class, we derive *CustomerNotFoundException*, which simply invokes its parent's constructor, passing *Nothing* for the customer because the customer could not be found.

```
Public Class CustomerNotFoundException
    Inherits CustomerException

    Public Sub New(ByVal Message As String)
        MyBase.New(Message, Nothing)
    End Sub
End Class
```

The second class derived from *CustomerException* is *CustomerNotDeleted-Exception*, which takes an additional parameter, *UserId*, and returns it in a property of the same name. A client handling this exception can use this *UserId* property to take other actions related to the customer.

```
Public Class CustomerNotDeletedException
    Inherits CustomerException

    Private m_UserId As String

    Public Sub New(ByVal Message As String, _
```

```
            ByVal ReqCustomer As Customer, ByVal UserId As String)

            MyBase.New(Message, ReqCustomer)
            Me.m_UserId = UserId
    End Sub
    Public ReadOnly Property UserId() As String
        Get
                Return Me.m_UserId
        End Get
    End Property
End Class
```

One other custom exception class, *EmployeeException*, inherits from *CRM-SystemException*. This exception is not used in the sample, but it could serve as the base for derived classes such as *EmployeeNotFoundException* and *Employee-NotDeletedException*.

```
Public Class EmployeeException
    Inherits CRMSystemException
    Public Sub New(ByVal message As String)
        MyBase.New(message)
    End Sub
End Class
```

Using the Custom Exceptions

The sample application's *frmMain* form has buttons for editing and deleting customers. In the following example, you're invoking the shared *EditCustomer* method, to which you pass the customer ID. In the sample, the customer is not found and the code catches the exception of type *CustomerNotFoundException* thrown by *EditCustomer*. Note that the code is also prepared to catch *Customer-Exception*, the parent of *CustomerNotFoundException*, as well as any other kind of exception that might be thrown.

```
Private Sub btnEdit_Click(...
    Dim c As Customer
    Try
        Dim i As Integer = 14213
        c = Customer.EditCustomer(i)
        ' do some work here if we get a valid customer back
    Catch exp As CustomerNotFoundException
        MessageBox.Show(exp.Message, exp.AppSource, MessageBoxButtons.OK, _
            MessageBoxIcon.Error)
    Catch exp As CustomerException
        MessageBox.Show(exp.Message, exp.AppSource, MessageBoxButtons.OK, _
            MessageBoxIcon.Error)
    Catch exp As Exception
        MessageBox.Show(exp.Message, exp.Source, MessageBoxButtons.OK, _
            MessageBoxIcon.Error)
    End Try
End Sub
```

When you try to delete a customer, the *DeleteCustomer* method throws a *CustomerNotDeletedException*. When you catch it, you can choose to work further with the *Customer* object that it returns. Keep in mind that because *DeleteCustomer* is a shared method, you don't need to instantiate a customer object to call it.

```
Private Sub cmdDelete_Click(...
    Try
        Dim i As Integer = 14213
        Customer.DeleteCustomer(i)
        MessageBox.Show(String.Format("Customer Id {0} was deleted.", _
            i), Me.Text, MessageBoxButtons.OK, MessageBoxIcon.Information)
    Catch ex As CustomerNotDeletedException
        Dim c As Customer
        c = ex.CustomerInfo
        ' We can now do something more interesting with
        ' the customer if we wanted to.
        MessageBox.Show(ex.Message, ex.AppSource, MessageBoxButtons.OK, _
            MessageBoxIcon.Error)
    Catch ex As CustomerException
        MessageBox.Show(ex.Message, ex.AppSource, MessageBoxButtons.OK, _
            MessageBoxIcon.Error)
    Catch ex As Exception
        MessageBox.Show(ex.Message, ex.Source, MessageBoxButtons.OK, _
            MessageBoxIcon.Error)
    End Try
End Sub
```

Global Exception Handler

Normally an untrapped error in Visual Basic 6 and earlier would produce a quick *MessageBox* dialog box, and then your process would shut down. Windows Forms, however, has injected a top-level error catch between the common language runtime and your code, presenting a dialog box that gives the user a chance to continue or quit. To see the global exception handler at work, run the sample application outside the debugger. (You can do this by pressing Ctrl+F5. If you run the code inside the debugger, you'll simply go into *Break* mode when there's an untrapped exception.) The special dialog box appears if the following three conditions are true:

- There's no active debugger.

- You don't have your own exception handler in place.

- You haven't turned on just-in-time (JIT) debugging in your application's config file.

The global exception handler is a welcome new capability, but you can take it further by attaching your own handler to take care of untrapped exceptions.

You do that by adding a handler for the exception *Application.ThreadException* and associating it with an *OnThreadException* procedure.

```
Private Sub cmdTrapped_Click(...
    ' Turn on our own global exception handler.
    AddHandler Application.ThreadException, _
        AddressOf Me.OnThreadException
    GenerateError()
End Sub
```

When an untrapped exception occurs, *OnThreadException* gets executed, and in it you can do any type of handling you care to. In fact, you can use this technique to centralize the handling of all your exceptions, thereby creating a global exception handler. By the way, there's no magic to the name *OnThreadException*; you can call the procedure anything you like as long as it has the correct signature.

```
Friend Sub OnThreadException(ByVal sender As Object, _
    ByVal t As System.Threading.ThreadExceptionEventArgs)
    Dim ex As Exception = t.Exception
    Dim exType As String

    If TypeOf ex Is ApplicationException Then
        exType = "ApplicationException"
    ElseIf TypeOf ex Is ArgumentException Then
        exType = "ArgumentException"
    ElseIf TypeOf ex Is CustomerNotFoundException Then
        exType = "CustomerNotFoundException"
    Else
        exType = "Exception"
    End If

    Dim msg As String
    msg = String.Format("We're sorry, an untrapped {2} has " & _
        "occurred.{0}The error message was:{0}{0}{1}", vbCrLf, _
        ex.Message, exType)
    MessageBox.Show(msg, "Global Exception Trap", _
        MessageBoxButtons.OK, MessageBoxIcon.Exclamation)
End Sub
```

When you no longer want the handler, just unhook it, as the following procedure does:

```
Private Sub cmdUntrapped_Click(ByVal sender As System.Object, _
    ByVal e As System.EventArgs) Handles cmdUntrapped.Click
    ' Turn our handler off and revert to the Windows Forms default.
    RemoveHandler Application.ThreadException, _
        AddressOf Me.OnThreadException
    GenerateError()
End Sub
```

Conclusion

Custom exceptions enhance the power of structured exception handling, making it an even more powerful weapon in the Visual Basic .NET developer's arsenal. Keep the following principles in mind:

- You create a custom exception by defining it in its own class.

- Base your custom exceptions on *System.ApplicationException*.

- Custom exceptions can be thrown and caught just like built-in exceptions.

- You will usually create custom exceptions to handle violations of business rules in your application, as opposed to run-of-the-mill errors, for which there is probably an exception class already defined.

- By exposing custom properties, your custom exceptions can provide additional information that might be useful to the client.

- Document your custom exceptions thoroughly so that a developer using your application knows what circumstances will trigger each exception, and what information it provides in addition to regular exception properties.

- To conform to convention, name your custom exceptions with a suffix of *Exception*.

- Consider attaching your own handler to *Application.ThreadException* to trap unhandled exceptions.

Application #6: Walking the Stack

This sample shows you how to programmatically access the call stack, which contains the sequence of procedures that led to the application's current execution point.

Building Upon...

Application #3: String Manipulation
Application #4: *Try...Catch...Finally*
Application #7: Object-Oriented Features

New Concepts

When an error occurs in your application, how do you determine the root cause? True, you can use *Try/Catch/Finally* blocks to provide information on the error, but you probably want more. This application introduces new ways for you to find out more.

Walking the Stack—Conceptual

When a procedure is called, it changes the flow of control in your application just like a *GoTo* statement does. But when the procedure is done, control returns to the statement following the original procedure call. The *stack* is a portion of memory that keeps track of the procedures that have been called in your application, noting those that are waiting to finish because calls they've made haven't been completed yet.

While you're debugging your application, or when you want to do some application profiling, you might want some way to determine which procedures your code passed through on its way to a particular problem. You'd like to know the procedure that called the current procedure, as well as the caller of that procedure, and so on, up the stack. This is commonly referred to as *walking the stack*, and it's simply a way to trace the sequence of procedures that haven't completed because they're waiting for the current one to finish its work. The sample application, shown in Figure 2-7, demonstrates how to walk the stack.

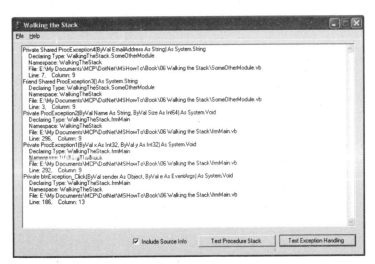

Figure 2-7   When you pass an *Exception* object to the constructor of the *StackTrace* class, you can show the code in your application that led up to the exception.

The *StackFrame* Class

To do a stack walk in Visual Basic 6, you're forced to use extraordinary measures—such as calling custom logging procedures—just to see which procedures got you to where you are. But with Visual Basic .NET it's far easier to get the information you need, thanks to the *StackTrace* class, found in the *System.Diagnostics* namespace.

A *StackTrace* object is a container for individual *StackFrame* objects, one for each method call on your application's stack. By using these objects, along with the *MethodInfo* and *ParameterInfo* classes (in the *System.Reflection* namespace), you can have access not only to the names of the procedures on the stack, but much more detailed information including the file and line number of the procedure, parameters of the various methods, and much more.

We'll show you how to use *MethodInfo* to identify the attributes of a method and gain access to its metadata. *ParameterInfo* lets you do the same for the method's parameters.

Code Walkthrough

The sample form has two buttons and a check box. The first button lets you traverse the complete stack, while the second button focuses on the portion of the stack that relates directly to an exception. Check the Include Source Info check box to see more information on each procedure listed. You'll see *DeclaringType*, which is the class or module in which the procedure is declared, *Namespace*, which is handy if you're tracing through more than one module or namespace. You'll also see the file name and line number of the procedure.

Test the Procedure Stack

The Test Procedure Stack button shows how to trace the entire stack all the way back to its beginning. It starts with the *btnStackTrace_Click* event procedure, which calls *ProcA*, which in turn calls *ProcB*.

```
Private Sub btnStackTrace_Click(...
    ProcA(1, 2, "Hello")
End Sub

Private Sub ProcA(ByVal Item1 As Integer, ByRef Item2 As Integer, _
    ByVal Item3 As String)
    Dim strResults As String = ProcB(String.Concat(Item1, Item2, Item3))
End Sub
```

When *ProcB* calls *GetFullStackFrameInfo*, there are three method calls on the stack, and the *GetStackFrameInfo* procedure shows how you can access their names and other information. *ProcB* passes a *StackTrace* object (with stack information at this point in the application) to *GetFullStackFrameInfo*.

You can include an optional *True* or *False* parameter in the constructor of the *StackTrace* object. If the parameter is *True*, information—including line and column number—is gathered on the file containing the code being executed. If it's *False* or omitted, no file information is provided.

```
Private Function ProcB(ByVal Name As String) As String
    GetFullStackFrameInfo(New StackTrace(chkIncludeSource.Checked))
End Function
```

GetFullStackFrameInfo loops through the stack frames, starting at the current procedure (which has an index of zero), and it retrieves the frames by number, using the *GetFrame* method. Note that there are more frames than the three methods pushed onto the stack so far by our application because *StackTrace* includes every frame on the stack, all the way to the initial *Sub Main* that started the application.

```
Private Function GetFullStackFrameInfo(ByVal st As StackTrace) As String
    Dim fc As Integer = st.FrameCount
    Dim i As Integer
    txtStackItems.Clear()
    For i = 0 To fc - 1
        ' Get info on a single frame.
        txtStackItems.Text &= GetStackFrameInfo(st.GetFrame(i)) & vbCrLf
    Next
End Function
```

GetStackFrameInfo gathers information about the method associated with a single stack frame. We've shown several method attributes, but there are still more available, including *IsConstructor*, *IsOverloaded*, and others.

```
Private Function GetStackFrameInfo(ByVal sf As StackFrame) As String
    Dim mi As MethodInfo = CType(sf.GetMethod(), MethodInfo)
    Dim output As String

    ' Show the method's access modifier
    If mi.IsPrivate Then
        output &= "Private "
    ElseIf mi.IsPublic Then
        output &= "Public "
    ElseIf mi.IsFamily Then
        output &= "Protected "
    ElseIf mi.IsAssembly Then
        output &= "Friend "
    End If

    ' Is it shared?
    If mi.IsStatic Then
        output &= "Shared "
    End If

    output &= mi.Name & "("
```

We're gathering information about the method's parameters, including the name, type, and whether the parameter is *ByVal* or *ByRef*. We could also have included whether the parameter was optional, as well as other information.

```
Dim piList() As ParameterInfo = sf.GetMethod.GetParameters()

    Dim params As String = String.Empty
    Dim pi As ParameterInfo
    For Each pi In piList
        params &= String.Format(", {0} {1} As {2}", _
            IIf(pi.ParameterType.IsByRef, "ByRef", "ByVal"), pi.Name, _
            pi.ParameterType.Name)
    Next pi

    ' Get rid of the first ", " if it exists.
    If params.Length > 2 Then
        output &= params.Substring(2)
    End If

    ' Get the procedure's return type and append it to the output string.
    Dim typ As Type = mi.ReturnType
    output &= ") As " & typ.ToString
```

Now we're optionally showing more detailed information about the method, such as its namespace, the module in which it's declared, the name of the file it lives in, and its line and column number in the file.

```
If chkIncludeSource.Checked Then
    ' Get the source file for the current method on the stack.
    Dim sourceFile As String = sf.GetFileName() & ""
    ' Give detailed info on the method
    If sourceFile.Length <> 0 Then
        ' Give detailed info on the method
        output &= String.Format("{0}    Declaring Type: {1}{0}" & _
            "     Namespace: {2}{0}    File: {3}{0}    Line: {4}," & _
            "     Column: {5}", vbCrLf, mi.DeclaringType, _
            mi.DeclaringType.Namespace, sourceFile, _
            sf.GetFileLineNumber, sf.GetFileColumnNumber)
    End If
End If
Return strOut
End Function
```

Test Exception Handling

Sometimes you might want to retrieve stack information only on the code in your application that led up to the exception. The Test Exception Handling button on the sample form demonstrates how you can optionally pass an *Exception* object to the constructor of the *StackTrace* class to accomplish this goal.

Note that, in this example, there is an exception handler in *btnException_Click* but none in the procedures it calls. When an exception is thrown in *ProcException4*, the .NET runtime walks back up the stack until it finds an active handler and uses it. Note also that you get access to the portion of the stack that relates to your exception by calling *GetFullStackFrameInfo* with a *StackTrace* object that includes the current *Exception* in its constructor. You'll notice that the stack information does include *ProcException1* through *ProcException4*, even though the exception handler is actually several frames higher on the stack.

ProcException3* and *ProcException4* are located in a separate module, and if you check the Include Source Info check box, the stack trace will reveal the module name as the Declaring Type.

```
Private Sub btnException_Click(...
    Try
        ProcException1(1, 2)
    Catch exp As Exception
        GetFullStackFrameInfo(New StackTrace(exp))
    End Try
End Sub

Private Sub ProcException1(ByVal x As Integer, ByVal y As Integer)
    ProcException2("Mike", 12)
End Sub

Private Sub ProcException2(ByVal Name As String, ByVal Size As Long)
    ProcException3()
End Sub

Friend Function ProcException3() As String
    Return ProcException4("mike@microsoft.com")
End Function

Private Function ProcException4(ByVal EmailAddress As String) As String
    Throw New ArgumentException("This is a fake exception!")
End Function
```

Conclusion

In this application you've seen that walking the stack lets you trace the route your code took to its current location. This process is valuable for debugging or profiling your application. You can walk the stack all the way to its beginning if you want to, or you can deal only with the portion that relates to the exception that just occurred.

When you don't need the kind of detail *GetStackFrameInfo* provides in this example, try using *StackFrame.ToString()*, which gives you a quick description of the current frame.

Keep in mind that you can get the stack frame information we've described here only when you've compiled in *Debug* mode.

Application #7: Object-Oriented Features

One criticism of Visual Basic 6 was that it was not a truly object-oriented language, which denied it membership among the premier development languages. That criticism no longer applies because Visual Basic .NET is fully object oriented. This sample application demonstrates some of the new object-oriented (OO) features in Visual Basic .NET.

Building Upon...

Application #3: String Manipulation
Application #8: Scoping, Overloading, Overriding

New Concepts

As you've no doubt heard over and over, Visual Basic .NET is an object-oriented language. What exactly does that mean? It means that the code you write manipulates a series of objects, each of which has certain characteristics and capabilities, and you make them do your will to get your work done.

Object Orientation Overview

You can think of an object as something like a robot that carries out actions on your behalf, like writing to a file or calculating a result from values you pass to it. To understand how objects work, we need to define a few basic terms:

- **Class**   A blueprint or design from which an object is created. A class spells out the abilities and characteristics the object will have when it's created.

- **Object**   An instance of a class. Just as a telephone is created from a design, so an object is created (instantiated) from a class.

You'll often hear the words *object* and *class* used interchangeably. Just remember that a class is an abstract definition of what the object will be, while the object is a concrete instance created from the class. Other important terms are:

- **Property**   A characteristic of a class. For a telephone, it could be *Color* or *Material,* each with a value like *Beige* or *Plastic*. A *Field* is similar to a property, but it can be changed more easily. Properties and fields are used to hold information related to the object.

- **Method**   Something the object can do or can be used to do. A telephone can *Dial*, for example.

- **Event**   An object's way of notifying you that something has happened. A telephone *Rings* when it gets an incoming signal.

Propeties, methods, and events are the class's *Members*, and by manipulating them you can make the object do your bidding. Three other terms we should note are:

- **Encapsulation**   An object's means of keeping its members self-contained, controlling how they are changed, and hiding from the user how it does its internal work.

- **Inheritance**   The ability to create a new class that's derived from an existing one (known as the base class). The derived class gets all the members of the base class, but it can add its own, modify the way its inherited members work, or both.

- **Polymorphism**   The ability to have multiple classes that can be used interchangeably, even though each class implements the same properties or methods in different ways.

Code Walkthrough

In the sample code, we'll demonstrate how to instantiate objects, use constructors, implement inheritance, and handle overloading, properties, and shared members.

Instantiating Objects

You instantiate an object using the *New* keyword. In the following example, you're instantiating a new *Customer* object and assigning it to the variable *cust*.

```
Private Sub cmdInstantiating_Click(...
    Dim cust As New Customer()
```

Once you have the object, you can assign values to its properties.

```
cust.AccountNumber = "1101"
    cust.FirstName = "Carmen"
    cust.LastName = "Smith"
```

You can use a method of the object (*GetCustomerInfo*) to do some work, such as gathering customer information.

```
Dim custInfo As String = cust.GetCustomerInfo()
```

Constructors

A *Constructor* is a procedure within a class that executes whenever an object is instantiated from that class. In Visual Basic .NET, the constructor is a *Sub* procedure named *New*. As with other procedures, the constructor might or might not require parameters to be passed to it.

Here's an example of a class with a constructor. It accepts three parameters and uses them to assign values to the object's properties. Instantiating the object and setting its properties all at one time is more efficient than setting the properties later.

```
Public Class CustomerWithConstructor
    ⋮
    Sub New(ByVal AccountNumber As String, ByVal FirstName As String, _
        ByVal LastName As String)
        Me.AccountNumber = AccountNumber
        Me.FirstName = FirstName
        Me.LastName = LastName
    End Sub
```

Here's the recommended syntax for using a single line of code to create an instance of a class that has a constructor:

```
Private Sub cmdConstructors_Click(...
    Dim cust As New CustomerWithConstructor("1101", "Carmen", "Smith")
```

Alternatively, you can declare the variable first and then instantiate the object:

```
    Dim cust2 As CustomerWithConstructor
    cust2 = New CustomerWithConstructor("1101", "Carmen", "Smith")
```

Figure 2-8 shows the sample application after the user has clicked the Constructors button, which causes the application to instantiate the *Customer-WithConstructor* class (and set its properties) using the class's constructor, as shown in the preceding code.

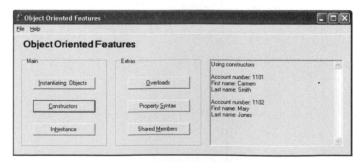

Figure 2-8 Passing initialization arguments to a constructor is more efficient than setting properties later.

Inheritance

Sometimes you have a class that's a perfect candidate for subclassing (deriving a new class from an existing one). For example, imagine that you've already defined a *Customer* class, but you have some customers with special characteristics: Government customers have a special government-issued number, and corporate customers need a special procedure for placing their orders.

To handle these situations, you can create derived classes that inherit from the base class, *Customer*. They get all the *Customer* members, but they can add members of their own, modify the way their inherited members behave, or both.

So you create the *GovtCustomer* and *CorpCustomer* classes. The *Inherits* keyword gives these classes all the characteristics of *Customer*, while allowing them to add their own members. *GovtCustomer* is given an additional property, *GovtNumber*, and *CorpCustomer* has an additional *PlaceCorpOrder* method.

```
Public Class GovtCustomer
    Inherits Customer
    Private m_GovtNumber As String
    Public Property GovtNumber() As String
        Get
            Return m_GovtNumber
        End Get
        Set(ByVal Value As String)
            _mGovtNumber = Value
        End Set
    End Property
End Class


Public Class CorpCustomer
    Inherits Customer
    Public Function PlaceCorpOrder(ByVal orderAmt As Single, _
        ByVal orderDate As Date) As String
        ' Process order and write data to database...
        Return "Order for $" & orderAmt & " placed on " & orderDate
    End Function
End Class
```

You use these classes just like you would use *Customer*, but in addition, you have access to their unique members.

```
Private Sub btnInheritance_Click(...
    Dim cust1 As New GovtCustomer()
    With cust1
        .GovtNumber = "9876543"
        .AccountNumber = "1103"
        .FirstName = "John"
        .LastName = "Public"
    End With
```

(continued)

```
Dim cust2 As New CorpCustomer()
With cust2
    .AccountNumber = "1104"
    .FirstName = "Mary"
    .LastName = "Private"
    Dim strOrderInfo As String = .PlaceCorpOrder(123.45, Today)
End With
```

Overloads, Property Syntax, and Shared Members

See the code in the sample application for demonstrations and extensive in-code comments on these topics, which are touched upon in even greater detail in Application #8: Scoping, Overloading, Overriding.

Conclusion

This application has shown that object-oriented programming resembles the way you used to play as a child, using bricks of different shapes and colors to construct the house of your dreams. Each brick is a separate object that contributes to the structure. When you need to change a brick, you either replace it with another or modify it, but you don't have to reconstruct the whole house.

■ You instantiate (create) an object by using the *New* keyword. An object is a concrete instance of a class, which is a blueprint or pattern that defines the object's characteristics.

■ A constructor in a Visual Basic .NET class is a *Sub* procedure named *New*, which might or might not accept parameters. It runs each time an object gets instantiated from the class, so it's a good place to initialize values of the new object.

■ Classes with parameterized constructors let you create the object and assign values to properties all in one action, a very efficient way to go.

■ When you find that you need a class that's very much like one you already have but needs some special properties or methods, create a new class that inherits from the original, and then add the members you need.

■ When you inherit, the original class is called the *base class* and the inherited one is called the *derived class*. This process is known as *subclassing*.

Application #8: Scoping, Overloading, Overriding

Not every member of every class needs to be publicly available to applications using that class. Some procedures, properties, and other members should be for the private use of the class itself, while others might be made available to derived classes. This sample shows how to set various levels of access to the members of a class, including *Public*, *Private*, *Protected*, and others. It also demonstrates how to extend derived classes with features such as *overloading* and *overriding*.

The application simulates a simple hiring system that allows you to hire full-time, part-time, and temporary employees. It uses a series of classes to do its work. *Employee* is a base class containing the features common to all employees, and *FullTimeEmployee*, *PartTimeEmployee*, and *TempEmployee* are all derived from *Employee*.

All employees have many things in common: they all get hired, all have salaries, each has a name, and so forth. But each employee type has specific features that set it apart from other kinds—for example:

■ Only full-time employees get annual leave.

■ Only temporary employees have an expected termination date when they are hired.

■ Part-time employees are required to work at least 20 hours per week.

To satisfy these needs, each derived class extends the *Employee* class in some way: by overriding methods of the base class, by implementing new methods or properties of its own, or by replacing (shadowing) members of the base class. There is also a *Friend* class named *EmployeeDataManager*, which simulates reading employee data to and writing employee data from a database.

Building Upon...

Application #3: String Manipulation
Application #4: *Try...Catch...Finally*
Application #7: Object-Oriented Features

New Concepts

Visual Basic .NET has some new rules regarding the visibility and access of classes and their members. This application illustrates a number of them.

Scoping

The application demonstrates *scoping* with the use of these keywords, which control the level of access allowed to a class and its members:

■ **Public** When a class or procedure is marked *Public*, any code that can get to it can use it with no restrictions.

- **Protected** Class members declared with the *Protected* keyword are accessible only from within their own class or from within a derived class.

- **Friend** Classes and procedures declared with the *Friend* keyword are accessible from within the program where they are declared and from anywhere else in the same assembly.

- **Private** Class members declared with the *Private* keyword are accessible only from within the class where they are declared.

- **Shared** Procedures declared with the *Shared* keyword can be used without necessarily having to create an instance of the class they belong to. You can call a shared procedure either by qualifying it with the class name (*EmployeeDataManager.WriteEmployeeData*) or with the variable name of a specific instance of the class (*edmManager.WriteEmployeeData*). You can also declare fields and properties as *Shared*.

The sample application, shown in Figure 2-9, illustrates these concepts.

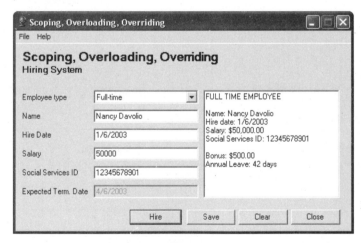

Figure 2-9 This application has a base class named *Employee*, from which *FullTimeEmployee*, *PartTimeEmployee*, and *TempEmployee* all inherit common characteristics. Each derived class has its own unique implementation of key features.

Overloading

In Visual Basic 6, you could declare a procedure with optional parameters. Code calling the procedure could then choose to include or omit those parameters. In Visual Basic .NET, you still can do that, but you can also *overload* a method. Overloading means having several versions of the same method, each with a different set of parameters.

Overriding

When a derived class implements its own version of a method in the base class, it is said to be *overriding* that method. Overriding is just one of the buzz words you'll need to be familiar with in the Visual Basic .NET world. The application demonstrates the use of the following statements and modifiers in classes and their members:

- ■ ***Inherits***   Tells you which base class the current class is inheriting from.

- ■ ***NotInheritable***   Prevents the class from being used as a base class.

- ■ ***MustInherit***   You can't create an instance of this class. The only way to use the class is to inherit from it.

- ■ ***Overridable***   Used to mark a property or method in a base class. It means derived classes can have their own implementation of the property or method. Public methods are *NotOverridable* by default.

- ■ ***Overrides***   Used in a derived class, it allows you to override a property or method that's defined in the base class.

- ■ ***NotOverridable*** (**default**)   Used in a base class, it prevents a property or method from being overridden in a derived class.

- ■ ***MustOverride***   Used on a property or method in the base class, it requires the derived class to override the property or method.

- ■ ***Shadows***   Used in a derived class, it lets you use the name of an inherited class member but replace it completely with your own implementation. The inherited type member is then unavailable in the derived class.

Code Walkthrough

Let's examine our classes and the relationships between them, beginning with the *Employee* class, which is the foundation for our application and from which three other classes are inherited. Note that all the classes are declared with the *Public* keyword.

The *Employee* Class

We want the *Employee* class to serve as a blueprint for other classes that will inherit from it, but we don't want users to create instances of *Employee*. By declaring the class with the *MustInherit* keyword, we ensure that no instances of this class can be created—it can only be inherited.

```
Public MustInherit Class Employee
    Protected c_HireDate As DateTime
    Protected c_Name As String
    Protected c_Salary As Decimal
    Protected c_SocialServicesID As String
```

The four variables we just declared will hold the internal values for the *HireDate, Name, Salary,* and *SocialServicesID* properties. Because they're declared with the *Protected* keyword, they're accessible only from within the *Employee* class and classes derived from it, such as *FullTimeEmployee* and *Part-TimeEmployee*. (If we had used the *Private* keyword, those variables would have been accessible only within *Employee*.) You can use *Protected* only at the class level, outside of any procedures. You cannot declare protected variables at the module, namespace, or file level.

Whenever an *Employee* object gets created, we want to set the default *HireDate* to today. We also want to allow the user to optionally include the name of the new employee. So *Employee* has two versions of its constructor, the procedure that runs whenever an instance of the class is created. You can use it to set up default values for certain properties, to establish database connections, or to perform any other initialization activities.

```
Public Sub New()
    Me.HireDate = Today
End Sub
```

The preceding procedure is the class's default constructor, which runs when an *Employee* object is instantiated with no parameters. The following version is an overload of the constructor—another version of the same procedure, with a different set of parameters. Because it accepts parameters, it's referred to as a *parameterized constructor*. This version runs when an *Employee* object is instantiated with a *String* parameter. Parameterized constructors allow data to be passed to the object at the same time it's instantiated. This requires less frequent access to the object and less code, and it results in better performance than individually setting properties later.

The following constructor lets you create an *Employee* object and set its *Name* property at the same time. (Caution: you might be tempted to set the *c_Name* variable directly in your constructor or other procedures, like this: *c_Name = strName*. Don't do it because it will bypass your *Name* property procedure. Using *Me.Name = strName* forces the property procedure to run and to execute any validation code it might contain.)

```
Public Sub New(ByVal strName As String)
    Me.Name = strName
```

```
        Me.HireDate = Today
    End Sub
```

Employee has several properties: *Bonus* is declared *ReadOnly*, so clients using the class can retrieve, but not set, its value. This lets you keep tight control over how much of a bonus employees receive. The *Get* procedure runs whenever a client retrieves the value of *Bonus*, which we provide by executing the *ComputeBonus* function. Each property has a data type; this one is a *Decimal*.

```
Public ReadOnly Property Bonus() As Decimal
    Get
        Return ComputeBonus()
    End Get
End Property
```

The *HireDate* property is a read/write *Date* property. When a value is retrieved from it, the *Get* procedure runs, and the *Set* runs when someone sets its value. In either of these procedures, we can enforce business rules. In this example, we won't accept a *HireDate* value later than the current date.

```
Public Property HireDate() As Date
    Get
        Return c_HireDate
    End Get
    Set(ByVal Value As Date)
        If Value <= Today Then
            c_HireDate = Value
        Else
            Throw New ArgumentException( _
                "Hire Date cannot be later than today", "HireDate")
        End If
    End Set
End Property
```

The *Name* property is also Read/Write and has no validation code.

```
Public Property Name() As String
    Get
        Return c_Name
    End Get
    Set(ByVal Value As String)
        c_Name = Value
    End Set
End Property
```

The *Salary* property is a special case, one that *must* be overridden by derived classes. We want each of the derived classes to implement its own means of assigning wages or salary, depending on the kind of employee it represents. To accomplish this, we declare the *Salary* property with the *MustOverride* keyword, which requires the derived class to override it and provide its own implementation code. Note that there is no *End Property* statement, nor any implementation statements.

```
Public MustOverride Property Salary() As Decimal
```

The *SocialServicesID* property is another special case, declared with the *Overridable* keyword. Because our company might have branches in other countries, we're using the generic term *SocialServicesID* to represent Social Security numbers in the U.S.A., as well as other social service–type IDs in other countries. The following example assumes that most of our employees are U.S. based. Consequently, we've decided that, unlike what we did with *Salary*, we'll include implementation statements to ensure that the *SocialServicesID* is numeric and exactly 11 characters long. Derived classes used in divisions of our company in other countries are free to override the property, implementing it as they choose to, but they are not *required* to do so, as they are with *Salary*.

```
Public Overridable Property SocialServicesID() As String
    Get
        Return c_SocialServicesID
    End Get

    Set(ByVal Value As String)
        If IsNumeric(Value) AndAlso Len(Value) = 11 Then
            c_SocialServicesID = Value
        Else
            Throw New ArgumentException( _
                "Social Security Number must be 11 numeric " & _
                "characters", "SocialServicesID")
        End If
    End Set
End Property
```

ComputeBonus is also declared with the *MustOverride* keyword, requiring derived classes to implement their own bonus calculation code.

```
Public MustOverride Function ComputeBonus() As Decimal
```

The *Hire* method that follows is an overloaded method, with three versions. When someone calls the *Hire* method, she must at least provide the name of the new employee. But two other versions of this method allow the user to optionally provide the employee's hire date and salary as well.

The argument list in each version of an overloaded method must be different from all the others, either in the number of arguments, their data types, or both. This allows the compiler to figure out which version of the method to use when the method is called. Derived classes might also have their own overloaded versions of the method, which must have their own unique list of arguments.

The first version here runs if *Hire* is called with just a *String* parameter—for example, *emp.Hire("Nancy Davolio")*. Version two runs if *Hire* is called with *String* and *Date* parameters—for example, *emp.Hire("Nancy Davolio", #12/5/2005#)*. The third version runs if *Hire* is called with *String*, *Date*, and *Decimal* parameters—for example, *emp.Hire("Nancy Davolio", #12/5/2005#, CDec(50000))*.

```
    Public Sub Hire(ByVal Name As String)
        Me.Name = Name
    End Sub

    Public Sub Hire(ByVal Name As String, ByVal HireDate As DateTime)
        Me.Name = Name
        Me.HireDate = HireDate
    End Sub

    Public Sub Hire(ByVal Name As String, ByVal HireDate As DateTime, _
        ByVal StartingSalary As Decimal)
        Me.Name = Name
        Me.HireDate = HireDate
        Me.Salary = StartingSalary
    End Sub
End Class
```

The *FullTimeEmployee* Class

FullTimeEmployee is derived from the *Employee* class, as indicated by the *Inherits* keyword. It therefore has all the properties, methods, and events of *Employee*, but it extends *Employee* by adding an *AnnualLeave* property and a *Compute-AnnualLeave* method and by implementing the *Salary* property and overriding the *ComputeBonus* method. Each of its constructors, shown in the following code, calls its counterpart in the base class by using the *MyBase* keyword.

```
Public Class FullTimeEmployee
    Inherits Employee

    Public Sub New()
        MyBase.New()
    End Sub

    Public Sub New(ByVal Name As String)
        MyBase.New(Name)
    End Sub
```

The *AnnualLeave* property is measured in days, and only the *FullTime-Employee* class has it, because neither part-time nor temporary employees are eligible for annual leave. It is *ReadOnly*, and we return a value from it by executing the *ComputeAnnualLeave* method.

```
Public ReadOnly Property AnnualLeave() As Integer
    Get
        Return ComputeAnnualLeave()
    End Get
End Property
```

This *Salary* property procedure provides the implementation for the *Salary* property that was declared but not implemented in the base class. It includes validation code that restricts the salary to a range between 30,000 and 500,000.

```
Public Overrides Property Salary() As Decimal
    Get
        Return c_Salary
    End Get
    Set(ByVal Value As Decimal)
        If Value < 30000.0 Or Value > 500000.0 Then
            Throw New ArgumentOutOfRangeException("Salary", _
                "Full-time employee salary must be between " & _
                "30,000 and 500,000")
        Else
            c_Salary = Value
        End If
    End Set
End Property
```

By implementing the *ComputeAnnualLeave* method, this class is extending *Employee*. The method does not appear in the base class, nor in the other classes derived from *Employee*. The method computes how long the employee has been with the company and determines his leave accordingly.

```
Public Function ComputeAnnualLeave() As Integer
    ' Code to compute annual leave would go here.
End Function
```

The following code implements the *ComputeBonus* method (which had no implementation in the base class) for full-time employees, who get an annual bonus of 1% of their salary.

```
Public Overrides Function ComputeBonus() As Decimal
    Return Me.Salary * CDec(0.01)
End Function
End Class
```

The *PartTimeEmployee* Class

This class also inherits from *Employee*, and it extends *Employee* in similar ways to *FullTimeEmployee*. It does have one item of note, the *Hire* method.

The *PartTimeEmployee* version of *Hire* overloads the already overloaded *Hire* method in the *Employee* base class. (There are now four versions of the

Hire method available in the *PartTimeEmployee* class.) This version of *Hire* makes the *StartingSalary* parameter optional and adds an optional *MinHours-PerWeek* parameter.

Note that, because these parameters are optional, they must be last in the parameter list and must each be given a default value, which will be used if the parameter is omitted.

```
Public Overloads Sub Hire(ByVal Name As String, ByVal HireDate As _
    DateTime, Optional ByVal StartingSalary As Decimal = 10000, _
    Optional ByVal MinHoursPerWeek As Double = 10)

    Me.Name = Name
    Me.HireDate = HireDate
    Me.Salary = StartingSalary
    Me.MinHoursPerWeek = MinHoursPerWeek
End Sub
```

The *TempEmployee* Class

This class has a couple of notable items. Temporary employees have an expected termination date, which is entered as an argument to the *Hire* method (shown later). *TempEmployee* uses a public variable rather than a property to hold that date. A public variable is called a *Field*, which acts like a property but can be written and read without a property procedure.

```
Public ExpectedTermDate As DateTime
```

Of course, when you use a *Field* you give up the validation and control that property procedures offer. Try setting *ExpectedTermDate* to a date in the past, for example, and it will be accepted because there's no validation being done to it.

The second notable item is the *TempEmployee* implementation of *Hire*, which *Shadows* the *Hire* method in *Employee*. In other words, this version of *Hire* completely replaces the *Hire* method in the base class, which is therefore not accessible at all to *TempEmployee*. It's a way of implementing a method in a completely different way than the base class, including having a different set of parameters, having a different return type, and in every way being independent of the original.

```
Public Shadows Sub Hire(ByVal Name As String, ByVal HireDate _
    As DateTime, ByVal StartingSalary As Decimal, ByVal _
    EmploymentEndDate As DateTime)

    Me.Name = Name
    Me.HireDate = HireDate
    Me.Salary = StartingSalary
    ExpectedTermDate = EmploymentEndDate
End Sub
```

Using the Classes

Fire up the sample form, and you'll be presented with data for a potential full-time employee. Click the Hire button, and the employee's data will be set and shown in the text box on the right. Click the Save button, and the application simulates writing the data to the database. To understand what's happening, put breakpoints on the first line of each of the following procedures: *HireFullTime-Employee*, *HireFullTimeEmployeeWithProperties*, *HirePartTimeEmployee*, *Hire-TempEmployee*, and *btnSave_Click*. Each procedure is liberally commented.

Look at the *EmployeeDataManager* class, which simulates writing data to the database. Note that it is declared with the *Friend* keyword, which means it's accessible to any code running within the same assembly. Also note its *Shared* methods, which can be used without creating an *EmployeeDataManager* object.

Conclusion

In this application, you've seen that inheritance lets you set a standard and then customize it in classes you derive from the base. An abstract class (declared with the *MustInherit* keyword) is a great way to set that standard. Derived classes get all the characteristics of the base class, but they can extend it with their own members.

- Don't confuse overloading and overriding. They sound alike, but they're very different. Overloading lets you have multiple versions of a method. Overriding lets a derived class implement a base class method in its own way.

- Only methods or properties that you declare as *Overridable* can be overridden in derived classes.

- When a method is overloaded, each version must have a unique combination of parameters. Overloading is one way of allowing a method to be called with different combinations of parameters. However, you can also make parameters optional with the *Optional* keyword.

- Always use the least public method that will meet your needs when you declare variables, methods, properties, and classes. The greater the scope of a variable, the more resources are required to carry it around, and the more likely it can be modified when you don't intend for it to be.

- Use property procedures rather than fields for holding object data. It's easier to implement a field (which you can do just by declaring a public variable), but property procedures let you control and validate the data values that are set and retrieved.

Application #9: Use Callbacks

This application demonstrates how to perform callbacks using both interfaces and delegates.

Building Upon...

Application #79: Use Thread Pooling
Application #84: Asynchronous Calls

New Concepts

Visual Basic .NET makes it easy for you to call a function by its address. This is an important feature because that's how you set up a callback.

Callbacks—Conceptual

What is a callback function, and why would you need one? A callback function is a reference to a method that you can pass to a second method. At some point, the second method invokes the reference, thereby *calling back* to the first method. You can use a callback to notify you when a job is done by calling a procedure in your code. First you initiate the action you want to happen, and then when it's done, it causes the callback procedure in your main code to be executed.

Let's say you want to delete a set of backup files, sort a group of objects, or perhaps enumerate all the files with a certain extension on your hard drive. You want to call a procedure to take care of these tasks, and you want that procedure to run another procedure once it's finished. That's when a callback fits the bill.

Creating and Using Callbacks

First you create the method you want the callback function to execute. This is usually a method that will take an action after some other action is complete. For example, suppose you want to create a call to a method that enumerates the *.vb files in your Microsoft Visual Studio Projects folder while your main code goes on to do something else. In addition, you want to be notified when the enumeration is done and create a list of the files that were found. You could write a procedure named *PrepareListAfterEnumeration* and make it your callback function.

The sample application, shown in Figure 2-10, contains code that illustrates how to create and use callbacks.

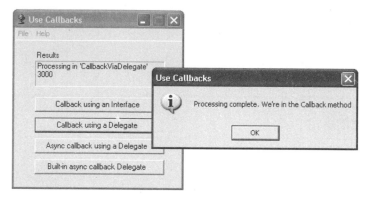

Figure 2-10   A callback function is a reference to a method you can pass to a second method. This process lets you determine, at run time, which method should be called.

Code Walkthrough

In this sample application, the callback function is simple—it just pops up a message box telling you that it's been executed. The *Implements* statement is there only because we want to be able to call this procedure via an interface, as well as directly.

```
Public Sub CallbackMethod() Implements ICallback.CallbackMethod
    MessageBox.Show("Processing complete. We're in the Callback method", _
        Me.Text, MessageBoxButtons.OK, MessageBoxIcon.Information)
End Sub
```

Using an Interface

If you care to, you can use an interface to call your callback function. You declare the interface like this:

```
Interface ICallback
    Sub CallbackMethod()
End Interface
```

Then you implement that interface on the callback procedure (shown in the preceding *CallBackMethod*), and set the whole thing up by registering your client class with the class that's going to do the work. In the following click event, we create an instance of the *CallbackViaInterface* class, register this class (*frmMain*) with the instance, and then call its *DoSomeProcessing* method. When that method is done, it calls back into the client via the *ICallback* interface. Finally, we unhook our class from the *CallbackViaInterface* class.

```
Private Sub cmdInterfaceCallback_Click(...
    Dim cvi As New CallbackViaInterface(lblResults)
```

```
        cvi.RegisterInterFace(Me)
        cvi.DoSomeProcessing()
        cvi.UnRegisterInterface()
End Sub
```

Here's what the *CallbackViaInterface* class looks like. A private field named *icb* will hold a reference to the *ICallBack* interface that we'll later use to call our callback procedure. Another private field, *ResultsLabel,* is initialized in the constructor and refers to a label on the demo form that will be updated while *DoSomeProcessing* is busy working.

```
Friend Class CallbackViaInterface
    Private icb As ICallback
    Private ResultsLabel As Label

    Public Sub New(ByVal lbl As Label)
        ResultsLabel = lbl
    End Sub
```

The following *DoSomeProcessing* method does the actual work the class is intended to accomplish. In this example, we're simply running a counter, but we could perform any number of other operations, such as sorting objects, deleting backup files, or counting the number of *.vb files in a folder. Once we're done processing, we invoke the interface's *CallBackMethod* method, which in turn calls the procedure in the client code that the interface is pointing to—we *call back* into the client code.

```
    Public Sub DoSomeProcessing()
        If Not icb Is Nothing Then
            Dim i As Integer
            For i = 1 To 3000
                ResultsLabel.Text = _
                    "Processing in 'CallbackViaInterface'" & vbCrLf _
                    & i.ToString()
                ResultsLabel.Refresh()
            Next
            icb.CallbackMethod()
        End If
    End Sub
```

For all the above to work, we had to register the calling class with the worker class. So the worker class has a procedure for that as well as an unregister procedure for unhooking the caller from the worker.

```
    Public Sub RegisterInterFace(ByVal cb As ICallback)
        icb = cb
    End Sub
        ⋮
End Class
```

Using Delegates

Another way to call the worker class and implement callbacks is through delegates. A delegate is a reference to a method that has the same signature as that method, but has no implementation. The advantage of a delegate is that you can use it to call any method whose signature it matches, allowing you to select different methods at run time based on input from the user or based on the results of previous processing.

In our example (which resembles our earlier interface-based technique), we create an instance of the *CallbackViaDelegate* class and then instantiate a *DelegateForCallback* object, passing it the address of the procedure we want it to execute later.

```
Private Sub btnDelegateCallback_Click(...
    Dim cvd As New CallbackViaDelegate(lblResults)
    Dim d As New DelegateForCallback(AddressOf Me.CallbackMethod)
    cvd.RegisterDelegate(d)
    cvd.DoSomeProcessing()
    cvd.UnRegisterDelegate()
End Sub
```

The *CallbackViaDelegate* class resembles the *CallbackViaInterface* class, but it uses a delegate rather than an interface. The delegate is declared outside the class and must be unique within the project. The following line of code shows how the delegate is declared. (Note that it takes no parameters, which means it can be a stand-in for any method that also takes no parameters, including our *CallbackMethod* procedure.)

```
Delegate Sub DelegateForCallback()
```

We use a private field to hold an instance of the delegate, and then assign it to the delegate that gets passed in to the *RegisterDelegate* procedure. Keep in mind that the delegate is now pointing to the address of our *CallbackMethod* procedure.

```
Private dell As DelegateForCallback
    :
Public Sub RegisterDelegate(ByVal d As DelegateForCallback)
    dell = d
End Sub
```

Our *DoSomeProcessing* method does some work and then uses the registered client reference (the delegate) to call back to the client. Note the optional argument indicating whether or not we want an asynchronous callback. If we don't, we call *Invoke*, which means, "Call the procedure that the delegate is pointing to." If we do want an asynchronous callback, we call *BeginInvoke*, which is similar to *Invoke*, except that the CLR uses a separate worker thread from its thread pool to call the delegate's target procedure. The procedure then runs parallel to this code.

```
Public Sub DoSomeProcessing(Optional ByVal async As Boolean = False)
    ⋮
        If async = False Then
            del1.Invoke()
        Else
            del1.BeginInvoke(Nothing, Nothing)
        End If
    ⋮
End Sub
```

Using Built-In Callbacks

There's still another technique you can use: built-in callbacks. Delegates have a built-in mechanism to call back to the client, as long as the signature of the method to be called back to matches the signature of the *AsyncCallback* delegate class (that is, it accepts a single parameter, of the *IAsyncResult* type). The *AsyncCallback* class is defined in the CLR specifically for calling back after an asynchronous invocation of a delegate.

This method will make an asynchronous call on a delegate and use its built-in callback to invoke the *BuiltInCallback* method. No user registration is needed because we're passing the callback delegate (*ac*) as an argument to the *BeginInvoke* method, which calls the delegate asynchronously.

```
Private Sub btnBuiltInCallback_Click(...
    Dim cvb As New CallbackViaBuiltIn(lblResults)
    Dim d As New DelegateForCallback(AddressOf cvb.DoSomeProcessing)
    Dim ac As New AsyncCallback(AddressOf Me.BuiltInCallback)
    d.BeginInvoke(ac, Nothing)
End Sub
```

Conclusion

Callbacks are perfect when you want to execute a method or series of methods and then have your calling code taking some action when the called code has finished its work.

■   Callbacks are useful for applications with long-running procedures, where you'd like your code to do something else in the meantime, but be notified when the lengthy operation is complete.

■   You might want to use a callback to keep you posted on the status of a long-running event, such as a File Transfer Protocol (FTP) download, by periodically updating a progress bar.

■   You can also use callbacks for notifying you when an event occurs, such as a form being closed, a numeric threshold being reached, or a long download being completed.

Application #10: Use XML Comments

Whereas C# developers revel in their built-in XML documentation capabilities, Visual Basic .NET developers have no such intrinsic documentation tool. This sample corrects that imbalance by providing a tool you can use to create XML documentation files for your library projects.

Building Upon...

Application #37: Use Menus
Application #66: Build a Custom Collection Class
Application #70: Reflection

New Concepts

Have you noticed how IntelliSense offers help on each class, method, and parameter as you type? Not only does it offer the available choices, it also provides a description of each item that helps to guide you. It seems to happen automatically for all the native .NET classes, but for the classes you create, it presents only the names of the items with no descriptions. Have you ever wished you could arrange to have such descriptions displayed for your classes? Well, you can, by creating an XML documentation file containing those descriptions.

When you add a reference to a component (let's say *foo.dll*), Visual Studio .NET searches the referenced component's folder for an XML file with the same base name (*foo.xml*). It reads the documentation from the file, and when you refer to classes, methods, and parameters from *foo.dll* in the code editor, the information about each one is displayed in IntelliSense. You can also use the Object Browser to view summary information, parameter information, and any remarks.

Code Walkthrough

The .NET documentation offers details on how an XML documentation file should be structured, but it provides little information on how to automate creating and managing such a file. This application lets you create and manage an XML documentation file for your component. Figure 2-11 shows an example of the XML Documentation Tool in action.

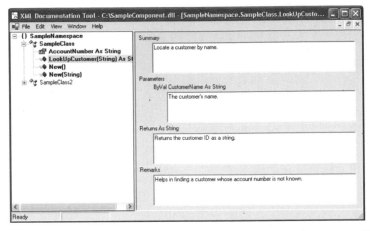

Figure 2-11   With this tool, you can add documentation to your library projects that will show up in the Object Browser and IntelliSense.

What's in the Solution

The solution contains both the XMLDocumentationTool project and a SampleComponent class library project to be used for demonstration. The SampleComponent library contains two classes, *SampleClass* and *SampleClass2*. Both classes are identical, but we've documented the *SampleClass* by using the XML Documentation Tool. Here's what *SampleClass* looks like:

```
Public Class SampleClass
    ' Store the account number internally.
    ' The XML documentation tool ignores private variables.
    Private m_AccountNumber As String

    Public Sub New()
        MyBase.new()
    End Sub

    ' Create a customer and assign their account number.
    Public Sub New(ByVal acctNum As String)
        MyBase.new()
        m_AccountNumber = acctNum
    End Sub

    Public Property AccountNumber() As String
        Get
            Return m_AccountNumber
        End Get
        Set(ByVal Value As String)
            m_AccountNumber = Value
        End Set
    End Property
```

(continued)

```
Public Function LookUpCustomer(ByVal customerName As String) As String
    ' Code to find customer by name in database.
End Function

Private Sub SomeOtherProcedure()
    ' A private procedure.
    ' The XML documentation tool ignores private procedures.
End Sub
End Class
```

Testing Existing Documentation

Now, let's see how some existing documentation shows up as you work. You'll need to be sure the XML documentation file is in the same folder as the DLL it documents. We've provided a starter XML file in the root folder of the XML Documentation Tool. To use it, follow these steps:

1. Build the *XMLDocumentationTool* solution.

2. Copy *SampleComponent.xml* from the root folder of the application to *SampleComponent\bin*. (You can do this in Visual Studio .NET if you want to.)

Now you want to test the documentation, so do the following:

1. Create a new Windows Application project. It must be in a separate solution from the component.

2. Set a reference to SampleComponent\bin\SampleComponent.dll.

3. Open the Object Browser, and select SampleComponent.

4. Expand SampleComponent, and select SampleNamespace.

You should see Summary And Remarks information for the namespace in the bottom pane. Now expand SampleNamespace, and select *SampleClass*. You'll see Summary And Remarks information for the class in the bottom pane and the members of the class in the right pane. Select each member in turn, and view the documentation below it. (For some items, the documentation will show only in IntelliSense, not in the Object Browser.)

Now let's see how IntelliSense uses the information you just saw. Double-click Form1 to get into its *Form_Load* event procedure, and declare a new instance of *SampleClass* by typing the following (being careful not to type the whole word *SampleNamespace*):

Dim samp As New SampleNamesp

Notice how IntelliSense selects SampleNamespace in the drop-down list and presents a ToolTip-type popup describing the namespace. Type a period and IntelliSense will complete the name and present a list of the classes in the namespace: *SampleClass* and *SampleClass2*. Click once on *SampleClass*, and you'll see a description of the class. Type an opening parenthesis and Intel-liSense will finish typing *SampleClass* and offer a list of its constructor over-loads. Notice that the popup includes a description of the *AcctNum* parameter.

Using the Documentation Tool

Now let's see how this information came to be available to IntelliSense and the Object Browser. Re-open the XML Documentation Tool solution, and press F5 to execute it. Select File | Open Assembly, and browse to SampleCompo-nent\bin. Choose SampleComponent.dll, and click Open and OK. *SampleNa-meSpace* appears.

Expand the *SampleNamespace* node, and you'll see the two classes it con-tains. Notice that *SampleClass* is shown in bold, which means it has documen-tation, while *SampleClass2* does not. Expand *SampleClass*, and you'll see its public members. Right-click each one and then choose Open, and you'll see the documentation we provided. Also examine the class and the namespace, which have their own documentation.

The data is saved in SampleComponent.xml, in the component's bin folder. The file looks like this:

```xml
<?xml version="1.0"?>


<doc>
    <assembly>
        <name>SampleComponent</name>
        <version>1.0.0.0</version>
        <fullname>SampleComponent, Version=1.0.0.0, Culture=neutral,
        PublicKeyToken=null</fullname>
    </assembly>
    <members>
        <member name="N:SampleNamespace">
            <summary>Sample component for demonstrating XML
            documentation.</summary>
            <remarks>This component is not functional. It's designed
            for demonstration purposes.</remarks>
        </member>
        <member name="T:SampleNamespace.SampleClass">
            <summary>Sample class for demonstration.</summary>
            <remarks>This class has methods and properties that are
            documented for demonstration purposes.</remarks>
        </member>
        <member name="P:SampleNamespace.SampleClass.AccountNumber">
            <summary>The customer's account number.</summary>
            <value>Value must be between 1 and 999.</value>
            <remarks>Although the account number is numeric, it is
            stored as a string.</remarks>
        </member>
        <member name="M:SampleNamespace.SampleClass.
        LookUpCustomer(System.String)">
```

(continued)

```
            <summary>Locate a customer by name.</summary>
            <param name="CustomerName">The customer's name.</param>
            <returns>Returns the customer ID as a string.</returns>
            <remarks>Helps in finding a customer whose account
            number is not known.</remarks>
        </member>
        ⋮
    </members>
</doc>
```

Now add some documentation of your own. Right-click on *SampleClass2*, and choose Open. Enter Summary and Remarks information, add any other documentation you want for the members of the class, and then press Save.

Test it in the Windows Application you created earlier. (If it's still open, you'll need to close and reopen it for Visual Studio to read the changed XML file.) You should see the additional documentation you entered.

You can open any existing component and document it. The tool will create a corresponding XML file and put it in the same folder as the DLL. As you work with the tool, note that:

- You can copy information from one node to another. Just select the first node and drag it onto the node you want to copy the information to.

- You can use the tool to edit documentation only for public and protected types and members that are exposed from the assembly file. *Private* and *Friend* methods or classes are not exposed and, therefore, are not viewable in the tree view.

- You can search for a specific member by selecting Find from the Edit menu.

- When there are conflicts between the information in the XML file and the assembly, the XML Documentation tool lists these conflicts as errors, along with the path to the node creating the error and a brief description of the error. The status bar displays the number of errors. Errors occur when the assembly and its XML documentation file are out of sync. See the tool's Help file for more details on possible errors.

Conclusion

The XML Documentation Tool makes it simple for you to document your component so that important information about it is available to IntelliSense and the Object Browser. Whereas C# programmers have a built-in capability for documenting their code directly in their classes, this tool gives equivalent functionality to the Visual Basic .NET developer. The tool can be used for assemblies built in languages other than Visual Basic .NET, as long as the assemblies are common language specification (CLS)–compliant managed-code assemblies, such as those created in C#.

Application #11: Key Visual Basic .NET Benefits

Visual Basic .NET offers a variety of innovations and enhancements over Visual Basic 6. This sample demonstrates several new features. They're described in much greater detail in other applications in this series, but we're providing a quick overview here just to whet your appetite. Figure 2-12 shows the sample application in action.

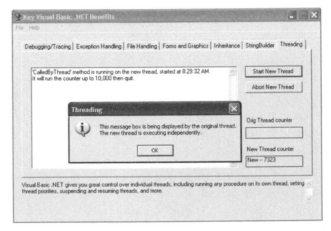

Figure 2-12   The sample application creates a thread and sends it off to run a particular procedure. Meanwhile, the original thread continues its work. It's easy to do with Visual Basic .NET.

Building Upon...

Application #3: String Manipulation
Application #4: *Try...Catch...Finally*
Application #5: Custom Exceptions
Application #7: Object-Oriented Features
Application #8: Scoping, Overloading, Overriding
Application #54: Work with Environment Settings
Application #55: Use the File System
Application #57: Use the Event Log
Application #73: Read From and Write To a Text File
Application #76: Create Trace Listeners
Application #79: Use Thread Pooling

New Concepts

Features shown in this sample include:

- **Debugging/Tracing**   You can use the *Debug* and *Trace* classes during development to help debug your application by writing variable values, status messages, and anything else you consider useful to a *Listener*. The *Listener* can be the console, a file, or the Event Log. *Debug* and *Trace* are almost mirror images of each other, except that the compiler removes *Debug* code when it produces a release build of your application but keeps *Trace* code.

- **Exception handling**   Visual Basic .NET structured exception handling outclasses *On Error GoTo* because you can manage errors more methodically. You can respond to generic exceptions, or you can easily target specific exceptions found in the .NET Framework. You can even create your own exceptions derived from the *Application-Exception* class.

- **File handling**   Reading from and writing to files is easier with the *StreamReader* and *StreamWriter* classes. You can manipulate files and get file information with the *FileInfo* and *FileVersionInfo* classes. And if you need a temporary file, it's readily available by using the *GetTempFileName* method of the *Path* class.

- **Forms and graphics**   If you ever wrote code to make controls resize when a user resized your form, you'll appreciate the simplicity of *Anchoring* and *Docking*. By setting a control's *Anchor* property, you can make it *elastic*, meaning it keeps its relationship to any of the four sides of the form. *Docking* lets you glue one or more edges of the control to one or more sides of the form. The new *Graphics* objects in Visual Basic .NET let you draw shapes and text wherever you care to, in any color and font.

- **Inheritance**   With inheritance, you can use any class as a base or template for new classes. See the classes named *Employee, Employee-DataManager, FullTimeEmployee, PartTimeEmployee,* and *Temp-Employee* for extensive comments on inheritance, overloading, overriding, and scoping.

- ***StringBuilder***   One of the most expensive operations your application can perform is manipulating strings. The *StringBuilder* provides a more efficient way to do it. The *StringBuilder* manipulates strings without repeatedly creating new strings, as happens when you use traditional string methods to do simple things such as concatenation. Whenever you expect to make multiple adjustments to a string, use the *StringBuilder*. It is orders of magnitude faster than traditional string manipulation.

- ■ **Threading**   The .NET Framework provides great control over individual threads. You can run any procedure on its own thread, set thread priorities, suspend and resume threads, and perform any number of other thread-related operations.

Code Walkthrough

We'll briefly discuss each feature.

Debugging/Tracing

You can easily write debugging information to the console, which is the default listener, with a simple *Write* or *WriteLine* statement:

```
Debug.WriteLine(strDebug)
```

When you want to write the debug information to a file, you can do so by creating a file for output and then creating a text writer and adding it to the debug listeners, like this:

```
Dim strFile As String = "C:\DebugOutput.txt"
Dim stmFile As Stream = File.Create(strFile)
Dim twTextListener As New TextWriterTraceListener(stmFile)
With Debug.Listeners
    .Clear()
    .Add(twTextListener)
End With
Debug.Write(strDebug)
Debug.Flush()
```

Writing to the Event Log is easy. Just create a listener for the event log, add it to the *Listeners* collection, and write to it.

```
Dim logdebugListener As New EventLogTraceListener(_
    "101 VB.NET Sample Applications:Why VB.NET is Cool")
With Debug.Listeners
    .Clear()
    .Add(logdebugListener)
End With
Debug.Write(strDebug)
Debug.Flush()
```

Exception Handling

Structured Exception Handling is much more robust and extensible than *On Error GoTo*. Here we're trying to open a file in a nonexistent directory. We can catch the specific exception associated with this type of situation, and we can accommodate other exceptions as well. The *Message* property is like the Visual Basic 6 *Err.Description*, and *StackTrace* shows the sequence of calls that got us here.

```
Private Sub ExceptionReadingFromFile()
    Try
        Dim sw As New StreamWriter("c:\12345678asdf\baddirectory.txt")
    Catch expDirNotFound As DirectoryNotFoundException
        txtExceptionHandlingResult.Text = "Message: " & _
        expDirNotFound.Message & vbCrLf & vbCrLf
        txtExceptionHandlingResult.Text &= "Stack Trace: " & _
            expDirNotFound.StackTrace
    Catch exp As Exception
        MsgBox(exp.ToString(), MsgBoxStyle.OKOnly Or _
            MsgBoxStyle.Critical, Me.Text)
    End Try
End Sub
```

File Handling

The .NET Framework has a variety of classes that make file and directory handling convenient, including *File*, *FileInfo*, *Directory*, *DirectoryInfo*, *StreamWriter*, *StreamReader*, *FileStream*, *Path*, and others. Reading from a file is as simple as:

```
Dim sr As New StreamReader(strFile)
txtFileResult.Text = sr.ReadToEnd()
sr.Close()
```

The following code shows how you can write to a file. (We're creating the file with *CreateText*, one of the shared methods of the *File* class.)

```
Dim sw As StreamWriter = File.CreateText(strFileWrite)
sw.WriteLine("The quick brown fox jumped over the " & _
    "lazy dogs.")
sw.Flush()
sw.Close()
```

The *FileInfo* class lets you copy, delete, move, and collect information about a file. In this case, we're simply checking the file's size:

```
Dim fi As New FileInfo(strFileWrite)
txtFileResult.Text = "Size of " & _
    strFileWrite.Substring(InStr("/", strFileWrite)) & ": " & _
    fi.Length.ToString + " bytes."
```

When you need a temporary file name, a simple method call provides it:

```
txtFileResult.Text = "Temp file name: " & Path.GetTempFileName
```

Forms and Graphics

On the sample form, *frmControls*, the Name text box is anchored to the Top, Left, and Right. This arrangement means that when the form is resized, the text box will automatically resize with the form, maintaining its relative position to those three points. The Address text box is anchored to the Top, Bottom, Left, and Right, so it will automatically resize all its dimensions with the form. The text box at the bottom is docked to the bottom of the form. Docking glues a control to one or more edges of the form so that the text box will maintain its original height, stay docked to the bottom, and expand or contract horizontally when the form is resized.

Working with graphics is easier than ever, but significantly different than in Visual Basic 6. Drawing a circle (in *frmGraphics*) involves creating a *Graphics* object, clearing the *PictureBox* control, and then creating a *Pen* object and drawing with it. Note how the graphics object is created by calling a method on the object it will later interact with, the *PictureBox*.

```
Dim g As Graphics = picDrawing.CreateGraphics()
g.Clear(Me.BackColor)
Dim p As New Pen(Color.Red, 3)
g.DrawEllipse(p, 120, 120, 100, 100)
g.Dispose()
```

Drawing a line or rectangle is equally simple. But you might be surprised to find that writing text graphically is much like drawing a shape. For example, the sample application creates some text in the *PictureBox* with the *DrawString* method of the *Graphics* object.

```
g.DrawString("VB.NET", New Font("Arial", 20), Brushes.Blue, 135, 135)
```

Inheritance

Inheritance lets you take an existing class and make it the prototype for derived classes. The sample application has an *Employee* class, from which are derived *FullTimeEmployee*, *PartTimeEmployee*, and *TempEmployee*. Each of the derived classes has all the characteristics of the original (base) class but can implement functionality of its own. See the code for extensive comments, and refer to Application #8: Scoping, Overloading, Overriding for much more information.

StringBuilder

The *StringBuilder* exists to speed up manipulation of strings. The sample repeatedly appends a string to the *StringBuilder*, an action that would create a separate *String* object for each concatenation if it were done the traditional way. Here are both methods. When you run the application, note how much faster the *StringBuilder* is.

```
tmr.Begin()
strConcatenated = strSBOrig
For i = 1 To intStrIterations
    strConcatenated = strConcatenated & strSBAppend
Next
tmr.End()
```

(continued)

```
tmr.Begin()
For i = 1 To intSBIterations
    sb.Append(strSBAppend)
Next
tmr.End()
```

Threading

The sample application creates a thread and sends it off to run a particular procedure. Meanwhile, the original thread continues its work. The *AddressOf* operator creates a delegate that references the *CalledByThread* procedure. When the *Start* method is invoked, the thread executes the procedure associated with the delegate.

```
newThread = New Thread(AddressOf CalledByThread)
newThread.Name = "New Demo Thread"
newThread.Start()
```

In this example, both the current thread and the new thread are doing some work—in this case, simply running a numeric loop. Note the use of *Application.DoEvents* method in each thread's loop, which ensures that the thread yields to other threads and does not monopolize the CPU's time while it's looping.

```
Dim i As Integer
For i = 0 To maxCount
    lblCurrCounter.Text = "Orig -- " & i.ToString()
    lblCurrCounter.Refresh()
    Application.DoEvents()
Next
```

Conclusion

Visual Basic .NET leverages a variety of features of the .NET Framework as well as language-specific features of its own to provide a language that is more robust and capable than Visual Basic 6 and that is truly object oriented.

Be sure to refer to other applications in this series for more detailed explanations of the features presented in this sample.

3

Data Access

The Microsoft .NET Framework introduces a new set of libraries that help you build robust data-centric applications. As you'll see in Application #25, these ADO.NET libraries do not necessarily *replace* legacy ADO for the COM developer. Rather, they represent a significant evolution of ADO for data access *from within managed code*. In short, ADO.NET is the API of choice for applications built using Microsoft Visual Basic .NET.

ADO was built for data access with relational databases that operate mainly in a connected, client-server environment; and although support for working with disconnected data and XML does exist, significant features are lacking. For example, the central object in ADO is the *RecordSet* object. It looks like a single table of data. In fact, if you want it to contain data from multiple database tables, you must use a JOIN query. The central object in ADO.NET is the *DataSet*. It stores data as a disconnected hierarchy of collections that represent the relational structure of its data source (for example, Microsoft SQL Server). Moreover, a *DataSet* can be easily shared with other applications because the data and relational structure serialize to XML and XML Schema, respectively. A *RecordSet* object, on the other hand, requires COM marshalling.

Although ADO.NET might seem more complex at first, the applications in this chapter will show that this next-generation ADO is a significant improvement that is well worth the effort required of you to make the transition.

Application #12: Use a *DataSet* and *DataView*

This sample introduces you to *DataSet* and *DataView*, two classes that are at the heart of ADO.NET. You'll learn how to connect to a database, retrieve data, use the *DataView* class's sorting and filtering capabilities to display ordered subsets of the data, and bind the *DataView* object to a *DataGrid* control. Figure 3-1 shows a screen shot of Application #12.

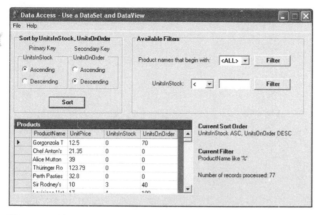

Figure 3-1   Application #12.

The sample application connects to the Northwind database and displays product information in a *DataGrid* control. You can sort the data in ascending or descending order on the primary key or secondary key. Controls are also available to filter the product information based on the first letter of the product name and the number of units in stock.

Building Upon...

Application #4: *Try/Catch/Finally*

New Concepts

ADO.NET was designed for data manipulation in a disconnected, distributed, XML-aware environment. The *DataSet* class is the principal abstraction of this architecture. The *DataView* class builds on it. Both reside in the *System.Data* namespace.

The *DataSet* class represents an in-memory, disconnected copy of data, with familiar class members that are consistent with a relational database model (for example, *DataTable*, *DataRow*, *DataColumn*, and *PrimaryKey*). It's both autonomous and aware. A *DataSet* object doesn't care where it came from or where it's going, but it remembers whence it came and is able to keep track of certain changes to its data.

The bridge between a *DataSet* object and a database is one of the concrete subclasses of the *DataAdapter* class. The *DataAdapter.Fill* method uses the SQL SELECT statement to retrieve data and populate the *DataSet* object. The *DataAdapter* class, in turn, employs a *DataReader* object to do the actual work of streaming the rows into the *DataSet* object. You'll learn more about the highly efficient *DataReader* class later in this chapter.

The *DataSet* class enjoys a close affiliation with XML. In fact, relational data can be abstracted and thus promoted to first-class .NET members via XML Schema mapping. This chapter, however, is concerned only with the generic, *untyped DataSet* object. Typed *DataSet* objects are an advanced topic and will be discussed later in this chapter.

Although you can use the *DataTable.Select* method to filter and sort the *DataRowCollection* object exposed by the *DataTable.Rows* property, a *DataView* object is typically preferred because it's easier to use, more flexible, and dynamically reflects any changes made to its underlying data source—that is, the *DataTable* object from which the *DataView* object was derived. With the *DataView* object, you can display multiple, dynamically updated views of the same disconnected data source, making it ideal for robust data-binding applications.

Code Walkthrough

The code that follows takes you through the main steps for working with a *DataSet* object and *DataView* object, including connecting to a database, retrieving data and filling a *DataSet*, creating a *DataView* for sorting and filtering purposes, and data binding to a *DataGrid* control to display the data.

Connecting to a Database

Most of the samples in this book use a *SqlConnection* object to connect to Microsoft SQL Server or the Microsoft Data Engine (MSDE). The *SqlConnection* class is optimized for use with SQL Server. The *OleDbConnection* class is also available for OLE DB–supported data sources.

The *SqlConnection* class is easy to use. Its second constructor takes a connection string. Two connection string constants are provided:

```
Protected Const SQL_CONNECTION_STRING As String = _
    "Server=localhost;DataBase=Northwind;Integrated Security=SSPI"

Protected Const MSDE_CONNECTION_STRING As String = _
    "Server=(local)\NetSDK;DataBase=Northwind;" & _
    "Integrated Security=SSPI"
```

Therefore, creating a connection to the database is as simple as setting *strConnection* to one of these connection strings and typing

```
Dim cnnNW As New SqlConnection(strConnection)
```

Creating and Filling a *DataSet*

The code to create and fill a *DataSet* object resides in the *Load* event of the form. It is wrapped in a *Try/Catch* block, which is not shown here for the sake of brevity. Following the instantiation of the *SqlConnection* class, a *SqlData-Adapter* object is created, passing the SQL SELECT statement and connection object to one of its constructors:

```
Dim daProducts As New SqlDataAdapter( _
"SELECT ProductName, UnitPrice, UnitsInStock, UnitsOnOrder " _
    & "FROM products", cnnNW)
```

The *Fill* method is then called to populate the *DataSet* object (instantiated earlier): daProducts.Fill(dsProducts, PRODUCT_TABLE_NAME). Because a *DataSet* object can hold multiple *DataTable* objects, you should name each one. In this case, the name is Products. This naming is, however, not required. As with any .NET collection, you can access its members by a key (Products) or a zero-based index—for example, DataSet.Tables(0).

> **Tip**   Manually create a *DataTable* object so that you can work more easily with any kind of data. A *DataTable* doesn't have to originate from a *DataSet*. You can instantiate it directly, add *DataColumn* and *DataRow* objects, and then fill the *DataTable* object in a variety of ways. For example, sorting an array has traditionally been programmatically difficult. Instead, you could populate a custom *DataTable* by iterating through an array. Then create a *DataView* and easily sort and filter its contents!

Creating and Working with a *DataView* Object

As mentioned earlier, the *DataSet* object is the underlying data source for a *DataView* object. (You cannot create a *DataView* object from a *DataReader* object.) To create a *DataView* object, you can either instantiate it directly or access a *DataView* object initialized to default settings via the *DefaultView* property of the *DataTable* class. You can then set the *RowFilter* and *Sort* properties to filter and sort a view of the underlying data:

```
dvProducts = dsProducts.Tables("Products").DefaultView
With dvProducts
    .RowFilter = DEFAULT_FILTER
    .Sort = DEFAULT_SORT
End With
```

The *RowFilter* property is a string value that takes the form of a column name followed by an operator and a value to filter on. This is similar to a SQL WHERE clause. In the previous code, DEFAULT_FILTER is set to "*ProductName like '%'*". This is equivalent to applying no filter at all.

> **Note**   There are numerous ways to construct a filter expression. See the *Expression* property of the *DataColumn* class in the .NET Framework software development kit (SDK) for more information.

> **Caution**   Filter expressions build on each other. If you want to reuse a *DataView* object that already has a filter applied, remember to reset the *RowFilter* property to its default (an empty string) prior to applying a new filter. If you do not, your resultset will not be what you intended. This is a common mistake that can trip up even experienced developers.

The *Sort* property works in a similar fashion. It's a string in the form of one or more column names each followed by ASC or DESC, for ascending or descending order, respectively. The default sort order is ascending, so you need only specify DESC. In this case, DEFAULT_SORT is "*UnitsInStock ASC, Units-OnOrder ASC*".

The sample application contains three *Button Click* event handlers that demonstrate how to apply a variety of filter and sort expressions. In each case, the principles are the same. It's left to you to explore this code further.

Data Binding to a *DataGrid* Control

The last step in the process of displaying a custom view of your disconnected data source is to data bind the *DataView* object to a control—in this case, a *DataGrid* control. Although the *DataGrid* control is a highly customizable and complex control, it's surprisingly easy to bind it to a data source and display its contents. You need only to set its *DataSource* property to an object that implements the *IList* or *IListSource* interface and the data is displayed (albeit in an unformatted manner you will typically want to change—but more on that in a later chapter). Here's the line of code relevant to our application:

```
grdProducts.DataSource = dvProducts
```

Conclusion

This has been a quick overview of the *DataSet* and *DataView* classes. You've learned some foundational ADO.NET concepts, such as how to

■   Connect to a database using a *SqlConnection* object

■   Retrieve data and fill a *DataSet* object by using a *SqlDataAdapter* object

■   Create a *DataView* object, and set its *Sort* and *RowFilter* properties

■   Data bind to a *DataGrid* control

Subsequent chapters will explore these and related concepts in more detail, building on what you have learned here.

Application #13: Use Stored Procedures

This sample shows you how to programmatically create stored procedures and then use them to retrieve data from SQL Server (or MSDE). The use of Microsoft Access queries is also demonstrated. A variety of stored procedures will be used. One requires an input parameter, another does not; and a third stored procedure makes use of input parameters, output parameters, and a return value. Figure 3-2 shows a screen shot of Application #13.

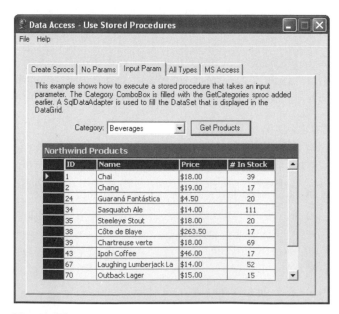

Figure 3-2   Application #13.

The sample application is divided into a series of tabbed demonstrations that each build on the other as you proceed from left to right. In the first tab, you'll create several custom stored procedures for the SQL Server or MSDE version of the Northwind database. The next three tabs demonstrate the use of these new stored procedures. The final tab shows you how to use an existing Microsoft Access query to generate a sales report. (The .mdb file containing the Access version of the Northwind database is included with the sample.)

Building Upon...

Application #4: *Try/Catch/Finally*
Application #12: Use a *DataSet* and *DataView*

New Concepts

Stored procedures are, in most cases, preferable to *ad hoc* SQL statements for a variety of reasons—such as data-tier logic encapsulation and performance gains. Discussion of these advantages is, however, beyond the scope of this chapter. It's assumed that you're already convinced of their importance. Additionally, you should already have a basic understanding of how stored procedures work and the SQL syntax involved with creating and using them. What remains is to show you how to work with them using ADO.NET.

Recall from the previous section that filling a *DataSet* object involves the following steps when using *ad hoc* SQL statements to retrieve data from SQL Server (or MSDE):

1. Connect to a database using a *SqlConnection* object.

2. Create a *SqlDataAdapter* object, passing in the SQL SELECT statement and the connection object.

3. Call the *DataAdapter.Fill* method, passing in the *DataSet* object.

   When using stored procedures, there are two additional steps:

4. Set the *SqlCommand.CommandType* property to *CommandType.StoredProcedure*. (The default, *CommandType.Text*, is for ad hoc SQL.)

5. If parameters are used, add *SqlParameter* objects to the *SqlParameterCollection* object exposed by the *SqlCommand.Parameters* property.

Although the *SqlParameter* class is indeed new, you've already implicitly used the *SqlCommand* class in the previous section when you passed the SQL SELECT statement to the *SqlDataAdapter* constructor. The data adapter used this statement to initialize a *SqlCommand* object that it exposes via its *SelectCommand* property. The *SqlCommand* class represents any SQL statement—whether it's *ad hoc* SQL text or a stored procedure. (A third, rarely used, option named *TableDirect* is also supported but not covered further.) It has a variety of methods to execute SQL statements. You'll get exposure to these methods in the upcoming section concerning the ADO.NET workhorse, the *SqlDataReader* class.

Code Walkthrough

Here we'll take a look at what's involved with the two additional steps previously mentioned for using stored procedures.

Calling a Parameterless Stored Procedure

The simplest use of a stored procedure involves no parameters. This is demonstrated in the No Params tab of the sample application. In the button's *Click* event handler, you'll find the following code:

```
Dim scnnNorthwind As New SqlConnection(SQL_CONNECTION_STRING)
Dim sda As New SqlDataAdapter("[Ten Most Expensive Products]", scnnNorthwind)
Dim dsProducts As New DataSet()
sda.SelectCommand.CommandType = CommandType.StoredProcedure
sda.Fill(dsProducts, "Products")
```

This code is identical to that which you saw in the previous section, with the following exceptions:

- The first argument to the data adapter's constructor is not a SQL statement, but rather it's the name of the stored procedure you want to execute. It is, in fact, the *CommandText* setting for the *SqlCommand* object exposed by the data adapter.

- The *CommandType* is explicitly set to *StoredProcedure* to indicate to the *SqlCommand* object what the *CommandText* refers to.

When you run the sample, the data is displayed in a generic gray *DataGrid* set to its default formatting. The other two samples involving a *DataGrid* use custom formatting set with *DataGridTableStyle* and *DataGridColumnStyle* objects. These are introduced in Chapter 4.

Adding an Input Parameter

A much more common scenario involves a stored procedure that uses an input parameter. Adding one is quite easy. The code in the *Click* event handler for the button on the Input Param tab shows how to do this. The first six lines declare and initialize the required variables. For demonstration purposes, the *SqlCommand* object is explicitly instantiated and passed to the *SqlDataAdapter*.

```
connectionString = SQL_CONNECTION_STRING
Dim scnnNorthwind As New SqlConnection(connectionString)
Dim scmd As New SqlCommand("GetProducts", scnnNorthwind)
Dim sda As New SqlDataAdapter(scmd)
Dim dsProducts As New DataSet()
Dim sparCatID As New SqlParameter()
```

SqlParameter object properties representing the input parameter are then set. Notice that the *ParameterName* property requires the @ symbol. (ADO.NET does not add this for you.) The SQL data types are conveniently encapsulated in a *SqlDbType* enumeration. In this case, you're passing a value of type *Int*. (You cannot use .NET Framework data types to set this property.) The actual value is taken from the selected item in the *ComboBox* control.

```
With sparCatID
    .ParameterName = "@CategoryID"
    .SqlDbType = SqlDbType.Int
    .Value = cboCategoriesInputParam.SelectedValue
End With
```

Once the parameter properties are set, you must add the *SqlParameter* object to the *SqlParameterCollection* object exposed by the *SqlCommand.Parameters* property:

```
With scmd
    .Parameters.Add(sparCatID)
    .CommandType = CommandType.StoredProcedure
End With
```

The preceding code could also be simplified and reduced to the following:

```
scmd.Parameters.Add(New SqlParameter("@CategoryID", _
    SqlDbType.Int)).Value = cboCategoriesInputParam.SelectedValue
```

Using an Output Parameter and Return Value

You'll often encounter scenarios in which you want to execute a SQL SELECT statement and get back additional values that aren't a part of the main result-set. You can do this in the sample application by using the All Types tab. The code for this tab uses a stored procedure created when you click the button in the Create Sprocs tab. The SQL statement used to programmatically create the stored procedure when you first run the application is as follows:

```
CREATE PROCEDURE GetProductCountAndAveragePrice
@CategoryID Int,
@AveragePrice Int OUT
AS
```

(continued)

```
DECLARE @SumProdPrices Money
SELECT @AveragePrice = SUM(UnitPrice)/COUNT(ProductID)
FROM Northwind.dbo.Products
WHERE CategoryID = @CategoryID
RETURN
(SELECT COUNT(ProductID)
FROM Northwind.dbo.Products
WHERE CategoryID = @CategoryID)
```

Notice in the third line that the *@AveragePrice* parameter is followed by the OUT (or OUTPUT) keyword. Its value is then set in the first SELECT statement. To retrieve this value from the database, you write the following code:

```
.Add(New SqlParameter("@AveragePrice", _
    SqlDbType.Money)).Direction = ParameterDirection.Output
```

The only difference between this code and the short notation in the previous section is the addition of a *ParameterDirection* enumeration value. The default is *Input*, so normally you don't need to set the parameter direction.

If you want to retrieve a SQL RETURN value from a stored procedure that is other than one of the five SQL Server return codes, use the *ReturnValue* enumeration. This will work only with an integer data type.

```
.Add(New SqlParameter("ReturnValue", _
    SqlDbType.Int)).Direction = ParameterDirection.ReturnValue
```

This code will store the return value from the SELECT statement following the RETURN keyword in the stored procedure.

Accessing the output and return parameter values is as easy as setting them. First, retrieve the parameter from the *SqlParameterCollection* object as you would when working with any other .NET collection: either by ordinal or key (parameter name). The *Value* property returns an *Object* type, so you must explicitly cast it to the desired type. Although this is straightforward, the syntax can get a little tricky if you want to apply string formatting, as in this code from the *Click* event:

```
CType(scmd.Parameters("@AveragePrice").Value, Double).ToString("c")
```

You can learn more about string formatting in other chapters.

Executing Microsoft Access Queries

Thus far, you have mostly been working with classes in the *System.Data.Sql-Client* namespace, optimized for use with SQL Server. Using Microsoft Access from ADO.NET requires a different data access provider, the classes for which are found in the *System.Data.OleDb* namespace. In the code for the final tabbed example, you'll notice that all classes used to connect to the database and retrieve data are in this namespace. Aside from the very different connection string (`"Provider=Microsoft.Jet.OLEDB.4.0;Data Source=..\North-wind.mdb"`), the code is almost identical to the previous examples.

Conclusion

This topic has shown you how to use stored procedures from ADO.NET. You learned how to call a stored procedure, use input and output parameters, and retrieve custom return values. These are core foundational tasks you'll likely use repeatedly as you develop .NET applications.

Application #14: Use a *SqlDataReader*

When performance is your chief concern, especially with large amounts of data, use a *DataReader* class. This abstract class is built for speed and roughly approximates the ADO *Recordset* when the latter uses a forward-only, read-only *firehose* cursor. The *DataReader* class is often used in Web applications, where performance concerns are paramount. In desktop applications, it finds more limited use because rich client interfaces that consume relational data often require the more robust functionality of the *DataSet* class. A more detailed comparison between the *DataReader* class and the *DataSet* class is offered later in this topic.

The sample application shows you how to use a *SqlDataReader* class, a concrete subclass of the *DataReader* class that is optimized for use with SQL Server. This class is found in the *System.Data.SqlClient* namespace. The sample application creates and executes a new stored procedure against the Northwind database. Two sets of results from the Products table are then displayed in a *TextBox* control. A *Label* control indicates the number of products in both resultsets. Figure 3-3 shows a screen shot of Application #14.

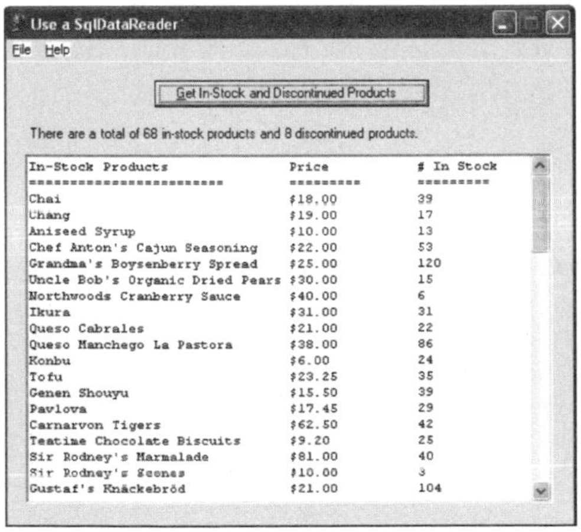

Figure 3-3   Application #14.

Building Upon...

Application #3: String Manipulation
Application #4: *Try/Catch/Finally*
Application #13: Use Stored Procedures

New Concepts

With ADO.NET, there are two main ways to retrieve data from a database. If you want to work with data offline—for example, in a disconnected manner—the *DataSet* class is your only choice. The connected world is served by the *DataReader* class. It communicates directly with the database. In fact, the *DataReader* class is used behind the scenes by the *DataAdapter* class to fill a *DataSet* object. One could say that the *DataReader* class is the real workhorse of ADO.NET.

> **Note**   Although the *DataReader* object does resemble the ADO *Recordset* object, you should keep two main differences in mind. First, ADO.NET has no support for server-side cursors. They aren't necessary because of the architecture of the *DataTable* class, which allows access to its rows in a *Collection* object via a key or index. Second, ADO.NET simplifies things by providing no equivalent to the *Recordset.MoveNext* method, a chief source of frustration for ADO developers in the past. Rather, the *DataReader.Read* method automatically advances the cursor to the next row, if one exists.

Because of the lightweight, connected nature of the *DataReader* class, you need to be aware of some restrictions and potential pitfalls in using it:

- Only one *DataReader* object can be used for any given connection object.

- The connection object cannot be used for any other purpose while the *DataReader* object is open. If you want to reuse the connection, you must first call the *DataReader.Close* method. In fact, you should always explicitly call the *Close* method instead of depending on the garbage collector. An open *DataReader* object ties up the existing connection, which is an expensive resource.

> **Tip**   If you want to tie the life of the connection to the *Data-Reader* object, use the *CommandBehavior.CloseConnection* enumeration when calling the *ExecuteReader* method. This will close the connection automatically when the *Data-Reader.Close* method is invoked. This is especially applicable to n-tier applications in which the calling tier doesn't have direct access to the underlying connection.

- The first row of data is not available until you call the *Read* method. (This is roughly equivalent to the ADO *RecordSet.MoveFirst* method.)

- If your stored procedure uses a return or output parameter, the parameter won't be available until after the *DataReader* object is closed. In this case, it's helpful to think of the stored procedure as a function. The code retrieving the data might have executed, but until the function ends, nothing is returned.

- There is no equivalent to the ADO *Recordset.RecordCount* property. In the following "Code Walkthrough" section you'll learn how to obtain the count using a batched query. Of course, you could also use a counter while iterating through the resultset.

- The data is retrieved forward-only. Once it is streamed in, you cannot go back through the rows in the *DataReader* unless you've stored the data in an object that supports this, such as an *ArrayList* object or a *DataTable* object.

- You cannot use a *DataReader* object for updates. The data is read-only.

- *DataReader* objects have no inherent support for XML serialization with a corresponding schema. You can call *ExecuteXMLReader* and retrieve an XML stream, but this is only if the T-SQL FOR XML clause is used in the query (SQL Server 2000 only). If you want to retrieve relational data that can be readily serialized as XML, you should use a *DataSet* object.

- A *DataReader* object cannot be used for data binding (that is, it doesn't support the *IList* or *IListSource* interface). For true data binding, you would first have to iterate through the *DataReader* object and then add the values to an object that supports one of these interfaces.

Performance Tips

If you elect to use a *DataReader* object over a *DataSet* object, your reasons are almost certainly performance-oriented. As such, you should be aware of a few things you can do to ensure that the *DataReader* object works optimally:

- Retrieve values in their native type instead of using the *Item* collection followed by an explicit cast. For example, `sdr.GetDecimal(1)` is more efficient than `CDbl(sdr.Item("UnitPrice"))`.

- If you want to use the *Item* collection, access the values by their index instead of by key (column name).

> **Caution**   Although accessing values using indices is faster than when using keys (because the type conversion penalty is not incurred), the performance advantage might be offset by maintenance issues and the greater potential for developer error. When keys are used, changes to the order of the columns in the resultset do not affect your code. When accessing values by indices, however, you run the risk of your application breaking if someone changes the ordering of columns in the database table or the SELECT statement. Additionally, the code is less readable when indices are used. For most applications, it's probably wise to use keys to avoid these pitfalls. Unfortunately, certain *DataReader* class methods such as *GetValue*, *GetDataType*, and *IsDbNull* do not allow keys. Exercise caution when using these methods.

- If you need only the data in the first column in the first row—for example, in a SELECT COUNT(*) statement—use *SqlCommand.ExecuteScalar* instead of *ExecuteReader*.

- When retrieving large rows, consider using the *CommandBehavior.SequentialAccess* enumeration.

Comparing the *DataSet* and *DataReader* Objects

Space limitations do not permit an extensive comparison of the *DataSet* object and *DataReader* object. Table 3-1, however, summarizes the major differences.

Table 3-1   Differences Between *DataSet* and *DataReader*

DataSet	*DataReader*
Disconnected	Connected
Supports data binding	Does not support data binding
Fully supports XML serialization	Limited serialization only with SQL Server 2000 and the *ExecuteXmlReader* method.
Access data in any direction	Access data in forward-only manner only
Supports data updates	Data is read-only
Can be cached to improve performance	Noncacheable
Data can be easily sorted and filtered	No support for sorting and filtering

Despite the vast differences between these two objects, it's often unclear which of the two is best for any given scenario. This is especially true for Web applications. The performance advantage is the number one reason given for choosing a *DataReader* object over a *DataSet* object, but in a recent MSDN article titled "Best Practices for Using ADO.NET," the authors made it clear that the performance gains might be negligible in most scenarios:

The DataAdapter uses the DataReader when filling a DataSet. Therefore, the performance gained by using the DataAdapter [sic—DataReader] instead of the DataSet is that you save on the memory that the DataSet would consume and the cycles it takes to populate the DataSet. This performance gain is, for the most part, nominal so you should base your design decisions on the functionality required.

In other words, for all but the most performance-critical scenarios, the feature-rich *DataSet* object is most likely your best choice.

Code Walkthrough

The code in this sample application, most of which resides in the button's *Click* event handler, is minimal and straightforward. Once a connection is established, the existing *GetProducts* stored procedure, if it exists, is dropped and then re-created. The stored procedure contains several SQL SELECT statements and a return value:

```
CREATE PROCEDURE GetProducts
AS
SELECT ProductName, UnitPrice, UnitsInStock
FROM Northwind.dbo.Products
```

(continued)

```
WHERE Discontinued = 0 AND UnitsInStock > 0
SELECT ProductName, UnitPrice
FROM Northwind.dbo.Products
WHERE Discontinued = 1
SELECT COUNT(ProductID)
FROM Products
WHERE Discontinued = 0 AND UnitsInStock > 0
RETURN (SELECT COUNT(ProductID)
FROM Northwind.dbo.Products
WHERE Discontinued = 1)
```

To execute the stored procedure, the *SqlCommand* object is reused as follows. The variable *sdr* has already been declared as a *SqlDataReader*. Notice that the connection is tied to the life of the *DataReader* object by using the *CloseConnection* enumeration.

```
With scmd
    .CommandText = "GetProducts"
    .CommandType = CommandType.StoredProcedure
    .Parameters.Add(New SqlParameter("ReturnValue", _
        SqlDbType.Int)).Direction = ParameterDirection.ReturnValue
    sdr = .ExecuteReader(CommandBehavior.CloseConnection)
End With
```

With the *SqlDataReader* object in hand, you can now call the *Read* method and iterate through the first resultset that it contains—in-stock products—building an output string for display later. The *Read* method returns a Boolean value: *True* if another row exists, and *False* if not. The high performance *StringBuilder* object, instantiated earlier, is used instead of traditional string concatenation.

```
While sdr.Read
    strProductName = sdr.GetString(0)
    sb.Append(strProductName)

    Select Case Math.Floor(strProductName.Length / 8)
        ' Case statements removed to conserve space.
    End Select

    sb.Append(sdr.GetDecimal(1).ToString("c"))
    sb.Append(vbTab)
    sb.Append(vbTab)
    sb.Append(sdr.GetInt16(2).ToString())
    sb.Append(vbCrLf)
End While
```

Notice that the values are accessed using the *GetDataType* method corresponding to the underlying data type. The product name, unit price, and units in stock are contained in the first (index 0), second, and third columns, respectively. One of the *ToString* overloads is used to format the decimal value to currency.

To jump to the resultset returned by the second SELECT statement in the stored procedure, use the *NextResult* method. The code is similar to what you've just seen, except that the values are accessed, for the sake of demonstration, through the *Item* property using the column name:

```
strProductName = sdr.Item("ProductName").ToString
sb.Append(CDbl(sdr("UnitPrice")).ToString("c"))
```

Notice that use of the *Item* property can be explicit or implicit. Typically, you will omit *Item*, as in the second line. Also, because the *DataReader* object returns a value of type *Object* when not using one of the *GetDataType* methods, you must explicitly cast it to the proper type. In the case of the unit price, you would cast it to a *Double* to take advantage of the currency formatter in its *ToString* method.

Access the final set of results in the same way. In this case, you are merely retrieving the total number of in-stock products:

```
sdr.NextResult()

While sdr.Read
    lblNumProducts.Text = "There are a total of " _
        & sdr.GetInt32(0).ToString & " in-stock products and "
End While
```

An alternative approach to retrieving the equivalent of the ADO *Recordset.RecordCount* property is to use a return value, as demonstrated in these closing statements of the *Click* event handler:

```
sdr.Close()

lblNumProducts.Text &= scmd.Parameters("ReturnValue").Value.ToString & _
    " discontinued products."
```

Recall that the *Close* method must be invoked prior to accessing the values in any output or return parameters.

Conclusion

This topic has shown you how to use a *SqlDataReader* object to retrieve and process data returned by a stored procedure containing batched SQL queries. Along the way, you learned that *DataReader* is a lightweight, high-performance class that efficiently serves the connected world. Being lightweight, however, it's not nearly as feature rich as the *DataSet* class. You should carefully weigh your application's current and future needs when considering whether to use a *DataReader* or a *DataSet*. When in doubt, do some performance testing to determine whether the inherent limitations of the *DataReader* class are worth the potential performance gains.

Application #15: Bind Data to a *ComboBox*

One of the most common Windows Forms controls is the *ComboBox* control. It's normally used to display data in a drop-down style control that is either editable (the *DropDownStyle* property set to *DropDown*) or noneditable (the *DropDownStyle* property set to *DropDownList*). A third, infrequently used style permits cycling through values without the drop-down effect (the *DropDownStyle* property set to *Simple*).

The *ComboBox* supports *complex data binding*, as opposed to the *simple data binding* covered in the next topic. Although it's *complex* under the hood, you'll see it's actually easy to implement. In fact, this topic is a slight departure from previous topics because there are few new concepts. Most of the discussion takes place in the "Code Walkthrough" section.

The sample application shows you how to bind a *ComboBox* control to a variety of data sources. Figure 3-4 shows a screen shot of Application #15.

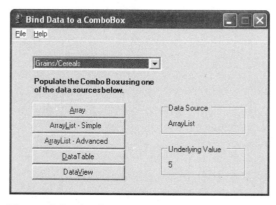

Figure 3-4   Application #15.

Building Upon...

Application #1: Use Arrays
Application #4: *Try/Catch/Finally*
Application #14: Use a *SqlDataReader*

New Concepts

Controls that permit binding to more than one data element—for example, multiple rows in two columns of a *DataSet* object—require complex data binding.

These controls, such as *ComboBox* or *DataGrid*, don't use the *Binding* class (covered in the next topic). Rather, they expose a *DataSource* property and other properties that, in turn, map to properties of the data source. For example, the *ComboBox* control uses the *DisplayMember* and *ValueMember* properties to set what the user sees for each item as well as the item's underlying value. Thus, implementing complex data binding is often as easy as setting a few properties of the control being bound. The "Code Walkthrough" section will explain this further.

> **Note** For a .NET type to qualify as a data source for complex data binding, it must implement or derive from the *IList* interface. Thus, arrays and most of the collection classes qualify.

Code Walkthrough

Each subheading that follows maps to an example in the sample application.

Arrays

One of the easiest ways to data bind a *ComboBox* control is to use an array. The code amounts to two lines:

```
Dim arrColors() As String = _
    {"AQUA", "BLACK", "BLUE", "GREEN", "RED", "WHITE", "YELLOW"}
cboDemo.DataSource = arrColors
```

The .NET data binding mechanism treats each item in the data source as an *Object* data type. By default, it will set both the text and value of each *ComboBox* item to the *ToString* equivalent of the *Object*.

ArrayList—Simple

As far as a *ComboBox* control is concerned, an *ArrayList* object is no different from an *Array* object. The twist with the simple *ArrayList* example is that it's filled by iterating through a *SqlDataReader*:

```
Dim strSQL As String = _
    "SELECT LastName + ', ' + FirstName As FullName " & _
    "FROM Employees"

cnnNW = New SqlConnection(strConnection)
cmd = New SqlCommand(strSQL, cnnNW)
Dim arlEmployees As New ArrayList()

cnnNW.Open()
dr = cmd.ExecuteReader(CommandBehavior.CloseConnection)
```

(continued)

```
While dr.Read
    arlEmployees.Add(dr("FullName"))
End While

dr.Close()
cboDemo.DataSource = arlEmployees
```

As you can see, the procedure for data binding to an *ArrayList* object is identical to that for an *Array* object. If you don't require each item in the *ComboBox* control to have an underlying value different from the displayed text, simply set the *DataSource* property and the .NET Framework does the rest.

ArrayList—Advanced

If you want to data bind to an *ArrayList* object as well as associate each item in the *ComboBox* control with an underlying value that is different from its display text, things get a little trickier. A typical implementation of this scenario is an *ArrayList* collection of custom objects that expose properties that are then mapped to the data binding mechanism via the *DisplayMember* and *ValueMember* properties.

This third example creates an *ArrayList* collection of custom *Category* objects. The *Category* class is implemented in the Category.vb class file. It exposes two public properties, *ID* and *Name*:

```
Class Category
    Dim _id As Integer
    Dim _name As String

    Sub New(ByVal intID As Integer, ByVal strName As String)
        _id = intID
        _Name = strName
    End Sub

    Public ReadOnly Property ID() As Integer
        Get
            Return _id
        End Get
    End Property

    Public ReadOnly Property Name() As String
        Get
            Return _Name
        End Get
    End Property
End Class
```

Several things are worth noting here. First, the properties must be declared as *Public*. Second, they must be *properties*, not fields. The reason for this is not documented. It basically boils down to an internal design decision by the .NET Framework team. It can be a source of frustration, however, because most classes in the .NET Framework treat fields and properties in the same way. Third, the properties don't have to be of type *String*. In this example, the *ID* property is an *Integer*. Recall that when the data binding occurs, the *ToString* equivalent of the object is displayed or used as the underlying value.

The code for this example is similar to that for a simple *ArrayList*:

```
Dim strSQL As String = _
    "SELECT CategoryID, CategoryName " & _
    "FROM Categories"

cnnNW = New SqlConnection(strConnection)
cmd = New SqlCommand(strSQL, cnnNW)
Dim arlCategories As New ArrayList()

cnnNW.Open()
dr = cmd.ExecuteReader(CommandBehavior.CloseConnection)

While dr.Read
    arlCategories.Add(New Category(dr.GetInt32(0), dr.GetString(1)))
End While

dr.Close()

With cboDemo
    .DataSource = arlCategories
    .ValueMember = "ID"
    .DisplayMember = "Name"
End With
```

The main difference is that, in addition to the *DataSource* property, the *DisplayMember* and *ValueMember* properties are also set. These are *String* values that map to the appropriate property of the objects contained in the data source.

DataTable and *DataView*

The final two examples are very similar. The SQL SELECT statement for both examples is shown in the following code. (The data source is acquired in the *frmMain_Load* event handler.)

```
Dim strSQL As String = _
    "SELECT ProductID, ProductName " & _
    "FROM Products"
```

Additionally, for both examples, the *DataSource*, *DisplayMember*, and *ValueMember* properties are set. The following code is for the *DataTable* example:

```
With cboDemo
    .DisplayMember = "ProductName"
    .ValueMember = "ProductID"
    .DataSource = dsProducts.Tables("PRODUCTS")
End With
```

As the data source is a *DataTable* object, it contains *DataRow* objects. You would normally access values in these objects using the following syntax: `DataRow.Item("ColumnName")`, or the shorthand `DataRow("ColumnName")`. Thus, it makes sense that the *DisplayMember* and *ValueMember* properties use the respective *DataRow* column names to map the values being bound. The same concept holds true when the data source is a *DataView* object.

Conclusion

This topic has shown you how to data bind a *ComboBox* control. You learned that there are two types of data binding in Windows Forms: simple and complex. The nomenclature belies the level of difficulty required to implement it. In fact, you'll find complex data binding to be quite simple to code. Acquire a data source that implements the *IList* interface, set a few properties, and let the .NET Framework do the rest. The next topic explores simple data binding in support of data navigation.

Application #16: Data Binding with Navigation

A feature often required for data-driven applications is the ability to step forward and backward through a set of records. *Data navigation*, as it is often called, requires that all controls involved with displaying the information be kept in sync with the current record. This topic will show you how to utilize data navigation in your Windows Forms applications.

The sample application is quite simple. Four *TextBox* controls display employee information from the Northwind database. You can use the navigation controls to step forward and backward through each record, or to jump to the beginning or end of the set of records. A *Label* indicates the number of the current record. Figure 3-5 shows a screen shot of Application #16.

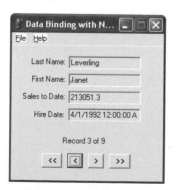

Figure 3-5   Application #16.

This topic is the first of three topics that build upon each other, culminating in a master-details Windows Form application. You'll see the user interface evolve as functionality is added. For example, in Figure 3-5, notice that the Sales To Date value is not formatted as currency. Also, the Hire Date would be best displayed in a shorter version, without the time. Custom formatting handlers are covered in the next topic, with the addition of two new fields to the interface.

Building Upon...

Application #4: *Try/Catch/Finally*
Application #12: Use a *DataSet* and *DataView*

New Concepts

In the previous topic, you learned about complex data binding. Ironically, this is often easier to implement than *simple* data binding.

Simple Data Binding and Windows Forms

With simple data binding you can bind any property of any control to almost any Framework type that contains data. Controls that expose one or two properties suitable for data binding, such as the *Text* and *Tag* properties of a *TextBox*, use simple data binding. Implementing this requires that you create a separate *Binding* object for each mapping. These objects are contained in the *ControlBindingsCollection* object that each control exposes through its *DataBindings* property.

CurrencyManager

After the controls are data bound, they must be kept synchronized as the user steps through the master list of records. Unlike legacy ADO, many possible .NET data sources, including *DataSet* objects, do not have the concept of a *current record*. Instead, this support is provided by the *CurrencyManager* class, one of the two implementations of the abstract *BindingManagerBase* class.

Despite the name, *CurrencyManager* has nothing to do with money or finances. Rather, it presides over all *Binding* objects associated with one particular data source. When the value of its *Position* property changes, the *CurrencyManager* object notifies all its associated *Binding* objects that they should update the data they are passing to their respective bound controls with the values at the new position in the data source. The *Position* property is read/write, so you can set it to advance or retreat through the data source. To obtain the current position, access the read-only *Current* property.

BindingContext

A *CurrencyManager* object exists for each data source used for simple data binding. As such, there can be more than one *CurrencyManager* object for any given control, either because the control is bound to more than one data source or because the control is a container for other controls that collectively use multiple data sources.

This is where the *BindingContext* object steps in: to encapsulate, as a collection, one or more *CurrencyManager* objects. To obtain a particular *Currency-Manager* object, simply pass the data source to the *BindingContext* property. Figure 3-6 illustrates how all of this works together.

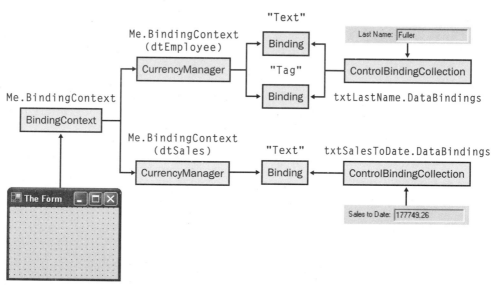

Figure 3-6 Simple data binding for a Windows form.

Notice that the Sales To Date *TextBox* control has a different *Currency-Manager* than the Last Name *TextBox* control. This is because each control is bound to a separate *DataTable* object within a single *DataSet* object (as you will see). Also notice that each *CurrencyManager* object was obtained via the form's *BindingContext* object. This is not required, however. All controls expose a *BindingContext* object. You could just as easily have obtained the same *CurrencyManager* object as follows:

```
txtLastName.BindingContext(dtEmployee)
```

Code Walkthrough

At a high level, the steps involved with implementing data binding with navigation are as follows:

■ Create *Binding* objects for each control using simple data binding.

■ Retrieve the *CurrencyManager* object for the data source that represents the set of records, and add a *PositionChanged* event handler.

■ Implement the *PositionChanged* handler to synchronize the controls.

The *DataSet* containing the employee records contains two *DataTable* objects: *dtEmployee* for general employee info and *dtSales* for employee sales data. Although the sales data could have gone in the same *DataTable* object as the employee info, it's worth demonstrating how to keep data current from multiple sources.

Creating the Bindings

Once the data source is created, you can proceed to create the *Binding* objects for each simple-bound control. To do this, simply call the *Add* method of the control's *DataBindings* collection, passing in the control property name, the data source, and the name of the *DataColumn* object that contains the actual data.

```
txtLastName.DataBindings.Add("Text", dtEmployee, "LastName")
txtLastName.DataBindings.Add("Tag", dtEmployee, "EmployeeID")
txtFirstName.DataBindings.Add("Text", dtEmployee, "FirstName")
txtHireDate.DataBindings.Add("Text", dtEmployee, "HireDate")
txtSalesToDate.DataBindings.Add("Text", dvSales, "SalesToDate")
```

Notice that *txtLastName* is the only control with two bindings. The *Tag* property stores the ID of the current employee. You'll see how this is used to keep the Sales To Date values synchronized.

Working with the *CurrencyManager*

The last block of code in the *CreateBindings* method obtains a *CurrencyManager* object for *dtEmployee* and then adds a handler for the *PositionChanged* event. A private class-level variable, *cmEmployee*, has already been declared:

```
cmEmployee = CType(Me.BindingContext(dtEmployee), CurrencyManager)
AddHandler cmEmployee.PositionChanged, _
    AddressOf EmployeeCurrencyManager_PositionChanged
```

With this code in place, all you need to do to navigate the employee records is change the value of the *Position* property of the *CurrencyManager* object when a navigation button is clicked (or a key is pressed, assuming you implement the *Form.KeyDown* event handler and the *Form.KeyPreview* property is set to *True*). For example, *NextRecord* increases the *Position* property by 1. This same method is used by the Next button and the right-arrow key:

```
Public Sub NextRecord()
    cmEmployee.Position += 1
End Sub
```

When the position changes, the *CurrencyManager* object fires the *Position-Changed* event and causes all its associated simple-bound controls to update. In this case, *txtLastName*, *txtFirstName*, and *txtHireDate* are all bound to *dtEmployee*. The *CurrencyManager* causes them to be updated automatically without further effort on your part.

If this was all you had, there would be no need to implement a *Position-Changed* event handler. In most scenarios, however, you need this handler to call other methods to update controls that are not under the aegis of *cmEmployee* or that use complex data binding—for example, a *DataGrid* control. In the sample application, *lblRecordNumber* and *txtSalesToDate* fall into this category.

The *PositionChanged* event handler is quite simple:

```
Protected Sub EmployeeCurrencyManager_PositionChanged( _
    ByVal sender As Object, ByVal e As System.EventArgs)
    ShowCurrentRecordNumber()
    ShowTotalSales()
End Sub
```

As you would expect, the handler merely calls methods to update the remaining controls that need to be kept in sync. These methods are as follows:

```
Protected Sub ShowCurrentRecordNumber()
    lblRecordNumber.Text = "Record " & _
        cmEmployee.Position + 1 & " of " & dtEmployee.Rows.Count
End Sub

Protected Sub ShowTotalSales()
    dvSales.RowFilter = "EmployeeID = " & txtLastName.Tag.ToString
End Sub
```

In *ShowTotalSales*, you can see that the *Tag* property is used to filter a *DataView* object.

> **Note** As Figure 3-6 illustrates, you could also obtain the *Currency-Manager* for *dtSalesToDate* to keep *txtSalesToDate* current. There is more than one way to implement data navigation.

Conclusion

This topic has taught you how to implement data binding with navigation. Although the concepts behind simple data binding might not seem so simple, it all boils down to the following main points:

■   There is a *CurrencyManager* object for each data source.

■   A *BindingContext* object manages the *CurrencyManager* object or objects.

■   A *CurrencyManager* object synchronizes all controls that are simple-bound to its associated data source.

■   A *PositionChanged* handler can be implemented to tie in all the remaining controls.

The *PositionChanged* handler is really the key to keeping everything synchronized. When this event fires, you can call any method you need and update simple or complex controls using a variety of data sources. In the final topic of this three-part series, "Application #18: Build a Master-Details Windows Form," you'll see how this handler is used to keep current two *DataGrid* controls that are hierarchically related to one another.

Application #17: Custom Data-Binding Format Handlers

In the previous topic, you saw how to implement data binding with navigation controls. For the purpose of taking a building-block approach, the controls lacked any formatting. Instead, the .NET data-binding mechanism used reflection to get the underlying type of the *Object* being bound and then called its default *ToString* method to render the value. This topic will show you how to implement custom format handlers—methods that are essential to most data-binding applications.

The sample application builds upon the previous topic. Two new controls are added so that you can learn how to handle *Boolean* and *Null* values in addition to *Currency* and *Date* values. Figure 3-7 shows a screen shot of Application #17.

Figure 3-7 Application #17.

Building Upon...

Application #4: *Try/Catch/Finally*

Application #12: Use a *DataSet* and *DataView*

Application #16: Data Binding with Navigation

New Concepts

This topic revolves around the *Binding* class. The .NET Framework documentation states that this class "represents the simple binding between the property value of an object and the property value of a control." In the previous topic, you saw *Binding* objects used implicitly when simple data binding was set up for each control. For example, consider the following:

```
txtFirstName.DataBindings.Add("Text", dtEmployee, "FirstName")
```

This code binds the *Text* property of the First Name *TextBox* control to the First-Name field in the data source.

This sample application works more closely with *Binding* objects, instantiating them directly and adding handlers for the *Format* event. This event is raised by the *Binding* object when:

- The property of a control is bound to a data value

- The *CurrencyManager.Position* property changes

- A *DataView* object is filtered or sorted, if this is the data source

Code Walkthrough

The code required to use custom data-binding format handlers is straightforward. In the sample application's *CreateBindings* method, you'll find the following code to establish a binding and formatting handler for the Sales To Date *TextBox* control. Code for the other controls is similar.

```
Dim dbnSalesToDate As New Binding("Text", dtSales, "SalesToDate")
AddHandler dbnSalesToDate.Format, AddressOf MoneyToString
txtSalesToDate.DataBindings.Add(dbnSalesToDate)
```

> **Caution**   Make sure you add the custom format handler prior to adding the *Binding* object to the *DataBindings* collection of the control. Design-time or run-time errors are not generated if you fail to do this. However, you might not notice until you step to another record for the first time that the data in the control does not format properly.

Thus, when the format event is raised by the *Binding* object for this control, the *MoneyToString* delegate will be invoked:

```
Protected Sub MoneyToString(ByVal sender As Object, _
    ByVal e As ConvertEventArgs)
    e.Value = CType(e.Value, Decimal).ToString("c")
End Sub
```

The data that is bound to the control is passed to this handler in a *Convert-EventArgs* object. Simply access its *Value* property, cast it to the appropriate type to have access to the type's special format codes (covered in Chapter 4, Application #32), and then reassign the *Value* property.

The same methodology is carried through for all the other controls. For example, to format the occasional NULL or empty string values that might exist in the data source for the Region *TextBox* control, you use the following code:

```
Protected Sub NullToString(ByVal sender As Object, _
    ByVal e As ConvertEventArgs)
    If IsDBNull(e.Value) Or e.Value.ToString.Trim.Length = 0 Then
        e.Value = "[N/A]"
    End If
End Sub
```

CheckBox control formatting is handled by the following simple subroutine:

```
Protected Sub SmallIntToBoolean(ByVal sender As Object, _
    ByVal e As ConvertEventArgs)
    Select Case e.Value
        Case 1
            e.Value = True
        Case Else
            e.Value = False
    End Select
End Sub
```

Finally, the employee's hire date can be formatted as follows:

```
Protected Sub DateToString(ByVal sender As Object, _
    ByVal e As ConvertEventArgs)
    e.Value = CType(e.Value, DateTime).ToShortDateString
End Sub
```

In all cases, the code and concepts are very similar.

Conclusion

This has been a short look at custom data-binding format handlers. The code and concepts are less involved and easier to understand than previous topics in this chapter.

Although not covered in this chapter, it's worth examining the *Parse* event, which is essentially the opposite of the *Format* event. The *Parse* event fires when data is read from the control and pushed back into its data source. Thus, you can allow the user to enter data in a format different from the format in which it will be stored.

You can see that the .NET Framework provides virtually unlimited flexibility for formatting data in your applications. Simply add a handler to the *Binding* object of a control, and then write code to display the data in any way you see fit.

Application #18: Build a Master-Details Windows Form

This is the final topic in a three-part series that includes data binding with navigation and custom format handlers. This sample application shows you how to build a master-details Windows Form. This type of interface is commonly used to navigate through a main resultset and allow the user to drill down into a particular record to view it, or related data, in greater detail. Figure 3-8 shows a screen shot of Application #18.

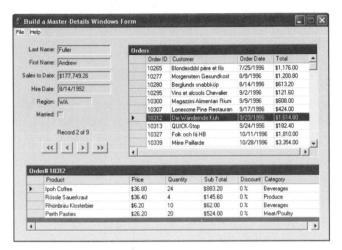

Figure 3-8   Application #18.

The upper portion of the application displays the master set of records. On the left, you can step through information from the Employees table of the Northwind database. Orders associated with each employee are displayed in the *DataGrid* control to the right. The product details for any specific order—selected by clicking its row in the Orders table—are displayed in the lower *DataGrid* control.

Building Upon...

Application #4: *Try...Catch...Finally*
Application #12: Use a *DataSet* and *DataView*
Application #16: Data Binding with Navigation
Application #17: Custom Data-Binding Format Handlers

New Concepts

There are no new concepts for this topic, as it builds entirely upon concepts presented in the previous two topics in this series. As a brief review, here are the main steps you take to implement a master-details application:

1.   Create one or more data sources.

2. Create *Binding* objects for each simple-bound control, adding custom formatting handlers if desired.

3. Create a *PositionChanged* event handler for the *CurrencyManager*.

Implementing a master-details application essentially amounts to adding two new custom methods to the *PositionChanged* event handler for data binding the *DataGrid* controls. The "Code Walkthrough" section will explain this in further detail.

Code Walkthrough

We begin the walkthrough by looking at the pivotal event hander in an application of this type. Here is a good place to put any methods you want invoked when the user steps to a different record:

```
Protected Sub EmployeeCurrencyManager_PositionChanged( _
    ByVal sender As Object, ByVal e As System.EventArgs)
    BindOrdersGrid()
    BindOrderDetailsGrid()
    ShowCurrentRecordNumber()
    ShowTotalSales()
End Sub
```

When comparing this with the previous topic in this series, you'll notice the addition of the *BindOrdersGrid* and *BindOrderDetailsGrid* methods. The former method displays all orders for the current employee in the upper right *DataGrid* control. The relevant code is as follows:

```
dvOrders.RowFilter = "EmployeeID = " & txtLastName.Tag.ToString

With grdOrders
    .CaptionText = "Orders"
    .DataSource = dvOrders
End With
```

The previously created *DataView*, named *dvOrders*, contains the orders for every employee in the database. Thus, to show only the orders for the current employee, we set the *RowFilter* property of the *DataView* object by using the *EmployeeID* value bound to the *Tag* property of the Last Name *TextBox* control. All that is left to do is assign the *DataView* object to the *DataSource* property.

The *BindOrderDetailsGrid* method is invoked next. The pertinent code in this subroutine is similar to what you've just seen:

```
Dim strCurrentOrderID As String = _
    dvOrders(grdOrders.CurrentRowIndex)("OrderID").ToString
dvOrderDetails.RowFilter = "OrderID = " & strCurrentOrderID

With grdOrderDetails
```

```
    .CaptionText = "Order# " & strCurrentOrderID
    .DataSource = dvOrderDetails
End With
```

As with the data source for the master *DataGrid* control, *dvOrderDetails* contains all order details in the database. To show only the details for the currently selected order, retrieve the Order ID from the *DataRowView* collection by using the *DataGrid.CurrentRowIndex* property. Then, use this value to create a statement for the *RowFilter* property.

If you were to build and run the application at this point, you'd see only partial functionality. The master-details relationship is set up between the two *DataGrid* controls. However, it works only for the first default record as you step through the employees. What is missing is the ability to click on a row in the master *DataGrid* control and have the order details change in the lower *DataGrid* control.

To implement this, you need to handle the *CurrentCellChanged* event raised by the master *DataGrid* control:

```
Private Sub grdOrders_CurrentCellChanged(ByVal sender As Object, _
    ByVal e As System.EventArgs) Handles grdOrders.CurrentCellChanged

    grdOrders.Select(grdOrders.CurrentCell.RowNumber)
    BindOrderDetailsGrid()
End Sub
```

This event fires when the user directly clicks a different cell or clicks the frame of the *DataGrid* control next to the row. To provide good feedback to the user, you should use the *Select* method to highlight the currently selected row.

> **Note**   You might think it would be more appropriate to handle the *DataGrid.Click* event. However, this fires only when the frame next to the row is clicked. Clicking in the cells will not raise the event and will not give you the master-details effect that you probably want.

Conclusion

This concludes a fast-paced, three-part series culminating in building a master-details Windows Forms application. In this final topic, you learned that establishing a master-details relationship between two *DataGrid* controls involves:

- Adding a couple of methods to bind the *DataGrid* controls to a filtered *DataView* object.

- Handling the *CurrentCellChanged* event.

In short, once the admittedly more complex foundation of data binding with navigation has been laid, it's not difficult to build on it.

You might also consider exploring a variation of the master-details user interface. This involves a single *DataGrid* control that is used to display both the orders and the order details, as in Figure 3-9.

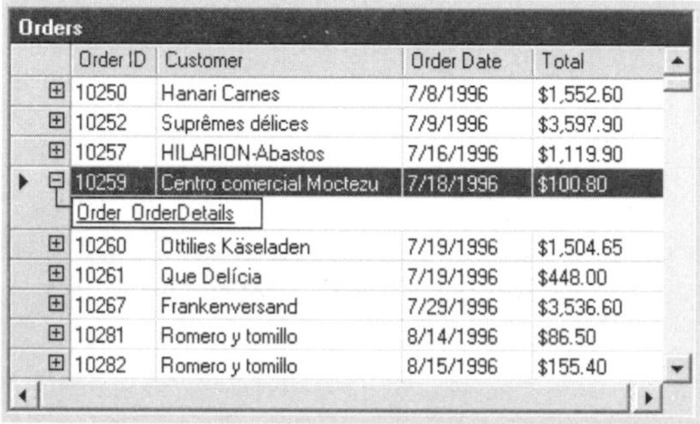

Figure 3-9   A close-up view of the Orders *DataGrid* when *DataRelation* objects are used in the data source.

Expanding the order row reveals a link to the Order Details table as shown in Figure 3-10. Clicking the link causes the same *DataGrid* control to display the order details.

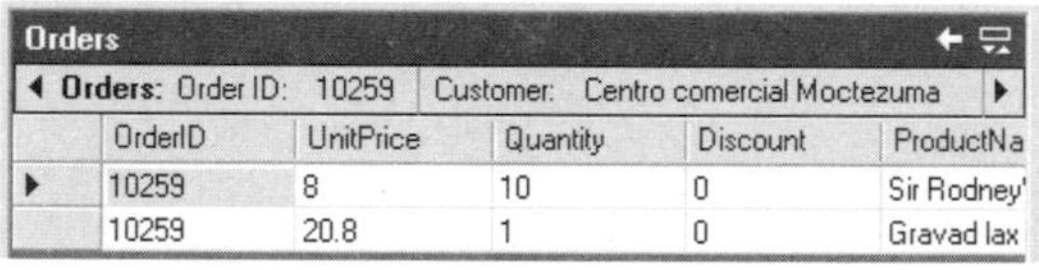

Figure 3-10   Rows from the OrderDetails *DataTable* as displayed in the Orders *DataGrid*.

Additionally, controls are added to the upper right corner of the *DataGrid* control to allow the user to return to the parent row, or to show or hide the parent row information. Although this type of layout requires the user to take an additional step in order to view details of a record, it does take up considerably less space.

To experiment with this implementation, uncomment the following line of code in the *CreateDataSet* method, which establishes a data relation between the Orders and Order Details *DataTable* objects:

```
dsEmployees.Relations.Add("Order_OrderDetails", _
    dtOrders.Columns("OrderID"), dtOrderDetails.Columns("OrderID"))
```

Application #19: Use a Typed *DataSet*

In the first application in this chapter, you were introduced to the concept of a *DataSet*, a core object of ADO.NET. In this next topic, you'll be adding to your knowledge of a generic, or *untyped, DataSet* its customizable subclass—known as a *typed DataSet*. You'll learn how it differs from the untyped *DataSet* from which it derives, and why you might want to use a typed *DataSet* instead of its generic parent. You'll also learn about the *SqlCommandBuilder* class and how it can be used in conjunction with the *SqlDataAdapter* class to update the data source of the *DataSet* object, pushing into SQL Server any changes that the *DataSet* object has been tracking.

The sample application shows you how to create and fill a typed *DataSet* object with products from the Northwind database, displaying them in a *ListBox* control. You can also add a new product, change the name of an existing product, or delete a product. Changes are tracked by the *DataSet* object until the time that you save them to the data source. The two buttons below the *ListBox* control allow you to repopulate the list from the database (using the *SqlDataAdapter.Fill* method) or to reconcile the *DataSet* object's changes with the database (using the *SqlDataAdapter.Update* method). Figure 3-11 shows a user updating the *DataSet* object in the sample application.

Figure 3-11   Application #19.

Building Upon...

Application #4: *Try/Catch/Finally*
Application #12: Use a *DataSet* and *DataView*

New Concepts

Recall that a *DataSet* object represents an in-memory, disconnected, and serializable copy of data. It contains various data-related collections that model a relational database, such as those for *DataTable*, *DataRelation*, *DataColumn*, and *Constraint* objects. A *DataSet* object is thus a robust and powerful object that will likely form the heart of your data-tier implementation.

A limitation of the untyped *DataSet* object, however, is that it uses late binding. To access values, the runtime engine uses an index or field name to look up and retrieve the object or value. Recall the syntax for accessing data in an untyped *DataSet* object:

```
DataSetObjectName.Tables("<TableName>" _
    or TableIndex).Rows(RowIndex)("<FieldName>" or FieldIndex)
```

An example of this format is

```
strCustomerName = ds.Tables(0).Rows(8)(2)
```

You could also use field names instead of indices, or a mix of the two—for example:

```
strCustomerName = ds.Tables("Customers").Rows(8)("LastName")
```

As you probably already know, late-bound access carries with it some disadvantages, including weakly typed variables and a performance degradation. This leads us to one of the main advantages of using a typed *DataSet* object. As the name implies, it strongly types the table and column information, making this information available through properties instead of via collection-based syntax.

Adding a Typed *DataSet* to Your Project

Microsoft Visual Studio .NET makes it very easy to add a typed *DataSet* to your project. Just follow these steps:

1.   In the Solution Explorer, right-click your project, point to Add, and then click Add New Item.

2. In the Add New Item dialog box, from the Templates pane select DataSet. Give it a name, and then click Open. You now have the design surface of an XML Schema file.

3. Open Server Explorer, and expand SQL Servers | <SQL Server instance name> | Northwind.

4. Expand the Tables, Views, or Stored Procedures node. Click and drag any of these database objects to the *DataSet* object's design surface. The XML Schema will be created based on the structure of a table and its relations, whether it be an actual table in the database or a table of results that were generated by a query.

5. Right-click the design surface, and make sure Generate DataSet is checked.

6. Press Ctrl+S to save the schema and automatically generate a typed *DataSet* class based on the schema. You are now ready to program against it!

7. If you want to actually view the typed *DataSet* class, in the Solution Explorer click on the project that contains the *DataSet* and then click the Show All Files icon. Then expand the typed *DataSet* icon in the project to view its *code-behind* files.

A typed *Dataset* class is thus defined as a class that extends its base *DataSet* class with members created from data-source information contained in an XML schema (.xsd file). In other words, a typed *DataSet* class provides all the inherent functionality of the untyped *DataSet* class, with the additional benefit of data objects that are first-class members. This structure provides the following benefits:

■ **Design-Time** An improved development experience

- ❑ The syntax for working with strongly typed *DataSet* class members provides type checking. (Make sure *Option Strict* is *On*.)

- ❑ Type mismatch errors are caught at compile time instead of at run time.

- ❑ Tables and columns (but not rows) can be accessed directly by name instead of by a collection-based lookup. Index or field name guesswork is virtually eliminated, and coding errors are reduced.

❑   Statement completion is ensured, as is IntelliSense support.

■ **Run-Time**   Better performance. In fact, code that accesses typed *DataSet* objects can often run twice as fast as code that accesses untyped *DataSet* objects using string-based collection lookups. However, the gap is narrowed considerably, if not eliminated, if you use a *DataColumn* object and proper type conversion code against an untyped *DataSet* object.

The syntax for working with a typed *DataSet* object takes the following form:

```
typedDataSetObjectName.DataTableName.Rows(RowIndexNumber).ColumnName
```

Therefore, if you were to use a typed *DataSet* to access the same data as in the preceding example, the syntax would read:

```
strCustomerName = tds.Customers.Rows(8).LastName
```

The "Code Walkthrough" section will afford you a much closer look at the syntax.

The *DataSet* object is disconnected from its data source. As such, when you make changes to rows in one or more of its *DataTable* objects, the changes are not reflected in the database until you push them back in. A *DataSet* object simply keeps track of all the changes and waits for you to propagate them back to the source. You can even invoke the *GetChanges* method to create a second *DataSet* object that contains only the changes made to the data thus far.

In the first application in this chapter, you learned that the *SqlDataAdapter* class is responsible for managing data between Microsoft SQL Server and a *DataSet* object. For example, to populate an empty *DataSet* object, you call the data adapter's *Fill* method. This involves a SQL SELECT statement. Similarly, to reconcile the changes in the *DataSet* object with SQL Server, you call the *Update* method.

As you know, database changes can involve inserting, deleting, and updating records. Each operation requires a different SQL statement. Being merely the bridge between the connected and disconnected realms of the ADO.NET world, the *SqlDataAdapter* object does not automatically generate these statements, leaving you with two options:

■ Manually set *InsertCommand*, *DeleteCommand*, and *UpdateCommand* properties of the data adapter to whatever you want.

■ Instantiate the *SqlCommandBuilder* class, and let it do the work for you.

If the *SelectCommand* property of the data adapter has been assigned to an instance of the *SqlCommand* class—and if this command object has its *CommandText* property set (for example, its SELECT statement)—the *SqlCommand-Builder* can infer the INSERT, DELETE, and UPDATE statements. For many scenarios, this approach is adequate. Just be aware that complex updates will likely require you to manually set the commands.

Code Walkthrough

When the Windows Form loads, the *FillTypedDataSet* method is invoked and the *ListBox* control is populated. The code to fill a generic *DataSet* object should look familiar to you by now. The difference for a *typed DataSet* object is that you instantiate the *DSTypedProducts* class instead of the *DataSet* class. (The variable *tdsNorthwind* has already been declared.)

```
Dim cnn As New SqlConnection(ConnectionString)
Dim cmd As New SqlCommand("SELECT * FROM ProductsTDS", cnn)
tdsNorthwind = New DSTypedProducts()
sdaTDS = New SqlDataAdapter(cmd)
sdaTDS.Fill(tdsNorthwind, tdsNorthwind.ProductsTDS.TableName)
```

Caution   Remember to pass the *DataTable* object's name to the *Fill* method if you're going to access the results using the strongly typed syntax. When the *Fill* method is called and the *DataTable* object is left unspecified, the data adapter will create a new *DataTable* object simply named Table. In other words, it will not fill the strongly typed table. No errors are generated. You are simply left scratching your head as to why you have an empty *DataTable* object. Accessing the *DataTable* object by using an ordinal-based collection lookup can also lead to confusion because the ordinal is off by the number of tables in your schema. When a typed *DataSet* object is instantiated, its *n* child *DataTable* objects are also created. Thus, although you thought the results would be in `tds.Tables(0)`, they're actually in `tds.Tables(0 + n)`.

The next line of code creates the *SqlCommandBuilder* object that will automatically generate the INSERT, UPDATE, and DELETE statements used later when we call the *SqlDataAdapter.Update* method.

```
Dim scbTDS As New SqlCommandBuilder(sdaTDS)
```

All that is required is instantiation. The data adapter will maintain a reference to it as we work with the *DataSet*.

To populate the *ListBox* control, iterate through the *Rows* collection of the typed *DataTable* object:

```
Dim dt As DSTypedProducts.ProductsTDSDataTable = tdsNorthwind.ProductsTDS
Dim dr As DSTypedProducts.ProductsTDSRow

lstResults.Items.Clear()
For Each dr In dt.Rows
    If Not dr.RowState = DataRowState.Deleted Then
        lstResults.Items.Add(dr.ProductName.ToString())
    End If
Next
```

Notice that you add to the list only those products that haven't been deleted from the *DataSet* object. *RowState* is one mechanism the *DataSet* object uses to keep track of the changes.

As mentioned earlier, the sample application allows you to add, delete, or modify a product. Let's take a closer look at the code needed to change a product's name. (Adding and deleting a product are similar and will not be covered further.) The key lines of code are as follows:

```
Dim tdr As DSTypedProducts.ProductsTDSRow = _
    CType(tdsNorthwind.ProductsTDS.Rows(lstResults.SelectedIndex), _
        DSTypedProducts.ProductsTDSRow)
Dim OriginalProductName As String
tdr.ProductName = txtUpdateProductName.Text
PopulateListFromTDS()
```

The first, rather lengthy, line of code initializes a strongly typed *DataRow* variable. The index of the selected item is used for an ordinal-based lookup in the *Rows* collection of the typed *DataTable* object. All that is left to do is assign a new value to the *ProductName* property. ProductName is one of the fields in the *DataTable* object. It has been converted to a property for the typed *DataSet* object.

The last bit of code we'll look at is in the *btnSaveToDataSource_Click* event handler. A single line of code is all that is required to push all changes made to the *DataSet* back into SQL Server:

```
sdaTDS.Update(tdsNorthwind, "ProductsTDS")
```

For your own instruction, I encourage you to try an update after commenting out the creation of the *SqlCommandBuilder* object, discussed earlier. Also, make changes to the *DataSet* object and then see what happens to those changes when you click the two buttons below the *ListBox* control.

Conclusion

Typed *DataSet* objects are a marvelous feature of ADO.NET. They're easy to create, and they offer many advantages over their untyped ancestor. During the development of your application, your life is made easier with statement completion and IntelliSense support for the typed data members. The improved syntax is also more intuitive. Design-time type checking pays off at run time, when type mismatch errors are all but eliminated. And performance gains can be considerable if you're used to doing string-based collection lookups. You should give strong consideration to widespread use of typed *DataSet* objects when building your next data-driven application.

Application #20: Build a Data-Entry Form

This data-entry application ties together in one convenient package numerous basic ADO.NET concepts you've been introduced to thus far. The interface consists of numerous *TextBox* controls and two *ComboBox* controls, with buttons to add, save, and delete a record. Figure 3-12 shows a screen shot of Application #20.

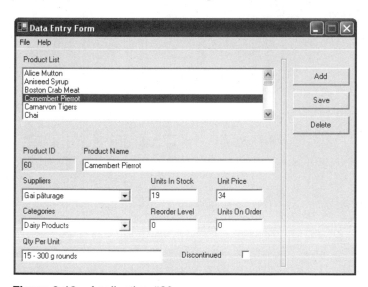

Figure 3-12   Application #20.

Building Upon...

Application #4: *Try/Catch/Finally*
Application #14: Use a *SqlDataReader*
Application #15: Bind Data to a *ComboBox*

New Concepts

There are no new concepts for this topic. It should be considered a review of several basic ADO.NET concepts that have already been covered.

Code Walkthrough

The code that follows shows you how to use a *SqlDataReader* object to populate various controls with data and then manipulate the data.

Populating the *ListControl*s

When the form first loads, it calls the following methods in its *Load* event handler:

```
PopulateCategoryCombo()
PopulateSupplierCombo()
PopulateProductList()
```

The code for all three methods is almost identical because the controls all derive from *ListControl*. As such, the first part of this walkthrough will deal with *PopulateCategoryCombo*.

The *PopulateCategoryCombo* method contains code for using a *SqlData-Reader* object to fill a *ComboBox* control with categories from the Northwind database:

```
strSQL = "SELECT CategoryID, CategoryName FROM Categories"

cnn = New SqlConnection(connectionString)
cmd = New SqlCommand(strSQL, cnn)

cnn.Open()
dr = cmd.ExecuteReader(CommandBehavior.CloseConnection)
```

Following the creation of a T-SQL SELECT statement, the *SqlConnection* and *SqlCommand* classes are instantiated. The connection is then opened, and a *SqlDataReader* variable (declared earlier) is used to receive the return from *ExecuteReader*. A *CommandBehavior* enumeration is used to conveniently close the connection when the data reader is closed.

```
cboCategories.Items.Clear()

Do While dr.Read()
    objListItem = New ListItem(dr.Item("CategoryName").ToString(), _
        CInt(dr.Item("CategoryID")))
    cboCategories.Items.Add(objListItem)
Loop

dr.Close()
```

After clearing the *ComboBox* control's *ObjectCollection* to make way for a new, updated set of items, a *Do/While* loop is used to iterate through the contents of the data reader and add new *ListItem* objects to the *ObjectCollection*. Although the *System.Web.UI.WebControls* namespace contains a *ListItem* class that represents a data item within a databound list control, there is no equivalent for a Windows Forms *ComboBox* class. Therefore, in this application, *List-Item* is a custom class that functions in an almost identical manner. Its constructor takes a *string* value and an *integer* value that are used, respectively, to display the item and give it an additional value (akin to the *DisplayMember* and *ValueMember* properties if you were data binding instead of simply filling the *ObjectCollection*):

```
Public Class ListItem
    Private mName As String
    Private mID As Integer

    Public Sub New(ByVal strName As String, ByVal intID As Integer)
        mName = strName
        mID = intID
    End Sub

    Public Sub New()
        mName = ""
        mID = 0
    End Sub

    Property ID() As Integer
        Get
            Return mID
        End Get
        Set(ByVal Name As Integer)
            mID = Name
        End Set
    End Property

    Property Name() As String
        Get
            Return mName
        End Get
```

(continued)

```
        Set(ByVal Name As String)
            mName = Name
        End Set
    End Property

    Public Overrides Function ToString() As String
        Return mName
    End Function
End Class
```

When *dr.Read* returns *False*, the application breaks out of the *Do/While* loop and then closes the data reader.

Populating the Remaining Form Elements

One line of code that is different among these three methods is contained in the *PopulateProductList* subroutine:

```
lstProducts.SetSelected(0, True)
```

This sets the selected *ListBox* item to the first product so that the user interface does not initialize with a lot of empty fields. When this is set, its *SelectedIndexChanged* event is fired, the handler for which contains code to initialize the rest of the application:

```
PopulateForm()
btnDelete.Enabled = True
btnAdd.Enabled = True
Mode = "Update"
```

PopulateForm is thus one of the key methods in this application. It gets called when the form is loaded and every time the user selects a new product from the *ListBox* control. The code in this method is straightforward:

```
objListItem = CType(lstProducts.SelectedItem, ListItem)

strSQL = "SELECT ProductID, ProductName, QuantityPerUnit, UnitPrice, " & _
    "UnitsInStock, UnitsOnOrder, ReorderLevel, Discontinued, " & _
    "SupplierID, CategoryID " & _
    "FROM Products " & _
    "WHERE ProductID = " & objListItem.ID

cnn = New SqlConnection(connectionString)
cmd = New SqlCommand(strSQL, cnn)

cnn.Open()
dr = cmd.ExecuteReader(CommandBehavior.CloseConnection)

If dr.Read() Then
    txtProductID.Text = dr.Item("ProductID").ToString()
    txtProductName.Text() = dr.Item("ProductName").ToString()
    txtQtyPerUnit.Text() = dr.Item("QuantityPerUnit").ToString()
```

```
    txtUnitPrice.Text() = dr.Item("UnitPrice").ToString()
    txtUnitsInStock.Text() = dr.Item("UnitsInStock").ToString()
    txtUnitsOnOrder.Text() = dr.Item("UnitsOnOrder").ToString()
    txtReorderLevel.Text() = dr.Item("ReorderLevel").ToString()
    chkDiscontinued.Checked = CType(dr.Item("Discontinued"), Boolean)
    SetSelectedItem(cboSuppliers, dr.Item("SupplierID").ToString())
    SetSelectedItem(cboCategories, dr.Item("CategoryID").ToString())
End If
dr.Close()
```

First a SELECT command is created that uses the product ID from the selected *ListBox* item in the WHERE criteria. Notice how the ID value is retrieved. The *SelectedItem* property returns the selected *ListItem* object. It is stored as a generic object, so it must be cast to the custom *ListItem* type before the *ID* property is accessible.

Next the data is retrieved and placed into a *SqlDataReader*, and the control properties are set to the various field values. The *ComboBox* controls use a custom *SetSelectedItem* helper method to cause the *ComboBox* to reflect the supplier and category associated with this product:

```
Private Sub SetSelectedItem(ByVal cbo As ComboBox, ByVal strID As String)
    Dim ListItem As ListItem
    Dim i As Int32

    While i <= cbo.Items.Count - 1
        ListItem = CType(cbo.Items(i), ListItem)
        If ListItem.ID = CInt(strID) Then
            cbo.SelectedIndex = i
        End If
        i += 1
    End While
End Sub
```

Finally the data reader is closed.

Inserting a New Product

The *AddProduct* method called in the *btnSave_Click* event handler has ADO.NET code similar to what you have just walked through:

```
strSQL = _
    "INSERT Products VALUES (" & _
    ScrubInput(txtProductName.Text) & "," & _
    CType(cboSuppliers.Items(cboSuppliers.SelectedIndex), _
    ListItem).ID & "," & _
    CType(cboCategories.Items(cboCategories.SelectedIndex), _
    ListItem).ID & "," & _
    ScrubInput(txtQtyPerUnit.Text) & "," & _
    txtUnitPrice.Text & "," & _
    txtUnitsInStock.Text & "," & _
    txtUnitsOnOrder.Text & "," & _
```

(continued)

```
            txtReorderLevel.Text & "," & _
            CType(IIf(chkDiscontinued.Checked, "1", "0"), String) & ")"

    cnn = New SqlConnection(ConnectionString)
    cmd = New SqlCommand(strSQL, cnn)

    cnn.Open()
    intRowsAffected = cmd.ExecuteNonQuery()
    cnn.Close()

    If intRowsAffected = 1 Then
        MessageBox.Show("Product successfully added.", Me.Text, _
            MessageBoxButtons.OK, MessageBoxIcon.Information)
    End If
```

Notice the *ScrubInput* helper function that is used to prepare certain entries. *ScrubInput* escapes single quotes, removes double quotes, replaces an empty string with NULL, and trims any white space:

```
strValue = strValue.Replace("'", "''")
strValue = strValue.Replace("""", "")

If strValue.Trim() = "" Then
    Return "NULL"
Else
    Return "'" & strValue.Trim() & "'"
End If
```

The code for updating and deleting a product is similar to that for inserting a new product, so this ends the "Code Walkthrough" section.

Conclusion

This has been a quick review of some basic ADO.NET code and concepts involved with building a simple data-entry form. The *SqlCommand* object was used exclusively to execute all T-SQL statements. Although a *DataSet* object was not involved, you could certainly elect to build the data-entry form using a *DataSet* object instead of a *SqlDataReader* object. Both options are open to you, and the right choice depends on the scenario you're trying to support.

Application #21: Build a Three-Tier Data Form

For most business applications, a well-known "best practice" is to organize your code into three tiers. Although there are differences of opinion about how a tier is defined and what goes where exactly, the typical model is as follows:

- An upper or presentation tier for the user-interface code

- A middle or business tier to house business rules and data-access logic

- A lower tier that contains the data storage—for example, a database

A three-tier architecture has a number of advantages, such as scalability and code reuse. For example, when the data-access logic is not tightly coupled with the presentation tier, it can easily be reused to serve many types of user interfaces, from a rich desktop client to a thin Web client.

This sample application will demonstrate how to build a simple master-details data form that follows this model. The presentation tier is comprised of a Windows Forms application that contains two *DataGrid* controls in a master-details relationship and buttons to update and refresh the data. Database requests from the presentation tier are handled by the middle tier, which contains a data-access layer. The term *layer* is defined as a logical grouping of code according to function. Multiple layers can exist within a tier. Because of this application's lack of complexity, a business rules layer is not needed. Figure 3-13 shows a screen shot of Application #21.

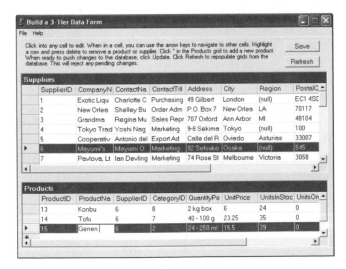

Figure 3-13   Application #21.

Building Upon...

Application #4: *Try/Catch/Finally*
Application #7: Object-Oriented Features
Application #12: Use a *DataSet* and *DataView*
Application #18: Build a Master-Details Windows Form
Application #19: Use a Typed *DataSet*

New Concepts

Several minor ADO.NET concepts are introduced in this sample and will be treated in the "Code Walkthrough" section. The majority of the code, however, should look familiar. What might be conceptually new to you is the way the application is set up in Visual Studio .NET.

The solution contains two projects, a Windows application and a class library named MiddleTier. The class library was added by right-clicking the solution in the Solution Explorer, pointing to Add, and then selecting New Project. Although both projects are indeed in the same solution, you must add a reference to the class library's DLL in the Windows application project or the application will not be able to access these middle-tier members.

If you right-click the MiddleTier project in the Solution Explorer and then click Properties, you'll see that the root namespace is set to MiddleTier. This means the fully qualified name of all the code in this class library begins with *MiddleTier*. Additional namespaces can be used to further organize the code. You'll see that the data access code is wrapped inside a block starting with *Namespace DataAccessLayer* and ending with *End Namespace*. (If logic for business rules were added, you could place it inside a *Namespace BusinessLayer/End Namespace* statement.) As a result, when accessing a method from the presentation tier, the fully qualified name is *MiddleTier.DataAccessLayer.Class-Name.MethodName*. This makes the code more organized and readable.

Finally, the middle-tier code comprises three classes: a data-access base class and two more specialized classes that derive from it. The *DALBase* class contains functions for getting a new *SqlConnection* object, returning a *DataSet* object to the presentation tier, and pushing *DataSet* changes back to the database. The other two classes, *Suppliers* and *Products*, are similar. Each has a constructor that creates a new *SqlDataAdapter* object, a read-only property that makes the *SqlDataAdapter* available to the base class, and a *GetData* method for filling a *DataTable* that is then added to the *DataSet* object returned by the base class.

Code Walkthrough

What follows is a discussion of the code in the presentation and middle tiers.

Presentation Tier

At the outset, the data-access layer base class is instantiated with class scope so that it can be shared by the rest of the class members:

```
Protected WithEvents dal As New MiddleTier.DataAccessLayer.DALBase()
```

Then, in the form's *Load* event handler, several methods are called to retrieve a *DataSet* object from the middle tier and subsequently bind each *DataTable* object in the *DataSet* object to its respective *DataGrid* control. In the *GetDataSet* method, you'll find the following code:

```
dsSupplierProducts = dal.GetDataSet()
dvSuppliers = dsSupplierProducts.Tables("Suppliers").DefaultView
dvProducts = dsSupplierProducts.Tables("Products").DefaultView
dvSuppliers.AllowNew = False
```

First, a method on the data-access layer by the same name is called and its return value is set to a local *DataSet* variable. Next, *DataView* objects are created to facilitate the master-details relationship using the *RowFilter* property, as you've seen in a previous topic. Finally, the user is prevented from adding a new supplier by setting the *AllowNew* property.

> **Tip**   Unlike when binding to a *DataTable* object, the *DataView* object also allows you to set restrictions on what the user can do in the *Data-Grid* control. By setting the *AllowNew*, *AllowEdit*, and *AllowDelete* properties, you can affect how the *DataGrid* control behaves.

The Save button *Click* event handler illustrates a couple of good points. The first line of code checks to see whether there have been any changes made to the *DataSet* control. If not, there is no reason to proceed with calling the middle tier:

```
If Not dsSupplierProducts.HasChanges Then Exit Sub
```

If there are changes to be pushed back into the database, a *Try/Catch* block is used to wrap code that calls the data-access layer:

```
Try
    Dim strResultsMsg As String =
        dal.SaveChanges(dsSupplierProducts.GetChanges)
```

(continued)

```
    MessageBox.Show(strResultsMsg, Me.Text, MessageBoxButtons.OK, _
        MessageBoxIcon.Information)
Catch exp As Exception
    MessageBox.Show(exp.Message, Me.Text, MessageBoxButtons.OK, _
        MessageBoxIcon.Error)
End Try
```

Notice that when the *DataSet* object is passed to the middle tier, *GetChanges* is invoked. This method creates a new *DataSet* object consisting only of the changes made since it was last loaded or since *AcceptChanges* was called. This is an important method to use, as it can greatly reduce your network traffic. Also, to provide feedback to the user, a results message is returned by the *SaveChanges* method and displayed using the *MessageBox* class. Finally, the presentation tier can receive error messages from the middle tier because *SaveChanges* throws a new exception when an error is encountered, as you will see shortly.

Middle Tier

The base class for the data-access layer has two primary methods: *GetDataSet* and *SaveChanges*. In each, the *Suppliers* and *Products* classes are first instantiated:

```
dalSuppliers = New Suppliers()
dalProducts = New Products()
```

Looking at the constructor for the *Products* class, you see that it contains familiar code for creating a *SqlDataAdapter* and setting the SELECT, INSERT, UPDATE, and DELETE commands that are used for transferring data back and forth between the *DataSet* object and the database:

```
Public Sub New()
    Dim cmdSelect As SqlCommand
    Dim cb As SqlCommandBuilder

    cnn = GetConnection()
    cmdSelect = New SqlCommand()
    With cmdSelect
        .CommandText = "SELECT * FROM ProductsDAL"
        .Connection = cnn
    End With

    m_daProducts = New SqlDataAdapter()
    m_daProducts.SelectCommand = cmdSelect

    cb = New SqlCommandBuilder(m_daProducts)
End Sub
```

With instances of these two classes in hand, their respective *GetData* methods are then called to retrieve two *DataTable* objects, which are then added to a new *DataSet* object to form a complete package that can easily be passed back to the presentation tier:

```
dtSuppliers = dalSuppliers.GetData
dtProducts = dalProducts.GetData

ds.Tables.Add(dtSuppliers)
ds.Tables.Add(dtProducts)
```

Before returning the *DataSet* object, however, a *DataRelation* object is added to the *DataSet* object to set up a parent-child relationship between the Suppliers and Products tables:

```
dcParent = dtSuppliers.Columns("SupplierID")
dcChild = dtProducts.Columns("SupplierID")

trSupplierProducts = _
    New DataRelation("SupplierProducts", dcParent, dcChild)

ds.Relations.Add(trSupplierProducts)
trSupplierProducts.ChildKeyConstraint.DeleteRule = Rule.Cascade
```

The last line of code is for instructional purposes only—specifically, to highlight the *Rule* enumeration. This enumeration is used to indicate the action that is taken when an ADO.NET *ForeignKeyConstraint* is enforced. The default value is *Cascade*, which means that related rows will also be updated or deleted. Thus, in this case the statement is not necessary because by default the *DeleteRule* (as well as the *UpdateRule*) is set to *Cascade*. If you wanted different behavior, you could use one of the other three *Rule* enumeration values: *None*, *SetDefault*, and *SetNull*.

Realize that without this *DataRelation* object there is no hierarchical relationship between the two tables in the *DataSet* object. In such a case, if the user were to delete a supplier from the master *DataGrid* control—which in turn marks them for deletion in its underlying *DataSet* object—any products associated with that supplier will remain in the *DataGrid* control and the *DataSet* object. Then, when the user attempts to save the changes back to the database, orphaned products will exist that will violate foreign-key constraints set in the lower data tier, causing an exception of type *SqlException* to be thrown. Try this for yourself. Run the application, click a supplier, look at its associated products in the lower *DataGrid* control, and then press Delete. Now comment the *DataRelation* code and repeat these steps. Notice that the products in the lower *DataGrid* control remain.

The *SaveChanges* function begins by declaring an integer variable for storing the number of rows changed when *SqlDataAdapter.Update* is called. Also declared is a *SqlTransaction* variable. This class represents a T-SQL transaction that is made in a SQL Server database. Use of a transaction is highly recommended. It ensures that all or none of the changes are pushed back to the database. In other words, if an error is encountered at any time during the update, the transaction can be rolled back and any partial changes can be undone. A two-phase transaction is used here: one phase to submit the changes to the database, and another to commit them if all goes well.

The update code is wrapped in a *Try/Catch* block. After obtaining and opening a new connection, a transaction is started by invoking the *BeginTransaction* method of the *SqlConnection* object:

```
cnn = GetConnection()
cnn.Open()
tranSQL = cnn.BeginTransaction()
```

Because the Products table is the child, its changes should be pushed to the database first. The *SqlDataAdapter* exposed by the *Products* class is accessed, and the Products table is passed to the *Update* method. Recall that the *Update* method will use the commands already generated by its *SqlCommandBuilder* object to queue the changes in the database for the final commit:

```
intNumRowsChanged = _
    dalProducts.DataAdapter.Update(ds.Tables("Products"))
```

Immediately following this line of code is similar code for the Suppliers table. Notice that the number of rows changed by this second update is added to the *intNumRowsChanged* variable to record the final number of rows changed:

```
intNumRowsChanged += _
    dalSuppliers.DataAdapter.Update(ds.Tables("Suppliers"))
```

If no exceptions have been thrown thus far, the transaction can be committed and a results message passed back to the presentation tier:

```
tranSQL.Commit() _
    Return intNumRowsChanged.ToString & " changes were made to the database."
```

However, if an error is encountered, the *Catch* block contains the following code to roll back the transaction and then throw a new exception that can be caught by the calling method:

```
tranSQL.Rollback()
Throw New Exception("The changes could not be saved due to the " & _
    "following error: " & exp.Message)
```

Finally, no matter what happens, the connection needs to be closed:

```
cnn.Close()
```

Conclusion

This sample has shown you how to build a simple master-details Windows application that is architected according to a three-tier model. The user interface resides in the presentation tier and does not have direct access to the database. Instead, it calls the middle tier, which acts as a broker between the lowest and highest tiers. Organizing and structuring your code in this way has many advantages. Using namespaces to further organize your code takes it one step further, making your code more usable, more readable, and easier to maintain.

Application #22: Build an Offline Application

This application builds upon the applications shown for data-entry forms and data binding with navigation by adding the ability to work offline as well as undo changes. By *offline* we mean that the application doesn't need to be connected to a database to persist changes between application executions. You'll see that this offline capability introduces several challenges and pitfalls. Figure 3-14 shows a screen shot of Application #22.

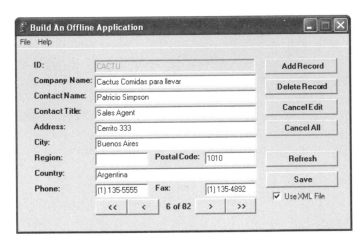

Figure 3-14   Application #22.

Building Upon...

Application #4: *Try/Catch/Finally*
Application #12: Use a *DataSet* and *DataView*
Application #16: Data Binding with Navigation
Application #19: Use a Typed *DataSet*
Application #20: Build a Data Entry Form
Application #21: Build a Three-Tier Data Form

New Concepts

The new concepts for this application center around how a *DataSet* object supports change tracking and offline operations using XML. At the beginning of this chapter, you learned that a *DataSet* object is an in-memory copy of data and the data's structure, or schema. When you query a database and store the results in a *DataSet* object, the object no longer needs to stay connected to the database. From this point, the *DataSet* object doesn't care where it came from. It's an intelligent, autonomous data cache. It inherently supports offline operations.

You need to understand two main aspects of the disconnected nature of the *DataSet* object. First, recall from an earlier topic that changes made to data in a *DataSet* object do not affect the object's data source until you call the *SqlDataAdapter.Update* method. How does the *DataSet* object keep track of changes? It uses a *DataRowState* enumeration. A *DataRow* object with no changes pending has the *Unchanged* enumeration value assigned to it. *DataRow* objects with changes pending are marked as *Modified*. Other enumeration values are *Detached*, *Added*, and *Deleted*. Note that these are all indicators of *pending* changes. That is, *pending reconciliation with the data source* (for example, a database). Until you reload the *DataSet* object or invoke either the *AcceptChanges* or *RejectChanges* method, the modifications are tracked using this *DataRow* enumeration in combination with an internal copy of the original *DataRow* object. Another related enumeration exposed by both the *DataRow* and *DataRowView* classes is *DataRowVersion*. This enumeration allows you to access the *Current*, *Original*, *Proposed*, or *Default* version of a *DataRow* object. The importance of this change-tracking concept will be underscored in the "Code Walkthrough" section, where you'll learn why use of the *DataView* class—with its *RowStateFilter* property—is essential if you must support the ability to persist and undo changes.

The second important aspect of the disconnected nature of the *DataSet* object is its exposure of numerous methods that support deserializing (reading) and serializing (writing) its data and schema to XML. Among these are *ReadXml* and *WriteXml*. Both have numerous overloads to work with *Stream*, *XmlReader*, and *XmlWriter* objects; *TextReader* and *TextWriter* objects; and other transport mechanisms. These methods also take an optional enumeration of type *XmlReadMode* that influences the deserialization or serialization process. Although the *XmlReadMode* enumeration values are mostly different between the two methods, one that is shared by both is *DiffGram*.

A *DiffGram* represents an XML format used by *DataSet* objects to track changes. Recall that a *DataSet* object automatically keeps track of all changes made to its data elements since it was last loaded or its *AcceptChanges* method was called. These changes can be serialized as a DiffGram, which takes the following form:

```
<?xml version="1.0"?>
<diffgr:diffgram
xmlns:msdata="urn:schemas-microsoft-com:xml-msdata"
xmlns:diffgr="urn:schemas-microsoft-com:xml-diffgram-v1"
xmlns:xsd="http://www.w3.org/2001/XMLSchema">

  <DataInstance>
  </DataInstance>

  <diffgr:before>
  </diffgr:before>

  <diffgr:errors>
  </diffgr:errors>
</diffgr:diffgram>
```

The *<DataInstance>* element is just a placeholder for the actual *DataSet* object (or *DataTable* object) that owns the DiffGram. This element contains children for each *DataRow* object, whether it has been modified or not. In other words, this is the data in its current state. Data elements that have been modified are identified by a *diffgr:hasChanges* annotation. This annotation can have three values: *inserted*, *modified*, or *descent*. The first value indicates a new row, the second value indicates an edited row, and the third value indicates a row for which one or more children from a parent-child relationship have been modified. The *<diffgr:before>* element contains the original version of the row. Finally, there is a *<diffgr:errors>* element that contains any errors for that row.

The following DiffGram contains several changes to the *DataSet* object used in this application. First, Customer 1 (ID ALFKI) was deleted. It does not appear as a child of the *<CustomersDataSet>* element, but it is present as a child of the *<diffgr:before>* element. Next, the Contact Name for Customer 2 (ID ANATR) was changed to *Pablo Taco*. The original Customer 2 data is also listed in the *<diffgr:before>* section. Finally, a new Customer 92 (ID PADAH) was added. This customer appears as a child of the *<CustomersDataSet>* element but not under *<diffgr:before>* because it was obviously not in the original *DataSet* object. Customers 3 through 89, as well as some of the fields, have been omitted for brevity. Also, DiffGram annotations are in bold.

```
<?xml version="1.0" standalone="yes" ?>
<diffgr:diffgram xmlns:msdata="urn:schemas-microsoft-com:xml-msdata"
xmlns:diffgr="urn:schemas-microsoft-com:xml-diffgram-v1">
  <CustomersDataSet>
    <Customers diffgr:id="Customers2" msdata:rowOrder="1"
    diffgr:hasChanges="modified">
      <CustomerID>ANATR</CustomerID>
      <CompanyName>Ana Trujillo Emparedados y helados</CompanyName>
      <ContactName>Pablo Taco</ContactName>
```

(continued)

```
            <ContactTitle>Owner</ContactTitle>
            <Phone>(5) 555-4729</Phone>
          </Customers>
          <Customers diffgr:id="Customers3" msdata:rowOrder="2">
            <CustomerID>ANTON</CustomerID>
            <CompanyName>Antonio Moreno Taquería</CompanyName>
            <ContactName>Antonio Moreno</ContactName>
            <ContactTitle>Owner</ContactTitle>
            <Phone>(5) 555-3932</Phone>
          </Customers>
          <Customers diffgr:id="Customers91" msdata:rowOrder="90">
            <CustomerID>WOLZA</CustomerID>
            <CompanyName>Wolski Zajazd</CompanyName>
            <ContactName>Zbyszek Piestrzeniewicz</ContactName>
            <ContactTitle>Owner</ContactTitle>
            <Phone>(26) 642-7012</Phone>
          </Customers>
          <Customers diffgr:id="Customers92" msdata:rowOrder="91"
          diffgr:hasChanges="inserted">
            <CustomerID>PADAH</CustomerID>
            <CompanyName>Paddy's Ale House</CompanyName>
            <ContactName>Patrick Barnes</ContactName>
            <ContactTitle>Owner</ContactTitle>
          </Customers>
        </CustomersDataSet>
        <diffgr:before>
          <Customers diffgr:id="Customers1" msdata:rowOrder="0">
            <CustomerID>ALFKI</CustomerID>
            <CompanyName>Alfreds Futterkiste</CompanyName>
            <ContactName>Maria Anders</ContactName>
            <ContactTitle>Sales Representative</ContactTitle>
            <Phone>030-0074321</Phone>
          </Customers>
          <Customers diffgr:id="Customers2" msdata:rowOrder="1">
            <CustomerID>ANATR</CustomerID>
            <CompanyName>Ana Trujillo Emparedados y helados</CompanyName>
            <ContactName>Ana Trujillo</ContactName>
            <ContactTitle>Owner</ContactTitle>
            <Phone>(5) 555-4729</Phone>
          </Customers>
        </diffgr:before>
      </diffgr:diffgram>
```

You are now ready for the code walkthrough.

Code Walkthrough

When the application loads, a copy of the Northwind Customers table is created (if it doesn't already exist); simple data bindings are cleared (if they exist) and then added to each *TextBox* control; and customer data is retrieved from the database and displayed. The rest of this section will discuss the code used for adding and deleting customer records, canceling modifications, and finally, saving the *DataSet* object to an XML file and loading the *DataSet* object from an XML file.

Adding a Record

The code for adding a record resides in the *btnAdd_Click* event handler. Although you could add a row directly to the *DataTable*, the syntax is easier if you go through the *DataView*, which will impart the change to its underlying *DataTable*:

```
Dim drv As DataRowView
drv = dvCustomers.AddNew
drv("CustomerID") = "[ID]"
drv("CompanyName") = "[Company Name]"
drv.EndEdit()
```

As the CustomerID and CompanyName fields do not accept NULL, a default value for each is provided. Following this, the *DataRowView.EndEdit* method is invoked. It is important to call *EndEdit* because if the user adds a row and then navigates elsewhere, the row is left in a *Detached RowState*. Leaving the row in a *Detached RowState* means that the *DataRow* has been created but is not yet a member of a *DataRowCollection*. A *DataRow* in this state can cause problems, so you should call *EndEdit* to append it to the *DataRowCollection*, which also marks it as a pending addition.

> **Caution**   The *CurrencyManager* also exposes methods for ending and canceling edits. Although using these methods might appear to work in certain situations, the .NET Framework documentation gives the following cautionary advice: "This property [*sic*] was designed to be used by complex-bound controls, such as the *DataGrid* control, to cancel edits. Unless you are creating a control that requires this same functionality, it is not recommended that you use this method."

Once the new row has been added, all that remains to be done is update the record number indication and move the position of the *CurrencyManager* to the new record so that the user can enter the data.

```
UpdateRecordNum()
cmCustomers.Position = dvCustomers.Count
```

The code in *UpdateRecordNum* contains a single line:

```
lblPosition.Text = cmCustomers.Position + 1 & " of " & dvCustomers.Count
```

You might think it would be acceptable to use the *Count* property of the *DataTable DataRowsCollection* instead of the *Count* property of the *DataView* object. The problem is that changes to the *DataTable* object are pending. Therefore, any additions or deletions will not be reflected in the total count. The *DataView* object, however, conveniently makes available a *RowStateFilter* property, the default for which is *CurrentRows*. This ensures that the user sees the current version of the rows—that is, the version that reflects the pending changes.

Further modifications to the record are handled automatically. When the user begins editing any item in the *DataRow* object, its *BeginEdit* method is implicitly called. Likewise, when the user navigates to another record, *EndEdit* is automatically invoked and the *DataSet* object records the pending changes.

Deleting a Record

Deleting a record can be done using three different methods. If you're not concerned about the *DataSet* object tracking changes (and thus having the ability to undo them), invoke *Remove* (if you have a reference to a specific *DataRow* object) or *RemoveAt* (if you have only the row's index in the *DataRowsCollection*). These methods permanently remove the row. They are equivalent to calling *Delete*, which merely marks a row for pending deletion, and then calling *AcceptChanges*.

This application supports change tracking and undoing, so in the *btnDelete_Click* event handler, you'll find the following code:

```
dvCustomers.Delete(cmCustomers.Position)
UpdateRecordNum()
```

Here is another example of the importance of working through the *DataView* object instead of with the *DataTable* object directly. It's reasonable to think you should be able to invoke *Delete* on the *DataRow* object and see the same results as when invoking it on the *DataRowView* object. However, for reasons not entirely clear at the time of this writing, when using the *DataTable* object, clicking the Delete button will only cause the current record to be marked for deletion. Subsequent clicks do nothing, unless you manually advance to the next record (and even this appears to function inconsistently). Perhaps there is a way around this pitfall that permits interaction directly with the *DataTable* object. Regardless, if you use the *DataView* object instead, everything works as you would expect.

Cancelling Modifications

Two buttons in this application permit modification cancellations: Cancel Edit and Cancel All. The *Click* event handler for the first button contains code to cancel edit operations on the current record:

```
dvCustomers(cmCustomers.Position).CancelEdit()
txtCustomerID.Enabled = False
```

This will undo any modifications made to the current record since *EndEdit* was called (either explicitly or implicitly). As mentioned earlier, it's best to invoke *CancelEdit* on the *DataRowView* object, not *CancelCurrentEdit* on the *Currency-Manager* object. The CustomerID *TextBox* control is also disabled when editing is cancelled. This control is editable only when adding a new customer.

The code for handling the Cancel All button is slightly different. Here, the *DataTable.RejectChanges* method is invoked to undo all pending changes to all *DataRow* objects. (There is no equivalent method for the *DataView* class.)

```
dvCustomers(cmCustomers.Position).CancelEdit()
dtCustomers.RejectChanges()
UpdateRecordNum()
```

Notice that you invoke *CancelEdit* (or *EndEdit*) prior to *RejectChanges*; if you didn't, modifications to the current record would not be undone. This is because the record is still in edit mode, and thus the changes have a *DataRow-Version* enumeration value of *Proposed* instead of *Current* (that is, pending).

Saving to and Loading from an XML File

The application allows you to save changes to the database or to an XML file. In the *btnSave_Click* event handler, you'll find the following code:

```
dvCustomers(cmCustomers.Position).EndEdit()

If dsCustomers.HasChanges Then
    If chkUseXML.Checked Then
        SaveCustomersToXML(dsCustomers)
    Else
        SaveCustomersToDatabase(CType(dsCustomers.GetChanges, _
            CustomersDataSet))
    End If
Else
    MsgBox("No changes to the DataSet were detected. Save aborted.", _
        MsgBoxStyle.Information, Me.Text)
End If
```

As you would expect by now, *EndEdit* is called before doing anything else so that the changes are marked as pending. Next, the *DataSet* object is checked for any changes. If any exist, an appropriate method is called based on the checked state of the Use XML File *CheckBox* control. If you're saving to a database, using the *GetChanges* method is advised so that only the changes get propagated back to the database, thus minimizing network traffic.

The *SaveCustomersToXml* method requires only one line of code to persist the *DataSet* object to XML:

```
dsCustomers.WriteXml("../dsCustomers.xml", XmlWriteMode.DiffGram)
```

An overload that accepts an *XmlWriteMode* enumeration is used to write the *DataSet* object in the DiffGram format. Similarly, in the *LoadCustomers-FromXml* method, you'll find the following code to load the *DataSet* object from the XML file:

```
dsCustomers.ReadXml("../dsCustomers.xml", XmlReadMode.DiffGram)
```

Experiment with the application to see how this works. Run it, make changes to various parts of it, check Use XML File, and then click Save. Then make some other changes, and click Refresh. You'll see the recent changes overwritten by the data from the XML file.

Conclusion

This is the longest discussion in this chapter. A fair amount of conceptual ground had to be covered to facilitate an adequate understanding of the code behind an offline application. Along the way, you were alerted to several pitfalls concerning the *DataTable* and *CurrencyManager* classes that could easily become a source of frustration. The bottom line is to remember the two most important points of this topic: avoid using the *CurrencyManager* methods, and when displaying data, in general think *DataView* and not *DataTable*. If you adhere to these rules of thumb, building a robust offline application should be smooth sailing.

Application #23: Use T-SQL to Create Database Objects

This sample application shows you how to create database objects by executing T-SQL statements from ADO.NET. The emphasis will be on constructing T-SQL statements to create a database and then add various database objects to it, such as a table, stored procedure, and view. The table will then be populated, a *DataSet* object filled with its contents, and the results displayed in a *DataGrid* control. Figure 3-15 shows a screen shot of Application #23.

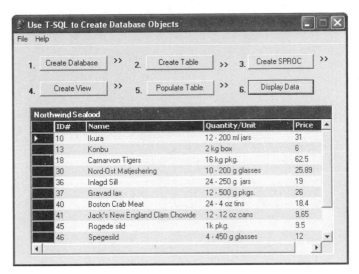

Figure 3-15   Application #23.

Building Upon...

Application #4: *Try/Catch/Finally*
Application #12: Use a *DataSet* and *DataView*

New Concepts

The new concepts are entirely related to SQL Server (or MSDE, which is a *lite* version of SQL Server and has the same internal architecture). The two main ADO.NET methods used in this application, *SqlCommand.ExecuteNonQuery* and *SqlDataAdapter.Fill*, have already been seen in previous topics. The former executes all T-SQL statements that create the new database and its associated objects. *Fill* is used only in the last step, to retrieve the data from the new database table and place it in a *DataSet* object.

As for SQL Server, you need to understand how it keeps track of its objects, both at the server and individual database levels. At the server level, the *master* database is all-important—every SQL Server instance has one. It stores all data that affects the operation of that instance, such as user accounts, other databases, and configuration settings. To create a database from code, you first need to check whether it already exists. You do this by querying the master..sysdatabases table. Objects residing in a particular database are found in the sysobjects table for that database.

Code Walkthrough

You'll now see how to query the sysdatabases and sysobjects tables and then use DROP, CREATE, and other T-SQL commands from ADO.NET.

Creating a Database

Although it's not required, you should find out whether the target SQL Server instance already contains a database of the same name. If you elect not to run this check, an exception of type *SqlException* could be thrown during the creation attempt. The following code, in the application's *CreateDatabase* method, demonstrates the syntax for writing a readable T-SQL statement that drops the App23Demo database if it exists and then creates it:

```
"IF EXISTS (" & _
"SELECT * " & _
"FROM master..sysdatabases " & _
"WHERE Name = 'App23Demo')" & vbCrLf & _
"DROP DATABASE App23Demo" & vbCrLf & _
"CREATE DATABASE App23Demo"
```

The T-SQL keyword EXISTS specifies a subquery that tests for the existence of a row. In this case, you're looking for the row in the sysdatabases table that contains information about the App23Demo database. EXISTS returns a *Boolean* value, so if the return value is *True*, use the DROP keyword to delete the database. In either case, you then use the CREATE DATABASE statement to create the App23Demo database.

The use of the carriage-return/line-feed constant (*vbCrLf*) is not necessary, but it can make your T-SQL statements more readable if you *Trace.Write* them for debugging purposes. If you omit carriage-return/line feed constants, make sure you add appropriate spaces at the end of each line to separate the various T-SQL statements.

Executing this and all other T-SQL statements in this sample that do not retrieve data is done using the following code:

```
Dim cnn As New SqlConnection(strConn)
Dim cmd As New SqlCommand(strSQL, cnn)
cnn.Open()
cmd.ExecuteNonQuery()
cnn.Close()
```

At this point in the chapter, these lines require no further comments. For the remaining T-SQL steps, this code is used to execute the statements.

Creating a Table

You are now going to be working at the database level and, thus, with the App23Demo..sysobjects table. In the *btnCreateTable_Click* event handler, you'll find the following T-SQL statement:

```
Dim strSQL As String = _
    "USE App23Demo" & vbCrLf & _
    "IF EXISTS (" & _
    "SELECT * " & _
    "FROM sysobjects " & _
    "WHERE Name = 'NW_Seafood' " & _
    "AND TYPE = 'u')" & vbCrLf & _
    "DROP TABLE NW_Seafood" & vbCrLf & _
    "CREATE TABLE NW_Seafood (" & _
    "   ProductID Int NOT NULL," & _
    "   ProductName NVarChar(40) NOT NULL," & _
    "   QuantityPerUnit NVarChar(20) NOT NULL," & _
    "   UnitPrice Money NOT NULL," & _
    "   CONSTRAINT [PK_Product] PRIMARY KEY CLUSTERED" & _
    "   (ProductID))"
```

The first line directs the server to use the App23Demo database for all subsequent commands. Following this line is the now-familiar use of the EXISTS keyword with a subquery against the sysobjects table. Notice that the object TYPE is added to the WHERE criteria. The value *u* indicates that it is a user table. It's wise to include the type in your criteria because it's possible for database objects of different types to share a name.

There are a number of statements involved with creating the NW_Seafood table. When using CREATE TABLE, you pass information about the columns the table will contain, as well as any constraints and other objects that define the table. In this sample, you see the column name, data type, and whether the table can contain NULL values. Lastly, a constraint is added to indicate that the ProductID column is the primary key.

Tip   An easy way to create a table and populate it with data is to use the SELECT INTO statement. For example, to create the table used in this sample, you could execute this T-SQL statement:

```
SELECT ProductID, ProductName, QuantityPerUnit, UnitPrice
INTO NW_Seafood
FROM Products Where CategoryID = 8
```

Keep in mind, however, that you'll then need to use ALTER TABLE to add constraints and other defining objects.

Creating a Stored Procedure and View

The T-SQL statement for creating a stored procedure looks similar to that for creating a table. In the *btnCreateSP_Click* event handler, you'll find the following code:

```
Dim strSQL As String = _
    "USE App23Demo" & vbCrLf & _
    "IF EXISTS (" & _
    "SELECT * " & _
    "FROM sysobjects " & _
    "WHERE Name = 'AddSeafood' " & _
    "AND TYPE = 'p')" & vbCrLf & _
    "DROP PROCEDURE AddSeafood"
```

The only difference worth mentioning between the preceding code and that used to create a table is that instead of type='u', you'll find type='p' (for *procedure*). Also, PROCEDURE is substituted for TABLE.

The T-SQL statement for creating a view is almost identical to the code just shown and requires no further comment:

```
Dim strSQL As String = _
    "USE App23Demo" & vbCrLf & _
    "IF EXISTS (" & _
    "SELECT * " & _
    "FROM sysobjects " & _
    "WHERE Name = 'GetSeafood' " & _
    "AND TYPE = 'v')" & vbCrLf & _
    "DROP VIEW GetSeafood"
```

Displaying the Data

To display the data in the *DataGrid* control, you must first populate the table with some products. You've created a stored procedure just for this purpose, *AddSeafood*, and this is executed in the *btnPopulate_Click* event handler by using the T-SQL statement EXECUTE App23Demo.dbo.AddSeafood.

Following this, in the *btnDisplay_Click* event handler, there is code for querying the previously created View and filling a *DataSet* object:

```
Dim strSQL As String = _
    "USE App23Demo" & vbCrLf & _
    "SELECT * " & _
    "FROM GetSeafood"
Dim cnn As New SqlConnection(strConn)
Dim cmd As New SqlCommand(strSQL, cnn)
Dim da As New SqlDataAdapter(cmd)
Dim dsSeafood As New DataSet()

da.Fill(dsSeafood, "Seafood")
```

The *DataGrid* control is then bound to the *DataSet* object for display:

```
With grdSeafood
    .CaptionText = "Northwind Seafood"
    .DataSource = dsSeafood.Tables(0)
    .Visible = True
End With
```

You'll also find *DataGrid* formatting code in this sample, but this is discussed in the next chapter.

Conclusion

This sample has given you an introduction to executing T-SQL statements that create a database and associated objects, all from ADO.NET. You learned that information about databases is contained in the master..sysdatabases table and that information about a database object is contained in that database's sysobjects table. You also learned that the EXISTS keyword can be used with a subquery to check for the existence of a database object before creating one anew.

Should you want to learn more about using T-SQL to create database objects, consider studying one of the lengthy scripts included with the .NET Framework. For example, you can find the instnwnd.sql script in C:\Program Files\Microsoft Visual Studio .NET\FrameworkSDK\Samples\Setup. By *reverse engineering* this script, you'll learn a lot about database object creation using T-SQL.

Application #24: Load Images from and Save Images to a Database

Sometimes you need to store images in a database instead of as physical files. This sample application, shown in Figure 3-16, will show you how to build a Windows Forms interface that allows you to do the following:

- Browse for an image on your hard disk

- Load the selected image into a *PictureBox* control for viewing

- Save an image displayed in the *PictureBox* control to the database

- Select an image from a *ListBox* control, and load it from the database

- Delete an image

Figure 3-16 Application #24.

Building Upon...

Application #4: *Try/Catch/Finally*
Application #12: Use a *DataSet* and *DataView*
Application #19: Use a Typed *DataSet*

New Concepts

The new concepts in this topic center around the abstract *Stream* class and how it's used to convert an image file to and from the *Image* data type that SQL Server uses to store images. Be sure not to confuse the *Image* data type with the word *image*, as if to imply that only images can be stored therein. Rather, the *Image* data type can store anything as variable-length binary data.

A byte array is used to send data to an Image field. Thus, the main question is: How does one convert an image file—whether a JPEG, Bitmap, or other format—into an array of bytes? There are several ways to accomplish this in .NET. One of the easiest ways is to use a concrete implementation of the *Stream* class. A stream in .NET is essentially an abstraction of a sequence of bytes, whether these bytes came from a file, a TCP/IP socket, a database, or wherever. *Stream* classes allow you to work with binary data, reading and writing back and forth between streams and data structures (such as a byte array).

Once the image is converted to a byte array, it's saved to a database by using coding practices you're already familiar with at this point in the book. The steps required to retrieve an image from a database essentially amount to reversing the process.

The "Code Walkthrough" section will explain these steps in further detail. You might also peek ahead to Chapter 8, which provides more in-depth information about working with streams.

Code Walkthrough

You'll first see how to browse for images on your hard disk and display them in a *PictureBox* control. Following this, you'll see code for reading and deleting images from, and saving images to, a database.

Browsing For and Displaying an Image

The first task is to find an image on your hard disk. To do this, use an *Open-FileDialog* object in conjunction with a standard *Button* control. In the *btnBrowse_Click* event handler, you can see how this is done. The first few lines of code merely set properties of the *OpenFileDialog* object.

```
With odlg
    .InitialDirectory = "C:\"
    .Filter = "All Files|*.*|Bitmaps|*.bmp|GIFs|*.gif|JPEGs|*.jpg"
    .FilterIndex = 2
End With
```

A pipe-delimited pair of file types is provided to determine the valid file types that can be accessed through the dialog box. Among other properties, you can also set *FilterIndex* to the default file type that you want to appear in the dialog box's Files Of Type menu. The index is not zero-based, so in this example, *Bitmaps* will appear as the default.

The dialog box is not actually opened until its *ShowDialog* method is called, which can be combined in an *If/Then* statement to check which button was pressed and perform follow-on tasks:

```
If odlg.ShowDialog() = DialogResult.OK Then
    With picSave
        .Image = Image.FromFile(odlg.FileName)
        .SizeMode = PictureBoxSizeMode.CenterImage
        .BorderStyle = BorderStyle.Fixed3D
    End With
    lblFilePath.Text = odlg.FileName
End If
```

Although an *OpenFileDialog* object contains an Open button instead of an OK button, there is no *DialogResult* enumeration for the Open button. Instead, use the *OK* enumeration. Once it's confirmed that the Open button has been clicked, properties of the *PictureBox* control are set. Notice how the *Image* property—which requires an object of type *System.Drawing.Image*—is assigned. The *Image* class is abstract and exposes a number of shared methods for working with images, one of which is *FromFile*. This method creates an *Image* object from a fully qualified path; and although the *OpenFileDialog.FileName* property might lead you to think that it contains only the file name, it actually has the full path.

Saving an Image

Now that your image file is represented by an *Image* object, you can use a stream to convert it to a byte array. In the *btnSave_Click* event handler, the first line of code creates a *MemoryStream* object:

```
Dim ms As New MemoryStream()
```

A *MemoryStream* object is simply a stream that uses memory as its backup store instead of some other medium. As a result, a *MemoryStream* object usually provides better performance. Streams are flexible. You could, for example, have used a *FileStream* object to open the image file directly and read it in. There are certainly numerous other ways, too. The implementation here, however, is simple and straightforward.

The *MemoryStream* is then passed as an argument to the *Save* method, another member of the *Image* class. You can optionally pass the image format—for example, by accessing the *Image*'s read-only *RawFormat* property:

```
picSave.Image.Save(ms, picSave.Image.RawFormat)
```

The actual byte array conversion comes in the next line. *GetBuffer* returns an array of unsigned bytes being held by the stream.

```
Dim arrImage() As Byte = ms.GetBuffer
ms.Close()
```

> **Tip** It's always best to manually close a stream as soon as possible instead of leaving it for the garbage collector. *Stream.Close* contains code that calls *GC.SuppressFinalize*, which means that the stream is not finalized and resources are released sooner. Also, if you are using a *FileStream* object, the underlying file cannot be moved or deleted until the stream is closed.

The last data-gathering task is to extract the filename from the full path, as there is no need to store the entire path in the database:

```
Dim strFilename As String = _
    lblFilePath.Text.Substring(lblFilePath.Text.LastIndexOf("\") + 1)
```

This might look a bit complex and convoluted, but all you're doing is indicating that you want a substring of the full path that starts after the last backslash.

With the filename extracted and the image converted to a byte array, you're now ready to use the ADO.NET practices you've already learned to push these to the database.

```
Dim cnn As New SqlConnection(connectionString)
Dim strSQL As String = _
    "INSERT INTO Picture (Filename, Picture)" & _
    "VALUES (@Filename, @Picture)"
Dim cmd As New SqlCommand(strSQL, cnn)

With cmd
    .Parameters.Add(New SqlParameter("@Filename", _
        SqlDbType.NVarChar, 50)).Value = strFilename
    .Parameters.Add(New SqlParameter("@Picture", _
        SqlDbType.Image)).Value = arrImage
End With
cnn.Open()
cmd.ExecuteNonQuery()
cnn.Close()
```

As you can see, at this point there is nothing new except the use of the *SqlDbType.Image* enumeration. Set the value of the *@Picture* parameter to the byte array, and execute the INSERT statement as you would with any other type of data.

Reading an Image

When the application's Manage tab is clicked, a *DataSet* object is automatically created and its contents bound to a *ListBox* control. This allows you to see what images are in the database. You can then select one to display it or delete it.

From this point forward, you're essentially reversing the process. To display an image, you have to convert it from a byte array to an *Image*, and then assign it to the *PictureBox.Image* property:

```
Dim arrImage() As Byte = _
    CType(dsPics.Tables(0).Rows(lstPics.SelectedIndex)("Picture"), Byte())
Dim ms As New MemoryStream(arrImage)

With picManage
    .Image = Image.FromStream(ms)
    .SizeMode = PictureBoxSizeMode.CenterImage
    .BorderStyle = BorderStyle.Fixed3D
End With
```

The *SelectedIndex* property of the *ListBox* control is used to to retrieve the contents of the associated Picture field in the *DataSet* object, which is then explicitly cast to a byte array. Following this, a *MemoryStream* is created by passing the byte array to its constructor. The last step is to invoke the shared *FromStream* method to convert the stream contents to an *Image*, and then assign this to the *PictureBox.Image* property.

Deleting an Image

Deleting the image is the simplest task of all. For this, the *SqlData-Adapter.Update* method is called after deleting the relevant row in the *Data-Table* object:

```
dsPics.Tables(0).Rows(lstPics.SelectedIndex).Delete()
da.Update(dsPics)
```

Finally, clean up the user interface to reflect the changes:

```
lblFileName.Text = ""
picManage.Image = Nothing
```

Conclusion

This application has shown you how to save images to and load images from a database. You learned that the save process involves the following progression: image file to *Image* to byte array to database. To load and display an image from the database, you reverse the process: database to byte array to *Image* to *PictureBox*. In addition to being introduced to the *OpenFileDialog* class, you were shown the *MemoryStream* class, which served as the in-memory conversion medium. You'll learn more about streams in Chapter 8.

Application #25: Use Legacy ADO

There are times when you might need to use legacy ADO from within your .NET application. For example, you could have a substantial investment in an ADO code base that you want to leverage in a .NET application. Or perhaps you want to set up a search engine on your Web site using the Windows 2000 Indexing Service, which at the present time returns search results only in an ADO RecordSet.

Fortunately, the .NET Framework makes it easy to work with ADO. This sample application will show you how to retrieve and manipulate data using ADO, as well as transfer data from a *RecordSet* to a *DataSet* object. Figure 3-17 shows a screen shot of Application #25.

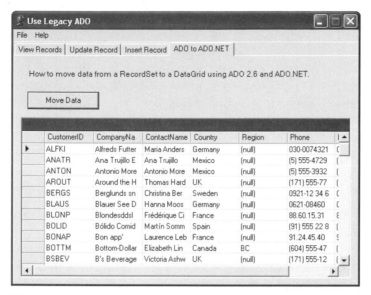

Figure 3-17   Application #25.

Building Upon...

Application #4: *Try/Catch/Finally*
Application #12: Use a *DataSet* and *DataView*
Application #15: Bind Data to a *ComboBox*
Application #16: Data Binding with Navigation

New Concepts

It is assumed you already have basic experience with ADO and just want to know how to use it from a .NET application. As such, using ADO within .NET and in conjuction with ADO.NET are the only new concepts.

ADO is made accessible to a .NET application through a COM Interop layer. This layer is actually a runtime-callable wrapper (RCW) that works with interoperability services of the .NET base class library. It's created especially for the ADODB DLL, making it appear to the .NET runtime as a native .NET component. Thus, an interop wrapper makes it appear as if you're working directly with the COM object. However, as with a proxy class for a Web service, you are actually calling members of the wrapper class, which handle the complex underlying communication details for you and forward your requests to the COM runtime.

There are two ways to create this wrapper class. The easiest way is to add a reference to a COM component in Visual Studio.NET. If it doesn't already have a COM interop wrapper built in—as is the case with the ADODB component—Visual Studio .NET will ask you for permission to create one. Alternatively, you can use the Type Library Importer utility (Tlbimp.exe) from the command line.

> **Caution** Some noteworthy instruction on this subject can be found in the .NET Framework Documentation: "When using ADO *Recordset* or *Record* objects in conjunction with .NET Framework applications, always call *Close* when you are finished. This ensures that the underlying connection to a data source is released in a timely manner, and also prevents possible access violations due to unmanaged ADO objects being reclaimed by garbage collection when existing references still exist. Note that the *OleDbDataAdapter.Fill* overload that takes a *DataTable* object and an ADO object implicitly calls *Close* on the ADO object when the *Fill* operation is complete."

Code Walkthrough

The first tab of the sample application shows how to navigate through an ADO Recordset. When the form loads, an ADO connection is created and opened in the *InitRecordNavigation* helper routine. A *RecordSet* object is then created using an *adOpenStatic* cursor to allow moving forward and backward through the records:

```
cnnADO.Open(ConnectionString)
Dim strSQL As String = _
    "SELECT CompanyName, ContactName, Phone " & _
    "FROM Customers"
rs.Open(strSQL, cnnADO, CursorTypeEnum.adOpenStatic)
' Advance to the first record.
rs.MoveFirst()
```

Although certainly not a best practice, the connection is left open for demonstration purposes so that it can be shared among the other examples. The code for displaying the *RecordSet* values in the *TextBox* controls is contained in the *PopulateSimpleNavigationForm* method. The syntax is similar to what you've seen when working with a *SqlDataReader* object or other ADO.NET data sources:

```
txtCompanyName.Text = CStr(rs.Fields("CompanyName").Value)
txtContactName.Text = CStr(rs.Fields("ContactName").Value)
txtPhone.Text = CStr(rs.Fields("Phone").Value)
```

When a navigation button is clicked, the button's *Click* event handler moves the *RecordSet* cursor and then updates the *TextBox* controls. For example, the *btnNext_Click* event handler contains the following code. Notice the code to ensure that there is a next record and not the end-of-file:

```
If Not rs.EOF Then
    rs.MoveNext()
    If rs.EOF Then
        rs.MovePrevious()
    End If
    PopulateSimpleNavigationForm()
End If
```

The second tab of the sample application shows how to fill a *ComboBox* control by iterating through a *RecordSet* object. Here, the default cursor *adOpenForwardOnly* is used because forward-only, read-only access is all that is needed. When this cursor is used, a *RecordSet* object is very similar to the ADO.NET *DataReader* object.

```
Dim strSQL As String = "SELECT CategoryName FROM Categories"
rs.Open(strSQL, cnnADO)
While Not rs.EOF
    cboCategoryName.Items.Add(rs.Fields("CategoryName").Value)
    rs.MoveNext()
End While
```

This example also shows how to execute a SQL command using ADO. The following code updates the category description and then checks the success/fail integer value returned as an object when the ADO Connection object's *Execute* method is called. (The SQL statement is omitted.)

```
Dim recordsAffected As Object
cnnADO.Execute(strSQL, recordsAffected)
If CInt(recordsAffected) = 1 Then
    MessageBox.Show("Update successful!", Me.Text, _
        MessageBoxButtons.OK, MessageBoxIcon.Information)
Else
    MessageBox.Show("A problem was encountered " _
        & "when updating the record!", Me.Text, _
        MessageBoxButtons.OK, MessageBoxIcon.Error)
End If
```

The code for the example in the third tab, which shows how to insert a record, is almost identical and is not covered further.

Finally, the example in the fourth tab demonstrates how to move data from a *RecordSet* object to a *DataSet* object. First, in ways similar to what you've already seen, a SQL command is executed by an ADO *Connection* object, returning a *RecordSet* object:

```
Dim strSQL As String = _
    "SELECT CustomerID, CompanyName, ContactName, Country, " & _
    "       Region, Phone, Fax " & _
    "FROM Customers"
rs = cnnADO.Execute(strSQL)
```

Next, a *DataSet* object is instantiated. This will be passed as an argument along with the *RecordSet* object to an *OleDbDataAdapter* object when the latter's *Fill* method is called.

```
Dim ds As New DataSet()
Dim da As New OleDb.OleDbDataAdapter()
da.Fill(ds, rs, "Customers")
```

Finally, the *DataGrid* control is bound to the *DataSet* object to display the transferred data:

```
grdMain.DataSource = ds
grdMain.DataMember = "Customers"
```

Conclusion

This topic has shown you how to work with legacy ADO classes from within a .NET application. You learned that the ADODB component is made available to managed code through a specialized COM interop wrapper that serves as an intermediary between the .NET and COM runtimes. Perhaps the most interesting example—showing the remarkable ability of ADO and ADO.NET to coexist with one another—was the final example, in which you saw how to fill a *DataSet* with data from a *RecordSet* by using a data adapter from the OLE DB .NET Data Provider.

Application #26: Use Crystal Reports

Crystal Reports is the standard reporting tool for Visual Studio .NET. It has enjoyed a long relationship with Microsoft, having shipped with Visual Basic since 1993. Crystal Reports .NET is the latest version. It was reengineered to take advantage of the .NET Framework and is a generational leap over preceding versions. This version is also not available as a standalone product. Rather, for the first time it has been fully integrated with the Visual Studio IDE.

With Crystal Reports, you have an integrated component that allows you to create a limitless number of professional-looking, custom reports that pull from a variety of data sources. You can then host these reports inside a Web or Windows application, or even publish them as a Web service.

Crystal Reports controls interact with other .NET controls to provide a rich user-interface experience with capabilities such as report filtering and drill down. Users can even export reports to Microsoft Word, Microsoft Excel, Adobe Acrobat, HTML formats, and more.

This sample shows you how to create a Windows Forms application that hosts four different reports providing various layouts and degrees of interaction. The Basic report simply shows tabular data. The Parameter report allows the user to select a company from a .NET *ComboBox* control and then view a report tailored to that company. The Dynamic Format report similarly takes parameters, but it uses them to format the results differently depending on the input. Finally, the Graph Drill Down report, shown in Figure 3-18, illustrates how to use bar graphs in conjunction with the drill-down feature of Crystal Reports.

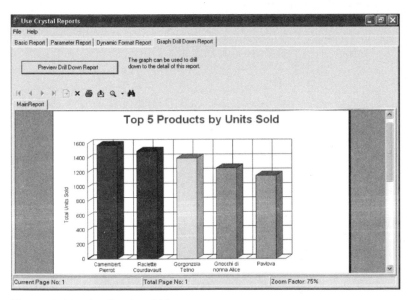

Figure 3-18   Application #26.

Building Upon...

Application #4: *Try/Catch/Finally*
Application #13: Use Stored Procedures
Application #14: Use a *SqlDataReader*
Application #15: Bind Data to a *ComboBox*
Application #19: Use a Typed *DataSet*

New Concepts

The new concepts we will focus on here center around the two data-access models used by Crystal Reports. Concepts involving the creation of reports are also briefly covered.

Data-Access Models

Crystal Reports use two different data-access models. With the Pull Model, a report handles everything, from connecting to the database, submitting the SQL commands, retrieving and formatting the data, and so on. Crystal Reports uses its own database drivers that support a variety of data sources. To many, this method is the easiest because no additional coding is required. Three examples in the sample application use the Pull Model.

The Push Model involves an intermediate data layer to handle retrieving data from the data source and passing it on to the report. For example, you could use ADO.NET to create a *DataSet* object and then bind (or *push*) the *DataSet* object to the report. This is more complex, but it gives you greater control over how data is retrieved (for example, with or without connection pooling) and what the report receives (for example, filtered further after retrieval). It also allows you to leverage existing code or skills instead of having to learn the Crystal Reports way of data access. The first example in the sample application uses the Push Model.

Creating Reports

Crystal Reports has an integrated Reports Designer to help you create the report files (*.rpt). As with other Visual Studio .NET integrated components that have supporting design tools, you can use the designer and its associated wizards (*experts*, as Crystal Reports refers to them) to set all the properties for connecting to a data source, retrieving the data, applying formatting, and so on. No additional code is required.

Alternatively, you can make minimal use of the designer, writing code to set properties at run time. To do this, Crystal Reports provides an extensive API that is well documented in the Visual Studio .NET integrated help.

Tip   One stumbling block for developers starting out with Crystal Reports .NET is how to get Stored Procedures to appear as an option in the Database Expert dialog box. By default, only Tables and Views will appear.

You can add Stored Procedures and change other settings for the Reports Designer as follows. First, open a report in Visual Studio .NET. Next, right-click on any white space in the report, point to Designer, and then click Default Settings. Click the Database tab, and then check Stored Procedures.

After you click OK, you still might not see Stored Procedures as an option in the Database Expert dialog box. If this happens, close and re-open Visual Studio .NET, and then reopen the Database Expert.

The Reports Designer has many features. It's beyond the scope of this topic to address them. Figure 3-19 depicts a report open in Visual Studio .NET, with the Field Explorer and Database Expert.

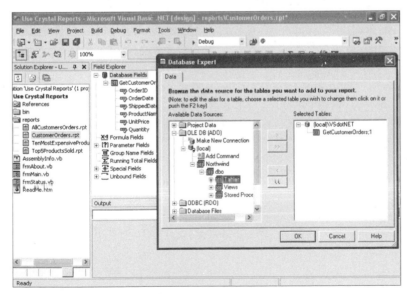

Figure 3-19   The Field Explorer and Database Expert are shown here for a Crystal report that is open in Visual Studio .NET.

In the "Code Walkthrough" section, you'll start with reports that have already been created.

Displaying Reports

The steps required to display a report in a Windows Forms application vary depending on how much you use the Reports Designer to configure the report. At a minimum, you simply add a Crystal Reports Viewer control to a form, create a *ReportDocument* object and call its *Load* method to load the desired report, and then set the viewer's *ReportSource* property (similar to .NET data binding with the *DataSource* property), effectively binding it to the report file.

A more code-intensive approach would involve interacting with members of the *CrystalDecisions.CrystalReports.Engine* namespace to set datasources, formatting, and many other things. You'll see some examples of this in the next section.

Code Walkthrough

This walkthrough is divided into two parts that represent the two data-access models used by Crystal Reports.

The Push Model Example

The first example you'll look at uses the Push Model. As such, the code is a bit more complex because the data retrieval is not handled by the report. In the *btnPreviewBasicReport_Click* event handler, you'll find the following variables initially declared:

```
Dim rptExpensiveProducts As New ReportDocument()
Dim dsTenMostExpProd As DSTenMostExpensiveProducts
Dim da As SqlDataAdapter
```

The *ReportDocument* class is found in the *CrystalDecisions.Crystal-Reports.Engine* namespace. As the name implies, it represents the report being displayed in the *CrystalReportViewer* control. The other two variables should be familiar to you from Application #19: Use a Typed *DataSet*.

The code needed to retrieve the data source and push it to the report comes next. The typed *DataSet*, created from the *Ten Most Expensive Products* stored procedure in Northwind, is first instantiated and filled:

```
dsTenMostExpProd = New DSTenMostExpensiveProducts()
da = New SqlDataAdapter("[Ten Most Expensive Products]", _
    ConnectionString)
da.Fill(dsTenMostExpProd, _
    dsTenMostExpProd.Ten_Most_Expensive_Products.TableName)
```

Next, the report is loaded by passing the path to the physical file created using the designer:

```
rptExpensiveProducts.Load("..\reports\TenMostExpensiveProducts.rpt")
```

Finally, the two source properties are set: the data source for the report, and the report source for the viewer:

```
rptExpensiveProducts.SetDataSource( _
    dsTenMostExpProd.Ten_Most_Expensive_Products)
crvBasic.ReportSource = rptExpensiveProducts
```

That's all there is to the more complex Push Model. The next example will illustrate the Pull Model.

The Pull Model Example

The Customer Orders report is displayed on the second *TabPage*, Parameter Report. This report takes a single parameter, the Customer Name from the *ComboBox* control, showing you how a data-bound .NET control can interact with a Crystal Reports control.

The variables declared and initialized inside the *btnPreviewCustomer-Report_Click* event handler are a bit different from the previous example. In addition to the *ReportDocument* variable, you'll find the following:

```
Dim tbCurrent As CrystalDecisions.CrystalReports.Engine.Table
Dim tliCurrent As CrystalDecisions.Shared.TableLogOnInfo
Dim pvCollection As New CrystalDecisions.Shared.ParameterValues()
Dim pdvCustomerName As _
    New CrystalDecisions.Shared.ParameterDiscreteValue()
```

The *Table* object represents a database table accessed by the report. You'll use this later to iterate through the *Tables* collection, setting connection-string properties encapsulated by the *TableLogOnInfo* class. The other two objects provide a container for parameters passed to the tables in the report. These are conceptually similar to the *SqlCommand.Parameters* collection and the *Sql-Parameter* object with which you're already familiar.

After the code for loading the report, you'll see code to set the connection information:

```
For Each tbCurrent In rptCustomersOrders.Database.Tables
    tliCurrent = tbCurrent.LogOnInfo
    With tliCurrent.ConnectionInfo
        .ServerName = ServerName
        .DatabaseName = "Northwind"
    End With
    tbCurrent.ApplyLogOnInfo(tliCurrent)
Next tbCurrent
```

This is largely for demonstration purposes. Remember that in the Pull Model the report will already have this information. However, you can override those settings at run time. If you know the connection information will not change, this code is not required.

The next few lines of code pass the parameter value to the report:

```
pdvCustomerName.Value = cboCustomers.Text
pvCollection.Add(pdvCustomerName)
rptCustomersOrders.DataDefinition.ParameterFields("@CustomerName"). _
    ApplyCurrentValues(pvCollection)
```

First, the *Value* property of the *ParameterDiscreteValue* object is set to the text of the selected *ComboBox* item. This parameter is then added to the parameters collection. Finally, the parameters collection is applied to the empty parameter field that has already been set in the report using the designer.

The code for the remaining two examples of the Pull Model is left for you to examine. The code for each contains only slight variations from the example you have just seen. Although they might look quite a bit different when displayed, most of these differences result from the design of the report, not the code behind it.

Conclusion

Crystal Reports .NET is a powerful, greatly overhauled version of a classic product that has, for a long time, served well the needs of many corporations. In this topic, you've gained a better understanding of how to display reports in a Windows Forms application. If your work is more Web-oriented, you'll be happy to know that the concepts and code involved with viewing Crystal Reports on the Web are almost identical. You've also learned more about the two types of data access models supported by Crystal Reports, and how to implement both.

Application #27: Compare Data Binding in Web and Windows Forms

This topic is a bit of a departure from the rest of this chapter in that the focus is on a comparison between two types of controls that are used in both Web and Windows Forms. The first type is a single-select control. In the *System.Web.UI.WebControls* namespace, one representation of this type is the *DropDownList* control. Its close relative in the Windows Forms family of controls is the *ComboBox* control. The second type is a multiselect control. In the

Web Forms family, one incarnation of this is the *CheckBoxList* control. Its Windows Forms relative is the *CheckBoxList* control. For those of you who develop both Windows and Web applications, awareness of these differences can help you save some cross-platform development frustration.

Application #27, shown in Figure 3-20, is a Web Forms application.

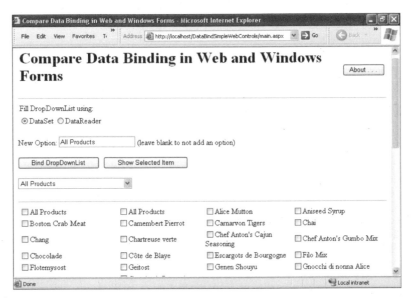

Figure 3-20   Web Forms application.

Building Upon...

Application #4: *Try/Catch/Finally*
Application #12: Use a *DataSet* and *DataView*
Application #14: Use a *SqlDataReader*
Application #15: Bind Data to a *ComboBox*

New Concepts

Although some code you haven't seen before will be discussed in the "Code Walkthough" section, there are no new concepts associated with using single-select and multiselect controls. The remainder of this topic will focus on the code differences when working across platforms.

Code Walkthrough

The code-behind for the Web Form shows two ways to data-bind a *DropDown-List*. In *BindDropDownListUsingDataSet*, you'll find the following code after the *DataSet* is acquired:

```
With cboProducts
    .DataTextField = "Name"
    .DataValueField = "ID"

    If Trim(txtNewOption.Text) <> "" Then
        .DataSource = Helper.UI.AddOption(dsProducts, .DataTextField, _
            .DataValueField, txtNewOption.Text, "0")
    Else
        .DataSource = dsProducts
    End If
    .DataBind()
End With
```

Astute readers should be able to pick out three distinct differences between this and similar code for data binding a *ComboBox* control. First, notice that instead of *DisplayMember* and *ValueMember* properties the *Drop-DownList* control uses *DataTextField* and *DataValueField* properties. This is merely a subtle syntax difference. More important, the *DropDownList* control permits you to data-bind directly to a *DataSet* object because it automatically defaults to the first *DataTable* object in the collection. Such is not the case with the *ComboBox* control, in which you must state which *DataTable* object in the collection is the data source. Finally, for Web controls, you must explicitly call the *DataBind* method or no data binding will occur and no exception is thrown. This is one of the chief causes of initial frustration for a Windows developer who is trying to leverage his skills in the Web Forms world.

The preceding code also contains a call to an *AddOption* method. What is this used for? Typically, you'll need to add an option to a control that is not stored in the database. For example, a common scenario is a *DropDownList* control that defaults to an All Options menu item, with each individual option listed below it. This is not as easy to accomplish as you might think because after a control is data-bound you normally cannot alter its collection of items. However, if you alter the control's data source after it is acquired but before the control is bound, you can achieve your goal. The *AddOption* method that resides in a separate Helper Class Library project does just that:

```
Shared Function AddOption(ByVal ds As DataSet, _
    ByVal strDisplayField As String, _
    ByVal strValueField As String, _
    ByRef strNewOptionText As String, _
    ByVal strNewOptionValue As String) As DataSet

    Dim dt As DataTable
    Dim drNew As DataRow
    dt = ds.Tables(0)
    drNew = dt.NewRow()
    drNew(strDisplayField) = strNewOptionText
    drNew(strValueField) = strNewOptionValue
    dt.Rows.InsertAt(drNew, 0)
    dt.AcceptChanges()
    Return ds
End Function
```

This function inserts an option into the top row of a *DataTable* object. It then returns a *DataSet* object, from which you will most likely want to create a *DataView* object to take advantage of its sorting and filtering capabilities. You can then use the *DataView* object as the data source. Note that if you want the additional option to appear at the top of the list as well as the data to appear in alphabetical order, it must be presorted. Creating and sorting a *DataView* object after the option is added might cause the additional option not to appear at the top. Thus, the data should be sorted at the database level in the SELECT statement.

The code in the method for data binding the *DropDownList* control to a *SqlDataReader* object is similar, as is the code for data binding the *CheckBoxList* control. These are not covered further, as no new comparison information is unveiled. Other differences, however, summarized in the "Conclusion" section, revolve around showing the selected item or items for these controls. Space limitations do not permit addressing these here. You are encouraged to experiment with the code and review the ample comments therein to verify what is summarized in the next section.

Conclusion

The results of the comparison between the single-select and multiselect control types are summarized in Table 3-2 and Table 3-3.

Table 3-2   Single-Select Control Comparison

ComboBox (in *DropDownList* mode, Windows Forms)	*DropDownList* (Web Forms)
DisplayMember and *ValueMember* are used to set the data bindings.	*DataTextField* and *DataValueField* are used to set the data bindings.
There is no *DataBind* method. Data binding occurs automatically. However, when the data source is a *DataSet*, you must explicitly set the *DataTable*—for example, `clstProducts.DataSource = dsProducts.Tables(0)`.	You must explicitly call the *DataBind* method. You can also bind directly to a *DataSet* unless it contains more than one *DataTable*, in which case you would need to explicitly set the *DataTable*.
Access information about the selected item using the *SelectedIndex*, *SelectedValue*, and *Text* properties.	Access information about the selected item using the *SelectedIndex*, *SelectedItem.Value*, and *SelectedItem.Text* properties.

Table 3-3   Multiselect Control Comparison

CheckBoxList (Windows Forms)	*CheckBoxList* (Web Forms)
The first two rows in Table 3-2 also apply to these controls.	
Selected means *highlighted*, which is different from *checked*.	*Selected* means *checked*.
Exposes a *SelectedItems* and *CheckedItems* collection. The former is not relevant because it contains 0 or 1 items.	Exposes only an *Items* collection. You must iterate through all items and check the value of the *Selected* property. (There is no *Checked* property.)
Objects in the *CheckedItems* collection are of type *DataRowView*.	Objects in the *Items* collection are of type *ListItem*.

Application #28: Work with the XML DOM

One of the most common ways to work with XML is via its Document Object Model, or DOM. The .NET Framework provides DOM-style support via classes in the *System.Xml* namespace. This sample application shows you numerous ways to work with the XML DOM. Through a series of examples, you'll become familiar with the *XmlDocument* class and the classes derived from the abstract *XmlNode* class. Figure 3-21 shows Application #28 in action.

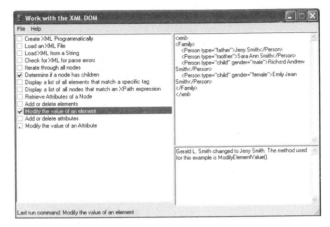

Figure 3-21   Application #28.

Building Upon...

Application #3: String Manipulation
Application #4: *Try/Catch/Finally*

New Concepts

An *XmlDocument* object represents an in-memory (cached) XML document that has been parsed as a tree of nodes to enable navigation and manipulation of its contents. According to the W3C specifications, each item in an XML document—whether it is an Element, Attribute, Text, etc.—is known as a node. Nodes are represented by the abstract *XmlNode* class. The *XmlDocument* class also extends *XmlNode*. You can get an idea of the various types of nodes that make up an XML document by perusing the members of the *XmlNode-Type* enumeration.

For example, consider the following simple XML document. Figure 3-22 shows how the document would be loaded into the DOM.

```
<?xml version="1.0"?>
  <books>
    <book>
      <author>Carson</author>
      <price format="dollar">31.95</price>
      <pubdate>05/01/2001</pubdate>
```

(continued)

```
    </book>
    <pubinfo>
      <publisher>MSPress</publisher>
      <state>WA</state>
    </pubinfo>
  </books>
```

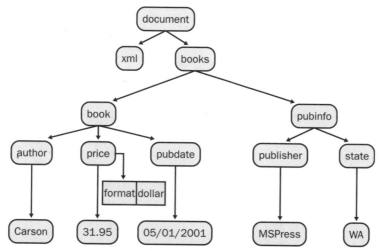

Figure 3-22 This figure shows how the memory is structured when the preceding XML data is read into the DOM structure (source: .NET Framework SDK Documentation).

Thus, working with XML using the DOM begins with becoming familiar with the members of the *XmlDocument* and *XmlNode* classes.

Code Walkthrough

You'll now see how to create an XML document programmatically, load an existing XML document, iterate through XML nodes using recursion, and find nodes using XPath expressions to modify their contents.

Creating an XML Document Programmatically

The *XmlDocument* class has methods that allow you to programmatically create an XML document. The *CreateXmlFile* method in the sample application contains code that demonstrates how to do this.

First, variables that represent the major parts of an XML document are declared and initialized. (For all the examples in the sample application, the most commonly used variables—such as xDoc—have already been declared at the class level.)

```
Dim xPI As XmlProcessingInstruction
Dim xComment As XmlComment
Dim xElRoot, xElFamily As XmlElement

xDoc = New XmlDocument()
```

You can now begin to build the document. Methods associated with each variable type are aptly named, making the code that follows self-describing:

```
xPI = xDoc.CreateProcessingInstruction("xml", "version='1.0'")
xDoc.AppendChild(xPI)

xComment = xDoc.CreateComment("Family Information")
xDoc.AppendChild(xComment)

xElRoot = xDoc.CreateElement("xml")
xDoc.AppendChild(xElRoot)
```

The only thing that requires some clarification is the use of *AppendChild*. As its name implies, this causes the passed node to be added to the end of the list of nodes for the document or node calling the method. You might think that *CreateElement* would suffice, but it only creates the element in memory and doesn't actually add it to the DOM. Thus *AppendChild* is conceptually similar to ADO.NET methods such as *DataTable.AcceptChanges*. Until *AcceptChanges* is invoked, new rows and other associated changes are not reflected in the *DataTable* object.

The remaining elements in this simple document are added as follows:

```
xElRoot = xDoc.CreateElement("xml")
xDoc.AppendChild(xElRoot)
xElFamily = _
    CType(xElRoot.AppendChild(xDoc.CreateElement("Family")), XmlElement)
xElFamily.AppendChild(xDoc.CreateElement("Father"))
```

Notice that *AppendChild* returns a reference to the node that was appended. This comes in handy when adding nodes in succession, as when the *Family* element is appended and then used in the next line for adding the *Father* element.

The final step is to save the cached XML in the DOM to a physical file. To do this, the *XmlDocument* class exposes an overloaded *Save* method. The overload used here takes the full physical path where the file will either be created or overwritten:

```
xDoc.Save(strModifyFile)
```

If you examine the file after saving it, you'll notice it's not very readable because of the lack of white space. By default, white space is stripped out when a document is saved. However, you can set the *XmlDocument.Preserve-WhiteSpace* property to *True* if you want the white space.

Loading XML

The *XmlDocument* class exposes two methods for loading XML. *Load* has four overloads that allow you to load XML into the DOM from a *Stream* object, an *XmlReader* object, or a *TextReader* object, or by providing a path to a physical file. In the sample application, the *LoadXmlFile* routine demonstrates the latter approach.

Alternatively, you can use *LoadXml* to load from a string. In the sample, *LoadXMLFromString* creates some XML content using a *StreamWriter* object and then loads it into the DOM using this line:

```
xDoc.LoadXml(sw.ToString())
```

Iterating Nodes Using Recursion

Sometimes there is a need to iterate through all nodes in a document. A good way to do this is with a method that uses recursion. In the sample's *Iterate-ThroughAllNodes* method, you see an example of this. After loading a document into the DOM, it invokes a private helper routine named *TraverseTreeAndWriteInfo*, which takes three arguments: a *StreamWriter* object, an *XmlNode* object, and an integer for tracking the node level so that proper indentation can be used to format the output:

```
Dim xNodeInLoop As XmlNode
Dim s As New String(CChar(vbTab), intLevel)
Dim strValues() As String = {s, xNode.Name, xNode.NodeType.ToString()}

sw.WriteLine("{0}{1} ({2})", strValues)

If xNode.HasChildNodes Then
    For Each xNodeInLoop In xNode.ChildNodes
        Me.TraverseTreeAndWriteInfo(sw, xNodeInLoop, intLevel + 1)
    Next xNodeInLoop
End If
```

The method determines whether the current node has any children. If it does, it calls itself recursively until all nodes in the document have been traversed. At each level, the node's name, type, and level are added to the array, which is then written to the *StreamWriter* object.

Finding and Manipulating Nodes

There are several ways you can find one or more nodes. The sample application uses XPath in conjunction with the *SelectSingleNode* and *SelectNodes* functions. These are exposed by *XmlNode* and return an *XmlNode* and *XmlNodeList*, respectively. In the sample's *ModifyElementValue* method, you'll find code that shows how to use an XPath expression to find an element:

```
xNode = xDoc.SelectSingleNode("//Person [.=""Gerald L. Smith""]")
If Not (xNode Is Nothing) Then
    xEl = CType(xNode, XmlElement)
    xEl.InnerText = "Jerry Smith"
End If
```

The value of this element is then changed by setting the *InnerText* property to a different string.

In the *ModifyAttributeValue* method, *SelectNodes* is used to retrieve an *XmlNodeList* object containing a collection of Person elements. This list is then iterated through, and the attribute values are changed for each element using *SetAttribute*:

```
xNodeList = xDoc.SelectNodes("//Person")
If xNodeList.Count > 0 Then
    For Each xNode In xDoc.SelectNodes("//Person")
        xEl = CType(xNode, XmlElement)
        Select Case xEl.GetAttribute("type")
            Case "father"
                xEl.SetAttribute("type", "parent")
                xEl.SetAttribute("gender", "male")
            Case "mother"
                xEl.SetAttribute("type", "parent")
                xEl.SetAttribute("gender", "female")
            Case "son"
                xEl.SetAttribute("type", "child")
                xEl.SetAttribute("gender", "male")
            Case "daughter"
                xEl.SetAttribute("type", "child")
                xEl.SetAttribute("gender", "female")
        End Select
    Next
End If
```

Another XPath example is in *DeleteNodesAndAddNodesWithAttributes*. After finding a specific element that has a *type* attribute equal to *parent*, the *age* attribute is deleted and the value of the *type* attribute is changed to *father*:

```
xNode = xDoc.SelectSingleNode("//Person[@type='parent']")
If Not (xNode Is Nothing) Then
    xEl = CType(xNode, XmlElement)
    xEl.Attributes.RemoveNamedItem("age")
    xEl.SetAttribute("type", "father")
End If
```

Last but not least, another good way to find a node is by its tag name, using the *GetElementsByTagName* method exposed by both *XmlDocument* and *XmlElement*. The following code in the sample's *DisplayElementsByTag* routine illustrates the use of this method. After getting a node list, the code iterates through all of its nodes and child nodes, passing information to the *Stream-Writer* object. Notice that to view the actual contents of the element—that is, what is between the element's tags—the contents were treated as a child of type *Text*:

```
xNodeList = xDoc.GetElementsByTagName(strTagSearchExp)
With sw
    .WriteLine("All text elements matching '{0}':", strTagSearchExp)
    .WriteLine(strLine)
    For Each xNode In xNodeList
        For Each xNodeChild In xNode.ChildNodes
            If xNodeChild.NodeType = XmlNodeType.Text Then
                .WriteLine(xNode.Name & ": " & xNodeChild.Value)
            End If
        Next
    Next
End With
```

For some of you, this might be easier than using XPath. However, it's more limiting because it returns only elements.

Conclusion

In the .NET Framework, Microsoft continues its extensive XML support with the DOM-style *XmlDocument* and *XmlNode* classes. Using these and derived classes, you can easily work with XML loaded into the DOM. After a brief overview of the DOM, you were taken on a quick survey of numerous examples in the sample application that demonstrate how to use the many members associated with these classes.

4

Building Windows Forms User Interfaces

Windows Forms is the name of the new forms package used in Microsoft Visual Basic .NET. As in Visual Basic 6.0, the basic unit of functionality is still the Form. As in Visual Basic 6.0, Windows Forms have properties, fields, events, and methods. However, unlike previous versions of Visual Basic, Visual Basic .NET forms are full-fledged classes that support visual inheritance.

Creating a Windows Forms application in Visual Basic .NET is as easy as it was in previous versions of Visual Basic: simply drag and drop controls onto your form, change their settings in the Properties window, add code behind the events, press F5, and go. Many of the controls you're familiar with in Visual Basic 6.0 are also present in Windows Forms: *Labels*, *TextBoxes*, *Menus*, *Toolbars*, *TreeViews*, *StatusBars*, and so on. Although they're similar, sometimes they work a little different, as in the case of the *ListBox* and *ComboBox* controls. In other cases, the controls are still there but are organized differently. For example, in Visual Basic 6.0, you had a single *CommonDialog* control, which encapsulated many different dialog windows. In Visual Basic .NET, these common dialog boxes have been better organized into separate controls, such as the *OpenFile-Dialog*, *SaveFileDialog*, *ColorDialog*, and *FontDialog*. In addition, many new controls have been added to the Visual Basic programmer's toolbox, including the *Splitter*, *NotifyIcon*, *ErrorProvider*, and *PrintPreviewDialog* controls.

All these topics, including visual inheritance, will be covered in this chapter.

Application #29: Use the *ListBox* and *ComboBox*

This sample shows you how to use the *ListBox* and *ComboBox* controls. It covers the basic functionality inherent in each control, as well as some improvements and new features available with these controls in Microsoft Visual Basic .NET.

As Figure 4-1 illustrates, the sample application consists of a single form with five tab pages. Each tab page covers a different topic related to the *ListBox* or *ComboBox* control. The Add Items tab demonstrates how to add items to a *ListBox* control from a list of objects. The Bind To DataTable tab populates a data table with a list of all files on the C: drive of your PC. That data table is then bound to a *ListBox* control. The Selection Mode tab allows you to test different styles of multiselect list boxes. The Bind To Array tab will bind a *ListBox* control to an array of objects representing all processes currently running on the machine. The final tab demonstrates a number of features of the *ComboBox* control, including how to bind to an ADO.NET *DataTable* object using the Northwind database.

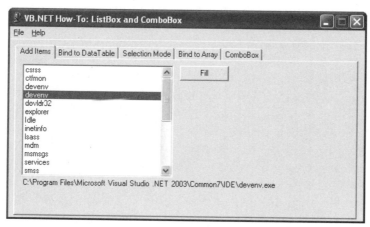

Figure 4-1   Sample application with the Add Items tab selected.

Building Upon...

Application #12: Using a *DataSet* and *DataView*
Application #15: Bind Data to a *ComboBox*
Application #16: Data Binding with Navigation
Application #20: Build a Data-Entry Form

New Concepts

If you've done any Visual Basic coding previous to .NET, you're most likely familiar with using *ListBox* and *ComboBox* controls, but there are a few new things to cover.

The *Items* Collection

Perhaps the most important new concept with the *ListBox* and *ComboBox* controls in .NET is that of the *Items* collection. In previous versions of Visual Basic, you could add only strings as an item. In Visual Basic .NET, however, items can be any type of object, not just strings. For example, if your application contains a set of customer objects, you can actually add these customer objects directly to a *ListBox* or *ComboBox* control. This lets you access each property and method of your customer objects directly from the *ListBox* or *ComboBox* control.

What's more, items are now a full-fledged collection, which gives you all the advantages inherent in using a collection. For example, to add a new item to the *Items* collection, simply call the *Items.Add* method. To remove a particular item from the *Items* collection, call the *Items.Remove* method. You can even determine whether an item exists by using the *Contains* method. Like any other collection, you can use a *For/Each* loop to iterate on the members and the *Count* property to determine the total number of items in the control.

Using *ListBox* and *ComboBox* Controls

The *ListBox* control allows you to display a list of items to the user. It is best suited for situations in which users need to see a large number of items at once or be able to select more than one item from a list. The *SelectionMode* property is used to enable the user to select multiple items.

The *ComboBox* control is essentially a *ListBox* control with the added benefit of a text box. To make a selection, the user can either choose an existing item from the list or enter text into the text box. This control is especially useful when screen real estate is limited, because you can set the list to drop down only when the user clicks the arrow button. The *DropDownStyle* property contains options to determine whether or not the list is displayed automatically and whether the text box is editable. If the list is always displayed and the text field is not editable, use a *ListBox* control instead.

Populating *ListBox* and *ComboBox* Controls

In Windows Forms applications, there are two basic ways of populating *ListBox* and *ComboBox* controls with data. The first way is to manually populate the *Items* collection using the *Add* method. The second way is to use data binding via the *DataSource*, *DisplayMember*, and *ValueMember* properties. Data sources include any objects instantiated from classes that implement the *IList* interface, such as the *Array* class, *Collection* class, and *DataView* class.

New Search Capabilities

Two new features that have been added to the *ListBox* and *ComboBox* controls in Visual Basic .NET are the *FindString* and *FindStringExact* methods. If you want to perform a search for a particular item, rather than manually looping through all the items, you can simply use the *FindString* and *FindStringExact* methods. The *FindString* method finds the first item that starts with a particular string, whereas *FindStringExact* searches for an exact match.

Code Walkthrough

This application contains five tabs for demonstrating the methods and properties of the *ListBox* and *ComboBox* controls. Each tab contains a Fill button, which populates the corresponding control with data. The five main topics covered include:

- Adding items to a *ListBox* control by using the *Items* collection

- Binding a *ListBox* control to a data table by using the *DataSource* property

- Using the *SelectionMode* property to change the style of a multiselect *ListBox* control

- Binding a *ListBox* control to an array of objects

- Binding a *ComboBox* control to a data source, and changing its properties to manipulate the control's behavior

Adding Items

In the *AddItems* subroutine, the *ListBox* control is cleared and populated from an array of *Process* objects by using the *Add* method. The *DisplayMember* property of the *ListBox* control is used to indicate which member of the *Process* object should be displayed in the control. Last, the items in the control are sorted by setting the *Sorted* property to *True*.

```
lstProcessesAddItem.Items.Clear()
lstProcessesAddItem.DisplayMember = "ProcessName"
For Each prc In Process.GetProcesses()
    lstProcessesAddItem.Items.Add(prc)
Next
lstProcessesAddItem.Sorted = True
```

Bind to *DataTable*

Earlier, it was mentioned that a second way of populating a *ListBox* control with data was to use data binding via the *DataSource*, *DisplayMember*, and *Value-Member* properties. Here, the *DataTable* object is populated with file names and bound to the *ListBox* control. (This data could have also come from a database table.) Again, the *DisplayMember* property indicates which field in the *DataTable* object will be displayed in the *ListBox* control. The *ValueMember* property dictates which item from the data table is used for the underlying value of each item. Finally, the *DataSource* property is set to the name of the data table.

```
Dim dt As DataTable = FillTable("C:\")
If Not (dt Is Nothing) Then
    With lstFiles
        .DisplayMember = "FileName"
        .ValueMember = "Length"
        .DataSource = dt
    End With
End If
```

In the *SelectedIndexChanged* event, the value associated with the selected item from the *SelectedValue* property is retrieved and displayed on the form. Remember, this value came from the *ValueMember* property indicated during the data binding process.

```
lblFileInfo.Text = "Length: " & lstFiles.SelectedValue.ToString
```

Selection Mode

In this Selection Mode tab, the *ListBox* control is populated from a file list, similar to the method used in the Bind To DataTable tab. The *SelectionMode* property is used to control how many items the user can select and how those items can be selected:

```
lstMultiSelect.SelectionMode = _
    CType(System.Enum.Parse(GetType(SelectionMode), _
    cboSelectionMode.Text), SelectionMode)
```

There are three ways with which a user can select items from a *ListBox* control. *SelectionMode.One* indicates that only a single item can be selected. *SelectionMode.MultiSimple* lets the user select one or more items using the mouse or Spacebar. Finally, *SelectionMode.MultiExtended* allows the user to select multiple items using the Shift key.

A great new feature of Visual Basic .NET is the ability to speed up the rendering of a control by preventing it from redrawing itself every time an item is added to it. This is done via the *BeginUpdate* and *EndUpdate* methods:

```
With lstSelectedItems
    .Items.Clear()
    .BeginUpdate()
    Dim fi As FileInfo
    For Each fi In lstMultiSelect.SelectedItems
        Items.Add(fi.Name)
    Next
    .EndUpdate()
End With
```

When an item is chosen from the *lstMultiSelect* control, the corresponding data for the selected item is added to the Selected Items *ListBox* control. This requires that the control be cleared and that all the selected items be re-added to it. Calling the *BeginUpdate* method just before adding the items back to the control prevents it from rendering each time an item is added. Once all the selected items have been added, the *EndUpdate* method is called and the control is rendered on the form.

Bind to an Array

Binding a control to an array is the simplest method of data binding. Just set the *DataSource* property of the control to the array and optionally specify a value for *DisplayMember*:

```
Dim prc As Process
With lstProcessesDataSource
    .ValueMember = "MainModule"
    .DisplayMember = "ProcessName"
    .DataSource = Process.GetProcesses()
End With
```

Because the *ValueMember* property was set, you can retrieve the *Selected-Value* property of the control. Here, the Process Module for the selected file is displayed:

```
lblFileName2.Text = CType(lstProcessesDataSource.SelectedValue, _
    ProcessModule).FileName
```

The ComboBox Tab

The ComboBox tab covers several important features of the *ComboBox* control in Visual Basic .NET. First, an ADO.NET *DataSet* object is populated from the Northwind database and the *ComboBox* control is bound to it:

```
Dim ds As New DataSet()
SqlDataAdapter1.Fill(ds)
cboDemo.ValueMember = "ProductID"
cboDemo.DisplayMember = "ProductName"
cboDemo.DataSource = ds.Tables(0)
```

Once the *ComboBox* is filled, the *cboDropDownStyle* control is used to select the *DropDownStyle* of the *ComboBox* control. Selecting *Simple* causes the drop-down list to display only a single value, and the text portion is editable. If *DropDown* is selected, the text portion is editable and the user can click the arrow button to display the list portion. The style *DropDownList* allows the user to click the arrow button to display the list portion, but the text box is not editable:

```
cboDemo.DropDownStyle = _
    CType(System.Enum.Parse(GetType(ComboBoxStyle), _
    cboDropDownStyle.Text), ComboBoxStyle)
```

In the *nudDropDownItems_ValueChanged* and *nudDropDown-Width_ValueChanged* event procedures, the maximum number of drop-down items and the width of the *ComboBox* control are set. The *MaxDropDownItems* property refers to the maximum number of items to be shown in the drop-down portion of the *ComboBox* control. The user would need to scroll with the arrows to see any items that are not within the visible portion of the drop-down list. The *DropDownWidth* property refers to how wide the drop-down portion of the *ComboBox* control is. You can specify this value to be larger than the width of the *ComboBox* control. This comes in handy when items in the drop-down list are expected to be long, but room for the *ComboBox* control is limited:

```
Private Sub nudDropDownItems_ValueChanged(ByVal sender As Object, _
    ByVal e As System.EventArgs) Handles nudDropDownItems.ValueChanged
    cboDemo.MaxDropDownItems = CInt(nudDropDownItems.Value)
End Sub

Private Sub nudDropDownWidth_ValueChanged(ByVal sender As _
    System.Object, ByVal e As System.EventArgs) Handles _
    nudDropDownWidth.ValueChanged
    cboDemo.DropDownWidth = CInt(nudDropDownWidth.Value)
End Sub
```

Conclusion

This has been a fairly quick overview of how to use *ListBox* and *ComboBox* controls in a Windows Forms application. Although the basics of using these two controls are already familiar to most Visual Basic programmers, there are some key new features to be aware of:

- ***Items* collection**   Both controls now use full-fledged collections for their items.

- **Searching**   You can perform a search for a particular string value on the items in either control.

- **Data binding**   These controls can be populated from a number of data sources, including arrays, collections, and ADO.NET *DataTables* objects.

Application #30: Use Common Dialog Boxes

This sample shows you how to use the *OpenFileDialog*, *SaveFileDialog*, *Color Dialog*, and *FontDialog* controls within your Windows Forms applications.

These dialog boxes are standard to Microsoft Windows operating systems, and they give your applications a common look and feel with which users will instantly be familiar. The sample application consists of a single form with two tab pages, as shown in Figure 4-2.

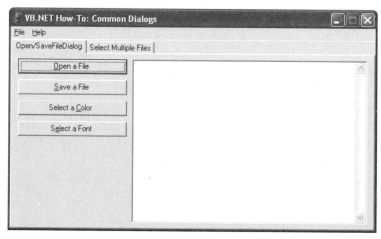

Figure 4-2   Common Dialogs sample application.

The first tab page lets the user select a text file by using the *OpenFile-Dialog* control. Once the user selects a text file, the file is opened and displayed in the *TextBox* control to the right. The user can then change how the text is displayed in the *TextBox* control. Clicking the Select A Color button brings up the *ColorDialog* control. Users can select whatever color they want, and the text box will be updated accordingly. Clicking the Select A Font button displays the *FontDialog* control. Here, the user is presented with a list of fonts currently installed on her machine. The text in the text box changes to the color that the user selects. Of course, the user is given the option of canceling out of these dialog boxes without any changes being made.

This sample application also uses the *SaveFileDialog* control to save the contents of the *TextBox* control to a new file.

The second tab page demonstrates how to use the *OpenFileDialog* control to let the user select multiple files.

New Concepts

In previous versions of Visual Basic, the open file, save file, font, and color dialog boxes were incorporated into a single ActiveX control named the Microsoft Common Dialog Control (Comdlg32.ocx). In Visual Basic .NET, each of these dialog boxes is its own control. This is part of the .NET emphasis on object-oriented design. To display a file-open dialog box, use the *OpenFileDialog* control;

to display a font dialog box, use the *FontDialog* control. This simplifies coding because each control represents a single entity.

Also, these controls are now intrinsic parts of the .NET Framework. There is no need to distribute a separate file to use these controls. Visual Basic 6.0 required an additional file, Comdlg32.ocx, to be distributed and registered on each client machine. With Visual Basic .NET, there are no additional requirements (other than that the .NET Framework be installed).

Ready-Made Functionality

There are two big advantages to using the common dialog controls in your applications. First, they are already done. There's no need for you to *roll your own* or re-create the wheel. Because you don't have to create these dialog controls from scratch, you spend less time on design, development, and testing.

Easier for Users

The second major advantage to using common dialog controls is that they are standard parts of the Windows operating system. Everything from word processors to graphics programs to MP3 players use these same common dialog controls. Users are instantly familiar with them and know how to use them. This makes your program easier to use.

DialogResult

Each of these common dialog controls uses the *DialogResult* enumeration. *DialogResult* enumerations are a set of predefined constants used to indicate how the user closes a dialog box. Table 4-1 lists the eight possible values, most of which are self-explanatory.

Table 4-1 *DialogResult* **Constants**

Constant	Value
Abort	The user aborted the dialog box, usually by clicking a button labeled Abort.
Cancel	The user canceled the dialog box, usually by clicking a button labeled Cancel.
Ignore	The user chose to ignore the dialog box, usually by clicking a button labeled Ignore.
No	The user responded in the negative, usually by clicking a button labeled No.
None	The user has not yet closed the dialog box.
OK	The user has a selection and is ready to proceed. In general, this button is labeled OK, but in the *OpenFileDialog* this button is labeled Open and in the *SaveFileDialog* it is labeled Save.

(continued)

Table 4-1 *DialogResult* **Constants** *(continued)*

Constant	Value
Retry	The user has chosen to retry the operation, usually by clicking a button labeled Retry.
Yes	The user responded in the affirmative, usually by clicking a button labeled Yes.

Code Walkthrough

The following sections describe, in some detail, the sample application's code for instantiating and using common dialog controls.

OpenFileDialog

The *btnOpenTextFile_Click* subroutine, which handles the Open A File button's *Click* event, begins by setting up the *FileOpenDialog*:

```
With odlgTextFile
    .CheckFileExists = True
```

To simplify coding, a *With/End With* block is used. The *OpenFileDialog* exposes a number of properties that allow you to customize it to suit your particular needs. *CheckFileExists* ensures that the user enters a file that actually exists. If the user were to enter a nonexistent file, the *OpenFileDialog* control would display a warning message box when the Open button is clicked. As long as this property is set to *True*, it's impossible for the user to enter a nonexistent file. This saves you the trouble of manually validating the file's existence.

```
.CheckPathExists = True
```

The *CheckPathExists* property works exactly the same for paths as *CheckFileExists* does for files. It should be noted that there is no need to set this property to *True* because, by definition, if a file exists its path must also exist.

```
.DefaultExt = "txt"
```

The *DefaultExt* property simply means that if the user fails to enter a file extension, the *OpenFileDialog* will automatically add one.

```
.DereferenceLinks = True
```

The *DereferenceLinks* property is useful for situations in which the user selects a shortcut (.lnk file) instead of a regular file. If this property is set to *True*, the file referenced by the shortcut is returned instead of the actual shortcut.

```
.Filter = "Text files (*.txt)|*.txt|All files|*.*"
```

The *Filter* property determines the items in the *Files of type* combo box. Each item consists of a pair of values separated by a vertical bar (|). The first part of each pair is a textual description of the file type. The second part of each pair is the actual file filter.

```
.Multiselect = False
```

The *Multiselect* property allows the user to select more than one file. For the Open A File button, this is set to *False*, but for the Retrieve Filenames button, this is set to *True*.

```
.RestoreDirectory = True
```

The *RestoreDirectory* property determines whether the dialog box should restore the current directory when the user closes the dialog box. By default, this is set to *True*.

```
.ShowHelp = True
```

The *ShowHelp* property indicates whether the Help button should be visible on the dialog box. If this is set to *True* and the user clicks the Help button, a *HelpRequested* event is raised where you can implement your own customized help.

```
.ShowReadOnly = False
```

The *ShowReadOnly* property indicates whether the Open As Read-Only check box should be visible on the dialog box.

```
.Title = "Select a file to open"
```

The *Title* property simply sets the caption that appears in the dialog box title bar.

```
.ValidateNames = True
```

The *ValidateNames* property ensures that the user enters only valid Win32 file names.

Once the *OpenFileDialog* object has been set up, the *ShowDialog* method is used to display the dialog box on the screen. If the user clicks the Open button, represented here by *DialogResult.OK*, the selected file's pathname is retrieved using the *Filename* property. Then the file's contents are read into a *StreamReader* object. Finally, the *StreamReader* object is used to fill the *TextBox*:

```
If .ShowDialog() = DialogResult.OK Then
    FileName = .FileName
    ts = New StreamReader(.OpenFile)
    txtFileContents.Text = ts.ReadToEnd()
End If
```

Figure 4-3 shows the dialog box that the *OpenFileDialog* object presents when the *ShowDialog* method is called.

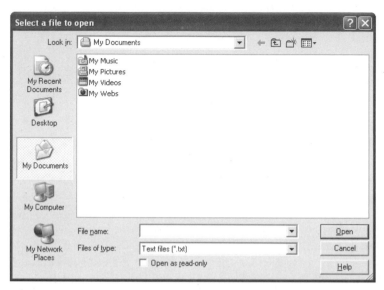

Figure 4-3 The *OpenFileDialog* object displays a dialog that allows the user to open a file.

ColorDialog

The *btnSelectColor_Click* subroutine, which handles the Select A Color button's *Click* event, begins by setting up the *ColorDialog*. First an array of integers is declared to store the user's custom colors:

```
Static CustomColors() As Integer = _
    {RGB(255, 0, 0), RGB(0, 255, 0), RGB(0, 0, 255)}
```

The array is initialized with a set of default values.

The next block of code is contained within a *With/End With* statement. Here, the *ColorDialog* object is initialized with a set of default values.

```
With cdlgText
    .Color = txtFileContents.ForeColor
```

The *Color* property represents the currently selected color. Here, the dialog box is set to match the color currently used by the *TextBox* control.

```
.CustomColors = CustomColors
```

The *CustomColors* property stores a set of custom colors as a set of ARGB (alpha, red, green, and blue) components.

```
.AllowFullOpen = True
```

The *AllowFullOpen* property expands the *ColorDialog* to reveal a section where the user can create custom colors. This can be set to *False* if you don't want to enable this functionality.

```
.AnyColor = True
```

The *AnyColor* property determines whether the dialog box displays all available colors in the set of basic colors.

```
.FullOpen = False
```

The *FullOpen* property determines whether the *ColorDialog* object's dialog box starts out expanded, revealing the custom colors section.

```
.SolidColorOnly = True
```

The *SolidColorOnly* property restricts the user to solid colors only. The default is *False*.

```
.ShowHelp = True
```

The *ShowHelp* property for the *ColorDialog* class works the same as it does for the *OpenFileDialog* class: the property determines whether the Help button is visible on the dialog box. If this is set to *True* and the user clicks the Help button, a *HelpRequested* event is raised, allowing you to implement your own custom help.

```
    If .ShowDialog() = DialogResult.OK Then
        txtFileContents.ForeColor = .Color
        CustomColors = .CustomColors
    End If
    cdlgText.Reset()
End With
```

Once the *ColorDialog* object has been set up, the *ShowDialog* method is used to display the dialog box (shown in Figure 4-4) on the screen. If the user presses OK, the foreground color of the *TextBox* control is changed to the color the user selected. The custom colors are then stored in the static array declared earlier.

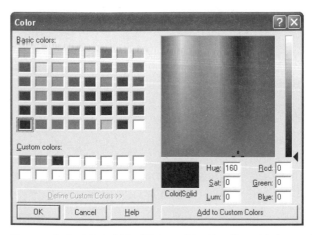

Figure 4-4   The *ColorDialog* object's *ShowDialog* method displays a Color dialog box that allows the user to specify a color.

FontDialog

The *btnSelectFont_Click* subroutine handles the Select A Font button's *Click* event. As with the previous two dialog boxes, this routine begins by setting up the various properties of the dialog box within a *With/End With* block:

```
With fdlgText
    .Font = txtFileContents.Font
```

The *Font* property simply sets the default font shown in the dialog box. Here it's initialized to the current font of the *TextBox* control.

```
.Color = txtFileContents.ForeColor
```

The *Color* property sets the default font color shown in the dialog box. Again, it's initialized to the current color of the *TextBox* control.

```
.ShowColor = True
```

The *ShowColor* property controls whether the user can select the font's color.

```
.ShowApply = True
```

The *ShowApply* property determines whether the Apply button on the *FontDialog* object is displayed. If this is set to *True* and the user clicks the Apply button, the *FontDialog* object raises an *Apply* event.

```
.ShowEffects = True
```

The *ShowEffects* property determines whether the strikethrough, underline, and text color options are available to the user.

```
.AllowScriptChange = True
```

The *FontDialog* has a combo box that lists the available language scripts for the specified font. When the user selects a different language script, the character set for that language becomes available for multilingual documents. The *AllowScriptChange* property determines whether the user can change the script in this combo box.

```
.AllowVectorFonts = False
```

The *AllowVectorFonts* property simply determines whether the *FontDialog* allows the user to select a vector font.

```
.AllowVerticalFonts = False
```

The *AllowVerticalFonts* property determines whether the dialog box displays vertical fonts. If this is set to *False*, only horizontal fonts are displayed.

```
.FixedPitchOnly = False
```

The *FixedPitchOnly* property determines whether the dialog box displays only mono-spaced fonts such as Courier New.

```
.FontMustExist = True
```

The *FontMustExist* property ensures that the user selects only an existing font. If the user tries to select a nonexistent font, an error message is displayed.

```
.MaxSize = 48
.MinSize = 8
```

The *MaxSize* and *MinSize* properties determine the upper and lower bounds for the size of the selected font. If the user selects a font size outside this range, the *FontDialog* object will display an error message.

```
    If .ShowDialog = DialogResult.OK Then
        ApplyFontAndColor()
    End If
End With
```

Finally, once all the *FontDialog* properties have been set, the *ShowDialog* method is used to display the dialog box (shown in Figure 4-5). If the user clicks the OK button, the selected font is applied to the *TextBox* control.

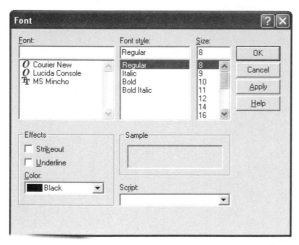

Figure 4-5   The *FontDialog* object represents a Font dialog box the user can use to select a font.

Conclusion

This sample covered how to use the *OpenFileDialog*, *SaveFileDialog*, *ColorDialog*, and *FontDialog* controls. There are two main advantages to using these common dialog controls. First, they are reusable components you can drag and drop onto your Windows Forms, saving you the time and trouble of re-creating them from scratch. Second, because they are standard functions of the Windows operating systems, users will be instantly familiar with how to use them, making your programs more user friendly.

Application #31: Validate Text Boxes

This sample demonstrates a technique for performing data validation on text boxes. Along the way, you'll see how to use regular expressions to perform data validation and how to create new user controls using inheritance. The sample application, shown in Figure 4-6, presents the user with five text boxes to enter the following data:

- ZIP Code (U.S.)

- E-Mail Address

- IP Address

- Social Security Number

- Phone Number (U.S.)

Figure 4-6   The Validating TextBoxes sample application demonstrates a technique for performing data validation on text boxes.

What makes this application unique is that each text box is self-validating. That is, all data validation is performed by the control itself. This makes creating your user interfaces much easier because you can drag and drop these controls right onto the form you're creating. Finding out whether the user entered valid data is as simple as checking the control's *IsValid* property. As an added touch, if the user enters invalid data, the text box will turn red (or whatever color you choose).

Building Upon...

Application #7: Object-Oriented Features
Application #8: Scoping, Overloading, Overriding

New Concepts

There are two new concepts that need to be explained before proceeding. The first concept is that of regular expressions. The second concept is how to take an existing control and use inheritance to create a brand new control.

Regular Expressions

Visual Basic has always been known as a great language for string handling. In fact, Visual Basic provides so many different string-handling features—all built into the language—that Visual Basic programmers sometimes take this ease of use for granted. For example, some languages, such as C, don't even have strings. Instead, C programmers use arrays of single characters to mimic strings. Regular expressions are a new feature in Visual Basic that provide powerful string-handling capabilities and require very little code.

So, what is a regular expression? A regular expression is a pattern of text used to search or perform matches against a string. In a sense, you might have already used a form of regular expressions when you used the *.* pattern when searching for a file on a computer using the Windows Search tool or the command-line *dir*. Regular expressions, however, provide a stricter, more powerful syntax.

For example, the regular expression to match a three-digit number is $\wedge\backslash d\{3\}\$$. At first that might seem a little confusing, so let's take it apart and examine it one step at a time. The $\wedge$ indicates the beginning of a string. The $\backslash d$ matches a digit character, 0 through 9. The $\{3\}$ is a subexpression that indicates the digit must occur three times. Finally, the $\$$ indicates the end of the string. So, to match a four-digit number, simply use this: $\wedge\backslash d\{4\}\$$. To match a two-digit number, use $\wedge\backslash d\{2\}\$$.

Let's take a look at another regular expression: $\wedge\backslash d\{3\}-\backslash d\{2\}-\backslash d\{4\}\$$. What does this do? Again, let's take it apart one piece at a time. The first part, $\wedge\backslash d\{3\}$, you've already seen before. This was the example used in the preceding paragraph that matched a three-digit number. The next part, -, simply means that a dash should come next in the string. The $\backslash d\{2\}$ indicates a two-digit number. The next part, -, indicates that a dash should come next. The $\backslash d\{4\}$ indicates a four-digit number. Finally, the $\$$ indicates the end of the string. So, to put $\wedge\backslash d\{3\}-\backslash d\{2\}-\backslash d\{4\}\$$ into English, this regular expression matches a string that begins with a three-digit number, followed by a dash, followed by a two-digit number, followed by a second dash, and finally a four-digit number. For example, 123-12-1234 would correctly match this pattern. In case you haven't guessed, this is a regular expression to match a Social Security number, and it's used to perform data validation on the Social Security number text box used in the sample application.

Regular expressions are quite powerful and allow you to do things that might otherwise take many lines of code. In fact, regular expressions are a language in and of themselves. An entire chapter or book could easily be written to explain all the possibilities. This has just been an introduction. As you delve deeper and deeper into regular expressions, you'll realize there are many different situations where you can use regular expressions. In addition to validating Social Security numbers, the sample application uses regular expressions to validate ZIP Codes, phone numbers, e-mail addresses, and IP addresses.

Creating a New *UserControl* Class by Using Inheritance

Inheritance has been one of the most requested features to be added to the Visual Basic language, and for good reason. Inheritance allows you to do things that otherwise would be impossible, or at least very difficult, and might require thousands of lines of code to accomplish. One area in particular where inheritance really stands out is in creating user controls. In previous versions of Visual Basic, to create a new control based on an existing control could require literally thousands of lines of code. This is because each property, method, and event of the control would have to be manually delegated from the new control to the original base control. Visual Basic .NET allows you to replace all this boilerplate code with just a couple lines of code:

```
Public Class RegExTextBox
    Inherits TextBox
```

The first line of code simply indicates the name of the user control. In Visual Basic .NET, a user control is a class. The second line indicates that this class inherits from the *TextBox* control. That's all there is to creating a new user control. Once these two lines of code are in place, you're ready to add properties, methods, or events to suit your particular needs. The sample application uses six different user controls.

Code Walkthrough

The file, RegExTextBox.vb, combines the two concepts of user controls and regular expressions to create a new user control. The *RegExTextBox* control inherits from the Windows Forms *TextBox* control and adds four new properties. The most important is the *ValidationExpression* property:

```
Public Property ValidationExpression() As String
    Get
        Return validationPattern
    End Get
    Set(ByVal Value As String)
        mValidationExpression = New Regex(Value)
        validationPattern = Value
    End Set
End Property
```

This property lets the developer specify the regular expression (as a string) that will be used to validate the text in the *TextBox* control. The *Regex* class is part of the .NET Framework, and it represents a regular expression.

The next most important property is the *IsValid* property:

```
Public ReadOnly Property IsValid() As Boolean
    Get
        If Not mValidationExpression Is Nothing Then
            Return mValidationExpression.IsMatch(Me.Text)
        Else
            Return True
        End If
    End Get
End Property
```

IsValid is quite simple. It returns *True* if the data matches the regular expression (or if no regular expression is supplied). Otherwise, it returns *False*.

The *RegExTextBox* control also has properties to set the error message and error color.

If the user enters invalid data, *RegExTextBox* changes its foreground color to red to alert the user that the data is invalid. To do this, *RegExTextBox* overrides the *TextBox* class's *Validated* event:

```
Protected Overrides Sub OnValidated(ByVal e As System.EventArgs)
    If Not Me.IsValid Then
        Me.ForeColor = mErrorColor
    Else
        Me.ForeColor = Me.DefaultForeColor
    End If

    MyBase.OnValidated(e)
End Sub
```

OnValidated works by calling the *IsValid* property. If *IsValid* returns *False*, it changes the value of the *ForeColor* property to red (or whatever color the user chooses). If *IsValid* returns *True*, the *ForeColor* property is reset to its normal color. Note that the final line of code inside this subroutine calls the base class *OnValidated* method. This is a good practice because it ensures that the base class, the original *TextBox* class, also receives the *Validated* event.

One of the great things about inheritance is that not only can you create a new user control based on an existing control, you can also create a second user control based on the first one. A class can inherit from another class, which inherits from another class, which inherits from another class, etc. In other words, you can have more than one level of inheritance. Of course, if the inheritance tree becomes too large, this can be unwieldy, so use this feature sparingly. The sample application uses *RegExTextBox* as the base control to create four more user controls: *EMailTextBox*, *IPAddressTextBox*, *PhoneTextBox*, and *SsnTextBox*.

Let's take a look at the *PhoneTextBox*:

```
Public Class PhoneTextBox
    Inherits RegExTextBox

    Public Sub New()
        MyBase.New()

        Me.ValidationExpression = "^((\(\d{3}\) ?)|(\d{3}-))?\d{3}-\d{4}$"
        Me.ErrorMessage = "The phone number must be " & _
            "in the form of (555) 555-1212 or 555-555-1212."

    End Sub
End Class
```

The Window Forms Designer code was removed from the listing. First, *PhoneTextBox* inherits from *RegExTextBox*. Inside the *New* method, default values are set for the *ValidationExpression* and the *ErrorMessage*. As you can see, this class is quite simple.

Now, let's look at *frmMain*. The *Click* event procedure for the Validate button performs all the data validation for the form. First, two variables are declared:

```
Dim genericControl As Control
Dim validationMessage As String
```

The variable *genericControl* is used to loop through the form's *Controls* collection using a *For Each* loop. The *String* variable, *validationMessage*, is used to build an error message that contains the error messages for all the controls on the form.

Because each user control has an *IsValid* property (from *RegExTextBox*), performing data validation is simple and elegant. The *For Each* loop is used to iterate on all the controls on the form. If the control is a *RegExTextBox*, the *IsValid* property is called:

```
For Each genericControl In Controls
    If TypeOf genericControl Is RegExTextBox Then
        Dim regExControl As RegExTextBox = _
            CType(genericControl, RegExTextBox)
```

```
        If Not regExControl.IsValid Then
            validationMessage &= regExControl.Name & ":" & _
                regExControl.ErrorMessage & vbCrLf
        End If
    End If
Next
```

The only line of code that needs explaining is the one with the *CType* statement. *CType* is used to cast the *genericControl* variable to a *RegExTextBox* object. This allows you to check the *IsValid* property.

Outside the loop, the text in *validationMessage* is checked to see whether it's empty. If it's not, the text in *validationMessage* is displayed on the form. If it's valid, "All controls contain valid input" is displayed:

```
If validationMessage <> "" Then
    txtInvalidControls.Text = "The following controls " _
        & "have invalid values : " _
        & vbCrLf & validationMessage
Else
    txtInvalidControls.Text = "All controls contain valid input"
End If
```

Conclusion

This sample presented one technique for validating text boxes. Regular expressions are patterns of text used to search or perform matches against strings. Inheritance allows you to create new user controls with a minimal amount of code. By combining regular expressions and user controls, you can create self-validating text boxes. Once these user controls have been created, you can drag and drop them onto any form you choose and greatly simplify the creation of your user interfaces.

Application #32: Use Format Codes to Format Data

Visual Basic .NET has many features that allow you to work with dates, times, and currencies of other cultures. This sample application shows how to display numeric, date-time, and enumeration values as strings, using a variety of standard and custom culture-specific format codes. The application, shown in Figure 4-7, consists of a main form with a three-tab control.

The first tab, *Numeric*, displays a number in currency, scientific (exponential), percent, number, fixed-point, and hexadecimal format. A combo box to the right lets the user choose a specific culture, such as "English - New Zealand" or "Portuguese - Brazil." The number is formatted to suit the particular culture the user selects. For example, in the United States, a period is used as a decimal separator, but in some nations a comma is used as a decimal separator. The second tab, *Date-Time*, works the same way as the first tab except it displays date-time values formatted to a user-selected culture. The third tab, *Enumeration*, displays the system enumeration *DayOfWeek.Friday*.

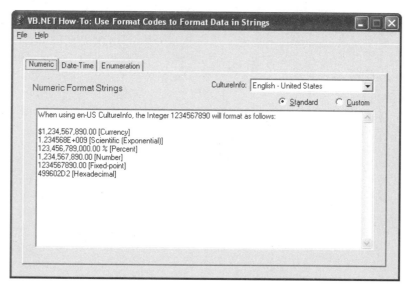

Figure 4-7   The Use Format Codes sample application.

Building Upon...

Application #7: Object-Oriented Features
Application #8: Scoping, Overloading, Overriding
Application #15: Bind Data to a *ComboBox*
Application #29: Use the *ListBox* and *ComboBox*

New Concepts

The sample application makes use of the *CultureInfo* class and the *ArrayList* class, which are discussed in the following sections.

CultureInfo

The *CultureInfo* class is part of the *System.Globalization* namespace, and it contains information about a particular culture. This includes the name of the culture, the calendar, and the writing system used. It also gives you access to culture-specific classes. These classes provide additional functions such as formatting dates and sorting strings. Culture names follow a standard convention consisting of a lowercase, two-letter abbreviation indicating the language followed by an uppercase, two-letter abbreviation indicating region. For example, *en-US* indicates the English language and the United States of America as the region, and *pt-BR* indicates the Portuguese language and Brazil as the region. Only the language is required; the region is optional. For example, *fr* simply means the French language without a specific region. Also, some culture names have prefixes that specify the script. For example, *Cy-sr-SP* indicates the Serbian language in the Serbia region using the Cyrillic script. Most culture names, however, do not have a script prefix. The .NET Framework documentation has a complete list of all culture names available.

ArrayList

One of the supporting classes used in the sample application is the *ArrayList* class. The *ArrayList* class is a specialized form of a collection that automatically grows and shrinks as you add and remove items. Part of the *System.Collections* namespace, the *ArrayList* provides advanced functionality beyond what you get with conventional Visual Basic arrays. For example, the *ArrayList* has a *Sort* method that sorts all the items in order. The *Contains* method determines whether a particular item exists. For searching capabilities, the *BinarySearch* method uses a binary search algorithm to locate a particular item in the *ArrayList* and returns its index if found. Finally, to erase the entire contents of the *ArrayList*, the *Clear* method is used.

Code Walkthrough

Inside *frmMain* is a user-defined class named *Culture*. This class simply exists to store a culture's name (ID) and description:

```
Public Class Culture
    Private _ID As String
    Private _desc As String

    Sub New(ByVal strDesc As String, ByVal strID As String)
        _ID = strID
        _desc = strDesc
    End Sub

    Public ReadOnly Property ID() As String
        Get
            Return _ID
        End Get
    End Property
```

(continued)

```
Public ReadOnly Property Description() As String
    Get
        Return _desc
    End Get
End Property
End Class
```

The *New* method is the class's constructor, and it allows you to pass the culture's name and description as the object is instantiated.

Inside the *frmMain_Load* event procedure, an *ArrayList* object is declared and populated with *Culture* objects:

```
Dim arlCultureInfo As New ArrayList()
With arlCultureInfo
    .Add(New Culture("English - United States", "en-US"))
    .Add(New Culture("English - United Kingdom", "en-GB"))
    .Add(New Culture("English - New Zealand", "en-NZ"))
    .Add(New Culture("German - Germany", "de-DE"))
    .Add(New Culture("Spanish - Spain", "es-ES"))
    .Add(New Culture("French - France", "fr-FR"))
    .Add(New Culture("Portuguese - Brazil", "pt-BR"))
    .Add(New Culture("Malay - Malaysia", "ms-MY"))
    .Add(New Culture("Afrikaans - South Africa", "af-ZA"))
End With
```

Because an *ArrayList* object is used, there is no need to redimension the array as new items are added.

After the array is populated, data binding is used to bind the *ArrayList* object to the two combo boxes that are located on the first two tabs:

```
'combo box on first tab
cboCultureInfoDateTime.DataSource = arlCultureInfo
cboCultureInfoDateTime.DisplayMember = "Description"
cboCultureInfoDateTime.ValueMember = "ID"

'combo box on second tab
cboCultureInfoNumeric.DataSource = arlCultureInfo
cboCultureInfoNumeric.DisplayMember = "Description"
cboCultureInfoNumeric.ValueMember = "ID"
```

The combo boxes let the user change the current culture for the application. As the culture changes, the display is updated to reflect the new culture. Formatting numbers and dates to a specific culture is surprisingly easy. This is because the *ToString* method is overloaded to be culturally aware. Consider the following code snippet from the *LoadNumericFormats* subroutine. *LoadNumericFormats* is called whenever the user changes the culture in one of the combo boxes:

```
With sb
    .Append(intNumber.ToString("C"))
    .Append(" [Currency]")
    .Append(crlf)
```

```
            .Append(intNumber.ToString("E"))
            .Append(" [Scientific (Exponential)]")
            .Append(crlf)
            .Append(intNumber.ToString("P"))
            .Append(" [Percent]")
            .Append(crlf)
            .Append(intNumber.ToString("N"))
            .Append(" [Number]")
            .Append(crlf)
            .Append(intNumber.ToString("F"))
            .Append(" [Fixed-point]")
            .Append(crlf)
            .Append(intNumber.ToString("X"))
            .Append(" [Hexadecimal]")
            .Append(crlf)
End With
```

sb is a *StringBuilder* object that allows for extremely fast string concatenations. *intNumber* is an integer that is set to a value of 1234567890. *crlf* is a string variable used to create line breaks within the string. When the *intNumber ToString* method is called, you can optionally set a format string. *C* indicates the currency format. *E* indicates exponential (or scientific) notation. *X* indicates hexadecimal format. The .NET Framework documentation has a complete list of all format codes that are available.

Changing the application's culture is also very easy, and it can be accomplished with just one line of code:

```
Thread.CurrentThread.CurrentCulture = New CultureInfo("en-US")
```

Conclusion

This sample application shows how to format numeric, date-time, and enumeration values to different cultures. As companies grow and expand into an increasingly global marketplace, creating applications that are globalized is becoming more important. This sample application provides only an introduction to the broader topic of globalization.

Application #33: Format a *DataGrid*

This sample shows how to display and format data in a *DataGrid* control. The data is retrieved from a SQL Server/MSDE database using ADO.NET. The data is loaded into a *DataSet* object, and the *DataGrid* control is populated by binding to this *DataSet* object. The controls on this form use anchoring so that the form resizes intelligently without the developer having to write any code. There are four button controls on the form, which is shown in Figure 4-8. Formatting the appearance of the *DataGrid* is accomplished using code in each button's *Click* event procedure. The buttons are named as follows (ranked in order of increasing control over formatting):

1. Default: Only default *DataGrid* formatting is used.

2. Grid Properties: Only *DataGrid* formatting properties are used.

3. Table Style: A *DataGridTableStyle* object is used to format the *Data-Grid* object.

4. Column Styles: *DataGridColumnStyle* objects are added to the *Data-GridTableStyle* object.

The formatting code implemented in each button's event procedure builds on the previous button.

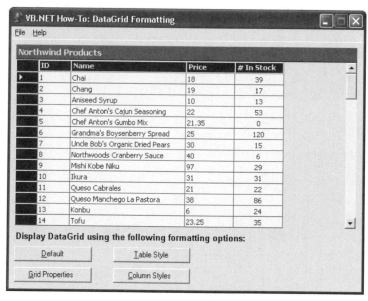

Figure 4-8   The *DataGrid* Formatting sample application as it appears after the Column Styles button has been clicked.

Building Upon...

Application #12: Use a *DataSet* and *DataView*
Application #18: Build a Master-Details Windows Form
Application #32: Use Format Codes to Format Data

New Concepts

This sample application introduces the *DataGrid* control and the *DataGridTableStyle* and *DataGridTextBoxColumn* classes. Each of these classes is discussed in more detail in the following sections.

Introducing the Windows Forms *DataGrid* Control

The *DataGrid* control is new to Visual Basic .NET. Part of the *Windows.Forms* namespace, a *DataGrid* presents data in a tabular or grid format similar to that of a worksheet in Microsoft Excel. The key to using the *DataGrid* is the *DataSource* property. The *DataSource* property specifies the source of data for the grid. A data source can be a *DataTable* object, a *DataView* object, a *DataSet* object, or a *DataViewManager* object. A data source can also be any other object that implements the *IList* or *IListSource* interfaces, such an *ArrayList* object or a *ListItemCollection* object. One thing to remember about the *DataGrid* control is that data must be bound in order to be displayed. That is, the *DataGrid* control does not support an *add item* mode or the ability to manually populate the grid row by row.

DataGridTableStyle

The *DataGridTableStyle* class represents the grid of a *DataGrid* control. Its function is to allow programmers to control the appearance of the *DataGrid* control. Using the *DataGridTableStyle* class is fairly straightforward. It exposes a set of properties you can set to control a *DataGrid* object's visual style. For example, the *BackColor* and *ForeColor* properties allow you to change the background and foreground color of the grid, respectively. The *Alternating-BackColor* property is great for making it easy for users to scan the grid at a glance by setting the background color of alternating rows. Every *DataGrid* object has a header row that shows the names of each column displayed. The *HeaderFont*, *HeaderBackColor*, and *HeaderForeColor* properties allow you to customize how the header row looks.

The *MappingName* property is key to using the *DataGridTableStyle* class in an application. The *MappingName* property indicates the name of the data source. This is needed because a *DataSet* can contain multiple resultsets. The *MappingName* identifies which resultset to use.

What's more, a *DataGrid* object can have multiple *DataGridTableStyle* objects, which are stored in the *DataGrid* object's *TableStyles* collection.

DataGridTextBoxColumn

The *DataGridTextBoxColumn* class hosts a *DataGridTextBox* control in a cell of a *DataGrid* object for editing strings. The *DataGridTextBoxColumn* and *DataGridTextBox* classes work together to allow users to directly edit values in the cells of a *DataGrid* object's column. The *DataGridTextBoxColumn* class allows you to customize how a *DataGridTextBox* object functions. For example, the *Format* property specifies how values should be displayed in the column using the format codes mentioned earlier in the chapter. (See the section "Application #32: Use Format Codes to Format Data.") The application's current *CultureInfo* setting is used to determine how to display the data correctly. You can also specify values for the *HeaderText* and *Width* properties of *DataGridTextBoxColumn*.

Code Walkthrough

Each of the buttons in the main form of the sample application demonstrates a way of formatting data in the *DataGrid* control.

The Default Button

The Default button populates the *DataGrid* control using the *DataGrid* control's default formatting properties. It simply connects to the database and does not change any settings of the *DataGrid* control:

```
Private Sub btnDefaultFormatting_Click(_
    ByVal sender As System.Object, _
    ByVal e As System.EventArgs) _
    Handles btnDefaultFormatting.Click
    ResetDemo()
    BindDataGrid()
End Sub
```

ResetDemo is a subroutine that restores the default settings of the *DataGrid* object. *BindDataGrid* is a subroutine that connects to the database server, fetches the data, and binds the data to the *DataGrid* control. Note that either Microsoft SQL Server or Microsoft Data Engine (MSDE) must be installed, and that the Northwind database must be present for the sample application to work. The *ResetDemo* and *BindDataGrid* subroutines are called for each button to ensure that everything is reset properly.

The Grid Properties Button

The Grid Properties button formats the *DataGrid* using only the *DataGrid* base property settings:

```
With grdProducts
    .AlternatingBackColor = Color.GhostWhite
    .BackColor = Color.GhostWhite
    .BackgroundColor = Color.Lavender
    .BorderStyle = BorderStyle.None
    .CaptionBackColor = Color.RoyalBlue
    .CaptionFont = New Font("Tahoma", 10.0!, FontStyle.Bold)
    .CaptionForeColor = Color.Bisque
```

```
        .CaptionText = "Northwind Products"
        .Font = New Font("Tahoma", 8.0!)
        .ForeColor = Color.MidnightBlue
        .GridLineColor = Color.RoyalBlue
        .HeaderBackColor = Color.MidnightBlue
        .HeaderFont = New Font("Tahoma", 8.0!, FontStyle.Bold)
        .HeaderForeColor = Color.Lavender
        .ParentRowsBackColor = Color.Lavender
        .ParentRowsForeColor = Color.MidnightBlue
        .SelectionBackColor = Color.Teal
        .SelectionForeColor = Color.PaleGreen
End With
```

Most of these properties should be self-explanatory. One thing you see repeatedly is the *Color* enumeration. *Color* is a part of the *System.Drawing* namespace, and it represents an ARGB color. ARGB stands for Alpha, Red, Green, and Blue. This is a 32-bit number that specifies a particular color. Fortunately, it's not necessary to know or memorize every color's ARGB number. *Color* is an enumeration that lets you specify a color's name rather than the actual number—for example, *Color.RoyalBlue* or *Color.PaleGreen*.

The Table Style Button

As with the previous two buttons, the Table Style button begins by calling the *ResetDemo* and *BindDataGrid* subroutines to ensure the *DataGrid* is properly re-initialized to default values. Then it sets some *DataGrid* properties directly, but only those that are not covered by *DataGridTableStyle* properties. Of particular interest here is the code that uses *DataGridTableStyle*. It begins by creating a new instance of the *DataGridTableStyle* class:

```
Dim grdTableStyle1 As New DataGridTableStyle()
```

After *grdTableStyle1* has been instantiated, its properties are set within a *With/End With* block:

```
With grdTableStyle1
        .AlternatingBackColor = Color.GhostWhite
        .BackColor = Color.GhostWhite
        .ForeColor = Color.MidnightBlue
        .GridLineColor = Color.RoyalBlue
        .HeaderBackColor = Color.MidnightBlue
        .HeaderFont = New Font("Tahoma", 8.0!, FontStyle.Bold)
        .HeaderForeColor = Color.Lavender
        .SelectionBackColor = Color.Teal
        .SelectionForeColor = Color.PaleGreen
        .MappingName = PRODUCT_TABLE_NAME
        .PreferredColumnWidth = 125
        .PreferredRowHeight = 15
    End With
```

Again, these properties should be self-explanatory. Once *grdTableStyle1* has been set up with the desired settings, it's added to the *DataGrid TableStyles* collection by using the *Add* method:

```
grdProducts.TableStyles.Add(grdTableStyle1)
```

The Column Style Button

After calling the *ResetDemo* and *BindDataGrid* subroutines, the Column Style button sets certain *DataGrid* properties directly, but only those that are not covered by *DataGridTableStyle* properties. Then a *DataGridTableStyle* object is created and populated. This part of the code is similar to the code for the Table Style button.

Next, four *DataGridTextBoxColumn* objects are created—one for each column of the *DataGrid* object. Because the code for each column is repetitive, let's just examine the code to create the first column:

```
Dim grdColStyle1 As New DataGridTextBoxColumn()
With grdColStyle1
    .HeaderText = "ID"
    .MappingName = "ProductID"
    .Width = 50
End With
```

The *DataGridTextBoxColumn* object allows you to format each column that you want to appear in the *DataGrid* control. In most cases, the *DataGrid-TextBoxColumn* class is appropriate. Notice that the column style properties available to you are more limited than those for the table style. For example, you cannot change the color of an individual column but you're allowed to change the width on a per-column basis. The *HeaderText* property specifies the name of the column, and the *MappingName* property maps the data of the column to a specific field in the *DataSource* object.

Finally, the four *DataGridTextBoxColumn* objects are added to the *Grid-ColumnStyles* collection of the *DataGrid* control by using the *AddRange* method:

```
grdTableStyle1.GridColumnStyles.AddRange _
    (New DataGridColumnStyle() _
    {grdColStyle1, grdColStyle2, grdColStyle3, grdColStyle4})
```

Conclusion

The Windows Forms *DataGrid* is a data-bindable control that displays data in a grid format. Many different objects can be used as data sources, including *DataTables*, *DataViews*, *DataSets*, *DataViewManagers*, or any other objects that implement the *IList* or *IListSource* interfaces. The *DataGridTableStyle* class represents the visual style of the grid itself. The *DataGridTextBoxColumn* class allows you to control the appearance and behavior of a column. The *DataGrid* control can be quite powerful, and by combining the *DataGrid* control's base properties with the *DataGridTableStyle* and *DataGridTextBoxColumn* classes, it's highly customizable as well.

Application #34: *DataGrid* Sorting and Filtering

This sample demonstrates how to sort and filter data being displayed in a Windows Forms *DataGrid* control. First ADO.NET is used to retrieve product information from a SQL Server (or MSDE) database. The data is loaded into a *DataSet* object, and the grid is populated by binding it to the *DataSet* object. ADO.NET is also used to filter the data. When the user clicks the Filter button, a *DataView* object is used to show only specified rows in the *DataGrid* control. The user can sort the data by clicking any column heading in the *DataGrid* control. Figure 4-9 shows the *DataGrid* Sorting and Filtering application running, after the user has clicked the Filter button.

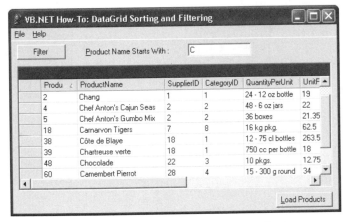

Figure 4-9   *DataGrid* Sorting and Filtering application.

Building Upon...

Application #7: Object-Oriented Features
Application #12: Use a *DataSet* and *DataView*
Application #33: Format a Data Grid

New Concepts

The next two sections explain how the sample code sorts and filters the data in the *DataGrid* control.

Sorting the *DataGrid*

Once a *DataGrid* control has been populated, sorting the data is extremely easy and requires absolutely no code. To sort a *DataGrid* control by a particular field, the user simply clicks the column header for that field. The data for the entire grid will be sorted in ascending order by that column. Clicking the same column header a second time will sort the grid in descending order. The user can toggle between ascending and descending order by clicking the same column header. This functionality is built into the *DataGrid* control itself; no actual code is required. If you would like to disable this feature, set the *DataGrid* object's *AllowSorting* property to *False*. By default, *AllowSorting* is set to *True*. A *DataGrid* control can also be sorted programmatically using the *Sort* property of the *DataView* object of the *Table* object to which the *DataGrid* control is bound. The *DataView* object is introduced in the next section.

Filtering the *DataGrid*

Unlike sorting, filtering a *DataGrid* control requires some code, but overall the process is fairly easy. To filter a *DataGrid* control, the sample application uses the *DataView* object. A *DataView* object is a data-bindable, customized view of a *DataTable* object that can be used not only for filtering, but also for sorting, searching, editing, and navigation. The key property used to filter data on a *DataView* object is *RowFilter*. The *RowFilter* property specifies the conditions for which data should be filtered. In a sense, the *RowFilter* property works in a manner similar to the WHERE clause in Structured Query Language (SQL). For example,

```
myDataView.RowFilter = "Age = 31"
```

would filter out all rows where *Age* isn't *31*.

You can also use compound conditions. For example,

```
myDataView.RowFilter = "Age = 31 AND Gender = 'Male'"
```

would filter out all rows where *Age* isn't *31* and *Gender* isn't *Male*. As part of ADO.NET, *DataView* objects can be used for both Windows Forms and Web Forms development. To simplify coding, each *Table* object of a *DataSet* object includes a *DataView* object built in by default. This object is named *Default-View*. Therefore, to filter a *DataGrid*, simply use the *DefaultView* property of the *DataSet* table that is bound to the *DataGrid* control. The code walkthrough will show an example of how this done.

Code Walkthrough

The declarations section of *frmMain* contains several module-level variables and constants that will be used throughout the form. Among the module-level variables is *ProductData*, a *DataSet* that holds order information returned from the database. PRODUCT_TABLE_NAME is a constant that holds the name of the table of information in the *ProductData DataSet*:

```
Protected ProductData As New DataSet()
Protected Const PRODUCT_TABLE_NAME As String = "Products"
```

Load Button

When the user clicks the Load button, a connection is established to SQL Server (or MSDE):

```
Dim northwindConnection As New SqlConnection(connectionString)
```

Next, a *SqlDataAdapter* object is used to move data from the database to the *DataSet* object:

```
Dim ProductAdapter As New SqlDataAdapter( _
    "select * from products", _
    northwindConnection)
```

The *DataSet* object is cleared and populated with the information from the products table of the Northwind database. Because a *DataSet* object can hold multiple result sets, you should name the result set when you populate the *DataSet* object. In this case, the result set is named using the PRODUCT_TABLE_NAMES constant:

```
ProductData.Clear()
ProductAdapter.Fill(ProductData, PRODUCT_TABLE_NAME)
```

Remember that *ProductData* is declared as a module-level variable in the *frmMain* declarations section.

Next, the *DataGrid* is bound to the products table in the *DataSet* by using the grid's *DataSource* property:

```
grdProducts.DataSource = ProductData.Tables(PRODUCT_TABLE_NAME)
```

Filter Button

Looking at the code from the top down, a *With/End With* block is used on the *ProductData.Tables(PRODUCT_TABLE_NAME)* object. Again, *ProductData* is the *DataSet* that holds the information retrieved from the database. The *RowFilter* property of the *DefaultView* object is used to filter the data so that only the product names starting with a specified string are shown. If no rows match the filter, a message box is displayed informing the user there are no matching rows. Finally, the *DataGrid* object is bound to the *DataView* object.

```
With ProductData.Tables(PRODUCT_TABLE_NAME)
    .DefaultView.RowFilter = "ProductName like '" & txtFilter.Text & "%'"

    If .DefaultView.Count = 0 Then
        MessageBox.Show("No matching rows.", _
            MESSAGEBOX_CAPTION, _
            MessageBoxButtons.OK, _
            MessageBoxIcon.Information)
    End If

    grdProducts.DataSource = .DefaultView
End With
```

Conclusion

This sample application demonstrates how to sort and filter data in a Windows Forms *DataGrid* control. The ability to sort data is provided automatically to the users when they click the column header of the column they want to sort by. A *DataGrid* control can also be sorted programmatically using the *Sort* property of the *DefaultView* property. *DefaultView* is a *DataView* object that is built in to every *DataSet* object. To filter a *DataGrid* control, use the *Filter* property of the *DefaultView* property of the *DataSet* object.

Application #35: Create an Explorer-Style Application

This sample application demonstrates how to create an application that uses the Windows Explorer–style interface. Windows Explorer–style applications came into popularity when Windows 95 introduced Windows Explorer, the 32-bit replacement for File Manager. Sporting a tree view to the left and a list view to the right, Windows Explorer introduced a new standard for user interfaces. The tree view was used to display the computer's drives. When you clicked a drive, it would expand to reveal its subdirectories. When you clicked a subdirectory, it too would expand to reveal its subdirectories. On the right was a list view control that displayed each directory's contents. As the directory selected on the left changed, the list view to the right changed accordingly. Best of all, the whole form was resizable. You could even resize the tree view and list view controls with a drag of the mouse. It was a model of simplicity and ease of use.

The sample application demonstrates how to create this type of interface, and what better example to use than a program that mimics the original Windows Explorer itself? The sample application does exactly that. It's a simplified version of the original Windows Explorer that lets you view the drives, directories, and files on your computer. It won't be as full featured, but it will definitely provide a great introduction to creating Windows Explorer–style interfaces.

Figure 4-10 shows what the sample application looks like.

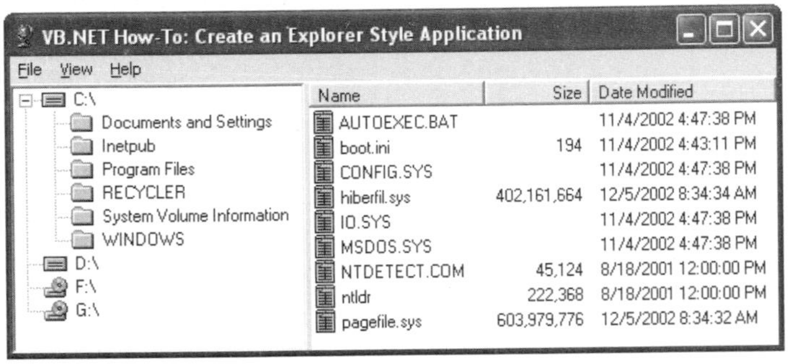

Figure 4-10   The Create A Windows Explorer–Style Application interface.

Building Upon...

Application #1: Use Arrays
Application #3: String Manipulation
Application #11: Key Visual Basic .NET Benefits
Application #32: Use Format Codes to Format Data
Application #37: Use Menus

New Concepts

This sample application describes the use of three new controls: the *TreeView* control, *ListView* control, and *Splitter* control.

The *TreeView* Control

The *TreeView* control displays items as a hierarchical collection of *TreeNode* objects. Each *TreeNode* object itself contains another collection of *TreeNode* objects. Each node has a *Text* property and can be associated with two bitmap images. The first bitmap image is for when the node is selected, and the second is for when the node is not selected. These images are kept in an *ImageList* control. The sample application demonstrates how to populate a *TreeView* control and associate images with each node.

The *ListView* Control

The *ListView* control is used for displaying lists of data. One advantage of using the *ListView* control is the flexibility in how the list is displayed. That is, there are four styles for displaying a list: *SmallIcon*, *LargeIcon*, *List*, and *Details*. In the sample application, the View menu is used to change how the *ListView* is displayed. Each list view item can have two bitmap images associated with it, a large icon and a small icon. What's more, each item can have subitems, which appear as columns in the *ListView* control, but these are displayed only when the *View* property is set to *Details*. In the sample application, the *ListView* control is used to display the files contained in the currently selected directory of the *TreeView* control.

The *Splitter* Control

The *Splitter* control is new to Visual Basic .NET. It allows the user to resize docked controls at run time. In the sample application, the *Splitter* control resides between the *TreeView* and *ListView* controls. When the user drags the *Splitter* control across the form, the *TreeView* and *ListView* controls resize accordingly. That is, as the *TreeView* expands, the *ListView* shrinks, and vice versa. This makes it easy for the user to resize the controls at run time to suit his particular needs.

To create a Windows Explorer–style interface, the following steps are used:

1. Add a *TreeView* to the form, and set its *Docking* property to *Left*.

2. Add a *Splitter* control to the form (to the right of the *TreeView* control).

3. Add a *ListView* control to the form, and set its *Docking* property to *Fill*.

Code Walkthrough

When the sample application starts, the first thing that needs to be done is populate the *TreeView* control with a list of drives on the user's machine. This work is performed by the *FillTreeView* subroutine. The first two lines of code inside this routine get this list of drives and store them in an array of *String*s:

```
Dim strDrives() As String
strDrives = System.Environment.GetLogicalDrives()
```

Once you have the list of drives, you can begin to populate the *TreeView* control. Remember that a *TreeView* control contains a collection of *TreeNode* objects. This collection is named *Nodes*, and each drive is added as a node to this *Nodes* collection:

```
TreeView1.BeginUpdate()
Dim x As Integer
For x = 0 To strDrives.Length - 1
    Dim objTreeNode As New TreeNode()
    objTreeNode.Text = strDrives(x)
    Select Case GetDriveType(strDrives(x))
        Case DRIVE_REMOVABLE
            objTreeNode.ImageIndex = 0
            objTreeNode.SelectedImageIndex = 0
        Case DRIVE_FIXED
            objTreeNode.ImageIndex = 1
            objTreeNode.SelectedImageIndex = 1
        Case DRIVE_CDROM
            objTreeNode.ImageIndex = 2
            objTreeNode.SelectedImageIndex = 2
        Case Else
            objTreeNode.ImageIndex = 0
            objTreeNode.SelectedImageIndex = 0
    End Select
    TreeView1.Nodes.Add(objTreeNode)
Next x
TreeView1.EndUpdate()
```

The preceding code requires a little more explanation. *GetDriveType* is a Win32 API function that returns an integer indicating the type of drive. This information is useful because the bitmap image used depends on whether the drive is a floppy disk, hard disk, or CD-ROM drive. A *Select Case/End Select* block uses the value returned from *GetDriveType* to determine which bitmap image to use. The *BeginUpdate* method is used to improve performance by preventing the control from repainting itself each time a new node is added. Calling the *EndUpdate* method enables redrawing of the control. Finally, note that when the form is first loaded, only the drives are loaded into the *TreeView*, not any directories. Loading individual directories is deferred to the point where the user clicks on the drive node. This delay is done intentionally because reading every single directory on every drive can be a very time-consuming process. By loading only directories that are needed, the application's perceived performance increases.

Therefore, when the user clicks on a node, its subdirectories must be loaded. This work is performed in the *TreeView* control *AfterSelect* event. The first thing to do inside this event is determine the full path of the currently selected directory. This is a little trickier than you might expect because the tree nodes are a hierarchy, and you have to account for how deep you are into the tree. This is where the *GetPathFromNode* function comes into play. It uses a *Do/Loop Until* loop to recursively determine the full path of the selected node:

```
Private Function GetPathFromNode(ByVal MyTreeNode _
    As TreeNode) As String
```

(continued)

```
    Dim objParent As TreeNode = MyTreeNode
    Dim strTemp As New System.Text.StringBuilder()
    Dim blnTopNode As Boolean

    Do
        strTemp.Insert(0, AppendDirSlash(objParent.Text))
        If TypeOf objParent.Parent Is TreeNode Then
            objParent = CType(objParent.Parent, TreeNode)
        Else
            blnTopNode = True
        End If
    Loop Until blnTopNode

    Return strTemp.ToString
End Function
```

Once you know the full path of the selected directory, getting its subdirectories is fairly straightforward and mirrors the technique used in the *FillTreeView* routine explained earlier:

```
TreeView1.SelectedNode.Nodes.Clear()
TreeView1.BeginUpdate()
Dim strFolders() As String
strFolders = Directory.GetDirectories(strFullPath)
Dim x As Integer
For x = 0 To strFolders.Length - 1
    Dim objTreeNode As New TreeNode()
    objTreeNode.Text = Path.GetFileName(strFolders(x))
    objTreeNode.ImageIndex = 4
    objTreeNode.SelectedImageIndex = 5

    TreeView1.SelectedNode.Nodes.Add(objTreeNode)
Next x
e.Node.Expand()
TreeView1.EndUpdate()
```

However, there are a few differences. First, the *TreeView* control *SelectedNode.Nodes.Clear* method is called to clear the contents of the selected node's *Nodes* collection. This is done in case the user has previously selected this directory. To get a list of the full pathnames of the node's subdirectories, the *Directory.GetDirectories* method is used. *Path.GetFileName* is used to strip off the path of these subdirectories so that only the name of the subdirectory is displayed in the *TreeView* control. As before, the *BeginUpdate* and *EndUpdate* methods are used for the sake of performance.

After the *TreeView* has been populated with the selected node's subdirectories, the final step is to populate the *ListView* control with all the files in the selected directory:

```
ListView1.BeginUpdate()
ListView1.Items.Clear()
```

```
Dim strFiles() As String
strFiles = Directory.GetFiles(strFullPath)
For x = 0 To strFiles.Length - 1
    Dim objListViewItem As New ListViewItem()
    With objListViewItem
        .Text = Path.GetFileName(strFiles(x))
        .ImageIndex = 6
        .StateImageIndex = 6
        .SubItems.Add(Format(FileLen((strFiles(x))), _
            "###,###,###,###"))
        .SubItems.Add(CStr(File.GetLastWriteTime(strFiles(x))))
    End With
    ListView1.Items.Add(objListViewItem)
Next x
ListView1.EndUpdate()
```

In many ways, the *ListView* control is programmatically similar to the *Tree-View* control. Instead of having a *Nodes* collection, it has an *Items* collection. Instead of having *TreeNode* objects, the collection contains *ListViewItem* objects. To add a new item to the collection, call the *Add* method. To re-initialize this collection, call the *Clear* method. When adding items, you can use the *BeginUpdate* and *EndUpdate* methods to improve performance. One key difference, however, is that *ListViewItems* have a *SubItems* collection. The objects in the *SubItems* collection correspond to the columns shown when the *ListView* control *View* property is set to *Details*. For the sample application, these subitems are the file's size in bytes and the date-time stamp of when the file was last modified.

Conclusion

The advantage of using the Windows Explorer–style interface is that it makes it very easy for the user to navigate and view information in a hierarchical fashion. Using the *Splitter* control, docked controls such as the *TreeView* and *List-View* controls are completely resizable, letting the user customize the application to her own preferences. This sample application should give you all you need to get started creating Windows Explorer–style applications.

Application #36: Create a System Tray Icon

A common task in Windows programming is adding an icon to the Windows system tray. In Visual Basic 6.0, there was no such built-in functionality. Developers either had to resort to using Win32 APIs or a third-party control. With the release of Visual Basic .NET, Visual Basic developers were finally able to use the system tray—right out of the box. This sample application demonstrates how to do exactly that: create an application that displays a notification icon in the system tray. Various properties and events will be demonstrated, including the ability to associate a context-sensitive menu with the icon. To make things a bit more interesting, the context-sensitive menu will be used to provide an introduction to the *System.Environment* class. Its menu items give the user access to selected functions, such as getting the current operating system version and the length of time since the user's computer was booted, using the *System.Environment* class. Figure 4-11 shows the simple form that the sample application displays when it starts.

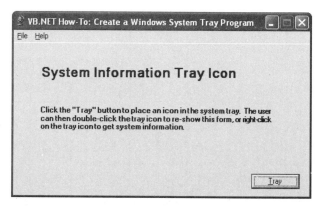

Figure 4-11   The sample application displays a dialog box that allows the user to place an icon in the system tray.

Building Upon...

Application #2: Use *DateTimes*
Application #7: Object-Oriented Features

New Concepts

This application introduces two new classes: The *NotifyIcon* class and the *System.Environment* class. These two classes are discussed in the sections that follow.

The *NotifyIcon* Control

The *NotifyIcon* control is a Windows Forms control that can be dragged and dropped onto any Windows Form. The *NotifyIcon* control is displayed in the component tray, which is part of the Windows Forms Designer and is located beneath the form. The component tray is used for any component that is part of a form but does not provide a visible surface at design time. At run time, the *NotifyIcon* control is displayed in the system tray. By default, the system tray is located at the bottom, far right of the Windows taskbar, although the user can change the location by moving the Windows taskbar. Programs such as antivirus software and the Windows Volume Control use this area for notification purposes or to provide users an easy way to access commonly used functionality.

The *NotifyIcon* control has only a handful of properties and methods. Among these is the *Icon* property. This is the icon that is displayed in the system tray. The *Text* property is the text that is displayed as a ToolTip when the user hovers the mouse over the icon. The *Visible* property is used to show and hide the icon. Finally, the *ContextMenu* property is used to associate a context menu with the control. This is the menu that pops up when the user right-clicks the icon in the system tray. The application starts with a simple form, shown in Figure 4-11, that contains a Tray button and some text. Clicking the Tray button causes the form to disappear and the application to display an icon in the system tray, as seen in Figure 4-12.

Figure 4-12   The *NotifyIcon* control appears in the Windows system tray at run time.

Accessing Machine Information via the *Environment* Namespace
The *System.Environment* is a static class that provides access to the current environment and platform. The sample application uses *System.Environment* to:

- Get the length of time elapsed since the user's machine was booted
- Get the version of the .NET Framework
- Get the version of the operating system

In addition, the *System.Environment* class can be used to get command-line arguments, set an exit code, and perform other useful tasks.

Code Walkthrough

Normally, the Windows Forms Designer–generated code is not something you need to worry about. However, in this instance, it's useful to examine this code to get a feel for how the *NotifyIcon* control works. All these properties were set at design time using the Properties window:

```
Me.ntfSystemInfo.ContextMenu = Me.mnuCtx
```

This line associates a context menu with the *NotifyIcon* control. It is this menu that pops up when the user right-clicks the icon in the system tray.

```
Me.ntfSystemInfo.Icon = _
    CType(resources.GetObject("ntfSystemInfo.Icon"), _
    System.Drawing.Icon)
```

This line sets the icon that will be displayed in the system tray.

```
Me.ntfSystemInfo.Text = _
    resources.GetString("ntfSystemInfo.Text")
```

This line sets the *Text* property of the *NotifyIcon*. This is the text that appears as a ToolTip when the user hovers the mouse over the icon in the system tray.

```
Me.ntfSystemInfo.Visible = _
    CType(resources.GetObject("ntfSystemInfo.Visible"), Boolean)
```

This line simply indicates whether the icon in the system tray should be visible or not. Again, all these properties were set using the Properties window. The point of going through the Windows Forms Designer–generated code was to get a better feel for what happens behind the scenes to get the *NotifyIcon* control to work.

The sample application is designed so that the notification icon is displayed only when the form is hidden. When the form is visible, the icon is not. Therefore, during the form's *Load* event, the *Visible* property of the *NotifyIcon* is set to *False*:

```
Private Sub frmMain_Load(ByVal sender As System.Object, _
    ByVal e As System.EventArgs) Handles MyBase.Load

    ntfSystemInfo.Visible = False
End Sub
```

Clicking the form's Tray button hides the form and displays the notification icon in the system tray:

```
Private Sub btnTray_Click(ByVal sender As System.Object, _
    ByVal e As System.EventArgs) Handles btnTray.Click
    Me.Hide()
    ntfSystemInfo.Visible = True
    ntfSystemInfo.Text = "System Information"
End Sub
```

Conversely, double-clicking the icon in the system tray hides the icon and displays the form:

```
Private Sub ntfSystemInfo_DoubleClick(ByVal sender As Object, _
    ByVal e As System.EventArgs) _
    Handles ntfSystemInfo.DoubleClick

    ntfSystemInfo.Visible = False
```

```
    Me.Show()
End Sub
```

When the user right-clicks the icon in the system tray, a context menu is displayed. The only thing you need to do to associate the context menu with the *NotifyIcon* control is simply set the *ContextMenu* property of the *NotifyIcon* control. No additional code is required. The context menu gives the user six choices:

- Current Date

- Current Time

- Time since last Restart

- Framework Version

- Current OS Version

- Exit

To get the current date, the sample application simply calls the *Now* method of the *DateTime* class. The date is displayed in long date format:

```
MessageBox.Show("Today's Date is: " + _
    DateTime.Now.ToLongDateString(), "Date", _
    MessageBoxButtons.OK, _
    MessageBoxIcon.Information)
```

To determine the current time zone, the sample application calls the *IsDaylightSavingTime* method of the *TimeZone.CurrentTimeZone* class. This method returns *True* or *False*. The *DaylightName* and *StandardName* properties are used to determine the actual name of the time zone:

```
If (TimeZone.CurrentTimeZone.IsDaylightSavingTime(DateTime.Now)) Then
    MessageBox.Show( _
        "The current time zone is: " + _
        TimeZone.CurrentTimeZone.DaylightName, _
        "Time Zone", _
        MessageBoxButtons.OK, _
        MessageBoxIcon.Information)
Else
    MessageBox.Show( _
        "The current time zone is: " + _
        TimeZone.CurrentTimeZone.StandardName, _
        "Time Zone", _
        MessageBoxButtons.OK, _
        MessageBoxIcon.Information)
End If
```

The Time Since Last Restart menu displays the length of time in minutes since the user's computer was last rebooted. The *TickCount* method of the

Environment class returns the number of milliseconds elapsed since the system started. This number is then converted to minutes:

```
Dim timeSinceLastRebootMinutes As Double = _
    ((Environment.TickCount / 1000) / 60)
```

The Framework Version menu displays the version number of the .NET Framework. The *System.Environment* makes this easy to do. Simply call the *Version* property:

```
MessageBox.Show("Framework Version: " + _
    Environment.Version.ToString(), _
    ".NET Framework Version", _
    MessageBoxButtons.OK, _
    MessageBoxIcon.Information)
```

Finally, the Current OS Version menu displays the name and version number of the underlying operating system:

```
MessageBox.Show("Framework Version: " + _
    Environment.Version.ToString(), _
    ".NET Framework Version", _
    MessageBoxButtons.OK, _
    MessageBoxIcon.Information)
```

Conclusion

In previous versions of Visual Basic, there was no built-in support for displaying an icon in the system tray. Most developers resorted to using the Win32 API or third-party controls. With the release of Visual Basic .NET, this ability is conveniently built into the .NET Framework with the *NotifyIcon* control.

Application #37: Use Menus

This sample application demonstrates how to use the *MainMenu* control, one of the most commonly used controls in Windows Forms. Various events are demonstrated, including the *Popup*, *Select*, and *Click* events. The sample applications also demonstrates how to use the *MdiList*, *RadioCheck*, and *Checked* properties. What's more, as you can see in Figure 4-13, the sample application uses the MDI paradigm for its interface. This provides an excellent opportunity to introduce how to create MDI applications in Visual Basic .NET. A few things have changed since Visual Basic 6.0, so this will explain some of the differences.

The sample application is a simple text editor that consists of two forms (not counting the About form). The first form, named *frmMain*, is the main form of the application and serves as the MDI parent form. The second form, named *frmEdit*, is the MDI child form. As is standard with MDI applications, there is one instance of the main form but there can be multiple instances of the child form open at the same time.

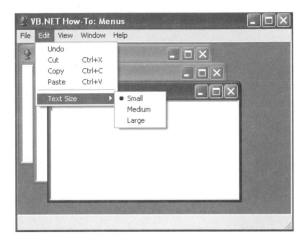

Figure 4-13   The Menus application in action.

Both *frmMain* and *frmEdit* use a *MainMenu* control. On *frmMain*, there are four top-level menu items: File, View, Window, and Help. Selecting New from the File menu creates a new instance of *frmEdit* where the user can enter and edit text. The View menu allows the user to toggle on and off a status bar displayed at the bottom of the form. The Window menu allows the user to tile the MDI child forms, either horizontally or vertically. The user can also cascade the child forms or even select a particular child form by using the *MdiList* property. Finally, selecting About from the Help menu brings up a standard About box. To exit the program, select Exit from the File menu.

frmEdit also has its own set of menus, which can be accessed by using a second *MainMenu* control. Its File menu allows the user to save and print files, and the Edit menu provides standard editing functions such as cut, copy, paste, and undo. The Text Size menu has a submenu that allows the user to change the size of text to small, medium, and large. At run time, the *frmEdit* menus are merged with the *frmMain* menus.

New Concepts

This sample application introduces the *MainMenu* control and MDI forms.

The *MainMenu* Control

The *MainMenu* control allows you to add menus to your Windows Forms. Simply drag and drop a *MainMenu* control from the toolbox to the design surface of your form. Then use the In-Place Menu Editor, shown in Figure 4-14, to add menus to your form.

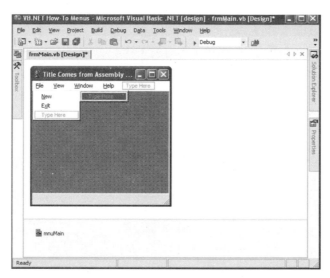

Figure 4-14 The In-Place Menu Editor.

MDI Forms

Multiple Document Interface (MDI) applications provide a methodology for creating a document-centric type of interface. MDI applications have a single container form that serves as the background for the application. As the user opens and creates new documents, each document is shown within its own child form. A user can have many documents open at the same time, or none at all. If the parent form is moved around the screen, all child forms move with the parent. Child forms can even be tiled or cascaded for ease of use. The multiple document interface is often used by text editing, word processing, and spreadsheet programs. Microsoft Visual Studio .NET, for example, uses MDI.

Code Walkthrough

Most of the code for this application is contained in *frmMain* and *fmEdit*. Both of these classes will be discussed in the sections that follow.

frmMain

As mentioned previously, *frmMain* is the container, or parent form, for the application. When the user selects a menu, the first handled event is the *Select* event. The *Select* event is useful for displaying a help string for the currently selected menu item in an application's status bar:

```
Dim strText As String

If sender Is mnuStatusBar Then
    strText = "Toggle display of the status bar"
ElseIf sender Is mnuAbout Then
    strText = "Display the About dialog box"
ElseIf sender Is mnuCascade Then
    strText = "Cascade child windows"
ElseIf sender Is mnuExit Then
    strText = "Exit demonstration"
ElseIf sender Is mnuNew Then
    strText = "Create new child window"
ElseIf sender Is mnuTileHorizontal Then
    strText = "Tile windows horizontally"
ElseIf sender Is mnuTileVertical Then
    strText = "Tile windows vertically"
Else
    strText = String.Empty
End If

WriteToStatusBar(strText)
```

The *WriteToStatusBar* subroutine simply sets the *Text* property of the *StatusBar* control.

The *Popup* event occurs when a list of menu items is about to be displayed. This event is often used for enabling/disabling, checking/unchecking, or even adding/removing menu items before the list of menu items is displayed. The View menu, for example, uses the *Popup* event to determine whether the Status Bar menu item should be checked or unchecked:

```
Private Sub mnuView_Popup(ByVal sender As Object, _
    ByVal e As System.EventArgs) Handles mnuView.Popup

    mnuStatusBar.Checked = sbarEdit.Visible
End Sub
```

When the user clicks the New menu item, a new instance of *frmEdit* is created. Remember that multiple instances of *frmEdit* can be created. Here's the code to do that:

```
Try
    Dim frm As New frmEdit()
    Static intChild As Integer

    intChild += 1
    frm.MdiParent = Me
    frm.Text = "Child " & intChild
    frm.Show()
Catch exp As Exception
    MessageBox.Show(exp.Message, Me.Text)
End Try
```

If you look past the error handling and the *intChild* code, you'll see that creating a new child form requires only three lines of code. The first line creates a new instance of *frmEdit*. The second line sets the parent form for the new instance of *frmEdit*. This is what the *MdiParent* property is for. Finally, to actually display *frmEdit*, call the *Show* method. What happens if you accidentally forget to set the *MdiParent* property? The form is still created and displayed, but not as an MDI child. Instead, *frmEdit* is displayed outside the parent container form. It cannot be tiled or cascaded, and if the parent form is moved, *frmEdit* doesn't move with it.

As for the *intChild* code, *intChild* is simply a static variable that counts the total number of times a new instance of *frmEdit* is created. This count is displayed in the title bar of *frmMain*.

The Window menu allows the user to rearrange all the child forms that are open in the application. The code to do this is extremely simple. All you have to do is set the *frmMain LayoutMdi* method. To arrange the child forms in cascade order, use *MdiLayout.Cascade*:

```
Me.LayoutMdi(MdiLayout.Cascade)
```

To tile the child forms horizontally, use *MdiLayout.TileHorizontal*:

```
Me.LayoutMdi(MdiLayout.TileHorizontal)
```

To tile the child forms vertically, use *MdiLayout.TileVertical*:

```
Me.LayoutMdi(MdiLayout.TileVertical)
```

It's that simple.

frmEdit

frmEdit is used as the application's child form and consists of a single *Main-Menu* control and *TextBox* control. When an MDI child is displayed on screen, the child's menus are merged with the parent form's menus. This merging process can get a little complicated. In particular, there are two properties of the *MainMenu* control that need to be set properly.

The first property is *MergeType*. There are four possible values that it can be set to: *Add*, *Replace*, *MergeItems*, and *Remove*. In the sample application, the File menu *MergeType* property is set to *MergeItems*. This way, the File menu on *frmMain* merges with the items on the File menu of *frmEdit* when it has the focus. On the other hand, the Edit menu on *frmEdit* has its *MergeType* property set to *Add*. This way, when it has the focus, its Edit menu gets added to the menus of its parent form.

The second property is *MergeOrder*. This property is used to determine the order in which menu items are merged with each other. The values in this property are relative. That is, the actual values don't matter, except in relation to other items. On *frmMain*'s File menu, the New menu item's *MergeOrder* is 0 and the Exit menu item's *MergeOrder* is 10. On *frmEdit*'s File menu, the Save menu item is set to 2 and the Print menu item is set to 3. The top and bottom dividers are set to 1 and 4. When you select New from the main form's File menu, the child form appears and its menus merge into the File menu on the main form. The same issues apply to the Edit menu of *frmEdit*. The top-level menu items on *frmMain* have their *MergeOrder* properties set to 0, 10, 20, 30, and 40. The Edit menu on *frmEdit* has its *MergeOrder* property set to 5. When an instance of *frmEdit* has the focus, its Edit menu appears between the first two menus on *frmMain* (because 5 is between 0 and 10).

Both *MergeType* and *MergeOrder* can be set directly in code or by using the Properties window. In the sample application, the Properties window was used, so this code can be found in the Windows Form Designer–generated code region. For *frmEdit*, here is the code for *mnuFile* and *mnuEdit*:

```
Me.mnuFile.MergeType = _
    System.Windows.Forms.MenuMerge.MergeItems
Me.mnuEdit.MergeOrder = 5
```

Note that the default value for *MergeType* is *Add* and for *MergeOrder* it is 0. To save space, the Windows Forms Designer creates only lines of code where the value is not the default.

Conclusion

The *MainMenu* control is one of the most commonly used controls in Windows Forms development. With the in-place menu editor, it's also one of the easiest to use. As you create more advanced Visual Basic .NET programs, you'll want to use the Multiple Document Interface (MDI) as the model for some of your applications, particularly if they are document-centric. Text editors and word processors make for great uses of MDI.

Application #38: Use Owner-Drawn Menus

This sample application demonstrates how to create an owner-drawn menu. An owner-drawn menu is one where you, as the programmer, override the default drawing behavior of a menu to add some sort of custom font or graphical effect. Specifically, this sample application creates an owner-drawn menu that displays an icon. To do this, a custom control is created, inheriting from the *MenuItem* control. Many newer applications, such as Microsoft Visual Studio .NET and Microsoft Office XP, display icons in their menus. By incorporating into your programs owner-drawn menus that display icons, your applications will have a more polished and professional look. The sample application shown in Figure 4-15 displays icons in its menu.

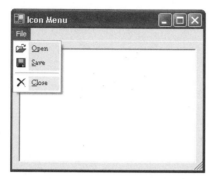

Figure 4-15   The sample application, Use Owner-Drawn Menus, uses owner-drawn menus to display menu items with an icon.

The sample application presents a simple text editor. Because the focus of this sample application is on how to create owner-drawn menus rather than how to create a text editor, the text editor itself doesn't do much beyond allowing the user to enter plain text. However, the text editor form has a *File* menu that uses a custom control named *IconMenuItem*. This is where most of the interesting code is located and is therefore the focus of this section.

Building Upon...

Application #7: Object-Oriented Features
Application #8: Scoping, Overloading, Overriding
Application #31: Validate Text Boxes
Application #37: Use Menus

New Concepts

This application introduces the concept of owner-drawn menus. Owner-drawn menus are objects derived from the *MenuItem* control that have their *OwnerDraw* property set to *True* and that override the base class's *OnDrawItem* method.

The *MenuItem* Control

The *MenuItem* control represents a submenu of a *MainMenu* control. As you know, adding a menu to a Visual Basic .NET Windows Forms involves adding a *MainMenu* control. Each submenu of this *MainMenu* control is a *MenuItem* control. Each *MenuItem* control in turn can have multiple submenu items. For example, the text editor form of the application contains File and Help submenus. These are actually implemented as *MenuItem* objects of the *MainMenu* control. The File *MenuItem* object has an Exit *MenuItem* object. The first release of Visual Basic .NET added many new exciting features to the language and integrated development environment (IDE). One of the most exciting improvements was the introduction of a great new menu editor. However, one feature that was left out of Windows Forms is the ability to associate an icon to a menu item. The owner-drawn feature of menus is used to add this ability to the sample application.

The *OwnerDraw* Property

OwnerDraw is a property of the *MenuItem* control that indicates whether the menu should be drawn by Windows or whether the application will programmatically draw the menu itself. By default, this property is set to *False*. When *OwnerDraw* is set to *True*, this tells .NET that you want to handle all the drawing yourself by overriding the *OnDrawItem* procedure. Place whatever custom code you want in the *OnDrawItem* event handler. The event argument for *OnDrawItem* includes a *Graphics* object. Use this *Graphics* object to manipulate the graphics displayed on screen.

Code Walkthrough

IconMenuItem is a custom control that inherits from the *MenuItem* control:

```
Public Class IconMenuItem
    Inherits MenuItem
```

Inside *IconMenuItem* are two module-level variables. Of particular significance is the *m_Icon* variable, which stores the icon to be displayed in the menu:

```
Private m_Icon As Icon
Private m_Font As New Font("Times New Roman", 8)
```

The *m_Icon* variable is set in the *IconMenuItem* constructor:

```
Public Sub New(ByVal Text As String, ByVal Icon As Icon, _
    ByVal onClick As EventHandler)
    MyBase.New(text, onClick)
    m_Icon = Icon
    MyBase.OwnerDraw = True
End Sub
```

The user passes the *Icon* to the constructor when the *MenuItem* is instantiated. Also, note that the constructor sets the *OwnerDraw* property to *True*. Again, this tells Windows that you'll supply the code to render the menu item yourself.

The next step in creating an owner-drawn menu is to override the *OnDrawItem* event handler:

```
Protected Overrides Sub OnDrawItem(ByVal e As DrawItemEventArgs)
```

The first line inside the *OnDrawItem* procedure calls the base class's *OnDrawItem* method. This begins the drawing process:

```
MyBase.OnDrawItem(e)
```

The *OnDrawItem* procedure has just one argument, *DrawItemEventArgs*, but it has several useful properties. The most important is the *Graphics* object. This represents a GDI+ drawing surface. The *Graphics* object provides various methods for drawing objects to a display device. For this particular sample application, the *Graphics* object will be used to draw the icon on the menu:

```
If Not m_Icon Is Nothing Then
    e.Graphics.DrawIcon(m_Icon, e.Bounds.Left + 2, e.Bounds.Top + 2)
End If

Dim myRect As Rectangle = e.Bounds
myRect.X += 22

Dim myBrush As Brush = SystemBrushes.Control

e.Graphics.FillRectangle(myBrush, myRect)
```

Note that *m_Icon* is checked to make sure it's not *Nothing*. This is to verify that *m_Icon* was properly set when it was passed into the *IconMenuItem* constructor. If *m_Icon* is *Nothing*, this code would still continue to work.

After the icon has been drawn, the next step is drawing the menu item's text. The next two lines are used to determine the length of space to leave for the accelerator key:

```
Dim myStrFormat As StringFormat = New StringFormat()
myStrFormat.HotkeyPrefix = System.Drawing.Text.HotkeyPrefix.Show
```

Finally, draw the menu text on the screen by using the *SolidBrush* object. *SolidBrush* is part of the *System.Drawing* namespace and simply defines a brush of a single color:

```
myBrush = New SolidBrush(e.ForeColor)
e.Graphics.DrawString(Me.Text(), m_Font, myBrush, _
    e.Bounds.Left + 25, e.Bounds.Top + 2, myStrFormat)
```

As mentioned previously, the *Graphics* object contains many useful properties and methods for drawing on a GDI+ design surface. Here, you see the *DrawString* method is used to draw the menu item's text on the *Graphics* object.

There's one final step before completing the *IconMenuItem* control. Before drawing the menu on the screen, you first need to know the size of a menu item. That's where the *OnMeasureItem* event comes into play. By over-riding *OnMeasureItem*, you can measure the string in the *MenuItem Text* prop-erty and use it to set the size of the menu item:

```
Protected Overrides Sub OnMeasureItem(ByVal e As MeasureItemEventArgs)
    Dim myStrFormat As New StringFormat()
    myStrFormat.HotkeyPrefix = System.Drawing.Text.HotkeyPrefix.Show
    MyBase.OnMeasureItem(e)
    e.ItemHeight = 22
    e.ItemWidth = CInt(e.Graphics.MeasureString(Me.Text(), _
        m_Font, 10000, myStrFormat).Width) + 10
End Sub
```

e is the argument passed into the *OnMeasureItem* routine. It has *Item-Height* and *ItemWidth* properties, which contain the size of the menu item.

There are a couple of new objects used in this code. *StringFormat* con-tains text layout information, such as alignment and line spacing. *StringFormat* is part of the *System.Drawing* namespace. *HotkeyPrefix* is an enumeration that specifies the type of display for hot-key prefixes for menu items.

Finally, the *MeasureString* method of the *Graphics* object is used to mea-sure the width of the string to be displayed. Note that the font of the string is passed in as one of the parameters.

Conclusion

Owner-drawn menus are a powerful feature of Visual Basic .NET. They allow the developer to control how the menu-drawing process works. This adds a new level of flexibility that in the past had eluded Visual Basic developers. In this sam-ple application, a custom control was created that displays icons in menu items. This is, undoubtedly, one of the more popular uses of owner-drawn menus in Visual Basic .NET. Using the technique presented in this sample application, you can create your own owner-drawn menus that perform custom actions, such as changing the color or font of a menu item or drawing a gradient.

Application #39: Use the Clipboard

Most applications for Windows support cutting or copying data to the Windows Clipboard and then pasting that data from the Clipboard into another application. The data formats of the copied information can vary depending on the task. This sample application, shown in Figure 4-16, demonstrates how to use the Windows Clipboard with data in multiple formats. It also demonstrates the primary classes, properties, and methods used when programming against the Clipboard.

The sample application uses a simple interface that has a series of menus for copying and pasting data within the application, and three controls that serve as containers for pasted data. A single image and some simple text (in several formats) are provided for copying. These items can be sent to the Clipboard in a single format or in multiple formats. Likewise, the user also has the ability to paste an item in a number of formats. These formats are determined dynamically according to the format or formats of the data that was copied in.

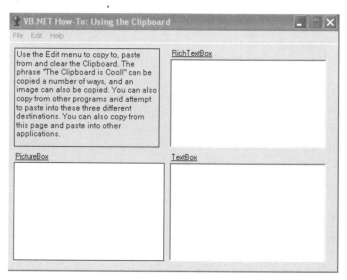

Figure 4-16   The main window of the Use The Clipboard application.

Building Upon...

Application #1: Use Arrays
Application #4: *Try/Catch/Finally*
Application #8: Scoping, Overloading, Overriding
Application #37: Use Menus

New Concepts

This application introduces the *Clipboard* class and describes how to use the class to copy data to the Windows clipboard.

The *Clipboard* Object

The *Clipboard* class resides in the *System.Windows.Forms* namespace, is *Not-Inheritable*, and has no public constructors. It is a simple class that represents the Windows clipboard and that has only two methods, which are used for sending and retrieving clipboard data. These methods are *SetDataObject* and *GetDataObject*. *SetDataObject* copies data to the clipboard. *GetDataObject* returns the data stored in the clipboard. This returned data is represented as an object that implements the *IDataObject* interface. What is *IDataObject*? *IDataObject* is an interface that provides a format-independent mechanism for transferring data. The data being transferred could be text, a bitmap, a wave audio file, or several other formats. The *DataFormats* class contains a list of predefined formats directly supported by the .NET Framework.

The *IDataObject* interface has four overloaded methods that are used when transferring data to and from the clipboard. The *SetData* method is used to store data in a specified format (such as text or bitmap). The *GetDataPresent* method is used to verify that the data in the clipboard is already in, or can be converted to, a given format. To retrieve data associated with a specified format, use the *GetData* method. Lastly, the *GetFormats* method returns a list of all formats the data is associated with, including formats the data can be converted to.

Copying Text to and from the Clipboard

Copying text items to and from the clipboard can be simple, as in the case of copying a string from one place in a document to another, or it can be as complex as copying text from a Web browser to another application that might or might not handle HTML tags. The latter situation makes it necessary to set data on the clipboard in several formats at once. The *SetData* method can be used to store multiple formats of a piece of data in the *DataObject* instance before it's moved to the clipboard. The *GetFormats* method discussed earlier can then be used to list the data formats available as the data is being retrieved, so that the application can use the most appropriate format before using the data. Be aware that no validation is done to ensure that an item being stored as HTML or RTF is truly in that format. The application receiving the data should not assume that the item being retrieved is necessarily in the format it was supposed to be in.

Copying Images to and from the Clipboard

Using images with the clipboard is done in a manner similar to using text. The same methods are used for populating, querying, and retrieving data from the clipboard. Multiple formats of an image can be copied for use by another application. Some data formats that can be used for images include *Bitmap*, *DeviceIndependentBitmap*, *MetafilePict*, *EnhancedMetafile*, and *TaggedImageFileFormat*.

Code Walkthrough

When *frmMain* is instantiated, five variables are initialized with values that will later be copied to and from the clipboard. These values will represent data items that contain a string, HTML, RTF, XML, and a bitmap.

```
Dim strText, strHTML, strRTF, strXML As String
Dim myImage As System.Drawing.Bitmap
```

mnuCopyTextAsRTF_Click

The *Edit* menu contains different submenus for moving information to and from the clipboard. There is a *Copy Text As* menu for copying a text item as Text, HTML, RTF, XML, and All Formats. Another menu, *Copy Image As*, copies an image as a bitmap. The *Paste As* menu item is used to paste the contents of the clipboard to the controls on the form. The formats available here will depend on the type of data that was copied in. Copying text to the clipboard as RTF is handled by the following lines of code:

```
Dim myDataObject As New DataObject()
myDataObject.SetData(DataFormats.Rtf, strRTF)
Clipboard.SetDataObject(myDataObject, True)
```

First a *DataObject* is created. Then the text is added to it with the proper format using *SetData*. The first parameter specifies the format of the data being stored, *DataFormats.RTF*. The second parameter is the data itself. Next, the *SetDataObject* method is used to copy the data object to the clipboard. Here the data object is passed in along with a Boolean value indicating whether or not the data should be retained once the application is closed.

mnuEdit_Popup

When this data is pasted, only the *Rich Text Format* menu is shown. This menu is actually populated based on the type of data that was copied to the clipboard. If the clipboard is not empty when the *Edit* menu is clicked, a list of supported formats is obtained using the *GetFormats* method of the *DataObject*:

```
If Not (Clipboard.GetDataObject() Is Nothing) Then
    strArray = Clipboard.GetDataObject().GetFormats()
```

Next, an array of these format types is created and populated. Each format type becomes a menu item that will be displayed when the user selects Paste As from the Edit menu.

```
ReDim myTypes(strArray.Length - 1)
For i = 0 To strArray.Length - 1
myTypes(i) = New MenuItem(strArray(i), _
    New System.EventHandler(AddressOf PasteAsMenuEventHandler))
Next i
```

Each menu item is set to point at a common routine, *PasteAsMenuEventHandler*, for handling paste events. This will be discussed next.

PasteAsMenuEventHandler

In *PasteAsMenuEventHandler*, variables are defined for retrieving the data from the clipboard and clearing the controls that will display the data. The selected format of the data is then determined and saved to a variable as a string:

```
strType = CType(sender, MenuItem).Text
```

The data object is inspected to determine whether the selected format is available in the clipboard:

```
If Clipboard.GetDataObject().GetDataPresent(strType) Then
```

The data is retrieved using the *GetData* method of the data object and is then saved to a local variable in the requested format:

```
obj = Clipboard.GetDataObject().GetData(strType)
```

If the data was retrieved successfully, it's copied to the first output control, a *RichTextBox* control using the control's *Paste* method:

```
If Not obj Is Nothing Then
    Me.rtbPaste.Paste(DataFormats.GetFormat(strType))
```

If there is a textual representation of the data in the clipboard, it can be pasted to the *TextBox* control as well. The *GetType* method of the retrieved object can be used to determine whether data can be pasted to a control:

```
If obj.GetType().ToString() = "System.String" Then
    Me.txtPaste.AppendText(CType(obj, String))
Else
    Me.txtPaste.AppendText(obj.GetType.ToString())
End If
```

Notice that the data is tested to see whether it's a *System.String*. This will determine whether or not the contents of the object need to be converted before being displayed in the *TextBox* control.

Conclusion

Most Windows applications support cutting or copying data to and from the Windows *Clipboard*. These applications might use different formats such as bitmap, RTF, and HTML. This sample application shows how the *Clipboard* class can be used to handle data in multiple formats by using the *IDataObject* interface.

Application #40: Use Drag-and-Drop

Previous versions of Visual Basic had two different and incompatible methods of adding drag-and-drop functionality to applications. The first method was known as standard drag-and-drop, and it was designed to support drag-and-drop operations between controls within a single application. While simple to code, standard drag-and-drop didn't work across multiple applications. The second method was known as OLE drag-and-drop. OLE drag-and-drop was slightly more complicated, but it worked across multiple applications. Unfortunately, OLE drag-and-drop was incompatible with standard drag-and-drop.

Visual Basic .NET simplifies all of this by settling on a single, standard way of performing drag-and-drop operations that works within a single application and across multiple applications. If you previously used OLE drag-and-drop, Visual Basic .NET drag-and-drop will seem very familiar.

The sample application demonstrates how to add drag-and-drop functionality to your programs. It consists of a main form with a two-paged tab control. The first tab page shows how to drag-and-drop items (as text) back and forth between two *ListBox* controls, as pictured in Figure 4-17.

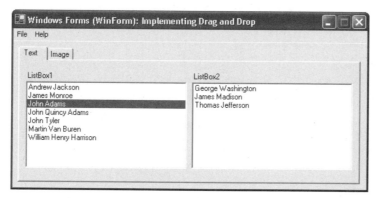

Figure 4-17   Application interface – Text tab.

The second tab page shows how to move an image back and forth between two *PictureBox* controls using drag-and-drop, as pictured in Figure 4-18.

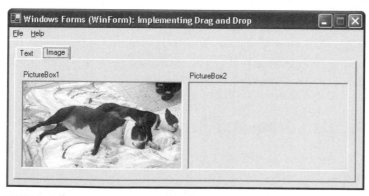

Figure 4-18   Application interface – Image tab.

Building Upon...

Application #29: Use the *ListBox* and *ComboBox*
Application #39: Use the Clipboard

New Concepts

Drag-and-drop in Visual Basic .NET is similar to OLE drag-and-drop in Visual Basic 6.0, although some of the names of methods and properties have changed.

The first step in enabling drag-and-drop in your application is to set each destination control's *AllowDrop* property to *True*. Generally, this is done in the *Form Load* event procedure or constructor. To begin an actual drag-and-drop operation, call the *DoDragDrop* method of the source control. Generally, the *DoDragDrop* method is called within the *MouseDown* event procedure. The *DoDragDrop* method accepts two parameters. The first parameter, *data*, is the object or data to be dragged. In the sample application, *data* is the text of a *ListBox* item (first tab) or a bitmap image (second tab). The second parameter, *allowedEffects*, is a bit field and is represented by the *DragDropEffects* enumeration. There are a total of six possible drag-and-drop effects:

Table 4-2   *DragDropEffects* Constants

Constant	Value
All	The data is copied, removed from the drag source, and scrolled in the drop destination.
Copy	The data is copied to the drop destination.
Link	The data is linked to the drop destination.
Move	The data is moved to the drop destination.
None	The drop destination does not accept the data.
Scroll	The drop destination will scroll.

The *DoDragDrop* method begins the drag-and-drop operation. The next step is to code the destination control *DragEnter* event procedure. The *DragEnter* event occurs when the user first drags the mouse over a possible destination control. This event is used to set which *DragDropEffects* the destination control will allow.

The final step to implementing drag-and-drop functionality in Visual Basic .NET is to handle the destination control *DragDrop* event. This event occurs when the user drags the mouse to the destination control and releases the mouse button. Use this event to place the dragged data into the destination control. The section that follows will walk you through this process step by step.

Code Walkthrough

The code walkthrough for this application focuses on four event procedures: *frmMain_Load*, *ListBox_MouseDown*, *ListBox_DragEnter*, and *ListBox_Drag-Drop*. The following sections discuss these event handlers in detail.

frmMain_Load

The first step to implementing endrange drag-and-drop functionality in Visual Basic .NET is to set each destination control's *AllowDrop* property to *True*. This property cannot be set at design time, so the form's *Load* event procedure is used:

```
Private Sub frmMain_Load(ByVal sender As System.Object, _
    ByVal e As System.EventArgs) Handles MyBase.Load

    ListBox1.AllowDrop = True
    ListBox2.AllowDrop = True
    PictureBox1.AllowDrop = True
    PictureBox2.AllowDrop = True

    FillListBoxWithPresidents(ListBox1)

    PictureBox1.Image = Image.FromFile("..\SleepingDogs.jpg")
End Sub
```

Note that both list boxes and both picture boxes have their *AllowDrop* properties set to *True*. This allows the user to drag-and-drop items from the first control to the second, and vice versa. Next, the first list box is populated with some sample data by calling the *FillListBoxWithPresidents* routine. Finally, the first picture box is populated with a sample image.

ListBox_MouseDown

Now that the form has been properly initialized, the source control *MouseDown* event procedure is used to begin the drag-and-drop operation. Because the code for dragging items from one list box to another is similar to dragging images to and from picture boxes, this walkthrough will focus on dragging and dropping items from the *ListBox* controls. First, examine the *ListBox_MouseDown* event procedure:

```
Private Sub ListBox_MouseDown(ByVal sender As Object, _
    ByVal e As System.Windows.Forms.MouseEventArgs) _
    Handles ListBox1.MouseDown, ListBox2.MouseDown
```

Note that the *Handles* clause specifies two events. This helps eliminate redundant code because it allows *ListBox1* and *ListBox2* to share the same event procedures.

Drag-and-drop operations begin when the user holds down the left mouse button while the mouse is hovering over a source control. The next line of code checks to makes sure the user clicked the left mouse button:

```
If e.Button = MouseButtons.Left Then
```

Then the generic *sender* object is cast to a *ListBox* object. Remember that both *ListBox1* and *ListBox2* will call this event procedure, so this also allows the same code to run for both controls:

```
Dim myListBox As ListBox = CType(sender, ListBox)
```

The next line of code makes sure that the user selected an item from the *ListBox*:

```
If myListBox.SelectedIndex > -1 Then
```

In the declarations section of *frmMain*, a variable named *m_SourceControl* was declared. This variable is used to keep track of which *ListBox* is the source for the current drag-and-drop operation. This variable is set in the *MouseDown* event procedure:

```
m_SourceControl = myListBox
```

Finally, the *DoDragDrop* method of the source *ListBox* is called:

```
myListBox.DoDragDrop(myListBox.Items(myListBox.SelectedIndex), _
    DragDropEffects.Move)
```

The first parameter is the text of the selected *ListBox* item. The second parameter indicates that this is a move operation.

ListBox_DragEnter

The *ListBox_DragEnter* routine sets the type of drag-and-drop effect for the destination list box. For this particular application, only *Move* is allowed, but other effects could be used, such as *Copy*, *Link*, and *Scroll*:

```
Private Sub ListBox_DragEnter(ByVal sender As Object, _
    ByVal e As System.Windows.Forms.DragEventArgs) _
    Handles ListBox1.DragEnter, ListBox2.DragEnter

    If e.Data.GetDataPresent(DataFormats.Text) = True Then
        e.Effect = DragDropEffects.Move
    Else
        e.Effect = DragDropEffects.None
    End If
End Sub
```

Again, note that the *Handles* clause specifies two events. This allows *ListBox1* and *ListBox2* to share the same event procedures. The *GetDataPresent* method is used to determine whether the data being dragged is text. This is done to ensure that the destination control can properly handle the data. If the dragged data was, for example, audio or a bitmap image, there would be no way for a normal *ListBox* to handle it.

ListBox_DragDrop

The *ListBox_DragDrop* event procedure completes the drag-and-drop process for the *ListBox* controls. It moves the selected item from the source list box to the destination list box:

```
Private Sub ListBox_DragDrop(ByVal sender As Object, _
    ByVal e As System.Windows.Forms.DragEventArgs) _
    Handles ListBox1.DragDrop, ListBox2.DragDrop

    Dim myListBox As ListBox = CType(sender, ListBox)

    Dim myText As String

    myText = e.Data.GetData(GetType(System.String)).ToString
    RemoveItemFromListBox(myText, CType(m_SourceControl, ListBox))
    myListBox.Items.Add(myText)
End Sub
```

The first few lines should be familiar, such as the *Handles* clause and casting the generic *sender* object to a specific type. Of particular importance is the *GetData* method of the *e.Data* object. The *e.Data* object is an argument passed into the *DragDrop* routine. *GetData* simply gets the data that has been dragged into the control. In this particular case, the data is text. The selected *Item* object is removed from the source list box and added to the destination list box.

Conclusion

The first step to adding drag-and-drop functionality to Visual Basic .NET programs is to set the *AllowDrop* property to *True* for each control that is to serve as a destination control. Then code the *MouseDown*, *DragEnter*, and *DragDrop* event procedures. The drag-and-drop metaphor is often used in Windows applications as a way to make it easier for users to interface with a program. Developers who used older versions of Visual Basic probably remember that Visual Basic had two different, and incompatible, ways of adding drag-and-drop functionality to their applications. Visual Basic .NET simplifies this by standardizing a single, yet robust method for implementing drag-and-drop.

Application #41: Simple Printing

This sample application demonstrates how to print from a Visual Basic .NET program. The main class that all .NET printing revolves around is known as the *PrintDocument* class. In addition to providing the *PrintDocument* class, Visual

Basic .NET also provides *PrintPreviewDialog*, *PrintDialog*, and *PageSetupDialog* classes. With these classes, you can add professional-quality printing support to your applications.

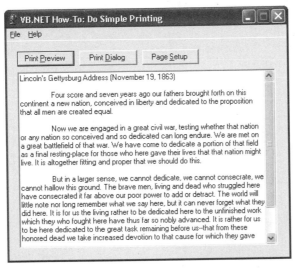

Figure 4-19   Main form of the sample application.

The sample application, shown in Figure 4-19, consists of a main form with a text box and three command buttons. When the form loads, the text box is populated with Abraham Lincoln's famous Gettysburg Address as sample data. The first button, Print Preview, will use the *PrintPreviewDialog* class to display a print preview of the document before it's sent to the printer. The second button, Print Dialog, will use the *PrintDialog* class to print the document. Finally, the Page Setup button will use the *PageSetupDialog* class to allow the user to change various page settings.

Building Upon...

Application #30: Use Common Dialog Boxes
Application #38: Use Owner-Drawn Menus

New Concepts

This sample application introduces the classes that the .NET Framework provides for adding print support to your application. The sample application's use of these classes, the *PrintDocument*, *PrintPreviewDialog*, *PrintDialog*, and *PageSetupDialog* classes, is described in the following sections.

The *PrintDocument* Class

As part of the *System.Drawing.Printing* namespace, the *PrintDocument* class is used to facilitate printing in Visual Basic .NET. To begin the printing process, the *Print* method of the *PrintDocument* object is called. This causes the *PrintDocument* to generate a *PrintPage* event. Inside the *PrintPage* event handler, include whatever code is needed to print the document using the *Graphics* object that is passed in as one of the arguments. Depending on what is to be printed, the code inside the *PrintPage* event handler can be very simple or very complex. Each time a new page is printed, a new *PrintPage* event occurs. Also passed into the *Print-Page* event handler is a flag named *HasMorePages*. When the document is done printing, this flag should be set to *False* to indicate that the print job is complete.

The *PrintPreviewDialog* Class

The *PrintPreviewDialog* class is used to display how a document will look when it's sent to the printer. This dialog control is fully featured and requires very little code to set up. To use it, simply set its *Document* property to the *PrintDocument* object that is to be printed, and call the *ShowDialog* method. The Print Preview dialog box, shown in Figure 4-20, displays on screen and allows the user to examine every page of the document, zoom in and out, and preview multiple pages at the same time. The user can choose to either close the dialog box or print directly from the preview dialog box.

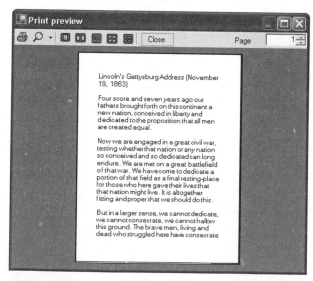

Figure 4-20 *PrintPreviewDialog* displaying the Gettysburg Address text from the sample application.

The *PrintDialog* Class

The *PrintDialog* class is used to display the standard Windows Print dialog box. This dialog box allows the user to change printers, select a print range, and set the number of copies to be printed. The user can click the OK button to send the document to the printer or click Cancel to exit the dialog box. Clicking the Properties button will display a second dialog box, the Printer Properties dialog box (seen in Figure 4-21), which is also standard in Windows. In the Printer Properties dialog box, the user can select myriad settings for the selected printer, such as layout and print quality. Like *PrintPreviewDialog*, *PrintDialog* is easy to use and requires very little code. Simply set its *Document* property to the *PrintDocument* object that is to be printed, and call the *ShowDialog* method. If the user clicks OK, the *ShowDialog* method will return *DialogResult.OK*. If the user clicks *Cancel*, the *ShowDialog* method will return *DialogResult.Cancel*.

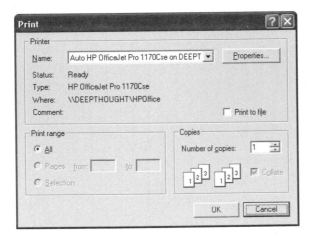

Figure 4-21   The standard Windows Print dialog box.

The *PageSetupDialog* Class

The *PageSetupDialog* class works in a manner similar to the previously explained print dialog boxes. Calling the *ShowDialog* method displays the Page Setup dialog box (shown in Figure 4-22). The *ShowDialog* method returns *DialogResult.OK* if the user clicks the OK button or *DialogResult.Cancel* if the user clicks the Cancel button. How is the *PageSetupDialog* different from the other dialogs? *PageSetupDialog* allows the user to change various settings related to how a page of a print document is to be printed. For example, the user can change the left, right, top, and bottom margins of a page or select the page size (legal, letter, envelope, index card, and so forth). The results of the user's selections are placed in a property named *PageSettings*. Use the *PageSettings* property to determine how the page should be printed.

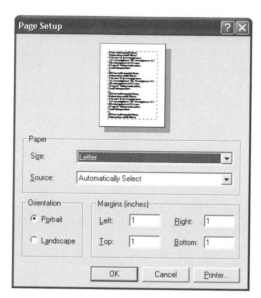

Figure 4-22   The Page Setup dialog box.

Code Walkthrough

The first thing the sample application does to enable print support is add an *Imports* statement to the *System.Drawing.Printing* namespace. Then a module-level variable is declared of type *PrintDocument*. These will be used to print the text in the *TextBox* control on the form:

```
Imports System.Drawing.Printing

Public Class frmMain
    Inherits System.Windows.Forms.Form

    Private WithEvents pdoc As New PrintDocument()
```

btnPrintPreview_Click

The code to show the Print Preview dialog box is simple. First an instance of the *PrintPreviewDialog* class is instantiated. Then the *PrintPreviewDialog Document* property is set to the module-level *PrintDocument* object that was declared in the *frmMain* declarations section. Finally, the *ShowDialog* method is called to display the dialog box. Note that a *Try/Catch/End Try* block is used to catch any errors. This is needed in case a printer is not installed:

```
Private Sub btnPrintPreview_Click(ByVal sender As System.Object, _
    ByVal e As System.EventArgs) Handles btnPrintPreview.Click
```

```
    Dim ppd As New PrintPreviewDialog()
    Try
        ppd.Document = pdoc
        ppd.ShowDialog()
    Catch exp As Exception
        MessageBox.Show("An error occurred while trying to load the " & _
            "document for Print Preview. Make sure you currently have " & _
            "access to a printer. A printer must be connected and " & _
            "accessible for Print Preview to work.", Me.Text, _
            MessageBoxButtons.OK, MessageBoxIcon.Error)
    End Try
End Sub
```

btnPrintDialog_Click

The *PrintDialog* class allows the user to select the printer they want to print to, as well as other printing options. To show the Print dialog box, simply create an instance of the *PrintDialog* class, tell it the document it is to print using the *Document* property, and call the *ShowDialog* method. If the user clicks the OK button, the document is printed by calling the *PrintDocument Print* method. Remember that the *Print* method will trigger a *PrintPage* event. The code to handle this event will be shown later.

```
Private Sub btnPrintDialog_Click(ByVal sender As System.Object, _
    ByVal e As System.EventArgs) Handles btnPrintDialog.Click

    Dim dialog As New PrintDialog()
    dialog.Document = pdoc

    If dialog.ShowDialog = DialogResult.OK Then
        pdoc.Print()
    End If
End Sub
```

btnPrintPageSetup_Click

The *PageSetupDialog* class lets the user alter settings such as the page size and orientation. To use *PageSetupDialog*, an instance of the *PageSetupDialog* class is created. Two of the *PageSetupDialog* object's properties are set before the *ShowDialog* method is called. First, the *Document* property is set to the *PrintDocument* that is to be printed. Again, this variable was declared in the *frmMain* declarations section. Second, the *PageSettings* property is set to the *DefaultPageSettings* of the *PrintDocument*. Then the *ShowDialog* method is called. If the user clicks the OK button on the Page Setup dialog box, the user's selections are copied to the *PrintDocument DefaultPageSettings* property:

```
Private Sub btnPageSetup_Click(ByVal sender As System.Object, _
    ByVal e As System.EventArgs) Handles btnPageSetup.Click
```

(continued)

```
      Dim psd As New PageSetupDialog()
      With psd
          .Document = pdoc
          .PageSettings = pdoc.DefaultPageSettings
      End With

      If psd.ShowDialog = DialogResult.OK Then
          pdoc.DefaultPageSettings = psd.PageSettings
      End If
End Sub
```

pdoc_PrintPage

Until now, the code for the sample application has been very straightforward. The code for the *PrintPage* event, however, is more involved. This is because the *PrintPage* event handler contains all the actual printing code. For the sample application, *pdoc_PrintPage* was designed to be very fast for printing plain text. *MeasureString* is used to calculate the text that can be fitted on an entire page. The *PrintPage* event handler begins by declaring two local variables. The first, *intCurrentChar*, holds the position of the last printed character. Remember that the *PrintPage* event occurs for every page that is printed. This variable is declared as static so that subsequent *PrintPage* events can use its value. The second variable, *font*, is the font that is to be used for printing:

```
Private Sub pdoc_PrintPage(ByVal sender As Object, _
    ByVal e As System.Drawing.Printing.PrintPageEventArgs) _
    Handles pdoc.PrintPage

    Static intCurrentChar As Int32
    Dim font As New font("Microsoft Sans Serif", 24)
```

Next, four more local variables are declared, *intPrintAreaHeight*, *intPrint-AreaWidth*, *marginLeft*, and *marginTop*. These contain the bounds of the printing area rectangle:

```
Dim intPrintAreaHeight, intPrintAreaWidth, marginLeft, marginTop As Int32
With pdoc.DefaultPageSettings
    intPrintAreaHeight = .PaperSize.Height - .Margins.Top - .Margins.Bottom
    intPrintAreaWidth = .PaperSize.Width - .Margins.Left - .Margins.Right
    marginLeft = .Margins.Left ' X coordinate
    marginTop = .Margins.Top ' Y coordinate
End With
```

If the user selects landscape mode, the printing area for height and width need to be swapped:

```
If pdoc.DefaultPageSettings.Landscape Then
    Dim intTemp As Int32
    intTemp = intPrintAreaHeight
```

```
    intPrintAreaHeight = intPrintAreaWidth
    intPrintAreaWidth = intTemp
End If
```

Next, the total number of lines in the document is calculated based on the height of the printing area and the height of the font:

```
Dim intLineCount As Int32 = CInt(intPrintAreaHeight / font.Height)
```

Then a rectangle structure that defines the printing area is created:

```
Dim rectPrintingArea As New RectangleF(marginLeft, marginTop, _
    intPrintAreaWidth, intPrintAreaHeight)
```

The *StringFormat* class encapsulates text layout information (such as alignment and line spacing), display manipulations (such as ellipsis insertion and national digit substitution), and *OpenType* features. The use of *String-Format* causes *MeasureString* and *DrawString* to use only an integer number of lines when printing each page, ignoring partial lines that would otherwise likely be printed if the number of lines per page did not divide up cleanly for each page (which is usually the case):

```
Dim fmt As New StringFormat(StringFormatFlags.LineLimit)
```

MeasureString is used to determine the number of characters that will fit in the printing area rectangle. *intCharFitted* is passed *ByRef* and used later when calculating *intCurrentChar* and *HasMorePages*. *intLinesFilled* isn't really needed for this sample except that it must be passed when passing *intChars-Fitted*. *Mid* is used to pass the segment of remaining text left off of the previous page of printing:

```
Dim intLinesFilled, intCharsFitted As Int32
e.Graphics.MeasureString(Mid(txtDocument.Text, intCurrentChar + 1), font, _
    New SizeF(intPrintAreaWidth, intPrintAreaHeight), fmt, _
    intCharsFitted, intLinesFilled)
```

Finally, the text is printed to the page using the *DrawString* method of the *Graphics* object:

```
e.Graphics.DrawString(Mid(txtDocument.Text, intCurrentChar + 1), font, _
    Brushes.Black, rectPrintingArea, fmt)
```

Before finishing, a few more things need to be done. First, *intCurrentChar* needs to be updated to include the number of characters that have been printed thus far. Because *intCurrentChar* is a static variable, its value is retained for the next *PrintPage* event:

```
intCurrentChar += intCharsFitted
```

Second, *HasMorePages* needs to be set to indicate whether the print document is complete. Remember that the *PrintPage* event will continue to fire until *HasMorePages* is set to *False*. Also, because *intCurrentChar* is a static variable, it must be explicitly reset in case there's another print job:

```
If intCurrentChar < txtDocument.Text.Length Then
    e.HasMorePages = True
Else
    e.HasMorePages = False
    intCurrentChar = 0
End If
End Sub
```

Conclusion

This sample application covered a lot of material. To review, the *Print-Document* class is used to send a document to the printer. When adding print support to your applications, the *PrintDocument* object should be declared as a module-level variable in the declarations section of the Windows Form. To begin the printing process, the *PrintDocument Print* method is called and the *PrintPage* event is raised for each page that is to be printed. The *PrintPage* event handler contains all the code that is necessary to print. In addition to providing the *PrintDocument* class, Visual Basic .NET also provides *PrintPreview-Dialog*, *PrintDialog*, and *PageSetupDialog* classes. The *PrintPreviewDialog* displays what the document will look like before it's sent to the printer. The *PrintDialog* class displays the standard Windows Print dialog box that allows the user to change printers, select a print range, and set the number of copies to be printed. Finally, the *PageSetupDialog* lets the user change various settings related to the printed page. This sample application only showed how to print simple text, but many other types of documents can be printed, such as reports, charts, and graphics. As you dig deeper into the *System.Drawing* namespace, you'll discover that printing with Visual Basic .NET is very powerful and that this sample only scratches the surface of what is possible.

Application #42: Associate Help with an Application

One of the most important things that developers can do for their end users is to provide them with a competent and easy-to-use help system for their applications. A number of controls are provided by the .NET Framework for building a help system. Among these are the *ToolTip*, *HelpProvider*, and *ErrorProvider* controls. This sample application, shown in Figure 4-23, will demonstrate how to use these controls to create a more helpful and user-friendly environment in a Windows Forms application.

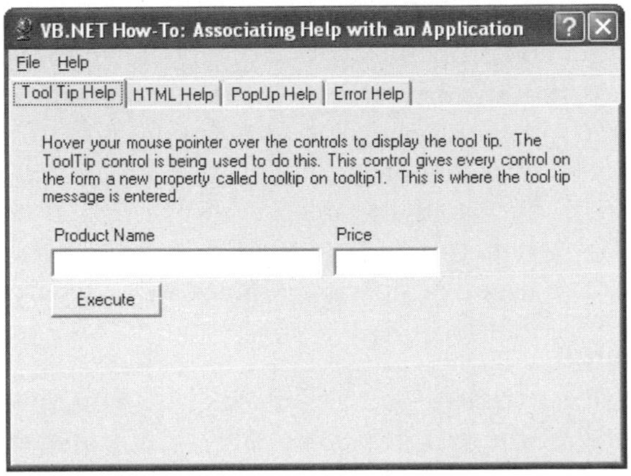

Figure 4-23 The main screen of Application #42, which demonstrates how to provide users of an application with an effective help system.

The sample application uses a simple interface that has a series of tab pages for demonstrating different methods of providing help to the user. Each tab page contains a number of controls along with one or more help features tied to them. The first tab page will demonstrate how the *ToolTip* class can be used to clarify the purpose of controls when the user hovers the mouse over them. The second tab uses the *HelpProvider* control to pop up messages for each control on the form as they are clicked. The third tab shows the ability of the *HelpProvider* control to provide links to compiled help documents or basic HTML help pages. The last tab demonstrates how the *ErrorProvider* control can be used to notify a user of invalid input.

New Concepts

This sample application introduces the *ToolTip* control, the *HelpProvider* control, and the *ErrorProvider* control. The following sections discuss these controls in more detail.

The *ToolTip* Control

The *ToolTip* control displays text to a user as a ToolTip when the user hovers the mouse over a control. A ToolTip can be associated with any control on a form (*Button*, *TextBox*, *PictureBox*, and so on) and should provide a short but meaningful explanation of the purpose of the control. A *ToolTip* control can handle multiple controls, so only one *ToolTip* control is needed for all items on a form.

The two main methods of the *ToolTip* control are *SetToolTip* and *GetToolTip*. The *SetToolTip* method is used to set the help text displayed for each control. *GetToolTip* retrieves the text associated with a specified control. The *ToolTip* control also has several properties that allow the developer to customize its behavior. For example, the *Active* property allows you to toggle the ToolTips on or off. The *InitialDelay* property is used to set the amount of time that the user must hover the mouse over a control before the ToolTip will appear. The *AutoPopDelay* property sets the length of time the ToolTip is shown. To change how long it takes for subsequent ToolTip windows to appear as the user moves the mouse from one control to the next, use the *ReshowDelay* property.

The *HelpProvider* Control

The *HelpProvider* control is used to associate help files with an application. The *HelpNamespace* property of the *HelpProvider* control indicates the path of a help document. As previously mentioned, these help files can be either compiled help documents (.chm) or HTML pages (.htm). The *Help* object is part of the *System.Windows.Forms* namespace and represents the HTML Help engine. It works in tandem with the *HelpProvider* control to provide help functionality to an application. The *Help* object has several shared methods that are used to launch the help files associated with the application.

There are several ways that the *HelpProvider* control can be used to provide help to an end user. First, context-sensitive help can be associated with individual controls on a Windows Form. Second, context-sensitive help can also be provided for a dialog box or controls within it. Finally, a help file can be opened at a specific location within the file, such as a table of contents or search area. The sample application demonstrates the first method.

The *ErrorProvider* Control

The *ErrorProvider* control provides an effective means of providing visual feedback during data validation. The *ErrorProvider* control will display an error icon next to each control that contains invalid data. The first advantage of using this control is that the error is displayed to the user until the invalid data has been corrected. The second, even more important advantage is that the *Error-Provider* control in no way interrupts users as they enter data. This contrasts strongly with the older, more conventional technique of displaying an error message in a message box. A message box is easy to code, but it has the unfortunate consequence of interrupting whatever the user might be doing. What's more, a user cannot proceed until the message box is dismissed. The *Error-Provider* control does not have these drawbacks. Plus, as Figure 4-24 shows, the *ErrorProvider* control shows the error message whenever the user hovers the mouse pointer over the error icon.

The most important properties of the *ErrorProvider* control are the *ContainerControl* and *Icon* properties. The *ContainerControl* property is set to the container that holds the controls to be validated, generally a Windows Form. The *Icon* property indicates the image that should be shown when an error needs to be communicated to the user. The *SetError* method is used to specify the error message to be displayed and where the icon should appear.

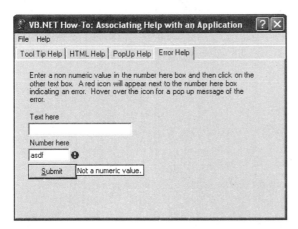

Figure 4-24   *ErrorProvider* control in action.

Code Walkthrough

This code walkthrough discusses the code for each of the sample application's tabs: Tool Tip Help, HTML Help, PopUp Help, and Error Help.

Tool Tip Help

The properties of the *ToolTip* control were set at design time, so the following code is found in the Windows Form Designer generated code:

```
Me.ToolTip1.SetToolTip(Me.btnExecute, "Execute the Query")
Me.ToolTip1.SetToolTip(Me.txtPrice, "Enter a price.")
Me.ToolTip1.SetToolTip(Me.txtProductName, "Enter a product name.")
```

The *SetToolTip* method is used to associate *ToolTip* messages with each control on the ToolTip Help tab.

HTML Help

As previously mentioned, the *HelpProvider* control and *Help* object work together to display .chm and .htm Help files to the user. First, the *ShowHelp* method is used in the *mnuContentsHelp_Click* event handler to display the contents of a help file:

```
Help.ShowHelp(Me, hpAdvancedCHM.HelpNamespace)
```

The first parameter indicates the parent control of the Help window. The second parameter is the *HelpNamespace* property of the *HelpProvider* control.

This property specifies the URL of the Help file. Next, *ShowHelpIndex* is used in the *mnuIndexHelp_Click* event handler to display the index for the Help file. These parameters are the same as for the *ShowHelp* method:

```
Help.ShowHelpIndex(Me, hpAdvancedCHM.HelpNamespace)
```

Finally, *ShowHelp* is again called, but this time two additional parameters are given. The following code is found in the *mnuSearchHelp_Click* event handler:

```
Help.ShowHelp(Me, hpAdvancedCHM.HelpNamespace, _
    HelpNavigator.Find, "")
```

The third parameter can be any one of the *HelpNavigator* enumerations. This enumeration specifies constants indicating which elements of the Help file to display and include *TableOfContents*, *Find*, *Index*, and *Topic*. *HelpNavigator.Find* indicates that the search page of the URL should be displayed. The last parameter references an object that contains the value of the specific topic within the Help file to display. If a *HelpNavigator* enumeration is supplied, this parameter should be empty.

Popup Help

The *SetHelpString* method of the *HelpProvider* control is used to associate a help string with a specified control. This string is displayed in a pop-up window when the user presses the F1 key while the specified control has focus. Again, inspect the Windows Form Designer–generated code:

```
Me.hpAdvancedCHM.SetHelpString(Me.rtbTextEntry, "This is the text " & _
    "entry area. Use this area to enter text which can be saved to " & _
    "an rtf file.")
Me.hpAdvancedCHM.SetShowHelp(Me.rtbTextEntry, True)
```

The *SetShowHelp* method is used to indicate whether or not a help message should be displayed for a given control. Pass in *True* to specify that the message should be shown and *False* to turn off the context-sensitive help feature.

Error Help

The last tab is the Error Help tab. Here, the value of *txtNumberValue* is validated at run time when focus is given to the *txtTextValue* text-box control. The *ErrorProvider* control is used to alert the user when invalid data is entered. In the *txtNumberValue_Validating* event handler, the value in the *txtNumberValue* text box is checked. Only numeric values are valid.

```
If Not IsNumeric(txtNumberValue.Text) Then
    ErrorProvider1.SetError(txtNumberValue, _
        "Not a numeric value.")
```

If the value entered is not numeric, the error message string is populated, causing the error icon to be displayed to the user. The string becomes a ToolTip for the error icon on the form. If the value is valid, the error message string is cleared, causing the icon to be hidden:

```
Else
    ErrorProvider1.SetError(txtNumberValue, "")
```

Conclusion

Windows applications should provide a means of giving help to the end users. This help can come in many forms. This sample demonstrated various ways that help features can be added to a Windows Forms application using the *ErrorProvider*, *HelpProvider*, and *ToolTip* controls. The *ToolTip* control provides ToolTips for controls on the form. The *HelpProvider* control supplies links to the help documents related to the application. Finally, the *ErrorProvider* control displays user-friendly error information to aid users in entering data.

Application #43: XP Theme Support

Windows XP introduced the concept of themes to the Windows user-interface experience. A theme is a set of icons, fonts, colors, and other elements that give a user's desktop a distinctive and unified appearance. Not only does this include a new look for the Start button and taskbar, it also changes the look of many standard Windows controls, such as the *Button*, *ComboBox*, *Radio*, and *TextBox* controls. As a Visual Basic .NET programmer, you might want to take advantage of Windows XP themes in your programs. This sample application will show you how to enable support for Windows XP themes by using Visual Basic .NET. Figure 4-25 shows how applications look without Windows XP themes enabled. Figure 4-26 shows how applications look with Windows XP themes enabled.

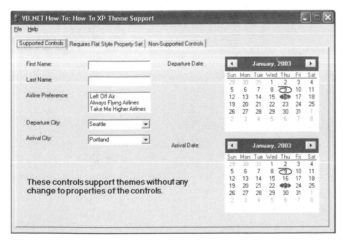

Figure 4-25   Application interface without Windows XP themes enabled.

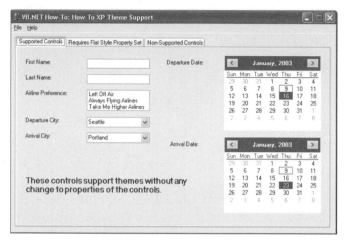

Figure 4-26 Application interface with Windows XP themes enabled.

Building Upon...

Application #28: Work with XML DOM
Application #29: Use the *ListBox* and *ComboBox*

New Concepts

This sample application shows you how to add support for Windows XP themes to your Visual Basic .NET applications. Adding this support is easy to do. In fact, there are only two steps required:

1. Set each control's *FlatStyle* property to *FlatStyle.System*.

2. Create a manifest file for the application.

The following sections discuss in more detail how to accomplish these tasks.

Setting *FlatStyle* to *FlatStyle.System*

The first step to enabling Windows XP theme support in Visual Basic .NET is to set every control that has a *FlatStyle* property to *FlatStyle.System*. This indicates that the operating system should use the default system style for each control, as illustrated in Figure 4-27.

Not all Windows Forms controls have a *FlatStyle* property—for example, the *TextBox* control doesn't have one. For these controls, you need to do nothing special.

Figure 4-27   Set the *FlatStyle* property to *System*.

You might be wondering why *FlatStyle.System* isn't the default for Windows Forms controls. The reason is that Windows Forms controls support additional features not available in the system default style. Certain properties such as background colors and background images cannot be used when *FlatStyle* is set to *FlatStyle.System*. Making *FlatStyle.Standard* the default value of the *FlatStyle* property allows you to use these properties out of the box.

Creating the Manifest File

The second step to enabling Windows XP theme support in Visual Basic .NET applications is to create a manifest file for your application. The manifest file is a simple text file that is used at run time by the operating system to enable Windows XP theme support. The manifest file should go into the same directory as the compiled application and should have the same name as the EXE plus a *.manifest* extension. For example, if an application's name is MyApp.exe, the manifest file should be named *MyApp.exe.manifest*. Only one manifest file is required per application, even if it consists of multiple dynamic-link libraries (DLLs).

Code Walkthrough

Because control properties are generally set at design time using the Properties window, there is very little code to walk through. So the code walkthrough for this sample application will focus on the manifest file. Here are the complete contents of the sample application's manifest file:

```
<?xml version="1.0" encoding="UTF-8" standalone="yes" ?>
<assembly xmlns="urn:schemas-microsoft-com:asm.v1" manifestVersion="1.0">
    <assemblyIdentity
        version="1.0.0.0"
        processorArchitecture="X86"
```

(continued)

```
            name="Microsoft.Winweb.MantaRay" type="win32"
    />
    <description>
        VB.NET How-To XP Theme Support
    </description>
    <dependency>
        <dependentAssembly>
            <assemblyIdentity
                type="win32"
                name="Microsoft.Windows.Common-Controls"
                version="6.0.0.0"
                processorArchitecture="X86"
                publicKeyToken="6595b64144ccf1df"
                language="*"
            />
        </dependentAssembly>
    </dependency>
</assembly>
```

The first and most obvious thing to note is that the manifest file is a standard text file containing XML. A manifest file contains run-time information about an application. It is used to indicate whether an application should bind to a certain version of a dependent file. This information is contained within the *<dependentAssembly>* tag. Note that the sample's manifest file says that the application should use *Microsoft.Windows.Common-Controls*, version 6.0.0.0. This is no coincidence, as this is the version that introduced support for Windows XP themes.

Also, this same manifest file will work with any Visual Basic .NET application for which Windows XP theme support is to be enabled. All you need to do is make sure the manifest is named properly and is in the correct directory. Again, the name of the manifest file should be the same as the executable with *.manifest* appended to it. For example, the sample application's executable filename is "VB.NET How-To XP Theme Support.exe" and the manifest filename is "VB.NET How-To XP Theme Support.exe.manifest". Both the executable and manifest files should reside in the same directory. By following these two steps, you can add Windows XP theme support to all your applications.

Conclusion

Enabling support for Windows XP themes is easy to do with Visual Basic .NET. First, for every control that has a *FlatStyle* property, simply change its value to *FlatStyle.System*. Second, create a manifest file and place it in the same directory as your application's executable file. You can copy the one supplied with the sample application for use in your program. All you have to do is make sure the manifest file is named correctly and is in the same directory as the executable. At run time, your application will automatically use the information contained in the manifest file to enable Windows XP theme support.

Application #44: Inherited Windows Forms

When designing an application that contains a large number of forms, it's often desirable to keep those forms consistent. Using forms inheritance can help to ensure that cross-project consistency is attained. It can also cut down on development time during your initial development phase and while maintaining and enhancing the application. Because a form is really just a class, a base form can be designed that will serve as a basis for all the forms in an application. Logos, menus, and standard command buttons can be coded once and then propagated throughout an application with very little effort. This sample application, shown in Figure 4-28, will demonstrate how visual inheritance is used with Windows Forms.

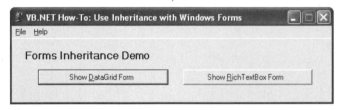

Figure 4-28   Application interface – Main Form.

The sample application includes several forms. The main form has two command buttons on it. The first button, ShowDataGrid Form, brings up a form that displays database information in a *DataGrid* control, as Figure 4-29 illustrates.

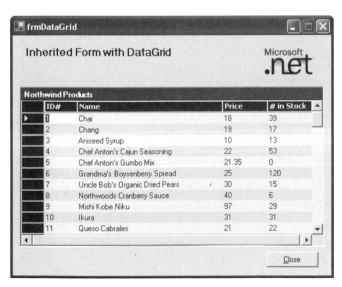

Figure 4-29   Inherited form with *DataGrid* control.

The second button, Show RichTextBox Form, brings up a form that displays the same database information as the first form, but uses a *RichTextBox* control, as shown in Figure 4-30.

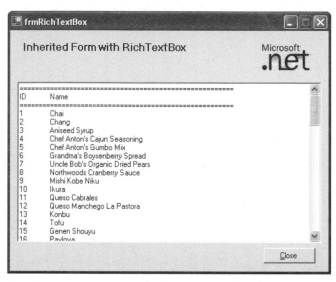

Figure 4-30   Inherited form with *RichTextBox* control.

Both forms inherit from a single base form named *frmBase*. This base form includes a *Button* control and several *Label* controls, has several properties set to customize its appearance, and includes a function for returning a *DataSet* object. The base form also has an empty area reserved so that it can be populated with database information by the derived forms.

Building Upon...

Application #7: Object-Oriented Features
Application #12: Use a *DataSet* and *DataView*

New Concepts

Visual inheritance can be thought of as the implementation inheritance of a visual object. This might seem complicated, but the idea is roughly similar to using an ActiveX control on a Visual Basic 6 form. The difference is that you now have reusability at the form level.

Inheriting forms allows for standardization across entire projects, a task that would have been difficult in the days of Visual Basic 6. This is a powerful new feature. Now, common elements of your forms can be encapsulated in a single base class that derives from *System.Windows.Forms.Form*. Forms that inherit from this base class are "born" with controls, properties, and functionality without the developer having to write any additional code. In addition, as changes are proposed for the common portions of your forms, they need to be changed in only one place rather than in all the forms in your application. Simply make the changes in the base class and recompile the application.

Creating a base class for a form is just like creating any other base class. Start with a Visual Basic Windows Application Project. Add to the base form any controls, functions, and property values that will be common throughout the application. Keep in mind that if the derived forms need to be able to change any inherited items, those items should be defined as *Protected* (or *Public*) in the base class. *Private* functions, properties, and controls will be inherited but cannot be altered by a derived class.

Once the base class has been defined, use the *Inherits* keyword to create a derived form. From within the derived form, you can modify and access all the public and protected controls of the base form, including making changes to their locations and properties. In the Visual Studio .NET Windows Forms designer, the inherited controls are identified by a small arrow that appears in the top-left corner of each control. Last, add any new controls or additional functionality to your derived form. You now have a new form that uses all the traits of the base form, plus any new functionality that is unique to this form.

Code Walkthrough

The sample application uses three forms to illustrate the creation and use of inherited Windows Forms: *frmBase*, *frmDataGrid*, and *frmRichTextBox*. The following sections discuss each of these forms in detail.

frmBase

In the sample application, *frmBase* serves as the base class from which other forms are derived. It therefore inherits from *System.Windows.Forms.Form*:

```
Inherits System.Windows.Forms.Form
```

Next, two connection strings are defined for accessing the database through either SQL Server or MSDE. If the connection string changes, only the code in the base class needs to be updated and all derived forms will automatically see the change.

```
Protected Const SQL_CONNECTION_STRING As String = _
    "Server=localhost;" & _
    "DataBase=Northwind;" & _
    "Integrated Security=SSPI"

Protected Const MSDE_CONNECTION_STRING As String = _
    "Server=(local)\NetSDK;" & _
    "DataBase=Northwind;" & _
    "Integrated Security=SSPI"
```

frmBase also contains a number of controls that will be inherited by derived classes. The control declarations can be found in the Windows Forms Designer–generated code:

```
Friend WithEvents lblTitle As System.Windows.Forms.Label
Friend WithEvents btnClose As System.Windows.Forms.Button
Friend WithEvents PictureBox1 As System.Windows.Forms.PictureBox
Protected WithEvents lblProtected As System.Windows.Forms.Label
Private WithEvents lblPrivate As System.Windows.Forms.Label
```

Controls defined using the *Friend* keyword are accessible from within the form that contains their declaration and from anywhere else in the same project. Controls defined as *Protected* are accessible only from within the base class or from within classes derived from the base class. Finally, controls defined as *Private* are accessible only from within the base class.

The data access function is accessible within the base class and all derived classes as well. Here, the *Protected* keyword is used:

```
Protected Function GetDataSource() As DataSet
```

All the controls, properties, and functionality defined in the base class will be inherited by derived forms. As previously mentioned, the new forms can also add new functionality to that which was inherited from the base class.

frmDataGrid

frmDataGrid is the first form that inherits from the *frmBase* base class. The *Inherits* keyword is used to specify the class being inherited from:

```
Public Class frmDataGrid
    Inherits frmBase
```

The *btnClose* control is one of the controls inherited from the base class. No event handler was defined in the base class, so the derived classes are responsible for providing that code. The *btnClose_Click* event handler contains code to close the form when the Close button is clicked:

```
Private Sub btnClose_Click(ByVal sender As Object, _
    ByVal e As System.EventArgs) Handles btnClose.Click
    Me.Close()
End Sub
```

The base class also provides the function for connecting to the database and retrieving information from it. In the *frmDataGrid_Load* event handler, the *GetDataSource* function that was inherited from the base class is called to populate the *DataGrid* control:

```
With dgProducts
    .CaptionText = "Northwind Products"
    .DataSource = GetDataSource().Tables(0)
End With
```

Finally, after the data has been retrieved and displayed in the *DataGrid* control, the title of the form is set:

```
lblTitle.Text = "Inherited Form with DataGrid"
```

frmRichTextBox

Like *frmDataGrid*, *frmRichTextBox* also inherits from the *frmBase* class:

```
Public Class frmRichTextBox
    Inherits frmBase
```

Again, the *GetDataSource* function that was inherited from the base class is called to populate the *RichTextBox* control. The following code can be found in the *frmRichTextBox_Load* event handler:

```
Dim ds As DataSet = GetDataSource()
```

Finally, the *lblTitle* control *Text* property is changed by the derived class:

```
lblTitle.Text = "Inherited Form with RichTextBox"
```

Conclusion

Visual inheritance is a powerful new feature of Visual Basic .NET. It allows a common set of features to be implemented across multiple forms in an application with minimal effort by developers. It also reduces the amount of time and effort involved in updating common elements across multiple forms in a large application. This sample demonstrates how visual inheritance can be used to standardize the look and feel of multiple forms in an application, as well as to effectively reuse large pieces of code.

Application #45: Create Top-Level Forms

Many document-based applications employ a user-interface paradigm that displays each document window as a top-level window. This makes it appear as if multiple instances of the same program are running at the same time but without wasting system resources. This sample application, shown in Figure 4-31, demonstrates a technique that allows you to use this interface model in your applications.

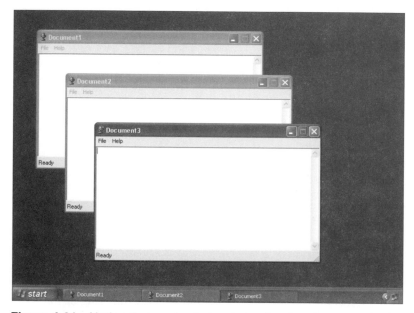

Figure 4-31 Notice that each window is top-level and appears in the taskbar as a separate program.

The sample application is a simple text editor. Each new document appears as a top-level window. The user can use the Windows taskbar or Alt+Tab to switch between document windows.

Building Upon...

Application #7: Object-Oriented Features

New Concepts

This application describes how to create applications with top-level forms. Top-level forms are sometimes used by document-centric applications, such as Microsoft Word and Microsoft Excel. Each time the user opens a new document or spreadsheet, it's shown as a top-level window. This enables the user to use Alt+Tab to switch between the documents as if they were each a separate process, but without the overhead incurred by loading each document into a separate process. The user can also switch between documents by using the Windows taskbar.

Creating Multiple Open Forms

The sample application starts in the *Sub Main* routine inside a class named *Forms*. This *Forms* class controls execution flow by launching and managing each document window. When the application begins, *Sub Main* sets the main thread to run outside the control of a particular form so that closing one document does not terminate the whole process. This is accomplished by calling the *Run* method of the *Application* object. Each time the user selects New from the File menu, the *Forms* class creates a new document window. When the user closes a document window by choosing Close from the File menu, an event is raised back to the *Forms* class. This lets the *Forms* class keep track of all the document windows. When the final document window is closed, the entire application shuts down. The user can also exit the program by selecting Exit from the File menu.

Code Walkthrough

The *Forms* class contains the *Sub Main* routine, which launches the application and manages program execution. This code walkthrough will begin by examining the declarations section of the *Forms* class:

```
Public Class Forms
    Private Shared m_Forms As New Collection()
    Private Shared m_FormsCreated As Integer = 0
```

m_Forms is a *Collection* object that manages a list of open document forms. Other forms such as the *About* form will not be in this list. Instead, only instances of *frmMain* will be added to this collection because only *frmMain* serves as the document window. *m_FormsCreated* is a counter for keeping track of the total number of document windows that have been opened. This counter is used in creating a default title for each new document window.

The *Forms* class *Sub Main* routine serves as the startup object for the sample application:

```
Public Shared Sub Main()
    Try
        NewForm()
    Catch exp As Exception
        MessageBox.Show("Sorry, we were unable to load a document", _
            "Application Main", MessageBoxButtons.OK, MessageBoxIcon.Error)
        Application.Exit()
    End Try

    Application.Run()
End Sub
```

NewForm is a routine that opens a document window. By calling this routine within *Sub Main*, the first document window is opened by default. A *Try/Catch/End Try* exception block is used to handle any possible errors. Finally, *Application.Run()* sets the application's main thread to run outside the control of a particular form so that closing one document window will not terminate the entire application.

The *NewForm* routine handles creating each new document window. *NewForm* is called when the application starts up (from *Sub Main*) and when the user selects New from the File menu:

```
m_FormsCreated += 1
Dim frm As New frmMain()
frm.Text = "Document" & Forms.m_FormsCreated.ToString()
m_Forms.Add(frm, frm.GetHashCode.ToString())
```

First, the *m_FormsCreated* counter is incremented. Then a new instance of *frmMain* is created and its caption text is set to display the document number. Finally, the document window is added to the *m_Forms* collection.

After the document window is created, a series of event handlers are wired to handle certain events of the document window. This lets *Forms* keep track of when each document window is closing and when the application is ending:

```
AddHandler frm.Closed, AddressOf Forms.frmMain_Closed
AddHandler frm.SaveWhileClosingCancelled, _
    AddressOf Forms.frmMain_SaveWhileClosingCancelled
AddHandler frm.ExitApplication, _
    AddressOf Forms.frmMain_ExitApplication
```

Finally, the *Show* method of the document window is called so that the form is displayed on screen:

```
frm.Show()
```

Users can open as many document windows as they would like without unduly consuming system resources.

Conclusion

Some document-based applications, such as Microsoft Word and Microsoft Excel support multiple windows, one per open document, displayed as top-level windows. This sample application demonstrates how to use this technique in your own document-centric applications.

Application #46: Dynamic Control Creation

This sample application demonstrates how to build a program that dynamically creates controls on the fly to generate its user interface. The sample application consists of two main forms. The first form allows the user to add *Button* and *TextBox* controls to the form at run time by clicking a *Button* control, as shown in Figure 4-32.

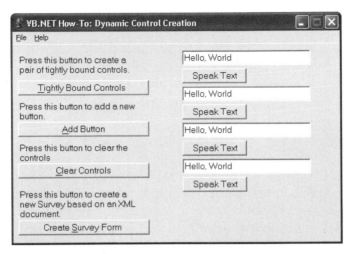

Figure 4-32 The main form of the sample application allows the user to dynamically create controls on the form.

The second form is a survey form that asks the user a series of questions. These questions are contained in a separate XML file. As the form is created, the application reads the data in the XML file to generate its user interface, as shown in Figure 4-33.

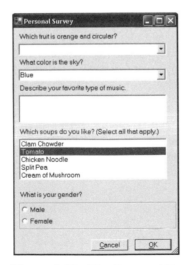

Figure 4-33 The Personal Survey form is dynamically created at run time.

> ## Building Upon...
>
> Application #7: Object-Oriented Features
> Application #29: Use the *ListBox* and *ComboBox*

New Concepts

This application illustrates the use of tightly bound controls, and adding and clearing controls. Each of these concepts is described in more detail in the following sections.

Tightly Bound Controls

Clicking the Tightly Bound Controls button will add two controls to the form— a *TextBox* control and a *Button* control. The user can type text into the *TextBox*, and when he clicks the *Button* control, a message box will be displayed showing what the user typed. Event handlers are declared beforehand and wired to the controls' events after the controls have been created. The "Code Walkthrough" section will demonstrate how this is done.

Adding and Clearing Controls

To add a control to a Windows Form at run time, first declare and instantiate an object of the type of control you want. For example,

```
Dim txtNewTextBox As New TextBox
```

creates a new *TextBox* control. Then set its properties, such as *Name*, *MultiLine*, and *MaxLength*. In particular, you need to set its *Size* and *Location* so that the control is properly sized and placed on the form. It is also recommended that each new control be added to the *Controls* collection of the form. This can be done using the *Add* method of the *Controls* collection. Finally, use the *AddHandler* statement to wire up any event procedures to the control's events.

To remove a control from a form, follow these steps. First, unwire any event procedures using the *RemoveHandler* statement. Second, remove the control from the *Controls* collection. Finally, call the control's *Dispose* method. This will allow the control to be unloaded from the form.

Code Walkthrough

The declarations section of the sample application's main form defines several variables and constants:

```
Private Const CONTROL_WIDTH As Integer = 300
Private Const CHARS_PER_LINE As Integer = 30
Private Const HEIGHT_PER_LINE As Integer = 19

Private m_ControlCount As Integer = 0
Private m_Location As New Point(10, 10)
```

The constants are used to properly position the controls on the form. The variable, *m_ControlCount*, is used to keep track of the number of tightly bound control pairs that are created. For simplicity's sake, the user is allowed to create only a maximum of five control pairs before the form runs out of room. The *m_Location* variable is used to keep track of the placement of the last control added to the form. This variable is needed to keep the controls from overlapping.

The Tightly Bound Controls Button

The *btnTightlyBoundControls_Click* subroutine handles the Tightly Bound Controls button's *Click* event by creating two tightly bound controls. The two controls created are the *Button* and *TextBox* controls. The subroutine uses event handlers that have been previously defined to handle the events. When the *Button* is pressed, the text in the *TextBox* is displayed in a message box.

Looking at the code, the first step is to declare and instantiate a *TextBox* object:

```
Dim txtSpeakText As New TextBox()
```

Then various properties for the *TextBox* need to be set:

```
txtSpeakText.Text = "Hello, World"
txtSpeakText.Name = "txtSpeakText"
txtSpeakText.Location = New Point(m_Location.X + 250, m_Location.Y)
txtSpeakText.Size = New Size(200, txtSpeakText.Height)
```

Next, the *TextBox* is added to the *Controls* collection:

```
Controls.Add(txtSpeakText)
```

m_Location is a module-level variable that keeps track of the position of the last control that was dynamically created. As mentioned previously, this positioning information is needed so that the controls don't overlap each other:

```
m_Location.Y += txtSpeakText.Height + 5
```

After creating the *TextBox* control, a *Button* control is created. As you can see, the code to dynamically create a *Button* control is the same as the code for dynamically creating a *TextBox* control:

```
Dim btnSpeakText As New Button()

btnSpeakText.Text = "Speak Text"
btnSpeakText.Name = "btnSpeakText"
```

(continued)

```
btnSpeakText.Location = New Point(m_Location.X + 250, m_Location.Y)
btnSpeakText.Size = New Size(100, btnSpeakText.Height)

btnSpeakText.Tag = txtSpeakText

Controls.Add(btnSpeakText)

m_Location.Y += btnSpeakText.Height + 5
```

Only one line of code is new. This sets the *Tag* property of the *Button* control to the newly created *TextBox* control. This is needed to keep track of which *Button* is associated with which *TextBox*.

Finally, the *AddHandler* statement is used to wire up the button's *Click* event procedure with the button's *Click* event:

```
AddHandler btnSpeakText.Click, AddressOf SpeakTextClickHandler
```

The Clear Controls Button

This *btnClearControls_Click* event procedure clears all the dynamically generated controls on the form. It does this by removing all the controls from the *Controls* collection and calling the *InitializeComponent* subroutine. *InitializeComponent* was automatically generated by the Visual Studio .NET Windows Forms Designer. This is an easy way of resetting a form to its original state. The *GetAssemblyAttributes* subroutine is used to reset the text of each form's caption to the name of the application. The module-level variables, *m_Location* and *m_ControlCount* are also re-initialized to default values:

```
Private Sub btnClearControls_Click(ByVal sender As System.Object, _
    ByVal e As System.EventArgs) Handles btnClearControls.Click

    Controls.Clear()

    InitializeComponent()

    GetAssemblyAttributes()

    m_Location = New Point(10, 10)

    m_ControlCount = 0

    Show()

End Sub
```

Conclusion

This sample application demonstrates how to perform dynamic control creation. It also shows how to add these controls to and remove these controls from the *Controls* collection of the *Form* and how to add and remove event handlers at run time. Using the techniques presented in this sample, you should be able to create dynamic user interfaces in your Visual Basic .NET applications.

5

Building Web Applications

One of the wonderful aspects of Microsoft .NET development is how easy it is to leverage your skills between the Microsoft Windows and Web Forms worlds. Much of the code is, of course, reusable; but even more important are the close similarities in development methodology. Thanks to new features in Microsoft Visual Studio .NET, developers with Windows Forms experience can quickly learn how to build Web applications.

What follows are two three-application series that endeavor to equip you with some foundational skills for building robust Web applications. You will first learn how to build various types of data manipulation interfaces that are centered mainly around the *DataGrid* control. The final three applications cover the topic of Web services. These are also Web applications. However, they primarily expose their application logic not to humans via a user-friendly interface, but rather to remote applications using cross-platform open standards such as XML, SOAP (Simple Object Access Protocol), and HTTP. In this regard, these applications are the *new COM* and provide a way to make the Internet a truly shared-application environment.

Application #47: Build Data-Entry Web Forms

Data entry in the form of a standard CRUD (Create, Read, Update, Delete) interface is an integral feature of many Web applications. This sample introduces you to ASP.NET and demonstrates how to build a data-entry Web form for products in the Northwind database. A *DataGrid* is used to display the products. Each row contains buttons to edit and delete the product. You can also click the Add New Item button located above the *DataGrid*. (See Figure 5-1.) Clicking the buttons to add or edit displays a simple entry form below the *DataGrid*.

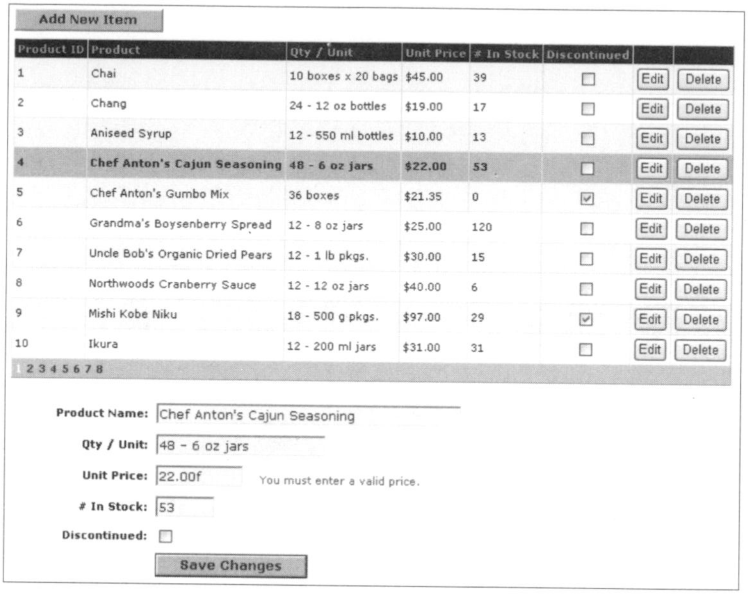

Figure 5-1 Application #47 showing the *DataGrid* and Add New Item Form controls.

Building Upon...

Application #4: *Try/Catch/Finally*
Application #12: Use a *DataSet* and *DataView*
Application #20: Build a Data-Entry Form
Application #27: Compare Data Binding in Web and Windows Forms

New Concepts

Space limitations for this book require us to assume you already have a basic understanding of foundational Web-application concepts such as the stateless nature of the Web and the life cycle of an ASP.NET Web Form. (If this isn't the case, see the upcoming "Tip.") Given this, building a Web-based data-entry application is conceptually identical to building a Windows Forms data-entry application. The data access logic is identical. (In fact, you may recall from Application #21 that one of the advantages of decoupling data-access code from the presentation tier is that you can reuse it with any type of front end.) And although a few differences in data-binding syntax exist, these were covered towards the end of Chapter 3. Therefore, the focus of this topic and the next two topics is on the "Code Walkthrough" sections so that ample space can be given to the implementation details.

> **Tip**   If you're new to ASP.NET or need to refresh your understanding of basic, yet critical, Web Forms development concepts, a great place to start is the series of pages in the Framework documentation under the heading "Introduction to Web Forms Pages." This documentation can be found by typing **Web Forms, about** in the Look For field of the Help browser's Index tab. Then click the Sync Contents button on the toolbar and you'll be shown how these introductory pages fit into the overall table of contents. Of particular importance is the document titled "Web Forms Page Processing" (vbconWebFormsPage-ProcessingStages.htm).

Code Walkthrough

This code walkthrough is divided into two main sections, "The .ASPX Page" and "The Codebehind Page." This is an arbitrary but convenient division that follows the practice of many Web developers who like to first lay out their controls on the Web Form and then wire them up by adding code to the .aspx.vb file.

> **Best Practices**   Although for logistical and pedagogical reasons the Framework Quickstart Tutorials include Visual Basic .NET code in the .aspx page itself, it's considered a best practice to put this code in the Web Form codebehind page whenever possible, restricting the contents of the .aspx page to markup elements such as HTML, CSS, and ASP.NET control-declaration syntax. Some programming tasks, however, are more cumbersome when using strongly typed code as opposed to ASP.NET tags and attributes. As a rule of thumb, if any given task is more difficult to implement in the codebehind, move it to the .aspx page. When you do this, however, keep in mind you might lose some of the benefits that strong typing affords, such as IntelliSense and precompiler error checking.

The .ASPX Page: *DataGrid*

The ASP.NET *DataGrid* is often the Web control of choice for displaying a set of records. With it, you can easily display data in a grid-like control that supports important data-interface features such as sorting and paging (topics that are covered in subsequent topics). The *DataGrid* is also flexible enough to allow ample control over how data in its cells is bound and formatted.

The ASP.NET syntax for working with a *DataGrid* can be quite simple. For example, if you were to change the code for this application's *DataGrid* control to the following, it would display Northwind products in a simple, yet fully functional, *DataGrid* that even supports paging:

```
<asp:datagrid id="grdProducts" runat="server" AutoGenerateColumns="True"
AllowPaging="True" />
```

If you were then to compare the *DataGrid* rendered using this line of code with the *DataGrid* in the previous screen shot, you would see that the only difference—aside from presentation style and data formatting—is the absence of the Edit and Delete button columns. Of course, these buttons are essential to a data-entry application. The point is that you can get pretty far with only one line of code. (The required codebehind logic, covered a bit later, would be identical.)

To configure a *DataGrid* for full use in a data-entry application, you must add and modify some *DataGrid* properties, as well as work directly with the *DataGridColumnsCollection* exposed by the *Columns* property. *DataGrid* properties are written as attributes of the *<asp:DataGrid>* tag:

```
<asp:datagrid id="grdProducts" runat="server" AutoGenerateColumns="False"
DataKeyField="ProductID" AllowPaging="True">
```

Following the standard *id* and *runat* attributes that accompany all ASP.NET controls, you find three additional attributes. Setting *AutoGenerate-Columns* to *False* will prevent the *DataGrid* from automatically displaying the data in bound columns. The default value is *True*, so if you want to create your own columns, this property must be set to *False*. (This is an all-or-nothing setting. You cannot set the *DataGrid* to autogenerate only a subset of the columns.) With the *DataKeyField* attribute, you can use a field in the data source as a key that can uniquely identify each row. You will see why this is important later in the code walkthrough. *AllowPaging* displays a subset of the records in the data source at any one time, allowing the user to page through the results. The *Link-Button* controls for paging appear at the bottom of the *DataGrid*. Javascript is automatically added to the page to invoke a *PageIndexChanged* event handler.

With these attributes set, you can get to work on writing the code that renders the columns. You do this by adding *DataGridColumn* objects to the *Data-*

GridColumnsCollection. The latter is declared on a Web Form by using the *<Columns>* tag. The *DataGridColumn* class is abstract. It serves as the base class for the column controls listed in Table 5-1.

Table 5-1   Implementations of the *DataGridColumn* Class

Class/Control Name	Purpose
BoundColumn	This is the most basic type of column that displays bound data. When *AutoGenerateColumns* is not set to *False*, the *DataGrid* automatically creates a *BoundColumn* control for each field in the data source and adds it to the *DataGrid-ColumnsCollection*.
ButtonColumn	Use this column to create a command button for each row in the *DataGrid*. Clicking a command button raises the *DataGrid.ItemCommand* event, which can be handled in the codebehind.
EditCommandColumn	Similar to a *ButtonColumn*, use this to add Edit, Update, and Delete command buttons for each row in the *DataGrid*. Each of these buttons is associated with a more specialized event, such as *UpdateCommand*.
HyperLinkColumn	This column renders its bound data as a hyperlink. Several properties are available to configure the hyperlink, such as *DataTextField* and *DataNavigateUrlField*. This is typically used for drill-down scenarios.
TemplateColumn	This column gives you the most control over how the data is presented. Use this when you need a custom solution that is not supported by the other column types.

This application uses five *BoundColumn* controls, a *TemplateColumn* control, and two *ButtonColumn* controls. Each control exposes a number of properties that can be set by using their equivalent tag attributes. To step through these in the order they appear in the *DataGrid*, you'd begin with the *BoundColumn* controls:

```
<Columns>
  <asp:BoundColumn DataField="ProductID" HeaderText="Product ID" />
  <asp:BoundColumn DataField="ProductName" HeaderText="Product" />
  <asp:BoundColumn DataField="QuantityPerUnit" HeaderText="Qty / Unit" />
  <asp:BoundColumn DataField="UnitPrice" HeaderText="Unit Price"
  DataFormatString="{0:c}" />
  <asp:BoundColumn DataField="UnitsInStock" HeaderText="# In Stock" />
```

The *DataField* attribute maps to a field in the data source for data binding. *DataFormatString* allows you to apply format codes to render the data in a variety of ways. Here, *c* denotes currency formatting.

Next is the *TemplateColumn*, which requires some explanation.

```
<asp:TemplateColumn ItemStyle-CssClass="Discontinued"
HeaderText="Discontinued">
  <ItemTemplate>
    <asp:CheckBox ID="chkDiscontinuedGrid" Runat="server"
    Checked='<%# CBool(Container.DataItem("Discontinued")) %>' />
  </ItemTemplate>
</asp:TemplateColumn>
```

Remember from Table 5-1 that this type of column gives you full control over the data binding and how it is rendered. A *TemplateColumn* was chosen here to display a *CheckBox* control that indicates whether a product has been discontinued. You can bind data to many different control properties, and the *Checked* property is no exception. Data-binding syntax takes the following form:

```
<%# CType(Container.DataItem("FieldName"), Type) %>
```

Notice the use of `<%# %>`, which delineates a data-binding expression. *Container.DataItem* will return an *Object* that you can then explicitly cast to the type needed. In the preceding code, the value of each row in the Discontinued column will be cast to a Boolean for binding to the *Checked* property.

Best Practices   You will often see an alternate form of data binding syntax: `<%# Databinder.Eval(Container.DataItem, "FieldName") %>`. *Databinder.Eval* always returns a string. (NULL values are converted to an empty string.) Although this consistency is a nice convenience for beginners, you should avoid using *Databinder.Eval* because it uses late binding for the string conversion. This can cause performance degradation.

Tip   One very nice feature of ASP.NET is the ability to data-bind to a function. This can open many doors, allowing you to implement complex logic to determine the data that ultimately gets rendered on the page. For example, you could write a *Public* function named *IsDiscontinued* that accepts a single argument of type *Object* and returns a *Boolean*. Your data-binding syntax would then look like this: `<%# IsDiscontinued(Container.DataItem("Discontinued")) %>`

The *ButtonColumn* controls use two self-explanatory attributes and a *CommandName* attribute that needs further elaboration:

```
<asp:ButtonColumn Text="Edit" ButtonType="PushButton"
CommandName="Edit" />
<asp:ButtonColumn Text="Delete" ButtonType="PushButton"
CommandName="Delete" />
</Columns>
```

The *DataGrid*, like the *DataList* and *Repeater* controls, supports *event bubbling*. This means that events raised in a child control *bubble up* to the containing control so that you don't have to write an event handler for each control in the container. The *DataGrid* and *DataList* support five events: *ItemCommand*, *UpdateCommand*, *EditCommand*, *DeleteCommand*, and *CancelCommand*. (The *Repeater* supports only *ItemCommand*.) You can associate a control with one of the five events by setting the *CommandName* attribute to the first word in the event. *ItemCommand* is the default event. If wired up, this event will always fire when a *Button* contained by the *DataGrid* is clicked. You will learn more about wiring and handling these events in the upcoming "The Codebehind Page" sections.

Changing the appearance of the *DataGrid* is easy using the *CssClass* and ___*Style* attributes as seen in the *<Columns>* listing shown earlier, or by using various style tags, as shown in the following code listing. These child tags can be placed anywhere inside the *<asp:DataGrid>* tag, one level deep:

```
<SelectedItemStyle CssClass="DataGrid_SelectedItemStyle" />
<ItemStyle CssClass="DataGrid_ItemStyle" />
<AlternatingItemStyle CssClass="DataGrid_AlternatingItemStyle" />
<HeaderStyle CssClass="DataGrid_HeaderStyle" />
<FooterStyle CssClass="DataGrid_FooterStyle" />
<PagerStyle CssClass="DataGrid_PagerStyle" Mode="NumericPages" />
</asp:datagrid>
```

Note that the *CssClass* attribute maps to classes in the .css file referenced in the HTML <HEAD> tag.

The .ASPX Page: Data-Entry Controls

If the Add New Item or Edit buttons are clicked, data-entry controls appear below the *DataGrid*. The *TextBox* containing the product price appears below. Associated with it are two validation controls, which provide client-side and server-side validation for the *TextBox*. The code for the other data-entry controls is similar.

```
<asp:textbox id="txtPrice" runat="server" MaxLength="8"
Columns="10"/> 
<asp:RequiredFieldValidator id="rfvPrice" runat="server"
ControlToValidate="txtPrice" Display="Dynamic"
```

(continued)

```
ErrorMessage="Required!" /> 
<asp:RegularExpressionValidator id="revPrice" runat="server"
ControlToValidate="txtPrice" Display="Dynamic"
ErrorMessage="You must enter a valid price."
ValidationExpression="\d+[.]?[\d]{0,2}" />
```

The *RequiredFieldValidator* control is used as its name implies and for a very common task: to make data entry required for the field associated with it. This association is made by setting its *ControlToValidate* attribute to the ID of the *TextBox*. The *RegularExpressionValidator* is wired up in a similar manner. With it, you can use regular expressions to validate data that is entered into the *TextBox*. In this case, the data must be numeric only, with an optional decimal and trailing digits up to two decimal places. Both controls have a *Display* attribute you can set to *Dynamic* so that they do not take up space on the page when there is no validation error. The default value is *Static*.

The Codebehind Page: *DataGrid*

This section explains how to wire up the event handlers to the child controls in the *DataGrid*. Click events that are raised by child *Button* controls and bubbled up to the containing *DataGrid* must be wired to their respective handler. (Setting the *CommandName* attribute for a *ButtonColumn* is only the first step.) You can do this in two ways. First, you can add an *OnEventNameCommand* attribute to the *DataGrid* tag in the .aspx page. For example, to wire the *Item-Command* event to a handler in the codebehind class, you would add the following code to the *DataGrid* tag:

```
OnItemCommand="grdProducts_ItemCommand"
```

Although it's a good idea to follow a *NamingContainer__EventName* nomenclature, the name of the handler routine can be anything you like. The only stipulation is that it must be a *Public* or *Protected* method with the proper argument signature.

Perhaps a more preferable way is to use the *Handles* clause with the handler. This reduces the code in the .aspx page. Additionally, if you use the convenient Class Name and Method Name drop-down menus in the Code Editor to create the shell of your handler, the *DataGrid* event-wiring attributes are redundant.

The code in the *ItemCommand* event handler is as follows:

```
Public Sub grdProducts_ItemCommand(ByVal source As Object, _
    ByVal e As DataGridCommandEventArgs) Handles grdProducts.ItemCommand
    If e.Item.ItemIndex > -1 Then
        intProductID = CInt(grdProducts.DataKeys(e.Item.ItemIndex))
    End If

    grdProducts.SelectedIndex = e.Item.ItemIndex
    btnSave.CommandArgument = ""
End Sub
```

Recall that this event is the default for all child *Buttons*. As such, it will fire any time one of the other four *DataGrid Command* events fires, or when it's explicitly used by setting the *CommandName* attribute to *Item*. This makes the *ItemCommand* event handler a good place to put any code that you would like to run across multiple controls. In this case, the handler does three things.

First, it retrieves the Product ID. Earlier you saw that the *DataKeyField* attribute is set to *ProductID* in the *DataGrid* tag. This fills the *DataKeyCollection* exposed by *DataKeys* with a list of Product IDs. These values are accessible using an index-based lookup. The index is contained in the *ItemIndex* property of the *DataGridItem* object exposed by the *DataGridCommandEventArgs* argument.

The trick here is that, because all *Button Click* events—including those raised by the sorting and paging *LinkButtons*—are first handled by the *ItemCommand* handler, you must check for a positive index prior to retrieving the Product ID. If the index equals *-1* (the value used by the Framework when nothing is selected), you know that an Edit or Delete *Button* was not clicked.

Second, it explicitly selects the associated row in the *DataGrid*. If you fail to do this, the *SelectedIndex* property will equal *-1* when you later try to use it in the *SaveItem* method to look up the Product ID. The *DataGrid* row will also not indicate a highlighted state, depriving the end user of some helpful feedback. (Row highlighting requires that you also include a *SelectedItemStyle* tag beneath the *DataGrid* tag, as you saw in an earlier listing.) Note that you could use *CommandName="Select"* in the *ButtonColumn* tag to cause row selection when the *Button* is clicked. However, the *Button* would lose its association with all but the *ItemCommand* event. See the "Conclusion" section for further remarks about this option.

The last line in the *ItemCommand* handler clears the *Save Button CommandArgument* property, which is set to *Add* in the *btnAddNew_Click* event handler as a way of implementing a quasi-modal operation.

All but the *EditCommand* event handler, discussed in the next section, are left for your own study. You should have no difficulty understanding the code if you're comfortable with what has been presented here and in the data-access topics upon which this topic builds.

The Codebehind Page: Data-Entry Controls

When you click the Edit button, data-entry controls appear with their values set to the data in each corresponding cell of the selected *DataGrid* row. How are these values retrieved? The answer is found in the *EditCommand* event handler:

```
Private Sub grdProducts_EditCommand(ByVal source As Object, _
    ByVal e As DataGridCommandEventArgs) Handles grdProducts.EditCommand
    txtProductName.Text = e.Item.Cells(1).Text
```

(continued)

```
    txtQtyUnit.Text = e.Item.Cells(2).Text
    ' Trim the dollar sign off the price.
    txtPrice.Text = e.Item.Cells(3).Text.TrimStart(New Char() _
        {CChar("$")}) txtInStock.Text = e.Item.Cells(4).Text
    chkDiscontinued.Checked = _
        CType(e.Item.Cells(5).FindControl("chkDiscontinuedGrid"), _
        CheckBox).Checked
    pnlForm.Visible = True
End Sub
```

The methodology is straightforward. Each row in the *DataGrid* has a collection of cells that can be accessed by a zero-based column index, numbered from left to right. Like the *ItemIndex* you saw earlier, the *Cells* property is accessible from the *DataGridItem* object. Currency formatting was used for the product price, so you have to trim the dollar sign. Also, to access properties of a control contained within a cell, you can use the *FindControl* method, passing the value of the control's *id* attribute. Cast the returned object to the control type.

Finally, to bring this lengthy code walkthrough to a close, a few points about the validation controls are worth mentioning. First, you'll notice in the codebehind class that these controls are not declared. If you were to place these controls onto the Web Form by using the Visual Studio .NET designer, variable declarations would be added automatically. There is, however, no need for such declarations because the codebehind class is not interacting with them programmatically. Thus, they were removed.

Second, placing validation controls on the page only ensures that you'll have client-side validation (assuming that you did not set the control's *Enable-ClientScript* property to *False* or that the user did not disable JavaScript for his or her browser). To take advantage of server-side validation, you have to check the page's *IsValid* property before calling the *SaveItem* method:

```
Private Sub btnSave_Click(ByVal sender As Object, ByVal e As EventArgs) _
    Handles btnSave.Click
    If IsValid Then
        SaveItem()
    End If
End Sub
```

Conclusion

This completes a rather ambitious introductory topic on building Web applications. The majority of the discussion centered around how to configure the *DataGrid* and wire up events fired by command *Buttons* contained within it. One of the more important things you learned is that the *ItemCommand* event is always fired when another *Command* event is raised. In fact, you could merge all the *Command* event handlers into a single *ItemCommand* handler that uses a *Select...Case* construct on *e.CommandName* for flow control. In this case, you would want to use *CommandName="Select"* in the *ButtonColumn* tag.

In the next two topics, you'll expand upon what you have learned here. The three topics together will serve to round out a basic suite of Web Form skills, equipping you with the knowledge and sample code you need to get off the ground quickly in the exciting arena of Web-application development.

Application #48: Implement *DataGrid* Sorting

This application is less complex than its immediate predecessor in Application #47, although it does build upon it. The focus of the discussion will be on how to implement sorting for a *DataGrid*. You'll also learn a variation on the master-details interface you saw in the previous topic—that is, you'll see how to *connect* several *DataGrid*s in a three-level master-details relationship: Customers, Orders, and Order Details. Clicking an Orders Button in the Customers *DataGrid* causes the Orders *DataGrid* on its right to show only the orders for the selected customer, as shown below in Figure 5-2. As the figure also shows, clicking a Details Button in the Orders *DataGrid* causes the Order Details *DataGrid* below it to show the products associated with the selected order.

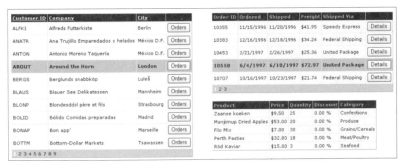

Figure 5-2   Application #48 showing the three related *DataGrid* controls presenting an increasing level of detail (clockwise from left).

Building Upon...

Application #4: *Try/Catch/Finally*
Application #12: Use a *DataSet* and *DataView*
Application #47: Build Data-Entry Web Forms

Code Walkthrough

The flow of the Code Walkthrough is similar to the previous topic. You will step through the code in the .aspx page and then complete the walkthrough in the codebehind page.

The .ASPX Page

The Customers *DataGrid* is the top-level master display control. It's the only one that allows sorting. The code for this control is similar to what you saw in the previous topic:

```
<asp:datagrid id="grdCustomers" runat="server" AllowSorting="True"
SortExpr="CustomerID" AutoGenerateColumns="False" AllowPaging="True"
DataKeyField="CustomerID">
  <SelectedItemStyle CssClass="DataGrid_SelectedItemStyle" />
  <ItemStyle CssClass="DataGrid_ItemStyle" />
  <HeaderStyle CssClass="DataGrid_HeaderStyle" />
  <FooterStyle CssClass="DataGrid_FooterStyle" />
  <PagerStyle CssClass="DataGrid_PagerStyle" Mode="NumericPages" />

  <Columns>
    <asp:BoundColumn DataField="CustomerID" SortExpression="CustomerID"
    HeaderText="Customer ID" />
    <asp:BoundColumn DataField="CompanyName" SortExpression="CompanyName"
    HeaderText="Company" />
    <asp:BoundColumn DataField="City" SortExpression="City"
    HeaderText="City" />
    <asp:ButtonColumn Text="Orders" ButtonType="PushButton"
    CommandName="Select" />
  </Columns>
</asp:datagrid>
```

When comparing this to the *DataGrid* in the previous topic, you'll see that the new feature here is sorting. To implement sorting, you must do three things. First, the *AllowSorting* property must be set to *True*. As with most properties of a Web control, this can be done using a tag attribute, as you see here, or by setting the property in the codebehind class. With *AllowSorting="True"*, the header text for each column renders as a *LinkButton*, the *Click* event for which bubbles up to the *DataGrid*, which in turn fires a *SortCommand* event on the *Button*'s behalf.

Second, if *AutoGenerateColumns* is set to *False*, you must supply a sort expression for every column that will support sorting. This is a data-source field name and is typically identical to the value of the *DataField* attribute. However, if, for example, you wanted to display a person's first and last name (that is, concatenated in the stored procedure into an aliased virtual column named FullName) but sort only on the last name, you could set *DataField* to FullName and *SortExpression* to LastName.

Realize that the *DataGrid* does not actually do the sorting. It merely passes the sort expression—contained in a *DataGridSortCommandEventArgs* object—to the *SortCommand* event handler. Thus, the third step in implementing *DataGrid* sorting is to add code to this handler. As you will see in the next section, this typically involves sorting a *DataView* and rebinding it to the *DataGrid*.

There can be a fourth step involved, which is optional but recommended. Because of the stateless nature of the Web, the sort expression will not persist during *DataGrid* paging (covered in the next topic). In other words, if the user sorted on the City column and then clicked a paging control, the sort order would revert to either some default expression hard-coded in the codebehind class or to the order inherent to the data source itself—for example, in a T-SQL ORDER BY clause. Moreover, the sort expression is not included as a member of the *DataGridPageChangedEventArgs* object. Therefore, when handling paging, you do not have access to the latest column-dependent sort expression unless you store it someplace.

This is where the custom *SortExpr* attribute comes in. *WebControl*—the base class for all Web controls—exposes an *AttributeCollection* object you can use to store custom key-value attribute pairs that do not correspond to a control property. This makes *AttributeCollection* a convenient container for any number of items, including custom JavaScript routines that provide user feedback. For example, if you wanted a confirmation dialog box to appear when a delete *Button* is clicked, you could add the following line to the page's *Load* event handler:

```
btnDelete.Attributes.Add("onclick", "if (!confirm(""Are you sure you ⇥
want to delete this?""))return false;return true;")
```

As you will see in the next section, the custom *SortExpr* attribute is used to store the latest sort expression, which can then be easily retrieved by any method to persist column sorting.

The methodology for setting up the master-details *DataGrid* relationships is similar to what you saw in the previous topic when data-entry controls were initialized to the values in a selected *DataGrid* row. The user clicks a *Button* in a *ButtonColumn*, which fires the *ItemCommand* event and another event determined by the *CommandName* property. Using the row's index, you can then retrieve an ID from the *DataGrid DataKeyCollection* object and set properties of child controls based on this value. The difference in this application is that instead of using the *CommandName* property to wire an additional event, the *Select* keyword is used:

```
<asp:ButtonColumn Text="Orders" ButtonType="PushButton"
CommandName="Select" />
```

This causes the row to be selected when the user clicks the *Button*. It also applies style attributes set in the *SelectedItemStyle* tag. Therefore, you don't have to explicitly select the row in the codebehind class.

The Codebehind Page

Handling the *SortCommand* event is usually quite simple. In this application, it involves two lines:

```
Public Sub grdCustomers_SortCommand(ByVal source As Object, _
    ByVal e As DataGridSortCommandEventArgs) Handles grdCustomers.SortCommand
    grdCustomers.Attributes("SortExpr") = e.SortExpression
    BindCustomersGrid()
End Sub
```

The first line obtains the latest sort expression from the *DataGridSort-CommandEventArgs* object and stores it in the *DataGrid AttributeCollection*. Following this, you are ready to reacquire the data source and bind it again to the *DataGrid*:

```
Sub BindCustomersGrid()
    Dim strSQL As String = _
        "SELECT c.CustomerID, c.CompanyName, c.City, " & _
        "   COUNT(o.OrderDate) AS OrderCount " & _
        "FROM Customers c " & _
        "INNER JOIN Orders o ON c.CustomerID = o.CustomerID " & _
        "GROUP BY c.CustomerID, c.CompanyName, c.City"
    Dim ds As DataSet = CreateDataSet(strSQL)
    Dim dv As DataView = ds.Tables(0).DefaultView

    dv.Sort = grdCustomers.Attributes("SortExpr")
    With grdCustomers
        .DataSource = dv
        .DataBind()
    End With
End Sub
```

Notice that the latest sort expression is retrieved from the *AttributeCollection* and assigned to the *Sort* property of the *DataView*. The sorting implementation is now complete.

As for the master-details feature, recall from the previous topic that *Data-Grid Command* events first flow through the *ItemCommand* event handler. Therefore, you have to ensure that code in this handler works properly, whether a *Button* in a *ButtonColumn* or a *LinkButton* in a column header is clicked. As an alternative to checking whether *e.Item.ItemIndex* equals *-1*, as was done in the previous topic, you can access *e.Item.ItemType*. This property contains a *ListItemType* enumeration value. If *ItemType* is *Pager*, you know that a paging control was clicked. *ListItemType.Header* indicates that a sorting control was clicked:

```
Private Sub grdCustomers_ItemCommand(ByVal source As Object, _
    ByVal e As DataGridCommandEventArgs) Handles grdCustomers.ItemCommand
    If e.Item.ItemType = ListItemType.Pager OrElse _
        e.Item.ItemType = ListItemType.Header Then Exit Sub
```

Following this check, you find code for displaying the Orders *DataGrid*. A *SqlParameter* object is created and then its value is initialized to the Customer ID retrieved from the *DataKeyCollection* of the Customers (master) *DataGrid*:

```
    Dim param As New SqlParameter("@CustomerID", SqlDbType.NChar, 5)
    param.Value = grdCustomers.DataKeys(e.Item.ItemIndex)
    BindOrdersGrid(param)
End Sub
```

The Order Details *DataGrid* is implemented similarly using the *Item-Command* event handler for its master, the Orders *DataGrid*.

Conclusion

This topic has shown you how to implement sorting and set up master-details relationships between *DataGrid*s. You learned that sorting involves three main steps:

1. Turn *DataGrid* sorting on.

2. Specify the sort expression for each sortable column.

3. Handle the *SortCommand* event.

An optional but recommended best practice is to persist the sort expression in the *AttributeCollection* for the *DataGrid*.

A common alternative to the master-details interface presented here is to use a *HyperLinkColumn* in the master *DataGrid* that links to a separate *details* Web Form page. To experiment with this, remove the first *BoundColumn* in the Customers *DataGrid* and replace it with the following:

```
<asp:HyperlinkColumn DataTextField="CustomerID"
DataNavigateUrlField="CustomerID"
DataNavigateUrlFormatString="details.aspx?id={0}"
SortExpression="CustomerID" HeaderText="Customer ID" />
```

Then add a Web Form named details.aspx to the Project and use the *id* querystring variable to set up the details *DataGrid*s.

Application #49: Implement *DataGrid* Paging

The ability to page through records instead of having to scroll through one large list is an essential feature of a Web-based data manipulation interface. This application builds upon what you've learned in the previous two topics by explaining how to implement *DataGrid* paging. We'll explain options that lead to four possible configurations: built-in paging, custom paging, built-in navigation controls, and custom navigation controls.

Figure 5-3   Application #49 showing the *DataGrid* with custom paging.

Building Upon...

Application #4: *Try/Catch/Finally*
Application #12: Use a *DataSet* and *DataView*
Application #16: Data Binding with Navigation
Application #47: Build Data-Entry Web Forms
Application #48: Implement *DataGrid* Sorting

New Concepts

The *DataGrid* offers tremendous support for paging. In its simplest incarnation, you need only to set a few properties and add a few lines of code to a *Page-IndexChanged* event handler, and the *DataGrid* takes care of the rest. With slightly more effort, you can use your own navigation controls instead of those built into the *DataGrid*.

How does the *DataGrid* do this? The internal nuts and bolts are beyond the scope of this book. Let it suffice to say that the *DataGrid* is able to pull from its data source only those records it needs for a *page* of results, as defined by the value of its *PageSize* and *CurrentPageIndex* properties. The only problem with built-in paging is that the data source must be filled with *all* the records, even if only 10 or 20 are shown at any one time. Caching the data source will help to a certain point. Use of the Application Cache mechanism is demonstrated in this sample. However, if your recordset contains millions—or even thousands—of rows, the resource requirements and probable performance degradation might prove unacceptable.

This is where custom paging comes in. With it, you can select from the data source the rows you want to display at any one time. This option will also work with the built-in or custom navigation controls. The only caveat is that you are most likely connecting to the database and retrieving data every time the user clicks a paging control. Database connections are expensive.

The bottom line is that *DataGrid* paging is flexible. With a little experimentation, and perhaps some stress testing, you can determine which implementation is best for your situation.

Code Walkthrough

As with the previous two topics, the walkthrough begins with the code in the .aspx page and then finishes with code in the codebehind page.

The .ASPX Page

Configuring a *DataGrid* for built-in paging requires that you set the *Allow-Paging* and *PageSize* properties. This is typically done on the .aspx page using attributes:

```
<asp:datagrid id="grdProducts" runat="server" PageSize="15"
AllowPaging="True" AutoGenerateColumns="False" AllowSorting="True"
SortExpr="ProductID">
```

The *PageSize* attribute defaults to 10. The setting here will allow 15 records to be displayed in the *DataGrid* at any one time.

Use the *PagerStyle* tag to set attributes that affect the appearance of the built-in navigation controls:

```
<PagerStyle CssClass="DataGrid_PagerStyle" Mode="NumericPages" />
```

Mode is the most important attribute. You have two options: *NextPrev* (the default) and *Numeric*. The former displays paging controls as *previous* and *next LinkButton*s. (You can specify the text.) *Numeric* displays a series of numbers. The default location is along the bottom of the *DataGrid*. However, this can also be changed using the *Position* attribute.

The code for the custom navigation controls requires no explanation. It's omitted here to conserve space.

Although it's permissible to display both the built-in and custom navigation controls, you'll probably want to turn off the built-in controls when displaying custom navigation. To do this, right-click the *DataGrid* when in the Design View and then click Property Builder. In the Properties dialog box, click Paging. Uncheck Show Navigation Buttons and then click OK.

The Codebehind Page

For built-in paging, you must handle the *PageIndexChanged* event. This typically involves setting the *DataGrid CurrentPageIndex* property to the *NewPageIndex* passed via the *DataGridPageChangedEventArgs* object and then rebinding the grid:

```
Private Sub productDetails_PageIndexChanged(ByVal source As Object, _
    ByVal e As DataGridPageChangedEventArgs) _
    Handles grdProducts.PageIndexChanged
    grdProducts.CurrentPageIndex = e.NewPageIndex
    intCurrentPage = e.NewPageIndex + 1
    BindGrid()
End Sub
```

The variable *intCurrentPage* has class scope and is used for the custom paging and navigation options. It's set here only to permit the built-in and custom paging controls to stay in sync when displayed simultaneously. Custom navigation is only slightly more complicated. Instead of handling *PageIndexChanged*, you handle the *Command* events raised by the *LinkButtons* and the *Click* event for the "Go!" *Button*. In this application, *intCurrentPage* is set in the handler and then assigned to the *CurrentPageIndex* property in the *SetCustomNavigation* method.

Custom paging involves three additional steps. First, both the *AllowPaging* and *AllowCustomPaging* properties must be set to *True*. For demonstration purposes, this is coded in the *chkUseCustomPaging_CheckedChanged* event handler. Normally you would simply add an *AllowCustomPaging* attribute to the *DataGrid* tag in the .aspx page.

In this application, the two remaining steps are completed in the *GetOnePageOfProducts* function. After some initial variable declarations, you find code for setting the *DataGrid VirtualItemCount* property:

```
Private Function GetOnePageOfProducts() As DataSet
    Dim strSQL As String
    Dim scnn As SqlConnection
    Dim scmd As SqlCommand
    Dim sda As SqlDataAdapter
    Dim ds As New DataSet()

    scnn = New SqlConnection(SQL_CONNECTION_STRING)
    scmd = New SqlCommand("", scnn)
```

```
If grdProducts.VirtualItemCount = 0 Then
    scmd.CommandText = _
        "SELECT COUNT(ProductID) FROM Products"
    scnn.Open()
    grdProducts.VirtualItemCount = CInt(scmd.ExecuteScalar)
    scnn.Close()
End If
```

The *DataGrid* needs to know the total number of records in the data source to set its *PageCount* property (data source record count / *Data-Grid.PageSize*) and accurately display the built-in navigation controls. With built-in paging, the *DataGrid* would determine this automatically from the data source. However, when you are only retrieving a subset of the records at any one time, you must inform the *DataGrid* via the *VirtualItemCount* property. Notice that this is done only once to avoid unnecessary trips to the database on each click of a paging control.

The last step is to retrieve a single page of records. If you enabled *Data-Grid* sorting, you'll want to move the sort expression to the T-SQL statement, as follows:

```
scmd.CommandText = _
    "SELECT ProductID, ProductName, UnitPrice, QuantityPerUnit, →
    UnitsInStock FROM Products ORDER BY " & _
    grdProducts.Attributes("SortExpr")
```

Then create a *SqlDataAdapter* and use the overloaded *Fill* method that accepts a start record and a maximum number of records to retrieve:

```
sda = New SqlDataAdapter(scmd)
sda.Fill(ds, grdProducts.CurrentPageIndex * grdProducts.PageSize, _
    grdProducts.PageSize, "products")

Return ds
End Function
```

This covers the key steps involved with implementing built-in and custom paging.

Conclusion

In this topic, you completed a three-part series on Web-application development that focused on data-manipulation interfaces involving the *DataGrid* control. You learned that the *DataGrid* offers flexible support for four configurations: built-in paging with built-in navigation controls (the easiest), built-in paging with custom navigation controls (almost as easy), custom paging with built-in navigation controls (more difficult, but only requires three additional steps), and custom paging with custom navigation controls. These configurations will support any scenario you can envision.

Application #50: Expose a Simple Web Service

You now begin another three-part series on Web-application development. In this topic, you'll learn how to build an XML Web service that exposes two methods. One method returns an untyped *DataSet* of the ten most expensive products from the Northwind database. The other, more complex, method returns an instance of a custom class containing a typed *DataSet* of products ordered by a customer, as well as the company name.

The Framework automatically renders a Web service test user interface when you load a Web service page (.asmx) in a browser. When the page first loads, you're presented with a list of links to the methods offered by the service. Clicking a link takes you to the method's test interface, as you can see in Figure 5-4.

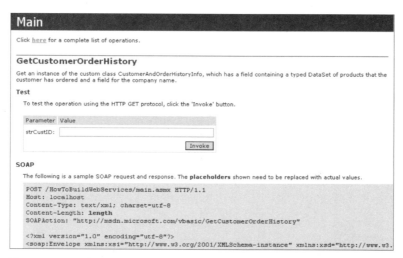

Figure 5-4   ASP.NET-generated Web service test page for Application #50.

Building Upon...

Application #4: *Try/Catch/Finally*
Application #12: Use a *DataSet* and *DataView*
Application #19: Use a Typed *DataSet*

New Concepts

The Framework documentation defines a Web service as "a programmable entity that provides a particular element of functionality, such as application logic, and is accessible to any number of potentially disparate systems using ubiquitous Internet standards, such as XML and HTTP." In other words, a Web service enables platform-independent remote procedure calls because it's based on widely accepted open standards.

This simple concept is spearheading the most significant evolution of the Internet since its inception. Using Web services, businesses can make application logic available to any client that can send and receive XML text messages. The potential, especially for business-to-business integration, is enormous.

The Framework has extensive support for Web services. It incorporates the Simple Object Access Protocol (SOAP) as its messaging protocol and the Web Services Description Language (WSDL) as its interface description language. It provides base classes, special attributes, and command-line utilities that take care of the low-level Web service implementation details, freeing you up to focus on the application logic. Visual Studio .NET takes it even further, offering many significant features that greatly facilitate building and consuming Web services.

Code Walkthrough

When creating an ASP.NET Web Service project in Visual Studio .NET, a number of tasks required for building a Web service are completed for you. It's important to understand these requirements. A good way to do this is by examining the simple "Hello World" Web service that Visual Studio .NET automatically generates for a new project. The main item of discussion is the Web service page (.asmx). Like a Web Form page (.aspx), a Web service page has a codebehind page associated with it (.asmx.vb). However, unlike Web Forms, the .asmx page contains only one line of code, in this case:

```
<%@ WebService Language="vb" Codebehind="main.asmx.vb"
Class="HowToBuildWebServices.Main" %>
```

Notice the @ *WebService* directive, which along with the .asmx extension, causes the ASP.NET runtime to process this page as a Web service.

The codebehind page contains the following code for the Web service class:

```
Imports System.Web.Services

<WebService(Namespace := "http://tempuri.org/")> _
Public Class Service1
    Inherits System.Web.Services.WebService
```

(continued)

```
<WebMethod()> Public Function HelloWorld() As String
    HelloWorld = "Hello World"
End Function
End Class
```

Notice the *Imports* statement. This refers to the Framework assembly of the same name, which is where the Web service base classes are found. The custom class, *Service1*, is like any other class you might build. Although Visual Studio .NET creates it to derive from *System.Web.Services.WebService*, this is not a requirement. It is, however, a good idea. *WebService* conveniently exposes numerous properties that make it easier to build your service. (As an interesting aside, *WebService* derives from *System.MarshalByRefObject*, which is the base class for .NET Remoting.) *Service1* is also declared with an optional *WebService* attribute that allows you to set several properties—such as a name, description, and namespace—for the Web service.

You should realize that the only code required to set up a Web service is the *WebMethod* attribute. By marking up a *Public* subroutine or function, you turn it into HTTP-accessible application logic. With this attribute, you can also set other method-level properties, including a description, cache duration, and even transaction options.

In the Web service for this topic, you find two Web methods. *GetTenMost-ExpensiveProducts* returns an untyped *DataSet*. Recall that *DataSet*s have native support for XML serialization. As such, they make an excellent return type for a Web method. The code for this method is as follows (with the data-access logic omitted to save space):

```
<WebMethod(Description:="Get an untyped DataSet of the ten most →
expensive products from the Northwind database.")> _
Public Function GetTenMostExpensiveProducts() As DataSet
    ' ... Data access logic...
    Dim sda As New SqlDataAdapter(scmd)
    ' Create and fill an untyped DataSet.
    Dim dsTenMostExpProds As New DataSet()
    sda.Fill(dsTenMostExpProds)
    Return dsTenMostExpProds
End Function
```

The code in this method is straightforward. In fact, there is no logic here that you haven't already seen in previous topics. The only addition is the *WebMethod* attribute. In other words, converting your application logic into a Web service is as simple as declaring it with the *Public* keyword and the *WebMethod* attribute!

The other Web method in this sample is *GetCustomerOrderHistory*. This function returns a custom type, *CustomerAndOrderHistoryInfo*, that contains two *Public* fields:

```
Public Class CustomerAndOrderHistoryInfo
    Public Orders As dsCustOrderHist
```

```
<XmlAttributeAttribute(AttributeName:="Company")> _
Public CompanyName As String
End Class
```

Orders is of type *dsCustOrderHist*, which is a typed *DataSet*. It was created by adding a *DataSet* to the project and then dragging the Northwind stored procedure CustOrderHist to its design surface. (See "Application #19: Use a Typed *DataSet*" in Chapter 3 for more information.) The other field, *CompanyName*, is a simple string that has been declaratively marked with an *XmlAttributeAttribute*. This attribute is not required. It's used merely to demonstrate how to *shape* the XML that is generated when this class is serialized as part of the XML SOAP message returned by the Web method.

The Web method contains the following code. Comments are supplied to help you follow along (with self-explanatory data-access logic again omitted):

```
<WebMethod(Description:="Get an instance of the custom class  ⇥
CustomerAndOrderHistoryInfo, which has a field containing a typed  ⇥
DataSet of products that the customer has ordered and a field for the  ⇥
company name.")> _
Public Function GetCustomerOrderHistory(ByVal strCustID As String) _
    As CustomerAndOrderHistoryInfo
    ' ... Data access logic...
    ' Create an instance of the custom return type.
    Dim cohi As New CustomerAndOrderHistoryInfo()
    ' Create and fill the typed DataSet.
    Dim dsOrderHistory As New dsCustOrderHist()
    sda.Fill(dsOrderHistory.CustOrderHist)
    ' Assign the typed DataSet to the Orders property.
    cohi.Orders = dsOrderHistory
    ' Retrieve the CompanyName and assign it to the other field in the
    ' return type.
    Dim objReturnVal As Object = scmd.ExecuteScalar()
    If Not IsDBNull(objReturnVal) Then
        cohi.CompanyName = objReturnVal.ToString
    End If
    ' Return the custom type.
    Return cohi
End Function
```

To test the Web service, build the project, open a browser, and then navigate to *http://localhost/HowToBuildWebServices/main.asmx*. Click a Web method link to access its test page. Then click the Invoke button to view the XML that is returned. Use **ALFKI** for the Customer ID when testing *GetCustomerOrderHistory*.

Conclusion

This has been a very quick explanation of Web services and how to build them. You learned how easy it is to convert existing application logic to a Web method and expose it to anyone who has access to the Web service address. All that is required is a *Public* routine—declared with the *WebMethod* attribute—residing in the codebehind page for a Web page with an .asmx extension and an @ *WebService* directive.

The next topic will show you how to build a client application to consume a Web service.

Application #51: Consume a Web Service

This second topic in the series on Web services focuses on how to consume a Web service. The sample application has four examples, each of which demonstrates interaction with real-world Web services. "Local Time By Zip" is the simplest example. It returns the local time at a Zip Code you enter. "Book Info By ISBN" shows how to retrieve the sales rank and current price from Amazon.com and Barnes & Noble for any book with an ISBN. "Dilbert (Async Demo)" is more advanced, demonstrating how to call the Daily Dilbert Web service asynchronously. (See Figure 5-5.) Finally, the "Failover (UDDI Demo)" simulates using the Microsoft UDDI Business Registry to provide failover support for another local time service.

Space limitations prohibit walking through the code for each example. Therefore, the discussion will focus on the Daily Dilbert service. You should, however, have no problem understanding the other examples because the methodology for consuming a Web service is the same in each.

Figure 5-5   Application #51 showing the asynchronous Web service invocation example.

Building Upon...

Application #4: *Try/Catch/Finally*
Application #12: Use a *DataSet* and *DataView*
Application #24: Load Images From and Save Images To a Database
Application #50: Expose a Simple Web Service

New Concepts

The concept of a *proxy* is important to understanding how a client application consumes a Web service. A proxy can be viewed as a class that represents, or stands in the place of, the Web service. Instead of working directly with the Web service's API, you will work with a high-level wrapper class that not only models the service's API but also provides inherited functionality that takes care of the low-level details involved with connecting to the service, creating and serializing SOAP request messages, and deserializing SOAP response messages.

A Web service proxy class is generated by a Framework command-line tool, WSDL.exe, or by Visual Studio .NET when you add a Web reference to your project. It does this by deserializing an XML document used for describing the Web service's API. This document uses the open-standard Web Services Description Language (WSDL). A Web service's WSDL document is generated automatically by the Framework by appending *?wsdl* to a Web service address. For example, the WSDL document for the Daily Dilbert service is located at *http://www.esynaps.com/WebServices/DailyDilbert.asmx?wsdl*. If you open this in your browser, you'll see an XML document that describes the service's interface.

You can view the code in the proxy class by taking the following steps. First, in the Solution Explorer, click the View All Files icon. Next, expand Web References | Esynaps | Reference.map. Finally, right-click the Reference.vb file and select View Code. While scrolling through the proxy class, note that it derives from *System.Web.Services.Protocols.SoapHttpClientProtocol*. This is where it gets the functionality for handling the low-level details. Next, notice that the *Url* property maintains a reference to the Web service address (.asmx).

If the Web service returns any complex types, such as a typed *DataSet* or custom class, you'll also find child classes representing them in the proxy. For example, if you view the code for the Book Info service (Web reference "PerfectXML"), you'll find the following class within the proxy class:

```
<System.Xml.Serialization.XmlTypeAttribute(→
[Namespace]:="http://www.PerfectXML.com/NETWebSvcs/BookService")> _
```

(continued)

```
Public Class All
    Public AmazonSalesRank As String
    Public AmazonPrice As String
    Public BNSalesRank As String
    Public BNPrice As String
End Class
```

In the code that consumes this Web service, you'll notice that a variable of type *PerfectXML.All* is created to contain the return value from the call to the service's *GetAll* Web method.

Proxy methods have also been generated for both the synchronous and asynchronous invocation of each Web method exposed by the service. Calling a Web method synchronously means that the client must wait for it to return before the thread can continue with other processes. This is often fine. However, if the Web method performs a time-consuming task, the wait might not be acceptable. By invoking the asynchronous proxy methods, you limit the amount of time the client thread is tied up.

There are two ways to conduct asynchronous operations:

- **Callback delegates**   The *AsyncCallback* is a pointer to a delegate that you want to invoke when the *Begin* Web method completes (more on *Begin* later). Use this if you are not concerned about how long it takes for the Web service to return.

- **Wait handlers**   The *ASyncWaitHandle* class allows you to set a time limit on the return. If the limit is exceeded, the call is abandoned.

Wait handlers are often the best approach. They're certainly the simplest. You'll see how to use them in the "Code Walkthrough" section.

Finally, a brief mention of UDDI is in order. UDDI is an acronym for Universal Description, Discovery, and Integration. As a key component of the Web services *stack*, it provides both a specification and a mechanism that facilitate the publication and discovery of businesses and services over the Internet. Windows Server 2003 also features native UDDI support for extranet and intranet scenarios. UDDI is extremely important for a variety of reasons, not the least of which is the ability to dynamically configure (for example, at run time) a client application for Web service consumption. Study the commented code in the "Failover" example and spend some time at *http://uddi.microsoft.com/developer/default.aspx* to learn more about UDDI.

Code Walkthrough

The Daily Dilbert Web service returns a different Dilbert cartoon each day in the form of a serialized byte array (Base64-encoded). In "Application #24: Load

Images From and Save Images To a Database" you learned how to convert a byte array to an image and display it in a *PictureBox*. The same concepts apply here. The only difference is that you're receiving the byte array from a deserialized SOAP response message instead of a database.

The code for consuming the Daily Dilbert Web service is contained in the *btnCartoon_Click* event handler.

```
Private Sub btnCartoon_Click(ByVal sender As System.Object, _
    ByVal e As EventArgs) Handles btnCartoon.Click

    If txtAsyncWaitPeriod.Text = "" Then
        MessageBox.Show("You must enter a number of seconds you wish ⟶
            to wait.", "Web Service Demo Information", _
            MessageBoxButtons.OK, MessageBoxIcon.Information)
        Return
    End If

    ' Create an instance of the Web service proxy class.
    Dim wsDailyDilbert As New Esynaps.DailyDilbert()
```

The first key step is to instantiate the Web service proxy class, as you see here. "Esynaps" is both the name of the Web reference and the proxy's namespace. When you add a Web reference, this defaults to a variation of the host's domain (for example, "com.esynaps.www"). You can, however, rename it in the Solution Explorer.

You are now able to invoke the Daily Dilbert Web method. If you were to do this synchronously, the code would appear as follows:

```
Dim arrPicture() As Byte
arrPicture = wsDailyDilbert.DailyDilbertImage
```

However, when calling asynchronously, several additional steps are required. Asynchronous proxy methods come in Begin-End pairs. Use *BeginWebMethodName* to invoke the Web method, and *EndWebMethodName* to retrieve the return value if the *Begin* method call completes in the time you specify. *Begin* methods return an object that implements the *IAsyncResult* interface. This object exposes an *ASyncWaitHandle* property of type *WaitHandle*, which you can use to specify the wait time:

```
Try
    Dim result As IAsyncResult = _
        wsDailyDilbert.BeginDailyDilbertImage(Nothing, Nothing)

    result.AsyncWaitHandle.WaitOne _
        (New TimeSpan(0, 0, CInt(txtAsyncWaitPeriod.Text)), False)
```

Here, the wait handler's *WaitOne* method is invoked. This will block the thread started by the *Begin* call until one of two things happens: a return value is received within the time specified in the *TimeSpan* structure, or the wait period exceeds the specified time.

To determine whether the call completed in time, check the value of the *IAsyncResult.IsCompleted* property. If the call was successful, invoke the corresponding *End* proxy method to retrieve the byte array:

```
If (result.IsCompleted) Then
    arrPicture = _
        CType(wsDailyDilbert.EndDailyDilbertImage(result), Byte())
```

The remaining code for displaying the image is omitted because it was explained in an earlier topic. Binary data manipulation is also the subject of the final Web service topic.

Conclusion

In this topic, you learned how to consume real-world Web services. The steps for conducting synchronous operations are simple. When you add a Web reference to your project, Visual Studio .NET creates a proxy class for you. All that remains to be done is to instantiate the proxy, call the Web method, and process the return value. In each example, you saw that the same methodology was followed.

You also learned about asynchronous operations. Although they're more difficult, you saw that only a few extra steps are required to limit how long the client application waits for the Web method to return its data.

Application #52: Transfer Binary Data from a Web Service

Capping off this three-part series on Web services is a fairly complex sample involving a Windows client application that displays images retrieved from a Web service. The sample ties into one package concepts and code that are sprinkled throughout the book. As such, what follows is not a comprehensive walkthrough, but rather a brief discussion of some key highlights.

The Web service exposes three Web methods. *Browse* returns an array of custom *ImageInfo* objects that contain information about images residing in a child images folder. This is used to fill a *ListBox* for selecting an image, as well as for displaying data such as image size and pixel format. *GetImage* accepts a filename and returns the corresponding image as a serialized byte array. *GetThumbnail* works similarly, but it returns a thumbnail instead of the full image. The Web service also contains other methods that support the Web methods but are not exposed as such.

With the client application, you can retrieve a list of available images and then click a filename to view the thumbnail and image information. (See Figure 5-6.) If you double-click a thumbnail or click the Display Image *Button*, a form appears that displays the full image and allows you to manipulate it in various ways. You can even save the image to your hard disk in one of several image formats.

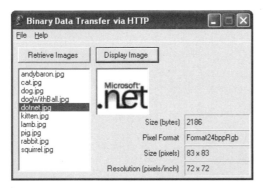

Figure 5-6   Application #52 showing a list of images retrieved from a Web service.

Building Upon...

Application #4: *Try/Catch/Finally*
Application #12: Use a *DataSet* and *DataView*
Application #20: Build a Data-Entry Form

New Concepts

Although Web services generally return XML as text, as you've already seen in the previous topic with the Daily Dilbert Web service, it's possible to have a Web Service return binary information. Because the SOAP serializer automatically serializes byte arrays using Base64 encoding, Web Services can easily return images, sounds, and much more. All you have to do is convert the source files into byte arrays and the Framework's serialization mechanism takes care of the rest. On the client side, the encoded string representing the image will be deserialized into a byte array, which must then be converted to a *Bitmap* object.

Code Walkthrough

As this sample consists of two applications, the Code Walkthrough first steps through the code in the Web service and then moves to the code in the Windows client that consumes the service.

The Graphics Service

As mentioned earlier, the *Browse* method returns an array of custom *ImageInfo* objects. For serialization, the *ImageInfo* class is declared as *Public* and contains *Public* fields:

```
Public Class ImageInfo
    Public Name As String
    Public Size As Long
    Public Height As Integer
    Public Width As Integer
    Public HorizontalResolution As Single
    Public VerticalResolution As Single
    Public PixelFormat As Imaging.PixelFormat
    Public Thumbnail As Byte()
End Class
```

Browse invokes *DirectoryInfo.GetFiles* on the images subfolder and then assigns *FileInfo* properties to *ImageInfo* objects:

```
<WebMethod(Description:="Retrieve an array of image file names.")> _
Public Function Browse() As ImageInfo()
    Dim i As Integer
    Dim fi As FileInfo
    Dim aImages As ImageInfo()
    Dim di As New DirectoryInfo(Server.MapPath("./Images"))
    Dim afi As FileInfo() = di.GetFiles("*.jpg")
    ReDim Preserve aImages(afi.Length - 1)

    For Each fi In afi
        aImages(i) = New ImageInfo()
        aImages(i).Name = fi.Name
        aImages(i).Size = fi.Length
        FillImageInfo(aImages(i), fi.Name)
        i += 1
    Next
    Return aImages
End Function
```

The Web method *GetImage* contains only one line of code, the return from a private helper function:

```
<WebMethod(Description:="Retrieve a single image.")> _
Public Function GetImage(ByVal FileName As String) As Byte()
    Return ReadFile(Server.MapPath("./Images/" & FileName))
End Function
```

ReadFile is where the source image is converted to a byte array:

```
Private Shared Function ReadFile(ByVal FilePath As String) As Byte()
    Dim fs As FileStream
    Try
        fs = File.Open(FilePath, FileMode.Open, FileAccess.Read)
        Dim lngLen As Long = fs.Length
        Dim abytBuffer(CInt(lngLen - 1)) As Byte
        fs.Read(abytBuffer, 0, CInt(lngLen))
        Return abytBuffer
    Finally
        fs.Close()
    End Try
End Function
```

First, a *FileStream* object is opened on the source file. *Read* is then invoked to read the binary data from the stream and write it to the supplied buffer.

The *GetThumbnail* Web method uses a helper function that is more involved. Consult the sample's ReadMe file and source-code comments for more information.

The Graphics Client

The code for retrieving the available images and displaying their filenames in a *ListBox* resides in the *btnRetrieve_Click* event handler. First, variables representing the Web service proxy class and the return type for the *Browse* Web method are declared. The proxy is then instantiated and the *ImageInfo* array variable *aInfo*, already declared at the class level, is assigned to the return value from the Web method:

```
Dim wsGraphics As GraphicsServer.ImageService
Dim info As GraphicsServer.ImageInfo
wsGraphics = New GraphicsServer.ImageService()
aInfo = wsGraphics.Browse()
```

All that remains is to clear the existing *ListBox* items and then iterate through the *ImageInfo* array to refill the control with the image filenames:

```
lstImages.Items.Clear()
For Each info In aInfo
    lstImages.Items.Add(info.Name)
Next
```

The code for displaying a full image resides in *DisplayImage*. The key lines for retrieving the image from the Web service are as follows:

```
wsGraphics = New GraphicsServer.ImageService()
strName = aInfo(lstImages.SelectedIndex).Name
bmp = GetImage(wsGraphics.GetImage(strName))
```

When the *GetImage* Web method is invoked, its return is passed to a private *GetImage* helper function on the client, which does the work of converting the deserialized byte array to a *Bitmap*:

```
Private Function GetImage(ByVal abyt() As Byte) As Bitmap
    Try
        Return New Bitmap(New MemoryStream(abyt))
    Catch exp As Exception
        MessageBox.Show(exp.Message, Me.Text)
    End Try
End Function
```

As you can see, it's a little easier to convert *from* a byte array than *to* a byte array. A *Bitmap* object is readily derived from a *MemoryStream* object.

The remainder of the code is not Web-service specific and is thus not covered further here.

Conclusion

This sample completes a three-part series on Web services and the discussion on building Web applications. You learned that binary data can be sent via HTTP because the Framework serialization mechanism converts a byte array to Base64-encoded text, which can then be contained in an XML SOAP message. Using the concepts and code presented here, you can quickly set up a Web service that can be used to serve up any type of binary content.

6

Working with Console Applications

Console applications are programs that operate from the command line, and like other applications you create with Microsoft Visual Basic .NET, they have full access to the .NET class library and to features such as inheritance, constructors, overloading, and initializers. They can also access other .NET applications. Console applications are lightweight and fast because they don't require a graphical user interface.

Application #53: Working with Console Applications

This sample application shows you how to create and use a console application. The application uses Microsoft SQL Server to read the Northwind database Products table into a dataset. When the application is run, it can accept a command-line argument or input from the user, which is either a Product ID or **QUIT**.

If a valid Product ID (integer format) is entered, its associated product information is displayed. If an invalid Product ID is entered, an exception message is displayed. You can continue to input Product IDs as long as you care to. When you type **QUIT** and press Enter, the application ends.

Building Upon...

Application #1: Use Arrays

Application #3: String Manipulation

Application #12: Use a *DataSet* and *DataView*

New Concepts

Microsoft Visual Basic .NET makes it easy to create and use console applications. Here's how.

Creating a Console Application

To create a console application in Microsoft Visual Studio .NET, simply select the Console Application template when you're creating a new project. Of course, as with any other .NET application, you could build it entirely in Notepad. Building it in Notepad, though, you'd need to do quite a bit more work, such as adding references yourself, compiling from the command line, and so on.

When you create the application in Visual Studio .NET, you'll get just two files, AssemblyInfo.vb and Module1.vb. In Module1.vb, you'll find a *Sub* procedure named *Main*. This is the entry point for your application. You can add other procedures as needed and call them from *Main*.

Reading to and Writing from the Console

Four methods of the *Console* class help you get data from the user and write to the console window: *Read*, *ReadLine*, *Write*, and *WriteLine*. Here's what they do:

- **Read**   Reads the next character from the input stream, which is usually the command line, but can be redirected

- **ReadLine**   Reads the next line of characters from the standard input stream

- **Write**   Writes data to the standard output stream

- **WriteLine**   Writes data to the standard output stream, followed by a line terminator

Uses for Console Applications

Console applications are useful in situations such as:

- Reading application or server log files

- Dumping collected data into a SQL Server or other database using INSERT and UPDATE commands

- Directly accessing .NET components

Console applications can conveniently be called from logon scripts or batch processes, and they can interact with both input and output files.

Code Walkthrough

The starting point for the console application is the *Sub Main* procedure, from which all other procedures can be called.

Handling Command-Line Arguments

In a console application *Sub Main* procedure, we can handle any command-line parameters the user entered. In the following code, we're allowing for one or more command-line arguments in an array named *args*. (The name is our choice.) If the *args* array has any elements, we'll use the first one (index zero) to find a matching product. Otherwise, we'll get input from the user at the command line. First, though, we'll connect to the database and populate a *DataSet* with data from the *Products* table.

```
Sub Main(ByVal args() As String)
    ⋮
    ConnectToDB()
    If args.Length > 0 Then
        FindProduct(args(0))
    Else
        Console.WriteLine("{0}{1}", vbCrLf, PROMPT_MESSAGE)
        Dim strInput As String = UCase(Trim(Console.ReadLine()))
```

We'll keep going until the user types **QUIT**, and we'll search for a matching product each time. We check to make sure the user has typed something before he has pressed the Enter key by testing the length of the input string.

```
While UCase(strInput) <> "QUIT"
    If Len(strInput) > 0 Then
        FindProduct(strInput)
    End If
```

Before reading the user's next input, we present the prompt message. Note that the *Write* and *WriteLine* methods accept a format parameter in just the same way as *String.Format* does. (See "Application #3: String Manipulation" in Chapter 2 for more information.)

```
    Console.WriteLine("{0}{1}", vbCrLf, PROMPT_MESSAGE)
    strInput = UCase(Trim(Console.ReadLine()))
End While
```

(continued)

```
        End
    End If
End Sub
```

To get the data the user wants, we need to connect to a database. In the following procedure, we'll first try to connect to the local SQL Server instance. If that doesn't work, we'll try a local Microsoft Data Engine (MSDE) installation (with the Northwind database).

```
Private Sub ConnectToDB()
    Dim strConnection As String = SQL_CONNECTION_STRING
    Dim IsConnecting As Boolean = True
    While IsConnecting
        Try
            Dim northwindConnection As New SqlConnection(strConnection)
            Dim ProductAdapter As New SqlDataAdapter("SELECT * FROM " & _
                "Products", northwindConnection)
            ProductAdapter.Fill(dsProducts, "Products")
```

Assuming the connection succeeded, we create a couple of *DataView*s, which let us sort as well as search the data in the *DataSet*. The first *DataView* will be used to find a product by its ID, and the second one will be used to find a product by its name.

```
            dvProductsByID = New DataView(dsProducts.Tables("products"), _
                "", "ProductID ASC", DataViewRowState.OriginalRows)
            dvProductsByName = New DataView(dsProducts.Tables( _
                "products"), "", "ProductName ASC", _
                DataViewRowState.OriginalRows)
```

If the attempt to connect with the first connection string fails, we try the alternate string.

```
        Catch exc As Exception
            If strConnection = SQL_CONNECTION_STRING Then
                strConnection = MSDE_CONNECTION_STRING
                Console.WriteLine("Attempting to Connect to MSDE")
            Else
                Console.WriteLine("To run this sample, you must have " & _
                    "SQL Server or MSDE with the Northwind database " & _
                    "installed. For instructions on installing MSDE, " & _
                    "view ReadMe.")
                End
            End If
        End Try
    End While
    Console.WriteLine("Connected to Database.")
End Sub
```

Finding Records

The *FindProduct* procedure searches for a matching product in the database, based on the user's input. It displays the product information if a valid ProductID or ProductName is found; otherwise, it displays an exception message. If the user enters a number, we search the *DataView* that's indexed on the ProductID. Otherwise, we search the ProductsByName *DataView*. We'll be writing data from the dvProducts *DataView* later, so we assign it to either the ID-related *DataView* or the Name-related one.

```
Private Sub FindProduct(ByVal strInput As String)
    Dim intItem As Integer
    If IsNumeric(strInput) Then
        intItem = dvProductsByID.Find(strInput)
        dvProducts = dvProductsByID
    Else
        intItem = dvProductsByName.Find(strInput)
        dvProducts = dvProductsByName
    End If
```

Once we're sure we've found a match (any result other than –1), we're ready to write the product information. The *Write* and *WriteLine* methods of the *Console* object accept a formatting parameter that lets you do a variety of things, such as aligning the output data into columns by specifying how many characters you want written. In this case, we're writing 17 chars in column 1. "{0}{1,-17}" means that we will write parameter zero, followed immediately by parameter 1, which is to be padded to 17 characters.

```
    If intItem = -1 Then
        Console.WriteLine("No product found.")
    Else
        Console.Write("{0}{1,-17}", vbCrLf, "Product ID: ")
        Console.WriteLine(dvProducts(intItem)("ProductID"))

        Console.Write("{0,-17}", "Product Name: ")
        Console.WriteLine(dvProducts(intItem)("ProductName"))
        ⋮
        Console.Write("{0,-17}", "Discontinued: ")
        If CBool(dvProducts(intItem)("Discontinued")) = False Then
            Console.WriteLine("False")
        Else
            Console.WriteLine("True")
        End If
    End If
End Sub
```

Conclusion

Console applications are in many ways as powerful as their more sophisticated counterparts, and they come in handy for many batch-oriented requirements. Keep the following in mind as you work with them:

- There's obviously no form associated with a console application. Instead, the entry point for your application is a public *Sub* procedure named *Main*.

- To get to a Command window, click the Start button, click Run, and then type **cmd**. Click OK.

- The *Console.ReadLine* method reads a line of characters and returns a string. The *Read* method returns a single character, followed by the new line character.

- *Console.Write* does not append a new line character to the output, allowing you to write more data to the same line. *WriteLine* outputs your data and then takes you to a new line.

7

Interacting with the Operating System

As you know, your .NET applications run inside an environment managed by the common language runtime (CLR). However, there are many cases where your application might need to communicate with underlying operating system features or services. This chapter examines some classes in the Base Class Library that allow you to interact with the operating system to perform tasks such as communicating with the COM port, launching and monitoring processes, and using Windows Management Instrumentation.

Application #54: Work with Environment Settings

This topic introduces two classes your applications can use to retrieve information about the current system configuration, such as the location of the TEMP directory, the current display size, and a list of available drives.

Building Upon...

Application #35: Create an Explorer-Style Application
Application #70: Reflection

New Concepts

The .NET Framework contains two classes in the *System* namespace that provide simple access to your system's environment settings. You can use this information to determine whether the current system meets your application's operational requirements. The *Environment* class exposes shared properties and methods dealing with the platform details, such as what operating system is running, what the current user name is, and the values for various environment settings. The *SystemInformation* class describes the operating system's current user-interface settings with properties such as *DoubleClickTime*, *MonitorCount*, and *WorkingArea*.

Code Walkthrough

The sample application displays information about the current system by invoking properties and methods of the *System.Environment* class. You can view the information by running the sample and selecting the various tabs.

Retrieving Environment Information

The *frmEnvironment_Load* event handler calls a set of utility procedures that populate the form's controls. The first call is to the *LoadList* procedure to populate the *lstFolders* list box with the names of each of the system's special folders. *LoadList* uses reflection to iterate over the members of the *Environment.Special-Folder* enumeration.

```
LoadList(lstFolders, GetType(Environment.SpecialFolder))
```

Another call to *LoadList* populates the *lstEnvironmentVariables* list box with the key values of the collection returned by *Environment.GetEnvironmentVariables*.

```
LoadList(lstEnvironmentVariables, _
    Environment.GetEnvironmentVariables.Keys)
```

The *LoadProperties* procedure simply populates some text boxes with various properties of the *Environment* class, and the *RunMethods* procedure displays the command-line arguments and local logical drives in some list boxes. Lastly, the *LoadSystemInformation* procedure uses properties of the *System-Information* class to populate the *lvwSystemInformation* list view control.

```
⋮
With lvwSystemInformation.Items.Add("DoubleClickTime")
    .SubItems.Add(SystemInformation.DoubleClickTime.ToString())
End With
⋮
```

On the Properties tab, you can click the Display Current Stack Trace button, which will display the stack trace in a message box by retrieving the *Stack-Trace* property of the *System.Environment* class.

```
MsgBox(Environment.StackTrace, MsgBoxStyle.OKOnly, Me.Text)
```

On the Methods tab, you can click the Expand button, which will parse the text in the Input text box and convert any environment variables delimited with percent symbols to their system values and display the results in the Results label. The *ExpandEnvironmentVariables* method of the *Environment* class performs all this work.

```
lblExpandResults.Text = _
    Environment.ExpandEnvironmentVariables(txtExpand.Text)
```

Conclusion

You can easily enforce platform run-time requirements for your applications by examining the information returned by the *Environment* and *SystemInformation* classes.

Application #55: Use the File System

This topic addresses how to retrieve information about a system's drive and directory structure. We also examine how to retrieve various attributes about files and directories from the file system. The sample application shows one way of creating an interface to navigate through drives, folders, and files.

Building Upon...

Application #1: Use Arrays
Application #73: Read From and Write To a Text File

New Concepts

The .NET Framework provides facilities for querying the file system through a number of different objects. You can find out what drives exist on a system, the contents of a directory, and various file attributes such as those displayed in the Window Explorer detail view.

DirectoryInfo and *FileInfo* Classes

The *DirectoryInfo* and *FileInfo* classes are available in the *System.IO* namespace. You can use instances of these classes to retrieve information about file-system objects. To create an instance of either, you must pass in a valid file-system path. With a *DirectoryInfo* instance, you can find out what that directory contains by using the *GetFiles* and *GetDirectories* methods. Each of these returns a string array containing the paths of the appropriate items. The *DirectoryInfo* and *FileInfo* classes also contain properties that expose file-system attributes such as *LastAccessTime*, *CreationTime*, and *LastWriteTime*.

TreeView Control

The *TreeView* control is commonly used to display directory structures to end users. The contents of a *TreeView* control consist of a hierarchy of *TreeNode* objects. You can add items to the *TreeView* by creating a new instance of the *TreeNode* class, setting its properties, and adding it to the *Nodes* collection of the *TreeView*. The *TreeNode* class has a number of properties that determine how it is displayed on screen. For most *TreeViews*, you'll want to set at least the *Text* property of each *TreeNode*, as this is what will display to the user. Also, any *TreeNode* with an item in its *Nodes* collection will automatically have an expand/collapse button next to it.

Code Walkthrough

The sample application uses various methods of the *DirectoryInfo* and *FileInfo* classes to create a file-system viewer. Users are able to expand directories and view metadata about various items. The file-system structure is displayed to the user through a *TreeView* control, and file-system object properties are displayed in the labels below the *TreeView*.

Retrieving Directory Contents

When the application starts, the *frmMain_Load* event handler calls the *LoadTreeView* method. The *LoadTreeView* method calls the shared *GetLogicalDrives* method of the *Directory* object. This returns an array of strings, each containing a drive letter. For each item in the array, a new *TreeNode* is added to the *TreeView*. In addition, each drive node is given a child node so that it appears with a plus sign next to it.

```
Dim strDrive As String
tvwRoot.Nodes.Clear()
For Each strDrive In Directory.GetLogicalDrives()
    With tvwRoot.Nodes.Add(strDrive)
        .Nodes.Add(DUMMY)
    End With
Next
```

The next activity occurs when a user clicks one of the plus signs to the left of the drive letters. The *BeforeExpand* event handler of the *TreeView* clears any existing child nodes and calls two functions, *AddFolders* and *AddFiles*, passing a reference to the node that is being expanded as a parameter.

```
e.Node.Nodes.Clear()
AddFolders(e.Node)
AddFiles(e.Node)
```

The *AddFolders* method retrieves the path for the passed-in *TreeNode* using the *FullPath* property. This string is then passed into the *GetDirectories* method of the *Directory* class. *GetDirectories* returns an array of strings containing the paths of the subdirectories. For each subdirectory, a child node is added to the current node. However, because we don't want the full path displaying in the *TreeView*, the *GetFileName* method of the *Path* class is used to extract the folder name.

```
Private Sub AddFolders(ByVal nod As TreeNode)
Dim strPath As String = nod.FullPath
Dim strDir As String
    For Each strDir In Directory.GetDirectories(strPath)
        ⋮
    Next
End Sub
```

Each child node added has its *Tag* property set to *ItemType.Directory*. *ItemType* is a private enumeration we are using to distinguish directories and files in the *TreeView*. This distinction will be important later in the application.

```
With nod.Nodes.Add(Path.GetFileName(strDir))
    .Tag = ItemType.Directory
    .Nodes.Add(DUMMY)
End With
```

The *AddFiles* method is almost identical to the *AddFolders* method except that it uses the *GetFiles* method of the *Directory* class and sets the *Tag* property of the child nodes to *ItemType.File*. Also, no *Dummy* child is added to the children because we don't want a plus sign to appear next to files in the *TreeView*.

```
Private Sub AddFiles(ByVal nod As TreeNode)
    Dim strPath As String = nod.FullPath
    Dim strFile As String
    For Each strFile In Directory.GetFiles(strPath)
        With nod.Nodes.Add(Path.GetFileName(strFile))
            .Tag = ItemType.File
        End With
    Next
End Sub
```

Retrieving Directory and File Information

When a user selects an item from the *TreeView*, that item's metadata is displayed. The *AfterSelect* event of the *TreeView* initiates this process. The *Tag* property for the selected node is interrogated to determine whether a file or directory item was clicked.

```
With e.Node
    Select Case .Tag
        Case ItemType.File
            ⋮
        Case ItemType.Directory
```

Within each *Case* statement, various controls are modified and a call to the *DisplayFSIProperties* method is made. Depending on whether a file or directory was selected, either an instance of the *FileInfo* or *DirectoryInfo* class is created and passed into the method call. The code for the file case is as follows:

```
Dim fi As New FileInfo(.FullPath)
lblLength.Text = fi.Length.ToString
DisplayFSIProperties(fi)
```

The *DisplayFSIProperties* procedure accepts a single parameter of type *FileSystemInfo*. Fortunately, both *FileInfo* and *DirectoryInfo* inherit from *FileSystemInfo*, so the procedure can operate on both object types. The procedure simply populates the interface with a variety of properties from the *FileSystemInfo* instance.

```
Private Sub DisplayFSIProperties(ByVal fsi As FileSystemInfo)
    lblAttributes.Text = fsi.Attributes.ToString
    lblCreationTime.Text = fsi.CreationTime.ToString
    lblLastAccessTime.Text = fsi.LastAccessTime.ToString
    lblLastWriteTime.Text = fsi.LastWriteTime.ToString
    lblExtension.Text = fsi.Extension
    lblFullName.Text = fsi.FullName
    lblName.Text = fsi.Name
End Sub
```

Conclusion

As you can see, not many steps are involved in retrieving file-system information. The majority of the work involved in creating a file-system viewing component deals with maintaining the *TreeView* control. Keep in mind that creating your own viewer is best suited to situations where you want to limit access to a specific set of directories. If you need an interface that allows a user to select a file or directory anywhere on the system, consider using one of the common dialog controls.

Application #56: Receive File Notifications

Many applications use the file system to maintain information. You can instruct the Framework to notify you when various aspects of the file system change. For example, you can design your application to automatically reload a configuration file whenever that file is updated rather than wait for the next application launch to apply the changes. This is a very useful feature for server applications where restarting the program might not be an option.

Building Upon...

Application #73: Read From and Write To a Text File

New Concepts

The Framework contains a class in the *System.IO* namespace named *FileSystem-Watcher*. This class allows you to specify what aspects of the file system you want to monitor and raises events when those aspects change. You identify the target directory by setting the *Path* property, and you specify what files to watch by setting the *Filter* property. Setting the *Filter* property to an empty string tells the watcher to watch all files. Assigning the *NotifyFilter* property an instance of the *NotifyFilters* enumeration determines what events the watcher will raise. Once all the properties are set, you can enable the watcher by setting the *EnableRaisingEvents* property to *True*.

Code Walkthrough

The sample application uses the *FileSystemWatcher* component to raise events when files in a specified location are manipulated. The list box displays messages from the *FileSystemWatcher* as you create, modify, and delete files in the specified directory. You can change the type of files to watch and the location to watch in by clicking the Enable Raising Events check box (it looks like a button) and selecting the events from the check-box list.

The *chkEvents_CheckedChanged* event handler calls the *GatherFSWProperties* procedure and then enables watching with *fsw.EnableRaisingEvents = blnIsRunning*. The *GatherFSWProperties* procedure sets the *Path*, *Filter*, *IncludeSubdirectories*, and *NotifyFilter* properties of the provided *FileSystemWatcher*.

```
Private Sub GatherFSWProperties(ByVal fsw As FileSystemWatcher)
    fsw.Path = txtPath.Text
    fsw.Filter = txtFilter.Text
    fsw.IncludeSubdirectories = chkIncludeSubdirectories.Checked
    fsw.NotifyFilter = CType(GetChecks(clstNotifyFilter), NotifyFilters)
End Sub
```

The *GetChecks* procedure is a utility function that converts the checked items in the check-box list into an instance of the *NotifyFilters* enumeration.

Once the *FileSystemWatcher* is enabled, it will raise events when the specified file-system changes occur. The *HandleChangedCreatedDeleted* event handler is configured to handle its *Changed*, *Created*, and *Deleted* events and post a message to the *lstEvents* list box.

```
Private Sub HandleChangedCreatedDeleted(ByVal sender As Object, _
    ByVal e As System.IO.FileSystemEventArgs) _
    Handles fsw.Changed, fsw.Created, fsw.Deleted
    Dim strText As String = String.Format("{0} was {1}", _
        e.Name, e.ChangeType)
    AddItem(strText)
End Sub
```

Conclusion

Responding to changes in the file system can make your applications more flexible and increase availability. The *FileSystemWatcher* provides a simple interface for connecting your application to the file system.

Application #57: Use the Event Log

Diagnosing and troubleshooting application errors are important parts of application maintenance. You can increase your ability to accurately diagnose application behavior by coding the application to report important conditions, such as errors or changes in configuration, to an external and convenient data store. The Event Log is an excellent place for such messages because it's fast, easily accessible, and built into the operating system.

New Concepts

The Windows event log system maintains a set of logs and a list of valid event sources. An event source is simply a string your applications use to identify themselves when sending event messages. Each source maps to a single log. This allows applications some flexibility in sending messages to the event log. An application can explicitly state what log to send the message to, or it can simply provide a source name, letting the operating system decide which log to use.

EventLog Class

The *EventLog* class in the *System.Diagnostics* namespace provides an interface for working with the system-defined logs and for creating your own custom logs. To work with a specific log, you create an instance of the *EventLog* class and provide the name of the log you want to use. You can optionally provide a machine name if the log resides on another machine. Once you have a reference to a log, you can read from it using the *Entries* property, which returns an *EventLogEntryCollection* object containing an *EventLogEntry* instance for each entry in the log. Entry details are available through properties such as *User-*

Name, *TimeWritten*, and *Message* as well as others. You use the *WriteEntry* method of the *EventLog* class to send a message to the log. At a minimum, you must provide a message and a message source, which is typically the name of your application. This method is heavily overloaded, so you can optionally specify a message type, category, and event ID.

You can let the operating system choose which log to use by providing an empty string for the *logName* parameter of the *EventLog* constructor. This forces the operating system to pick a log based on the source name you provide when sending a message with the *WriteEntry* method. The following code demonstrates this approach:

```
Dim el As New EventLog("", Environment.MachineName, mySource)
el.WriteEntry(myMessage)
```

In general, applications can write messages to the Application event log. However, you might decide that your application should have its own log. This is useful during development when you might be generating an unusually high number of log messages while testing. It's also useful in production when you want each application to have its own log.

> **Tip**   Consider abstracting the event log name to the application configuration file. That way you can easily change what log the application writes to. See "Application #72: Configuration Settings" in Chapter 8 for information on using configuration files.

Use the shared *CreateEventSource* method to define a new log. This method requires a log name and the name of an event source that can write to the log. Keep in mind that a source can point to only one log, so if you want to point an existing source to the new log you'll first need to delete the existing source mapping. The *DeleteEventSource* method will do this.

> **Important**   You'll need to reboot your machine for any event-source mapping changes to take effect.

Code Walkthrough

The sample application demonstrates how to read from and write to event logs as well as create and delete custom application logs. After adding an entry or creating a new log, click the Read From The Event Log button to verify your changes.

Writing to an Event Log

The *btnWriteEntry_Click* event handler on *frmWrite* sends a message to the event log system with a source value of "VB.NET How To: Using the Event Log". The system will put this message in whatever log is currently mapped to that source. When you first run the application, this is an unmapped source, so the system will automatically map it to the Application log. After you create a custom log and reboot as described later, the messages will go to the custom log.

```
Dim ev As New EventLog("", Environment.MachineName, _
    "VB.NET How To: Using the Event Log")
ev.WriteEntry(txtEntry.Text, entryType, CInt(txtEventID.Text))
ev.Close()
```

Reading from an Event Log

The *btnViewLogEntries_Click* event handler in *frmRead* creates a reference to the log identified in the *logType* variable. *logType* is set when you select a log from the list box. You don't need to specify an event source because this reference will not be used to write to the log.

```
Dim ev As New EventLog(logType)
```

Next, we loop backward through the *Entries* collection and output information for each *EventLogEntry*. The loop uses a *Step* value of –1 because the items in the *Entries* property are ordered by date and we want to display the ten latest entries.

```
Dim entry As EventLogEntry
:
Dim i As Integer
For i = ev.Entries.Count - 1 To LastLogToShow Step -1
    Dim CurrentEntry As EventLogEntry = ev.Entries(i)
    rchEventLogOutput.Text &= "Event ID : " & _
        CurrentEntry.EventID & vbCrLf
    rchEventLogOutput.Text &= "Entry Type : " & _
        CurrentEntry.EntryType.ToString() & vbCrLf
    rchEventLogOutput.Text &= "Message : " & _
        CurrentEntry.Message & vbCrLf & vbCrLf
Next
```

Managing Event Logs

The *btnCreateLog_Click* event handler in *frmCreateDelete* creates a new log and remaps the "VB.NET How To: Using the Event Log" source to the new log. First, we check the existence of the log and the source. If the source exists, we must delete it before it can be mapped to the new log.

```
If EventLog.SourceExists("VB.NET How To: Using the Event Log") Then
    EventLog.DeleteEventSource("VB.NET How To: Using the Event Log")
End If
```

Now we can create the new log and map the source to it with a call to *CreateEventSource*.

```
EventLog.CreateEventSource("VB.NET How To: Using the Event Log", & _
    txtLogNameToCreate.Text)
```

Remember, if you send a message to the event log with this source, it will continue to go to the Application log until you reboot the machine.

The *btnDeleteLog_Click* event handler in *frmCreateDelete* checks the existence of the specified log and deletes it.

```
If EventLog.Exists(txtLogNameToDelete.Text) Then
    EventLog.Delete(txtLogNameToDelete.Text)
```

Conclusion

Reporting application status to the Event Log allows users and administrators to more easily troubleshoot your applications. The degree to which the event log is useful is dependent on the quality of information you choose to have your application place in it. Fortunately, the *EventLog* class makes it very easy to supply rich error data with little impact on performance.

Application #58: Read and Write Performance Counters

Performance counters provide an extremely valuable mechanism for monitoring the performance and health of a machine or a specific application. Your applications can even create their own custom counters in which to output detailed performance metrics.

Building Upon...

Application #1: Use Arrays
Application #7: Object-Oriented Features

New Concepts

The *System.Diagnostics* namespace contains classes for working with performance counters. Counters are organized into categories, and there can be multiple instances within a category. Each instance contains its own set of counters. For example, there is a category named *.NET CLR Data*. This category maintains a default instance named *_global_* and another instance for each process hosted by the runtime. Each instance contains its own set of counters, such as "SqlCli-ent: Total # failed connects", and the *_global_* instance maintains totals across all instances. When retrieving counter data, you must first get a reference to a cate-gory with the *PerformanceCounterCategory* class. You can call the *GetCounters* method to retrieve an array of *PerformanceCounter* objects for that category. If the category contains multiple instances, you must provide the instance name to the *GetCounters* method. The following code demonstrates this:

```
Dim cat As PerformanceCounterCategory = _
    New PerformanceCounterCategory(".NET CLR Data")
Dim counters As PerformanceCounter() = cat.GetCounters("someInstance")
```

Once you have a *PerformanceCounter* instance, you can retrieve its value by calling the *NextValue* method. If the counter is a custom counter, you can mod-ify its value with the *Increment*, *IncrementBy*, and *Decrement* methods.

Code Walkthrough

The sample application demonstrates how to enumerate through all the perfor-mance counters on a system and how to modify the values of custom counters. You'll also see how to determine whether a counter is built-in or custom.

Retrieving Counter Information

The *frmMain_Load* event handler populates the *cboCategories* combo box with the names of all the performance counter categories. First, we retrieve the cat-egories on the system by calling the shared *GetCategories* method.

```
Dim myCategories() As PerformanceCounterCategory
myCategories = PerformanceCounterCategory.GetCategories()
```

Next, the name of each category is added to the *myCategoryNames* array.

```
Dim myCategoryNames(myCategories.Length - 1) As String
Dim i As Integer = 0 ' Used as a counter
For Each myCategory In myCategories
    myCategoryNames(i) = myCategory.CategoryName
        i += 1
Next
```

After sorting the array, each name is added to the combo box.

```
Array.Sort(myCategoryNames)
Dim nameString As String
For Each nameString In myCategoryNames
    Me.cboCategories.Items.Add(nameString)
Next
```

The *cboCategories_SelectedIndexChanged* event handler runs when you select a category from the category combo box. The first step in retrieving all the counters for a category is to determine whether the category has any instances. We do this by calling the *GetInstanceNames* method and checking the length of the returned array. If the length is zero, no instances are defined and we can just retrieve the counters by calling *GetCounters*.

```
myCategory = New PerformanceCounterCategory( _
    Me.cboCategories.SelectedItem.ToString())
myCounterNames = myCategory.GetInstanceNames()
If myCounterNames.Length = 0 Then
    myCounters.AddRange(myCategory.GetCounters())
```

However, if there are instances defined, we must loop through the instances and retrieve each instance's counters by passing the instance name into *GetCounters*.

```
Else
    Dim i As Integer
    For i = 0 To myCounterNames.Length - 1
        myCounters.AddRange( _
            myCategory.GetCounters(myCounterNames(i)))
    Next
End If
```

Now that the *myCounters* array is populated, we can add the items to the *cboCounters* combo box. However, we have created a utility class named *CounterDisplayItem*. This class wraps a *PerformanceCounter* instance and overrides the *ToString* method to return instance and counter name information as a single string. For each counter in our array, we create an instance of *CounterDisplayItem* populated with the current counter and add it to the combo box. When the combo box renders, it calls the *ToString* method on each of its items.

```
Me.cboCounters.Items.Clear()
Me.cboCounters.Text = ""
For Each myCounter In myCounters
    Me.cboCounters.Items.Add(New CounterDisplayItem(myCounter))
Next
```

The *cboCounters_SelectedIndexChanged* event handler retrieves the counter from the currently selected *CounterDisplayItem* and outputs the counter's properties to the form.

```
Dim myCounterDisplay As CounterDisplayItem
myCounterDisplay = CType(cboCounters.SelectedItem, CounterDisplayItem)
m_Counter = myCounterDisplay.Counter
Me.txtCounterType.Text = m_Counter.CounterType.ToString()
Me.txtCounterHelp.Text = m_Counter.CounterHelp.ToString()
Me.sbrStatus.Text = ""
```

The controls for modifying counter values are enabled or disabled depending on whether the current counter is a custom counter, because only custom counters can be modified. Unfortunately, there is no *IsCustom* property on the *PerformanceCounter* class. Instead, we have created an *IsCustom* property in the *CounterDisplayItem* utility. This method sets the counter's *ReadOnly* property to false and then attempts to retrieve the counter's value. This operation will throw an error if the counter is not a custom counter.

```
Dim isReadOnly As Boolean = m_Counter.ReadOnly
Try
    m_Counter.ReadOnly = False
    m_Counter.NextValue()
    Return True
Catch exc As Exception
    Return False
Finally
    m_Counter.ReadOnly = isReadOnly
End Try
```

Modifying Counter Values

Once you have identified that a counter is a custom counter, you can modify its value using the *Increment* and *Decrement* methods of the *PerformanceCounter* class. These each modify the current value by 1. If you want to modify by a value larger than 1, you can use the *IncrementBy* method, supplying negative numbers if you want to decrement the counter.

Conclusion

Performance counters offer an easy way for your applications to export real-time performance and fault metrics to the operating system. The types in the *System.Diagnostics* namespace provide a complete framework for working with these counters and even creating your own.

Application #59: Use the *Process* Class and Shell Functionality

This topic discusses how to start additional processes from a .NET application. This can be useful in scenarios where one application needs to selectively enlist the help of another application or service.

Building Upon...

Application #55: Use the File System
Application #73: Read From and Write to a Text File

New Concepts

The *System.Diagnostics* namespace contains the *Process* class, which contains a variety of methods for spawning processes. The easiest way to launch a process is to call the shared *Start* method and provide the file path to the executable or file of interest. You can specify any file type that has an executable mapped to its Open action. The *Start* method is overloaded, so you can optionally specify command-line arguments to pass to the new process. If you want even greater control over how the new process is started, you can create an instance of the *ProcessStartInfo* class and pass it into the *Start* method. The *ProcessStartInfo* class provides many properties that affect how an application is launched. The *WindowStyle* property determines how the new process will display: *Maximized*, *Minimized*, *Normal*, or *Hidden*. The *Arguments* property provides another way to supply command-line arguments. An especially powerful member is the *Verb* property. Setting this property allows you to perform an action on the file other than opening it. The only restriction is that the verb you supply must be defined for that file type on the system.

Code Walkthrough

The sample application demonstrates how to use the *Process* class to launch applications. The *btnStartProcess_Click* event handler simply launches Notepad using the shared *Start* method.

```
Process.Start("notepad.exe")
```

The *btnProcessStartInfo_Click* event handler also launches Notepad, but it uses the *ProcessStartInfo* class to specify that it should be maximized.

```
Dim startInfo As New ProcessStartInfo("notepad.exe")
startInfo.WindowStyle = ProcessWindowStyle.Maximized
Process.Start(startInfo)
```

The *btnUseVerb_Click* event handler creates a text file and then creates a *ProcessStartInfo* object for the file.

```
Dim sw As New System.IO.StreamWriter("demofile_shell.txt")
sw.WriteLine("Eureka! You've printed!")
sw.Close()
Dim startInfo As New ProcessStartInfo("demofile_shell.txt")
```

Next, we indicate that we want to print the document instead of opening it.

```
startInfo.Verb = "print"
```

This time, when we start the process we'll maintain a reference to the returned *Process* instance so that we can call *WaitForExit*, which will force our application to block until the printing finishes.

```
Dim p As Process = Process.Start(startInfo)
p.WaitForExit()
```

Finally, we can delete the sample file and display a message box with the *ExitCode* of the process. In general, an exit code of 0 indicates a success and a nonzero number indicates some error condition.

```
System.IO.File.Delete("demofile_shell.txt")
MessageBox.Show("Printing finished with an exit code of " + _
    p.ExitCode.ToString())
```

The *btnCommandLine_Click* event handler uses the *Arguments* property of the *ProcessStartInfo* object to send a command-line argument to a new instance of Windows Explorer.

```
Dim startInfo As New ProcessStartInfo("explorer.exe")
startInfo.Arguments = "/n"
Process.Start(startInfo)
```

Conclusion

The *Process* class provides a simple way to interact with other applications with very little overhead. This is especially convenient for interaction with applications whose only automation interface might be through the command line.

Application #60: View Process Information

Viewing process information can be an extremely useful feature for administrative tools and utilities. With the appropriate information, you can better diagnose problematic machine behavior. For example, you can identify how much of your system's resources a particular application is consuming, such as memory or processor time.

Building Upon...

Application #3: String Manipulation
Application #35: Create an Explorer-Style Application

New Concepts

The *Process* class in the *System.Diagnostics* namespace provides a detailed interface for retrieving information about the processes currently running on a machine. The shared *GetCurrentProcess*, *GetProcessByID*, and *GetProcessBy-Name* methods each return a single *Process* object. The *GetProcesses* method, however, returns an array of *Process* objects, each associated with the appropriate resource. You can identify how much processor time a process is using with the *PrivilegedProcessorTime*, *UserProcessorTime*, and *TotalProcessorTime* properties. *PrivilegedProcessorTime* is the amount of CPU time a processor spends executing core operating system code, while *UserProcessorTime* is the amount of time spent executing application code. *TotalProcessorTime* equals the sum of the two. If memory usage is what you're interested in, you should use the *WorkingSet* property to determine how much physical memory a process is consuming.

The *Process* class has an unusual behavior related to its property values. The properties of the class are organized into groups. The first time you access a member of a group, the class retrieves all the property values for the group and caches them. The group's values are not updated again until you call the *Refresh* method.

Sometimes, you might need to know how specific threads or modules within a process are affecting the system. The *Process* class has a *Threads* property, which returns an array of *ProcessThread* objects containing thread-specific CPU usage properties. The *Process* class's *Modules* property returns an array of *Process-Module* objects identifying each module's file location and memory consumption.

Code Walkthrough

The sample application demonstrates how to use the *Process* class to view information about all the running processes on a machine. Clicking one of the listed processes displays resource-use statistics in the right pane and thread information in the bottom pane. You can view which code modules a process has loaded by right-clicking the process and choosing *View Modules*.

Reading Process Data

The *frmMain_Load* event handler calls the *EnumProcesses* method, which retrieves an array of process objects by calling the shared *GetProcesses* method of the *Process* class.

```
Dim Processes() As Process
    ⋮
Processes = Process.GetProcesses()
```

Each process is then added to the module-level collection *mcolProcesses*, and some CPU usage–related properties are retrieved.

```
For Each p In Processes
    mcolProcesses.Add(p, p.Id.ToString())
    tppt = p.PrivilegedProcessorTime
    tupt = p.UserProcessorTime
    tpt = p.TotalProcessorTime
```

The statistics of the current process are added to variables to maintain some total usage information.

```
mtpt = mtpt.Add(tpt)
mtppt = mtppt.Add(tppt)
mtupt = mtupt.Add(tupt)
```

After some formatting of the CPU usage numbers, the statistics are added to the *lvProcesses* list view control.

```
With Me.lvProcesses.Items.Add(p.ProcessName & " (0x" & _
  Hex(p.Id).ToLower() & ")")
    .SubItems.Add(p.Id.ToString())
    .SubItems.Add(strTPT)
    .SubItems.Add(strPPPT)
    .SubItems.Add(strPUPT)
End With
```

Finally, a custom entry is added to the list view containing the calculated CPU usage totals.

```
⋮
With Me.lvProcesses.Items.Add(PROCESS_NAME_TOTAL)
    .SubItems.Add(PID_NA)
    .SubItems.Add(mstrTPT)
    .SubItems.Add(mstrPPPT)
    .SubItems.Add(mstrPUPT)
End With
```

Selecting a process from the list view invokes the *lvProcesses_Selected-IndexChanged* event handler. This procedure retrieves the process ID from the selected item and then resets some interface properties.

```
Dim lv As ListView = CType(sender, ListView)
If lv.SelectedItems.Count = 1 Then
    Dim strProcessId As String = lv.SelectedItems(0).SubItems(1).Text
⋮
```

Next, the appropriate process is retrieved from the process collection and passed into calls to *EnumProcess* and *EnumThreads*.

```
p = CType(mcolProcesses.Item(strProcessId), Process)
p.Refresh()
EnumProcess(p)
EnumThreads(p)
```

The *EnumProcess* method makes a series of calls to the *AddNameValue-Pair* method to add numerous process properties to the *lvProcessDetail* list view. Many of these property calls are wrapped in *Try/Catch* blocks to handle various exceptions.

```
⋮
Dim lv As ListView = Me.lvProcessDetail
lvProcessDetail.Items.Clear()
mits = lvProcessDetail.Items

Const NA As String = "Not Authorized"
    Try
        AddNameValuePair("Start Time", p.StartTime.ToLongDateString() & _
          " " & p.StartTime.ToLongTimeString())
        AddNameValuePair("Responding", p.Responding.ToString())
```

The *EnumThreads* method outputs the properties of each *ProcessThread* in the process's *Threads* collection of the process. CPU usage statistics, priority settings, and thread start time are output to the *lvThreads* list view control.

```
For Each t In p.Threads
    tppt = t.PrivilegedProcessorTime
    ⋮
    With Me.lvThreads.Items.Add(t.Id.ToString())
        .SubItems.Add(t.BasePriority.ToString())
        .SubItems.Add(t.CurrentPriority.ToString())
    ⋮
```

The *mnuModules_Click* event handler retrieves the appropriate process from the process collection and calls its *Refresh* method to ensure we get up-to-date information.

```
⋮
Dim p As Process
p = CType(mcolProcesses.Item(strProcessId), Process)
⋮
p.Refresh()
```

Next, a call to the *Count* property of the *Modules* property is used to determine whether you are able to access the modules for the process. If not, this action will result in a *Win32Exception*.

```
Try
    Dim i As Integer = p.Modules.Count
Catch exp As System.ComponentModel.Win32Exception
    MessageBox.Show("Sorry, you are not authorized to read this ⟶
        information.", Me.Text, MessageBoxButtons.OK, _
        MessageBoxIcon.Exclamation)
    Exit Sub
End Try
```

The actual work for displaying the module data occurs in *frmModules*. This form has a *ParentProcess* property to which we assign the current process reference before making a call to *RefreshModules*.

```
If mfrmMod Is Nothing Then
    mfrmMod = New frmModules()
End If
mfrmMod.ParentProcess = p
mfrmMod.RefreshModules()
mfrmMod.ShowDialog(Me)
```

The *RefreshModules* method resets the interface and calls the *EnumModules* method.

```
Me.sbInfo.Text = "Process = " & mParentProcess.ProcessName
Me.lvModDetail.Items.Clear()
EnumModules()
```

EnumModules loops through the array returned by the *Modules* property, adding each *ProcessModule* to the *mcolModules* collection and each module name to the *lvModules* list view.

```
⋮
Dim m As ProcessModule
For Each m In mParentProcess.Modules
    Me.lvModules.Items.Add(m.ModuleName)
    Try
        mcolModules.Add(m, m.ModuleName)
⋮
```

Upon selecting a module, the *lvModules_SelectedIndexChanged* event handler calls *EnumModule*, which clears the *lvModDetail* list view and displays a set of the *ProcessModule* property values.

```
Me.lvModDetail.Items.Clear()
Try
    AddNameValuePair("Base Address", Hex(m.BaseAddress.ToInt32).ToLower())
    AddNameValuePair("Entry Point Address", _
        Hex(m.EntryPointAddress.ToInt32).ToLower())
⋮
```

Conclusion

The system's Task Manager is useful for viewing process statistics but does not expose thread or module details. It is also viewable only on the local machine. With the *Process* class, you have greater control over what information you want to expose and through what interface you want to expose it.

Application #61: Use WMI

The Windows Management Instrumentation (WMI) framework provides a standardized model for retrieving operating system, hardware, and application information. Using WMI can reduce the number of unique APIs you need to learn and simplify your coding effort.

Building Upon...

Application #35: Create an Explorer-Style Application

New Concepts

WMI is built into the Windows operating systems and is accessible through the classes in the *System.Management* namespace. WMI is intended to provide a single API for retrieving system data across an enterprise. Each type of resource that exposes data through WMI is identified by a WMI Class. For example, *Win32_DisplayConfiguration* describes a system's display capabilities, and *Win32_NetworkAdapter* describes the properties of a physical network adapter. You retrieve data through WMI by executing queries that indicate the class of data you're interested in. The *ManagementObjectSearcher* provides one way to submit a query. The constructor can take a query in the form of a string or an *ObjectQuery* instance. Call the *ManagementObjectSearcher Get* method to execute the query. The *Get* method returns an instance of the *ManagementObject-Collection* containing one *ManagementObject* instance for each entity matching your query criteria. The *ManagementObject* contains a key/value collection named *Properties* from which you can retrieve information about that entity. The following code shows how to issue a query and display a property for each returned item:

```
Dim sQuery as string = "SELECT * FROM Win32_networkadapter"
Dim mosSearcher As New ManagementObjectSearcher(sQuery)
Dim moItem As ManagementObject
For Each moItem In mosSearcher.Get()
    MessageBox.Show(moItem.Properties("ProductName").Value.ToString())
Next
```

Similar to database access, some WMI queries can return large amounts of data and take a significant amount of time to execute. In these cases, it's sometimes desirable to execute the query asynchronously. The *ManagementObject-Searcher Get* method has an overload that accepts a *ManagementOperation-Observer* instance as a parameter. A call to this overload does not block, allowing your application to continue executing. The *ManagementOperation-Observer* raises events as the status of the query changes. You must make sure you have connected some event handlers before you execute the *Get* method.

Code Walkthrough

The sample application demonstrates how to retrieve some commonly used information about the operating system, machine BIOS, and hardware. The Asynchronous Enumeration tab shows how to perform asynchronous queries, and the WMI Classes tab shows how to retrieve a list of all the WMI classes installed on the system.

Synchronous Queries

The *btnOperatingSytem_Click* event handler defines a query as a string to retrieve operating system information with the *Win32_OperatingSystem* class.

```
Dim search As New _
    ManagementObjectSearcher("SELECT * FROM Win32_OperatingSystem")
```

The results of the query are output to the *txtOutput* text box.

```
Dim info As ManagementObject
For Each info In search.Get()
    txtOutput.Text = "Name: " & info("name").ToString() & CRLF
    ⋮
Next
```

The *btnProcessor_Click* event handler is almost identical except it uses a *SelectQuery* instance to define a query to retrieve processor information. The *SelectQuery* object reduces the complexity of the query you need to define by requiring only the class of the entities you want to retrieve.

```
Dim query As New SelectQuery("Win32_processor")
Dim search As New ManagementObjectSearcher(query)
⋮
```

Asynchronous Queries

The *btnStartEnum_Click* event handler asynchronously executes a query by connecting the *OnEnumObjectReady* method as an event handler to a *Management-OperationObserver* object. After defining the query, you should create an instance of the *ManagementOperationObserver* and attach event handlers to any of the events you're interested in. The *ObjectReady* event fires once for each object returned by the query and will be handled by the *OnEnumObjectReady* method.

```
⋮
Dim observer As New ManagementOperationObserver()
AddHandler observer.ObjectReady, AddressOf OnEnumObjectReady
```

When you're ready to execute the query, pass the *ManagementOperation-Observer* instance to the *ManagementObjectSearcher Get* method.

```
search.Get(observer)
```

The *OnEnumObjectReady* procedure uses the *ObjectReadyEventArgs* parameter *NewObject* property to reference the returned *ManagementObject*.

```
If Not IsNothing(e.NewObject("VolumeName")) Then
    item.SubItems.Add(e.NewObject("VolumeName").ToString())
    item.SubItems.Add(e.NewObject("Size").ToString() & " bytes")
    If e.NewObject("FreeSpace").ToString() <> "0" Then
        item.SubItems.Add(e.NewObject("FreeSpace").ToString() & " bytes")
    Else
        item.SubItems.Add("(none)")
    End If
End If
```

Conclusion

The WMI framework can be leveraged to expose a tremendous amount of information about systems on your enterprise. The majority of the work involved in querying the WMI data stores is handled by the classes in the *System.Management* namespace, allowing you to focus on learning the names of the specific WMI entities and properties your applications need.

Application #62: Respond to System Events

A robust application should be able to react automatically to changes in system configuration. Many aspects of a system can change at run time and affect how your application operates. Designing your application to automatically react to these changes makes it easier to use and more reliable.

New Concepts

The *Microsoft.Win32* namespace contains a class named *SystemEvents*. This class exposes many shared events that are raised in response to various system changes. The *UserPreferenceChanged* event is raised when a user modifies system properties such as mouse, keyboard, or display appearance settings. The *LowMemory* event notifies your application when the system is running out of free RAM. Other events notify you of a system shutdown, user log off, and system time changes.

You can attach to these events using the normal *Handles* statement, but you might want some flexibility in determining when your application should respond to these events. The *AddHandler* and *RemoveHandler* functions allow you to selectively attach and detach event handlers to a particular event.

> **Important**   *AddHandler* and *RemoveHandler* can be used with any event, not just those exposed by *SystemEvents*.

AddHandler requires a reference to an event for the first parameter and a delegate to an event handler as the second parameter. You can manually create the delegate or use the *AddressOf* operator to automatically create the delegate for you. You must make sure the signature of the event handler is identical to that of the event you are attaching to. Use the *RemoveHandler* function to detach an event handler from an event using the same parameters as your call to *AddHandler*.

Code Walkthrough

The sample application uses the *AddHandler* and *RemoveHandler* functions to dynamically attach and detach from the shared events exposed by the *System-Events* class. The application will display a notification message in the text box for any system event that is selected in the list of check boxes. For example, check the Handle Time Changes check box and then change the system time through the Date/Time Properties control panel. A message will appear indicating receipt of the system event.

The *chkTimeChanges_CheckedChanged* event handler uses the *AddHandler* function to assign the *TimeHandler* procedure as an event handler for the *SystemEvents.TimeChanged* event.

```
Private Sub chkTimeChanges_CheckedChanged(ByVal sender As System.Object, ByVal
e As System.EventArgs) Handles chkTimeChanges.CheckedChanged
    If chkTimeChanges.Checked Then
        AddHandler SystemEvents.TimeChanged, _
            AddressOf TimeHandler
```

If the check box is deselected, we remove the *TimeHandler* procedure from the *SystemEvent.TimeChanged* event handler list with a call to the *RemoveHandler* function.

```
RemoveHandler SystemEvents.TimeChanged, _
    AddressOf TimeHandler
```

The application performs an identical set of actions for each demonstrated system event.

Conclusion

Responding to system events requires very little code because the *SystemEvents* class handles all low-level communication with the operating system. Although their use is not required, the *AddHandler* and *RemoveHandler* functions can increase application performance by allowing you to selectively respond to events only when necessary.

Application #63: Use the COM Port

Modern computers contain many types of interfaces to communicate with hardware devices. Even with newer interfaces like USB and FireWire, the COM port continues to be heavily supported by hardware manufacturers for devices ranging from home PC peripherals to industrial factory machines. Communicating with COM ports is a great way to extend the power of your applications beyond the desktop.

Building Upon...

Application #7: Object-Oriented Features
Application #79: Use Thread Pooling

New Concepts

Unlike the other topics in the chapter, there is no Framework namespace or class for communicating with COM ports. Unfortunately, this means the only means .NET provides is through calls directly to the operating system. Even worse, you need to be familiar with some 22 system functions to successfully open, write to, read from, and close a COM port. On the bright side, this topic and its associated sample application provide a wrapper class that has all the operating system code already written. This class is named after the original specification developed in the 1960s, *Rs232*.

Rs232 Class

You need to be familiar with a number of hardware communication topics—such as parity, baud rate, and stop bits—to use the system APIs for COM port communication. Fortunately, the *Rs232* class handles these nasty details and requires only that you assign the *Port* property an integer to identify the specific COM port you want to work with and call the *Open* method. You can override the default settings through properties such as *BaudRate*, *BufferSize*, and *Parity*. The *Open* method throws an exception if it's unable to connect to the port.

The *Write* method allows you to send a *String* or *Byte* array to the connected device and does not return a value. If you expect your device to respond, you need to set up a mechanism to monitor for responses. The *Read* method attempts to read the specified number of bytes from the port. It returns an integer indicating how many bytes were actually read, with a -1 indicating that no data was read. The new data can be retrieved through the *InputStream* property. A call to *Read* throws an exception if the port isn't in a valid state for reading, such as being closed before the *Read* method is called.

Although you don't need to explicitly make Win32 API calls to use the *Rs232* class, an understanding of the basic mechanics will help you should you choose to dive into the inner workings of the class. As mentioned earlier, *Rs232* uses a number of functions in the Kernel32 system DLL. Kernel32 is known as a C-style DLL because it doesn't expose any of the COM interfaces. To gain access to its functions, you have to use the *DllImportAttribute* class defined in the *System.Runtime.InteropServices* namespace. First, you declare a function with a signature matching the DLL's function. You can then place the *DllImport* attribute on the function declaration and indicate what DLL the function resides in. The following code imports the *GetLastError* function from Kernel32:

```
<DllImport("kernel32.dll")>
Private Shared Function GetLastError() As Integer
End Function
```

Once a function is imported, you can call it just like any other .NET function. The Framework's Platform Invoke system handles the marshalling of parameters and return values to the DLL and back.

Code Walkthrough

The sample application uses the *Rs232* class to check for available ports, check for modems on those ports, and send messages to a modem if one is found. The *frmMain Form* maintains an *Rs232* instance in a module-level variable named *m_CommPort*. The *btnCheckForPorts_Click* event handler uses this instance to check whether any devices are connected to COM ports 1 through 4 by calling the *IsPortAvailable* function for each port number. The *IsPortAvailable* function attempts to open a connection to the specified port by invoking the *Open* method of the *m_CommPort* object.

```
Try
    m_CommPort.Port = ComPort
    m_CommPort.Open()
    m_CommPort.Close()
    Return True
Catch
    Return False
End Try
```

The *btnCheckModems_Click* event handler calls the *IsPortAModem* method for each of the available ports. This is accomplished by opening the port and sending an "*AT*" command to the device with the *Write* method. The string "*AT*" is converted to an ASCII byte array as it is passed into the *Write* method.

```
m_CommPort.Port = ComPort
m_CommPort.Open()
m_CommPort.Write(Encoding.ASCII.GetBytes("AT" & Chr(13)))
```

A modem will acknowledge the "*AT*" command with an "*OK*". This procedure blocks execution for 200 milliseconds to give the device a chance to respond.

```
System.Threading.Thread.Sleep(200)
Application.DoEvents()
```

You can call the *Read* method to determine whether the device responded. If it didn't, the *Read* method will throw an error. In this case, it doesn't matter what data was returned by the device, so retrieving data from *InputBuffer* is not necessary.

```
Try
    Dim b As Byte
    m_CommPort.Read(1)
    m_CommPort.ClearInputBuffer()
    m_CommPort.Close()
    Return True
Catch exc As Exception
    m_CommPort.Close()
    Return False
End Try
```

The *btnSendUserCommand_Click* event handler opens the port that a modem was found on and executes whatever command you enter in the *txtUserCommand TextBox*. Some valid commands to try are **ATI3**, **ATI4**, and **ATI7**. These all return information about the installed modem.

```
m_CommPort.Port = (m_ModemPort)
m_CommPort.Open()
m_CommPort.Write(Encoding.ASCII.GetBytes(Me.txtUserCommand.Text & Chr(13)))
```

After sending the message, you need to enable some mechanism to watch for responses. You could manually start another thread or use the *Timer* control. This procedure uses a *Timer* instance named *tmrReadCommPort*.

```
Me.tmrReadCommPort.Enabled = True
```

The *tmrReadCommPort_Tick* event handler fires every 100 milliseconds and attempts to read from the port. If no data is available, the *Catch* block simply catches the thrown exception. If data is available, it is read in one byte at a time and displayed in the *txtStatus TextBox* by the *WriteMessage* procedure.

```
While (m_CommPort.Read(1) <> -1)
    ' Write the output to the screen.
    WriteMessage(Chr(m_CommPort.InputStream(0)), False)
    m_ResponseReceived = True
End While
```

After outputting the received data, the event handler finishes by closing the port and disabling the timer and enabling the command button.

Conclusion

Although the details of COM port communication are rather involved, the *Rs232* class encapsulates most of that complexity and provides an easy-to-use interface.

Application #64: Interact with Services

Although Windows server operating systems provide mechanisms for viewing and manipulating the services running on a computer, you might need to write your own code to manage some services. Server applications often need to ensure that prerequisite services exist and are running before executing, or you might have a system that needs to periodically send custom commands to a service.

Building Upon...

Application #78: Create a Windows Service

New Concepts

The *System.ServiceProcess* namespace contains a class named *ServiceController*. This class allows you to interrogate and manipulate Windows service applications running on your network. Using the constructor, you specify the name of the service and the machine it's running on. The returned instance exposes information about the state of the service through properties such as *Status* and *ServiceType*. You can start, stop, pause, and resume a service by using the like-named methods. There are also properties that tell you whether the service can be manipulated, such as *CanStop* and *CanPauseContinue*. You should check these properties before attempting to change the service.

The *ExecuteCommand* method allows you to tell the service to perform some predefined task. The service doesn't have to be running to call this method. *ExecuteCommand* does not return a value, and the only input parameter is an integer indicating what command you want to execute. The commands available are determined by the service developer.

Code Walkthrough

The sample application demonstrates how to create your own service administration program. It displays a list of all the installed services and their current status. You can start, pause, resume, and stop services using the provided buttons. The application starts by calling the *EnumServices* procedure when the form loads. *EnumServices* retrieves an array of *ServiceController* objects by calling the shared *GetServices* method on the *ServiceController* class.

```
:
Dim svc As ServiceController
Dim svcs As ServiceController() = ServiceController.GetServices()
```

You can display the service information by iterating over the array and adding items to the *lvServices ListView* control.

```
For Each svc In svcs
    With Me.lvServices.Items.Add(svc.DisplayName)
        .SubItems.Add(svc.Status.ToString())
```

```
        .SubItems.Add(svc.ServiceType.ToString())
    End With
⋮
```

You should also persist references to the *ServiceControllers* in a separate collection.

```
⋮
    mcolSvcs.Add(svc, svc.DisplayName)
Next svc
```

Selecting an item in the *lvServices* list view executes the *UpdateUIFor-SelectedService* procedure, which retrieves the appropriate *ServiceController* from the *mcolSvcs* collection based on the name of the selected item.

```
⋮
strName = lvServices.SelectedItems(0).SubItems(0).Text
mSvc = CType(mcolSvcs.Item(strName), ServiceController)
```

The *Enabled* state of the command buttons are set based on the values of the *CanStop*, *CanPauseAndContinue*, and *Status* properties.

```
With mSvc
    cmdStart.Enabled = (.Status = ServiceControllerStatus.Stopped)
    cmdStop.Enabled = (.CanStop AndAlso _
      (Not .Status = ServiceControllerStatus.Stopped))
    cmdPause.Enabled = (.CanPauseAndContinue AndAlso _
      (Not .Status = ServiceControllerStatus.Paused))
    cmdResume.Enabled = (.Status = ServiceControllerStatus.Paused)
End With
⋮
```

The form has a *Timer* control named *tmrStatus*. The *tmrStatus_Tick* event handler calls the *UpdateServiceStatus* procedure, which loops through our persisted *ServiceController* collection calling the *Refresh* method on each controller and updating that item's status in the list view.

```
⋮
Dim lvi As ListViewItem
For Each lvi In Me.lvServices.Items
    mSvc = CType(mcolSvcs.Item(lvi.Text), ServiceController)
    mSvc.Refresh()
    lvi.SubItems(1).Text = mSvc.Status.ToString()
Next lvi
⋮
```

Each of the command buttons executes the appropriate method on the selected *ServiceController* and displays any exceptions in a message box.

Conclusion

Creating your own service manipulation scripts or applications can simplify an administrator's task of managing your application, and the *ServiceController* class makes this very easy.

Application #65: Interact with a Windows Service

The Windows Registry provides a convenient place to store user-configuration settings. While .NET provides facilities for application-configuration files, these files have no concept of user-specific settings. The Registry, on the other hand, has a structure well suited for storing user-specific information.

Building Upon...

Application #35: Create a Windows Explorer–Style Application
Application #67: Understand the Garbage Collector

New Concepts

The *Microsoft.Win32* namespace provides the *Registry* class as an entry point to the system Registry. The *Registry* class contains shared properties for each of the Registry's major hives: *CurrentUser*, *LocalMachine*, *ClassesRoot*, *Users*, and *CurrentConfig*. Each of these properties returns an instance of the *RegistryKey* class. The *RegistryKey* class has properties and methods for reading and manipulating the contents of a key. The names of a key's subkeys and values can be retrieved by the *GetSubKeyNames* and *GetValueNames* methods, respectively. These methods return an array of strings. The *OpenSubKey* method returns another *RegistryKey* instance when provided with the name of the subkey to open. The *GetValue* method returns the data in the registry for the specified value. You can modify the Registry structure with the *CreateSubKey*, *DeleteSub-Key*, *SetValue*, and *DeleteValue* methods.

Code Walkthrough

The sample application allows you to browse your system Registry and modify the string values of existing keys. The *AddChildNode* procedure accepts a *Tree-Node* and a *RegistryKey* as parameters. The *Name* property of the key is provided to the node's constructor so that it will be displayed as the text for the node. A reference to the key itself is persisted in the node's *Tag* property for future use.

```
Dim newNode As New TreeNode(key.Name)
newNode.Tag = key
```

If the key has subkeys, a placeholder child node is added to the current node. This placeholder ensures that an expand icon will appear next to the node in the *TreeView*.

```
If key.SubKeyCount > 0 Then
    newNode.Nodes.Add("placeholder")
End If
```

Finally, the new node is added as a child of the provided parent node.

```
parent.Nodes.Add(newNode)
```

The *frmMain_Load* event handler makes a call to *AddChildNode* for each root-level key in the registry.

```
AddChildNode(tvReg.TopNode, Registry.ClassesRoot)
⋮
```

Expanding an item causes the *tvReg_BeforeExpand* event handler to fire before the item is expanded on screen. This procedure retrieves the *RegistryKey* instance stored in the selected item's *Tag* property and adds a child node for each of that instance's subkeys. Before adding the child nodes, you should clear the *Nodes* collection because it currently contains the placeholder node added earlier.

```
⋮
Dim key As RegistryKey = CType(e.Node.Tag, RegistryKey)
node.Nodes.Clear()
Dim subKeyName As String
For Each subKeyName In key.GetSubKeyNames()
    Try
        AddChildNode(node, key.OpenSubKey(subKeyName, True))
    Catch
    End Try
Next
```

The *tvReg_AfterCollapse* event handler fires when you collapse an expanded item. In an effort to conserve memory, this application clears the *Nodes* collection of the collapsed node. This relinquishes all those child nodes and the *RegistryKey* instances associated with them to the garbage collector.

```
Dim node As TreeNode = e.Node
If node.Text = "Registry" Then Exit Sub
node.Nodes.Clear()
node.Nodes.Add("placeholder")
```

A call to the garbage collector *Collect* method forces that memory to be returned to the system.

```
GC.Collect()
```

Tip   With Task Manager running, repeatedly expand and collapse the HKEY_CLASSES_ROOT node and monitor the application's memory usage. Do so again with the *GC.Collect* line commented out.

When you select a key in the *TreeView*, the *tvReg_AfterSelect* event handler displays that key's values in the *lvValues ListView* to the right. The *GetValueNames* method of the current *RegistryKey* returns an array of strings. For each name in the array, you can call the key's *GetValue* method and place the return from *ToString* in the *ListView*.

```
⋮
Dim key As RegistryKey = CType(e.Node.Tag, RegistryKey)
If key.ValueCount > 0 Then
    Dim sValName As String
    Dim sVal As String
    For Each sValName In key.GetValueNames()
        sVal = key.GetValue(sValName, String.Empty).ToString()
        With lvValues.Items.Add(sValName)
            .SubItems.Add(sVal)
        End With
    Next
End If
```

You can double-click an entry in the *ListView* to edit that value. The *lvValues_DoubleClick* event handler determines whether the selected value is an array. This application does not support editing an array, so it simply exits the procedure.

```
⋮
If lvValues.SelectedItems.Count = 1 Then
    Dim sValName As String = lvValues.SelectedItems(0).Text
    Dim sVal As String = lvValues.SelectedItems(0).SubItems(1).Text

    If sVal = "System.Byte[]" Or sVal = "System.String[]" Then Exit Sub
```

If the value is not an array, the user is presented with an instance of the *frmEditValue* dialog box and the returned value is written to the Registry by using the *SetValue* method of the current *RegistryKey*.

```
⋮
Dim key As RegistryKey = CType(tvReg.SelectedNode.Tag, RegistryKey)
key.SetValue(sValName, sVal)
```

The procedure ends by updating the *ListView* with the new setting value.

```
lvValues.SelectedItems(0).SubItems(1).Text = sVal
```

Conclusion

The *Registry* and *RegistryKey* classes provide a simple mechanism for working with the system Registry. While application-configuration files provide a convenient place for most of an application's general settings, the Registry is often better suited for user-specific information.

8

Working with the .NET Framework

The .NET Framework contains an enormous set of prebuilt classes in its Base Class Library. These classes expose a wide range of functionality from user-interface components to server memory management. This chapter explores many Framework features you can use to make your applications more powerful and flexible, such as HTTP communication, regular expressions, reflection, and Microsoft Message Queue.

Application #66: Build a Custom Collection Class

This topic shows how to create custom collection classes by inheriting from *System.Collections.CollectionBase*. While the .NET Framework has many general-purpose collection classes, they are not *type-safe* because they are designed to contain objects of any type. If you want a collection that contains only objects of a specific type, you need to create a custom collection.

Building Upon...

Application #7: Object-Oriented Features
Application #8: Scoping, Overloading, Overriding

New Concepts

The first step in designing a custom collection is to identify which framework collection class is most suitable to serve as your custom collection's base class. Each collection type maintains at least one internal list in which it stores the items added to it. The collections differ in the methods they expose for retrieving, adding, and deleting items from the list. For example, the *Microsoft.VisualBasic.Collection* class is intended to duplicate the behavior of the *Collection* object found in Visual Basic 6. As such, it's limited to simple methods for adding an item with or without an associated key and for retrieving items by index or by key. It doesn't contain any methods for searching for a particular item in the list. On the other hand, the *System.Collections.Hashtable* class requires that items be added with a key, does not support retrieval by index, and has methods for searching.

Once you've identified the framework collection class to serve as your base, you can begin creating your custom collection class. First, define a new class that inherits from your chosen framework collection class. Next, override all members of the base class that have a parameter or return value of the object type. Make sure the parameters and return values of your overrides use your custom type. For example, if you want to create a collection for storing *Widget* objects and your base class exposes an *Insert(item as Object)* method, you should override it with an *Insert(item as Widget)* method. This ensures that only *Widgets* can be inserted into the collection. Very often, the override can simply call the corresponding method in the base class.

System.Collections.CollectionBase

If you want to create your own collection class completely from scratch, you can start with the *CollectionBase* class. This is an abstract class that contains a protected *ArrayList* for storing members named *InnerList*, a *Count* property, and a *RemoveAt* method. It has no other methods, so you are free to implement whatever functionality you need. At a minimum, you'll want to implement methods for adding, retrieving, and removing items from the collection.

Code Walkthrough

The sample application demonstrates how to create a type-safe collection named *Customers* that stores instances of a *Customer* class. The *Customer* class is a simple class with four properties: three that expose private fields and a fourth, *DisplayData*, that returns a string containing all the customer data.

```
Public ReadOnly Property DisplayData() As String
    Get
        Return Me.custAccount & ": " & Me.FirstName & " " & Me.LastName
    End Get
End Property
```

Creating a Type-Safe Collection

The *Customers* class is our type-safe collection and inherits from the *Collection-Base* class.

```
Public Class Customers
    Inherits System.Collections.CollectionBase
```

An internal *ArrayList* is available through the *InnerList* property. You have to implement some methods to allow *Customer* objects to be added to it. The first is an *Add* method that accepts an instance of the *Customer* class. This method simply wraps a call to the *Add* method of the *InnerList*.

```
Public Overloads Function Add(ByVal Value As Customer) As Customer
    Me.InnerList.Add(Value)
    Return Value
End Function
```

It's entirely up to you to decide how flexible your collection class should be. To make this class even easier to use, a second *Add* method accepts strings for the customer's first name, last name, and account number. This method creates an instance of the *Customer* class and populates it with the passed-in values. Finally, the new *Customer* object is returned from the method.

```
Public Overloads Function Add(ByVal FirstName As String, _
    ByVal LastName As String, _
    ByVal AccountNum As String) As Customer

    Dim cust As New Customer()
    cust.FirstName = FirstName
    cust.LastName = LastName
    cust.AccountNumber = AccountNum
    Me.InnerList.Add(cust)
    Return cust
End Function
```

Now that *Customer* objects can be added to the list, we need to expose methods for retrieving them. Two *Item* methods are defined. One accepts an *Integer* to allow lookup by index position. This method wraps a call to the *Item* method of the *InnerList* and casts the return value to a *Customer* object.

```
Public Overloads Function Item(ByVal Index As Integer) As Customer
    Return CType(Me.InnerList.Item(Index), Customer)
End Function
```

The second *Item* method takes a *Customer* object as a parameter and performs a lookup using the *IndexOf* method of the *InnerList*. This method checks the list to see whether the passed-in *Customer* exists and, if it does, retrieves and returns it. An exception will be thrown if the passed-in *Customer* is not in the list.

```
Public Overloads Function Item(ByVal cust As Customer) As Customer
    Dim myIndex As Integer
```

(continued)

```
    myIndex = Me.InnerList.IndexOf(cust)
    Return CType(Me.InnerList.Item(myIndex), Customer)
End Function
```

Finally, you need methods to remove *Customer* objects. The *Customers* collection inherits the *RemoveAt* method from *CollectionBase*. No override for this method is necessary, as it is already type-safe, accepting just an *Integer* as a parameter. However, an additional *Remove* method that accepts a *Customer* object and removes it from the *InnerList* has been added for additional functionality.

```
Public Overloads Sub Remove(ByVal cust As Customer)
    Me.InnerList.Remove(cust)
End Sub
```

You now have a type-safe collection class that exposes methods that deal only with *Customer* objects. Figure 8-1 shows the final list of members for the class.

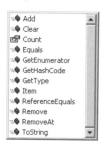

Figure 8-1 *Customer* Members.

Manipulating a Collection

The *frmMain* form uses an instance of the *Customers* class named *myCustomers*. The *Form_Load* event adds *Customer* objects to the *myCustomer* collection. After adding each item, it also adds the returned *Customer* object to the *lstItems* list box.

```
lstItems.DisplayMember = "DisplayData"
cust = myCustomers.Add("Tom", "Slick", "1234567890")
listNumber = lstItems.Items.Add(cust)
```

Notice also that the return value is not cast from the call to the *Add* method. This is because the casting is done inside the collection. This results in simplifying the code needed to modify and access the items in the collection.

Conclusion

You can see that creating a basic type-safe collection is mostly a matter of wrapping the methods of the *InnerList* member of *CollectionBase* with your own custom members. However, more powerful custom collections can be created by inheriting from other classes in *System.Collections* and overriding their members. You can focus your base-class selection by examining what the primary feature set your custom class requires. Common behaviors to consider include the ability to associate a key with each value, choose whether the items are stored in a sorted order or in an add order, and specify what size list the class is optimized for.

Application #67: Understand the Garbage Collector

This topic explores an aspect of the .NET Framework's memory management system known as the Garbage Collector (GC). You'll see how the GC reclaims memory from your application and how you can make your applications more memory efficient by creating GC-aware classes and by interacting directly with the GC.

New Concepts

Unlike some other runtime environments, memory management for managed code is nondeterministic. This means that although your code can indicate when it is finished using an object by setting a reference to *Nothing*, it can not explicitly remove that object from memory. The common language runtime (CLR) is responsible for determining when to actually remove the object from memory. The part of the CLR that handles this is known as the Garbage Collector.

The Garbage Collector

The CLR asks the Garbage Collector to reclaim memory by collecting any unused objects when it needs memory. An unused object is one that cannot be reached by following references from the application. You should set your references to *Nothing* as soon as you are done with them to ensure your objects are eligible for collection as soon as possible.

Finalization

A memory-savvy application should also make sure each object is capable of cleaning up any resources it might acquire during its lifetime. In general, resources should be released as soon as possible, often in the same method call that acquired them. Sometimes though, an object might need to acquire a resource when it's created and might not want to release the resource until it's being destroyed. The simplest way to do this is to implement a finalizer by overriding the *Finalize* method. The *Finalize* method is a special-case procedure that, if implemented, is automatically called by the GC just before the object is destroyed. This provides a very convenient place to put clean-up code to perform tasks such as destroying database connections and file handles.

The benefit of a finalizer is that it's *guaranteed* to run; however, a major drawback is that you don't know *when* it will run. You could destroy a reference to an object, but the GC might not collect the object for many minutes, depending on the memory requirements of the system. In this scenario, your object is still holding on to its resources even though your application is not using them. Another problem with finalizers is that they slow down the garbage-collection process, which can have a significant impact on application-wide performance. To resolve these problems, you should also implement an explicit way for an application to tell your object to clean up its resources.

Disposing of an Object

The act of cleaning up resources an object is using is referred to as disposing of the object. It's such a common task that the .NET Framework has an interface named *IDisposable* for objects to implement. The *IDisposable* interface defines a single method named *Dispose*. You might have seen this method implemented on some common Framework types, such as the *Form* and *DataSet*. The *Dispose* method is generally implemented so that if it's called on an object, it will clean up that object's resources and might even call *Dispose* on any child objects that are disposable.

If you implement *IDisposable*, you need to take one other issue into account. Imagine that you call *Dispose* on an object and then destroy your reference to it. A little while later, the GC calls *Finalize* on that object and tries to clean up its resources *again*. This is likely to cause errors and is completely unnecessary, as the object already cleaned itself up when it was disposed of. To avoid this situation, you need to tell the GC not to call *Finalize* when it collects the object. You can do this by calling the *SuppressFinalize* method of the GC class in your *Dispose* method. By implementing the *Finalize* and *Dispose* methods correctly, you'll have a class that can be explicitly instructed to release its resources by a client or automatically by the GC.

Manipulation of the Garbage Collector

As indicated in the last section, even though the GC operates in the background and can pretty much be left to run on its own, you'll want to manipulate it directly in some cases. For example, suppose you're finished with a very large object and want to immediately reclaim the memory that object was using rather than waiting for the GC collection. You can force the GC to collect the object by calling the *Collect* method. This method will cause the GC to collect any unreferenced objects and call their finalizers. Keep in mind that the memory used by these objects will not be released until after the finalizers have finished.

Taking the last example a bit further, suppose you plan to immediately load another large object after calling *GC.Collect*. You might want to wait until all the finalizers have finished just to be sure that enough memory will be available for the new object. This can be done by calling the GC *WaitForPendingFinalizers* method, which will block client processing until all finalizers have finished.

Code Walkthrough

The sample application works with a class named *GcTest* to demonstrate the relationship between disposing, finalizing, and the GC. In addition, various methods of the GC are used to show how to force a collection. First we'll look at the clean-up functionality of the *GcTest* class.

> **Note**   The *GcTest* class is a recursive class, meaning it contains a child that is also an instance of *GcTest*. Many methods in the class used to populate the object hierarchy and raise events back up to the form are beyond the scope of this discussion.

Finalizing a Class

The *GcTest* class has overridden the *Finalize* method and implements a call to the *CleanUp* method. The *CleanUp* method is where the real work of releasing resources occurs. This work is contained in its own procedure, so it can be called by both the finalizer and the *Dispose* method. In this application, the *CleanUp* method just sends a message indicating that it was called. Most methods in *GcTest* also raise the *ObjectGcInfo* event, which is used by the application to send messages up to the form.

```
Protected Overrides Sub Finalize()
    CleanUp()
    RaiseEvent ObjectGcInfo(m_Name + " Finalized")
End Sub
```

To test the finalizer, run the application and click the Create Objects button. This generates a hierarchy of *GcTest* objects and displays their names in the list box. A reference to the topmost *GcTest* object is stored in the *m_TestObject* variable.

```
m_TestObject = New GcTest("TestObject", OBJECT_DEPTH)
```

Now select the first item in the list box, and click the Kill Selected Object button. This will set the form's *m_TestObject* variable to *Nothing*, making it available for garbage collection.

```
m_TestObject = Nothing
```

Finally, click the Run GC button. The *btnRunGC Click* event forces the Garbage Collector to collect any unreachable objects.

```
GC.Collect()
GC.WaitForPendingFinalizers()
```

Remember that even though the objects in the hierarchy contain references to each other, none of them are reachable because we destroyed the reference to the topmost object. The activity log should show that the finalizer on each object was called, an action which in turn resulted in each object's *CleanUp* method being called. Figure 8-2 shows the application's Activity Log display after running the Garbage Collector.

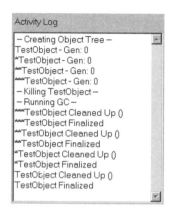

Figure 8-2 Activity Log.

Disposing of a Class

The *GcTest* class has also been designed to allow for explicit cleanup by implementing the *IDisposable.Dispose* method. The *Dispose* method first prevents the GC from calling the finalizer by calling *GC.SuppressFinalize* and passing in a reference to itself. Then *Dispose* is called on its child if it has one. Finally, the *CleanUp* method is called.

```
Implements IDisposable
Sub Dispose() Implements IDisposable.Dispose
    GC.SuppressFinalize(Me)
    If Not m_Child Is Nothing Then
        m_Child.Dispose()
        m_Child = Nothing
    End If
    CleanUp()
    RaiseEvent ObjectGcInfo(m_Name + " Disposed ()")
End Sub
```

Test the dispose functionality by running the application and creating the objects. Then select the first item in the list box, and click the Dispose Selected Object button. The *btnDisposeObject Click* event is almost identical to the *btnKillObject Click* event except that it calls *Dispose* on the selected object before destroying the reference to it.

```
m_TestObject.Dispose()
m_TestObject = Nothing
```

Notice in the activity log that each object was cleaned up. Now click the Run GC button, and you'll see that no finalizers are called as a part of garbage collection. Figure 8-3 shows the Activity Log output.

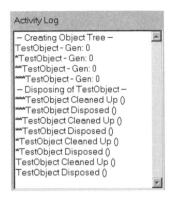

Figure 8-3   Activity Log output.

You can continue to experiment with the application by killing and disposing of objects further down in the hierarchy.

Conclusion

You've now seen how to create a class that can interact with the Garbage Collector and can reliably release its resources. When designing and using your classes, keep in mind that while finalizers are a convenient construct, explicitly calling *Dispose* will almost always result in a higher level of performance for your system.

Application #68: Partition an Application

This topic discusses the benefits of and steps involved in partitioning an application into multiple components. Learning how to separate application logic into components is very useful for stand-alone application developers, and it's the first step to creating distributed enterprise applications. The sample application compares various ways of partitioning your logic and examines the development trade-offs of each.

Building Upon...

Application #33: Format a *DataGrid*
Application #73: Read From and Write To a Text File

New Concepts

Partitioning an application basically means dividing your code into separate projects based on the type of work the code performs. Each project generates an application component when compiled. Up to now, you've been creating single-component applications, which consist of just an .exe file. This might be adequate for simple applications written by a single developer, but for larger applications or projects involving multiple developers, partitioning is often a necessity.

A partitioned application is one that contains two or more components. For a WinForms application, there is a primary component: the application .exe, which uses any number of supporting code libraries, or DLLs. The first step in partitioning an application is determining how many components are appropriate for your application and what code should go in each. One of the most common ways to take advantage of partitioning, even in a simple application, is to separate all code related to data access into a separate code library, often referred to as a data-access layer.

Partitioning is extremely valuable because it offers various benefits throughout an application's lifetime. These benefits can make development, deployment, and maintenance of an application easier and more flexible. Let's take a minute to look at some of these benefits in detail.

Code Reuse

This is perhaps the most common reason for initially partitioning your applications. Just as functions allow you to reuse code within a single application, partitioning allows you to share code between multiple applications. When you put code into a code library separate from your application's .exe, it gets compiled into a separate DLL. Because it's a separate file, you can reference it and use it in any number of other applications.

For example, imagine you have to build a WinForms application and an ASP.NET application that manipulate the same database. If you don't use partitioning, you'll have to duplicate all the code that reads from and writes to the database in both applications. However, if you were to put all the data-access code into its own code library, you could write the library once and use it in both applications. This results in reduced development time for the second application and less code to maintain. Also, the code in both applications is simpler because all the complex data-access code is encapsulated in the component.

Code Maintenance

In addition to there being *less* code to maintain, the resulting code is also generally *easier* to maintain. This is because the complex task an application performs is divided into discrete substeps that can be quickly located and changed. For example, if you need to update some code in response to database schema changes, you can more quickly locate the appropriate code because you know you only have to look in the data component. Or if you need to change the way a piece of data is formatted on-screen or a control used for user input, you can limit your search to just the UI component. Without partitioning, all your code exists in one project, making it harder to locate any single piece of code.

Partitioning Steps

Ideally, partitioning should become an implicit part of designing an application. Remember that a partitioned design can greatly increase your ability to meet future requirements even when the current specifications might not necessitate multiple components. The steps involved in partitioning an application include:

- Identify your application components. For example:
  - ❏ Primary UI component
  - ❏ Supporting user-interface component
  - ❏ Business rules component
  - ❏ Data-access component
- Implement each component in a separate project.
  - ❏ Windows Application for the primary UI component
  - ❏ Windows Control for the supporting UI component
  - ❏ Class library for the business rules and data-access component
- Add references between each project and its dependent projects.
- Implement code in the primary project to use the partitioned classes and controls.

Code Walkthrough

The sample application contains a tab control with three tabs labeled Form, Component, and User Control. Each tab contains a button labeled Get Customers, which performs the same set of tasks. The tasks are:

- Load and parse data from a comma-separated values text file, Customers.csv
- Add the data to a *DataTable*
- Display the results in a *DataGrid* by binding to the *DataTable*

The three tabs vary in the way their code is separated into components. The Form tab uses no components. The Component tab uses a component named *DataAccessComponent*. And the User Control tab uses a component named *CSVControls*, which in turn uses the *DataAccessComponent*. Let's first look at the nonpartitioned version.

No Partitioning

The code used by the Form tab is contained completely inside the *Click* event of the *btnLoadDataGridForm* button. This procedure begins by defining the variables needed for reading the text file. The *StreamReader* provides read access to the .csv file, and the *strLine* and *strColumns* variables are used during the parsing of the file.

```
Dim objStreamReader As StreamReader = _
    New StreamReader(strCustomersFile)
Dim strLine As String
Dim strColumns() As String
```

Next, the *DataTable* is defined and columns for the pieces of data in the .csv file are added to it:

```
Dim dtCustomers As New DataTable()
Dim drCustomer As DataRow
dtCustomers.Columns.Add("CustomerID")
dtCustomers.Columns.Add("CompanyName")
dtCustomers.Columns.Add("ContactName")
dtCustomers.Columns.Add("Phone")
```

Once the *DataTable* is defined, the contents of the .csv file are read line by line. Each line is parsed into a string array named *strColumns* and added to the *DataTable*. This process continues until there are no more lines in the text file.

```
strLine = objStreamReader.ReadLine
Do While (Not strLine Is Nothing)
    drCustomer = dtCustomers.NewRow
    strColumns = Split(strLine, ",")
    drCustomer.ItemArray = strColumns
    dtCustomers.Rows.Add(drCustomer)
    strLine = objStreamReader.ReadLine
Loop
```

Finally, the data is displayed by binding the *DataTable* to the *DataGrid* named *grdCustomersForm*.

```
grdCustomersForm.SetDataBinding(dtCustomers, "")
```

This code, while functionally sufficient, is not at all reusable. In particular, you can imagine that you might need to load customer data from a .csv file into a *DataTable* in many applications. Unfortunately, with this code, the best you could do would be to copy and paste it into the new application.

> **Important** Copying and pasting large amounts of code between applications is one of the biggest indicators that you should consider partitioning that logic into a separate component.

Data-Access Partition

To make the .csv parsing code reusable, it needs to be placed in a separate component. You can see that there is another project in the solution named DataAccessComponent. This project was created by adding a new Class Library project. In the project is a *CustomersDB* class. This class contains a method named *GetCustomers*, which loads the .csv file data into a *DataTable* and returns the *DataTable*. The rest of the code is virtually identical to the code presented in the previous section.

```
Public Function GetCustomers() As DataTable
    Return dtCustomers
End Function
```

Also, to make this component more flexible, a string property named *File-Name* has been added so that you can pass in the location of the .csv file just before calling *GetCustomers*.

```
Protected m_FileName As String
Public Property FileName() As String
    Get
        Return m_FileName
    End Get
    Set(ByVal Value As String)
        m_FileName = Value
    End Set
End Property
```

To use this component, a reference has to be made between the Partition An Application project and the DataAccessComponent project. Figure 8-4 shows the reference to the DataAccessComponent.

Figure 8-4 Reference to the DataAccessComponent assembly.

Now that the component has been implemented and a reference has been set, we can use the functionality provided by the component. The *Click* event for the *bnLoadDataGridComponent* button contains the code that uses the component to retrieve the data. First a *DataTable* to store the returned data and an instance of the *CustomersDB* class are instantiated.

```
Dim dtCustomers As DataTable
Dim oBusiness As DataAccessComponent.CustomersDB = _
    New DataAccessComponent.CustomersDB()
```

To retrieve data, the component user simply has to set the *FileName* property, call *GetCustomers*, and bind the *DataTable* to the *DataGrid*.

```
oBusiness.FileName = strCustomersFile
dtCustomers = oBusiness.GetCustomers()
grdCustomersComponent.SetDataBinding(dtCustomers, "")
```

You can see that partitioning your application does not mean you have to write a lot more code. In fact, in the long run you end up writing much less code. After compiling, you could now use this *CustomersDB* class from any application.

The User Interface and the Data-Access Partition

Partitioning the data-access code for your application is a great start, but you might also have reason to create reusable interface components. The third tab, User Control, uses a custom user control named *grdCustomersUserControl*. This control is an instance of the *CustomerGrid* defined in the CSVControls project. This user control exposes a *BindCustomers* method, which uses the *DataAccessComponent* to get a *DataTable* and binds the *DataTable* to the *dgData* constituent *DataGrid*.

```
Sub BindCustomers()
    Dim dtCustomers As DataTable
    Dim oBusiness As DataAccessComponent.CustomersDB = _
        New DataAccessComponent.CustomersDB()
    oBusiness.FileName = m_FileName
    dtCustomers = oBusiness.GetCustomers
    dgData.SetDataBinding(dtCustomers, "")
End Sub
```

With this code, the *CustomerGrid* control is a fully self-contained UI component that can load and display customer data. Any WinForms application can now use it by simply setting a reference to the DLL and implementing two lines of code. The Partition An Application project has a reference to the CSVControls project, and the *Click* event of the *bnLoadUserControl* button implements the code to use the custom control.

```
grdCustomersUserControl.FileName = strCustomersFile
grdCustomersUserControl.BindCustomers()
```

Conclusion

Partitioning is an easy way to make your code more reusable, manageable, and distributable. The majority of the work involved consists of identifying what portions of your application should be partitioned and being diligent in implementing the correct code in the correct partition. Once you are comfortable encapsulating your data-access code in a separate component, you might consider taking the next step by separating your business rules into yet another component.

Application #69: Send and Receive Data

This topic explores how to send and receive text and binary data over HTTP. Although the .NET Framework and Microsoft Visual Studio .NET provide first-class support for Web services, there might be cases where you want to use Internet resources that are not Web services. For example, if you're creating a .NET application that needs to make calls to classic ASP pages, you can't use the Web services functionality. You'll need to know how to manually issue an HTTP request and process the response.

Building Upon...

Application #73: Read From and Write To a Text File

New Concepts

For any interaction with an HTTP server, you must be able to populate a request with data to send to the server and read the data returned by the server. You can use the *WebRequest* and *WebResponse* classes in conjuction with the *StreamReader* and *StreamWriter* classes to perform these tasks.

Working with *WebRequest* and *WebResponse* Classes

The *WebRequest* and *WebResponse* classes are located in the *System.Net* namespace and provide client-side Internet functionality. You can use the *WebRequest* object to make requests to Internet resources. The benefit of these classes is that they hide all the complex details of the underlying protocols. So you can make a request to a Web page without having to know the inner workings of HTTP. In fact, you can make a call to a Web page in as little as three steps:

1. Create the *WebRequest* instance, and set its URL.

2. Set the request method to **GET** or **POST**.

3. Issue the request.

The *WebRequest* object handles the work of making the HTTP connection to the server and sending the request message. The response sent back by the server is provided to you as an instance of the *WebResponse* class. In many cases, you'll need to pass data to the server and read the response sent back. The *WebRequest* and *WebResponse* classes each expose a *Stream* object to allow you to populate the request and consume the response.

Working with Streams

The .NET Framework uses the *System.IO.Stream* class as a base for many data transfer needs. If you need to work with the file system, an external device, or Internet resources, you'll use some implementation of the *Stream* class to transfer your data. The fundamentals of working with streams involve creating the stream and using the *Read* and *Write* methods. The *Read* and *Write* methods provide byte-level access to the underlying data. Both methods provide parameters you can use to determine how much data to work with at a time. This flexibility allows you to work with large amounts of data in more manageable chunks. Each implementation of the *Stream* class reads and writes its data from different locations. For example, the *FileStream* exposes data in a file, the *MemoryStream* allows you to read and write from a memory buffer, and the streams exposed by *WebRequest* and *WebResponse* read from and write to the Internet. The sample application demonstrates many ways of using the various types of streams.

Code Walkthrough

The sample application contains four buttons that examine various ways of exchanging data with a Web site. The top three buttons send files to and retrieve files from the Web site, while the bottom button sends the text entered into the *TextBox* to the server. The Web site consists of four ASPX pages that provide the server-side functionality for the application. You must expose these files through a virtual directory before you can run the sample application.

> **Note**   While this application uses ASP.NET pages hosted in Internet Information Services (IIS), the mechanisms described in this walkthrough will work with any HTTP server technology.

Creating Virtual Directories

Creating a virtual directory allows you to expose a file system directory as a Web resource. For this application, we need to create a virtual directory on the local machine named VDir1 that points to the VDir1 file system directory. Implement the following steps to create the virtual directory:

1. Open Internet Information Services.

2. Expand the machine name node.

3. Right-click Default Web Site, and select New, Virtual Directory.

4. Click Next.

5. Enter **VDir1** for the Alias field.

6. Click Next.

7. Browse to the Application Directory / VDir1.

8. Click Next.

9. Click Finish.

10. Close Internet Information Services.

Copying Streams

Before we look at sending data to the Web site, we need to first understand a utility procedure named *CopyData*, which transfers data from one stream to another. This procedure is important because most code in the application is centered around moving data into and out of the streams provided by the *WebRequest* and *WebResponse* classes. The *CopyData* procedure has two *Stream* object parameters, one named *FromStream* that acts as the data source and another named *ToStream* that is the data destination.

```
Private Sub CopyData(ByVal FromStream As Stream, ByVal ToStream As Stream)
```

The retrieval of data from *FromStream* is done by calling its *Read* method. This method fills the byte array passed in to the first parameter with data. The number of bytes to retrieve is defined by the third parameter. In this case, we're retrieving data in blocks of 4096 bytes. In addition to filling the byte array with data, the *Read* method also returns an integer indicating how many bytes were actually read into the array. This value will be 0 once we reach the end of the stream. The second parameter allows you to specify an offset from which to begin reading, but it's not used in this application.

```
Dim intBytesRead As Integer
Const intSize As Integer = 4096
Dim bytes(intSize) As Byte
intBytesRead = FromStream.Read(bytes, 0, intSize)
```

After reading a chunk, we check to see whether any data was returned, and if so, we write it to the destination stream by using the *Write* method and passing in the chunk of data and the integer indicating how much data is in the chunk. This read/write process continues until no data is left in the source stream.

```
        While intBytesRead > 0
            ToStream.Write(bytes, 0, intBytesRead)
            intBytesRead = FromStream.Read(bytes, 0, intSize)
        End While
End Sub
```

Once the procedure is finished, the entire contents of *FromStream* will have been copied into *ToStream*. This procedure is extremely useful because the parameters are typed as *Stream*. That means we can use it to transfer data between any two objects that inherit from *Stream*, including file streams, network streams, and memory streams. Now let's see how we can use streams to get data to and from a Web server.

Send Text

The *cmdPassText_Click* event handler takes text entered into the *txtDataPassed TextBox* and sends it to the PassText.aspx page in the Web site. The Web page processes the text and returns a message, which is displayed in the *txtData-Returned TextBox*. Instances of the *WebRequest* and *WebResponse* classes are declared to handle this round-trip exchange.

```
Dim req As WebRequest
Dim rsp As WebResponse
```

The *WebRequest* instance is created by calling the *WebRequest* shared *Create* method and passing in the URL to be invoked. Keep in mind that this does not invoke the URL at this time; it simply verifies that your address is a valid Uniform Resource Identifier (URI).

> **More Info** You can find out more about what qualifies as a valid URI by looking up the *System.Uri* class in online help.

We also need to specify how the contents of our request should be sent to the server by assigning a value of GET or POST to the *Method* property. Using POST assures that the data will be sent in the body of the HTTP message.

```
req = WebRequest.Create("http://localhost/VDir1/PassText.aspx")
req.Method = "POST"
```

Now that our *WebRequest* instance is configured, we can identify what data to send to the server by populating the request stream. The *GetRequest-Stream* method returns a reference to a *Stream* object that could be used directly, but because we want to write some text to the stream, we create a *StreamWriter* instance and pass the *Stream* into the *StreamWriter* constructor.

```
Dim sw As New StreamWriter(req.GetRequestStream())
```

We can now use the text-friendly methods of the *StreamWriter* to pass in the data from the *txtDataPassed TextBox*. Once we are done filling the request, we can close the *StreamWriter*.

```
sw.WriteLine(txtDataPassed.Text())
sw.Close()
```

Our *WebRequest* is now configured and populated with data, so we can finally issue the request to the server by calling the *GetResponse* method. This sends an HTTP request message containing our data to the URL specified earlier and returns a *WebResponse* instance we can use to retrieve the server's response.

```
rsp = req.GetResponse()
```

Retrieving and working with the response from the server is similar to working with the request. We get the response stream by calling *GetResponse-Stream* on our *WebResponse* instance and passing the stream into the constructor for a *StreamReader* instance. This allows us to work with the stream as text instead of having to work byte by byte.

```
Dim sr As New StreamReader(rsp.GetResponseStream())
txtDataReturned.Text = sr.ReadLine()
```

As a final bit of error handling, you should make sure your request and response streams are closed once you are done with them.

```
If Not req Is Nothing Then req.GetRequestStream().Close()
If Not rsp Is Nothing Then rsp.GetResponseStream().Close()
```

Send a File

The *cmdSendFileData_Click* event handler sends a file, datafile.txt, to the server. The type of file sent in this manner is not limited to text files and can actually be of any type. The process starts by creating a new *FileStream* object referencing the file that you want to send.

```
fs = New FileStream("datafile.txt", FileMode.Open)
```

Next, the *WebRequest* object is created just like in the previous example; however, this time we point to the SendData.aspx page.

```
req = WebRequest.Create("http://localhost/VDir1/SendData.aspx")
req.Method = "POST"
```

Finally, we populate the request by copying the contents of the *FileStream* to the *WebRequest* request stream and send the file by calling *GetResponse*.

```
CopyData(fs, req.GetRequestStream())
⋮
Dim rsp As WebResponse = req.GetResponse()
```

Receive Files

Receiving files from a server is basically the same as sending a file but in reverse. The *cmdReceiveDataFile_Click* event handler invokes the ReceiveData.aspx page to retrieve an .xml file from the server. Creating and configuring the *WebRequest* object is the same except that, in this case, we're using the HTTP GET method instead of POST because we're not sending any data to the server.

```
req = WebRequest.Create("http://localhost/VDir1/ReceiveData.aspx")
req.Method = "GET"
```

GetResponse is called to invoke the page and store the returned *Web-Response*.

```
Dim rsp As WebResponse = req.GetResponse()
```

The *WebResponse* instance contains the XML data returned by the server. Because we want to store this data in a file, we create an instance of the *FileStream* class and copy the contents of the response stream into the file.

```
fs = New FileStream("ReceivedXMLFile.xml", FileMode.Create)
CopyData(rsp.GetResponseStream(), fs)
```

The final step is to ensure that both the response and file streams are closed.

```
If Not rsp Is Nothing Then rsp.GetResponseStream.Close()
If Not fs Is Nothing Then fs.Close()
```

After running this part of the sample, you should have a file named ReceivedXMLFile.xml in the bin directory.

Receive Images

The process for retrieving image data from a server is identical to that for retrieving any kind of file. However, sometimes you might want to display that image directly in a *PictureBox* control instead of saving it to a file. The *cmdReceiveImageFile_Click* event handler does just that. Retrieving the data from the server is no different than before, except you copy the returned data into a *MemoryStream* instance instead of a *FileStream*.

```
ms = New MemoryStream()
CopyData(rsp.GetResponseStream(), ms)
```

The *MemoryStream* instance can then be passed into the shared *FromStream* method of the *Image* class. This reads the contents of the stream and returns an *Image* object that can be assigned to the *Image* property of the *PictureBox*.

```
picDownloadImage.Image = Image.FromStream(ms)
```

When you run this part of the sample, an image of clouds should appear in the picture box.

Conclusion

You can see that sending and receiving data over HTTP has much more to do with understanding streams and the kind of data your are exchanging than understanding the inner workings of HTTP. By issuing your own Web requests, you can create clients that can easily interact with any Web resource, even if it's not a true Web service.

Application #70: Reflection

Reflection is the process of interrogating an assembly at run time to discover information about the types that the assembly contains. You can find out all kinds of information, such as what members a type has; the type accessibility of those members; and the number, type, and order of any parameters a member might require. Development tools and configuration utilities often make use of reflection to display this type metadata to users. Visual Studio .NET, for example, uses reflection to display the member signature ToolTips and member drop-down lists while you code. The .NET Framework provides many classes for retrieving assembly and type metadata. This topic examines some of these classes.

New Concepts

The primary class used to retrieve information about classes is the *Type* class. You create a *Type* object and tell it what class you want to examine. So if you want to reflect the *Foo* class, you need to have an instance of the *Type* class that is *Foo* specific. From that *Type* instance, you could then find out what methods *Foo* has, whether *Foo* is public, or what interfaces *Foo* implements. There are two simple ways to get a *Type* instance. One is to call the *GetType* method on an instance of the object you want to reflect. All .NET objects have a *GetType* method. For our *Foo* example, the code could look like the following:

```
Dim f As New Foo()
Dim t As Type = f.GetType()
```

You can also get a type reference by calling the shared *GetType* method of the *Type* class and passing in the name of the class to reflect as a string. For example:

```
Dim t as Type = Type.GetType("Foo")
```

The major limitation of this method is that you can get type information only for classes in the current assembly. We will look at reflecting other assemblies later in this topic.

Once you have a *Type* instance, you can call a variety of *GetXXX* methods—such as *GetMethods*, *GetProperties*, and *GetInterfaces*—to retrieve information about those aspects of the target class. There is also a set of *IsXXX* properties, such as *IsPublic* and *IsSerializable*. The return value from methods such as *GetProperties* or *GetMethods* is an array of *XXXInfo* classes such as *PropertyInfo* or *MethodInfo*. You can then use the properties of these *XXXInfo* objects to find out information such as what the return type of the target property is or what parameters the target method takes.

> **Note** Remember that while the *Type* class exists in the *System* namespace, the other reflection classes, such as *MethodInfo* and *PropertyInfo*, are in the *System.Reflection* namespace.

> **More Info** Reflection is also often used to dynamically invoke members on a class. The *Type* class contains methods for this, but they are beyond the scope of this topic. For more information, look up *Type.InvokeMember* in online help.

Examining Loaded Assemblies

As mentioned earlier, the *GetType* method of the *Type* class allows you to reflect only classes in the currently executing assembly. Sometimes you'll need to reflect classes in other loaded assemblies. The *System* namespace provides a class named *AppDomain* that you can use to find out what assemblies are currently loaded in your application. The shared property *CurrentDomain* of the *AppDomain* class returns a reference to your application domain. You can then call the *GetAssemblies* method of your *AppDomain* object to return an array of *Assembly* objects.

Once you identify which assembly contains the type you want to reflect, you can call the *GetType* method of the appropriate *Assembly* object and pass in the name of the class you want to reflect. If we assume that our *Foo* class exists in a loaded assembly named *BarAssembly*, we could reflect *Foo* with the following:

```
Dim asm As [Assembly]
For Each asm In AppDomain.CurrentDomain.GetAssemblies()
    If asm.GetName.Name = "BarAssembly" Then Exit For
Next
Dim t As Type = asm.GetType("Foo")
```

> **More Info**   If you need to reflect a type that is in an assembly that isn't loaded, you can use a variety of methods of the *Assembly* class to load it. See *Assembly.LoadFrom* in online help for more information.

Code Walkthrough

The sample application allows you to view information about all the currently loaded assemblies and the types in those assemblies. You can start by clicking the List Loaded Assemblies button, which will display the names of the currently loaded assemblies in the list box. Then select an assembly, and click the Show Detail button to display the types contained in that assembly. You can then click on a type to display the members contained by that type. The following sections examine the code in detail.

Listing Loaded Assemblies

The application has a class-level variable named *CurrentAsm* that is used to store a reference to the currently selected assembly.

```
Private CurrentAsm As [Assembly]
```

The *cmdListLoadedAssemblies_Click* event handler starts by declaring an array of *Assembly* objects, and it populates the array by calling the *GetAssemblies* method of the current *AppDomain*.

```
Dim asms() As [Assembly]
asms = AppDomain.CurrentDomain.GetAssemblies()
```

We then loop through each *Assembly* in the array and display their names. The *GetName* method returns an instance of the *AssemblyName* class, which contains version and culture information in addition to the simple name.

```
lstLoadedAssemblies.Items.Clear()
Dim asm As [Assembly]
For Each asm In asms
    lstLoadedAssemblies.Items.Add(asm.GetName.Name)
Next
```

The rest of the procedure resets the interface and sets the *CurrentAsm* variable to *Nothing*.

Displaying Assembly Contents

The *ShowAssemblyDetail* method displays assembly information in response to clicks on the *btnAssemblyDetail* button and double-clicks on the *lstLoadedAssemblies* list box.

```
Private Sub ShowAssemblyDetail(ByVal sender As System.Object, _
    ByVal e As System.EventArgs) Handles lstLoadedAssemblies.DoubleClick, _
    btnAssemblyDetail.Click
```

After checking to make sure an item is selected in the assembly list, we loop through the loaded assemblies to get a reference to the one with the selected name.

```
Dim asm As [Assembly]
For Each asm In AppDomain.CurrentDomain.GetAssemblies()
    If asm.GetName.Name = lstLoadedAssemblies.Text Then Exit For
Next
CurrentAsm = asm
```

After displaying the *FullName* and *Location* properties on screen, we display the full name of each of the *Types* defined in the current assembly by looping through the array of *Types* returned by the *GetTypes* method of our *CurrentAsm* object.

```
txtDisplayName.Text = CurrentAsm.FullName
txtLocation.Text = CurrentAsm.Location

Dim t As Type
For Each t In CurrentAsm.GetTypes
    lstTypes.Items.Add(t.FullName)
Next
```

Displaying a Type's Members

The *lstTypes_SelectedIndexChanged* event handler is responsible for displaying all members of the selected *Type*. First, a *Type* instance is created by calling the *GetType* method of our currently selected assembly.

```
Dim t As Type = CurrentAsm.GetType(lstTypes.Text)
```

Finally, we display the *Name* and *MemberType* properties of each *MemberInfo* object in the array returned by the *GetMembers* method of the *Type* object.

```
Dim mi As MemberInfo
For Each mi In t.GetMembers()
    lstMembers.Items.Add(mi.Name & " - " & mi.MemberType.ToString)
Next
```

Conclusion

This topic has shown you how to reflect information about the types contained in the currently loaded assemblies. With this information, you can create more powerful tools and utilities.

Application #71: Use MSMQ

Microsoft Message Queue (MSMQ) provides applications with a powerful yet simple mechanism for transferring data between two applications in an asynchronous fashion. The .NET Framework has the *System.Messaging* namespace to provide you with a set of classes that make sending and receiving messages from MSMQ queues remarkably easy. This topic examines some of those classes.

Building Upon...

Application #72: Configuration Settings
Application #78: Create a Windows Service
Application #79: Use Thread Pooling
Application #82: Serialize Objects
Application #84: Asynchronous Calls

New Concepts

Working with a queue is focused around the *MessageQueue* class. This class provides methods for connecting to a queue, interrogating its contents, sending a message to it, and retrieving messages from it. You can add a MessageQueue instance to your code manually or drag one onto a design surface from the Toolbox.

Configuring the *MessageQueue* Component

When you create a *MessageQueue* instance, you have to provide at least two pieces of information before you can send or receive messages. You must specify the path to the actual queue in the enterprise by providing a string to the *Path* property. A path that would connect to a private queue named *Foo* on the local machine would look like the following:

```
FormatName:DIRECT=OS:.\private$\foo
```

> **More Info** The help documentation for the *MessageQueue.Path* property has some examples of other valid queue paths.

You also need to tell the *MessageQueue* component how to serialize objects when you send them to the queue. You do this by providing a value for the *Formatter* property. The two main choices here are the *XmlMessageFormatter* and the *BinaryMessageFormatter*. The *BinaryMessageFormatter* creates compact messages that can be used only by a receiving application that is also using the *BinaryMessageFormatter*. This limits your consuming applications to being .NET applications. The *XmlMessageFormatter* serializes your object to an XML string. Because XML is not .NET specific, your consuming application can be anything that can talk to the queue and process XML. The basic message transfer process is displayed in Figure 8-5.

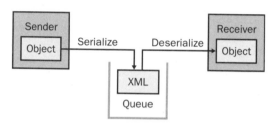

Figure 8-5   The message transfer process for an object using the *XmlMessageFormatter* and MSMQ.

Sending and Receiving Messages

Once you have your *MessageQueue* component configured, you can use its methods to send and receive messages from the queue. The *Send* method provides a simple mechanism to submit objects to the queue. At a minimum, you need to provide the object you want to send, and you can optionally provide a label for the message and define transaction behavior if you're sending to a transactional queue. The component will then pass your object to the selected formatter and then pass the serialized data on to the queue. Your application will continue after the message is placed in the queue.

You can retrieve all the messages in a queue by calling the *GetAllMessages* method. This returns an array of *Message* objects that you can then process. If you want to retrieve messages one at a time, you can use the *Receive* method to perform a synchronous retrieval or use *BeginReceive* and *EndReceive* to perform asynchronous reads. The *Message* object contains *Body* and *Label* properties you can use to retrieve the content of the message.

Code Walkthrough

The sample application demonstrates how to send information from one application to another by using MSMQ as the transport mechanism. The application consists of three projects. The Server project contains the definition for the

MSMQOrders class. This class defines a simple business object that contains product order information. The Client project provides a user interface for populating an instance of the *MSMQOrders* class and sending it to a private message queue named *Orders*. The WindowService project defines a Microsoft Windows service application that consumes messages in the *Orders* queue. You can find the setup instructions for the application in the ReadMe.htm file in the root application directory.

The *MSMQOrders* class contains three public fields to store order information. There is also a *Process* method that uses a tracing method so that we can verify it is consumed. This has been added solely for the requirements of this sample application and is not a requirement for using MSMQ in general.

```
Public Class MSMQOrders
    Public Number As Integer
    Public Customer As String
    Public RequiredBy As Date
    Public Sub Process(ByVal State As Object)
        Trace.WriteLine(Number & " - " & Customer & " - " & RequiredBy)
        Threading.Thread.Sleep(2000)
    End Sub
End Class
```

When you run the *Client* application and send a message, it will go to the queue and be consumed by the installed service. You can verify that the message was sent by examining the journal for the *Orders* queue.

Defining the Queue

MSMQ integration is provided to the Client application through the *MessageQueue* component on the *frmMain* design surface. This component was added from the Components tab of the toolbox. Two properties that have been set are worth pointing out. The *Formatter* property is set to use the *XmlMessageFormatter*. This ensures any objects sent to the queue will be serialized into XML before going to the queue. Also, the *Path* property is configured to retrieve its value from the *qOrders.Path* item in the application's configuration file. You can see this by expanding *DynamicProperties* in the Property window.

Writing to the Queue

Once the queue is configured, we can send objects to it. The *cmdSend_Click* event handler starts by creating an instance of the *MSMQOrders* class and populating it with values from the interface.

```
Dim o As New Server.MSMQOrders()
o.Number = CInt(Me.txtOrderNumber.Text)
o.Customer = Me.txtCustomer.Text
o.RequiredBy = CDate(Me.txtReqDate.Text)
```

Sending the object consists of calling the *Send* method of the queue object and passing in our order object as the first parameter and some text as the label.

```
Me.qOrders.Send(o, "New Order: " & o.Number)
```

Remember that at this point the Framework serializes our object to XML and sends it to the *Orders* queue with the label we specified.

Reading from the Queue

The WindowsService application contains a service defined in the Watch-MSMQ.vb file. It has a *MessageQueue* component configured the same as the component in the Client project. The process of consuming messages from the *Orders* queue begins when the service is started and the *OnStart* method fires. This method calls the *HookQueue* procedure, where we determine whether our queue component has been instantiated yet. This component needs to be instantiated to support the pause/continue behavior of Windows services.

```
If Me.qOrders Is Nothing Then
    Me.qOrders = New System.Messaging.MessageQueue(Me.m_Path)
End If
```

After ensuring that we have a *MessageQueue* object, we start retrieving messages asynchronously by calling the *BeginReceive* method.

```
Me.qOrders.BeginReceive()
```

Each time a message is retrieved, the queue's *ReceiveCompleted* event is raised. Our event handler, *qOrders_ReceiveCompleted*, handles that event and processes the retrieved message. We get the message by calling the *EndReceive* method of the queue and passing in the *AsyncResult* property of the *Receive-CompletedEventArgs* parameter. This returns a *Message* object, the body of which is our serialized *MSMQOrders* object.

```
Dim m As Message
m = qOrders.EndReceive(e.AsyncResult)
```

The body of the message needs to be converted to an *MSMQOrders* object, which we do with a simple use of the *CType* function.

```
Dim o As Server.MSMQOrders
o = CType(m.Body, Server.MSMQOrders)
```

At this point, your application can do whatever it wants with the retrieved object. This application calls the order object *Process* method on a separate thread. Because the call is made on another thread, our service can continue listening for additional messages in the queue without having to wait for the current order to finish processing.

```
ThreadPool.QueueUserWorkItem(AddressOf o.Process)
Me.qOrders.BeginReceive()
```

Listing Messages in the Queue

In addition to retrieving messages from the queue, you can also find out what messages are in the queue without consuming them. The Client application has a List Messages In Queue button that displays in a list box the labels of all the messages in the queue. This is done in the *cmdScanQ_Click* event handler by iterating over the *MessageQueue* component.

```
Dim m As Message
For Each m In Me.qOrders
    Me.lstMessages.Items.Add(m.Label)
Next
```

Conclusion

The .NET Framework makes it easy to use MSMQ as a transport mechanism between applications. With a few lines of code, you can add a powerful messaging system with transaction, acknowledgement, security, and auditing features to your programs.

Application #72: Configuration Settings

This topic examines the purpose of the *appSettings* section of .NET application configuration files and how to read from and write to it in your applications. By the end of the topic, you'll understand how to use configuration settings and how to create reusable custom classes for standardizing your *appSettings*-related code.

Building Upon...

Application #28: Work with XML DOM
Application #35: Create an Explorer-Style Application
Application #67: Understand the Garbage Collector
Application #73: Read From and Write To a Text File

New Concepts

Virtually every application needs to store configuration information outside of compiled code that can be used at run time. Whether it's user settings or a database connection string, this information needs to be easily accessible from code and updatable. In the past, this information was mostly stored in either the system

Registry or in .ini files, but this is no longer the case in .NET. For .NET applications, you store these settings in an Application Configuration File. This configuration file is simply an XML document that complies with the configuration file schema. An example of a simple configuration file is shown in Figure 8-6.

```
<?xml version="1.0" encoding="Windows-1252"?>
<configuration>
  <appSettings>
    <add key="DB.UserID" value="NancyDavino" />
    <add key="DB.Password" value="asdfjkl;" />
    <add key="DB.ConnectOnStart" value="True" />
  </appSettings>
</configuration>
```

Figure 8-6   Example Application Configuration File.

More Info   Configuration files can actually contain more than just custom application settings. For more information on all the things configuration files can be used for, see *ms-help://MS.VSCC/MS.MSDNVS /cpguide/html/cpconapplicationconfigurationfiles.htm.*

The Framework supplies some easy-to-use utility classes for reading your application's configuration file. However, to use them, your configuration file must reside in the application's root directory and be named ExecutableAssemblyName.exe.config. So, if your application is named Foo.exe, your configuration file must be named Foo.exe.config and exist in the same directory as Foo.exe.

Tip   In Visual Studio, add an Application Configuration File named app.config to your project. When you run the project, Visual Studio will automatically rename it and copy it to the Debug directory for you.

The *System.Configuration* namespace contains a class named *ConfigurationSettings*. This class has a single shared property named *AppSettings* that automatically loads your application configuration file and reads in the items in the *appSettings* section. This information is made available to you in a read-only *NameValueCollection*. This is very convenient because you don't have to load, parse, or validate the configuration file. However, because the access provided by the *AppSettings* property is read-only, you are not able to make any changes to the configuration file.

The *AppSettings* Class

Most applications need the ability to change configuration settings from time to time, either as the result of a change in user preferences or sometimes because of environmental changes. In addition, you might want to have multiple configuration files for your application. You'll have to write your own code to perform these tasks because the built-in mechanisms described earlier cannot handle these requirements. The sample application illustrates one possible way to implement an application-settings manager with the following features:

- Load settings from anywhere on the file system

- Add new settings

- Update existing settings

- Optionally, automatically save when changes are made

Code Walkthrough

The sample application allows you to view application settings in the default application configuration file. The Custom tab uses the custom *AppSettings* class discussed earlier to manipulate the settings in any available configuration file. The following walkthrough describes how to work with the built-in application settings and how to create the utility classes.

> **Note**   When running the sample application from Visual Studio, changes will not be saved between sessions. This is because Visual Studio overwrites the configuration file each time you run the application. To see your changes persisted, run the compiled application directly from the file system.

Accessing the *AppSettings* Property

The AppSettings tab allows you to load and display the settings in the application configuration file. The loading takes place in the *cmdLoadAS_Click* event handler by getting a reference to the *AppSettings* property of the *Configuration-Settings* class. Remember that the *ConfigurationSettings* class is available in the *System.Configuration* namespace.

```
mAppSet = ConfigurationSettings.AppSettings
```

We can display the individual settings either by index or key value. The *cmdListByKey_Click* event handler retrieves an array of key values and loops through this array using each key as the input to the *Item* method of the *App-Settings* reference. The return is added to the list box.

```
If Not mAppSet Is Nothing Then
    Me.lstSettings.Items.Clear()
    Dim keys() As String
    keys = mAppSet.AllKeys
    Dim key As String
    For Each key In keys
        Me.lstSettings.Items.Add(key & ": " & mAppSet.Item(key))
    Next
End If
```

The *cmdListByIndex_Click* event handler also displays the settings, but it does so by looping through the *Items* by index.

```
If Not mAppSet Is Nothing Then
    Me.lstSettings.Items.Clear()
    Dim i As Integer
    For i = 0 To mAppSet.Count - 1
        Me.lstSettings.Items.Add(mAppSet.GetKey(i) & ": " & _
            mAppSet.Item(i))
    Next
End If
```

The Custom *AppSettings* Wrapper

The Custom tab provides controls for loading a configuration file and manipulating its contents through an instance of the custom *AppSettings* class. Each setting in the configuration file is exposed through an instance of the custom *AppSetting* class.

The *AppSetting* Class

The *AppSetting* class maintains three pieces of information: a key, a value, and a reference to the *AppSettings* instance it belongs to.

```
Private mParent As AppSettings
Private mstrKey As String
Private mstrValue As String
```

mstrKey and *mstrValue* are exposed through public properties named *Key* and *Value*, respectively. When setting the *Value* property, we call the *Update-Parent* method after storing the new value.

```
mstrValue = Value
Me.UpdateParent()
```

The *UpdateParent* method calls the parent's *Update* method and passes in a reference to itself. This signals the parent that a setting has changed. We will examine the parent's update behavior later in this walkthrough.

```
Private Sub UpdateParent()
    If Not Me.mParent Is Nothing Then
        Me.mParent.Update(Me)
```

```
      End If
End Sub
```

AppSettings Class

The *AppSettings* class wraps access to a configuration file's *appSettings* section. The class's constructor requires that you provide a path to the configuration file you want to manage and a Boolean indicating whether the class should automatically save after every change.

```
Public Sub New(ByVal ConfigFile As String, _
    ByVal AutoSave As Boolean)
```

After some validation, the specified file is loaded into a module-level *Xml-Document* instance named *cfg*.

```
cfg.Load(ConfigFile)
```

If no exceptions are thrown, we know that the file was well-formed XML, but we still need to make sure it contains an *appSettings* section in the appropriate place. We use the XPath query defined in the APPSETTINGS_ELEMENT constant to retrieve a node reference. If this reference is *Nothing*, the file does not contain the necessary structure.

```
xAS = cfg.SelectSingleNode(APPSETTINGS_ELEMENT)
```

Retrieving Items

The *Item* method accepts a string containing the key for the setting you want to retrieve and returns an instance of the *AppSetting* class. The key you pass in is injected into the XPath query contained in the XPATH_KEY_ADD_KEY constant by using *String.Format*.

```
Public Function Item(ByVal Key As String) As AppSetting
    Dim xNode As XmlNode
    Dim strSearch As String = XPATH_KEY_ADD_KEY
    xNode = xAS.SelectSingleNode(String.Format(strSearch, Key))
```

If a node is found, we retrieve the second attribute and construct a new instance of *AppSetting*.

```
    Return New AppSetting(Key, _
        xNode.Attributes.Item(1).Value, Me)
```

Iterating All Items

The *GetAllItems* function returns all of the setting data through an array of *AppSetting* instances. An *XmlNodeList* is populated with *XmlNode* references retrieved by using the XPath query defined in the XPATH_KEY_ADD constant.

```
Dim xNode As XmlNode
Dim xNodeList As XmlNodeList
Dim atts As XmlAttributeCollection
xNodeList = xAS.SelectNodes(XPATH_KEY_ADD)
```

We then loop through the list, creating a new *AppSetting* instance for each node. The first attribute of each node contains the setting key and the second attribute contains the value.

```
Dim xa As XmlAttribute
Dim asa(xNodeList.Count - 1) As AppSetting
Dim i As Integer = -1
For Each xNode In xNodeList
    i += 1
    atts = xNode.Attributes
    With atts
        asa(i) = New AppSetting(.Item(0).Value, .Item(1).Value, Me)
    End With
Next
Return asa
```

Updating a Setting

So far we have basically re-created the functionality provided by the Framework's *ConfigurationSettings* class. However, this class also contains methods for adding new settings and changing existing settings. Earlier we examined the *Update* method of the *AppSetting* class. That method simply called the *Update* method on the parent *AppSettings* class and passed in a reference to itself. The *Update* method of the *AppSettings* class takes the passed-in *AppSetting* and copies its data into the underlying XML configuration file. The first step is to make sure there is a setting with the specified key already in the configuration file. We take the *Key* property of the passed-in *AppSetting* and inject it into the XPath query defined by the XPATH_KEY_ADD_KEY constant.

```
Dim xNode As XmlNode
Dim strSearch As String = XPATH_KEY_ADD_KEY
xNode = xAS.SelectSingleNode(String.Format(strSearch, _
    NewSetting.Key))
```

If the setting is found, we populate its value attribute with the *Value* property of the *AppSetting* instance.

```
If xNode Is Nothing Then
    ⋮
Else
    xNode.Attributes.Item(1).Value = NewSetting.Value
End If
```

Finally, we indicate that the settings have changed by setting the *mblnDirty* variable to *True* and call the *Save* method if *AutoSave* is equal to *True*. Remember, the value of *AutoSave* was set when the *AppSettings* instance was first created.

```
Me.mblnDirty = True
If Me.AutoSave Then
```

```
    Me.Save()
End If
```

We will examine the use of the *Save* method later in the walkthrough.

Adding a Setting

To add a new setting to the configuration file, we have to create the appropriate XML structure, populate it with data, and add it to the *appSettings* section of the file. The *Add* method performs these tasks by accepting two strings—one for the key and one for the value of the new setting—and returning an *AppSetting* instance for the newly created setting.

```
Dim newElem As XmlElement
Dim newAttr As XmlAttribute
newElem = cfg.CreateElement(NEWELEMENT)
newAttr = cfg.CreateAttribute("key")
newAttr.Value = Key
newElem.Attributes.Append(newAttr)
newAttr = cfg.CreateAttribute("value")
newAttr.Value = Value
newElem.Attributes.Append(newAttr)
xAS.AppendChild(newElem)
```

After the setting is added, we perform the same saving-related tasks as in the *Update* method.

```
Me.mblnDirty = True
If Me.AutoSave Then
    Me.Save()
End If
```

Saving

In the last two sections, we've seen calls to the *Save* method. This method simply calls the *Save* method of the *XmlDocument* instance *cfg* and sets the dirty flag to *False* after the save completes.

```
Public Sub Save()
    cfg.Save(Me.mstrFileName)
    Me.mblnDirty = False
End Sub
```

Conclusion

Application configuration files provide an easy and standardized way of exposing configuration information to your programs. The built-in Framework classes in the *System.Configuration* namespace allow you to easily read these values, while creating your own settings wrapper classes allows you to add any other configuration-related functionality you need.

Application #73: Read From and Write To a Text File

This topic describes some of the functionality provided by classes in the *System.IO* namespace for working with text files. The sample application examines various ways of reading text data and saving changes back to the file.

> **Note**   See "Application #55: Use the File System" in Chapter 7 for information on how to retrieve file-system information about files and directories.

Building Upon...

Application #30: Use Common Dialog Boxes

New Concepts

The *System.IO* namespace contains many types for working with text files such as the *File*, *StreamReader*, and *StreamWriter* classes.

Using the *File* Class

The *System.IO.File* class provides a number of shared methods for working with both binary and text files. In general, these methods require the path to the file of interest to be passed in as a parameter. There is a general-purpose method named *Open* that allows you to specify what kind of access you want to the file and what kind of access other applications should have while your code is using the file. There are also some helper methods such as *CreateText*, *Append-Text*, and *OpenText* that open files with the appropriate access settings already set. *OpenText* returns a *StreamReader* instance, and *CreateText* and *AppendText* return *StreamWriter* instances. In many cases, you'll want to check whether a file exists before you read it or attempt to edit its contents. You can do this by calling the *Exists* method of the *File* object.

Using the *StreamReader* Class

The *StreamReader* class allows you to retrieve data from a text file either all at once or piece by piece. If you want to retrieve all the data in the file at once, you can easily do so by calling the *ReadToEnd* method. Sometimes you might want to read a file line by line—for example, if you were reading a data file that uses carriage returns as the row delimiter. The *ReadLine* method returns all the characters up to the next new line or to the end of the file if there are no more new line characters. Once all the data has been read, calls to *ReadLine* will return *Nothing*. The last action you must be sure to do after reading your data is release the file by calling the *Close* method. This will ensure that your application releases any locks on the file.

Using the *StreamWriter* Class

The *StreamWriter* instance returned by the *CreateText* and *AppendText* methods can be used to send string data to the file. The *Write* method simply adds the specified text to the file, while the *WriteLine* method adds the text and a new line character. The *StreamWriter* contains an internal buffer to reduce the number of times the underlying stream is actually accessed. To make sure all your data is sent from the buffer to the file, you should call the *Flush* method before calling the *Close* method.

Code Walkthrough

The sample application allows you to create, read, and append to text files. The first step in executing any of these tasks is to identify the path of the file you want to work with. You can do this by manually entering the path in the *File Name* text box or using the dialog boxes presented by the New File and Open File buttons. You can read from a file by clicking the appropriate button or write to a file by first entering text in the *File Text* text box and clicking either Create New File or Append To File.

Reading Files

The *btnStreamReaderReadFromFile_Click* event handler implements the code for reading the entire contents of the text file in one shot. By passing a file path into the *OpenText* method of the *File* object, we get an instance of the *StreamReader* class.

```
Dim myStreamReader As StreamReader
myStreamReader = File.OpenText(txtFileName.Text)
```

The *ReadToEnd* method of the *StreamReader* instance is used to populate a text box with the entire contents of the file.

```
Me.txtFileText.Text = myStreamReader.ReadToEnd()
```

Finally, the *StreamReader* is closed before the procedure ends.

```
If Not myStreamReader Is Nothing Then
    myStreamReader.Close()
End If
```

The *btnStringReaderReadFileInLines_Click* event handler reads a file line by line and prepends line numbers before displaying the text. Variables for temporarily storing a line of text and a row counter are declared in addition to *StreamReader*.

```
Dim myStreamReader As StreamReader
Dim myInputString As String
Dim rowCount As Integer = 0
```

The code for opening the file is identical to the last procedure, but this time we call *ReadLine* instead of *ReadToEnd*. The returned string contains just the text up to the next new line character in the document.

```
myStreamReader = File.OpenText(txtFileName.Text)
txtFileText.Clear()
myInputString = myStreamReader.ReadLine()
```

Because the *ReadLine* method will return *Nothing* when there is no more data, you should check for *Nothing* before attempting to process the text.

```
While Not myInputString Is Nothing
```

As long as there is text, we prepend the current value of the row counter and add the line to the text box. The row counter is then incremented, and the next line is read.

```
txtFileText.Text += rowCount.ToString() + ": " + _
    myInputString + vbCrLf
rowCount += 1
myInputString = myStreamReader.ReadLine()
```

The last way we read text is character by character, as demonstrated in the *btnStreamReaderReadInChars_Click* event handler. Just as before, we declare a *StreamReader* and a variable to store each character as it is read in. Notice that this variable, *myNextInt*, is an *Integer* not a *String*. This is because the read method returns an integer character code that will be converted to a *String*.

```
Dim myStreamReader As StreamReader
Dim myNextInt As Integer
```

Next, the file is opened and the first character is read into *myNextInt* by calling the *Read* method of our *StreamReader* instance.

```
myStreamReader = File.OpenText(txtFileName.Text)
txtFileText.Clear()
myNextInt = myStreamReader.Read()
```

Just as in the last example, we have to make sure data was returned, but this time we do it by checking whether *myNextInt* is not equal to –1. If it isn't, then it contains a character code that must be converted using the *ChrW* function. Then the next character is read and the process is repeated.

```
While myNextInt <> -1
    txtFileText.Text += ChrW(myNextInt)
    myNextInt = myStreamReader.Read()
    txtFileText.Refresh()
    System.Threading.Thread.CurrentThread.Sleep(100)
End While
```

> **Note**   The *System.Threading.Thread.CurrentThread.Sleep(100)* statement causes execution to pause for 100 milliseconds. This statement is used solely to give the output a typewriter-like appearance and is not required for reading text by character.

Writing To Files

The *btnStreamWriterCreateFile_Click* event handler uses a *StreamWriter* instance to write the contents of the *txtFileText TextBox* to the specified file. However, before writing the data, we determine whether the file already exists by calling the *Exists* method of the *File* class. If it does exist, we prompt the user to specify whether she wants to overwrite it.

```
If File.Exists(txtFileName.Text) Then
    If MsgBox("That file exists. Would you like to overwrite it?", _
        MsgBoxStyle.YesNo) = MsgBoxResult.No Then
        Return
    End If
End If
```

The *CreateText* method of the *File* class is used to create a new text file or overwrite an existing one. It returns a *StreamWriter* instance that is used to transfer data to the file.

```
myStreamWriter = File.CreateText(txtFileName.Text)
```

The *Write* method of the *StreamWriter* instance copies the contents of the text box into the writer's buffer. The *Flush* method sends the buffered data to the file.

```
myStreamWriter.Write(txtFileText.Text)
myStreamWriter.Flush()
```

Appending to an existing file is demonstrated in the *btnStreamWriter-AppendToFile_Click* event handler. The code for appending is essentially the same as the last example except that the *AppendText* method of the *File* class is used instead of the *CreateText* method. This ensures that all data written to the file is added to the end of the file.

```
myStreamWriter = File.AppendText(txtFileName.Text)
```

Conclusion

You can see that working with text files requires learning only a couple classes and methods. Remember that the methods of the *File* class discussed here are all shared methods. If you want to maintain a reference to a file, consider using the *System.IO.FileInfo* class.

Application #74: Use Temporary Resources

It's quite common for an application to need to store some information for use later on. Ideally, we would like to store everything in memory, but often this is not possible because system resources are limited or the amount of data we want to store is very large. In these situations, you can use a file to temporarily store the information.

Building Upon...

Application #73: Read From and Write To a Text File

New Concepts

An application that uses temporary files needs to select a reasonable location for creating the files that does not clutter the user's system. The Framework provides mechanisms to ensure that your application uses temporary files responsibly.

Locating Temporary Locations

Technically, you could create your temporary file wherever you want, but we suggest you create your temporary files in the system-defined Temp directory. The exact location of this directory varies across platforms, so you need to retrieve the path at run time. The *System.IO.Path* class has a couple methods specialized for working with temporary files. One of them is the *GetTempPath* method, which returns the path to the system's Temp directory as a string.

Creating Temporary Files

Once you know where the Temp directory is located, you can create files in it as you would create files in any other location. However, the *Path* class has another utility function, *GetTempFileName*, that automatically creates a temporary file and returns the path to the file. Immediately after creating the file, you should set the file's *Temporary* attribute. Setting this attribute allows the runtime to optimize its use of the file. You can then work with the file as necessary.

Code Walkthrough

The sample application allows you to locate the system's Temp directory and create, use, and destroy temporary files. In addition, you'll see how to mark your temporary files so that the runtime can optimize its use of them.

Working with Temporary Files

Before we can create a temporary file, we need to retrieve the path to the Temp directory. The *btnFindTempDirectory_Click* event handler retrieves the Temp path by calling the *GetTempPath* method of the *Path* class. This call is made within a *Try/Catch* block, so we can catch any exceptions. Notice that in addition to normal I/O-related exceptions, you should also handle any security-related exceptions.

```
Try
    tempPathString = Path.GetTempPath()
Catch sex As Security.SecurityException
    Me.sbrStatus.Text = "You do not have the required permissions."
Catch exc As Exception
    Me.sbrStatus.Text = "Unable to retrieve TEMP directory path."
End Try
```

The *btnCreateTempFile_Click* event handler creates a temporary file by calling the *GetTempFileName* method of the *Path* class. Remember that although this method returns a string, it actually creates a file at the path returned.

```
m_FileName = Path.GetTempFileName()
```

After creating the file, we set the file's *Temporary* attribute by creating a *FileInfo* instance that points to the file and modifying the *Attributes* property.

```
Dim myFileInfo As New FileInfo(m_FileName)
myFileInfo.Attributes = FileAttributes.Temporary
```

Now that the temporary file exists, we can use it just like any other file. The *btnUseTempFilebtnUseTempFile_Click* event handler creates a *StreamWriter* to the new file and writes out some text.

```
Dim myWriter As StreamWriter = File.AppendText(m_FileName)
myWriter.WriteLine("Data written to temporary file.")
```

You should always make sure you flush and close your file-access classes even when using temporary files.

```
myWriter.Flush()
myWriter.Close()
```

The final task is to make sure our application deletes any temporary files that it created. You can do this simply by calling the shared *Delete* method of the *System.IO.File* class and passing in the path to the file. The *btnDeleteTempFile_Click* event handler does exactly this.

```
File.Delete(m_FileName)
```

Conclusion

Working with temporary files is identical to working with any other file except that you ask the system for the location to create it in. Remember to treat temporary files just as you would any other resource by destroying them once you are done with them.

Application #75: Send Mail

Whether you are using it to send an administrative alert or an action confirmation to a user, e-mail has become an important facet of most applications. The Framework makes sending e-mail to a Simple Mail Transport Protocol (SMTP) server very easy by wrapping up all e-mail functionality in a couple simple classes.

Building Upon...

Application #3: String Manipulation
Application #30: Use Common Dialog Boxes
Application #64: Interact with Services
Application #72: Configuration Settings

New Concepts

The *System.Web.Mail* namespace contains three classes that can be used to create and send e-mail messages to an SMTP server. The *SmtpMail* class exposes a shared property named *SmtpServer* that you use to specify the host name or IP address of the target SMTP server. The *Send* method accepts either a *MailMessage* instance or a series of strings, and sends the message to the specified server. The *MailMessage* class exposes properties for defining the common aspects of an e-mail message, such as *Subject*, *Body*, *BodyFormat*, *From*, and *To*. If you want to add attachments to your message, you can create instances of the *MailAttachment* class and add them to the *Attachments* property of the *MailMessage*. You simply provide a file path to the *Filename* property, and the class will handle the reading, encoding, and transmission of the file for you.

Code Walkthrough

The sample application demonstrates how to create an e-mail message, add attachments, and send the message to an SMTP server.

Setting Up an SMTP Mail Server on Windows XP

To run the sample, you must have a running SMTP server available. If there is already one you can use, just change the application setting in app.config to point to it. Otherwise, you can install the SMTP service locally.

If you are running Windows XP Professional on your computer, you can install for free the Microsoft Web server, Internet Information Services 5.1 (IIS), from the Windows XP Pro installation CD and configure it to run on your system. To do this, open the Add Or Remove Programs control panel and click Add/Remove Windows Components.

If you don't have IIS installed, select the Internet Information Services (IIS) check box, leaving all the default installation settings intact. If you do have IIS installed and just need to add SMTP support, select Internet Information Services and click the Details button. Select the SMTP Services check box.

With IIS installed, you will find the Internet Information Services console in the Performance And Maintenance section of the Administrative Tools control panels. Double-click the Internet Information Services icon.

Once the Internet Information Services console is open, you'll see any IIS Web services you have running on your machine, including the SMTP server. You'll also have a mailroot/Drop directory structure under the InetPub directory. This is the directory where your messages will appear when you send them from your application.

Defining Attachments

Before we create and send an e-mail message, we need to identify some files to send as attachments to the message. The *btnBrowse_Click* event handler allows you to select a file from an Open dialog box. A new *MailAttachment* object is created with the path to the selected file and added to the *arlAttachments ArrayList*.

```
With odlgAttachment
    ⋮
    arlAttachments.Add(New MailAttachment(.FileName))
    Dim strFileName() As String = _
        .FileName.Split(New Char() {CChar("\")})
    strFileName.Reverse(strFileName)
    lstAttachments.Items.Add(strFileName(0))
```

We examine the use of this *ArrayList* when sending a message in the next section.

Sending Mail

The *btnSend_Click* event handler is invoked after the user fills out the e-mail information on the form. The e-mail addresses are validated by passing in their values to the *ValidateEmailAddress* function. The *ValidateEmailAddress* method performs a simple check to make sure that an "@" and a "." both exist in the entered value.

```
Try
    ValidateEmailAddress(txtFrom)
Catch ex As Exception
    txtFrom.Select(0, txtFrom.Text.Length)
    erpEmailAddresses.SetError(txtFrom, ex.Message)
    Exit Sub
End Try
```

> **Tip**   You could implement more powerful validation by using the regular expression techniques described later in the "Application #77: Use Regular Expressions" section.

Once the e-mail addresses are validated, we can build the body for the e-mail message. In this case, we are using a *StringBuilder* to concatenate the body contents.

```
Dim sb As New StringBuilder()
sb.Append("The following email was sent to you from " & _
    "the Send Mail How-To sample application:")
sb.Append(vbCrLf)
sb.Append(vbCrLf)
sb.Append("MESSAGE: ")
sb.Append(Trim(txtBody.Text))
sb.Append(vbCrLf)
```

Creating the message entails creating an instance of the *MailMessage* class and populating its properties with the entered values.

```
Dim mailMsg As New MailMessage()
With mailMsg
    .From = txtFrom.Text.Trim
    .To = txtTo.Text.Trim
    .Cc = txtCC.Text.Trim
    .Bcc = txtBCC.Text.Trim
    .Subject = txtSubject.Text.Trim
    .Body = sb.ToString
    .Priority = CType(cboPriority.SelectedIndex, MailPriority)
```

The last bit of information to define for our message is its attachments. Each item in the *arlAttachments ArrayList* is added to the *Attachments* collection of our *MailMessage* object.

```
If Not IsNothing(arlAttachments) Then
    Dim mailAttachment As Object
    For Each mailAttachment In arlAttachments
        .Attachments.Add(mailAttachment)
    Next
End If
End With
```

We can now send our message by calling the shared *Send* method of the *SmtpMail* class. Before doing this though, we read a value named *Smtp-Mail.SmtpServer* from the application configuration file and assign it to the *SmtpServer* property of the *SmtpMail* class.

```
SmtpMail.SmtpServer = _
Configuration.ConfigurationSettings.AppSettings.Item("SmtpMail.SmtpServer")
Try
    SmtpMail.Send(mailMsg)
```

Conclusion

The Framework makes it easy to send e-mail from your applications. As long as you have an SMTP server available, you can use the classes in the *System.Net.Mail* namespace to create and send messages with attachments.

Application #76: Create and Use Trace Listeners

Monitoring run-time health and behavior is an important part of application development and maintenance. The Framework contains an easy-to-use class in the *System.Diagnostics* namespace named *Trace* that you can use to output messages to a group of trace listeners. The listeners then send the messages to some observable location such as the Event Viewer, a file, or a database. This topic examines some of the members of the *Trace* class and how to implement some of the provided listeners. Finally, we will look at how to extend your diagnostic ability by creating your own custom listeners.

Building Upon...

Application #7: Object-Oriented Features
Application #8: Scoping, Overloading, Overriding

New Concepts

Getting started with tracing is remarkably easy because Visual Studio automatically hooks up a trace listener that sends trace messages to the Output window in the integrated development environment (IDE). All you have to do is call the shared *WriteLine* method of the *Trace* class and provide the message you want output. There are a couple other write-related methods you can use—such as *Write*, which doesn't include a line feed. *WriteLineIf* and *WriteIf* allow you to specify an expression and message. They output the message only if the condition is *True*. You can also indicate that you want a portion of your output to be indented by calling the *Indent* method. All messages written after calling *Indent* will be indented until you call *Unindent*. Once your application is done tracing, you should be sure to call the *Close* method to force all listeners to flush any contents they might have buffered and close themselves.

Using the Event Log Trace Listener

While the default trace listener might be sufficient during development, you'll likely want to send your messages to some external store once your application is in production. The event log is one option that is convenient because it can easily be monitored remotely. To implement event log tracing, you should create an instance of the *EventLogTraceListener* class and provide a reference to the log you want to write to the constructor. The listener will start receiving trace messages after you add the instance to the shared *Listeners* collection of the *Trace* class.

Creating a Custom Trace Listener

In some cases, you might want to write trace messages to some custom location or in a custom format. For example, you might want to have your trace messages stored in a database or sent via e-mail to an administrator. To do this, you need to create your own listener by implementing a class that inherits from the *TraceListener* class. At a minimum, you must implement the *Write* and *WriteLine* methods to determine where and how your listener sends its messages.

Code Walkthrough

The sample application illustrates how to use various types of trace listeners, including the *DefaultTraceListener*, *EventLogTraceListener*, and *TextWriterTraceListener*. In addition, a custom listener that writes to an HTML file is demonstrated.

Default Trace Listener

The *cmdTraceToOutput_Click* event handler uses the *WriteLine*, *Indent*, *WriteLineIf*, and *Unindent* methods of the *Trace* class to send messages to the Output window of the IDE. Remember, the listener that writes to the Output window is automatically added to the *Listeners* collection, so we don't have to add it in code.

```
Trace.WriteLine("****** Trace Output Start ******")
Trace.WriteLine("Output window trace information")
Trace.Indent()
Trace.WriteLine("This line is indented")
Trace.WriteLine("Product Type = " & ProductType)
Trace.WriteLine("Price = $" & Price)
Trace.WriteLineIf(Price > 1800, "Price > $1800")
Trace.Unindent()
Trace.WriteLine("****** Trace Output End ******")
```

Figure 8-7 shows output displayed in the Output window.

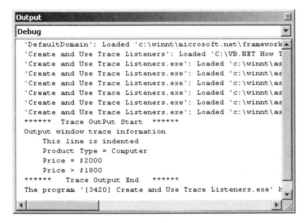

Figure 8-7   Trace output in the Output window.

Event Log Trace Listener

The *cmdTraceToEventLog_Click* event handler sends a message to the event log. It starts by creating an instance of the *EventLog* class and setting its *Source* property.

```
Dim myLog As New EventLog()
myLog.Source = Me.Text
```

This *EventLog* instance is then passed in to the constructor of the *Event-LogTraceListener* class.

```
Dim tlEventLog As New EventLogTraceListener(myLog)
```

Before we add the event log listener to the *Listeners* collection, we need to remove the default trace listener by calling the *Clear* method of the *Listeners* collection.

```
Trace.Listeners.Clear()
```

Now we can add the event log listener.

```
Trace.Listeners.Add(tlEventLog)
```

Finally, we call *WriteLine*. Once this procedure completes, you can view the message in the event log.

```
Trace.WriteLine("This is a test of event log tracing")
```

TextWriterTraceListener

The *cmdTraceToFile_Click* event handler uses an instance of the *TextWriter-TraceListener* to send trace messages to a text file. The path to the file is provided to the listener's constructor.

> **Note**   The *TextWriterTraceListener* can be used to write to any stream, not just files. You could, for example, use it to send messages to a network stream.

```
Dim tlTextFile As New TextWriterTraceListener("TraceOutput.txt")
```

We then remove the default listener and add the new one just as in the previous section.

```
Trace.Listeners.Clear()
Trace.Listeners.Add(tlTextFile)
```

The rest of the procedure sends messages as normal, but now the messages are being written to the TraceOutput.txt file in the application directory. The final line in the procedure opens the new trace file in Notepad.

```
System.Diagnostics.Process.Start("Notepad.exe", "TraceOutput.txt")
```

Creating an HTML Trace Listener

The sample application defines a custom trace listener named *HTMLTraceListener* that writes messages to an HTML file. Because the *TextWriterTraceListener* already contains all the functionality for writing to a file, we chose to inherit from it instead of from *TraceListener*.

```
Public Class HTMLTraceListener
    Inherits System.Diagnostics.TextWriterTraceListener
```

There is a constructor that accepts a file name and passes that information on to the base-class constructor.

```
Public Sub New(ByVal fileName As String)
    MyBase.New(fileName)
End Sub
```

There is also a method named *WriteHeader* that is intended to be called before the listener starts receiving trace messages. This method writes some HTML to give the document a title.

```
Public Sub WriteHeader(ByVal Title As String)
    Writer.WriteLine("<head>")
    Writer.WriteLine("<title>" & Title & "</title>")
    Writer.WriteLine("</head>")
    Writer.WriteLine("<H2>" & Title & "</H2>")
    Writer.WriteLine("<P><HR>")
End Sub
```

The protected *WriteIndent* method is overridden because creating indentations in HTML is different from doing so in a plain text file. *IndentLevel* and *IndentSize* are public properties you can read to determine how much of an indentation to write out.

```
Dim i As Integer
Dim j As Integer
If IndentLevel > 0 Then
    For i = 1 To IndentLevel
        For j = 1 To IndentSize
            Writer.Write(" ")
        Next j
    Next i
End If
```

The *WriteLine* method is overridden so that each message is preceded by a timestamp and followed by an HTML line break.

```
Writer.Write("<B>" & Now() & " - ")
If NeedIndent Then
    WriteIndent()
End If
Writer.WriteLine(message & "</B><BR>")
```

Using the HTML Trace Listener

The process for using our new *HTMLTraceListener* is almost identical to how we used the *TextWriterTraceListener* as illustrated in the *cmdTraceToHTML_Click* event handler. The only difference is that after creating the listener, we call the *WriteHeader* method to create a title in the output file.

```
Dim tlHTMLFile As New HTMLTraceListener("TraceOutputHTML.htm")
tlHTMLFile.WriteHeader("HTML Trace Output for " & Me.Text)
```

The rest of the procedure sends tracing messages and closes the listeners as we've seen before. The procedure completes by launching the HTML trace file in your default browser.

Conclusion

Tracing is a simple and easy way of monitoring the status of your applications. In many cases, the provided trace listeners should be sufficient, but you can always enhance your tracing capability by creating your own trace listeners.

Application #77: Use Regular Expressions

This topic explores the basics of using regular expressions to validate data entered by an end user. We examine the *Regex* class and some regular-expression syntax.

New Concepts

At some point or another, you have probably written code to make sure the data entered by a user matched some sort of pattern. In the past, this type of validation was often accomplished by parsing the piece of data character by character and checking a set of rules to determine whether each character was appropriate. Regular expressions provide us with an alternative way of performing these kinds of validation tasks. The .NET Framework has regular-expression support built in through the *Regex* class that allows us to perform very complex validations with very little code.

A regular expression is a string that describes a character pattern that another string must match. You provide your expression string and your data string to the *Regex* class, and it tells you whether the data string matches the pattern defined in the expression string. The majority of your development effort in working with regular expressions will involve learning the regular-expression syntax. The sample application walkthrough provides you with an introduction to this syntax.

Code Walkthrough

The sample application demonstrates how to use regular expressions to validate some common types of data patterns, such as zip codes, dates, and e-mail addresses.

Validating Data

If you look through the code for the *btnValidate_Click* event handler, you should notice that there isn't much code to review. This is exactly the point of regular expressions. The majority of the validation work is done by the *Regex* class that we pass our data and validation expression to. The *IsMatch* method returns a Boolean indicating whether or not our data is valid according to the expression. Each expression used in the procedure is explained in the following sections.

Zip Codes

The first expression used defines a zip code containing either five digits or five digits followed by a dash and another four digits.

```
^(\d{5}|(\d{5}-\d{4}))$
```

The construction of this expression can be broken down as follows. The ^ specifies that nothing can precede the matching text. The \d means we expect a digit, and the {5} indicates that we expect five of them. The | says that we can have either the pattern before it or the pattern after it. The (starts a pattern group. The - represents a literal dash, and the \d{4} matches the last four digits. Finally, the $ indicates that nothing can follow the matching data. With this pattern, values of 13254 and 13253-8657 would both be valid.

Dates

The next expression is one that matches month, day, and year numerical dates separated by either a / or a -.

```
^\d{1,2}(/|-)\d{1,2}\1(\d{4}|\d{2})$
```

The expression is broken down as follows: The \d{X,Y} matches a sequence of digits where the number of digits is between X and Y. So \d{1,2} would match one or two digits. The /|- indicates that either a / or a - must appear next. Notice that this choice is wrapped in parentheses. This is important because the parentheses declare this choice as a group. After the \d{1,2} pattern for the days, the next value is a \1. This is a reference to the first group in the pattern, which is the /|- choice we just saw. This group reference means that the next value must be the same as whatever satisfied the referenced group pattern. So, if a / is what satisfied the first group pattern, the next value after the days must be a / also. The last group, (\d{4}|\d{2}), means we can specify years with either four or two digits. You can't use \d{4,2} here because three digits would satisfy that expression.

E-mail Addresses

The last expression used in this procedure is one that validates e-mail addresses. It's a flexible pattern that accounts for the period-separated format of both user and domain names.

```
^([\w-]+\.)*?[\w-]+@[\w-]+\.([\w-]+\.)*?[\w]+$
```

Let's start with the expression to the left of the @ that defines valid user names. The first group, ([\w-]+\.), is broken down into the following. The \w represents any word character, which is any alphanumeric character or an underscore. The + means we can have one or more of the word characters, and the \. means that this set of word characters must be followed by a period. The *? that follows the group means that the preceding group is optional and can repeat. The

+ after the next [\w-] means we can have any number of word characters but must have at least one. This ensures that you couldn't have an e-mail address with a period just before the @. The following are examples of valid e-mail user names according to this pattern: john.doe, jdoe, and j.d.1.

The rest of the pattern uses similar constructs to define valid e-mail domains.

Conclusion

Regular expression allow us to perform complex validation with very little code. You have now seen examples of some common expressions and how they are used with the *Regex* class to validate data entered by a user.

9

Advanced .NET Framework

One of the most exciting things about Visual Basic .NET is the newfound power it gives to Visual Basic programmers. In previous versions of Visual Basic, certain types of applications were often difficult or impossible to write, or required third-party toolkits and complicated Win32 API calls. As a result, many of these advanced techniques were often the exclusive domain of C++ programmers. Visual Basic .NET changes all that. Advanced programming techniques, such as creating Windows Services and thread pooling, are now accessible to Visual Basic programmers. This chapter attempts to cover some of these advanced topics.

Application #78: Create a Windows Service

This sample application demonstrates how to create a Microsoft Windows service (formerly Windows NT Service) using Microsoft Visual Basic .NET. There are three projects in the solution. The first project, VB.NET How-To Creating a Windows Service, provides a user interface for accessing the Windows service. The second project, VB.NET How-To Windows Service Demo, is the actual Windows service. The Windows service itself is fairly simple. Whenever the service starts, pauses, resumes, or ends, a message is written to the event log. Finally, the third project, VB.NET How-To Windows Service - Time Track Install, is used to demonstrate the creation of an installation package for a Windows service.

Building Upon...

Application #2: Use *DateTimes*
Application #7: Object-Oriented Features
Application #8: Scoping, Overloading, Overriding

New Concepts

A Windows service is a special type of application that runs in the background and has no user interface. A Windows service can run without any user being logged on to the computer and can be started, stopped, paused, resumed, or disabled. Microsoft SQL Server and Internet Information Services (IIS) are two examples of programs that run as services.

Creating a Windows Service

The easiest way to create a Windows service using Visual Basic .NET is to use the Windows Service project template. Using this template, Visual Studio .NET will automatically create a *Service1* class that contains the skeleton code needed to implement a Windows service.

The *Service1* class inherits from the *System.ServiceProcess.ServiceBase* class. At a bare minimum, a service should override the *OnStart* and *OnStop* methods. As you can probably guess, the *OnStart* method is called when the service is to start and the *OnStop* method is called when the service is to stop. In addition, the *ServiceBase* class provides *OnContinue, OnPause, OnShutdown*, and various other methods. Depending on the specifics of what tasks the service is to perform, these methods might or might not be needed.

Create an Installer for a Windows Service

To create an installer for a Windows service, right-click on the design surface of the class that inherits from *ServiceBase* and select the Add Installer menu. Visual Studio .NET will add a new class to your project named *ProjectInstaller*. By default, this class has two components to it: *ServiceProcessInstaller1* and *ServiceInstaller1*. Both are called by installation utilities when installing the Windows service. Among other things, *ServiceProcessInstaller1* specifies the name of the account under which the service should run and *ServiceInstaller1* specifies the display name of the service. These can be set in code or in the Properties window. To actually install a Windows service, you can either create a setup project or use the InstallUtil.exe utility. The sample application uses the former method. This is where the VB.NET How-To Windows Service - Time Track Install project comes into play. It creates an .msi file, which serves as the installation package for the application. To install the Windows service, simply double-click VB.NET How-To Windows Service - Time Track.msi in Windows Explorer.

Code Walkthrough

As stated previously, there are three projects in the sample application. The code walkthrough will focus on the VB.NET How-To Windows Service Demo project. This service does nothing more than keep track of the time it is running. Although it is simple, it demonstrates the fundamentals of creating Windows services in Visual Basic .NET.

Service1.vb (default)

To better understand how the code in the sample application works, first take a look at how the *Service1* class appears before any code is changed or added:

```
Imports System.ServiceProcess

Public Class Service1
    Inherits System.ServiceProcess.ServiceBase

' Component Designer generated code

    Protected Overrides Sub OnStart(ByVal args() As String)
        ' Add code here to start your service. This method
        ' should set things in motion so your service
        ' can do its work.
    End Sub

    Protected Overrides Sub OnStop()
        ' Add code here to perform any tear-down necessary
        ' to stop your service.
    End Sub
End Class
```

The first line of code imports *System.ServiceProcess*. This namespace provides the classes that allow you to implement, install, and control Windows service applications. Next, an empty stub for *OnStart* has been provided. This method is overridden, and it's where you place the code to run when the service is started. Next is an empty stub for the *OnStop* method. Place any code that is needed to stop the service into the *OnStop* routine.

VB.NET How-To TimeTracker Windows Service.vb

In the sample application, the *Service1* class was renamed to *VB_NET_HowTo_ TimeTrackerService*:

```
Imports System.ServiceProcess

Public Class VB_NET_HowTo_TimeTrackerService
    Inherits System.ServiceProcess.ServiceBase
```

The declarations section contains several module-level variables:

```
Private timeStart As DateTime
Private timeEnd As DateTime
Private timeElapsed As New TimeSpan(0)
Private timeDifference As TimeSpan
Private isPaused As Boolean = False
```

The *timeStart* and *timeEnd* variables are used to keep track of the times the service starts and ends. The *timeElapsed* and *timeDifference* variables are both *TimeSpan* objects. The *timeDifference* variable is used to calculate the difference between *timeStart* and *timeEnd*. The *timeElapsed* variable is used to keep a running total of time elapsed. Finally, *isPaused* is a Boolean that indicates whether the service is currently in a paused state.

The *OnStart* method is called whenever the service is started:

```
Protected Overrides Sub OnStart(ByVal args() As String)

    timeElapsed = New TimeSpan(0)

    timeStart = DateTime.Now()
    isPaused = False

    EventLog.WriteEntry("The VB.NET How-To Service was Started at " + _
        timeStart.ToString())

End Sub
```

Inside *OnStart*, *timeElapsed* is reset to zero. This is necessary because the service can be restarted without pausing or stopping. Then, *timeStart* is initialized to the current time by using *DateTime.Now*. Next, *isPaused* is set to *False*. Finally, a message is written to the event log indicating the time the service has been started.

The *OnStop* method is called whenever the service is stopped. This provides an opportunity to perform whatever clean-up code your application needs:

```
Protected Overrides Sub OnStop()

    timeEnd = DateTime.Now()
    If Not isPaused Then
        timeDifference = timeEnd.Subtract(timeStart)
        timeElapsed = timeElapsed.Add(timeDifference)
    End If

    EventLog.WriteEntry("The VB.NET How-To Service was Stopped at " + _
        timeEnd.ToString())
    EventLog.WriteEntry("The VB.NET How-To ran for a total time of " + _
        timeElapsed.ToString())
End Sub
```

For the sample application, this means calculating the elapsed time and writing it out to the event log. Note that the code checks to make sure the service isn't paused. This needs to be done to make sure the time the service is paused isn't counted as part of the total elapsed time.

Of course, the *ServiceBase* base class provides more than just the *OnStart* and *OnStop* methods. For example, the *OnPause* method is used when the service is to be paused. The sample application uses the *OnPause* method to calculate the total elapsed time so far, set *isPaused* to *True*, and write a message to the event log:

```
Protected Overrides Sub OnPause()

    timeEnd = DateTime.Now()
    If Not isPaused Then
        timeDifference = timeEnd.Subtract(timeStart)
        timeElapsed = timeElapsed.Add(timeDifference)
    End If
    isPaused = True

    EventLog.WriteEntry("VB.NET How-To Service was Paused at " + _
        DateTime.Now().ToString())
End Sub
```

Finally, *OnContinue* occurs when a paused service is supposed to continue:

```
Protected Overrides Sub OnContinue()
    If isPaused Then
        timeStart = DateTime.Now
    End If
    isPaused = False

    EventLog.WriteEntry("VB.NET How-To Service Continued at " + _
        DateTime.Now().ToString())
End Sub
```

The *OnContinue* method begins by setting *timeStart* to the current time. Because the service is resuming, *isPaused* must be set back to *False*. Finally, a message is written out to the event log to indicate the service has resumed.

Conclusion

A Windows service is a special type of application that runs in the background and has no user interface. To create a Windows service in Visual Basic .NET, begin by creating a new solution using the Windows Service template in Visual Studio .NET. At a minimum, implement the *OnStart* and *OnStop* methods. Additional methods exist such as *OnPause* and *OnContinue*. To create an installer for a Windows service, right-click the design surface of the class that inherits from the *System.ServiceProcess.ServiceBase* class. In the popup menu, select Add Installer. Visual Studio .NET will add a new class to your project named *ProjectInstaller*. Use this class to set the various properties of the *ServiceProcessInstaller1* and *ServiceInstaller1* components so that installation utilities can install the Windows service.

Application #79: Use Thread Pooling

The ability to use threads within Visual Basic has long been a requested feature because threads allow you to create a multitasking application that runs smoothly. However, if an application requires a design where threads must be constantly created and destroyed, performance might actually suffer. Thread pooling is a technique that streamlines the performance of these types of applications. When a thread is no longer needed, rather than being terminated, the thread is saved to a pool where it can be reused later. Conceptually, this is similar to database connection pooling. Thread pooling improves performance because it eliminates the overhead of repeatedly creating and destroying threads.

This sample application demonstrates how to use a thread pool in Visual Basic .NET. It consists of a main form with three *TabPages*. The first *TabPage*, Queued Functions (shown in Figure 9-1), compares performance by running three processes in sequential order, in three discrete threads. It demonstrates the *ThreadPool* function *QueueUserWorkItem* to queue a task to a thread. The second *TabPage*, Timers, shows how to use the *Threading.Timer* class to set up timed events. The third *TabPage*, Synchronization Objects, demonstrates how to use the synchronization objects *Mutex*, *ManualResetEvent*, and *Auto-ResetEvent* to manage functions on separate threads.

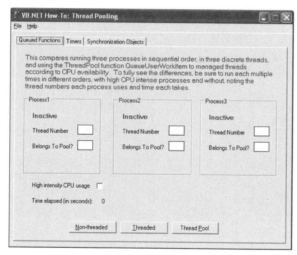

Figure 9-1   The application interface for the Thread Pooling demonstration.

Building Upon...

Application #7: Object-Oriented Features
Application #8: Scoping, Overloading, Overriding
Application #9: Use Callbacks
Application #11: Key Visual Basic .NET Benefits

New Concepts

This sample introduces three new concepts: function queuing, timers, and synchronization objects.

Function Queuing

Creating a thread pool can be a tricky task. Fortunately, Visual Basic .NET provides a built-in *ThreadPool* object that does much of the hard work for you. Part of the *System.Thread* namespace, the *ThreadPool* object provides a pool of threads that can be used for various application tasks. When a thread is terminated or goes into a sleep state, it's placed into the thread pool. Visual Basic .NET manages assigning a work item to a thread automatically. You only need to queue the work item by using the *QueueUserWorkItem* method of the *ThreadPool* object. To use *QueueUserWorkItem*, simply pass it a delegate to the function to call when the thread is available. This is known as *function queuing*. By default, the *ThreadPool* has a maximum limit of 25 threads per processor.

Timers

The *Timer* class provides a way to execute a routine at specified time intervals. This is handy when you want to perform a particular task at regular intervals. For example, the *Timer* class could be used in a client e-mail application to check a server for incoming e-mail messages every five minutes. When using the *Timer* class, you set the amount of time to wait before the first time the routine is executed and the amount of time to wait between subsequent invocations. When you're done with the *Timer* class, be sure to call the *Dispose* method to free all allocated resources. *Timer* is also part of the *System.Thread* namespace.

Synchronization Objects

When two or more threads need to access a shared resource at the same time, a synchronization object is used to guarantee that only one thread uses the resource. Thus, synchronization objects are used to gain exclusive access to a shared resource. Visual Basic .NET has three types of synchronization objects: *Mutex*, *ManualResetEvent*, and *AutoResetEvent*. All three derive from the *WaitHandle* class, which serves as the base class for synchronization objects. The *Mutex* synchronization object is used to gain exclusive access to a shared resource. Only one thread at a time can hold a *Mutex*. All other threads are suspended until the *Mutex* is released.

The *ManualResetEvent* and *AutoResetEvent* synchronization objects are also used for synchronization and are similar to each other. They both have two states, signaled and unsignaled. *Signaled* means the shared resource has been locked and no other thread can use it. *Unsignaled* means the shared resource is available to be used by another thread. To signal and unsignal the *Manual-*

ResetEvent and *AutoResetEvent* objects, use the *Set* and *Reset* methods, respectively. The key difference between the *ManualResetEvent* and *AutoResetEvent* objects is that *AutoResetEvent* is automatically reset to unsignaled by the system after a single waiting thread has been released. The sample application demonstrates how to use all three objects on the Synchronization tab page.

Code Walkthrough

The sample application consists of one main form and two helper classes, *ProcessGroup* and *TimerGroup*. The *ProcessGroup* class is used to simulate a two-second process using thread pooling. The *TimerGroup* class is used to demonstrate the *Threading.Timer* class.

frmMain Declarations

The declarations section of *frmMain* contains several module-level variables:

```
Private autoResetEvent1 As Threading.AutoResetEvent
Private manualResetEvent1 As Threading.ManualResetEvent
Private mutex1 As Threading.Mutex

Private processGroup1 As ProcessGroup
Private processGroup2 As ProcessGroup
Private processGroup3 As ProcessGroup
```

The first three variables—*autoResetEvent1*, *manualResetEvent1*, and *mutex1*—represent the three types of synchronization objects available in Visual Basic .NET. Then three *ProcessGroup* objects are declared. These objects will be used to simulate work items that will be queued to the thread pool.

frmMain_Load

When *frmMain* loads, the three *ProcessGroup* objects are instantiated. Each *ProcessGroup* has a *Completed* event, which occurs when the work item has been completed. An event handler named *OnProcessesCompleted* is hooked to each *ProcessGroup*'s *Completed* event. Next, the *ProcessGroup*'s shared *PrepareToRun* method is called to initialize the *ProcessGroup* objects:

```
Private Sub frmMain_Load(ByVal sender As System.Object, _
    ByVal e As System.EventArgs) Handles MyBase.Load

    processGroup1 = New ProcessGroup(lblProcess1Active, _
        lblProcess1ThreadNum, lblProcess1IsPoolThread)
    processGroup2 = New ProcessGroup(lblProcess2Active, _
        lblProcess2ThreadNum, lblProcess2IsPoolThread)
    processGroup3 = New ProcessGroup(lblProcess3Active, _
        lblProcess3ThreadNum, lblProcess3IsPoolThread)

    AddHandler processGroup1.Completed, AddressOf OnProcessesCompleted
    AddHandler processGroup2.Completed, AddressOf OnProcessesCompleted
```

```
    AddHandler processGroup3.Completed, AddressOf OnProcessesCompleted

    ProcessGroup.PrepareToRun()

    timerGroup1 = New TimerGroup(lblTimer1Output, lblTimer1ThreadNum, _
        lblTimer1IsThreadPool)
    timerGroup2 = New TimerGroup(lblTimer2Output, lblTimer2ThreadNum, _
        lblTimer2IsThreadPool)
End Sub
```

Thread Pool Button

When the user clicks the Thread Pool button, the process begins. First, all the buttons on the tab page are disabled. Next, the *PrepareToRun* method is called to reinitialize the *ProcessGroup* objects. Then, the *StartPooledThread* method is called:

```
Private Sub btnThreadPool_Click(ByVal sender As System.Object, _
    ByVal e As System.EventArgs) Handles btnThreadPool.Click

    btnNonthreaded.Enabled = False
    btnThreaded.Enabled = False
    btnThreadPool.Enabled = False

    ProcessGroup.PrepareToRun()

    processGroup1.StartPooledThread()
    processGroup2.StartPooledThread()
    processGroup3.StartPooledThread()
End Sub
```

Queuing a Function

The *StartPooledThread* method itself is very short. The first line creates a callback to the subroutine *RunPooledThread*. The second line performs the actual function queuing. As explained previously, to queue a work item to the thread pool, use the *QueueUserWorkItem* method of the *Threading.ThreadPool* object:

```
Sub StartPooledThread()
    Dim callback As New Threading.WaitCallback(AddressOf RunPooledThread)
    Threading.ThreadPool.QueueUserWorkItem(callback, Nothing)
End Sub
```

OnProcessesCompleted

When the task finally completes, the *OnProcessesCompleted* event procedure is triggered. This routine calculates the number of seconds the task took to complete and displays the result in a label on the form. Then it re-enables the buttons that were disabled in the *btnThreadPool_Click* routine. Finally, the *PrepareToRun* method is called to reinitialize the *ProcessGroup* objects:

```
Private Sub OnProcessesCompleted()
    Dim secondsElapsed As Double = ProcessGroup.GetTicksElapsed / 1000
```

(continued)

```
        lblSecondsElapsed.Text = secondsElapsed.ToString

        btnNonthreaded.Enabled = True
        btnThreaded.Enabled = True
        btnThreadPool.Enabled = True

        ProcessGroup.PrepareToRun()
    End Sub
```

Conclusion

Visual Basic .NET provides a built-in thread-pool object named *ThreadPool* as part of the *System.Threading* namespace. To queue a function to *ThreadPool*, use the *QueueUserWorkItem* method. To execute a routine at specific time intervals, use the *System.Threading.Timer* class. Finally, synchronization objects are used to make sure that no more than one thread can access a shared resource at the same time. Visual Basic .NET provides three such synchronization objects: *Mutex*, *ManualResetEvent*, and *AutoResetEvent*. Threading is a powerful tool in the Visual Basic .NET programmer's toolbox, and thread pooling is useful in situations where an application constantly creates and destroys new threads.

Application #80: Use Sockets

This sample application demonstrates how to create a simple chat program by using sockets. Support for using sockets within Visual Basic .NET is provided by the *System.Net* and *System.Net.Sockets* namespaces. Broken into two different solutions, the sample application features a chat server (shown in Figure 9-2) and a chat client. It demonstrates three important aspects of sockets communication using the *TcpClient* and *TcpListener* classes:

- **Server-to-client communication**   The server application allows you to enter text to broadcast to all attached clients. To run this demonstration, run the server and at least one instance of the client.

- **Client-to-client communication**   This shows how to send text from a client application to all other attached clients. To run this demonstration, run the server with at least two instances of the client running.

- **Client-to-server request with server response**   This demonstrates the client sending the server a request for a list of all users that are in the chat. When the client receives the response, it fills a list-box control with the users. To run this demonstration, run the server and at least one instance of the client.

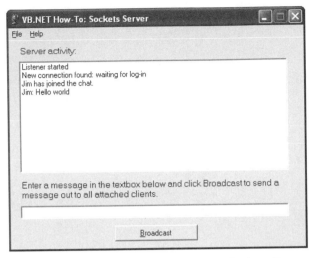

Figure 9-2   Application Interface for the Sockets Server project.

Building Upon...

Application #7: Object-Oriented Features
Application #8: Scoping, Overloading, Overriding
Application #11: Key Visual Basic .NET Benefits

New Concepts

This sample application introduces three new concepts: sockets, TCP clients, and TCP listeners.

Sockets

Simply speaking, a socket is an endpoint for communication between two computers. In Visual Basic .NET, the *Socket* class is part of the *System.Net.Sockets* namespace and serves as a wrapper around the Winsock32 API. The *Socket* class supports both synchronous and asynchronous modes. In synchronous mode, network calls such as *Send* and *Receive* wait until the operation completes before returning control to the calling program. In asynchronous mode, these calls return immediately and a callback is used to indicate when the operation completes. To use a socket, you must know the connected computer's IP address and TCP port number. In the sample application, the TCP port number is defined as a constant so that both client and server use the same port. Sending data across the connection is accomplished by using the *Send* or *SendTo* method. To read data from the socket, use the *Receive* or *ReceiveFrom* method.

TcpClient Class

The *TcpClient* class is a type of socket that provides TCP services for client access. To send and receive data, you use a *NetworkStream* object, which provides an underlying stream of data for the network. The *TcpClient GetStream* method returns this *NetworkStream* object. For example, *TcpClient.GetStream.Read* would receive a message from a connected client. *TcpClient* is capable of both synchronous and asynchronous communications. The *Read* and *Write* methods are synchronous, while the *BeginRead, BeginWrite, EndRead,* and *EndWrite* methods are asynchronous. When you're done with your *TcpClient*, use the *Close* method to release its resources.

TcpListener Class

The *TcpListener* class is also a type of socket and listens for connections from TCP clients. Once a *TcpListener* object has been instantiated, use the *Start* method to begin listening for network requests. There are two ways to detect a request. One way is to use the *Pending* method to detect incoming connection requests. You can also use the *AcceptSocket* or *AcceptTcpClient* method to block until a connection request arrives. The sample application uses the *AcceptTcpClient* method. When the *TcpListener* is done listening for network requests, the *Stop* method is used.

Code Walkthrough

The sample application is divided into two solutions: a server solution and a client solution. This code walkthrough will focus on the server solution.

The Server Solution—*frmMain*

First, examine the declarations section of *frmMain*, the main form of the application:

```
Imports System.Net.Sockets

Public Class frmMain
    Inherits System.Windows.Forms.Form

    Const PORT_NUM As Integer = 10000

    Private clients As New Hashtable()
    Private listener As TcpListener
    Private listenerThread As Threading.Thread
```

First, the *System.Net.Sockets* namespace is imported to the file to reduce the amount of typing required. A constant, PORT_NUM, is used to specify the port number the application will use. A PORT_NUM constant is also defined in the client solution. *clients* is a *Hashtable* that is used to keep track of all clients that connect to the server. As each client connects, a new item is added to the *Hashtable*. When a client disconnects, it's removed from the collection. The *listener* object is the *TcpListener* object that listens for and connects to client applications. Finally, a thread is declared that will be used later in conjunction with the *listener* object. Although using a thread to listen for client requests is not a requirement for programming with sockets, it can make the application more responsive.

The Server Solution—*frmMain_Load*

When *frmMain* loads, it starts the background listener thread and updates the status list box to indicate the server is now available for client requests:

```
Private Sub frmMain_Load(ByVal sender As System.Object, _
    ByVal e As System.EventArgs) Handles MyBase.Load

    listenerThread = New Threading.Thread(AddressOf DoListen)
    listenerThread.Start()
    UpdateStatus("Listener started")
End Sub
```

The Server Solution—*frmMain.DoListen*

The *DoListen* subroutine is used by the background listener thread so that clients can connect to the server without slowing down the user interface:

```
Private Sub DoListen()
    Try
        listener = New TcpListener(PORT_NUM)
        listener.Start()
        Do
            Dim client As New UserConnection(listener.AcceptTcpClient)
            AddHandler client.LineReceived, _
                AddressOf OnLineReceived
            UpdateStatus("New connection found: waiting for log-in")
        Loop Until False
    Catch
    End Try
End Sub
```

Inside *DoListen*, a new *TcpListener* object is created to listen for client requests. Note that the port number is passed into its constructor and the *Start* method is used to begin the listening process. A *Do/Loop* is used to continuously monitor for client requests. If a request is received, the *OnLineReceived* method is invoked.

OnLineReceived acts as an event handler and is triggered when a client sends a command to the server. The sample application defines four types of commands: "CONNECT", "CHAT", "DISCONNECT", and "REQUESTUSERS". The command is sent over the network stream as a text message. A vertical bar (|) is used as a delimiter to separate the type of command from the content of the message. For example, consider "CHAT|Hello World". "CHAT" is the type of command, and "Hello World" is the actual message content. To parse the message, the *Split* method of the *String* object is used:

```
Private Sub OnLineReceived(ByVal sender As UserConnection, _
    ByVal data As String)

    Dim dataArray() As String

    dataArray = data.Split(Chr(124))

    Select Case dataArray(0)
        Case "CONNECT"
            ConnectUser(dataArray(1), sender)
        Case "CHAT"
            SendChat(dataArray(1), sender)
        Case "DISCONNECT"
            DisconnectUser(sender)
        Case "REQUESTUSERS"
            ListUsers(sender)
        Case Else
            UpdateStatus("Unknown message:" & data)
    End Select

End Sub
```

Now that the client is connected, the chat program is operational for clients to send messages back and forth to each other.

Conclusion

This sample application shows how to use sockets within Visual Basic .NET applications. Support for sockets is provided by the *System.Net* and *System.Net.Sockets* namespaces. The sample application uses two basic types of sockets, *TcpClient* and *TcpListener*. The *TcpClient* class provides client connections for TCP network services. The *TcpListener* class listens for connections from TCP clients. When running the sample application, remember to run both the server and client solutions at the same time.

Application #81: Work with Resource Files

This sample application shows how to work with resource files to create forms that are localized to specific cultures. A resource file contains nonexecutable data such as strings and graphics that can be embedded into the portable executable (PE) file for an application. Windows Forms have *Localizable* and *Language* properties, which allow a form to share application code for all cultures while allowing the form to easily display culture-specific strings and images. The sample application contains a form, *frmDataEntry*, that uses these properties and resource files for four different cultures: France, Italy, Spain, and the United States. The user can select from these four cultures simply by clicking a command button, as shown in Figure 9-3. When the button is clicked, *frmDataEntry* displays the culture the user selected, as shown in Figure 9-4.

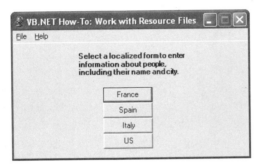

Figure 9-3   The main form lets you choose between four different cultures.

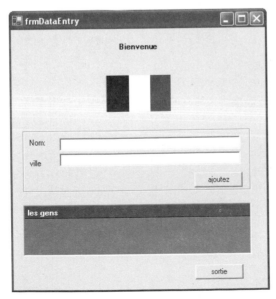

Figure 9-4   The data entry form localized to French.

Building Upon...

Application #7: Object-Oriented Features
Application #8: Scoping, Overloading, Overriding
Application #32: Use Format Codes to Format Data

New Concepts

This sample application introduces two new concepts: globalization and localization. To support these concepts in your applications, Windows Forms provides *Localizable* and *Language* properties.

Globalization and Localization

Visual Basic .NET provides built-in support for creating global, culturally aware applications. These days, many companies are expanding their markets across the world. Users in other parts of the globe have various standards for formatting numbers, dates, and currencies, and they speak various languages. To make your applications usable to these people, you must design them to take into account the concepts of globalization and localization. Globalization is the process of formatting data based on the selected culture. For example, in the United States, a period is used as a decimal place and a comma as a thousands separator. But in other countries, a comma is used as a decimal place and a period is used as a thousands separator. Localization is the process of displaying languages and graphics based on the selected culture. In the sample application, the text and graphics on *frmDataEntry* change according to the selected culture.

Localizable and *Language* Properties

Creating a localized form in Visual Basic .NET is straightforward. First, set the form's *Localizable* property to *True*. This tells Visual Basic .NET the form will be localized to one or more cultures. Next, each Windows Form has a *Language* property that indicates the current localizable language. By default, this property is set to *(Default)*. After you've set *Localizable* to *True*, change the *Language* property to whatever language you want to localize to and then make whatever culture-specific changes that need to be made to the form. Visual Studio .NET automatically handles the creation of all appropriate resource files. Then change the *Language* property to the next culture you want to localize to, and make the culture-specific changes to the form for that language. Repeat these steps for as many cultures as there are to be localized.

Code Walkthrough

Because the actual localization takes place at design time when you're creating your user interface, there is very little code to walk through. The *frmMain* form contains four button controls: Italy, France, Spain, and US. Each of these buttons will display the *frmDataEntry* form localized to one of these cultures. For example, here is the click event procedure for the France button:

```
Private Sub btnFrance_Click(ByVal sender As System.Object, _
    ByVal e As System.EventArgs) Handles btnFrance.Click

    Thread.CurrentThread.CurrentUICulture = New CultureInfo("fr-FR")
    Dim frmData As New frmDataEntry()
    frmData.ShowDialog()
End Sub
```

Thread.CurrentThread.CurrentUICulture represents the current culture for the user interface. The culture code for the French language and the region France is "fr-FR". By changing *Thread.CurrentThread.CurrentUICulture*, you are effectively telling Visual Basic .NET to render your form for this culture.

Conclusion

As the world seems to get smaller and smaller, there is a greater need to create applications that can be sold and used across the global marketplace. Globalization and localization are two related but different concepts. Globalization is the process of formatting the same data based on the current culture, whereas localization is the process of displaying different languages and images based on the current culture. To create a localized form, set the form's *Localizable* property to *True* and customize the user interface for each culture using the form's *Language* property. A resource file containing all localizable data (such as strings and graphics) is automatically embedded into the binary file of an application. Using the *Localizable* and *Language* properties, Visual Studio .NET will create these resource files for you.

Application #82: Serialize Objects

Serialization is the process of converting an object into a linear sequence of bytes. This is a powerful technique that has several practical uses, such as persisting an object's state to disk. For example, a word-processing document might exist as an object. Using serialization, the word-processing document can be saved to a file on disk for later retrieval. When the user wants to reopen the document, it's deserialized and the document is restored. Other uses include cloning objects and remoting.

The sample application, shown in Figure 9-5, allows the user to serialize a class by using either SOAP or binary format. The six grouped command buttons are for serializing and deserializing. The bottom two buttons allow the user to view the SOAP envelopes for the serialized objects. The text boxes on the right allow the user to specify the initial data for the instances. The read-only text boxes on the far right allow the user to see the new field values after deserialization.

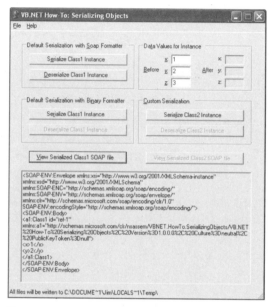

Figure 9-5 The application interface for the Serialization demonstration.

Building Upon...

Application #7: Object-Oriented Features
Application #8: Scoping, Overloading, Overriding

New Concepts

There are two ways to mark a class as being serializable: using the *<Serializable>* attribute, or implementing the *ISerializable* interface.

Using the *<Serializable>* Attribute

The *<Serializable>* attribute is the easiest way to mark a class as being serializable. Simply add this attribute to a class, and all module-level fields in a class are marked as being serializable. This includes all public and private fields.

Implementing *ISerializable*

A second way to mark a class as serializable is to implement the *ISerializable* interface. *ISerializable* has only one method that must be implemented: *GetObjectData*. *GetObjectData* accepts two parameters and has no return value. The first parameter, *SerializationInfo*, holds all the data needed to serialize or deserialize an object. The second parameter, *StreamingContext*, indicates the source or destination of the information. Because you implement *GetObjectData* yourself, you can specify exactly which fields are to be serialized.

Formatters

Regardless of how a class is marked as being serializable—either by using the *<Serializable>* attribute or the *ISerializable* interface—the data is serialized using a formatter. Visual Basic .NET provides two built-in formatters: the *BinaryFormatter* and the *SoapFormatter*. The *BinaryFormatter* is used to serialize and deserialize an object in binary format. The *SoapFormatter* uses XML format. You can also create your own formatters, which can be customized in any way you want.

Marking a Class as Serializable

The sample application contains a class named *Class1*, which is used as the object to be serialized:

```
<Serializable()> Public Class Class1

    Public x As Integer
    Private y As Integer
    <NonSerialized()> Public z As Integer

    Public Sub New(ByVal argx As Integer, ByVal argy As Integer, _
        ByVal argz As Integer)
        Me.x = argx
        Me.y = argy
        Me.z = argz
    End Sub

    Public ReadOnly Property GetY() As Integer
        Get
            Return y
        End Get
    End Property
End Class
```

As you can see, *Class1* is marked with the *<Serializable>* attribute. Normally, this means that all fields in the class—public and private—will be serialized. However, if there is a particular field you don't want to be serialized, you can mark it with the *<NonSerialized>* attribute. In this case, the variable *z* is marked with the *<NonSerialized>* attribute.

Serialization Using the *SoapFormatter*

Now that you've seen the class that is to be serialized, here is the code that serializes an instance of *Class1* to an XML file using the *SoapFormatter*:

```
Private Sub cmdStandardSerializationSoap_Click( _
    ByVal sender As System.Object, _
    ByVal e As System.EventArgs) _
    Handles cmdStandardSerializationSoap.Click

    Dim c As New Class1(CInt(txtX.Text), CInt(txtY.Text), CInt(txtZ.Text))
    Dim fs As New FileStream(strFileName1, FileMode.OpenOrCreate)
    Dim sf As New SoapFormatter()

    sf.Serialize(fs, c)

    fs.Close()

End Sub
```

First, an instance of *Class1* is created and populated with sample data. Then a *FileStream* is created. This will be used to save the XML to a file on disk. Next, an instance of the *SoapFormatter* is created. Now that all the variables have been set up, the *Serialize* method of the *SoapFormatter* is called to perform the actual serialization. Note that the *FileStream* and *Class1* objects are both passed into the *Serialize* method. Finally, the file is closed.

Deserialization Using the *SoapFormatter*

The code for deserializing an object is similar to the serialization code:

```
Private Sub cmdStandardDeserializationSoap_Click( _
    ByVal sender As System.Object, _
    ByVal e As System.EventArgs) _
    Handles cmdStandardDeserializationSoap.Click

    Dim c As Class1
    Dim fs As New FileStream(strFileName1, FileMode.Open)
    Dim sf As New SoapFormatter()

    c = CType(sf.Deserialize(fs), Class1)

    fs.Close()

End Sub
```

Again, an instance of *Class1* is declared, but this time it won't be instantiated until later. Then a *FileStream* object is created to read the XML text file. Next, an instance of a *SoapFormatter* is created. To perform the actual deserialization, the *Deserialize* method of the *SoapFormatter* object is called. This is when *Class1* is instantiated. Finally, the file is closed.

Conclusion

Serialization is the process of converting an object into a linear sequence of bytes. To mark a class as serializable, use either the *<Serializable>* attribute or implement the *ISerializable* interface. To perform serialization, use a formatter. Visual Basic .NET provides two built-in formatters: *SoapFormatter* and *Binary-Formatter*. You can also create your own custom formatter. The *Serialize* method is used to serialize an object, and the *Deserialize* method is used to deserialize an object.

Application #83: Use TCP Remoting

This sample is designed to show how to use .NET Remoting with Visual Basic .NET. Because .NET Remoting is an architecture for distributed applications, this sample is divided into three solutions: server, host, and client. The server solution is named RemoteCustomer, and it exposes three types of server objects: client-activated, single-call, and singleton.

Before running the demo, you need to build all three solutions. You should build them in the following order:

1. RemoteCustomer

2. Host

3. Client

Once the binaries have been built, start the Host application first to make sure your objects are available for remoting. Then start the client, which is shown in Figure 9-6.

Building Upon...

Application #7: Object-Oriented Features
Application #72: Configuration Settings
Application #82: Serialize Objects

Figure 9-6   The application interface for the Client project.

New Concepts

This sample application introduces several new concepts: .NET Remoting, and single-call, singleton, and client-activated objects.

.NET Remoting

.NET Remoting is the process of communicating between different processes, usually across a network. .NET Remoting is the .NET replacement for DCOM in Visual Basic 6.0, only it's more powerful and flexible. For example, with .NET Remoting, you have the power of actually moving an object across the network from one machine to the next using the Visual Basic .NET built-in serialization capabilities. There were no built-in facilities for serialization in DCOM, so this had to be done manually. .NET Remoting is also very flexible. You can choose between HTTP and TCP for your transfer mechanism, and SOAP and binary formats for the data encoding. What's more, you can switch between these by simply changing a couple of lines in a configuration file. No recompilation is necessary.

Single-Call and Singleton Objects

Single-call and singleton objects both run on the server and service client requests. The key difference between them is that a single-call object serves just one request and then is destroyed upon completion, whereas a singleton object serves multiple clients and multiple requests. Thus, a single-call object is stateless and a singleton object is stateful. Further, only one singleton object exists at a time. Multiple single-call objects can be running in memory simultaneously.

Client-Activated Objects

Client-activated objects also run on the server and service client requests. Unlike single-call objects, client-activated objects are stateful. Also, client-activated objects are different from singleton objects in that multiple client-activated objects can exist at the same time, serving multiple clients. If you're familiar with DCOM in Visual Basic 6.0, client-activated objects are the most similar of the .NET Remoting objects to DCOM.

Code Walkthrough

As mentioned previously, this application comprises three solutions. The code walkthrough will focus on two of these solutions: first, on the server solution and then the client solution.

The Server Solution—Defining the Server Classes

The server solution, *RemoteCustomer*, exposes three types of server objects: client-activated, single-call, and singleton. Note that all three inherit from the *MarshalByRef* object:

```
Public Class Customer
    Inherits MarshalByRefObject
    ⋮

Public Class SingleCallCustomer
    Inherits MarshalByRefObject
    ⋮

Public Class SingletonCustomer
    Inherits MarshalByRefObject
    Implements IDisposable
    ⋮
```

The Client Solution—Accessing a *SingleCall* Object

There's a lot of code contained in these three solutions, more than can be shown here. So, the rest of the walkthrough will focus on the code to access a *SingleCall* object. Take a look at the event procedure for the Single Call Debug Data button:

```
Private Sub cmdSingleDebug_Click(ByVal sender As System.Object, _
    ByVal e As System.EventArgs) Handles cmdSingleDebug.Click

    Dim args() As Object
    Dim scCust As SingleCallCustomer

    Try
        scCust = _
            CType(Activator.CreateInstance _
            (GetType(RemotingSample.SingleCallCustomer), _
            args), RemotingSample.SingleCallCustomer)
        With Me.lstResponses.Items
```

(continued)

```
                .Add("Debug data follows:")
                .Add(String.Format(" Creation Time: {0}", _
                scCust.DebugCreationTime.ToString))
                .Add(String.Format(" Code Base: {0}", scCust.DebugCodeBase))
                .Add(String.Format(" Fully Qualified Name: {0}", _
                scCust.DebugFQName))
                .Add(String.Format(" Remote Host Name: {0}", _
                scCust.DebugHostName))
                .Add(String.Format(" Creation Time: {0}", _
                scCust.DebugCreationTime.ToString))
                .Add("End Debug Data")
            End With

        Catch exp As Exception
            Dim txt As String
            txt = "I was unable to access the remote customer object." _
                & vbCrLf & vbCrLf & _
                "Detailed Error Information below:" & vbCrLf & vbCrLf & _
                " Message: " & exp.Message & vbCrLf & _
                " Source: " & exp.Source & vbCrLf & vbCrLf & _
                " Stack Trace:" & vbCrLf & _
                exp.StackTrace

            MessageBox.Show(txt, "Generic Exception", MessageBoxButtons.OK, _
                MessageBoxIcon.Stop)

        End Try

    End Sub
```

Again, single-call objects live only for the life of one method call. Each time the button is clicked, a new instance of the object is created. Note that to create a single-call object, the code uses *Activator.CreateInstance*. The *Activator* object is used to create types of objects locally or remotely, or to obtain references to existing remote objects. The first parameter to *CreateInstance* is the type of object you want to create. The second parameter is the arguments to be passed into the object's constructor. Although *SingleCallCustomer* is expecting no arguments, it is a required parameter, so you must pass something. In this case, *args* is defined as an array of objects. There is no need to initialize the array. Simply pass it in as is. Once the object has been instantiated, a series of diagnostic messages are written to the list box on screen. The code is enclosed within a *Try/Catch/Finally* block to trap for errors. If an exception is thrown, it is caught, and an appropriate error message displays on screen.

Conclusion

.NET Remoting is a powerful technology for enabling the distributing of .NET applications. Objects can live solely on a single machine or be transferred across the network. Out of the box, .NET Remoting provides two methods of data transfer—HTTP and TCP—and two methods of encoding—SOAP and binary. You can also plug in your own data-transfer and encoding objects. There are three types of server objects: singleton, single-call, and client-activated. The most similar of these to classic DCOM is the client-activated object. .NET Remoting is such an advanced technology that you'd need an entire book to explain it in detail. Hopefully, this sample will give you a good start. For more information, consult the .NET documentation.

Application #84: Asynchronous Calls

This sample application demonstrates how to use threads to create a responsive application while executing a processor-intensive or lengthy task in the background. This application allows the user to fire a long-running process on various types of threads. The main form contains three command buttons. The first button runs the task on the same thread as the main application, effectively blocking the user from interacting with the main form until the task is finished. The second and third buttons run the task on a second thread, allowing the user to continue interacting with the main form. The difference is that the second button runs the task on a thread from the worker pool, whereas the third button uses a newly created Win32 thread. This example does not include synchronization because no data is being accessed by multiple threads.

Figure 9-7   The application interface of the Asynchronous Calls demonstration.

Building Upon...

Application #7: Object-Oriented Features
Application #79: Use Thread Pooling

New Concepts

This sample application introduces two new concepts: the *DebuggerStep-Through* attribute and delegates.

DebuggerStepThrough Attribute

The *DebuggerStepThrough* attribute is used several times in the sample application to tell the Visual Studio .NET debugger to skip over a routine while it's executing. You can, however, still set a breakpoint in the routine. The *DebuggerStepThrough* attribute is used because attempting to step through multithreaded code can sometimes lead to inconsistent results.

Delegates

A delegate is a special kind of data type that allows you to pass a routine as a parameter to a method. In a sense, delegates are new to Visual Basic developers, but in reality, this mechanism has been prevalent all along. Behind the scenes, events are implemented as delegates. To create your own delegate, use the *Delegate* keyword. For example:

```
Public Delegate Sub MyDelegateType(ByVal i As Integer, ByVal s As String)
```

This creates a new delegate named *MyDelegateType* with two parameters, an integer and a string, in that order. The signature is important because any procedure assigned to this delegate must have the same signature to keep your code type-safe. Once a delegate type has been declared, you can create instances of it by passing in the address of the routine you want to assign it to. For example:

```
Public Sub MyProcedure(ByVal i As Integer, ByVal s As String)
    ' Do something
End Sub

Dim dt As New MyDelegateType (AddressOf MyProcedure)
```

The sample application uses a delegate in the *Click* event procedure for the Run On Worker Pool Thread button.

Code Walkthrough

The focal point of the code walkthrough will be on *frmMain*. In particular, it will examine the *TheLongRunningTask* subroutine and the *cmdSameThread_Click*, *cmdWorkerPoolThread_Click*, and *cmdRunOnNewWin32Thread_Click* event handlers.

TheLongRunningTask Subroutine

Before taking a look at the actual threading code, first look at the *TheLongRunningTask* subroutine. The first thing to notice is that this subroutine doesn't do any real work. Its only purpose is to simulate a long-running process. The *Sleep* method of the *Thread.CurrentThread* object is used to simulate a long-running piece of code:

```
Private Sub TheLongRunningTask()

    Dim f As New frmTaskProgress()
    f.Show()
    f.Refresh()

    Dim i As Integer
    For i = 1 To 10
        f.prgTaskProgress.Value += 10
        Thread.CurrentThread.Sleep(500)
    Next

    f.Hide()
    f.Dispose()
End Sub
```

The *Sleep* method inserts a half-second delay. To keep the user apprised of its progress, this subroutine displays a form with a progress bar on it. As the *For/Next* loop iterates, the progress bar is incremented. *TheLongRunningTask* takes 5 seconds to run.

The Run On Same Thread Button

When the user clicks the Run On Same Thread button, the *TheLongRunning-Task* subroutine is executed directly. No threading is used. In other words, this is "normal" code:

```
<DebuggerStepThrough()>_
Private Sub cmdSameThread_Click(ByVal sender As System.Object, _
    ByVal e As System.EventArgs) _
    Handles cmdSameThread.Click

    TheLongRunningTask()

End Sub
```

Also, note that when this button is clicked, the whole application is unresponsive until the task completes.

TaskDelegate

TaskDelegate is a delegate used by the Run On Worker Pool Thread button:

```
Delegate Sub TaskDelegate()
```

The Run On Worker Pool Thread Button

The Run On Worker Pool Thread button executes the *TheLongRunningTask* subroutine on a thread from the thread pool. This is performed asynchronously using the *TaskDelegate* declared previously. The *AddressOf* operator passes the memory address of the *TheLongRunningTask* subroutine into the delegate, and then the *BeginInvoke* method starts execution:

```
<DebuggerStepThrough()>_
Private Sub cmdWorkerPoolThread_Click( _
    ByVal sender As System.Object, _
    ByVal e As System.EventArgs) _
    Handles cmdWorkerPoolThread.Click

    Dim td As New TaskDelegate(AddressOf TheLongRunningTask)
    td.BeginInvoke(Nothing, Nothing)

End Sub
```

Note that when this button is clicked, the application itself remains responsive.

The Run On New Win32 Thread Button

Finally, the Run On New Win32 Thread button runs the same subroutine as the previous two buttons. But this time the task is run on a newly created operating system thread (not on a thread from the thread pool):

```
<DebuggerStepThrough()>_
Private Sub cmdRunOnNewWin32Thread_Click( _
    ByVal sender As System.Object, _
    ByVal e As System.EventArgs) _
    Handles cmdRunOnNewWin32Thread.Click

    Dim t As New Thread(AddressOf TheLongRunningTask)
    t.Start()
End Sub
```

Again, when this button is clicked, the application remains responsive.

Conclusion

Visual Basic .NET allows you to run code asynchronously using free threading. Free threading lets you write an application that performs a task on a separate thread, keeping your user interface free and responsive. You can even use multiple threads to run multiple tasks simultaneously. This technique is very useful when you're trying to create an application that scales. As more clients connect, or as the workload increases, you can add more threads.

10

GDI+

GDI+ is a graphics device interface that lets you present information on a screen or on a printer. Like its predecessor, GDI, it lets you display information without having to talk directly to the device involved. However, GDI+ is even easier to use than GDI because you simply use the classes and methods provided by the *System.Drawing* namespace to get your work done. Not only won't you need to know how to talk to any specific hardware device, but you won't have to be concerned with device contexts, pen positions, and other requirements that GDI imposed on you.

Using GDI+, you can draw lines and shapes, fill closed shapes such as rectangles and ellipses, display text on a screen or a printer, animate images, and create screen savers. In the samples that follow, we'll demonstrate these capabilities.

Application #85: Work with GDI+ Pens

This sample demonstrates most of the features available when using the GDI+ *Pen* object, which you use to draw lines and shapes. In succeeding samples, we'll look at working with brushes, text, images, screen savers, and animation.

Building Upon...

Application #1: Use Arrays
Application #29: Use the *ListBox* and *ComboBox*

New Concepts

To draw lines or curves, you need two objects: a *Graphics* object and a *Pen* object. The *Graphics* object has methods such as *DrawLine, DrawEllipse, DrawRectangle*, and others. A *Graphics* object is always associated with a specific object—such as a form or a *PictureBox*—that you can think of as the canvas on which it draws. You can think of the *Graphics* object as something like your hand, which you use to draw lines and shapes.

Like your hand, a *Graphics* object needs a drawing instrument to actually do a drawing. That's where the *Pen* object comes in. It has properties that let you determine its width, its color, the style of line it draws, how intersecting lines should be joined, and much more. Some key properties of the *Pen* object include the following:

- **Alignment**   Determines which side of the designated line the pen should draw on. For instance, Inset will cause the pen to draw on the inside of a circle.

- **DashCap**   Determines the cap that should be put on both ends of any dashes in a line drawn by the pen. For example, caps can be round, flat, or triangular.

- **DashStyle**   Determines the look of the line. It can be solid, dashes, dots and dashes, or even custom.

- **EndCap**   Determines the cap that should be put on the end of a line drawn by the pen.

- **LineJoin**   Determines how two adjacent lines should be joined. For instance, the join can be rounded, beveled, or mitered.

- **MiterLimit**   Determines when the miter edge of two adjacent lines should be clipped. The default is 10.0.

- **StartCap**   Determines the cap that should be put on the start of a line drawn by the pen.

- **Width**   The width of the pen, in pixels.

One other object that will figure largely in your GDI+ work is the *Point* object. It represents a single point on the drawing surface, indicated by x- and y-coordinates, expressed as integers. A companion object, *PointF*, accepts floating-point numbers for its coordinates. Figure 10-1 shows three lines drawn using several of these key properties.

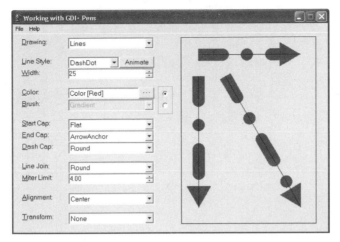

Figure 10-1   With GDI+ pens, you can choose from a wide variety of line styles, start and end caps, and more.

Code Walkthrough

The heart of the sample is the *RedrawPicture* procedure, which collects all the user-defined information and uses it to create a *Pen* object. The *Pen* object is then used to draw one of three different kinds of drawings. As you can see in the following code, this procedure handles almost all events triggered by the user interface, specifically the change events of combo boxes and other controls for which the user makes choices.

```
Private Sub RedrawPicture(ByVal sender As System.Object, _
    ByVal e As System.EventArgs) _
    Handles MyBase.Activated, comboShape.SelectedIndexChanged, _
    updownWidth.ValueChanged, txtColor.TextChanged, _
    comboAlignment.SelectedIndexChanged, _
    comboStartCap.SelectedIndexChanged, comboEndCap.SelectedIndexChanged, _
    comboDashCap.SelectedIndexChanged, _
    comboLineJoin.SelectedIndexChanged, _
    comboLineStyle.SelectedIndexChanged, updownMiterLimit.ValueChanged, _
    comboTransform.SelectedIndexChanged, comboBrush.SelectedIndexChanged
```

To draw, we must first create the *Graphics* object that we'll use to draw on the *PictureBox* (which is named *pbLines*). Then we use the *Graphics* object *Clear* method to remove anything that might already be in the picture box. Next, we get rid of any current transform on the *Pen* object, and we set the *DashPattern* that will be implemented when the user selects a custom line style.

```
m_graphic = pbLines.CreateGraphics()
m_graphic.Clear(pbLines.BackColor)
pbLines.Refresh()
m_Pen.ResetTransform()
m_Pen.DashPattern = New Single() {0.5, 0.25, 0.75, 1.5}
```

A pen can have either a color or a brush assigned to it, but not both. We determine which of the two to use depending on the user's choice in the *radio-Color* check box. If Brush is checked, we'll select the kind of brush the user indicated in the Brush combo box. There are four choices, which are described in the following paragraph.

A Solid brush is just what it sounds like. A Hatch brush can have a variety of styles, including *Horizontal* (a pattern of horizontal lines), *ZigZag* (horizontal lines composed of zigzags), and *Plaid* (the style used in our sample application). The Texture brush "paints" using an image as its base "pigment." The Gradient brush in this example contains Alice Blue in the upper left corner of the *PictureBox* and ends with Dark Blue in the lower right, with a gradual transition in between.

> **Tip**   Assigning a *Color* to a pen is identical to assigning it a *Solid-Brush*.

```
If radioColor.Checked Then
    m_Pen.Color = m_penColor
Else
    Select Case comboBrush.Text
        Case "Solid"
            m_penBrush = New SolidBrush(m_penColor)
        Case "Hatch"
            m_penBrush = New HatchBrush(HatchStyle.Plaid, m_penColor)
        Case "Texture"
            m_penBrush = New TextureBrush( _
                New Bitmap("..\WaterLilies.jpg"), WrapMode.Tile)
        Case "Gradient"
            m_penBrush = New LinearGradientBrush( _
                New Point(0, 0), _
                New Point(pbLines.Width, pbLines.Height), _
                Color.AliceBlue, Color.DarkBlue)
    End Select

    m_Pen.Brush = m_penBrush
End If
```

Now we set the properties of the pen. Together, these properties give us complete control over the look of the lines that will be drawn with the pen. Notice that, because we loaded the combo boxes with shared constants from pen-related enumerations, we're able to use the selected item from each combo box directly. If we had loaded them with text strings, we would have had to do something like a *Select Case* to use their values.

```
m_Pen.Width = updownWidth.Value
m_Pen.DashStyle = CType(comboLineStyle.SelectedItem, DashStyle)
m_Pen.MiterLimit = updownMiterLimit.Value
m_Pen.StartCap = CType(comboStartCap.SelectedItem, LineCap)
m_Pen.EndCap = CType(comboEndCap.SelectedItem, LineCap)
m_Pen.DashCap = CType(comboDashCap.SelectedItem, DashCap)
m_Pen.LineJoin = CType(comboLineJoin.SelectedItem, LineJoin)
m_Pen.Alignment = CType(comboAlignment.SelectedItem, PenAlignment)
```

Transforms are used for some advanced features of pens. You can, for instance, create a calligraphic-style pen with *ScaleTransform*. In this sample, if the user chooses None, we remove any transforms that might previously have been applied to the pen, restoring it to normal. If Scale is chosen, we make the width of the pen half as thin as normal and double its height. This yields a calligraphic look.

For Rotate, we rotate the brush by 45 degrees, and for Translate, we apply a transformation that expands the drawn object horizontally by a factor of 2 and vertically by a factor of 4. Both *RotateTransform* and *TranslateTransform* take effect only if the underlying brush supports them.

```
Select Case comboTransform.Text
    Case "None"
        m_Pen.ResetTransform()
    Case "Scale"
        m_Pen.ScaleTransform(0.5, 2)
    Case "Rotate"
        m_Pen.RotateTransform(45)
    Case "Translate"
        m_Pen.TranslateTransform(2, 4)
End Select
```

Now that the *Pen* has been defined and its properties have been set, we can use the *Graphics* object *DrawLine* to draw the desired lines on the *PictureBox*. We'll also draw matching thin black lines, using the same coordinates, to let the user see where the line was intended to go and to show what various properties do.

In the following code, we draw three simple lines using the user-defined pen. The *DrawLine* method has several overloads, including one which accepts a *Pen* object, followed by x- and y-coordinates for the beginning point of the line and x- and y-coordinates for its ending point. So our first line starts at pixel 35 on both the x- and y-axes, and it extends to a point 35 pixels less than the width of the *PictureBox* and 35 pixels down on the y-axis. In short, it's a straight horizontal line. The second line is a vertical line, and the last one is a diagonal line.

Then we'll draw the same three lines using the thin black pen (declared earlier at the class level) so that the user can see the effects.

```
If Me.comboShape.Text = "Lines" Then
    With m_graphic
        .DrawLine(m_Pen, 35, 35, pbLines.Width - 35, 35)
        .DrawLine(m_Pen, 35, 80, 35, pbLines.Height - 35)
        .DrawLine(m_Pen, 90, 80, pbLines.Width - 35, _
            pbLines.Height - 35)
    End With

    With m_graphic
        .DrawLine(m_BlackThinPen, 35, 35, pbLines.Width - 35, 35)
        .DrawLine(m_BlackThinPen, 35, 80, 35, pbLines.Height - 35)
        .DrawLine(m_BlackThinPen, 90, 80, pbLines.Width - 35, _
            pbLines.Height - 35)
    End With
```

In our next option, we create a more complex shape by using an array of *Points* to define a multisegment line. Note that even though this line has several segments, it is a single line. If several independent lines were used instead, even if they connected, the end and start caps (if any) would be placed on each independent line. Here they are placed only on the beginning and end of the compound line.

We use the *DrawLines* method of the *Graphics* object (not to be confused with *DrawLine*), which lets you draw a continuous line that connects a series of points. To do that, it accepts a *Pen* object and an array of *Point* or *PointF* objects. As you might recall, a point on our drawing surface is represented by a pair of x- and y-coordinates. We're using *PointF* objects because they allow floating-point coordinates, unlike *Point* objects, which allow only integers. We might need floating-point numbers because we're doing math with the *Picture-Box* width and height.

```
ElseIf Me.comboShape.Text = "Intersecting Lines" Then
    Dim ptArray(5) As PointF
    ptArray(0) = New PointF(35, 35)
    ptArray(1) = New PointF(70, pbLines.Height - 75)
    ptArray(2) = New PointF(100, 35)
    ptArray(3) = New PointF(pbLines.Width - 40, pbLines.Height \ 2)
    ptArray(4) = New PointF(pbLines.Width \ 2, pbLines.Height \ 2)
    ptArray(5) = New PointF(pbLines.Width - 25, 25)

    m_graphic.DrawLines(m_Pen, ptArray)
    m_graphic.DrawLines(m_BlackThinPen, ptArray)
```

Our final option is to draw a circle and a curve. The *DrawEllipse* method will produce the circle if we provide it with a pen and a *Rectangle* object that will form a bounding box for the ellipse. Or we can give it starting x- and y-coordinates and the width and height of the imaginary bounding rectangle, which is what we've chosen to do here. The *DrawArc* method is identical to *DrawEllipse*, except that we must additionally tell it where to start and stop drawing the arc. So we give it a *StartAngle*, which tells it how many degrees from the x-axis to start drawing, and a *SweepAngle*, which represents the number of degrees from the *StartAngle* to the end of the arc.

```
    ElseIf Me.comboShape.Text = "Circles and Curves" Then
        m_graphic.DrawEllipse(m_Pen, 25, 25, 200, 200)
        m_graphic.DrawArc(m_Pen, 25, 25, CInt(pbLines.Width * 1.5), _
            pbLines.Height - 55, 90, 180)

        m_graphic.DrawEllipse(m_BlackThinPen, 25, 25, 200, 200)
        m_graphic.DrawArc(m_BlackThinPen, 25, 25, CInt(pbLines.Width * _
            1.5), pbLines.Height - 55, 90, 180)
    End If
End Sub
```

Conclusion

In this sample application, we've shown you how GDI+ makes working with graphics even simpler than it was with GDI. It does so by using .NET Framework classes and methods. You've seen that to draw lines and curves, you need a *Graphics* object, which provides the drawing methods, and a *Pen* object, which holds the characteristics of the line you're going to draw. A *Graphics* object is always associated with a specific object, such as a form or a *PictureBox*.

Application #86: Work with GDI+ Brushes

In the previous sample, we showed how .NET gives us easy access to GDI+ via a comprehensive set of classes and methods from the *System.Drawing* namespace. You saw that to draw you need a *Graphics* object and a *Pen*. In this sample, we'll show you how to use the *Brush* object to fill closed shapes such as rectangles and ellipses.

Building Upon...

Application #85: Work with GDI+ Pens

New Concepts

Whereas you use a pen to draw the outline of a shape, you use a brush to fill the interior of such a shape. You can choose to have both a border and a fill or to have only one of the two. To fill a shape, you need a *Graphics* object and a *Brush*. The *Graphics* object provides methods such as *FillRectangle* and *FillEllipse*, while the *Brush* gives you a way to specify the color, pattern, and other properties of the fill.

Five kinds of brushes are available, two in the *System.Drawing* namespace and three in *System.Drawing.Drawing2D*. They are as follows:

- **System.Drawing.SolidBrush**   A brush composed of a single color. Use this brush to fill a shape with a solid color.

- **System.Drawing.TextureBrush**   A brush that uses an image as its source. Use this brush to fill a shape from an image. For example, you might fill an oval shape from a portrait to imitate the look of an old-fashioned picture.

- **System.Drawing.Drawing2D.HatchBrush**   A rectangular brush composed of three elements: a foreground color, which specifies the color of the lines in the hatch; a background color, which represents the color of the spaces between the lines; and a hatch pattern, which includes such choices as checkerboards, diagonals, diamonds, and zigzags.

- **System.Drawing.Drawing2D.LinearGradientBrush**   A brush that lets you create a fill that transitions smoothly from one color to another. The *Blend* property of the brush lets you determine the relative intensity of the colors at each point along the gradient.

- **System.Drawing.Drawing2D.PathGradientBrush**   Whereas the *LinearGradient* color transition goes from one edge of the shape to the other, the shading with this brush starts in the center of the shape and transitions to the outside. It can be used on simple shapes such as rectangles and ellipses, as well as on the more complex shapes represented by *GraphicsPath* objects.

Figure 10-2 shows a *TextureBrush* being used to fill a pair of ellipses using a photograph as its drawing source.

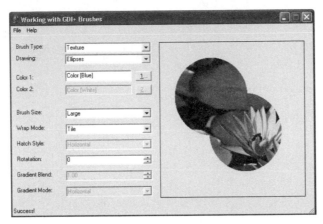

Figure 10-2   A *TextureBrush* lets you use a graphical image as the source for your drawing.

Code Walkthrough

The *RedrawPicture* procedure provides the meat of the demonstration. It creates one of the five types of brushes and assigns the appropriate user-defined properties to the brush. The brush is then assigned to *m_Brush*, which is used to draw one of three different shapes. There is also code to ensure that the user interface (UI) displays only the options that are appropriate for the type of brush being used. As you'll notice, this procedure handles virtually all events fired by the UI.

```
Private Sub RedrawPicture(ByVal sender As System.Object, _
    ByVal e As System.EventArgs) Handles MyBase.Activated, _
    cboBrushType.SelectedIndexChanged, cboDrawing.SelectedIndexChanged, _
    txtColor1.TextChanged, cboWrapMode.SelectedIndexChanged, _
    cboHatchStyle.SelectedIndexChanged, txtColor2.TextChanged, _
    cboGradientMode.SelectedIndexChanged, nudRotation.ValueChanged, _
    nudGradientBlend.ValueChanged, MyBase.Resize
```

After clearing the picture box and the status bar, we're ready to get to the business of creating a brush.

SolidBrush

The first option is a solid brush, based on the user-selected color. We'll assign it to *m_brush*, our class-level brush variable, because doing that will make IntelliSense help available on the brush object.

```
Select Case cboBrushType.Text
    Case "Solid"
        ⋮
        Dim mySolidBrush As New SolidBrush(m_Color1)
        m_Brush = mySolidBrush
```

HatchBrush

The second option is to create a new *HatchBrush* using the user-selected colors for foreground and background color settings. Because the *HatchStyle* property is read-only, it must be set as we instantiate the *HatchBrush*.

```
Case "Hatch"
    ⋮
    Dim myHatchBrush As New HatchBrush( _
        CType(cboHatchStyle.SelectedItem, HatchStyle), _
        m_Color1, m_Color2)
    m_Brush = myHatchBrush
```

TextureBrush

The third option is to create a new *TextureBrush* based on a bitmap picture of water lilies. The bitmap can also be a pattern you've created. The *WrapMode* determines how the brush will be tiled if it's not spread over the entire graphics area. The *RotateTransform* method rotates the brush by the user-specified amount. We could also have used a *ScaleTransform* to re-shape the brush. For example, this statement cuts the width of the brush in half and doubles the height: `myTextureBrush.ScaleTransform(0.5F, 2.0F)`

> **Caution** Be cautious when creating a *TextureBrush*. If you define a *Rectangle* larger than the bitmap, it will trigger an *OutOfMemory* exception.

```
Case "Texture"
    ⋮
    Dim myTextureBrush As New TextureBrush( _
        New Bitmap("..\WaterLilies.jpg"), m_BrushSize)
    myTextureBrush.WrapMode = CType(cboWrapMode.SelectedItem, _
        WrapMode)
    myTextureBrush.RotateTransform(nudRotation.Value)
    m_Brush = myTextureBrush
```

LinearGradientBrush

Our next option is to create a new *LinearGradientBrush*. The brush is based on a size defined by a rectangle. In this case, we're using the user-defined *m_BrushSize*. Two colors are used, one for defining the start color of the gradient and one for defining the end color.

> **Tip**   You can create more advanced gradients by using the *Blend* property, which lets you specify the relative intensity of each of the colors along the gradient path.

We define the *LinearGradientMode* in the constructor. This controls the direction of the gradient. We could have used an angle, but for simplicity that isn't done here. The *WrapMode* determines how the gradient will be tiled if it is not spread over the entire graphics area. The *LinearGradientBrush* can use all values for *WrapMode* except *Clamp*.

To set the point where the blending will focus, you can use any value between 0 and 1. The default is 1.

```
Case "LinearGradient"
    ⋮
    Dim myLinearGradientBrush As New LinearGradientBrush( _
        m_BrushSize, m_Color1, m_Color2, _
        CType(cboGradientMode.SelectedItem, LinearGradientMode))
    If CType(cboWrapMode.SelectedItem, WrapMode) <> _
        WrapMode.Clamp Then
        myLinearGradientBrush.WrapMode = _
            CType(cboWrapMode.SelectedItem, WrapMode)
    Else
        Me.sbrDrawingStatus.Text += _
            "A Linear Gradient Brush cannot use the " & _
            "Clamp WrapMode."
    End If
    myLinearGradientBrush.RotateTransform(nudRotation.Value)
    myLinearGradientBrush.SetBlendTriangularShape( _
        nudGradientBlend.Value)
    m_Brush = myLinearGradientBrush
```

For more advanced uses, you can use the *SetSigmaBellShape* method to set where the center of the gradient occurs, as in this line of code: `myLinear-GradientBrush.SetSigmaBellShape(0.2)`

PathGradient
The last option lets us create a path by defining a set of points and then follow that path by using *PathGradient*. In cases like this, you'll often define and use a *GraphicsPath* object instead of a set of points, but in this case, we're using a simple triangle. Once we've defined the triangle, we create a new *PathGradientBrush* based on the path just created. Anything not bounded by the path will be transparent instead of containing coloring.

The colors for the *PathGradient* are defined differently than other gradients because we can use different colors for each side. In this case, we're using only one color, but we could assign a different color to each side of the path. The *CenterColor* is the color that the edges blend into. *SurroundColors* is an array of colors that defines the colors around the edge. We could also set the *CenterPoint* property somewhere other than the center of the path (even outside the rectangle bounding the path)—for example: myPathGradientBrush.CenterPoint = New PointF(50, 50)

```
Case "PathGradient"
    ⋮
    Dim pathPoint() As Point = {New Point(0, m_BrushSize.Height), _
        New Point(m_BrushSize.Width, m_BrushSize.Height), _
        New Point(m_BrushSize.Width, 0)}
    Dim myPathGradientBrush As New PathGradientBrush(pathPoint)
    myPathGradientBrush.CenterColor = m_Color1
    myPathGradientBrush.SurroundColors = New Color() {m_Color2}
    myPathGradientBrush.WrapMode = _
        CType(cboWrapMode.SelectedItem, WrapMode)
    myPathGradientBrush.RotateTransform(nudRotation.Value)
    myPathGradientBrush.SetBlendTriangularShape( _
        nudGradientBlend.Value)
    m_Brush = myPathGradientBrush
```

Conclusion

In this sample application, we've shown you how to use a *Brush* to fill the interiors of shapes. A *HatchBrush* is a brush with a variety of possible patterns. A *TextureBrush* is one whose source is an image. Gradient brushes let you create fills that transition smoothly from one color to another.

Application #87: Work with GDI+ Text

You might find it surprising that to display text on a form, *PictureBox*, or some other surface you need to *draw* it—but that's exactly the way it is. This sample shows some of the many features available when using GDI+ to work with text.

Building Upon...

Application #85: Work with GDI+ Pens

New Concepts

Fonts and text are rendered by means of GDI+, and the major method you'll use to display text to the screen is the *DrawString* method of the *Graphics* object. You need four essential items to display text using *DrawString*:

- The text to be displayed
- A font in which you want the text displayed
- A brush to draw with
- The location where it should be displayed, which can be x and y coordinates or a rectangle within which the text will be displayed

Whereas you use a *Pen* to draw lines and curves, you need a *Brush* to draw text. As always, the *Brush* is a holder for characteristics of the drawing, while the *Graphics* object provides the methods for doing the drawing.

You have a variety of options when displaying text. You always display text within a bounding rectangle, within which you can use hatch brushes, texture brushes, gradient brushes, and of course, solid brushes. You must carefully measure the size of the text you intend to display, because the size of the bounding rectangle will determine whether the text is appropriately positioned on the screen and whether it will fit in the space provided. Figure 10-3 shows text reflected by the *TranslateTransform* method.

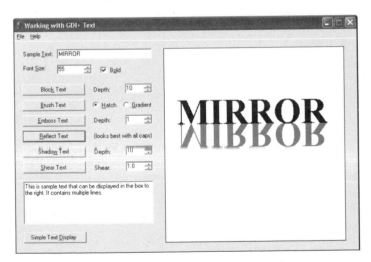

Figure 10-3   When you draw text with GDI+ brushes, you can use transformations to show the text in a variety of orientations.

Code Walkthrough

We'll examine several options for displaying text on a drawing surface, illustrating the point we made earlier—that text must be drawn.

Block Text

Our first option creates the sample text with a block appearance. We begin by setting up the brushes we'll use for the foreground and background. We need a font object for the text, so we create one, using the values the user has set. Notice how we've used the *CheckState* of the *chkBold* check box. *CheckState.Checked* is equal to 1 and *Unchecked* is 0. *FontStyle.Bold* is equal to 1 and *Regular* is 0. So we simply cast the check state of the check box to a font style and we've declared whether we want boldface type or not. Then we create a *Graphics* object from the picture box and clear the box.

```
Private Sub btnBlockText_Click(...
    Dim myForeBrush As Brush = Brushes.Aquamarine
    Dim myBackBrush As Brush = Brushes.Black
    Dim myStyle As FontStyle = CType(chkBold.CheckState, FontStyle)
    Dim myFont As New Font("Times New Roman", Me.nudFontSize.Value, _
        myStyle)
    Dim g As Graphics = picDemoArea.CreateGraphics()
    g.Clear(Color.White)
```

We need to determine the size that will be required to draw the sample text. The *MeasureString* method provides the exact dimensions of the provided string, so you can determine whether it will fit in the area where you want to display it. *MeasureString* returns its results in a *SizeF* structure, which has *Width* and *Height* properties. Using those properties, we calculate the x- and y-coordinates for the starting point of our display.

```
    Dim textSize As SizeF = g.MeasureString(Me.txtSample.Text, myFont)
    Dim xLocation As Single = (picDemoArea.Width - textSize.Width) / 2
    Dim yLocation As Single = (picDemoArea.Height - textSize.Height) / 3
```

Now we're ready to display the text. We'll draw the black background first. To get the block effect, we draw the text repeatedly from the offset in the lower left up to the point where the main text will be drawn. Because people tend to think of light as coming from the upper left, we've subtracted the offset depth from the x dimension instead of adding it. If we had added it, the block might look more like a shadow.

```
    Dim i As Integer
    For i = CInt(nudBlockDepth.Value) To 0 Step -1
        g.DrawString(txtSample.Text, myFont, myBackBrush, _
            xLocation - i, yLocation + i)
    Next
```

Finally, we draw the white main text over the black text. Note how we provide the *DrawString* method with the text we want to display, the font to use, the brush to draw with, and the coordinates at which to draw.

```
    g.DrawString(txtSample.Text, myFont, myForeBrush, xLocation, _
        yLocation)
End Sub
```

Brush Text

Here we'll display the sample text by using either a *Hatch* or *Gradient* brush. In creating a *HatchBrush*, we must specify the style of hatch we want (in this case, Diagonal Brick), as well as foreground and background colors. Before we create the *LinearGradientBrush*, we want to provide a boundary within which the gradient will be displayed. So we create a rectangle that's the size of our text. Then we pass that rectangle as the first argument to the constructor of the *LinearGradientBrush*, along with the starting and ending colors of the gradient and the orientation of the gradient (in this case, Forward Diagonal).

```
Private Sub btnBrushText_Click(...
    ⋮
    Dim textSize As SizeF = g.MeasureString(Me.txtSample.Text, myFont)
    Dim myBrush As Brush
    If Me.optHatch.Checked Then
        myBrush = New HatchBrush(HatchStyle.DiagonalBrick, _
            Color.Yellow, Color.Blue)
    Else
        Dim gradientRectangle As New RectangleF(New PointF(0, 0), textSize)
        myBrush = New LinearGradientBrush(gradientRectangle, Color.Blue, _
            Color.Yellow, LinearGradientMode.ForwardDiagonal)
    End If
    g.DrawString(txtSample.Text, myFont, myBrush, _
        (picDemoArea.Width - textSize.Width) / 2, _
        (picDemoArea.Height - textSize.Height) / 3)
End Sub
```

Embossed Text

The following procedure creates the sample text with an embossed look. To create the effect, the sample text is drawn twice. It's drawn first in black, offset slightly from the drawing starting point, and then drawn again in white, the current background color. This gives the impression that the text is raised. To give the impression of engraving instead of embossing, simply use the negative of the offset value.

```
Private Sub btnEmboss_Click(...
    Dim myBackBrush As Brush = Brushes.Black
    Dim myForeBrush As Brush = Brushes.White
    ⋮
```

(continued)

```
Dim textSize As SizeF = g.MeasureString(Me.txtSample.Text, myFont)
xLocation = (picDemoArea.Width - textSize.Width) / 2
yLocation = (picDemoArea.Height - textSize.Height) / 3
```

We'll draw the black background first. (Note: if you subtract the *nudEmboss-Depth* value instead of adding it, you'll get an Engraved effect. Try it with the Depth control on the form.) Finally, we draw the white main text over the black text.

```
g.DrawString(txtSample.Text, myFont, myBackBrush, _
        xLocation + Me.nudEmbossDepth.Value, _
        yLocation + Me.nudEmbossDepth.Value)
    g.DrawString(txtSample.Text, myFont, myForeBrush, xLocation, yLocation)
End Sub
```

Reflected Text

This example reflects text around the baseline of the characters. It's more advanced than most of the other examples and requires careful measurement of the text. Because we'll be scaling, and scaling effects the entire *Graphics* object not just the text, we need to reposition the origin of the *Graphics* object from (0,0) to the (*xLocation, yLocation*) point. If we don't, when we attempt to flip the text with a scaling transform, it will merely draw the reflected text at (*xLocation, –yLocation*), which is outside the viewable area.

```
Private Sub btnReflectedText_Click(...
    Dim myBackBrush As Brush = Brushes.Gray
    Dim myForeBrush As Brush = Brushes.Black
    ⋮
    g.TranslateTransform(xLocation, yLocation)
```

Reflecting around the origin still poses problems. The origin represents the upper left corner of the text's bounding rectangle. This means the reflection will occur at the *top* of the original drawing. This is not how people are used to seeing reflected text. So we need to determine where to draw the text, and we can do that only when we've calculated the height required by the drawing.

This is not as simple as it might seem. The *Height* returned from the *MeasureString* method includes some extra spacing for descenders and white space. But we want *only* the height from the *baseline* (which is the line on which all caps sit). Any characters with descenders drop below the baseline. To calculate the height above the baseline, we need to use the *GetCellAscent* method. Because *GetCellAscent* returns a *Design Metric* value, it must be converted to pixels and scaled for the font size.

```
Dim lineAscent As Integer
Dim lineSpacing As Integer
Dim lineHeight As Single
Dim textHeight As Single
```

```
lineAscent = myFont.FontFamily.GetCellAscent(myFont.Style)
lineSpacing = myFont.FontFamily.GetLineSpacing(myFont.Style)
lineHeight = myFont.GetHeight(g)
textHeight = lineHeight * lineAscent / lineSpacing
```

> **Tip**   Reflection looks best with characters that can be reflected over the baseline nicely—like capital letters. Characters with descenders look odd. To fix that, factor in the height of the descenders as you calculate the text height, and then you'll reflect across the lowest descender height. Here's how:
>
> ```
> Dim lineDescent As Integer
> lineDescent = myFont.FontFamily.GetCellDescent(myFont.Style)
> textHeight = lineHeight * (lineAscent + lineDescent) / lineSpacing
> ```

We'll draw the reflected text first so that we can demonstrate the use of the *GraphicsState* object. A *GraphicsState* object maintains the state of the *Graphics* object as it currently stands. You can then scale, resize, and otherwise transform the *Graphics* object. You can immediately go back to a previous state by using the *Restore* method of the *Graphics* object. Had we drawn the main one first, we would not have needed the *Restore* method or the *GraphicsState* object.

First we'll save the graphics state so that we can restore it later. To draw the reflection, we'll use the *ScaleTransform* method with a negative value. Using −1 will reflect the text with no distortion. Then we restore the previous state and draw the main text.

```
    Dim myState As GraphicsState = g.Save()
    g.ScaleTransform(1, -1.0F)
    g.DrawString(txtSample.Text, myFont, myBackBrush, 0, -textHeight)
    g.Restore(myState)
    g.DrawString(txtSample.Text, myFont, myForeBrush, 0, -textHeight)
End Sub
```

Shadowed Text

This example draws the sample text with a solid brush and a shadow. To create the shadow, the sample text is drawn twice. The first time it's offset and drawn in gray, and then it's drawn again normally in black.

```
Private Sub btnShadowText_Click(...
    Dim myShadowBrush As Brush = Brushes.Gray
    Dim myForeBrush As Brush = Brushes.Black
    ⋮
    g.DrawString(txtSample.Text, myFont, myShadowBrush, _
        xLocation + Me.nudShadowDepth.Value, _
        yLocation + Me.nudShadowDepth.Value)
```

(continued)

```
    g.DrawString(txtSample.Text, myFont, myForeBrush, xLocation, yLocation)
End Sub
```

Sheared Text

The following procedure shears the text so that it appears angled. This requires the use of a *Matrix*, which will define the shear. Because we'll be scaling, and scaling affects the entire *Graphics* object and not just the text, we need to reposition the origin of the *Graphics* object from (0, 0) to the (*xLocation, yLocation*) point.

```
Private Sub btnShearText_Click(...
    ⋮
    g.TranslateTransform(xLocation, yLocation)
```

Now we set a reference to the *Transform* object for the current *Graphics* object, *Shear* it by the specified amount, and finally, draw the main text.

```
    Dim myTransform As Matrix = g.Transform
    myTransform.Shear(nudSkew.Value, 0)
    g.Transform = myTransform
    g.DrawString(txtSample.Text, myFont, myForeBrush, 0, 0)
End Sub
```

Simple Text

The following procedure simply takes the lines of text in the text box and places them in the *picDemoArea PictureBox*. The text will word wrap as necessary, but it will not scroll.

```
Private Sub btnSimpleText_Click(...
    ⋮
    g.DrawString(txtLongText.Text, myFont, myForeBrush, _
        New RectangleF(0, 0, picDemoArea.Width, picDemoArea.Height))
End Sub
```

Conclusion

In this sample application, you've seen that you display text within a bounding rectangle, whose size you must measure with the *MeasureString* method to determine whether the text is appropriately positioned on the screen and whether it will fit in the space provided. You've also seen that you can use any font on your system when you're drawing text. Powerful scaling and transformation methods let you twist, bend, shear, and distort text into a variety of shapes.

Application #88: Work with GDI+ to Manipulate Images

This sample shows you how to manipulate images using GDI+, including changing the size of an image and rotating, zooming, and cropping an image.

Building Upon...

Application #85: Work with GDI+ Pens

New Concepts

GDI+ provides new ways to work with images. This example illustrates several of them.

Changing the Size of an Image

Once you've loaded your image into a *PictureBox*, you can apply one of four *SizeMode* settings to the *PictureBox*:

- **AutoSize**   The *PictureBox* size is adjusted to match the size of the image in it.

- **CenterImage**   The image is displayed in the center of the *Picture-Box*. If the image is larger than the *PictureBox*, its outside edges are clipped.

- **Normal**   The image is located in the upper left corner of the *Picture-Box*. Its right and bottom edges are clipped if it is larger than the *PictureBox*.

- **StretchImage**   The opposite of *AutoSize*. The image is stretched or shrunk to fit the size of the *PictureBox*.

Rotating Images

The *Image* class *RotateFlip* method lets you rotate an image, flip it, or both. You provide the method with a *RotateFlipType* argument (for example, *Rotate180FlipX*) that determines how many degrees you want to rotate the image and the axis, if any, on which you want to flip it. Choices include rotation by 90, 180, and 270 degrees; flipping on the x-axis, y-axis, or both; and combinations of all these options. Rotation is always clockwise.

Zooming and Cropping Images

Zooming means resizing the image so that it appears that the user's perspective has changed by being either brought closer to or moved farther away from the picture.

Cropping consists of creating a new image at a size you specify and filling it with the portion of the old image that will fit the dimensions of the new one.

If you want to allow the user to undo the crop, you need to create a variable that holds a copy of the bitmap before it's cropped. Figure 10-4 shows an image that is both rotated and cropped.

Figure 10-4   The WaterLilies.jpg, which is bigger than the *PictureBox*, is centered within it, and its edges are cropped. The inset shows a portion of the image after it is rotated by 90 degrees.

Code Walkthrough

Let's examine some ways we can manipulate an image, starting with resizing it.

Image Sizing

All four size settings mentioned previously are represented by four Size Mode radio buttons on the sample form. The *SizeModeRadioButtons_CheckedChanged* procedure handles the *CheckedChanged* events of all four radio buttons, and it adjusts the *PictureBox.SizeMode* property accordingly. Each radio button stores one of the values of the *PictureBoxSizeMode* enumeration (whose values are 0 through 3) in its *Tag* property.

```
Private Sub SizeModeRadioButtons_CheckedChanged(...
    Dim opt As RadioButton = CType(sender, RadioButton)
    Dim sm As PictureBoxSizeMode = CType(opt.Tag, PictureBoxSizeMode)
    If opt.Checked Then
        picImage.SizeMode = sm
```

You must manually reset the *PictureBox* to its original size if *AutoSize* has been set. It will not automatically return to the size set in the designer.

```
            If sm = PictureBoxSizeMode.AutoSize Then
                btnFit.Enabled = False
            Else
                btnFit.Enabled = True
                picImage.Width = PICTUREBOX_WIDTH
                picImage.Height = PICTUREBOX_HEIGHT
            End If
        End If
    End If
End Sub
```

The *Fit* procedure makes the image fit properly in the *PictureBox*. You might think that *AutoSize* would make the image appear in the *PictureBox* according to its true aspect ratio within the fixed bounds of the *PictureBox*. But *AutoSize* simply expands or shrinks the *PictureBox* itself. So the *Fit* procedure determines whether the image is smaller than the *PictureBox*. If it is, and if *Fit* was called by the Zoom In button, it centers the image.

```
Private Sub Fit()
    If picImage.Image.Width < picImage.Width And _
        picImage.Image.Height < picImage.Height Then
        If Not IsFitForZoomIn Then
            picImage.SizeMode = PictureBoxSizeMode.CenterImage
        End If
    End If
    CalculateAspectRatioAndSetDimensions()
End Sub
```

Image Rotation

As we mentioned earlier, rotation is always clockwise when you use the *Rotate-Flip* method, and in *btnRotateRight_Click* in the following code, we're simply rotating the image by 90 degrees. In *btnRotateLeft_Click*, we're achieving the left rotation by rotating the image by 270 degrees, which is the same as if we had rotated it counter-clockwise by 90 degrees. Note that in each case we need to refresh the *PictureBox* after the rotation.

```
Private Sub btnRotateRight_Click(...
    picImage.Image.RotateFlip(RotateFlipType.Rotate90FlipNone)
    picImage.Refresh()
End Sub

Private Sub btnRotateLeft_Click(...
    picImage.Image.RotateFlip(RotateFlipType.Rotate270FlipNone)
    picImage.Refresh()
End Sub
```

Zooming

To zoom, we resize the image, as shown in the following procedure. When zooming in or out, the *SizeMode* controls on the sample form are disabled. Otherwise, the zooming won't work as anticipated. The following *If* test ensures that the initial Zoom In transition is smooth. Without the test, if the *SizeMode* is something other than *AutoSize*, the image can appear to Zoom Out on the first click, and then Zoom In on subsequent clicks.

```
Private Sub btnZoomIn_Click(...
    If grpSizeMode.Enabled Then
        picImage.SizeMode = PictureBoxSizeMode.AutoSize
    End If
    grpSizeMode.Enabled = False
    btnFit.Enabled = True
    IsFitForZoomIn = True
```

The *StretchImage* mode works best for zooming because the image is forced to conform to the size of the *PictureBox*. Zoom works best if you first fit the image according to its true aspect ratio. (See *CalculateAspectRatioAndSetDimensions.*)

When it's time to actually do the zoom, you do it by simply adjusting the image's dimensions up or down—in this case, by 25 percent. You could, of course, choose any increment you want, including letting the user enter it.

```
    picImage.SizeMode = PictureBoxSizeMode.StretchImage
    Fit()
    picImage.Width = CInt(picImage.Width * 1.25)
    picImage.Height = CInt(picImage.Height * 1.25)
End Sub

Private Sub btnZoomOut_Click(...
    grpSizeMode.Enabled = False
    btnFit.Enabled = True
    Fit()
    picImage.SizeMode = PictureBoxSizeMode.StretchImage
    picImage.Width = CInt(picImage.Width / 1.25)
    picImage.Height = CInt(picImage.Height / 1.25)
End Sub
```

The following procedure calculates and returns the image's aspect ratio and sets its proper dimensions. It's used by the *Fit* procedure and also for saving thumbnails of images.

```
Private Function CalculateAspectRatioAndSetDimensions() As Double
    Dim ratio As Double
    If picImage.Image.Width > picImage.Image.Height Then
        ratio = picImage.Image.Width / _
                picImage.Image.Height
        picImage.Height = CInt(CDbl(picImage.Width) / ratio)
    Else
        ratio = picImage.Image.Height / _
                picImage.Image.Width
        picImage.Width = CInt(CDbl(picImage.Height) / ratio)
```

```
        End If
        Return ratio
End Function
```

Cropping

In our example, we accept upper left x- and y-coordinates from the user, along with the width and height of the desired new image. Then we create a rectangle defined by those coordinates (relative to the upper left corner of the *Picture-Box*) and the desired width and height.

```
Private Sub btnCrop_Click(...
    If IsValidCropValues() Then
        imgUndo = picImage.Image
        btnUndo.Enabled = True
        Dim recSource As New Rectangle(CInt(txtXCoord.Text), _
            CInt(txtYCoord.Text), CInt(txtWidth.Text), _
            CInt(txtHeight.Text))
```

Caution   You might be tempted to create a *Graphics* object off the *PictureBox* (rather than a new *Bitmap*) and then to clear the *PictureBox* and draw the cropped image onto it, like this:

```
Dim grPicImage As Graphics = picImage.CreateGraphics
grPicImage.Clear(picImage.BackColor)
grPicImage.DrawImage(picImage.Image, 0, 0, recSource, _
    GraphicsUnit.Pixel)
```

This will appear to work, but as soon as you use any of the other controls on the form you'll see that the *PictureBox* actually still contains the original image, not the cropped one.

Then we create a new, blank *Bitmap* on which we will draw the cropped image. We get a *Graphics* object from the *Bitmap* for drawing, and we draw the image in the upper left corner of the *Bitmap*. Finally, we set the *PictureBox* image to the new cropped image.

```
        Dim bmpCropped As New Bitmap(CInt(txtWidth.Text), _
            CInt(txtHeight.Text))
        Dim grBitmap As Graphics = Graphics.FromImage(bmpCropped)
        grBitmap.DrawImage(picImage.Image, 0, 0, recSource, _
            GraphicsUnit.Pixel)
        picImage.Image = bmpCropped
    End If
End Sub
```

Conclusion

In this sample application, we've shown you that an image in a *PictureBox* can be resized several ways by setting the *SizeMode* property of the *PictureBox*. You've seen that you can rotate and flip an image at the same time, and the *RotateFlip* method accepts a variety of *RotateFlipType* arguments that let you turn and flip an image in any direction you want. Zooming means resizing the image. Be careful about the first user click after choosing Zoom In if the *SizeMode* is something other than *AutoSize*.

Application #89: Create a Screen Saver with GDI+

You might think there's something mysterious about a Microsoft Windows screen saver, but it's really nothing more than a Windows application in disguise. You can easily build your own screen saver by creating a regular Windows application with a form that's displayed in dialog mode, maximized to fill the screen, and waiting for a cue to be dismissed. The cue can be a mouse click or a movement of the mouse. This sample shows you how to create and deploy a screen saver with Visual Basic .NET.

Building Upon...

Application #82: Serialize Objects
Application #85: Work with GDI+ Pens
Application #86: Work with GDI+ Brushes
Application #88: Work with GDI+ to Manipulate Images

New Concepts

You'll want your screen saver form not to have a title bar, not to show up in the taskbar, and not to be "touchable" in any way by the user (except to dismiss it with a mouse click or a mouse movement). So you'll need to set the following form properties:

- *FormBorderStyle = None*

- *ControlBox = False*

- *MaximizeBox = False*

- *MinimizeBox = False*

- *ShowInTaskbar = False*
- *SizeGripStyle = Hide*
- *TopMost = True*
- *WindowState = Maximized*

> **Tip**   While you're developing the screen saver, set the form's size to a fraction of the screen's size, set the *ControlBox* property to *True*, and set the *WindowState* property to *Normal*. That way the form won't cover the entire screen, you can see your code for debugging purposes, and the form will have a title bar so that you can move it around.

Code Walkthrough

The sample solution has two projects: Create a Screensaver with GDI+.vbproj and GDI+ Screen Saver.vbproj. The second one is the screen-saver project, while the first is a small installation program to install your screen saver once you've completed it. The procedures we'll describe next are in the screen-saver project, except for those in the "Deploying the Screen Saver" section. Figure 10-5 shows the screen saver form during development, small and sizeable.

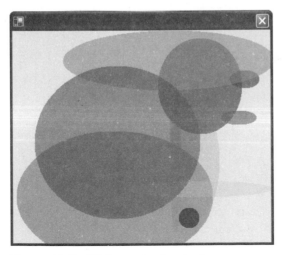

Figure 10-5   While you're developing your screen saver, keep the form small and sizeable so that you can test and debug it easily.

Application Entry Point

Sub Main is the entry point into our application, the first procedure that executes when the screen-saver program is run. The *STAThread* attribute means this application will run in a single-threaded apartment, and it's needed for COM interoperability reasons. Windows will pass parameters to this program whenever a user is setting up the screen saver using the Display Properties | Screen Saver property screen. The parameters will be passed in an array named *args*, and Windows will pass a */p*, */c*, or */s* argument, depending on how the screen saver should behave. We'll explain each argument in the following paragraphs.

First we need to determine whether an argument was passed and, if so, which one. A */p* argument means we're being asked to show a preview of the screen saver. We haven't implemented the preview functionality here because it involves creating and joining threads and is beyond the scope of this sample, so we'll simply exit the application.

```
<STAThread()> Shared Sub Main(ByVal args As String())
    If args.Length > 0 Then
        If args(0).ToLower = "/p" Then
            Application.Exit()
        End If
```

If the screen saver should offer a form for user options, Windows passes a */c*, so we'll create and display a *frmOptions* form, and then exit when the form is closed. If the screen saver should simply execute normally, Windows passes a */s*, so we'll create and display a *screenSaverForm* and then exit when the form is closed.

```
        If args(0).ToLower.Trim().Substring(0, 2) = "/c" Then
            Dim userOptionsForm As New frmOptions()
            userOptionsForm.ShowDialog()
            Application.Exit()
        End If
        If args(0).ToLower = "/s" Then
            Dim screenSaverForm As New frmSceenSaver()
            screenSaverForm.ShowDialog()
            Application.Exit()
        End If
```

If there are no arguments, we'll simply execute the screen saver normally, because it means that the user double-clicked the .scr or .exe file or ran it from within Visual Studio. We know this because otherwise Windows would have passed a parameter to the application.

```
    Else
        Dim screenSaverForm As New frmSceenSaver()
        screenSaverForm.ShowDialog()
```

```
        Application.Exit()
    End If
End Sub
```

Normal Operation

When the screen-saver form is loaded, we initialize it by creating the *Graphics* object we'll use for drawing, loading the user's saved options (creating an options file if one does not exist), setting the speed based on the user-defined options, and enabling the timer. The speed setting dictates how quickly shapes will be displayed when the screen saver is active.

```
Private Sub frmSceenSaver_Load(...
    m_Graphics = Me.CreateGraphics()
    m_Options.LoadOptions()
    Select Case m_Options.Speed
        Case "Slow"
            Me.tmrUpdateScreen.Interval = 500
        Case "Fast"
            Me.tmrUpdateScreen.Interval = 100
        Case Else
            Me.tmrUpdateScreen.Interval = 200
    End Select
    Me.tmrUpdateScreen.Enabled = True
End Sub
```

All subsequent operations are in response to events. When the timer ticks, a new shape is drawn on the screen, and this continues until a mouse button is clicked or the mouse is moved over the form.

```
Private Sub tmrUpdateScreen_Tick(...
    DrawShape()
End Sub
```

The *DrawShape* subroutine draws a randomly colored, randomly sized shape to the screen, based on some user-defined parameters. It starts by computing the largest possible values for the screen, as indicated by the form width and height. (Remember that the form is maximized.) Note that *x1*, *x2*, *y1*, and *y2* are coordinates for random points to be generated later, *myRect* is the rectangle within which the shapes will be drawn, and *myColor* is the color to be used to draw the shapes.

```
Private Sub DrawShape()
    Dim maxX As Integer = Me.Width
    Dim maxY As Integer = Me.Height
    Dim x1, x2, y1, y2 As Integer
    Dim myRect As Rectangle
    Dim myColor As Color
```

Next we generate some random numbers ranging between zero and the maximums we determined earlier, and we create a rectangle based on the generated coordinates.

```
x1 = m_Random.Next(0, maxX)
x2 = m_Random.Next(0, maxX)
y1 = m_Random.Next(0, maxY)
y2 = m_Random.Next(0, maxY)
myRect = New Rectangle(Math.Min(x1, x2), Math.Min(y1, y2), _
    Math.Abs(x1 - x2), Math.Abs(y1 - y2))
```

We'll select a color at random for the shape we're about to draw. If the user wants transparent shapes, we'll allow the transparency to be randomly generated as well. If not, we'll set the *Alpha* to 255 (the maximum). *Alpha,* which is the first argument to the *Color.FromArgb* function, determines how opaque the shape will be.

```
If m_Options.IsTransparent Then
    myColor = Color.FromArgb(m_Random.Next(255), m_Random.Next(255), _
        m_Random.Next(255), m_Random.Next(255))
Else
    myColor = Color.FromArgb(255, m_Random.Next(255), _
        m_Random.Next(255), m_Random.Next(255))
End If
```

Finally, we draw an ellipse or rectangle based on user-defined options.

```
If m_Options.Shape = "Ellipses" Then
    m_Graphics.FillEllipse(New SolidBrush(myColor), myRect)
Else
    m_Graphics.FillRectangle(New SolidBrush(myColor), myRect)
End If
End Sub
```

Ending the Application

When the user clicks a button or moves the mouse, we want the screen saver to quit. The following routines accomplish that. The first one simply exits if any mouse button is clicked on the screen saver form.

```
Private Sub frmSceenSaver_MouseDown(...
    Application.Exit()
End Sub
```

The second one responds to a mouse movement. Because the *MouseMove* event can sometimes be fired by very trivial moves of the mouse, we'll verify that the mouse has actually been moved by at least a few pixels before exiting. To do that, we store the current location of the mouse, turn on a switch that shows we're tracking the mouse movements, and exit only if the mouse has been moved at least 10 pixels.

```
Private Sub frmSceenSaver_MouseMove(...
    If Not m_IsActive Then
        Me.m_MouseLocation = New Point(e.X, e.Y)
        m_IsActive = True
    Else
        If Math.Abs(e.X - Me.m_MouseLocation.X) > 10 Or _
            Math.Abs(e.Y - Me.m_MouseLocation.Y) > 10 Then
            Application.Exit()
        End If
    End If
End Sub
```

Setting Options

We want the user to be able to choose screen-saver options such as how fast
shapes should be drawn on the screen, whether they should be rectangles or
ellipses, and whether the shapes should be transparent. So we provide an
Options form, which gets called when the screen-saver program is invoked
with the */c* argument.

We've defined a class named *Options* (which you can see in *Options.vb*) to
hold the preferences as properties and provide methods for loading and saving
the preferences. Creating a class makes it easy to save the options to disk in
XML format by serializing the class and then later retrieving them by deserialization. (See "Application #82: Serialize Objects" for more details.)

The *btnOK_Click* procedure in *frmOptions* creates an *Options* object and
sets its values to the user-selected values on the form. It then saves the choices
to disk.

```
Private Sub btnOK_Click(...
    Dim myOptions As New Options()
    If Me.optEllipses.Checked Then
        myOptions.Shape = "Ellipses"
    Else
        myOptions.Shape = "Rectangles"
    End If
    myOptions.IsTransparent = Me.chkTransparent.Checked
    myOptions.Speed = Me.cboSpeed.Text
    myOptions.SaveOptions()
    Me.Close()
End Sub
```

The *Form_Load* event procedure of *frmOptions* loads the current user-
defined options and sets the controls on the form accordingly. The *Load*
method of the *Options* class always returns values, even if the options file
doesn't currently exist.

```
Private Sub frmOptions_Load(...
    Dim myOptions As New Options()
    myOptions.LoadOptions()
```

(continued)

```
        Me.cboSpeed.Text = myOptions.Speed
        Me.chkTransparent.Checked = myOptions.IsTransparent
        If myOptions.Shape = "Ellipses" Then
            Me.optEllipses.Checked = True
        Else
            Me.optRectangles.Checked = True
        End If
    End Sub
```

Deploying the Screen Saver

Screen savers live in the Windows System directory, which by default is C:\Windows\System32. To install your new screen saver, you simply have to copy the .exe application file to the System directory, changing the extension from .exe to .scr. In the sample solution, we've provided a project that copies the file to its correct location. It assumes you have a copy of "101 VB.NET Sample Applications Screensaver.scr" in the root directory of the 89 Create a Screensaver with GDI+ project.

If you don't, copy "101 VB.NET Sample Applications Screensaver.exe" from GDI+ Screen Saver\bin to the root directory of the 89 Create a Screensaver with GDI+ project and change the extension to .scr.

Once you're sure the screen-saver file is in place, the *btnInstall_Click* procedure of *frmMain* handles the installation for you. Notice the use of *Environment.CurrentDirectory* (the folder where the executable is running) and *Environment.SystemDirectory* (the Windows System directory).

```
    Private Sub btnInstall_Click(...
        Dim fileName As String = _
            "101 VB.NET Sample Applications Screensaver.scr"
        Dim sourceFile As String = _
            Environment.CurrentDirectory & "\..\" & fileName
        Dim destFile As String = Environment.SystemDirectory & "\" & fileName
        Try
            File.Copy(sourceFile, destFile, True)
        Catch ex As Exception
            MsgBox(ex.ToString(), MsgBoxStyle.Exclamation, Me.Text)
        End Try
    End Sub
```

Conclusion

In this sample application, you've seen that a screen saver is simply a Windows Application in disguise. Once you change its file extension from .exe to .scr and put it in the Windows System directory, it will show up on the list of screen savers in Control Panel | Display. You've seen that Windows passes */p*, */c*, or */s* arguments to the screen saver to indicate how it should behave. They indicate

Preview, Set Options, and Normal, respectively. We've also shown you that generating random colors and even random levels of transparency is easy with the *Random* class and the *FromArgb* function of the *Color* class.

Application #90: Animation

This application demonstrates how to do animation with GDI+, including classic frame animation, drawing and moving a shape on the screen, and animating text with a gradient fill. The sample form offers three animations: a winking eye, a bouncing ball, and a text animation. (The text animation is shown in Figure 10-6.)

Building Upon...

Application #85: Work with GDI+ Pens
Application #86: Work with GDI+ Brushes
Application #88: Work with GDI+ to Manipulate Images

Figure 10-6   Creating an animated gradient in text or any other shape is easy—you simply change its point of origin in a loop.

New Concepts

Once you know how to manipulate images with the Framework GID-related classes, you'll probably want to make some of them come alive with animation. With a few carefully chosen methods and some basic mathematical skills, you can bring an image to life. We'll demonstrate the principles in the code walk-through.

Code Walkthrough

The animations shown here require a timer whose *TimerOnTick* procedure triggers the image's movement. Before starting the motion, however, some initial preparation is required, including clearing existing drawings when switching from one animation to another, computing the size of the bouncing ball, and so on.

Setting Up

The *OnResize* procedure fills the bill in handling the setup chores. This method overrides the *OnResize* method in the base *Control* class. *OnResize* raises the *Resize* event, which occurs when the control (in this case, the *Form*) is resized. That means it will be called when the form is loaded because the *Resize* event fires as a part of that process. We will also call this procedure whenever a radio button is clicked to change animations.

First, if *Wink* is chosen, we'll simply clear the form.

> **Tip**   To clear the form, you could also use *grfx.Clear(Me.BackColor)* or *Me.Invalidate()*.

```
Protected Overrides Sub OnResize(ByVal ea As EventArgs)
    If optWink.Checked Then
        Dim grfx As Graphics = CreateGraphics()
        Me.Refresh()
        grfx.Dispose()
```

If the user selects the Bouncing Ball, we have much more to do. First we erase any existing drawings. Next, we determine the size of the ball by setting the radius of the ball to a fraction of either the width or height of the client area, whichever is less. Then we set the width and height of the ball by multiplying the radius we calculated earlier by the horizontal and vertical resolution of the *Graphics* object.

```
    ElseIf optBall.Checked Then
        Dim grfx As Graphics = CreateGraphics()
        grfx.Clear(Me.BackColor)
        Dim dblRadius As Double = Math.Min(ClientSize.Width / grfx.DpiX, _
            ClientSize.Height / grfx.DpiY) / intBallSize
        intBallRadiusX = CInt(dblRadius * grfx.DpiX)
        intBallRadiusY = CInt(dblRadius * grfx.DpiY)
        grfx.Dispose()
```

Now we'll set the distance the ball moves to 1 pixel or a fraction of the ball's size, whichever is greater. This means that the distance the ball moves each time it is drawn is proportional to its size, which is, in turn, proportional to the size of the client area. Thus, when the client area is shrunk, the ball slows down, and when it is increased, the ball speeds up—resulting in an apparent constant speed no matter what size the form is set to.

```
intBallMoveX = CInt(Math.Max(1, intBallRadiusX / intMoveSize))
intBallMoveY = CInt(Math.Max(1, intBallRadiusY / intMoveSize))
```

Notice that the value of the ball's movement also serves as the margin around the ball, which determines the size of the actual bitmap on which the ball is drawn. So the distance the ball moves is exactly equal to the size of the bitmap, which permits the previous image of the ball to be erased before the next image is drawn—all without an inordinate amount of flickering. We determine the actual size of the *Bitmap* on which the ball is drawn by adding the margins to the ball's dimensions.

```
intBitmapWidthMargin = intBallMoveX
intBitmapHeightMargin = intBallMoveY
intBallBitmapWidth = 2 * (intBallRadiusX + intBitmapWidthMargin)
intBallBitmapHeight = 2 * (intBallRadiusY + intBitmapHeightMargin)
```

Now that we have the size of the ball, we create a new bitmap, passing in the dimensions we just calculated. Then we obtain the *Graphics* object exposed by the *Bitmap*, clear the existing ball, and draw the new ball. Finally, we reset the ball's position to the center of the client area.

```
myBitmap = New Bitmap(intBallBitmapWidth, intBallBitmapHeight)
grfx = Graphics.FromImage(myBitmap)
With grfx
    .Clear(Me.BackColor)
    .FillEllipse(Brushes.Red, New Rectangle(intBallMoveX, _
        intBallMoveY, 2 * intBallRadiusX, 2 * intBallRadiusY))
    .Dispose()
End With
intBallPositionX = CInt(ClientSize.Width / 2)
intBallPositionY = CInt(ClientSize.Height / 2)
```

In the final choice in the *If* statement, we simply clear the form if the user selects the Animated Text option.

```
ElseIf optText.Checked Then
    Dim grfx As Graphics = CreateGraphics()
    grfx.Clear(Me.BackColor)
End If
End Sub
```

Frame Animation

Now that the setup is done, the bulk of the work is passed to the following *TimerOnTick* procedure, which handles the *Tick* event for the *Timer*. This is where the animation takes place, so it's the heart of our application.

The first option handles the winking eye. To create the illusion of winking, we'll display a sequence of four images stored in an array, each one showing a different stage of the wink. We draw each image with the *DrawImage* method of a *Graphics* object, using overload #8, which takes the image to be displayed, the x- and y-coordinates (which in this case will center the image in the client area), and the width and height of the image. Note *intCurrentImage*, a class-level counter that begins at 1 and determines which of the four images in the array will be displayed as the animation progresses.

```
Protected Overridable Sub TimerOnTick(...
    If optWink.Checked Then
        Dim grfx As Graphics = CreateGraphics()
        Dim img As Image = arrImages(intCurrentImage)
        grfx.DrawImage(img, CInt((ClientSize.Width - img.Width) / 2), _
            CInt((ClientSize.Height - img.Height) / 2), img.Width, _
            img.Height)
```

Each time the timer ticks, we bump up the image counter *intImage-Increment,* which is a class-level variable that lets us control the animation order. When we get to the last image of the four, we reverse the order so that the eye closes, and when we get back to the first image, we reverse the animation order again so that the eye re-opens.

```
        intCurrentImage += intImageIncrement
        If intCurrentImage = 3 Then
            intImageIncrement = -1
        ElseIf intCurrentImage = 0 Then
            intImageIncrement = 1
        End If
```

Bouncing Ball

The next option enables the bouncing ball. First we create a *Graphics* object, and then we use it to draw the bitmap containing the ball on the *Form*. Then we increment the ball's position by the distance it has moved in both the x and y directions after being redrawn.

```
    ElseIf optBall.Checked Then
        Dim grfx As Graphics = CreateGraphics()
        grfx.DrawImage(myBitmap, _
            CInt(intBallPositionX - intBallBitmapWidth / 2), _
            CInt(intBallPositionY - intBallBitmapHeight / 2), _
            intBallBitmapWidth, intBallBitmapHeight)
        grfx.Dispose()
        intBallPositionX += intBallMoveX
        intBallPositionY += intBallMoveY
```

> **Tip**   You should always call *Dispose* for objects that expose this method instead of waiting for the Garbage Collector to do it for you. This almost always increases your application's performance.

When the ball hits a boundary, we want to reverse its direction. So when its x-axis position puts it beyond the width of the form, or less than zero, we invert *intBallMoveX*, which controls its direction. We do the same for the y-axis (inverting *intBallMoveY*), but we set the upper boundary at 40 instead of zero so that the ball doesn't bounce into the controls at the top of the form.

```
If intBallPositionX + intBallRadiusX >= ClientSize.Width _
    Or intBallPositionX - intBallRadiusX <= 0 Then
    intBallMoveX = -intBallMoveX
    Beep()
End If
If intBallPositionY + intBallRadiusY >= ClientSize.Height _
    Or intBallPositionY - intBallRadiusY <= 40 Then
    intBallMoveY = -intBallMoveY
    Beep()
End If
```

Animated Text

For the final option, animating a gradient with text, we begin by setting the font type and the text to be displayed, and we determine the size of the text with the *MeasureString* method. Keep in mind that *MeasureString* returns its results in a *SizeF* structure, which has *Width* and *Height* properties. Using those properties, we calculate the x- and y-coordinates for the starting point of our display, which in this case is the center of the client area.

```
ElseIf optText.Checked Then
    Dim grfx As Graphics = CreateGraphics()
    Dim font As New font("Microsoft Sans Serif", 96, _
        FontStyle.Bold, GraphicsUnit.Point)
    Dim strText As String = "GDI+!"
    Dim sizfText As New SizeF(grfx.MeasureString(strText, font))
    Dim ptfTextStart As New PointF( _
        CSng(ClientSize.Width - sizfText.Width) / 2, _
        CSng(ClientSize.Height - sizfText.Height) / 2)
```

We'll set the start point of the gradient to the upper left of the text's boundary rectangle. We'll set the end point's x coordinate to a changing value so that we can achieve the animation effect. Once we've instantiated the *LinearGradientBrush*, we draw the text using Blue for the gradient's starting color and use the form's background color for the ending color.

```
Dim ptfGradientStart As New PointF(0, 0)
Dim ptfGradientEnd As New PointF(intCurrentGradientShift, 200)
Dim grBrush As New LinearGradientBrush(ptfGradientStart, _
    ptfGradientEnd, Color.Blue, Me.BackColor)
grfx.DrawString(strText, font, grBrush, ptfTextStart)
grfx.Dispose()
```

Now we'll animate the gradient by moving its starting point based on the value in *intCurrentGradientShift*, which is incremented or decremented by *intGradientStep* each time this procedure gets called. Once *intCurrentGradientShift* gets to 500, we reverse its direction.

```
    intCurrentGradientShift += intGradientStep
    If intCurrentGradientShift = 500 Then
        intGradientStep = -5
    ElseIf intCurrentGradientShift = -50 Then
        intGradientStep = 5
    End If
    End If
End Sub
```

Conclusion

In this sample application, you've seen that you can achieve image animation just by drawing a sequence of images to the screen. You've also seen that you might sometimes need more complex computations when you need to precisely place an image in a series of progressive locations, as with our bouncing ball example. We showed you that to clear a form, you can use *Graphics.Clear(Me.BackColor)*, *Me.Refresh()*, or *Me.Invalidate()*. And you saw that creating an animated gradient is easy. You simply change its origin in a loop.

11

Building Enterprise Services Applications

Enterprise Services is the Microsoft .NET Framework term for COM+ Services. More accurately, Enterprise Services is the name given to the classes in the *System.EnterpriseServices* namespace. These classes form a wrapper around COM+ Services, providing a much improved COM API. By combining Enterprise Services with features of the common language runtime (CLR), building COM+ applications has never been easier.

Application #91: Create an Enterprise Services Component

This topic can be considered part one of a two-part series on building a simple Enterprise Services component. We assume that you have a basic understanding of COM+, or Enterprise Services as it is referred to in the .NET Framework. Therefore, this topic focuses on the steps required to build an Enterprise Services component.

At the outset, it's important to clarify some terminology. From the perspective of managed code, the term *application* takes on its traditional meaning. Also from this perspective, the term *serviced component* means a component that uses COM+ Services. Thus, for this topic, there is a Windows Forms application (that does not use COM+ directly), which consumes a serviced component. From the perspective of COM+, however, a serviced component is known as a *COM+ application*. You'll see this term in the Component Services management console. Keep this in mind as you continue reading.

The Microsoft Windows application simulates a data entry form for Northwind products. It does little more than instantiate the serviced component and call appropriate methods. A Class Library project contains the code and the strong name key for the serviced component. Although for instructional purposes a connection string is set in the component class, *Product*, there is no actual connection to a database. Instead, trace statements are written to the Output window. A *StatusBar* on the host application is also employed to confirm user actions.

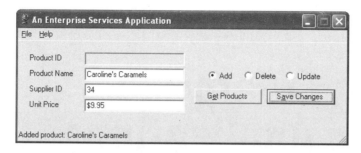

Part two of this series will extend the component to support method-level role-based security.

Building Upon...

Application #4: *Try/Catch/Finally*
Application #70: Reflection

New Concepts

In the past, it has been quite difficult to build COM+ applications. With the advent of the .NET Framework, however, the COM programming model has been extensively overhauled, due mainly to features inherent in the CLR. Among these features are the following:

■ **Greatly improved API** The CLR can be viewed as a replacement for COM because of the wrapper classes in the *System.EntepriseServices* namespace. Of course, the CLR doesn't replace COM+ itself, as this is the component runtime environment that provides numerous middle-tier services not presently found in the .NET Framework.

■ **Accessible assembly metadata** Binaries, or *assemblies* as they are referred to in the .NET Framework, can be declaratively marked with a variety of attributes. This permits serviced components to run under COM+ services without you having to manually configure them by using the Component Services snap-in. This metadata is accessible at precompile time, compile time, and run time via the *System.Reflection.Assembly* class.

Thus, assuming you have an understanding of COM+, implementing these features in Microsoft Visual Basic .NET basically amounts to learning the associated attributes and how to use them declaratively.

In addition to writing the code you'll see in the code walkthrough, you must also perform two other tasks when building a serviced component:

■ **Strong-name the assembly**   All serviced components must be signed with a public-private key pair. To generate a key pair you use the sn.exe utility from a command prompt, as follows:

```
sn.exe -k MyComponent.snk
```

The path to this key is then referenced in the AssemblyInfo.vb file for the component.

■ **Deploy the assembly**   You deploy an assembly by placing the assembly in the global assembly cache (recommended) or by registering the assembly with COM+. The latter option can take three forms:

❏   Manual registration using the regsvcs.exe utility

❏   Programmatic registration using the *RegistrationHelper* class

❏   Dynamic (also known as *lazy*) registration

The third option is typically used during development. The component is automatically registered when it is first accessed (causing a slight performance degradation). This is the type of deployment used for the two applications in this series.

You'll now step through the code for a serviced component.

Code Walkthrough

The walkthrough is divided into two parts. You begin with the *Product* class, where most of the code resides. In the second half, you'll learn about the assembly attributes that are needed to properly configure the application for COM+ Services.

The *Product* Class

The most basic step involved with building a serviced component is to derive from the base class provided by the .NET Framework for all classes that use COM+ Services. This base class is *ServicedComponent*, and it resides in the *System.EnterpriseServices* namespace.

```
Imports System.EnterpriseServices

Public Class Product
    Inherits ServicedComponent
End Class
```

At this point, you have the basis of a COM+ component. All that remains to be done is set the required *AssemblyKeyFile* attribute in the AssemblyInfo.vb file. Further code for this class does not need to be written in any particular way. Of course, in most cases you want to take advantage of various COM+ features and change the default COM+ runtime settings. This is where attributes come in.

In this application, attributes are used at the assembly, component-class, and method levels. You'll see how the assembly attributes are set in the next section. The class is declaratively marked as follows to require transactions, to enable both Just-in-Time activation (that is, instantiation) and object pooling, and to set a construction string:

```
<Transaction(TransactionOption.Required), _
    JustInTimeActivation(True), _
    ObjectPooling(Enabled:=True, MinPoolSize:=2, MaxPoolSize:=10), _
    ConstructionEnabled(Default:= _
    "Server=localhost;DataBase=Northwind;Integrated Security=SSPI")> _
    Public Class Product
        Inherits ServicedComponent
    End Class
```

When this component is registered with COM+ Services, these attributes will determine related settings that can be viewed in the component's Properties dialog box. In Figure 11-1, the Properties dialog box for the Product component shows the activation settings that were set via the *ObjectPooling* and *ConstructionEnabled* attributes.

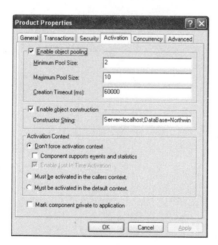

Figure 11-1   The Properties dialog box for the Product component shows the activation settings that were set via the *ObjectPooling* and *ConstructionEnabled* attributes.

The only attribute used at the method level is *AutoComplete*. This marks the method for auto completion, which means that if the procedure exits with no exception, *SetComplete* is automatically called; otherwise, *SetAbort* is called.

```
' Simulates a call to a stored procedure to update a product.
<AutoComplete(True)> _
    Public Sub Update( _
        ByVal ProductID As Integer, _
        ByVal ProductName As String, _
        ByVal SupplierID As Integer, _
        ByVal UnitPrice As Decimal)
        ⋮
        Try
            'cmd = New SqlCommand("Update", cnn)
            ⋮
            'cmd.ExecuteNonQuery()
            DoTracing("Product.Update called at " & _
                DateTime.Now.ToLongTimeString)
        Catch exp As Exception
            Throw New Exception(exp.Message, exp.InnerException)
        End Try
    End Sub
```

The methods for adding, deleting, and getting products are similar to *Update*. When examining the class, you'll also see various base-class methods overridden, such as *Deactive* and *CanBePooled*.

The Assembly Metadata

As mentioned earlier, the only line of code that needs to be added to the component's AssemblyInfo.vb file is the following, which associates ("strong-names") the assembly with the key you generate using the sn.exe utility:

```
<Assembly: AssemblyKeyFile("..\..\KeyFile.snk")>
```

If you fail to add this statement, a *RegistrationException* is thrown when the component is instantiated.

Although it's not required, the *ApplicationName* attribute is important. If you don't give the application a name, it will register as *ServicedComponent*:

```
<Assembly: ApplicationName("My Sample COM+ Application")>
```

You'll also want to identify the application in a more unique way than a friendly name. For this, use the *ApplicationID* attribute and pass a GUID to its constructor:

```
<Assembly: ApplicationID("F3F4E0DA-6712-4AA9-9F48-871A81FD2844")>
```

This component also adds a description using the *ApplicationDescription* attribute. (When you read *application* here, think "from the perspective of COM+." These attributes are specifying COM+ Services settings, not CLR settings.)

Finally, to indicate that the component should run in a system process (dllhost.exe), pass the *ActivationOption.Server* enumeration value to the *ApplicationActivation* attribute.

```
<Assembly: ApplicationActivation(ActivationOption.Server)>
```

If you would rather run the component in the creator's process, pass the *Library* enumeration value.

Conclusion

This topic introduced you to building a serviced component (also known as a COM+ application) by using classes in the *System.EnterpriseServices* namespace. These classes form a wrapper around COM+ Services, providing a greatly improved API. Add to this some special COM+ attributes, as well as to metadata via the way that .NET Framework assemblies support access to metadata via reflection, and your life as a COM+ application developer has become much easier.

The next topic will extend this application to support method-level, role-based security.

Application #92: Implement Role-Based Security

This topic continues where the previous topic left off by extending its serviced component to support role-based security at the method level. If you haven't already read the "Application #91" section, you should do so before proceeding.

Building Upon...

Application #4: *Try/Catch/Finally*
Application #70: Reflection
Application #91: Create an Enterprise Services Component

New Concepts

There are no new concepts for this topic. We've assumed that you already have a basic understanding of COM+ concepts such as marshaling and roles. As with the previous topic, the discussion will focus on the Enterprise Services attributes used to declaratively mark up the serviced component.

Code Walkthrough

The code walkthrough begins with the *Product* class and then proceeds to a review of the attributes used in the AssemblyInfo.vb file.

The *Product* Class

To support role-based security at the method level, several changes have been made to the *Product* class for the serviced component (class members are omitted to conserve space):

```
<ComponentAccessControl(True), _
    SecureMethod(), _
    Transaction(TransactionOption.Required), _
    JustInTimeActivation(True), _
    ObjectPooling(Enabled:=True, MinPoolSize:=2, MaxPoolSize:=10), _
    ConstructionEnabled(Default:= _
    "Server=localhost;DataBase=Northwind;Integrated Security=SSPI")> _
    Public Class Product
        Inherits ServicedComponent
        Implements IMyInterface
    End Class
```

Notice the addition of two attributes. *ComponentAccessControl* serves as the component's security "master switch." In COM+ parlance, *access control* is the term used for authorization. Thus, marking this class with the *ComponentAccess-Control* attribute means that authorization is enabled for the component.

The *SecureMethod* attribute enables authorization at the method level. When you use this attribute, you must implement an interface. In this application, *IMyInterface* serves this purpose:

```
Public Interface IMyInterface
    Sub Add( _
        ByVal ProductName As String, _
        ByVal SupplierID As Integer, _
        ByVal UnitPrice As Decimal)

    Sub Delete(ByVal ProductID As Integer)

    Sub Update( _
        ByVal ProductID As Integer, _
        ByVal ProductName As String, _
        ByVal SupplierID As Integer, _
        ByVal UnitPrice As Decimal)

    Function GetProducts() As DataTable
End Interface
```

At this point, all that remains is to apply *SecurityRole* attributes to the *Product* class methods you want to secure.

> **Warning**   If you apply the *SecurityRole* attributes to the method decla-
> rations in the interface, they will not be set properly in COM+ Services.
> As the Framework documentation states, "Security roles can be speci-
> fied at the component level, per interface and per method." However,
> "As with other method attributes, security configuration is not currently
> shared between interface definition and method implementation."

In this application there are two roles, Managers and Clerks. The former
basically has administrative rights. Managers can retrieve products as well as
add, update, or delete a product. Clerks, on the other hand, have limited rights.
They can only retrieve products or add a new product. Thus, you want to associate the *Add* method with both roles, as follows:

```
<AutoComplete(True), _
    SecurityRole("Managers"), SecurityRole("Clerks")> _
    Public Sub Add( _
        ByVal ProductName As String, _
        ByVal SupplierID As Integer, _
        ByVal UnitPrice As Decimal) Implements IMyInterface.Add
        ⋮
        Try
            'cmd = New SqlCommand("Add", cnn)
            ⋮
            'cmd.ExecuteNonQuery()
            DoTracing("Product.Add called at " & _
                DateTime.Now.ToLongTimeString)
        Catch exp As Exception
            Throw New Exception(exp.Message, exp.InnerException)
        End Try
    End Sub
```

Associating the *Add* method with both roles will allow members of both the
Managers and Clerks roles to add a product. The *Delete* and *Update* methods
use only the *SecurityRole("Managers")* attribute, which denies access to users
who are only members of the Clerks role.

Figure 11-2 illustrates the effects of using these attributes. The left pane
shows the expanded tree view for the Product component. The Update Properties dialog box shows the three roles used in the application as a whole. (The
special Marshaler role is covered on page 471.) Only the Managers role is per-
mitted access to this method.

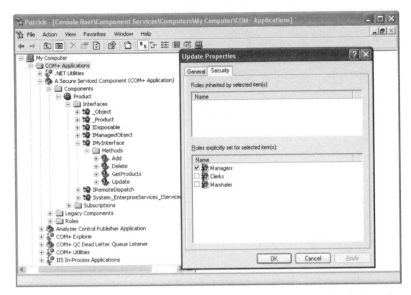

Figure 11-2   Various roles set in COM+ Services as a result of using the *SecureMethod* and *SecurityRole* attributes.

Finally, if you want only component-level access control, you can apply *SecurityRole* attributes to the class instead of the methods. In this case, you would not need to implement an interface.

The Assembly Metadata

To support role-based security, three attributes are added to the AssemblyInfo.vb file used in the "Application #91" section. The first attribute added is the *ApplicationAccessControl* attribute, which acts just like the *ComponentAccessControl* attribute but at the COM+ application level. This is the "master security switch" for the application as a whole. If this attribute is not set, security checks are not enabled for other members of the application.

```
<Assembly: ApplicationAccessControl _
    (AccessChecksLevel:=AccessChecksLevelOption.ApplicationComponent)>
```

The *AccessChecksLevelOption* enumeration has two members, *Application* and *ApplicationComponent*. The latter is the default, so the preceding statement could simply be written as follows:

```
<Assembly: ApplicationAccessControl()>
```

Role settings at the COM+ application level can be specified using the *SecurityRole* attribute, as follows:

```
<Assembly: SecurityRole("Managers", _
    Description:="Managers have complete access.", _
    SetEveryoneAccess:=False)>
<Assembly: SecurityRole("Clerks", _
    Description:="Clerks have limited method-level access.", _
    SetEveryoneAccess:=False)>
```

The use of these attributes here is not required. If application authorization is enabled, roles used in any of the components are automatically added to role lists that appear elsewhere in the COM+ application's settings. The benefit of using the attributes in AssemblyInfo.vb is that you can also pass arguments to set the *Description* and *SetEveryoneAccess* properties. If the latter is set to *True*, the Everyone user group is automatically added as a member to the role. In this application, the component is fully secured from the outset. You will have to manually add user accounts to the roles in the COM+ Services console. This is discussed in more detail in the next section.

You can see the result of using these attributes in Figure 11-3. It depicts the Properties dialog box for the serviced component, which appears in the snap-in as a "COM+ Application." (See comments on terminology in the previous topic.)

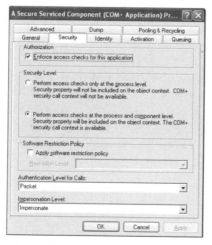

Figure 11-3   The effect of using security-related *EnterpriseServices* attributes in the AssemblyInfo.vb file is shown in this serviced component Properties dialog box.

In the Security tab, you see that Enforce Access Checks For This Application is checked. Also, the second Security Level option is selected. These settings correspond to the *ApplicationAccessControl* attribute and the *AccessChecksLevel-Option.ApplicationComponent* enumeration value, respectively.

The Windows Application

The only change made to the Windows application that consumes the serviced component is to trap an *UnauthorizedAccessException* and display instructions for adding users to the roles in COM+ Services. For example:

```
Catch expSec As UnauthorizedAccessException
    MsgBox("You are not currently authorized to retrieve products. " & _
            "To remedy this, take the following steps: 1. Close the " & _
            "application. 2. Open the COM+ snap-in and add your user " & _
            "account to the Clerks role. If not already a member, also " & _
            "add your account to the Marshaler role. 3. Restart the " & _
            "application.", MsgBoxStyle.OKOnly, Me.Text)
```

Figure 11-4 shows the Roles node expanded for the COM+ application and the author's user account after manually adding it to the Managers role.

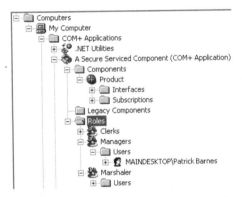

Figure 11-4   A Windows user account is made a member of the Managers role.

Notice the presence of an additional role, Marshaler. As the article "Building Secure ASP.NET Applications" explains:

The Enterprise Services infrastructure uses a number of system-level interfaces that are exposed by all serviced components. These include IManagedObject, IDisposable, *and* IServiceComponentInfo. *If access checks are enabled at the interface or method levels, the Enterprise Services infrastructure is denied access to these interfaces. As a result, Enterprise Services creates a special role called Marshaler and associates the role with these interfaces. At deployment time, application administrators need to add all users to the Marshaler role who need to access any methods or interface of the class.*

The authors then go on to write that you can automate the process of adding users by using various custom scripts.

As you experiment with the sample application and the COM+ snap-in settings, be aware that you must cycle the application for the changes to take effect. To do this, right-click the application's node in COM+ Services and then click Shut Down. Right-click the node again, and then click Start. Closing and rerunning the Windows application will achieve the same results.

Conclusion

This concludes a brief two-part series on building Enterprise Services applications. In this second installment, you learned how to apply Enterprise Services attributes to enforce role-based security at the method level. This involved several new attributes as well as an interface. For real-world deployment, it would also involve custom scripts to automate adding users to the COM+ Services roles.

12

COM Interop/PInvoke

The .NET Framework has a remarkable collection of several thousand classes, designed to handle almost every conceivable programming need. Yet there are times when the developer needs a little extra flexibility or performance and turns to legacy applications or low-level system calls. In fact, until all programs are rewritten to .NET standards, you'll probably have a continuing need to interoperate with the COM world and unmanaged code.

Although you pay a performance penalty whenever you interoperate (data marshaling and additional instructions being the culprits), you sometimes either have no choice because the required functionality doesn't yet exist in a .NET application, or you simply prefer the legacy applications or functions. This chapter describes how you can make your .NET applications use Microsoft Excel, Microsoft Word, and Microsoft Internet Explorer and how you can call unmanaged dynamic-link library (DLL) functions from managed code.

Application #93: Automate Office via COM Interop

This sample application shows you how to automate Microsoft Office from .NET.

Building Upon...

Application #7: Object-Oriented Features

New Concepts

Not every application can be all things to all people, so sometimes you'll find that you need the help of another program to accomplish your goals. For example, you might have some raw numbers you're processing in your Microsoft Visual Basic .NET application, and you decide that you need some sophisticated statistical computations done on the data. One way to meet the need is to use an Excel workbook to process the numbers.

However, you don't have to click a shortcut to call up Excel because, like all the major Microsoft Office programs, Excel exposes its object model to other programs, which can then invoke and manipulate it programmatically.

This process is known as Automation, and it lets one application (the client) create an instance of another (the server) and use the commands from the server's object model to perform a variety of tasks. This sample application shows how you can use Automation to access Microsoft Office applications from a Visual Basic .NET application.

Automation lets you use a program such as Word or Excel like a component, so you must first set a reference to the Word or Excel object library. Then you can programmatically create an instance of Word or Excel and get some work done with it.

Adding a Reference to a COM object

If you want to set a reference to Excel, for example, choose Project | Add Reference. In the Add Reference dialog box, choose the COM tab (because Office applications live in the COM world). Find the reference you need, such as *Microsoft Excel 10.0 Object Library*, click Select, and then click OK. The reference will be set and will show up in your References folder as *Excel*.

Behind the scenes, however, Microsoft Visual Studio has performed a little sleight of hand on your behalf by creating a runtime callable wrapper (RCW) around the COM component and setting the reference to the wrapper rather than to the COM component itself. The wrapper is needed because your .NET application has no idea how to interact with a COM component, which requires that you access it via interfaces—and that's just not the .NET way.

The RCW bridges the gap between .NET and COM by serving as the broker between the two worlds, translating calls from your application into the format the COM component wants and marshalling data back and forth between the two entities.

You can create an RCW in a couple ways. One is by using a command-line utility named *tlbimp* (type library importer), which is located in your FrameworkSDK\bin folder. Once you create the wrapper you can set a reference to it and access the COM component through it.

But it's much easier to simply set a reference to the COM component from within Visual Studio .NET, as described earlier, because Visual Studio .NET automatically creates the wrapper and also sets the reference to it.

If you created the reference to the Excel object library just described, here's how you can see the wrapper that was created for you. Click on the Project menu, and choose Show All Files. Then in the Project Explorer, expand the bin folder. You'll see a file named Interop.Excel.dll and, if you have other COM component references, possibly other files beginning with *Interop*.

Now that you have the wrapper and the reference, you're ready to go to work by instantiating an Excel *Application* object and using its methods. That's what we'll describe in the code walkthrough. Figure 12-1 shows the sample lunch menu, ready to be exported to Excel, where the calorie average of the foods listed will be calculated.

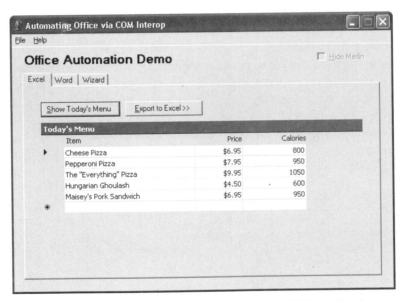

Figure 12-1   With Automation, your Visual Basic .NET application can use Microsoft Office programs such as Microsoft Excel to do work on its behalf.

Code Walkthrough

We'll show how to use Excel to perform calculations and how to use Word to do spelling checking.

Automating Excel

This code creates and fills a *DataSet* from an XML document and then binds it to a *DataGrid*. Then it exports the contents of the *DataSet* to an Excel spreadsheet and runs an Excel function that calculates the average of values in a column. First, we'll load the grid with items on a fictitious lunch menu contained in an XML document.

```
Private Sub btnGetMenu_Click(...
    ⋮
    dsMenu = New DataSet()
    dsMenu.ReadXml(Application.StartupPath & "\..\menu.xml")
    With grdMenu
        .CaptionText = "Today's Menu"
        .DataSource = dsMenu.Tables(0)
    End With
    ⋮
    btnExport.Enabled = True
End Sub
```

Now we want to export the contents of the *DataGrid* to Excel, and then run a simple *Average* function to determine the calorie average for all the foods. The Excel object model has a hierarchy from *Application* to *Workbook* to *Worksheet*. We first instantiate an *Application* object, which means we're creating an instance of Excel. Then we create a workbook and a get a reference to the first worksheet within that workbook. Note the use of *CType*, which is needed because excelBook.Worksheets(1) returns an *Object*, which then has to be cast as a worksheet object.

We make the Excel instance visible so that the user can see the data being entered into the spreadsheet. If we don't do that, all the operations will proceed, but Excel will operate invisibly. (We'll see an example of that in the Word demo.)

```
Private Sub btnExport_Click(...
    Dim excelApp As New Excel.Application()
    Dim excelBook As Excel.Workbook = excelApp.Workbooks.Add
    Dim excelWorksheet As Excel.Worksheet = _
        CType(excelBook.Worksheets(1), Excel.Worksheet)
    excelApp.Visible = True
```

Now we use properties and methods of the *Worksheet* object to set the column headers and to format the cells and columns. We use the Excel *Range* object to refer to the set of cells we're about to work on, and then we apply changes as needed.

```
    Dim rng As Excel.Range = excelWorksheet.Range("A1")
    With rng
        .ColumnWidth = 21.71
        .Value = "Item"
        .Font.Bold = True
    End With

    rng = excelWorksheet.Range("B1")
    With rng
        .ColumnWidth = 9
```

```
        .HorizontalAlignment = Excel.Constants.xlRight
        .Font.Bold = True
        .Value = "Price"
    End With

    rng = excelWorksheet.Range("C1")
    With rng
        .ColumnWidth = 9
        .HorizontalAlignment = Excel.Constants.xlRight
        .Font.Bold = True
        .Value = "Calories"
    End With
```

Now we're ready to export the data from our *DataGrid*. We'll use a counter that starts at 2 so that the data will be placed beginning in row 2 of the worksheet, following the column headers. Then we'll loop through the *Rows* collection of the *DataSet* and write the data in each row to the cells in Excel.

```
    Dim i As Integer = 2
    With excelWorksheet
        Dim dr As DataRow
        For Each dr In dsMenu.Tables(0).Rows
            .Range("A" & i.ToString).Value = dr("Item")
            .Range("B" & i.ToString).Value = dr("Price")
            .Range("C" & i.ToString).Value = dr("Calories")
            i += 1
        Next
    End With
```

We want to format the bottom row differently from the data, so we select row 8 from column A to column C and make it Red and Bold. We also set the first cell in the range to *Average Calories*. Note that *A1* in this case doesn't mean the first cell of the *Worksheet*, but the first cell of the range in question, A8 to C8.

```
    rng = excelWorksheet.Range("A8:C8")
    With rng
        .Font.Color = RGB(255, 0, 0)
        .Font.Bold = True
        .Range("A1").Value = "Average Calories"
    End With
```

Finally, we select the cell that will display the calorie average, and then set the *Average* formula using the *FormulaR1C1* property, which uses numbers to label both rows and columns and makes it easy for us to refer to the current row minus 6 through the current row minus 2. Then we *AutoFit* all columns and go to the first cell of the sheet. The user is provided with the average calorie count of the items in his lunch menu.

```
    With excelWorksheet
        .Range("C8").Select()
        excelApp.ActiveCell.FormulaR1C1 = "=AVERAGE(R[-6]C:R[-2]C)"
        .UsedRange.Columns.AutoFit()
```

(continued)

```
        .Range("A1").Select()
    End With
End Sub
```

Automating Word

If you want to add spelling checking capability to any application, one way to do it is by using the Microsoft Word spelling checker. This example shows how to do that.

The *btnSpellCheck_Click* event procedure lets the user run the Word spelling checker against whatever text is in the *RichTextBox* control (loaded earlier with the *btnBrowseWord_Click* procedure). First, we instantiate the Word *Application* object. Notice that, unlike the Excel example, we don't make Word visible, because it doesn't need to be seen to do a spelling check. We want to let the user either check the entire document or choose a portion of the document to be checked, so we test the length of the *RichTextBox* selected text. If it's greater than zero, we check only that portion; otherwise, we check the entire document.

```
Private Sub btnSpellCheck_Click(...
    Dim wordApp As New Word.Application()
    Dim hasNoSpellingErrors As Boolean
    Dim portionChecked As String

    If Len(rtfDocument.SelectedText) > 0 Then
        portionChecked = "text"
        hasNoSpellingErrors = _
            wordApp.CheckSpelling(rtfDocument.SelectedText)
    Else
        portionChecked = "document"
        hasNoSpellingErrors = wordApp.CheckSpelling(rtfDocument.Text)
    End If

    Dim spellCheckResponse As String
    If hasNoSpellingErrors Then
        spellCheckResponse = "Congratulations, your " & portionChecked & _
            " has no spelling errors."
    Else
        spellCheckResponse = "Your " & portionChecked & _
            " has spelling errors."
    End If

    MessageBox.Show(spellCheckResponse, "Spelling Check Results", _
        MessageBoxButtons.OK, MessageBoxIcon.Information)
End Sub
```

This example simply displays a dialog box telling you whether your spelling check succeeded or failed. However, you could enhance this functionality to create a more feature-rich application that mimics the Word spelling checker, including such features as allowing the use of custom dictionaries, and more.

Conclusion

When Visual Basic .NET doesn't do all that you need, you can enlist the services of other applications, such as those in the Microsoft Office suite. Once you set a reference to the object library you need, Visual Studio .NET automatically creates the necessary runtime callable wrapper to let your .NET application interoperate with the COM component. There's almost no limit to what you can do with such interoperation if you're willing to learn the object models of the applications you choose to automate.

Application #94: Automate Internet Explorer via COM Interop

This sample application demonstrates two ways of automating Internet Explorer.

Building Upon...

Application #9: Use Callbacks
Application #84: Asynchronous Calls
Application #93: Automate Office via COM Interop

New Concepts

Just as you can automate Microsoft Office applications such as Word and Excel (as shown in the "Application #93" section), you can also automate Internet Explorer. You might want to allow a user to browse the Web directly within your application, or you might want to let the user open Internet Explorer to a Web site of her choice from within your application. This sample application demonstrates how to do both.

Using the ActiveX Internet Explorer Web Browser Control

You're probably familiar with using ActiveX controls in Microsoft Visual Basic 6, and the procedure for using them in .NET is very similar. You need to add the Microsoft Web Browser control to your Toolbox so that you can place it on a form. To do this, select the Toolbox tab on which you want the control to appear. Then right-click the Toolbox and choose Add/Remove Items. The Customize Toolbox dialog box appears, with tabs containing COM components and .NET Framework components. On the COM Components tab, locate Microsoft Web Browser and check the box beside it. Click OK.

The control appears on your Toolbox with the name Microsoft Web Browser and a globe icon. Now you can place the control on a form and use its properties and methods, which we'll describe in the code walkthrough.

When you put the Microsoft Web Browser control on a form, Visual Studio .NET adds a couple references (AxSHDocVw and SHDocVw) to Microsoft Internet Controls in the project References folder and creates runtime callable wrappers for them both. (See the "Application #93" section for more information on RCWs.)

Automating Internet Explorer

Automating Microsoft Internet Explorer is much like automating Word or Excel, as demonstrated in the "Application #93" section. You set a reference to the object library of the COM application you intend to automate, and then you manipulate it programmatically. To set the reference, right-click your References folder, and choose Add Reference. In the Add Reference dialog box, select the COM tab and locate Microsoft Internet Controls. Click the Select button and the OK button. Visual Studio .NET adds SHDocVw to your References folder and creates an RCW for it. Note that if you had previously put the Microsoft Web Browser control on a form in the project, the SHDocVw reference would already have been set and you'd be ready to go.

Microsoft Internet Explorer offers you a number of ways to customize its user interface, including whether or not to display the address bar, the toolbar, and the status bar. The browser can be displayed in full-screen mode, in which the status bar, toolbar, menu bar, and title bar are hidden. It also offers a theater mode option, which is similar to the full-screen option but which includes minimal navigational buttons and a status bar in the upper right corner.

Code Walkthrough

Now let's see how we can put these concepts into action.

Coding the Web Browser Control

The Microsoft Web Browser control has a number of methods that let you navigate the Internet just as if you were using a full-scale, standalone browser. The first illustration of that is the following procedure, which uses the *Navigate* method of the control to display a Web page, based on the URL entered in a text box:

```
Private Sub btnGo_Click(...
    axBrowser.Navigate(txtAddress.Text)
End Sub
```

It's important for you to know when the document has been loaded into the browser control so that you can begin to work with the document. The *DocumentComplete* event provides the necessary notification by firing when the document has been completely loaded. In the following code, we assign the loaded document to *axDoc*, which was declared at the class level as an *mshtml.IHTMLDocument2* interface object. This is an interface you can use to retrieve information about the document, and to examine and modify the HTML elements and text within the document.

> **Caution**   Be careful that you don't attempt to assign *axDoc* somewhere other than this handler because you'll get a null object reference if the document has not been completely loaded.

```
Private axDoc As mshtml.IHTMLDocument2 ' declared at the class level
  ⋮
Private Sub axBrowser_DocumentComplete(ByVal sender As System.Object, _
    ByVal e As AxSHDocVw.DWebBrowserEvents2_DocumentCompleteEvent) _
    Handles axBrowser.DocumentComplete
    axDoc = CType(axBrowser.Document, mshtml.IHTMLDocument2)
    txtAddress.Text = axDoc.url
    HandleNavButtons()
End Sub
```

To enable the user to navigate backward and forward through the history list, the *HandleNavButtons* procedure determines whether the history has entries and enables or disables the back and forward buttons accordingly. The *history* property is a member of the *mshtml.IHTMLWindow2* interface, so we access it through the *parentWindow* property of *axDoc*.

```
Protected Sub HandleNavButtons()
    If axDoc Is Nothing OrElse axDoc.parentWindow.history.length = 0 Then
        btnBack.Enabled = False
        btnForward.Enabled = False
    Else
        btnBack.Enabled = True
        btnForward.Enabled = True
    End If
End Sub
```

Now that we've set up all the prerequisites, moving backward and forward is easy. We simply use the *history* property *go* method to move one step ahead or one step backward in the history list.

```
Private Sub btnBack_Click(...
    axDoc.parentWindow.history.go(-1)
    txtAddress.Text = axDoc.url
End Sub

Private Sub btnForward_Click(...
    axDoc.parentWindow.history.go(+1)
    txtAddress.Text = axDoc.url
End Sub
```

Coding Internet Explorer as a Standalone Browser

We want to enable the user to set display options before opening the browser, including window size and position and which bars to display. Figure 12-2 shows the available choices as well as the result after navigating to a site on the Web.

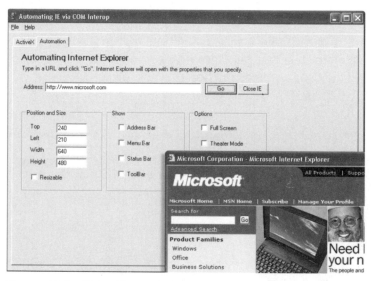

Figure 12-2   Using Automation, your application can launch Microsoft Internet Explorer and navigate the World Wide Web.

If the user chooses either the full-screen or theater-mode option, it's not appropriate to try to set the window size or the bars to be displayed. So we'll disable those option groups accordingly, using the *Options_CheckedChanged* procedure, which is an event handler for both the *chkFullScreen* and *chkTheaterMode* check boxes. We also want to prevent full-screen and theater mode from being selected together, but we don't want to use radio buttons, so we handle the issue in the following code by unchecking either one when the other is checked.

```
Private Sub Options_CheckedChanged(ByVal sender As System.Object, _
    ByVal e As System.EventArgs) Handles chkFullScreen.CheckedChanged, _
    chkTheaterMode.CheckedChanged
    Dim isChecked As Boolean = chkFullScreen.Checked _
        Or chkTheaterMode.Checked
    grpShow.Enabled = Not isChecked
    grpPosition.Enabled = Not isChecked

    Dim sndr As CheckBox = CType(sender, CheckBox)
    If sndr.Name = "chkFullScreen" Then
        If chkFullScreen.Checked Then
            chkTheaterMode.Checked = False
        End If
    ElseIf sndr.Name = "chkTheaterMode" Then
```

```
        If chkTheaterMode.Checked Then
            chkFullScreen.Checked = False
        End If
    End If
End Sub
```

With the *btnGo2_Click* procedure, we'll open Microsoft Internet Explorer and configure its user interface based on the options selected by the user. We begin by instantiating an *SHDocVw.InternetExplorer* object, provided it doesn't already exist.

```
Private Sub btnGo2_Click(...
    If ieBrowser Is Nothing Then
        ieBrowser = New SHDocVw.InternetExplorer()
    End If
```

Now we get to customize the user interface before launching the browser. Note that both the address bar and the menu bar will be displayed only if the toolbar is also displayed.

```
    With ieBrowser
        If grpShow.Enabled Then
            .AddressBar = chkAddressBar.Checked
            .MenuBar = chkMenuBar.Checked
            .StatusBar = chkStatusBar.Checked
            .ToolBar = CInt(chkToolBar.Checked)
        End If
        .FullScreen = chkFullScreen.Checked
        .TheaterMode = chkTheaterMode.Checked
        If grpPosition.Enabled Then
            If IsNumeric(txtTop.Text) Then
                .Top = CInt(txtTop.Text)
            End If
            ⋮
            .Resizable = chkResizable.Checked
        End If
    End If
```

Finally, we make the browser visible and navigate to the URL the user entered. Note the use of the hourglass cursor and of the overloaded *Show* method of the status form, which takes a message-to-be-displayed parameter.

> **Important**   Remember to set the *Visible* property of the browser object or else it won't show up.

```
        Me.Cursor = Cursors.WaitCursor
        frmStatus = New frmStatus()
        frmStatus.Show("Connecting to Web page and processing HTML. " & _
            " Please stand by...")
```

(continued)

```
            .Visible = True
            .Navigate(txtAddress2.Text)
      End With
End Sub
```

We want to know when the document has completely loaded, and the *DocumentComplete* event provides that notification. However, its event procedure gets executed on a different thread from the one that created the form. This poses a challenge: we can modify the user interface only through the same thread that created it because the underlying user-interface classes are not thread safe. To solve this dilemma, we've marshaled the information back to the main thread by using the form's *Invoke* method to use a delegate to call the *HideStatus* method, which hides the status form and restores the cursor to normal. (See the "Application #9: Use Callbacks" section in Chapter 2 and the "Application #84: Asynchronous Calls" section in Chapter 9 for more information on asynchronous calls and delegates.)

```
Private Sub ieBrowser_DocumentComplete(ByVal pDisp As Object, _
    ByRef URL As Object) Handles ieBrowser.DocumentComplete
    Me.Invoke(New HideStatusDelegate(AddressOf Me.HideStatus))
End Sub

Delegate Sub HideStatusDelegate()
Protected Sub HideStatus()
    frmStatus.Hide()
    Me.Cursor = Cursors.Default
End Sub
```

Conclusion

You can let your user have free access to the Internet directly from your application with Microsoft Internet Explorer. You can either use the ActiveX Web Browser control, which becomes a part of your form, or invoke Internet Explorer in standalone mode. In either case, the object model is the same, except that the Web Browser control ignores properties such as *FullScreen* and *TheaterMode* that make sense only in the full browser.

Application #95: Make Win32 API Calls

This sample application demonstrates how to use Win32 API function calls in Visual Basic .NET.

New Concepts

Although the .NET Framework provides thousands of classes, designed to meet almost every programming requirement, you might occasionally want to access low-level operating system functions more directly. In such situations, it's time for placing a call to the Win32 API. Platform Invoke, or PInvoke, is a service provided by the .NET Framework to enable managed code to call unmanaged functions in DLLs.

Uses for Win32 API Calls

Imagine that you want to determine all the processes that are currently executing, you'd like a list of all active windows, or you want to make a window's title bar flash to alert the user. Instead of writing code for these tasks, you can take advantage of the large number of functions already existing as part of the operating system. These functions are found in a number of DLLs, of which the most commonly used are *Kernel32.dll*, which offers functions for managing memory and resources; *User32.dll*, which lets you manage messages, menus, and communications; and *GDI32.dll*, which has device output functions such as those for drawing and font management.

Collectively, they're referred to as the *Win32 API*, and each of these DLLs is brimming with useful functions you can use right away. But before you rush into using them, be aware that calling DLL functions can be complex, the code in the functions is unmanaged, and the .NET Framework offers many of the same capabilities in an easier-to-use package.

Using the Declare Syntax

To use a Win32 API function, you must first declare it, either with a *Declare* statement or with the *DLLImport* method attribute. A *Declare* statement lets your application know that you want to use an external function found in a DLL. The syntax looks like this:

```
Public Declare Function GetWindowsDirectory _
    Lib "kernel32" _
    Alias "GetWindowsDirectoryA" _
    (ByVal lpBuffer As StringBuilder, ByVal nSize As Long) As Long
```

The *GetWindowsDirectory* function retrieves the path to the current Windows directory. *Lib* specifies the name of the DLL in which the function lives. *Alias* refers to the actual name of the function within the DLL, a feature that lets you *Declare* using any name you want to, as long as you *Alias* to the actual function name. So our example function could have been named *FindWindowsFolder*, for example, and that's the name we'd use when calling it.

When a Win32 API function accepts a string parameter, the DLL has two versions of the function: an ANSI version that ends in *A* (for example, *GetWindowsDirectoryA*), and a Unicode version that ends in *W* (for example, *GetWindowsDirectoryW*).

Once you've declared your function, you can use it to find out where Windows lives. You call your function by passing it two parameters: *lpBuffer*, which is a *String* (or *StringBuilder*, as in our previous example), and *nSize*, which is a *Long* that you'll set to the size of the buffer you're providing. When the function returns, it places the path to Windows in the buffer and returns the size of the path. You could call it as shown in the following example, which you could put in a wrapper class for convenience.

```
Private Function LocateWindowsDir() As String
    Dim sb As New StringBuilder(255)
    Dim bufSize As Long = 255
    Dim winSize As Long
    Dim winFolder As String

    winSize = GetWindowsDirectory(sb, bufSize)
    If winSize > 0 Then
        winFolder = sb.ToString().Substring(0, winSize)
    End If
    Return winFolder
End Function
```

Win32 API declarations must be done in a class or module. In many cases, you'll find it convenient to create a class that serves as a wrapper around your declared functions, making it easy to call the functions as methods of the class. We've taken that approach in this sample application

As an alternative to *Declare*, you can also use *DLLImport*, an attribute you can apply to a method that points to an external DLL. See the sample code and the additional reference material for uses of *DLLImport*. Figure 12-3 shows the ability to uses a Win32 API call to find and display an active window.

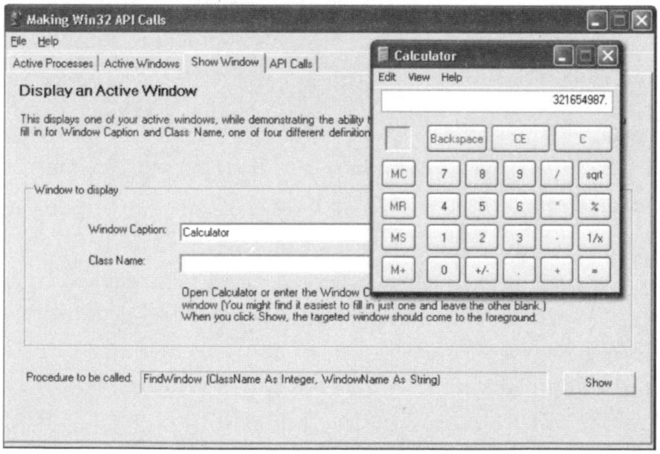

Figure 12-3 Platform Invoke makes it possible for your application to make calls to functions in unmanaged Win32 API DLLs, including listing active processes, displaying selected active windows, and gathering system information.

Passing Structures

Some DLL functions expect more than simple parameters. Many of them provide a wealth of information, and the easiest way to return it compactly is via a *Structure*, which is a type that you define that is a lot like a class. You can create an instance of a *Structure,* and it can have constructors, constants, fields, methods, properties, and more. However it's different from a class in that you can't inherit a *Structure*, nor can it inherit from another class.

One function that requires a *Structure* to be passed to it is *GetVersionEx*, which reports on the operating system's version information, and whose required *Structure* looks like this:

```
<StructLayout(LayoutKind.Sequential)> _
Public Structure OSVersionInfo
    Public OSVersionInfoSize As Integer
    Public majorVersion As Integer
    Public minorVersion As Integer
    Public buildNumber As Integer
    Public platformId As Integer
    <MarshalAs(UnmanagedType.ByValTStr, SizeConst:=128)> _
    Public versionString As String
End Structure
```

When you're about to call *GetVersionEx*, you instantiate an *OSVersionInfo* object and call it as shown in the following example. When the function call returns, you have access to all the properties of the *versionInfo* structure. (See the documentation for information on the *StructLayout* and *MarshalAs* attributes.)

```
Private Sub btnGetOSVersion_Click(...
    Dim versionInfo As New ApiWrapper.OSVersionInfo()
    versionInfo.OSVersionInfoSize = Marshal.SizeOf(versionInfo)
    ApiWrapper.GetVersionEx(versionInfo)
    txtFunctionOutput.Text = "OS Version is: " & _
        versionInfo.majorVersion.ToString() & "." & _
        versionInfo.minorVersion.ToString() & vbCrLf
    txtFunctionOutput.Text += "Build Number is: " & _
        versionInfo.buildNumber.ToString()
End Sub
```

Code Walkthrough

Now let's see how we can use these concepts to get a variety of information about the operating system, currently active windows and processes, and more. We'll examine each tab of the sample application in turn.

Show Active Processes

The *btnRefreshActiveProcesses_Click* procedure fills a list box with all the currently active processes. It does this by calling the *APIWrapper* function *Enum-Windows*, which is a wrapper for the Win32 API function of the same name. It uses a delegate to specify that the *FillActiveProcessesList* function should be called once per active process. Because *EnumWindows* is unmanaged code, you have to create a delegate to allow it to call *FillActiveProcessesList*, which is managed code. All three procedures are shown in the following code.

```
Private Sub btnRefreshActiveProcesses_Click(...
    lvwProcessList.Items.Clear()
    ApiWrapper.EnumWindows(New _
    ApiWrapper.EnumWindowsCallback(AddressOf _
        FillActiveProcessesList), 0)
End Sub

Public Declare Function EnumWindows Lib "user32.dll" _
    Alias "EnumWindows" (ByVal callback As EnumWindowsCallback, _
    ByVal lParam As Integer) As Integer

Public Delegate Function EnumWindowsCallback(ByVal hWnd As Integer, _
    ByVal lParam As Integer) As Boolean
```

To provide a list of active processes, the following function is called once by *EnumWindows* for each active process. It gets the Window caption and class name and updates the *ListView* of the active processes. Take a look at the Win32 API functions in the *APIWrapper* class, and note that they're declared differently than in Visual Basic 6. All *Long*s have been replaced with *Integer*s, and *String*s have been replaced with *StringBuilder*s.

```
Function FillActiveProcessesList(ByVal hWnd As Integer, _
    ByVal lParam As Integer) As Boolean
    Dim windowText As New StringBuilder(STRING_BUFFER_LENGTH)
    Dim className As New StringBuilder(STRING_BUFFER_LENGTH)

    ApiWrapper.GetWindowText(hWnd, windowText, STRING_BUFFER_LENGTH)
    ApiWrapper.GetClassName(hWnd, className, STRING_BUFFER_LENGTH)

    Dim processItem As New ListViewItem(windowText.ToString, 0)
    processItem.SubItems.Add(className.ToString)
    processItem.SubItems.Add(hWnd.ToString)
    lvwProcessList.Items.Add(processItem)

    Return True
End Function
```

Show Active Windows

Here we're doing almost exactly what we did in the preceding example, except this time we want to show only those processes that represent active, visible windows. So we call the *FillActiveWindowsList* procedure via *API-Wrapper.EnumWindowsDllImport*, which works just like *EnumWindows* except that it's defined using *DllImport* instead of *Declare*.

```
Private Sub btnRefreshActiveWindows_Click(...
    lstActiveWindows.Items.Clear()
    APIWrapper.EnumWindowsDllImport(New _
    APIWrapper.EnumWindowsCallback(AddressOf _
        FillActiveWindowsList), 0)
End Sub

<DllImport("user32.dll", EntryPoint:="EnumWindows", SetLastError:=True, _
CharSet:=CharSet.Ansi, ExactSpelling:=True, _
CallingConvention:=CallingConvention.StdCall)> _
Public Shared Function EnumWindowsDllImport(ByVal callback _
As EnumWindowsCallback, ByVal lParam As Integer) As Integer
End Function
```

This function is called once for each active process by *EnumWindows*. It passes the handle of the process to *ProcessIsActiveWindow* to verify that it is a valid window, and it updates the active windows *Listbox* if it is. You should review the sample code's *ProcessIsActiveWindow* procedure, which calls various *APIWrapper* functions to determine whether a windows process is a valid active window.

```
Function FillActiveWindowsList(ByVal hWnd As Integer, _
    ByVal lParam As Integer) As Boolean
    Dim windowText As New StringBuilder(STRING_BUFFER_LENGTH)
    ApiWrapper.GetWindowText(hWnd, windowText, STRING_BUFFER_LENGTH)
    If ProcessIsActiveWindow(hWnd) Then
        lstActiveWindows.Items.Add(windowText)
    End If
    Return True
End Function
```

Show an Active Window

When you want an active window to be displayed in the foreground, you can use the *ShowWindow* Win32 API call to make it so. The following procedure finds an active window based on the values in the Window Caption and Class Name text boxes and then brings it to the foreground. It calls one of four overloads for the Win32 API function *FindWindow* in the *APIWrapper* class that allow either a *String* or an *Integer* to be passed to the class name and window name. If either of the fields is blank, passing a 0 to the parameter marshals NULL to the function call.

```
Private Sub btnShowWindow_Click(...
    Dim hWnd As Integer
```

(continued)

```
     If txtWindowCaption.Text = "" And txtClassName.Text = "" Then
         hWnd = ApiWrapper.FindWindowAny(0, 0)
     ElseIf txtWindowCaption.Text = "" And txtClassName.Text <> "" Then
         hWnd = ApiWrapper.FindWindowNullWindowCaption(txtClassName.Text, 0)
     ElseIf txtWindowCaption.Text <> "" And txtClassName.Text = "" Then
         hWnd = ApiWrapper.FindWindowNullClassName(0, txtWindowCaption.Text)
     Else
         hWnd = ApiWrapper.FindWindow(txtClassName.Text, _
             txtWindowCaption.Text)
     End If

     If hWnd = 0 Then
         MsgBox("Specified window is not running.", _
             MsgBoxStyle.Exclamation, Me.Text)
     Else
         ApiWrapper.SetForegroundWindow(hWnd)
         If ApiWrapper.IsIconic(hWnd) Then
             ApiWrapper.ShowWindow(hWnd, ApiWrapper.SW_RESTORE)
         Else
             ApiWrapper.ShowWindow(hWnd, ApiWrapper.SW_SHOW)
         End If
     End If
End Sub
```

FindWindow searches for a window by class name and window name. *FindWindowAny* takes two *Integer* parameters and finds any available window. *FindWindowNullClassName* attempts to locate a window by window name alone. *FindWindowNullWindowCaption* attempts to locate a window by class name alone.

Various API Calls

On the final tab of the sample form, you'll find a variety of useful Win32 API calls. Set breakpoints behind each button, and see how they utilize the Win32 API calls.

Conclusion

In this sample application, we've shown that although the .NET Framework has almost every functionality you might need, sometimes you just have to get back to basics and do a low-level call. You've seen that Platform Invoke (PInvoke) is a way for managed code to call unmanaged functions located in DLLs. Keep in mind that because Win32 API functions are case sensitive, you should alias the function names to fit your own naming conventions. You can use *StringBuilders* instead of *String* for most Win32 API function calls. We recommend that you build a wrapper class around your Win32 API function calls. It will make calling them much easier.

13

Visual Studio .NET

Microsoft Visual Studio .NET offers a powerful development environment right out of the box. However, you can make it even more powerful by creating custom Add-ins to extend its features. This chapter examines how to create and deploy Add-ins for Visual Studio .NET.

Application #96: Create a Visual Studio .NET Add-In

During a development project, you might find yourself creating assorted utilities to perform various coding or resource management tasks. Often, these utilities end up as stand-alone applications that require you to leave the Microsoft Visual Studio integrated development environment (IDE) to use them. Add-ins provide a powerful way for you to incorporate custom functionality into the IDE. The Add-ins can even interact with and modify the IDE.

Building Upon...

Application #4: *Try/Catch/Finally*
Application #7: Object-Oriented Features

New Concepts

Visual Studio .NET provides a set of classes that allow you to automate and extend the IDE's features. The *EnvDTE* and *Extensibility* assemblies expose namespaces by the same names that contain the class interfaces necessary for creating Visual Studio .NET Add-ins.

> **Tip** The *EnvDTE* and *Extensibility* documentation is part of the Visual Studio documentation, not the .NET Framework SDK.

The *IDTExtensibility2* Interface

The *IDTExtensibility2* interface defines the methods that allow your Add-in to respond when Visual Studio loads and unloads. The interface exposes five methods: *OnConnection, OnDisconnection, OnAddInsUpdate, OnStartup-Complete*, and *OnBeginShutdown*. *OnConnection* fires when the Add-in is loaded, and *OnDisconnection* fires when it is unloaded. *OnAddInsUpdate* fires in both cases. *OnStartupComplete* fires when Visual Studio is done starting up and *OnBeginShutdown* fires when Visual Studio is closing. The most important of these is *OnConnection*, as this is where your Add-in is initialized and can modify toolbars and menus to make itself accessible to the user.

The *IDTCommandTarget* Interface

The *IDCommandTarget* interface allows your Add-in to receive named commands from Visual Studio. The interface exposes two methods, *QueryStatus* and *Exec*. The environment uses *QueryStatus* to determine what commands are valid on an Add-in. For a simple Add-in, all commands might always be valid, but for more complex Add-ins, you can enable and disable commands as necessary. For example, a particular command might be valid only if text is currently selected in a code window. Visual Studio calls the *Exec* method in response to a user action and passes in the name of the command to execute. Your Add-in can then perform its work.

The *DTE* Class

The hosting environment passes in an *EnvDTE.DTE* instance when it calls your Add-in's *OnConnection* method. This reference serves as the entry point to the Visual Studio automation object model. Your Add-in code uses this reference to affect the design-time environment. The *DTE* class exposes aspects of the environment through properties such as *Documents, Commands, Solution*, and *StatusBar*. After learning the two interfaces just discussed, you should focus on learning the *DTE* object model.

Debugging and Installation

Once you have implemented the necessary interfaces, you'll start debugging your Add-in. When you run your project, a new instance of Visual Studio will launch and your Add-in will load, depending on the settings you chose in the

Add-In Creation wizard. Invoke your Add-in through the commands defined, and debug your code as normal.

The Add-In Creation wizard creates a setup project for installing your Add-in. The installer copies the Add-in's assembly to the target machine and edits the registry to expose the Add-in to Visual Studio. Anytime you make a change to your Add-in that would affect the registry—such as modifying code that affects the IDE's command bars—you should rebuild and reinstall the Add-in. This will ensure that the registry is kept up to date with your Add-in.

> **Tip**   If your Add-in's buttons are not appearing as expected, you should close all instances of Visual Studio and run the Add-in's installer from the file system. This will ensure that all the necessary registry settings are set correctly.

Code Walkthrough

The sample application demonstrates how to use the Add-In Creation wizard and implement the *IDTExtensibility2* and *IDTCommandTarget* interfaces to create a Visual Studio .NET Add-in. The Add-in provides an interface for modifying text selected in the code editor.

The Add-In Wizard

If you want to create your own Add-in from scratch, you can create the starting point for the sample Add-in by creating a new Add-in project. The Visual Studio .NET Add-in type is in the Other Projects/Extensibility Projects folder. On page one of the wizard, select Visual Basic. On page two, uncheck Microsoft VSMacros IDE, as this Add-in will run only in Visual Studio. On page three, enter a user-friendly name and description. This information will appear in the Visual Studio Add-In Manager. On page four, check the check box for creating a Tools menu item. Accept the defaults for the rest of the wizard.

Using the *IDTExtensibility2* Interface

The sample application Add-in builds upon the code generated by the Extensibility wizard. Visual Studio passes in a reference to itself in the *application* parameter of *OnConnect*. This reference provides the entry point back into Visual Studio that your code uses to modify the environment. The *OnConnect* method starts by storing this reference in a module-level variable named *applicationObject*. A reference to the environment's *AddIn* object is also stored in the *addInInstance* variable.

```
applicationObject = CType(application, EnvDTE.DTE)
addInInstance = CType(addInInst, EnvDTE.AddIn)
```

The next line identifies when this Add-in is being launched by comparing the value of the *connectMode* parameter with some values from the *Extensibility.ext_ConnectMode* enumeration. You can use this comparison, for example, to determine whether the Add-in is being launched through the command line.

```
If connectMode = Extensibility.ext_ConnectMode.ext_cm_UISetup Or _
    connectMode = ext_ConnectMode.ext_cm_AfterStartup Then
```

The Add-in next deletes any existing commands that the environment might have installed for it by looping through the *applicationObject Commands* collection. Call the *GetEnumerator* method to retrieve this collections enumerator.

```
Dim coll As IEnumerator = _
    applicationObject.Commands.GetEnumerator()
Do While coll.MoveNext
    CommandObj = CType(coll.Current, Command)
    If CommandObj.Name = _
        "101Utilities.Connect.ChangeCase" Then
        CommandObj.Delete()
    End If
Loop
```

Adding a command to the environment is a two-step process. First you define a *Command* object using the *AddNamedCommand* method of the *EnvDTE Commands* property. This method requires the name of the command, a reference to the *AddIn* to execute the command on, and numerous display options such as button text, ToolTips, and image. The last parameter determines whether the command will be enabled by default when the Add-in is loaded. This Add-in specifies that the command should be disabled by default.

```
CommandObj = applicationObject.Commands.AddNamedCommand(objAddIn, _
  "ChangeCase", "Change Case", _
  "Executes the command for 101Utilities", True, 59, Nothing, _
  vsCommandStatus.vsCommandStatusUnsupported)
```

The second step is to add a control to the interface for the newly created command. The following code adds a control to the Tools menu of the IDE:

```
CommandBarControlObj = _
  CommandObj.AddControl(applicationObject.CommandBars.Item("Tools"))
```

Using the *IDTCommandTarget* Interface

Visual Studio passes in the name of a command to the *QueryStatus* method of the *IDTCommandTarget* interface. Your code should evaluate whether that command is valid at that time and assign an appropriate value from the *EnvDTE.vsCommandStatus* enumeration. The sample Add-in's *101Utilities.Con-*

nect.ChangeCase command is valid only if text is selected in the editor. First, try to get a *TextSelection* reference.

```
Dim tsSelectedText As TextSelection
Try
    tsSelectedText = CType(applicationObject.ActiveDocument.Selection, _
      TextSelection)
Catch
    statusOption = vsCommandStatus.vsCommandStatusUnsupported
End Try
```

Now that we have a *TextSelection*, check to make sure there is text in it, as it's possible to have a *TextSelection* with a length of zero. If there is text selected, enable the command by indicating that it's both supported and enabled.

```
If tsSelectedText.Text.Length > 0 Then
    statusOption = CType(vsCommandStatus.vsCommandStatusEnabled + _
      vsCommandStatus.vsCommandStatusSupported, vsCommandStatus)
End If
```

The environment calls the *Exec* method to invoke a command on an Add-in. This method retrieves the currently selected text and passes it to an instance of the *MainForm* dialog.

```
Dim tsSelectedText As TextSelection
Try
    tsSelectedText = CType(applicationObject.ActiveDocument.Selection, _
      TextSelection)
Catch x As Exception
    MessageBox.Show("You must have selected text to perform this action.")
    Exit Sub
End Try
Dim frmMain As New MainForm()
frmMain.StringValue = tsSelectedText.Text
```

The *MainForm* form provides a visual interface for a user to convert the supplied text to an uppercase or lowercase format. If the user clicks OK, the edited text is supplied to the *TextSelection* in the IDE.

```
If frmMain.ShowDialog() = DialogResult.OK Then
    tsSelectedText.Text = frmMain.StringValue
End If
```

Conclusion

Visual Studio .NET provides a rich extensibility framework and automation API. You can use these features to create powerful extensions to the IDE that are easily distributable with the included setup project.

14

Securing Applications

Security is paramount, and in this chapter, we'll show how you can use a user's Microsoft Windows identity and role membership to control access to protected resources. We'll also demonstrate how you can implement your own custom authentication schemes. We'll walk you through using hash algorithms to uniquely identify documents, messages, or both. And finally, we'll show how you can enhance security by implementing encryption.

Application #97: Implement Windows Role-Based Security

This sample application shows you how to retrieve the identity and group membership for a Windows user of your application. The sample application demonstrates how to selectively enable certain application features (such as controls) based on the user's identity. The sample form has two tabs. The first tab shows how you can gather information about the user's identity and the groups the user belongs to. The second tab demonstrates selective access to a protected form, based on the groups the user belongs to.

Building Upon...

Application #4: *Try/Catch/Finally*
Application #7: Object-Oriented Features

New Concepts

The .NET Framework provides a coordinated set of classes for managing security, making it easier than ever to control access to protected resources and to specific portions of your code.

Leveraging Windows Security

The techniques we'll demonstrate in this sample application give you access to the Windows identity of the current user, and they show you how to apply security measures based on the user's identity and group membership. The classes we'll focus on are found in the *System.Security.Principal* and *System.Security.Permissions* namespaces, and they are as follows:

- ■ *WindowsIdentity*   A class that represents a user account.

- ■ *WindowsPrincipal*   A class that incorporates both the user's identity and group membership.

- ■ *PrincipalPermission*   A class that lets you stipulate that the current operation can be carried out only by one or more principals that you specify. For example, you can stipulate that only User1 can run a particular procedure, or that only members of Group1 can do so. Further, you can specify that User1 can run the procedure only if she is also a member of Group1. You can also combine requirements for multiple identities, groups, or both through methods such as *Intersect* and *Union*. See the code walkthrough for examples.

Windows Principals

Once you have identified who the user is and which groups she belongs to, you can authorize her to take further actions. But first you must be sure you know who she is. To accomplish that, you can start with the *WindowsIdentity* class, which represents the identity of the current user. This class gets its information from the operating system and its key properties include the following:

- ■ *AuthenticationType*   Indicates how the user was authenticated

- ■ *IsAnonymous*   Indicates whether the system considers the user to be anonymous

- ■ *IsAuthenticated*   Indicates whether Windows has authenticated the user

- ■ *IsGuest*   Indicates whether the user is using a Guest account

- ■ *IsSystem*   Indicates whether the user is using a System account

- ■ *Name*   Specifies the name with which the user logged on to Windows

- ■ *Token*   Specifies the user's Windows account token

You can use these properties to make decisions on whether and how to grant a user access to sensitive resources. For example, you might choose to allow such access only if the user has been authenticated by Windows and is not using a Guest account. Figure 14-1 shows the result of a successful demand that the current user be part of the Administrators group.

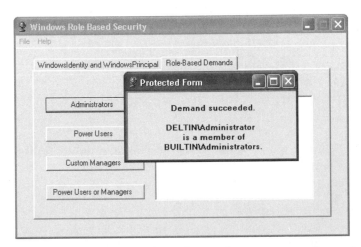

Figure 14-1 With role-based security, you can easily control user access to resources based not only on user identities but also on the groups (roles) to which they belong.

With the *WindowsIdentity* in hand, you can create a *WindowsPrincipal* object based on the identity. The *WindowsPrincipal*, which also gets its data from the operating system, will contain not only the user's identity but also the groups to which the user belongs. With these elements, you're able to authorize the user based either on her identity or on her group membership, as we'll describe in the next section.

Code Walkthrough

First, at the class level, we use the *GetCurrent* method to create a *Windows-Identity* object that represents the current user. Then we create a *Windows-Principal* object based on the *WindowsIdentity* object.

```
Private m_idWindows As WindowsIdentity = WindowsIdentity.GetCurrent()
Private m_prinWindows As WindowsPrincipal = _
    New WindowsPrincipal(m_idWindows)
Private m_strIdentity As String = m_idWindows.Name
```

Retrieving User Information

Now that we have the *WindowsPrincipal* object, we can determine the user's group memberships. In the *btnRetrieveUserInfo_Click* procedure, we'll set the

Checked property of each *Checkbox* control based on whether the user is a member of a specific group (role). To see whether the user is a member of a built-in group, we use the *IsInRole* method, passing it one of the members of the *WindowsBuiltInRole* enumeration, which has entries for such groups as Administrators, Power Users, and more.

```
Private Sub btnRetrieveUserInfo_Click(...
    chkAdministrator.Checked = _
        m_prinWindows.IsInRole(WindowsBuiltInRole.Administrator)
    chkPowerUsers.Checked = _
        m_prinWindows.IsInRole(WindowsBuiltInRole.PowerUser)
    chkUsers.Checked = _
        m_prinWindows.IsInRole(WindowsBuiltInRole.User)
```

> **Note** Members of the *WindowsBuiltInRole* enumeration are spelled a little differently than the Windows groups they represent: they have no spaces, and they don't have a closing *s*.

If you prefer, you can use the BUILTIN keyword with the group name, which must be spelled the same way it is in Windows. The equivalent of *WindowsBuilt-InRole.Administrator* would be "BUILTIN\Administrators"—for example: `chk-Administrator.Checked = prinWindows.IsInRole("BUILTIN\Administrators")`.

To test for membership in a custom group, we must concatenate the computer name with the name of the custom group.

```
    chkManagers.Checked = _
        m_prinWindows.IsInRole(m_machineName & "\Managers")
```

Finally, we display the *WindowsIdentity* properties, whose contents help us determine how much to permit this user to do on our system.

```
    With m_idWindows
        txtLogin.AppendText(String.Format("Name: {0}{1}", _
            .Name, ControlChars.CrLf))
        txtLogin.AppendText(String.Format("AuthenticationType: {0}{1}", _
            .AuthenticationType, ControlChars.CrLf))
        ⋮
        txtLogin.AppendText(String.Format("IsSystem: {0}{1}", _
            .IsSystem, ControlChars.CrLf))
        txtLogin.AppendText(String.Format("Token: {0}{1}", _
            .Token, ControlChars.CrLf))
    End With
End Sub
```

Implementing Authorization

Once we have access to the current principal, we can impose demands that specify what that user can do.

In this example, we have a form that we want only selected users, groups, or both to be able to display. It's displayed by a procedure named *ShowProtectedForm*, which accepts the name of a group that will be allowed to see the form. In the following example, we'll display the form if the current user is a member of the Administrators group:

```
Private Sub btnAdminRun_Click(...
    ShowProtectedForm("BUILTIN\Administrators")
End Sub
```

> **Note**   You can't use the *WindowsBuiltInRole* enumeration here. You must pass a string using the BUILTIN keyword and the Windows group name.

In the *ShowProtectedForm* procedure, we're using the *PrincipalPermission* object to run a security check against the active principal. We're requiring that the principal be part of the group provided in *strGroup*, or else they cannot execute the procedure.

```
Private Sub ShowProtectedForm(ByVal strGroup As String)
    ⋮
    Dim ppTest As New PrincipalPermission(Nothing, strGroup)
```

Because we're passing *Nothing* as the first parameter to the *Principal-Permission* constructor, any member of the specified group will be allowed access. However, you can specify both an identity and a role (the identity would be the first parameter), in which case the current principal must meet both criteria.

Once the *PrincipalPermission* object is created, we use its *Demand* method to require that the user meet the stated criteria. If the criteria are not met, a security exception is thrown, and we handle it gracefully in a *Try/Catch* block.

```
    Try
        ppTest.Demand()
        Dim frm As New frmProtected()
        frm.Show()
        frm.txtProtected.Text = String.Format( _
            "{0}Demand succeeded.{0}{0}{1}{0}is a member of{0}" & _
            "{2}.", ControlChars.CrLf, m_strIdentity, strGroup)
    Catch ex As System.Security.SecurityException
        txtDisplay.Text = String.Format("Security Exception:" & _
            "{0}{3}{0}{1} is not a member of{0}{2}.", ControlChars.CrLf, _
            m_strIdentity, strGroup, ex.Message)
    End Try
End Sub
```

What if you want to allow members of more than one group to have access to the protected resource? You can implement a *Demand* that checks for multiple groups by using the *Union* method. The following example requires the user to be a member of either the built-in Power Users group or the custom Managers group. If the user is not a member of either one, a security exception will be thrown.

```
Private Sub btnUnion_Click(...
    :
    Dim ppPower As New PrincipalPermission(Nothing, "BUILTIN\PowerUsers")
    Dim ppMgr As New PrincipalPermission(Nothing, m_machineName & _
        "\Managers")
    Try
        ppPower.Union(ppMgr).Demand()
        Dim frm As New frmProtected()
        frm.Show()
        frm.txtProtected.Text = String.Format( _
            "Demand succeeded.{0}{1}{0}is a member of either{0}Power " & _
            "Users or Managers.", ControlChars.CrLf, _
            m_strIdentity)
    Catch ex As System.Security.SecurityException
        :
    End Try
End Sub
```

Conclusion

Using the *WindowsIdentity*, *WindowsPrincipal*, and *PrincipalPermission* classes, you can easily control access to protected resources, based on the current user's identity and membership in specific groups (roles).

Application #98: Create a Login Dialog Box

This sample application demonstrates how to create a login dialog box to authenticate users and restrict access to selected features of the application. The user must first log in, within three attempts, using either custom authentication or Windows authentication. After the user logs in, his role membership is checked. If the user is a member of either the custom Managers group or the built-in Administrators group, the main form displays a list of the application's users from the Users.XML file; otherwise, the main form is left blank.

Building Upon...

Application #12: Use a *DataSet* and *DataView*
Application #92: Implement Role-Based Security
Application #97: Implement Windows Role-Based Security

New Concepts

In the "Application #97: Implement Windows Role-Based Security" section, we demonstrated the use of the *WindowsIdentity* and *WindowsPrincipal* classes, which give us access to the identity and group membership of a user. In this sample application, we'll demonstrate the use of two sister classes: *GenericIdentity* and *GenericPrincipal*, both found in the *System.Security.Principal* namespace.

Principals and Roles

Whereas the *WindowsIdentity* and *WindowsPrincipal* classes represent authentication data gathered from the operating system, the *GenericIdentity* and *GenericPrincipal* classes represent user authentication data that results from custom authentication mechanisms.

For example, you can implement your own custom authentication for your application, accepting credentials from users in a custom dialog box and validating them against your own database of usernames and passwords. Once you've authenticated a user, you can create generic identity and principal objects for that user and implement authorization based on them.

A principal is an object that contains information about both the user's identity and his group membership. Armed with a principal, you can restrict use of a form to only users who belong to custom groups such as Managers or Executives, or to a built-in group such as Administrators or Power Users. Figure 14-2 shows a successful login based on custom authentication.

Figure 14-2   By using *GenericIdentity* and *GenericPrincipal* objects, you can "roll your own" user authentication while still having access to the Windows-authenticated user and role information.

Generic Principals

Whereas a *WindowsPrincipal* is instantiated based only on the user's Windows-authenticated identity, and gathers the user's group membership from the operating system, a *GenericPrincipal* is created from the user's identity coupled with an array of one or more roles to which the user belongs. You'll find *GenericIdentity* and *GenericPrincipal* perfectly suited to custom authentication schemes because you can create your own set of identities and create your own roles at will.

This sample application shows you how you can use both the *Windows* and *Generic* classes, implementing custom authentication via user credentials stored in an XML file, but also accessing Windows authentication data.

Code Walkthrough

First, the application presents a custom Login dialog box that asks for a username and password. The dialog box also has a check box that allows the user to bypass the custom authentication if the user is a member of the built-in Administrators group. When the user clicks the OK button, the following routine swings into action to validate him.

Step one is to instantiate an object from the *CustomUser* class. This class has three methods: *IsAdministrator*, *GetPrincipal*, and *ValidateUser*, each of which will be explained shortly. If the user claims to be an Administrator and truly is, no further authentication is needed, so we display the main form. Otherwise, we notify the user that authentication failed.

```
Private Sub btnOK_Click(...
    Dim objUser As New CustomUser()
    If chkAdministratorAccount.Checked Then
        If objUser.IsAdministrator Then
            ShowMainForm()
        Else
            LimitLoginAttempts("Current user is not an Administrator. " & _
                "Please provide a Username and Password.")
        End If
    Else
```

If the user doesn't claim to be an Administrator, we determine whether the user account exists, based on the submitted username and password. The *ValidateUser* method can return one of four results, and we take action accordingly:

```
Dim strName As String = txtUserName.Text
    Dim strPassword As String = txtPassword.Text
    Select Case objUser.ValidateUser(strName, strPassword)
```

If the user's credentials are valid, we get a *GenericPrincipal* object associated with the user's identity, and show the main form.

```
Case ValidationResult.ValidUser
    Dim prinGenPrincipal As GenericPrincipal
    prinGenPrincipal = objUser.GetPrincipal(strName, _
        strPassword)
    Thread.CurrentPrincipal = prinGenPrincipal
    ShowMainForm()
```

If the user has presented invalid credentials, we warn the user and handle multiple login attempts.

```
            Case ValidationResult.InvalidUser
                LimitLoginAttempts("Invalid credentials. Please " & _
                    "try again.")
            ⋮
        End Select
    End If
End Sub
```

Custom Authentication

The *CustomUser* class encapsulates the essentials for authenticating the user, based on credentials in the XML user data file, a portion of which is shown in the following code sample. Note that a user can belong to more than one role.

```
<users>
    <user>
        <name>Bob</name>
        <password>pass</password>
        <role>Managers</role>
        <role>Executives</role>
    </user>
    ⋮
</users>
```

ValidateUser Method

The *ValidateUser* method verifies whether the user account exists in the XML user data file, and it returns a *ValidationResult* (an enumeration we created for the purpose). First we read the XML into a *DataSet* and filter on the user-name and password.

```
Function ValidateUser(ByVal strName As String, ByVal strPassword As String) _
    As ValidationResult
    Dim dsUsers As New DataSet()
    Dim drRows() As DataRow
    Try
        dsUsers.ReadXml("..\Users.xml")
        drRows = dsUsers.Tables(0).Select("name = '" & _
            strName & "' and password = '" & strPassword & "'")
```

> **Important** If the filtered collection contains one row, a record was found. Otherwise, the user either doesn't exist or there's a duplicate. If you plan to use the filtering technique shown here, you'll need to ensure, when adding new users to the list, that there are no two users with the same credentials.

```
        Select Case drRows.Length
            Case 1
                Return ValidationResult.ValidUser
            Case 0
                Return ValidationResult.InvalidUser
            Case Else
                Return ValidationResult.DuplicateUser
        End Select
    Catch ex As FileNotFoundException
        Return ValidationResult.UserDataNotFound
    End Try
End Function
```

IsAdministrator Method

The *IsAdministrator* method verifies whether the currently logged-in Windows user is an Administrator. If you expect repeated role-based validation, set the principal policy as shown in the following code sample. The *SetPrincipalPolicy* method sets Windows principals as the default result whenever threads in this application domain attempt to bind to principals.

```
Function IsAdministrator() As Boolean
    AppDomain.CurrentDomain.SetPrincipalPolicy( _
        PrincipalPolicy.WindowsPrincipal)
```

Note   If you expect only a single instance of role-based validation, you can use the following syntax, rather than setting the principal policy:

```
Dim prinWinPrincipal As New _
    WindowsPrincipal(WindowsIdentity.GetCurrent())
```

We convert the current principal, of whatever type, into a *Windows-Principal* and then check whether the user account belongs to the *Administrators* group.

```
    Dim prinWinPrincipal As WindowsPrincipal = _
        CType(Thread.CurrentPrincipal, WindowsPrincipal)
    If prinWinPrincipal.IsInRole(WindowsBuiltInRole.Administrator) Then
        Return True
    Else
        Return False
    End If
End Function
```

GetPrincipal Method

The *GetPrincipal* method returns a *GenericPrincipal* representing a user account. First we create a *GenericIdentity* representing the user. Then we read the XML user list into a *DataSet* and filter the *DataSet* to produce a *DataRows* collection (which should have only one row) containing the user's credentials.

```
Function GetPrincipal(ByVal strName As String, ByVal strPassword As String) _
    As GenericPrincipal
    Dim idGenIdentity As New GenericIdentity(strName)
    Dim dsUsers As New DataSet()
    dsUsers.ReadXml("..\Users.xml")
    Dim drRows() As DataRow = dsUsers.Tables(0).Select("name = '" & _
        strName & "' and password = '" & strPassword & "'")
```

The *DataSet* has two tables. Table(0) contains the user name and password, and Table(1) has the roles. The *DataSet* considers Table(1) to be a child table of the Table(0) because the *role* element is repeated in the XML file. The *DataSet* creates a default relationship between the two tables named *user_role*. Using that relationship, we retrieve child rows containing the user's roles.

```
    Dim drChildRows() As DataRow = drRows(0).GetChildRows("user_role")
```

We create a string array to hold the roles the user belongs to. The array will have as many elements as there are rows in *drChildRows*. Therefore, its upper bound will be one less than the number of rows in *drChildRows*.

```
    Dim strRoles(drChildRows.Length - 1) As String
    Dim i As Integer = 0
    Dim dr As DataRow
    For Each dr In drChildRows
        strRoles(i) = dr.Item(0).ToString()
        i += 1
    Next
```

Finally we combine the identity and the roles to create the *GenericPrincipal*, which we'll use for authorization.

```
    Dim prinGenPrincipal As New GenericPrincipal(idGenIdentity, strRoles)
    Return prinGenPrincipal
End Function
```

Restricting the User

Having authenticated the user, we can now determine what the user is allowed to do—that is, implement *Authorization*. The main form has a *DataGrid* that lists the application user accounts. We intend to make that list available only to members of the built-in Administrators group or to the custom Managers role.

In the *Load* event procedure of the form, we check the user's role membership, accessing both Windows and generic roles. If the user is either a

Manager or an Administrator, we'll load and display the current user accounts. Otherwise, we won't.

```
Private Sub frmMain_Load(...
    If Thread.CurrentPrincipal.IsInRole("Managers") Or _
       Thread.CurrentPrincipal.IsInRole("BuiltIn\Administrators") Then
        Dim dsUsers As New DataSet()
        dsUsers.ReadXml("..\users.xml")
        With dgUsers
            .CaptionText = "User Accounts"
            .DataSource = dsUsers.Tables(0)
        End With
    Else
        MessageBox.Show("You must be a member of either the Managers " & _
            "or Administrators role to view user account information.", _
            "Insufficient Permissions", MessageBoxButtons.OK, _
            MessageBoxIcon.Exclamation)
    End If
End Sub
```

Conclusion

It's just as easy to use the generic identity and principal objects as the Windows versions. Having them available means that you can implement your own custom authentication schemes while still taking advantage of the Framework's extensive security features.

Application #99: Cryptographic Hash Algorithms

This sample application demonstrates how to use hash functions to ensure data integrity. It simulates the transmission of data over a network or the Internet, with the recipient being able to verify that the received data was not corrupted in transit.

When you run the application, an XML data document of all the Northwind products is created by querying the Microsoft SQL Server Northwind database and persisting the *DataSet* to XML. This simulates the sender's creation of the source document. The contents of this document are then read into a *StreamReader* and converted to a string to be displayed in a *TextBox*. This simulates your receiving the transmitted document.

When the main form is loaded, an MD5 hash digest is created to be used as an original "key" by which you can validate the transmitted XML. You can click the Compare button to compare the hash digest for the products sent over the wire (displayed) with the hash digest sent from Northwind. If you alter the contents of the *TextBox* by even one character and click Compare, you'll see

that the hash digests no longer match. Examples of three different hash types—
MD5, SHA1, and SHA384—are provided.

Building Upon...

Application #12: Use a *DataSet* and *DataView*
Application #22: Build an Offline Application
Application #73: Read From and Write To a Text File

New Concepts

Because data transmitted over a network is susceptible to interception and corruption, you need a means of verifying that the data you receive is the same as
the original. Hash digests let you do that.

Hashing Algorithms

Hash values (also known as message digests) are unique and extremely compact numerical representations of a piece of data. Changing even one character
in a source file can result in huge differences in the hash value. It's considered
to be computationally infeasible that any two messages can produce the same
hash value, or that a message can be produced to match an existing hash value.

Because a hash value is like a fingerprint for the original message, hashes
are extremely valuable for ensuring data integrity. For example, if you compare
the hash value generated before a message is sent with the hash value generated from the message you receive, you can determine whether the message
has been corrupted. Some of the more commonly used hashing algorithms, all
found in the *System.Security.Cryptography* namespace, are as follows:

- **MD5 hashing algorithm**   The MD5 algorithm accepts an input
  message and produces a 128-bit hash value. MD5 is often used for
  digital signatures.

- **SHA1 hashing algorithm**   Like MD5, SHA1 also produces a message digest. SHA1 output, however, is 160 bytes long, as opposed to
  128 bits for MD5.

- **SHA384 hashing algorithm**   SHA384 is a big brother to SHA1,
  producing a 384-bit message digest.

Figure 14-3 shows a successful comparison between the original hash
digest of a message and the hash digest after it is received.

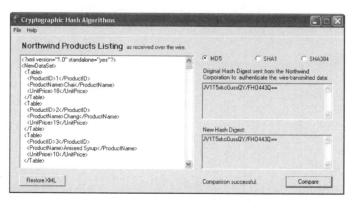

Figure 14-3   A hash value (or message digest) serves as a digital finger-print of a file. When you send the file and the message digest to someone else, the recipient can verify whether the data arrived uncorrupted.

Code Walkthrough

When the main form is loaded, its *Form Load* event calls the *CreateOriginal-ProductsList* procedure to create the original XML document, reads in the XML, displays it in the large *TextBox*, and then calls a function to generate an MD5 hash digest to display in the upper right *TextBox*.

First we create the XML document, simulating the original products list sent by the Northwind Corporation. The XML document is stored in the application's root folder. Then we open the XML document and convert it to a string. This simulates transferring the product listing over the wire to a client.

```
Private Sub frmMain_Load(...
    CreateOriginalProductsList()
    Dim sr As New StreamReader("..\products.xml")
    strOriginalXML = sr.ReadToEnd
    sr.Close()
```

Next we display the transmitted XML and the hash digest that is used for authenticating the transmitted XML. This digest is generated from the contents of the original document, not from the XML displayed in the *TextBox*.

```
    txtXML.Text = strOriginalXML
    txtHashOriginal.Text = GenerateHashDigest(strOriginalXML)
    txtHashForCompare.Text = COMPARE_INSTRUCTIONS
    ⋮
End Sub
```

Generating the Digest

The *GenerateHashDigest* function performs the work of encryption, generating each of the three hash digest types. We begin by creating an *Encoding* object so that we can use its convenient *GetBytes* method. *GetBytes* creates a byte array from the source text passed as an argument. To create the hash, we simply call the *ComputeHash* method of the desired cryptographic provider, passing it the byte array we just generated. Finally the function returns a Base64-encoded version of the hash. Base64 is a method of encoding binary data as ASCII text.

```
Function GenerateHashDigest(ByVal strSource As String) As String
    Dim uEncode As New UnicodeEncoding()
    Dim bytProducts() As Byte = uEncode.GetBytes(strSource)
    Select Case True
        Case optMD5.Checked
            Dim md5 As New MD5CryptoServiceProvider()
            hash = md5.ComputeHash(bytProducts)
        Case optSHA1.Checked
            Dim sha1 As New SHA1CryptoServiceProvider()
            hash = sha1.ComputeHash(bytProducts)
        Case optSHA384.Checked
            Dim sha384 As New SHA384Managed()
            hash = sha384.ComputeHash(bytProducts)
    End Select
    Return Convert.ToBase64String(hash)
End Function
```

> **Tip**   In addition to accepting a complete byte array, *ComputeHash* can do its work on a portion of a byte array, or it can accept a *Stream*.

Comparing the Hashes

To verify data integrity, you need to compare the original hash value with the hash value produced from the received text. The *btnCompare_Click* routine does just that. It compares, byte for byte, the original hash digest with the hash digest generated from the contents of the *TextBox*. First we create an *Encoding* object so that we can use the *GetBytes* method to obtain byte arrays. Then we create a byte array from the original XML file sent by the Northwind Corporation.

```
Private Sub btnCompare_Click(...
    Dim uEncode As New UnicodeEncoding()
    Dim bytHashOriginal As Byte() = uEncode.GetBytes(txtHashOriginal.Text)
```

Now we generate a hash digest from the contents of the large *TextBox* containing the XML. The contents simulate the XML received from the Northwind Corporation over the wire. We want to compare the new hash with the original hash to make sure the XML has not been corrupted in transit. So from the new hash digest we create a byte array for comparison with the original hash digest byte array.

```
Dim strHashForCompare As String = GenerateHashDigest(txtXML.Text)
Dim bytHashForCompare As Byte() = uEncode.GetBytes(strHashForCompare)
```

We loop through all the bytes in the hashed values and compare them, byte for byte. If any pair fails to match, we display an appropriate message and exit the loop. Otherwise, we indicate success.

```
txtHashForCompare.Text = strHashForCompare
Dim i As Integer
For i = 0 To bytHashOriginal.Length - 1
    If bytHashOriginal(i) <> bytHashForCompare(i) Then
        lblResults.Text = "Data has been corrupted!"
        Exit For
    Else
        lblResults.Text = "Comparison successful."
    End If
Next i
End Sub
```

Conclusion

Cryptographic hash values or message digests provide a simple way for you to ensure that two versions of a data item are identical. Various hashing algorithms are available, each with varying message digest sizes. The larger the digest size, the more secure the fingerprint. Naturally, you'll need to use the same algorithm (MD5, SHA1, SHA384, or other) that was used on the original data. You'll probably use this technique most often to verify that transmitted data arrived without modification.

Application #100: Encrypt and Decrypt Data

This sample application shows you how to encrypt and decrypt data using symmetric encryption, in which you and your recipient use the same key both to encrypt and to decrypt the data. The application lets you load a document, create a key, encrypt the document, and decrypt the document. You can choose between two popular encryption standards: *Rijndael* and *TripleDES*.

Building Upon...

Application #73: Read From and Write To a Text File

New Concepts

When you need to transmit data securely, one useful option is to encrypt it. Encrypting ensures that the data remains confidential, protects it from being altered, and helps to assure the recipient that it truly originated from you. Private-key encryption, also known as symmetric encryption, requires you and your recipient to have the same key, which is used both to encrypt and to decrypt the data. Naturally, you'll need to protect this key because anyone who gets it can decrypt intercepted messages.

> **Note**   Another kind of encryption, public-key or asymmetric encryption, utilizes a public-private key pair. You encrypt data with your private key, and then give your public key to your recipient. The public key is used to decrypt the data, and it can decrypt only data that was encrypted with your private key, assuring your recipient that the data came from you.

One advantage of symmetric encryption is that it's very fast compared to the other alternative, public-key encryption, and is therefore ideal for large amounts of data.

> **Tip**   You can take advantage of the strengths of both encryption technologies by sending your main document (which could be quite large) encrypted symmetrically, and sending the private key (which will be quite small) encrypted asymmetrically.

The symmetric encryption key is generated from a secret password, which serves as the cryptographic *seed* for the key. It's conceivable that someone might guess the password and generate his own copy of the key, or that an intruder might use a *dictionary attack*, in which multiple possible passwords are tried until the correct one is sniffed out. To prevent such security breaches, you can *salt* the password before generating the key. The salt is in the form of random bytes added to the password, which makes the generated key harder to duplicate.

Further, the Framework encryption classes use a technique known as *cipher block chaining* (CBC), in which data is encrypted a block at a time, with each block ranging from 8 to 32 bytes. Data from the previous block is mixed into the encryption of the current block to further ensure randomness, even when encrypting identical blocks. The first block is encrypted using an Initialization Vector (IV). You can generate both the salt and the IV and save them in a file that you can send to your recipient. Using the password and the salt/IV file, your recipient can generate the key to be used for decryption.

The Framework encryption classes (found in the *System.Security.Cryptography* namespace) are stream-based, which means that an input stream of data can be passed to an encryption stream and on to an output stream without having to be saved to disk in between.

TripleDes

TripleDES is a block cipher based on the Data Encryption Standard (DES). It applies the DES algorithm to the data three successive times and can use either two or three 56-bit keys.

Rijndael

Rijndael is a block cipher that allows block lengths up to 256 bits. Its keys can also range up to 256 bits.

Figure 14-4 shows the sample form with a loaded text file ready to be encrypted. Note the use of both a password and a key file.

Figure 14-4   The .NET Framework classes make it easy for you to encrypt files. Using your chosen password, a salted key file and one of the available cryptographic providers, you can create an encryption that will be tough to break.

Code Walkthrough

When the main form loads, we first instantiate *m_crpSample*, an instance of the *SampleCrypto* class, passing the name of the default crypto type. *SampleCrypto* is a custom class within our project designed to handle encryption functions. *m_crpSample* was declared earlier at the class level as `Private m_crpSample As SampleCrypto`. Next we set paths for the files that will contain the keys used for encryption.

```
Private Sub frmMain_Load(...
    ⋮
    m_crpSample = New SampleCrypto("Rijndael")
    Dim strCurrentDirectory As String = _
        Microsoft.VisualBasic.Left(Environment.CurrentDirectory, _
        Len(Environment.CurrentDirectory) - 3)
    m_strRijndaelKeyFile = "C:\Rijndael_key.dat"
    m_strTripleDESKeyFile = "C:\TripleDES_key.dat"
    txtRijndaelKeyFile.Text = m_strRijndaelKeyFile
    txtTripleDESKeyFile.Text = m_strTripleDESKeyFile
    ⋮
End Sub
```

Next we need a file to encrypt. The *btnLoad_Click* procedure lets us locate one, and then retrieves its contents and places them into the *TextBox* by using the code `txtCrypto.Text = ReadFileAsString(m_strSourcePath)`. The following *ReadFileAsString* procedure converts the contents of the file first to a byte array, and then to a string for display.

```
Private Function ReadFileAsString(ByVal path As String) As String
    Dim fs As New FileStream(path, FileMode.Open, FileAccess.Read, _
        FileShare.Read)
    Dim abyt(CInt(fs.Length - 1)) As Byte
    fs.Read(abyt, 0, abyt.Length)
    fs.Close()
    Return UTF8.GetString(abyt)
End Function
```

> **Note** Even though in this sample application we're using only text files for demonstration, the encryption mechanism works on files of any kind.

We need to generate an encryption key, so when the user fills in a password to be used as the seed for the key and clicks the Create Key File button, *btnCreateKey_Click* starts the creation of a salt/IV file with the following method call: `m_crpSample.CreateKeyFile(m_strCurrentKeyFile)`.

The *CreateKeyFile* procedure creates the key file as shown in the following sample code. After initializing each byte array to the proper length for the particular crypto class we're using, we create a *FileStream* object to write the salt and IV to a file.

```
Public Function CreateKeyFile(ByVal strSaveToPath As String) As Boolean
    ReDimByteArrays()
    Dim fsKey As New FileStream(strSaveToPath, FileMode.OpenOrCreate, _
        FileAccess.Write)
```

To generate a random value for salting the key, we use a random number generator. These random bytes are appended to the password before the key is derived from it, making a dictionary attack much more difficult. The *Password-DeriveBytes* class lets us generate a key using the password and the salt. Once we've generated a new random IV, we're ready to write the results to the key file.

```
    Dim rng As RandomNumberGenerator = RandomNumberGenerator.Create()
    rng.GetBytes(m_abytSalt)
    Dim pdb As New PasswordDeriveBytes(m_strPassword, m_abytSalt)
    m_abytKey = pdb.GetBytes(m_abytKey.Length)
    m_crpSym.GenerateIV()
    m_abytIV = m_crpSym.IV
    Try
        fsKey.Write(m_abytSalt, 0, m_abytSalt.Length)
        fsKey.Write(m_abytIV, 0, m_abytIV.Length)
        m_strSaltIVFile = strSaveToPath
        Return True
    Catch exp As Exception
        Throw New Exception(exp.Message)
    Finally
        fsKey.Close()
    End Try
End Function
```

With the target file loaded, its path stored in *m_strSourcePath*, and our key file created, we can now begin the encryption process, which is initiated by the *EncryptDecrypt_Click* procedure, with the method call `m_crpSample.EncryptFile()`. The actual encryption is done by the *EncryptFile* method of the *SampleCrypto* class, which is shown in the next section.

Encrypting Data

Step one for encrypting data is to get the salt and IV information from the key file. Then we create a *FileStream* object and read the source file into a byte array (*abytInput*). This is similar to how we earlier loaded the *TextBox*.

```
Public Sub EncryptFile()
    GetSaltAndIVFromKeyFile()
    Dim fsInput As New FileStream(m_strSourceFile, FileMode.Open, _
```

```
    FileAccess.Read)
Dim abytInput(CInt(fsInput.Length - 1)) As Byte
fsInput.Read(abytInput, 0, CInt(fsInput.Length))
fsInput.Close()
```

Next we create a second *FileStream* object that will write the data to a temporary file once it's encrypted. We create a *CryptoStream* object that points to the file stream and will operate in *Write* mode. Note the use of the *Create-Encryptor* method of the *SymmetricAlgorithm* class, which creates a symmetric encryptor object that will actually perform the encryption.

```
Dim fsCipherText As New FileStream("temp.dat", FileMode.Create, _
    FileAccess.Write)
fsCipherText.SetLength(0)
Dim csEncrypted As New CryptoStream(fsCipherText, _
    m_crpSym.CreateEncryptor(), CryptoStreamMode.Write)
```

Finally, to perform the encryption and write the data out, we invoke the *Write* method of the crypto stream, passing in the unencrypted byte array from the source file. The encryption takes place, and the encrypted data is passed to the file stream and written to the temporary file. Thus, the logic flow is as follows: byte array → *CryptoStream* → *FileStream*.

```
csEncrypted.Write(abytInput, 0, abytInput.Length)
csEncrypted.FlushFinalBlock()
```

> **Important** When you use this technique and the bytes are all written, you must call *FlushFinalBlock* to indicate to the crypto stream that you've finished using it and that it should finish processing any bytes remaining in its buffer. Typically this involves padding the last output block to a complete multiple of the crypto object's block size (for Rijndael this is 16 bytes, or 128 bits), encrypting it, and then writing this final block to the memory stream.

Finally we clean up by closing the crypto stream, which automatically closes the file stream. Then the *SwapFiles* procedure copies the temporary file to the original one and deletes the temp file.

```
    csEncrypted.Close()
    SwapFiles(False)
End Sub
```

Decrypting Data

If someone has sent you an encrypted file, along with a password and a key file containing the salt and the IV, you need to install that key file on your machine and begin the decryption process. The first part of the process is the same as for encryption: you load the target file and enter the password. Then you'll load the key file, and click the Decrypt button. The *EncryptDecrypt_Click* procedure calls the *m_crpSample.DecryptFile* method, and the *DecryptFile* method swings into action, as shown in the following code.

To decrypt the file, we get the salt and IV information from the key file. Then we read the encrypted file into the *fsCipherText FileStream*, pass it to the *csDecrypted CryptoStream*, pass the decrypted data to the *srReader Stream-Reader* and on through the *fsPlainText FileStream* and the *swWriter Stream-Writer* to the output file. Finally we close the streams and clean up.

```
Public Sub DecryptFile()
    GetSaltAndIVFromKeyFile()
    Dim fsCipherText As New FileStream(m_strSourceFile, FileMode.Open, _
        FileAccess.Read)
    Dim csDecrypted As New CryptoStream(fsCipherText, _
        m_crpSym.CreateDecryptor(), CryptoStreamMode.Read)
    Dim srReader As New StreamReader(csDecrypted)
    Dim fsPlainText As New FileStream("temp.dat", FileMode.Create, _
        FileAccess.Write)
    Dim swWriter As New StreamWriter(fsPlainText)
    Try
        swWriter.Write(srReader.ReadToEnd)
    Catch expCrypto As CryptographicException
        Throw New CryptographicException()
    Finally
        csDecrypted.Close()
        srReader.Close()
        swWriter.Close()
    End Try
    SwapFiles(True)
End Sub
```

Conclusion

In this sample application, we've shown you how the .NET Framework cryptography classes make it simple for you to encrypt data for secure transmission. You've also seen that TripleDES and Rijndael are only two of the Framework symmetrical encryption options, which also include RC2 and DES. Symmetric encryption (which this sample has focused on) is fast, and therefore, suited for large amounts of data. Asymmetric encryption is more secure but slower and, therefore, more suited for smaller data sizes.

15

Coding Conventions

The topic of coding conventions (or coding standards) comes up a lot. You can always find it as a recent topic in the *microsoft.public.dotnet.languages.vb* newsgroup. A search on Google for "Coding Conventions" returns 170,000 hits. Why such interest? I think people simply want to know *the way* to format code.

With that said, there is no single way of authoring Microsoft Visual Basic code that is universally agreed upon. Microsoft defines a set of coding conventions that are adopted to a large or small degree by many development teams, but it's very common for different sets of developers to follow, at least slightly, different rules.

Why Are Coding Conventions Important?

You might wonder why we have conventions at all if nobody can agree on them. The reason, in a word, is consistency. At a minimum, code should be consistent with itself. This means that if you have multiple developers working on a given application, they should all be following the same rules. This can happen only if the rules are documented and agreed upon.

Ideally, all the code in an organization is consistent—although in practical terms, this virtually never happens. If the code that's currently being written is consistent with code that's developed in other departments, developers are more portable within the organization.

Coding conventions also affect code maintenance. Over the lifetime of a given application, more resources will be used to enhance and maintain the application than were originally used to develop the application. Also, applications are not typically maintained exclusively by the original authors. If the application uses consistent coding conventions, it's easier to decipher and modify. For these reasons alone, coding conventions have value.

The true value of coding conventions is that they convey additional information not by what is written, but by how it's written. Based on a given set of coding conventions, you can tell certain things by looking at the following statements:

```
currentUser = NextUser()
If currentUser.IsValid Then
    txtUserIsValid.Text = "Yes"
End If
```

What could you tell about this code? Based on the conventions that will be outlined in this chapter, you would know that *currentUser* is a private or protected variable and not a public property. You would know that *IsValid*, on the other hand, is a public property that returns a Boolean value. You would also know that *txtUserIsValid* is a user-interface element, and more specifically, a *TextBox*. Compare this case with the following code:

```
CurrentUser = NextUser()
If CurrentUser.CheckValid Then
    UserIsValid.Text = "Yes"
End If
```

In this case, you can't make any assumptions. There's no way to tell whether *CurrentUser* is a public property or an internal variable. You know that *UserIsValid* is some kind of object, but is it a user-interface object? There's no way to be certain, as any class could expose a *Text* method. If you do assume that it's a user-interface element, you don't know whether it's a *Label*, a *TextBox*, or something else. Left to maintain this code, you would have a certain amount of spelunking to do just to figure out what you're looking at.

I want to repeat that coding conventions described in this book are not the only ones that work. You could have standards where *_currentUser*, *currentUser*, *current_user*, *sCurrentUser*, and CURRENT_USER would all denote completely different things. The point is simply to have standards because doing so will enhance the readability and maintainability of your code.

How Much Is Too Much?

Once you've decided that you're going to institute coding conventions, you can either define a few guidelines or attempt to define a rule for nearly every conceivable coding scenario. If you want a truly minimalist approach, just remember, "It's more important to be consistent than to be right." This philosophy has a number of ramifications. It means that if you're maintaining existing code, you simply follow the coding conventions used by the original author. Also remember that it's never a good idea to fix the coding conventions of an entire application, unless the application is already being rewritten for some other reason.

Coding Recommendations

If you want something a little more structured, I'll offer what I consider to be the most important conventions for Microsoft Visual Basic .NET.

Option Strict On

Option Strict On was used for all the samples in this book simply because it results in safer, more reliable, often better performing, and more explicit code. Almost all production code should be authored with *Option Strict On*. There is one exception: if you're specifically trying to leverage the late-binding feature of Visual Basic .NET, it's OK to use *Option Strict Off*. However, this code should be contained within its own file, and the majority of the application should still use *Option Strict On*.

Camel Casing

Camel casing means the first letter is a lowercase letter and then the beginning of each subsequent word is an uppercase letter. For example: *currentUser*, *firstCustomer*, and *myDocumentsFolder*. You should use camel casing for parameters passed to methods, for local variables, and for private or protected class variables. Using this convention makes it easy to see that something is an internal variable and not externally accessible.

Pascal Casing

Pascal casing means that you capitalize the first letter of every word. For example: *GetCustomer*, *SaveChanges*, and *FirstName*. Pascal casing should be used for all classes, enumerations, methods, properties, public fields, namespaces, etc. In other words, Pascal casing is used for everything except the few cases where you use camel casing.

This use of Pascal and camel casing is consistent with all the classes you'll find in the base class library of the .NET Framework.

Comments

You should comment every procedure. This commenting should include at a minimum the purpose of the method, a description of the arguments, and the meaning of the value returned. You should also comment all variables and properties, and all logical blocks of code. The most important rule of commenting is that the comments should describe the code, not repeat the code. Consider the following two sections of code:

```
' open a text file
Dim sr As New StreamReader("c:\somefile.txt")
' declare an integer
Dim i As Integer
' loop on reading each line
While sr.ReadLine()
    ' increment i
    i += 1
End While

' Count the lines in a file
Dim sr As New StreamReader("c:\somefile.txt")
Dim i As Integer
While sr.ReadLine()
    i += 1
End While
```

Which is more informative? The first example comments every line. However, the comments don't tell you anything you don't already know. They're just repeating the code. Sometimes, less is more. In the second example, the comment explains what the code does, not how it does it. This is the purpose of comments. If you feel you have to comment *how* the code is doing something, perhaps because a certain code block is extremely complex, consider rewriting the code to simplify it. Remember, comments are designed to give additional information to a programmer who already has the ability to read code.

Do Things the Visual Basic Way

When dimensioning a variable, it's better to say `Dim cn As New SqlConnection()` than to say `Dim cn As SqlConnection = New SqlConnection()`. This approach also means it's preferable to use *Len* instead of *String.Length*, *MsgBox* instead of *MessageBox.Show*, and *Declare* instead of *DllImport*. It's also worth noting that conversion functions such as *CInt* and *CBool* are not really functions; they are language keywords and are actually faster than `CType(x, Integer)`.

There is a great misunderstanding about the intrinsic Visual Basic methods. People have the impression that if you use *Len*, you're not writing "pure" .NET code. This is completely untrue. *Len* is simply a method in the *Microsoft.VisualBasic* namespace. This namespace is part of the core Framework. By using these methods, you aren't burdening your application with carrying around something equivalent to the Visual Basic 6 runtime. The exception to this is the *Microsoft.VisualBasic.Compatability* namespace. This exists only for migrating Visual Basic 6 code to Visual Basic .NET, and it should never be used for new development.

Use Meaningful and Consistent Names

You should pick names that are readable and mean something. You should use variables such as *i*, *j*, and *k* only for trivial loops. If you have a property or variable that stores a Boolean value, its name should contain *Is* to denote a *True* or *False* value or yes/no—for example, *IsValid* or *IsAuthorized*.

Constants and Enumerations

Your code should never contain magic numbers or strings. You should use constants and enumerations instead. For example:

```
' Bad
Dim bufferSize(1024 * 1024) As Byte

' Good
Const K_BYTE As Integer = 1024
Const MEG_BYTE As Integer = 1024 * K_BYTE
Dim bufferSize(MEG_BYTE) As Byte
```

In the first example, who knows what the code means? In the second example, it's obvious that the code is creating a 1-megabyte buffer. The only raw numbers that should appear in your code are 0 and 1. Anything else should be defined as a constant or enumeration. It is also a matter of convention to declare constants in all capital letters with an underscore separating each word.

Enumerations can also make your code more readable and maintainable. Compare the following:

```
Public Enum Priority
    Low
    Medium
    High
End Enum

' Bad
Mail.Priority = 1

' Good
Mail.Priority = Priority.Medium
```

Using the enumeration obviously makes the code more readable. Enumerations in .NET have the added advantage of allowing you to easily convert them to strings. For example: `lblPriority.Text = Mail.Priority.ToString()`.

Hungarian Notation

When you use Hungarian notation, you prefix each variable declaration with mnemonics that denote the type. For example, *m_sUserName* indicates a private or protected member variable of the *String* data type. In Visual Basic 6, this type of Hungarian notation was sometimes used. What was almost universal, however, was to prefix all user-interface elements with a three-character prefix: *txt* for *TextBox*, *lbl* for *Label*, and so on.

In Visual Basic.NET, *m_* should be used only for private or protected members that are accessed through a public property procedure. Other protected member variables should simply be given a camel-case name. Primitive data types should not be prefixed, so you should simply use *customerName*, and not *sCustomerName* or *strCustomerName*.

Microsoft originally recommended against using any form of Hungarian notation; however, the prefixes for user-interface elements are so ingrained and useful that they're now accepted. If you're building an application that has a *user name* label, text box, and member variable, you can run out of creative names quickly. However, with prefixes for the user interface elements, it's obvious what *lblUserName*, *txtUserName*, and *userName* are in your code.

Table 15-1 shows the recommended prefixes for user-interface elements:

Table 15-1 Standard Controls

Class	Prefix
Button	*btn*
CheckBox	*chk*
CheckedListBox	*clst*
ColorDialog	*cdlg*
ColumnHeader	*chdr*
ComboBox	*cbo*
ContextMenu	*cmnu*
CrystalReportViewer	*crv*
DataGrid	*grd*
DateTimePicker	*dtp*
DomainUpDown	*dud*
ErrorProvider	*erp*
FontDialog	*fdlg*
Form	*frm*
GroupBox	*grp*
HelpProvider	*hlp*
HScrollBar	*hsb*
ImageList	*img*
Label	*lbl*
LinkLabel	*lnk*

Table 15-1   Standard Controls

Class	Prefix
ListBox	lst
ListView	lvw
Menu	mnu
MonthCalendar	cal
NotifyIcon	nico
NumericUpDown	nud
OpenFileDialog	odlg
PageSetupDialog	psd
PictureBox	pic
PrintDialog	pdlg
PrintDocument	pdoc
PrintPreviewControl	ppc
PrintPreviewDialog	ppd
ProgressBar	pbr
RadioButton	rad
RadioButtonList	rbl
RichTextBox	rtf
SaveFileDialog	sdlg
Splitter	spl
StatusBar	sbr
StatusBarPanel	sbr
TabControl	tab
TabPage	pge
TextBox	txt
Timer	tmr
ToolBar	tbr
ToolBarButton	tbb
ToolTip	tip
TrackBar	trk
TreeNode	nod
TreeView	tvw
VScrollBar	vsb

Because data objects are so common, they're also sometimes prefixed. If you decide to prefix data objects, you should use the conventions listed in Table 15-2.

Table 15-2   Data Objects

Class	Prefix
Connection	*cnn*
Command	*cmd*
CommandBuilder	*cb*
DataAdapter	*da*
DataColumn	*dcl*
DataReader	*dr*
DataRow	*drw*
DataSet	*ds*
DataTable	*dt*
DataView	*dv*

Use Good Object-Oriented (OO) Practices

Visual Basic 6 is an event-driven programming language. If you have a structured programming background, you know that in Visual Basic 6 you simply had to think differently to solve the same problems.

In addition to being event driven, Visual Basic .NET is fully object oriented. Guess what? This means thinking differently to solve the same problems. The purpose of this book isn't to teach the concepts of object-oriented (OO) languages. Many great titles exist that cover the concepts quite adequately. The point I want to make is that you no longer have a choice about doing or not doing OO. All Visual Basic .NET code is OO by nature. When you create a Web page or a form, it shows up in your code as a class. The Framework itself makes extensive use of inheritance, polymorphism, and other OO concepts. In addition, the Framework was specifically designed to assume that you would inherit portions of it and implement interfaces as *the way* to build solutions.

Visual Basic 6 was not OO, and you might not be used to thinking this way. I strongly recommend learning object-oriented analysis and design practices and using them in your applications.

Some Things Were Bad, Are Bad, and Always Will Be Bad

Goto, *Option Explicit Off*, and *On Error Resume Next* have generally never been good ideas. They still aren't. But, the list of "bad things" has actually grown with

Visual Basic .NET. You should now avoid the *On Error* construct completely. Instead, you should use structured error handling in your code:

```
Try
    Dim x As Integer
    x = x / 0
Catch ex As Exception
    MsgBox(ex.Message)
Finally
    ' This code always runs
End Try
```

When handling errors this way, you wrap the code that might fail in a *Try* block. If an exception occurs, execution will jump to the *Catch* block, where the error can be dealt with appropriately. Code in the *Finally* block will always run, whether an exception occurs or not. For a detailed description of structured exception handling, see the related sample. It suffices to say that structured exception handling should be used in place of *On Error*, in every case.

You should also avoid type characters when declaring variables. So instead of using

```
Dim s$
```

you should use

```
Dim s as String
```

One exception to the "has always been bad" rule is variable declaration. You used to pay a performance penalty if you dimensioned variables using *As New*:

```
Dim cnn As New SqlConnection()
```

This is now the recommended mechanism for instantiating objects.

User Interface

You can do some simple things to make your application more accessible. The easiest thing to do is to add accelerators for all menus, labels, buttons, and so forth. Each application should also contain an About form on the Help menu that at a minimum explains where the user can get support.

When naming user-interface elements, it's not a crime to have *Label1* and *Panel1*, unless those objects will be accessed by code. Any object that is accessed by code—either to access properties or methods, or handle events—should have a meaningful name.

Conclusion

Coding conventions are all about making code that's more readable and ultimately more maintainable. You can almost think of conventions as metadata for your code, as they convey additional information beyond the code itself. While this section has outlined many common and agreed-upon coding conventions for Visual Basic .NET, you might need additional or different conventions within your organization. That's fine. What is critical is that within your organization you adopt conventions that everyone agrees to. Conventions are simply a mechanism for consistency.

16

Windows Server 2003 for .NET Developers

This chapter discusses new and enhanced features in Windows Server 2003 that affect application development and application support on the platform. The goal of this chapter is to point out features and services that have changed from previous versions, problems that have been resolved, and new features that developers can take advantage of when writing and deploying applications on Windows Server 2003.

Windows Server 2003 as an Application Server

Microsoft Windows Server 2003 is designed to be an industry-leading application server. As such, Windows Server 2003 supports a broad range of standards, protocols, and communication interfaces. What sets Windows Server 2003 apart from other server platforms are the features you get out-of-the-box that allow developers to both build and deploy robust, scalable, and reliable applications. This chapter will introduce you to those features.

.NET Framework 1.1

The Microsoft .NET Framework is included with Windows Server 2003 source files and can be installed to allow either .NET development or hosting.

Internet Information Services (IIS) 6.0

Internet Information Services (IIS) is the Microsoft Web server. As connectivity to the Internet and between organizations and individuals increases, Web-based applications and services have become the preferred way of sharing data and interacting with customers and partners. Internet Information Services is, therefore, an important part of the application support services offered by Windows Server 2003. This section covers the new architecture and features of IIS 6.0 (which is included with Windows Server 2003) and discusses how developers can take advantage of them.

IIS Architecture

IIS 6.0 has been completely rearchitected to be faster, to be more reliable, and to provide administrators and application developers with more control over how Web applications run. This new architecture radically changes how HTTP requests are sent and received, how Web server processes are managed, and how Web server processes communicate with one another. The changes include three new IIS-related components: HTTP.SYS, a kernel-mode HTTP listener; worker processes that execute Web application code; and the WWW Service Administration and Monitoring component, which manages worker processes.

HTTP.SYS—Kernel-Mode HTTP Listener

The first of these components is a kernel-mode HTTP Listener/Responder, HTTP.SYS. This kernel-mode driver is part of the network subsystem, starts at boot time, and is always running. By default, HTTP.SYS is not configured to listen on any ports and does not expose a security risk. HTTP.SYS will begin listening for requests only when the Internet Information Services component is added and Web sites are configured. When Web sites are configured, inetinfo and other IIS 6.0 components communicate with HTTP.SYS to fulfill HTTP requests. This is different from previous versions, which used winsock for these services. HTTP.SYS sends and receives HTTP traffic, and it routes requests to the IIS worker process responsible for a given Web site or application. HTTP.SYS does not run any application code or perform processing steps required to generate responses to any HTTP requests; it only routes HTTP requests and responses. HTTP.SYS maintains a kernel-mode cache. Therefore, it will cache responses that are cacheable and will attempt to service new requests from cache if possible. HTTP.SYS has a namespace routing table that maps URLs to the worker processes in which the corresponding sites and applications are running. HTTP.SYS uses this namespace routing table to route incoming HTTP requests.

HTTP.SYS is also responsible for performing logging functions and implementing Quality of Service (QoS) functions such as connection limits and timeouts, queue-length limits, and bandwidth throttling.

Worker Processes

Worker processes are user-mode processes that are responsible for processing Web requests. The name of each spawned worker process is W3WP.EXE. They replace the DLLHOST.EXE process from Windows 2000 and the MTX.EXE process from Windows NT 4.0. Worker processes are associated with application pools. An application pool has at least one worker process assigned to it. Web sites, virtual directories, and applications are assigned to application pools based on the desired level of application isolation, performance, monitoring, recycling, and so forth. The worker process associated with a given pool processes all Web requests for the applications that are members of that pool. When HTTP.SYS receives a request for a URL, it uses its namespace routing table to determine which application pool supports the application associated with the URL. HTTP.SYS then submits the request to the worker process (or processes) associated with the application pool. The worker process might perform any number of actions to fulfill the request, including returning static pages, invoking ISAPI extensions, running Common Gateway Interface (CGI) handlers, and running application code such as ASP.NET. Worker processes send responses to HTTP.SYS, which will send the response the originating address. (HTTP.SYS might also cache the response.)

WWW Service Administration and Monitoring Component

The WWW Service Administration and Monitoring component (W3SVC) is a user-mode component of the World Wide Web service and is responsible for managing worker processes throughout their lifecycle. When Inetinfo.exc starts the World Wide Web service, the W3SVC reads the Metabase and initializes the HTTP.SYS namespace routing table, which maps URLs to the correct worker process running the corresponding site or application. Once the namespace routing table is initialized, HTTP.SYS can forward requests to the worker processes. The W3SVC is responsible for starting worker processes and will do so when the first request for a namespace supported by a worker process is received.

The W3SVC also manages worker processes through their lifetime by monitoring, starting, stopping, and recycling worker processes as configured. You'll learn more about worker processes when you read about application pools a little later in this chapter. Figure 16-1 shows how the components and processes of Internet Information Services work together.

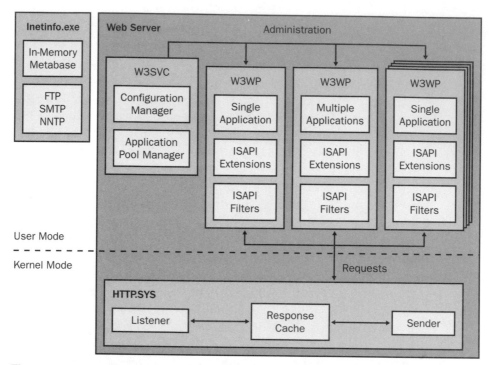

Figure 16-1   This figure shows the components and processes used by IIS to listen for, process, and respond to Web requests and manage worker processes.

IIS 6.0 Application Isolation

Application isolation is critically important in a Web server environment. Both internal (intranet) and public (Internet) Web servers typically host multiple Web sites and a variety of applications that support those Web sites. Much of the code run by applications is run on the Web server itself. Application code that is poorly written or ill-behaved might be prone to crashing. Depending on how well an application is isolated, and the version of IIS, the crash of a single application might affect nothing else running on the Web server or it might take down the entire Web server, necessitating a reboot.

To understand application isolation, you have to understand how the operating system controls processes and how application processes are managed by IIS. A process is the smallest unit of control for the operating system. A process has a range of memory addresses assigned to it and can put threads on the processor for execution and so forth. The operating system can terminate a nonresponsive process; other processes are unaffected and continue to run.

Evolution of Application Isolation in IIS 4.0 and 5.0

The communications architecture of IIS 4.0 lent itself to running applications in-process. This meant that Web requests, and any application code run as the result of a Web request, were executed in the same process space as the Inetinfo.exe (IIS) process. Applications ran much faster in-process because no overhead was incurred by crossing process boundaries to communicate with Inetinfo or by contacting ISAPIs (which also ran in the Inetinfo process space). Unfortunately, if an in-process application crashed, it took down the entire Web server. In IIS 4.0, you could run applications out-of-process. This approach was used to isolate a single application to a single process. Applications that were mission critical or prone to crashing were isolated to protect themselves and the Web server. Unfortunately, out-of-process applications suffered from decreased performance due to the amount of communication required to cross process boundaries and talk to the Inetinfo process, and ISAPIs running in the Inetinfo process space. Moreover, running many applications out-of-process resulted in a performance penalty on the server as a whole because of the increased overhead related to managing additional processes.

IIS 5.0 was a huge improvement over IIS 4.0. First, the communications architecture was improved so that running applications out-of-process incurred a smaller performance penalty. Next, application pools were introduced. In IIS 5.0, you could run applications in-process or out-of-process, or you could run multiple applications in a single out-of-process pool. An IIS 5.0 Web server had one, and only one, application pool. This setup provided the best performance-to-reliability trade-off. Typically, administrators would put all their well-behaved applications in the pool to protect the Web server service (inetinfo.exe) in case one of those applications crashed. That ensured the Web server would continue to run and could restart the application pool and applications automatically after a crash. This minimized service interruption, but it still meant the applications running in the pool were vulnerable to each other's malfunctions. If one application in the pool crashed, the pool process was terminated and restarted, which would interrupt other applications running in the pool. There were some additional issues with IIS 5.0. Specifically, ISAPIs still ran in-process, which meant a poorly written ISAPI could still crash the Web server service.

IIS 6.0 Isolation Modes

This brings us to the discussion of isolation modes in IIS 6.0. IIS 6.0 supports two isolation modes for application isolation. The first isolation mode is IIS 5.0 isolation mode. In this mode, IIS 6.0 emulates the architecture of IIS 5.0. IIS still uses the HTTP.SYS kernel-mode services for request queuing and caching, but each Web request must traverse Inetinfo.exe. Applications are configured to run in-process, out-of-process, or in a single out-of-process pool, and ISAPIs run in-process with Inetinfo.exe. IIS 5.0 isolation mode is for backward compatibility for Web applications only and can be used to ensure applications previously supported on IIS 5.0 continue to run.

The preferred IIS 6.0 isolation mode is Worker Process isolation mode. This isolation mode takes full advantage of the new IIS 6.0 architecture. In this mode, the Web server service (inetinfo.exe process) is completely isolated from application code and ISAPIs. Everything needed to fulfill Web requests, including ISAPIs, are loaded into the process space of the worker processes fulfilling the requests. All user code is handled by worker processes. Processing is fast because most request steps can be fulfilled from within the worker process, and applications can be completely isolated from each other and from the server. If a worker process fails or hangs, the W3SVC simply shuts down the failing worker process and starts a new one to replace it. In addition, in IIS 6.0 Worker Process isolation mode there is no concept of in-process or out-of-process—there are simply multiple application pools (as many as you want to create). In addition, you can assign as many or as few applications to a pool as you want.

IIS 6.0 cannot support both modes simultaneously, and the default isolation mode is different depending on whether IIS 6.0 is installed new or as an upgrade. If IIS 6.0 is upgraded from a previous version of IIS, the isolation mode is set to IIS 5.0 isolation mode. If IIS 6.0 is installed new, the initial isolation mode is set to Worker Process isolation mode. The isolation mode can be changed by selecting or deselecting the Run WWW Service In IIS 5.0 Isolation Mode check box on the service tab of the Web Sites object properties in the Internet Information Services (IIS) Manager MMC snap-in, or by configuring the *IIS5isolationModeEnabled* parameter in the metabase. HTTP.SYS operation is unaffected by isolation mode settings. Changing the isolation mode requires that Internet Information Services be restarted.

Table 16-1 lists the default modes for each installation type. Table 16-2 compares isolation modes.

Table 16-1   Default Isolation Mode by Installation Type

Installation	Isolation Mode
New installation	Worker process
Upgrade of IIS 6.0	Current mode preserved
Upgrade from IIS 4.0 or 5.0	IIS 5.0 isolation mode

Table 16-2   Isolation Modes Compared

IIS Function	IIS 5.0	IIS 5.0 Iso Mode	Worker Process Iso Mode
IIS Metabase	Inetinfo.exe	Inetinfo.exe	Inetinfo.exe
HTTP.SYS configuration	n/a	W3SVC	W3SVC
Worker process management	n/a	n/a	W3SVC
Worker process	n/a	n/a	W3WP.EXE
Running in-process ISAPI extensions	Inetinfo.exe	Inetinfo.exe	W3WP.EXE
Running out-of-process ISAPI extensions	DLLHost.exe	DLLHost.exe	n/a
Running ISAPI filters	Inetinfo.exe	Inetinfo.exe	W3WP.EXE
HTTP protocol support	Inetinfo via Winsock	HTTP.SYS	HTTP.SYS
FTP, NNTP, SMTP	Inetinfo.exe	Inetinfo.exe	Inetinfo.exe
IIS Metabase	Inetinfo.exe	Inetinfo.exe	Inetinfo.exe
HTTP.SYS configuration	n/a	W3SVC	W3SVC
Worker process management	n/a	n/a	W3SVC
Worker process	n/a	n/a	W3WP.EXE
Running in-process ISAPI extensions	Inetinfo.exe	Inetinfo.exe	W3WP.EXE
Running out-of-process ISAPI extensions	DLLHost.exe	DLLHost.exe	n/a
Running ISAPI filters	Inetinfo.exe	Inetinfo.exe	W3WP.EXE
HTTP protocol support	Inetinfo via Winsock	HTTP.SYS	HTTP.SYS
FTP, NNTP, SMTP	Inetinfo.exe	Inetinfo.exe	Inetinfo.exe
IIS Metabase	Inetinfo.exe	Inetinfo.exe	Inetinfo.exe

Isolation-Mode Recommendations

Remember that IIS 6.0 defaults to IIS 5.0 isolation mode when a previous version of IIS is upgraded. If you simply upgrade your existing IIS servers, you won't get many of the advantages of the new architecture until you change modes. The goal should be to run in Worker Process isolation mode. Before upgrading servers, you should create a test server running in IIS 6.0 in Worker Process isolation mode. Migrate the applications to the test server, and test them running in that mode. Once all applications have been tested and verified to work in Worker Process isolation mode, upgrade production servers and switch to Worker Process isolation mode.

IIS 6.0 Application Pools

At this point, you've heard a lot about application pools and even learned the history of application isolation from IIS 4.0 to the current generation Web server, IIS 6.0. In addition to the performance and reliability enhancements offered in Worker Process isolation mode, you also get more granular application management because you can configure multiple application pools.

You can create as many application pools as you like and configure as many or as few applications in each pool as you like. In Worker Process isolation mode by default, a single application pool is created (named *DefaultAppPool*) and all applications run in that application pool. If you want to isolate an application, simply create a new application pool and configure the application you want to isolate to run in the new pool. In Worker Process Isolation mode, application pool names appear in the Application Pool drop-down list box on the Home Directory tab of a Web site, or the Virtual Directory tab of a Virtual Directory, which allows you to select from among the configured pools. Application pools also have lots of configuration options, which allow administrators to configure how the applications running in the pool are managed, monitored, and optimized. You can group applications in pools based on these requirements.

Application-Pool Health Monitoring

Application pools can be monitored by the WWW Service Administration and Monitoring component (W3SVC). The W3SVC uses worker process pinging to send messages to the worker process through a named pipe. The worker process is supposed to respond to the ping. The W3SVC will consider an application to be unhealthy if the application has crashed or if all available threads are blocked. The W3SVC will terminate the unhealthy worker process or invoke Rapid Fail Protection, depending on the configuration.

Rapid Fail Protection protects your Web server from an application that is failing repeatedly. With Rapid Fail Protection, you specify a number of failures (such as 5) over a given interval (such as 5 minutes). If the application pool exceeds the specified number of failures in the time interval, it is taken out of service and will not be restarted. HTTP.SYS returns a 503 Service Unavailable out-of-service message to any requests to URLs serviced by that application pool. IIS will not restart the application. By not restarting, the application is prevented from consuming resources during restart and failure, which could lead to widespread disruptions.

Application-Pool Recycling

Application pools can also be configured to periodically recycle. Recycling is configured on the Recycling tab and works the same way as ASP.NET application recycling, except it's configured on a per–application pool basis. You can configure application pools to be recycled after a specified number of seconds, after a specified number of requests, at specified times during the day, or when virtual or used memory exceeds thresholds you specify.

Recycling provides an automated way to periodically reset applications. Some poorly written applications can benefit from periodic restart, and recycling can provide added stability while problems are corrected. Application-pool recycling can replace periodic reset scripts that are run on some Web servers to accomplish the same task. The W3SVC is responsible for recycling application pools and uses overlapped recycling. The old worker process remains active long enough to finish servicing existing requests, or until the Shutdown Time Limit (configured on the Application Pool's Performance tab) is reached. A new worker process is created and added to the namespace routing table in HTTP.SYS, and all new requests for the application pool are directed to the new worker process.

Application-Pool Performance

Application pools can also be configured to conserve system resources by using the Performance tab of the Application Pool properties. You can specify an idle time-out, which allows the application pool to shut down if no request has been made of the pool in the specified interval. This saves server resources by terminating unused worker processes. This allows you to better manage the resources when the processing load is heavy or when certain applications are consistently idle.

You can also specify to restrict the number of requests that are allowed to be queued for an application pool. If the number of requests exceed the allowed maximum, the server returns a 503 Service Unavailable error. This prevents large numbers of requests from queuing up and overloading your server. This would happen only if requests couldn't be processed quickly enough. If this happened consistently, you should address the problem by scaling up the server (such as by adding processors), by off-loading tasks to other servers, or by moving the sites or applications being overloaded to separate, faster servers.

You can enable CPU monitoring and specify a maximum percentage of CPU utilization the application pool is allowed to consume over a given time interval. The W3SVC can log an event or terminate the worker processes associated with the pool.

You can also assign multiple worker processes to the application pool. By default, application pools have only one worker process assigned. If you configure multiple worker processes to support the pool, you create a Web Garden. Having multiple worker processes assigned to a pool can increase scalability for long-running applications that have many more simultaneous connections. They can also increase scalability on heavily used application pools. You can also use them to reduce the chance of service disruptions due to blocks on multiprocessor systems. If one of the worker processes experiences a block, the other worker processes can continue to function. Web Gardens are not recommended when the application pools are only lightly loaded, when normal health management provides adequate reliability, and when applications running in the pool cannot be multi-instanced.

Application-Pool Identities

Finally, you can configure the account the application pool runs under on the Identities tab of the application pool properties. You can choose one of three predefined accounts or specify an account you have created. The three predefined accounts are the Network Service account (the default), which has a low level of privilege; the Local Service account, which has a lower level of privilege because it has no outbound credentials and can't act as a machine on the network (it accesses the network as ANONYMOUS); and the Local System account, which is a highly privileged account. You should use an account with the lowest level or privilege that is able to perform processing tasks for applications in the pool. If you decide to designate a user-defined account for the pool, you can browse to the account from this tab. Any accounts you create to be used as an application-pool account should be added to the IIS_WPG group on the local system.

Application-Pool Scenarios and Recommendations

There are several theories for how you can group applications into application pools on IIS 6.0. For example, you could put all sites and applications from a single branch or customer in the same pool. In a hosted environment, you could create an application pool for each department or customer. You could create a Problem Child application pool with aggressive recycling settings for all your ill-behaved applications. Remember that there is not a one-to-one mapping between IIS 4 and IIS 5 isolation modes and application-pool configuration, so review each application individually. In general, it's best to put mission-critical applications in their own pool, put applications that share common requirements (for example, Health Monitoring, Recycling, and Performance or Identity settings) in the same pool, and put well-behaved, noncritical applications in the same pool.

XML Metabase

One of the most important changes in IIS 6.0 is the introduction of the XML Metabase. The Metabase stores all the configuration information for IIS. The

Metabase was introduced in IIS 4.0 because it was more extensible than the Windows NT registry, and it has been with us ever since. The problem with the Metabase until now has been that it has been a black hole for administrators and developers alike. Prior to IIS 6.0, you had to use proprietary tools such as Metaedit.exe or complicated APIs to access and manipulate the Metabase directly. With IIS 6.0, Metabase information is stored in a plain text file. Information in the Metabase is stored in XML format, meaning the document starts with an XML declaration, logical units of information (such as IIS Web Service configuration and application pool configuration) are XML elements, and the actual configuration parameters are attributes of the corresponding elements. All information is surrounded by the appropriate start and end tags. Metabase files are located in the %SystemRoot%\system32\inetsrv\ folder. The MBSchema.xml file contains the Metabase Schema, and the Metabase.xml contains the Metabase.

The XML Metabase provides many advantages, the biggest of which is that you can edit the Metabase with simple text editors. You don't need to learn ADSI or WMI APIs, although both ADSI and WMI scripting providers are supported and, in most cases, pre-IIS 6.0 administration scripts will still work fine. The change in format has not hurt performance. Metabase read and write performance is equivalent to IIS 5.0. If you enable Direct Metabase Edit on the properties page of the server object, or set the *EnableEditWhileRunning* metabase attribute, you can edit the Metabase.xml file while IIS is running, and most changes will take effect immediately. The Metabase configuration can also be easily exported using the IISCNFG.vbs script, which allows administrators to create server-independent configuration files. This allows you to easily configure duplicate IIS servers in scenarios where Network Load Balancing is used.

Metabase History

The new Metabase History feature significantly simplifies testing and implementation rollback. It's very simple. IIS tracks changes to the Metabase, and each time the Metabase is written to disk, copies of the Metabase Schema and Metabase.XML files are saved to %SystemRoot%\system32\inetsrv\history. Each version is marked with a unique number. By default, ten sets of history files (Metabase and Schema) are stored in the history folders; you can adjust this default setting with the *MaxHistoryFiles* setting in the Metabase. The history feature allows you to easily roll back any changes made to the Metabase. To restore the Metabase to its previous state, simply select Backup/Restore Configuration from the All Tasks context menu of the server object, or copy, paste, and rename one of the copies from the History folder. Now developers can easily make changes to test or tune applications, and then quickly, easily, and safely roll back to the original configuration.

Enterprise UDDI Services

Universal Description, Discovery, and Integration (UDDI) is a standard for listing and describing Web services and other applications. Support for UDDI is growing on a broad basis, and Microsoft has included Enterprise UDDI services with Windows Server 2003 to provide out-of-the-box support for UDDI services targeting intranet and extranet scenarios. This section will explain what UDDI is and how it is used to locate, describe, and connect Web services and applications.

What Is UDDI?

UDDI has been called a directory for applications that don't have a user interface. Users and search engines will use UDDI to locate information about Web services and other applications on a network. UDDI components describe what services and applications do, and provide information about how to connect to the services. UDDI can be used to advertise public applications and services, as well as internal applications and services in intranet and extranet scenarios.

Developers and companies will register Web services and other applications along with metadata describing and categorizing the services and applications. Other developers, customers, partners, and search engines will locate the services and applications using UDDI. Companies deploying or planning to deploy Web services and applications they want to share internally with partners or customers should start looking into UDDI. Developers should know about UDDI because it helps them find, share, and reuse Web services and other applications and to build smart applications that can search UDDI to locate those services. UDDI might also be of interest to IT professionals because it will help them categorize network applications. End users don't have to know UDDI and might not realize they're using it when they use a Web-based interface or a search engine that connects to UDDI servers.

Enterprise UDDI Services

Microsoft offers Enterprise UDDI services on Windows Server 2003 (all versions except Web Server Edition). Enterprise UDDI Services is compliant with versions 1 and 2 of the UDDI standard and is designed to target intranet scenarios to facilitate Web services, application visibility, and sharing of code. Enterprise UDDI Services also targets extranet scenarios to support the discovery and description of services used between partner organizations, as well as to enable construction of smart (UDDI-aware) applications. Microsoft Enterprise UDDI Services is a Web application (not a Windows Server 2003 service) and requires IIS 6.0 and MSDE or Microsoft SQL Server.

The State of UDDI

Version 3.0 of UDDI was just released and is being reviewed. Information about the UDDI standard can be found at *http://www.uddi.org*. You can visit the Microsoft UDDI directory and listing of public applications at *http://uddi.microsoft.com*.

Active Directory

Active Directory is a directory service based on X.500 directory structure concepts, which support reliable synchronization (replication) of directory objects, is extensible, and supports industry-standard protocols such as Lightweight Directory Access Protocol (LDAP) and Kerberos authentication.

The primary role of Active Directory is to provide centralized authentication, authorization, account management, and directory lookup services for Microsoft network environments. Because of the ubiquitous nature of Active Directory's primary role, domain controllers and global catalog servers are typically deployed to every location in a company. In many instances, multiple domain controllers or global catalog servers are deployed in a location to provide redundancy or increase performance. Everyone needs to be able to authenticate and access corporate services, so Active Directory needs to be everywhere and available all the time.

The Active Directory schema can also be extended to support additional objects in support of applications and services. Active Directory is excellent for applications such as Microsoft Exchange 2000 and Exchange 2003 that require a directory service and must be supported throughout an organization. Exchange 2000 and Exchange 2003 benefit from Active Directory by being able to use the existing directory structure without requiring organizations to deploy and maintain an additional directory service.

Applications also have an impact on the directory service because they require additional hardware to support increased directory lookup activity, add to replication overhead, and increase the size of the Active Directory database. Network administrators are often reluctant to allow developers to use the corporate Active Directory to support applications that require directory services. Often, developers have deployed ad hoc solutions—such as Access database lookups or network-based XML file lookup to support applications—rather than using a directory service.

In Windows Server 2003, Microsoft has enhanced Active Directory to make it easier for applications to use. Microsoft has also added a new capability—Active Directory Application Mode—to make it easier for developers to deploy applications that use directory services independently from the traditional Active Directory infrastructure.

Active Directory Application Partitions

In Windows 2000, some application data was stored in the Domain partition in the Active Directory database, which meant that all domain controllers in the domain stored the data, and global catalog servers throughout the forest stored some of the data. More commonly, application data was stored in the Active Directory Configuration partition, which meant that all domain controllers in the forest stored all the data. This increased overhead on domain controllers and increased directory replication traffic. There was no way to control which domain controllers stored a copy of the data for an application. No matter where the application was deployed, the directory service data went everywhere.

In Windows Server 2003, Active Directory supports application partitions. Application partitions are separate from domain partitions, so data is isolated from domain and configuration data. Furthermore, replicas must be manually designated so that administrators can control which domain controllers hold copies of the application data. This also means administrators can control replication issues related to application data.

In short, with application partitions administrators can feel comfortable that they can control the impact Active Directory–enabled applications have on the Directory Service infrastructure. In addition, developers can feel more comfortable writing applications that use Active Directory.

Active Directory Application Mode

To provide a solution for developers who simply don't have or don't want to use the corporate Active Directory infrastructure (and for administrators who would rather the developers didn't as well), Microsoft has developed Active Directory Application Mode (AD/AM).

AD/AM (pronounced *Adam*) runs as a non-operating-system service and doesn't need to be deployed on a domain controller. You can run multiple instances simultaneously on a single box, with each instance being independently configurable. AD/AM allows an application to store directory data in a *private* directory service that supports only that application, potentially on the same server as the application. If required, additional copies of AD/AM can be deployed and a replication topology can be configured to support the AD/AM instance. The schema for the directory service can be tailored to meet the needs of the application. AD/AM can be managed by local-server or application administrators, or it can be centrally managed. Moreover, AD/AM can be used to provide robust directory services in Windows NT 4.0 domains, which do not support traditional Active Directory. Both corporate developers and independent software vendors (ISVs) can use AD/AM to build directory service–enabled applications.

AD/AM can be installed on any version of Windows Server 2003. It can also be installed on Windows XP Professional for application development and testing.

COM+ 1.5

COM+, an extension to the Component Object Model, consists of managed component services that have traditionally provided middleware services in support of applications built on components or requiring transaction handling. The COM+ support found in Windows 2000 has been carried over to Windows Server 2003 and extended with COM+ version 1.5. New features in COM+ 1.5 include the following:

- **Applications as services**   You can now configure COM+ applications as services. Implementing COM+ applications as services provides better startup control, and component DLLs are loaded into memory at boot time. This makes the application highly available and more reliable.

- **COM+ application partitions**   COM+ application partitions allow multiple versions of COM components to be installed on the same computer. You can completely isolate the applications of one department or customer from another and reduce infrastructure costs by consolidating COM+ applications onto a single server.

- **Component aliasing**   COM+ 1.5 now supports component aliasing. With component aliasing, you can configure physical implementations of a component multiple times.

- **Process recycling**   COM + 1.5 allows for COM+ applications to be recycled (gracefully restarted). Process recycling can be configured through the COM+ user interface or programmatically. Similar to process recycling in ASP.NET applications and in IIS 6.0 application pools, processes can shut down and restart based on criteria you specify, including elapsed time since application start, number of requests, and memory used.

- **Public/Private components**   COM+ 1.5 allows you to specify that components are public or private. Public components can be seen and activated by any application. Private components can be seen and activated only by other components in the same application, and can be configured to block access from outside of the application. Private components can still use COM+ services.

■ **Advertising COM+ applications as Web services** You can expose COM+ components directly as Web services or as components that can be consumed through remoting. This can allow requests to pass through the firewall when they might otherwise be blocked.

Microsoft Message Queue (MSMQ) 3.0

Microsoft Message Queuing Service (MSMQ) 3.0 is included in Windows Server 2003. MSMQ allows applications to communicate with one another asynchronously for simple communication and in support of transactions.

MSMQ 3.0 provides three major enhancements over previous versions of MSMQ: one-to-many messaging, messaging over the Internet using XML and SOAP messages over HTTP, and programmable management. These enhancements allow for applications that utilize MSMQ to leverage the HTTP protocol to exchange messages through firewalls and to use HTTPS (Encrypted HTTP) to provide secure message transfer.

Index

A

Access, queries, 100–105
accessing
  call stack, 58–63
  class members, setting levels, 69–78
Active Directory, Windows Server 2003, 541–543
Active Directory Application Mode (AD/AM), 542–543
active processes, showing, 488
active windows, showing, 488–489, 490
ActiveX controls, Microsoft Web browser control, 479
AD/AM (Active Directory Application Mode), 542–543
Add Web Reference dialog box
  browsing UDDI nodes, 3
  enhanced in Visual Studio .NET 2003, 1–3
AddHandler function, 336
Add-In Creation wizard, 493
add-ins, creating in Visual Studio .NET, 491–495
ADO
  legacy. *See* legacy ADO
  RecordSet object, 95
ADO.NET
  classes. *See individual classes by name*
  DataSet, typed, 129–135
  DataSet object, 95
  managed code, 95
AllowPaging attribute, 278
animation. *See* GDI+, animation
AppDomain class, 366
AppendText, 381
application isolation, 532–536
Application object, EnableVisualStyles method, 20
application servers, Windows Server 2003, 529
ApplicationAccessControl attribute, 469
applications
  COM+, defined, 461
  console, 307–312
    command-line arguments, 309–310
    Console class methods, 308
    Creating, 308
    finding records, 311

help, 254–259
  Error help, 258
  ErrorProvider control, 256–257
  HelpProvider control, 256
  HTML help, 257
  Popup help, 258
  ToolTip control, 255, 257
  interacting, 326–328
  isolation, IIS (Internet Information Services) 6.0, 532–536
  partitioning, 353–359
    code maintenance, 354
    code reuse, 354
    copying and pasting code, 356–357
    data access partitions, 357–358
    steps, 355
  partitions, Active Directory, 542
  pools, IIS (Internet Information Services) 6.0, 536–538
AppSettings class, 375, 376–377
AppSettings property, 375–376
appSettings section (.NET Application Configuration File), 373–379
  iterating items, 377–378
  retrieving items, 377
  saving, 379
  updating settings, 378–379
AppSettings wrapper, 376
Architecture, IIS (Internet Information Services), 530–532
  HTTP.SYS, 530–531
  W3SVC (WWW Service Administration and Monitoring Component), 531
  worker processes, 531
arguments, command-line, and console applications, 309–310
ArrayList class, 207
ArrayList object, advanced, 114–115
ArrayList object, simple, 113–114
arrays, 113–116
  ArrayList object, advanced, 114–115
  ArrayList object, simple, 113–114
  binding controls to, 190

The 3 Leaf Solutions Authoring Team Biographies

Bob Carver began working in IT in the late 1980s with the U.S. Army Corps of Engineers, deploying and supporting electronic mail and network technologies. He has continuously worked in those areas since that time. After leaving the Army in 1998, Bob joined ARIS Corporation as an instructor, focusing on Microsoft Exchange, Microsoft Windows, and Internet Information Services (IIS)–related courses. At 3 Leaf Solutions, Bob heads many large consulting operations. His recent major consulting projects included designing and deploying Active Directory and managing an upgrade of Exchange 5.5 to Exchange 2000 for Nautilus Group Inc.

Bob is also active in developing and delivering content for Microsoft. Bob has created many technical sessions for the TechNet group, covering Operating Systems, Exchange, IIS, BizTalk, and other topics. Bob also developed content for the Microsoft Network Service Provider/High-Volume-Hosting/Prescriptive Architecture Group, including Windows Web Hoster Workshops on IIS 5.0 scalability, reliability, and migration topics. He is also the key developer behind the 3 Leaf curriculum on migrating to and administering Microsoft Windows .NET Server.

As a Senior Principal of 3 Leaf Solutions, Bob spends his time helping companies integrate emerging Microsoft platforms and server products into their company infrastructures.

Sean Campbell began his career as a college instructor in the early 1990s at Purdue University. He has continued to work with a wide range of Microsoft technology since leaving Purdue. Sean then began to pursue consulting and training engagements with a well-known Chicago franchise: *http://chicago.cubs.mlb.com /NASApp/mlb/chc/homepage/chc_homepage.jsp*. In 1998, Sean joined ARIS Corporation and taught Microsoft Visual Basic and Microsoft SQL Server courses, and he worked on consulting engagements centered on these technologies.

Sean has been one of the principal sources of .NET Development and SQL Server expertise at 3 Leaf Solutions, as well as a leading expert on code development in C#, Visual Basic .NET, and T-SQL. Sean has also been the author of many seminars for Microsoft on technologies such as SQL Server, ASP.NET, .NET Remoting, .NET Security, MMIT, and the .NET Compact Framework. He has led many consulting projects at 3 Leaf Solutions, including SQL Server installations and configurations, a large GIS application upgrade from DAO and Microsoft Access to ADO and SQL Server, as well as numerous .NET projects.

As a Senior Principal at 3 Leaf Solutions, Sean specializes in investigating new technologies for 3 Leaf in a variety of areas related to his expertise. Sean gets most of his kicks from working with new Microsoft product releases early in their development, prior to release to the general public.

When he's not writing code, Sean loves spending time with his family, taking in the Pacific Northwest, reading (history primarily), and taking in any baseball game *http://mlb.mlb.com* game he can.

Scott Swigart has more than 12 years of development experience, starting with authoring low-level hardware diagnostics in C++ for the ADP corporation. Since then, Scott has developed a wide variety of applications (Web applications, desktop, console, and so forth), using more than 20 programming languages. Today, Scott is completely focused on Microsoft .NET (both Visual Basic .NET and C#), as he believes that Microsoft.NET is the best application framework available today.

In addition to development experience, Scott also has extensive experience teaching and presenting at large events, such as DevDays and TechEd. As the e-visionary for 3 Leaf, Scott is constantly focused on analyzing the emerging technologies to determine which will be core to future solutions. With this knowledge, Scott works with companies that seek to obtain a competitive advantage by adopting technologies early in their life cycle.

Patrick Barnes is an independent developer, an author, and a consultant living in America's heartland—Cedar Rapids, Iowa. After leaving the U.S. Navy in 1994 as an FA-18 fighter pilot and combat veteran, Patrick opted for four years of relative serenity at Microsoft. This eventually led to the formation of Development Insites, a company that specializes in building applications and educational materials that leverage the .NET Framework. Patrick has been building production ASP .NET Web sites and Web services since the Beta 1 release in 2000. He is also the author of numerous courses, articles, and technical presentations on SQL Server and .NET technologies.

Jim Pragit is an independent consultant working out of beautiful Glen Ellyn, Illinois. Jim began his IT career in the mainframe world doing COBOL and Assembler development for the IBM 370 series mainframe.

Shortly after graduating in 1997, he permanently switched from mainframes to PCs and has never looked back. With over five years of real-world development experience with Visual Basic under his belt, Jim has been specializing in all things .NET since before it was even called .NET. He has authored numerous presentations, demonstrations, and Knowledge Base articles on the .NET platform. Jim especially enjoys working with Windows Forms, ASP.NET, and the .NET Compact Framework.

Kris Horrocks is an independent developer, a trainer and an author from Charlotte, North Carolina. He started working with Microsoft technologies while pursuing an MCSD instead of graduate school, but he owes his love of programming to a third-grade Olympics of the Mind competition for Basic programming on a Commodore 64. When not glued to his laptop creating .NET content for early adopters, he can be found wakeboarding or singing too much karaoke.

Oz Rugless is a consultant, a developer, and a trainer who travels across the United States teaching and consulting on the latest Microsoft technologies. Oz is principal of the Rugless Group, Inc., an Orlando, Florida consulting firm whose clients range from large corporations to small businesses and private organizations. Oz holds Microsoft certifications, including MCSD, MCSE, MCDBA, and MCT.

Get a **Free**
e-mail newsletter, updates,
special offers, links to related books,
and more when you

register online!

Register your Microsoft Press® title on our Web site and you'll get a FREE subscription to our e-mail newsletter, *Microsoft Press Book Connections.* You'll find out about newly released and upcoming books and learning tools, online events, software downloads, special offers and coupons for Microsoft Press customers, and information about major Microsoft® product releases. You can also read useful additional information about all the titles we publish, such as detailed book descriptions, tables of contents and indexes, sample chapters, links to related books and book series, author biographies, and reviews by other customers.

Registration is easy. Just visit this Web page and fill in your information:

http://www.microsoft.com/mspress/register

Microsoft®

Proof of Purchase

Use this page as proof of purchase if participating in a promotion or rebate offer on this title. Proof of purchase must be used in conjunction with other proof(s) of payment such as your dated sales receipt—see offer details.

101 Microsoft® Visual Basic® .NET Applications
0-7356-1891-7

CUSTOMER NAME

Microsoft Press, PO Box 97017, Redmond, WA 98073-9830